Angelo Antonio Scotti

Meditations for the use of the clergy for every day in the year

Volume III.

Angelo Antonio Scotti

Meditations for the use of the clergy for every day in the year
Volume III.

ISBN/EAN: 9783742814456

Manufactured in Europe, USA, Canada, Australia, Japa

Cover: Foto ©Thomas Meinert / pixelio.de

Manufactured and distributed by brebook publishing software
(www.brebook.com)

Angelo Antonio Scotti

Meditations for the use of the clergy for every day in the year

MEDITATIONS

FOR THE USE OF THE CLERGY,

for Every Day in the Year.

ON THE GOSPELS FOR THE SUNDAYS.

FROM THE ITALIAN OF MGR. SCOTTI, ARCHBISHOP OF THESSALONICA.

REVISED AND EDITED BY THE OBLATES OF ST. CHARLES.

VOL. III.

FROM THE FIFTH SUNDAY AFTER EASTER
TO THE ELEVENTH SUNDAY AFTER PENTECOST.

LONDON: BURNS AND OATES,
PORTMAN STREET AND PATERNOSTER ROW.
MDCCCLXXIV.

INDEX. I.

INDEX. II.

OF THE MEDITATIONS ON THE MOTHER OF GOD.

INDEX. I.

INDEX. II.

OF THE MEDITATIONS ON THE MOTHER OF GOD.

FIFTH SUNDAY AFTER EASTER.

PRIESTS MUST INSTRUCT THE FAITHFUL IN THE DUTY OF PRAYER.

I. THEY MUST SHEW ITS EFFICACY.
II. THEY MUST INSIST ON ITS NECESSITY.
III. THEY MUST EXPLAIN ITS CONDITIONS.

"Amen, amen, I say to you: if you ask the Father anything in My Name, He will give it you."—*St. John* xvi. 23.

1. *Amen, Amen, I say to you.* St. Alphonsus Liguori writes as follows:—"I say, and repeat, and will continue to repeat as long as I live, that all our salvation depends on prayer; and, therefore, that all spiritual writers in their books, all preachers in their sermons, all confessors in administering the sacrament of Penance, should inculcate nothing more strongly than continual prayer. They should be continually crying aloud, ' Pray, pray, never cease from prayer!'" This same Saint has indeed put together innumerable passages of Holy Scripture setting forth this great duty of prayer. It is, however, sufficient for our purpose to call to mind those words which form the subject of our meditation. In them (says St. Thomas) our Saviour promises to make prayer the means of obtaining our requests. He promises, as it were, by an oath: "Amen, Amen, I say to you," and so exhibits (as Cornelius à Lapide points out) the gravity, the sublimity, and the certainty of this .truth. Let us call to mind those other words: "All things, whatsoever you ask, when

ye pray, believe that you shall receive, and they shall come unto you" (St. Mark xi. 14). " For every one that asketh receiveth; and he that seeketh findeth " (St. Luke xi. 10). Prayer is the means of obtaining all good things. It is, says St. Chrysostom, the anchor of the wavering, the treasure of the poor, the medicine for diseases, the safeguard of health. All evils disappear through prayer, says St. Augustin. If the Faithful did but persuade themselves that God is "rich unto all that call upon Him " (Rom. x. 12), they would blame themselves alone for the evils which befall them on account of their neglect of this great means of salvation ; and thus they would be speedily brought back to the way of holiness and justice.

2. *He will give it you.* It is the office and the duty of Priests to impress on each one of the Faithful that prayer is necessary by necessity of precept. Jesus Christ has said, "Ask, and it shall be given you ; seek, and you shall find ; knock, and it shall be opened to you " (St. Matt. vii. 7). The reason of this is evident ; for, if we can do no good thing without the assistance of Divine grace, and yet are bound to do good works, we are therefore bound to procure the requisite grace. Now, all grace, with the exception of the first grace, called by theologians '*gratia excitans*,' is given to him only who asks for it. God wills to give, (says St. Augustin), but he gives only to him who asks. Further, let Priests make the Faithful understand that prayer is necessary '*necessitate medii*,' as a means of overcoming temptations, and of procuring our salvation. After baptism, says St. Thomas, continual prayer is necessary to man in order that he may enter heaven. For, although by baptism our sins are re-mitted, there still remain concupiscence to assail us from within, and the world and the devil to ensnare us from without. The reason, then, which makes us certain of the necessity of prayer is this—that in order to be saved we must contend and conquer ; but without the Divine assistance we cannot resist so many and such powerful enemies, and this assistance, in the ordinary course of Providence, is only granted in answer to prayer. Therefore, let us take every opportunity of insisting on this great lesson—that men "ought always to pray, and not to faint "

(St. Luke xviii. 1). But we shall never inculcate this truth as we ought if we of ourselves love not prayer—if we are not, in fact, men of prayer.

3. *If you ask the Father anything in My Name.* We must explain tô the Faithful the conditions of prayer, lest the words be fulfilled, "You ask, and receive not, because you ask amiss" (St. James iv. 3). In the sentence proposed for our present meditation we find (according to St. Thomas) that those conditions are seven—viz., that it be made (1) for spiritual goods; (2) with perseverance; (3) with concord; (4) that it proceed from filial affection; (5) that it be made with humility; (6) at a right season; (7) for oneself. But, above all, we must inculcate humility; for "the prayer of him that humbleth himself shall pierce the clouds, and he will not depart till the Most High behold" (Eccls. xxxv. 21). We must also recommend confidence in the goodness of God, and in the merits of our Redeemer; mindful of the words, "Let him ask in faith, nothing wavering" (St. James i. 6);—and, again, perseverance: "Pray without ceasing" (1 Thes. v. 17). All the holy Fathers and Doctors of the Church, all zealous Preachers and Directors of souls, have ever insisted on this point, as of the utmost importance. Let us imitate them; let us ever keep before us the great truth expressed by St. Liguori,—viz., that he who prays obtains grace and is saved; but that the number of those saved is few, because few only pray. The Rogation days afford a most suitable opportunity for speaking on this subject.

"Blessed be God, who hath not turned away my prayer, nor His mercy from me."
—*Ps.* lxv. 20.

"Lord, teach us to pray."—*St. Luke* xi. 1.

MONDAY.

THE PRIVATE PRAYERS OF PRIESTS AS COMPARED WITH THOSE OF THE LAITY.

I. THEIR GREATER PERFECTION.

II. THEIR GREATER LENGTH.

III. THEIR EXEMPLARY CHARACTER.

" Hitherto you have not asked anything in My Name. Ask, and you shall receive, that your joy may be full. These things I have spoken to you in proverbs. The hour cometh when I will no more speak to you in proverbs, but will show you plainly of the Father."—*St. John* xvi. 24, 25.

1. *The hour cometh when I will no more speak to you in proverbs.* The conditions of perfect prayer ought to be well known to a Minister of the Sanctuary. He, moreover, is able to fulfil them better than the laity, who are ready to excuse themselves by saying, " We know not what we should pray for as we ought " (Rom. viii. 26). From his earliest years the Priest has learnt these conditions, so that it would be a disgrace to him to merit St. Basil's reproof—"Sometimes you ask and do not receive, because you have asked wrongly, or unfaithfully, or lightly, or without due consideration, or without perseverance." Moreover, prayer is an act of that virtue which is called religion; for, says St. Thomas, by prayer man shows reverence to God, inasmuch as he submits himself to Him, and in praying confesses that he needs Him as the author and giver of all the good things which he possesses. Every one must be aware that this virtue of religion is especially required of Priests. Surely, then, they are

bound above all others to perfect themselves in prayer. Again, the Holy Spirit is the author of prayer, and how many times has not this Spirit come to them? It is their own fault if the Spirit Himself asketh not for them " with unspeakable groanings" (Rom. viii. 26). If we had ardent charity, our prayers would be perfect; for St. Augustin fitly says, " the Spirit—that is, charity—groans ; charity prays." Now, if it be a disgrace to a Priest that the laity should equal him in this exercise, how much more if he be inferior to those many devout women who pray with such fervour !

2. *Ask, and you shall receive.* The Angelical Doctor points out that prayer should be long continued. Surely Priests, above all others, should be conspicuous in this respect, seeing they have before their eyes the great High Priest, Who passed the whole night in the prayer of God (St. Luke vi. 12). St. Anselm observes that St. Luke, who sets forth our Lord in His Priestly character, speaks more frequently than the other Evangelists of His prayers. Moreover, our Lord Himself, when He announced to the Apostles their election to the Priesthood, represented to them prayer as one of their chief aims: "I have chosen you . . . that, whatsoever you shall ask of the Father in My Name, He may give it you" (St. John xv. 16). Thus the Apostles committed to the seven Deacons the distribution of alms, in order that they might not be withdrawn from prayer: "But we will give ourselves continually to prayer, and to the ministry of the word" (Acts vi. 4). Thus, also, St. Paul taught Timothy that prayer is the means for sanctifying every creature; " for it is sanctified by the word of God, and prayer " (1 Tim. iv. 5)—nay, he set before him prayer as his chief occupation: "I desire, therefore, first of all, that supplications, prayers, intercessions, and thanksgivings, be made for all men" (1 Tim. ii. 1). Let us consider that one of the reasons for which Christ gave the counsel of Virginity, and for which we are bound to celibacy, is, that we may freely give ourselves to prayer: "which may give you power to attend upon the Lord without impediment" (1 Cor. vii. 35). St. Chrysostom says, that if we did but pray well and continuously we should never sin; and (as the same Father tells us in another place) the dev'

assails us when he beholds us stripped of this armour, but when he sees us well furnished with it he flies from us.

3. *Hitherto you have not asked anything.* If we have cause to reprove numbers of Christians for their negligence in praying, the fault is in great part ours, because we do not give them a right example. It is true that we must not imitate the Pharisees, who prayed at the corners of the streets, that they might receive praise, "feigning long prayer" (St. Luke xx. 47; St. Matt. vi. 5); but our light should "shine before men, that they may see our good works, and glorify our Father Who is in heaven" (St. Matt. v. 16). Men know that we are the friends, the Ministers, of Christ, the deputies of His love; they know that we are celibate, freed from secular affairs, and therefore that our lives are specially suited for prayer. They know that we preach the necessity and the immense advantages of prayer. What will they say, then, if they see us wearied by prayer, distracted in prayer? What will they of our household say if they see us go away when they are reciting the holy Rosary, if they perceive that we do not fulfil that precept of Christ, "Enter into thy chamber, and, having shut the door, pray to thy Father" (St. Matt. vi. 6). In this way we may be found to lack that which St. Augustin calls "the column of virtue, the ladder by which to ascend to God." Thus, also, will our people become deficient in that which St. Chrysostom calls their great treasure, their great harbour and place of refuge.

"I cried with my whole heart, hear me, O Lord."—*Ps.* cxviii. 145.

"Let Thy ears be attentive, and Thy eyes open, to hear the prayer of Thy servant."—2 *Esd.* i. 6.

TUESDAY.

———

ON THE PRIEST'S PUBLIC PRAYERS, ESPECIALLY
ON THE RECITAL OF THE DIVINE OFFICE.

I. The sublime character of this obligation.

II. The reason of its being laid upon Ecclesiastics.

III. The mode in which it should be fulfilled.

———

"In that day you shall ask in My Name, and I say not to you that I will ask the Father for you, for the Father Himself loveth you, because you have loved Me, and have believed that I came out from God."—*St. John* xvi. 26, 27.

1. *In that day you shall ask in My Name.* If all prayers are to be offered to the Father in the Son's Name, this is especially the case in regard to the Divine Office. For it is recited by Priests in the name of the Church—that is, of the mystical Body of Christ; and it is to be recited "all the days," or as long as the Church lasts, "even to the consummation of the world." Thus, St. Basil calls Psalmody "the voice of the Church, the function performed by the whole heavenly commonwealth;" and St. Peter Damian speaks of the seven Canonical Hours as the seven cleansing fountains placed in the bosom of the Holy Church. The Priest, then, should bear in mind that in reciting the Office he is speaking as the Ambassador of the Church, and with the voice of the Church; as St. Augustin says. Let him put to himself the questions suggested by St. Bernard,—viz., (1) Who has imposed the obligation? It is the Church, who is the Spouse of Christ, our Mother and our Queen. (2) On whom is it im

posed ?   Upon us, sinners, who in the discharge of this duty are associated with the Angels; for psalmody is the work of those ministering spirits who stand before the Throne of God.   (3) What is its purport ?   The salvation of the Faithful, for whom this sacrifice of praise is offered ; for the Divine Office is, as it were, a peculiar sacrifice, says Cassian.   (4) In what does this duty consist ?   It consists in coming before that God before Whom the Angels cover their faces (Isaias vi. 2), tremble, and dread (Job xxvi. 2).   Surely, if the Cleric would reflect on these great truths before the recital of the Canonical Hours, his soul would be well disposed for prayer, and he would not be "as a foolish man that tempteth God " (Eccl. xviii. 23).

2. *For the Father Himself loveth you.* This sublime charge is laid upon Priests for seven reasons especially,—viz., (1) because they are supposed to be the friends of God (St. John xv. 14), and it is the duty of friends to act as reconcilers, and to obtain grace for all; (2) because they are supposed to be holy (Isaiah xx. 7) ; and the prayers of holy persons are more readily granted (Ps. cxlix. 9); (3) because they are, as St. Bernard says, mediators between God and the people, and it pertains to a mediator to interpose himself between two parties, in order to obtain peace and preserve it (Gal. iii. 19); (4) because they are Ambassadors to God; and most fitly so, as sent by God Himself to treat with men in His behalf (Eph. vi. 20) ; (5) because they are free from secular cares (2 Tim. ii. 4), and for that reason can fulfil this important duty better than others ; (6) because they are well acquainted with the needs of the Faithful, —being dispensers of the House of God (as St. Prosper says)— and because they can with greater earnestness advocate the cause of the needy, whom they bear on their shoulders (as St. Eucherius says); (7) because they understand the necessity, efficacy, and conditions of prayer better than other men, and therefore are better able to carry out the injunction of St. Ambrose, " Let thy faith cry aloud ; let thy affection cry aloud ; let thy blood cry aloud."   Let us therefore thank God, Who through His Church has destined us to so noble and important an office.   How many ᵛre condemned to spend their whole time in mean employments,

in order to gain a loaf of bread! Might not such lot have been ours?

3. *Because you have loved Me.* The love which we ought to bear to Jesus Christ is the grand secret of the worthy recital of the Divine Office; for, in proportion as our love is more fervent, so will our friendship towards God be more sincere, our intercourse with Him more grateful, our recollection of mind more lasting. So shall we pray, as the Church enjoins, "worthily, attentively, and devoutly." Let us consider in the first place this word "worthily." We have to plead before the Throne of God (as St. Chrysostom reminds us) the cause, not only of a whole city, but of the whole world—of all mankind—of the living and of the dead. What sanctity is required in those who fulfil so august an Embassy! Next, let us consider the word "attentively." Almighty God requires a reasonable service from us, and therefore He would not be honoured only with the lips, nor would He that His work be done negligently. Therefore the Council of Cologne enjoins that the Priest should fulfil this, his daily and nightly task, with inward affection and mind fixed on God alone; for "cursed is he who doeth the work of God negligently." Lastly, let us consider the meaning of the term "devoutly." Let us endeavour to imitate St. Augustin, who felt himself inflamed with love by the words of the Psalms: "Oh, what accents did I utter unto Thee!" he says, "in those Psalms; and how was I by them kindled towards Thee, and on fire to rehearse them, if possible, through the whole world, against the pride of mankind!" What great merit should we gain before God if we did but recite the Canonical Hours with due reverence and devotion! What great merit, says St. Alphonsus, is the devout recital of one single Office!

"Let my prayer come in before Thee; incline Thy ear to my petition."—*Ps.* lxxxvii. 2.

"I will speak to my Lord, whereas I am dust and ashes."—*Gen.* xviii. 27.

WEDNESDAY.

HOW PRIESTS GROW WEARY OF RECITING THE DIVINE OFFICE.

I. BECAUSE OF THE CORRUPTION OF THE HUMAN WILL.
II. BECAUSE OF THE OBSCURITY OF THE PSALMS.
III. BECAUSE OF THE FORCE OF THE OBLIGATION.

"I came forth from the Father, and am come into the world: again, I leave the world, and I go to the Father. His disciples say to Him, Behold, now Thou speakest plainly, and speakest no proverb. Now we know that Thou knowest all things, and Thou needest not that any man should ask Thee. By this we believe that Thou comest forth from God."—*St. John* xvi. 28—30.

1. *I leave the world, and I go to the Father.* Such are precisely the resolutions which the Priest ought to make when he prepares to recite the Divine Office: "I leave the things of this world, and go to the throne of the Eternal Father." But this is often distasteful, because of the corruption of the human will, which finds a difficulty in good works. This difficulty is the penalty of our corrupt nature—a penalty which remains even in the heart of those who are regenerated in Baptism, and who thus experience in themselves a continual conflict. The mind knows what is good, but feels repugnance in doing it: it wills, and it wills not, to serve and honour God. "The mind commands itself" (says St. Augustin), "and is resisted. When I was deliberating upon the immediate fulfilment of my long-made resolution of serving God, it was I, myself, who willed—I myself who willed not. My will to do it was imperfect; my will not to do it was imperfect; and thus was I at strife with myself." It is indeed an awful

thought that the wicked " run to evil" without delay; " they make haste to shed blood" (Prov. i. 16), whilst we, on the contrary, are only brought with the greatest difficulty and reluctance to perform a work so noble and excellent, as is the prayer made in the name of the Church. We find no difficulty in wasting our time in building castles in the air, or in frivolous talking—" our thoughts are unprofitable thoughts" (Is. lix. 7)—and yet it wearies us to think of God, to praise God, to speak with God; whereas, as St. Augustin says, to fix the mind for a little while on God is great blessedness. Let us resolve to overcome, with the help of grace, this vice of our nature : let us " put off the old man," and put on Jesus Christ, Who prayed so often and so willingly. Let us say to God, " Of Thee shall I continually sing" (Ps. lxx. 6).

2. *Thou speakest plainly, and speakest no proverb.* The Disciples so little understood the language which the Messias then used that (says St. Augustin) they did not even perceive that they understood it not. But some Priests are aware that they do not understand the Psalms, and it is this which renders such an occupation wearisome to them. This is a fault in all those who are able, and who therefore ought, to make the Holy Scriptures their delight. They ought to remember that Holy Scriptures, and especially the Psalms, deserve to be studied before undertaking the recital of them ; and that they are, as St. Gregory says, the fountain in which Priests should wash themselves before they enter the Sanctuary. Then would they fulfil that Divine precept, " Sing ye wisely" (Ps. xlvi. 8) ; then would the Psalms be both " sweetness to the heart, and food to the mouth," according to the expression of St. Bernard. Hence, with good reason, St. Alphonsus exclaims, " What illumination is received from these divine words ! how many holy maxims does not the soul imbibe from them ! how many holy acts of love, confidence, humility, repentance, may be made by reciting them !" If only we recited the Office with faith and fervour, what treasures of grace might we thus lay up for ourselves ! Let us reflect seriously on these truths, and make earnest resolutions of amendment in this all-important matter.

3. *Thou needest not that any man should ask Thee.* Christ, without inquiry of any man, replied freely to the thoughts of His Disciples; but neither could the Disciples, nor can we, freely say and do all that pleases us. Our liberty is regulated by the law, and has been restrained by the vow, which we made when we received the Subdiaconate, to recite the Divine Office. This seems an intolerable weight to carnal men—a chain which ever binds, a monotonous occupation which wearies them. " We languish with weariness," says St. Gregory. But spiritual men consider the greater merit which is gained by doing a good work under a vow. They consider how true is the maxim of St. Augustin, that the necessity which compels us to a higher aim is, indeed, a blessing. They look upon the Divine Office as a prelude of Paradise, as St. Gregory Nazianzen calls it; for then they are united to the Angels, who praise God together with them; for the service of the Angels is to be always praising God, says St. Ambrose. They rejoice in this occupation as in a sacrifice of praise, and fulfil it according to St. Bernard's rule, who teaches us that in offering the sacrifice of praise we should unite the sense to the words, our affection to the sense, joy to our affection, seriousness to joy. Lastly, let us use the Psalter as a compendium of the Holy Scriptures, containing, as St. Augustin says, a treasure of doctrine, and furnishing to each one that which is necessary for him. Are these our sentiments ? Let us endeavour that they may be so: let us repent if they have not been so hitherto.

" Praise ye the Lord, because psalm is good : to our God be joyful and comely praise."—*Ps.* cxlvi. 1.

" O Lord, save me, and we will sing our psalms all the days of our life."— *Is.* xxxviii. 20.

ASCENSION DAY.

THE THREEFOLD GAIN TO OUR SACERDOTAL MINISTRY DERIVED FROM THE ASCENSION OF OUR LORD.

I. Joy.
II. Glory.
III. Efficacy.

"And the Lord Jesus, after He had spoken to them, was taken up into Heaven, and sitteth on the Right Hand of God. But they, going forth, preached everywhere, the Lord working withal, and confirming the word with signs that followed."—*St. Mark* xvi. 19, 20.

1. *Was taken up into Heaven.* The source and the Head of our Priesthood is Christ. He has ascended into Heaven in order that our joys might be exceeding great through the hope of attaining the same good. For (says St. Chrysostom) as is the Head such is the body; as is the source, such is the end. Venerable Bede makes this reflection—that St. Luke, who was destined by the Holy Spirit to set forth more fully than the other Evangelists the Priesthood of Christ, began his Gospel with the Priesthood of Zachary, and ended it with the joy of the Apostles (the Priests of the new dispensation) at their Master's Ascension, and the praises which they gave to God in the Temple for this event. For he concludes his Gospel with these words—"They went back to Jerusalem with great joy, and they were always in the Temple, praising and blessing God" (St. Luke xxiv. 52, 53). They rejoiced, and we also ought to rejoice, at the glorification

of our Master, at the humiliation of the devil, at the confusion of the Jews, at the redemption of the human race, at the reparation of the fall of the Angels. So Cardinal Hugo. We, then, who are better instructed than the laity in this mystery, ought to surpass them in spiritual joy; inspired by the hope that, after having followed our great High Priest in the consummation of His work, we shall follow Him also to eternal happiness. Let us imitate the Apostles, who, in the fulness of their joy, prepared to follow their ascended Lord on His great journey; as St. Cyprian says.

2. *Sitteth on the Right Hand of God.* The Founder of our Priesthood—He who has constituted us His Ministers—sits at the Right Hand of the Father. Now, the glory of a Minister consists in four things, viz., (1) the glory of the King whose Minister he is; (2) the importance of the functions entrusted to him; (3) the familiar intercourse with which the King honours him; (4) the reward which is reserved for him. In the Ascension of our Saviour all these conditions concur for the ennobling of our Ministry. He sits at the Right Hand of the Father in order to associate our humanity with the Divine glory, as St. Leo points out; and, in comparison with this King of Glory, what is the glory of earthly kings, and the glory of their ministers? " His glory is dung and worms; to-day he is lifted up, and tomorrow he shall not be found" (1 Mach. ii. 62, 63). In the next place, this King has confided to us the things which He preferred to His very life—that is, the glory of His Father, and the salvation of souls. He destines us to this work on earth, and thereby associates us with those seven noble Spirits, the Princes of the Angelic hosts, who are ever employed for the same object in Heaven, and who are represented as His eyes, and as the Ministers of His strength : " Behold in the midst of the throne and of the four living creatures, and in the midst of the ancients, a Lamb standing as it were slain, having seven horns and seven eyes, which are the seven Spirits of God, sent forth into all the earth" (Apoc. v. 6). Further, although He is crowned with glory and honour, He treats us with the greatest familiarity. He admits us, as Assuerus admitted Esther, to plead the cause of

the people. He sends us in His Name, saying, "He that heareth you heareth Me ; he that despiseth you despiseth Me" (St. Luke x. 16). Jesus descends into our hands, allows us to touch Him, to feed on Him, and to dispense Him to others. Lastly, the reward which He promises to His Ministers is worthy of His magnificence; for, says St. Augustin, He grudges us not Heaven, but says to us, Be My faithful Ministers if you wish to reign with Me. Therefore, let us represent this great mystery to the Father, especially in Holy Mass, during which we so frequently refer to it; and let us pronounce those words with confidence and fervour.

3. *The Lord working withal.* · Our Saviour ascended into Heaven in order to leave Priests upon earth as stewards and dispensers of the gifts which (as St. Thomas says) He sends from His eternal throne in Heaven, where He sits as God and Lord. What wonder, therefore, if He blessed the labour of the Apostles by His grace, and still continues to bless the efforts of His Priests? Well does St. Augustin remark, that He promised His assistance to us in the person of the Apostles; and He will give it, if only we refuse not to execute His commands. All the world saw the assistance given by Christ to His Disciples, when it beheld the miracles which they worked even by their mere shadow (Acts v. 15); and, if visible miracles are less frequent in these days than they were in the first ages of Christianity (because the plant of Faith is now securely rooted, and no longer needs to be nourished with this Heavenly water), yet spiritual miracles are still of frequent occurrence; for (says St. Gregory) Holy Church now works in spiritual things what the Apostles did in corporal things. In truth, Her Ministers cast out the devil from the souls of the Faithful; they speak with that tongue of the Apostles which is not spoken by others; they take up serpents—that is to say, those vices which creep about the world, and would induce penitents to fall again into sin; in Sacramental Confession they drink in with the ear the poison of sinful narratives, and this poison does not hurt them; they cure the sick —that is to say, those who are tormented with spiritual maladies. So St. Bernard. And these miracles are greater than corporal

miracles, inasmuch as they are concerned with men's souls, with grace, with eternity; which are more precious than the body, and nature, and time, says St. Gregory. Therefore, let us rejoice in the Lord that we are destined to such great works, and let us strive to do them always well. Let us confide in the protection of Him Who, having worked in former ages many visible miracles, now works, by means of us, miracles of equal power, and of greater mercy; as St. Augustin declares.

"Be thou exalted, O Lord, in Thy own strength; we will sing and praise Thy power."—*Ps.* xx. 14.

"Pray for us to the Father that He would keep us, and keep us from evil."—From *St. John* xvii. 12, 15.

FRIDAY.

THE PRIESTHOOD OF CHRIST AT THE RIGHT HAND OF THE FATHER.

I. Its GLORY IS ETERNAL.

II. Its POWER IS ABSOLUTE.

III. Its EXERCISE IS PERFECT.

"Sitteth on the Right Hand of God."—*St. Mark.* xvi. 19.

1. *To sit on the Right Hand of the Father* is the property of Christ alone; nor has it ever been said to any creature, however noble, "Sit on My Right Hand" (Heb. i. 13). For, says St. Thomas, this glory belongs to Him, inasmuch as, according to the Divine nature, He is equal to the Father, and,

according to the human nature, He exceeds all creatures in the Divine gifts which He possesses. The Father has sworn that this, His Son's glory, shall never be dissevered from the Priestly office, and He has sworn it to Him alone, and to none else; " for the others, indeed, were made Priests without an oath, but this with an oath, by Him that said unto Him, The Lord hath sworn, and He will not repent, Thou art a Priest for ever according to the order of Melchisedeck " (Heb. vii. 20, 21). Therefore the Apostle looked upon Jesus at the Right Hand of the Father as a Priest, carrying on His office in the Holy of Holies, and having care of the true Tabernacle, the Tabernacle founded by God—that is, of the whole Church: " We have such an High Priest, who is set on the Right Hand of the throne of majesty in the Heavens, a Minister of the Holies, and of the true Tabernacle, which the Lord hath pitched, and not man" (Heb. viii. 1, 2). He it is Who offers perpetually the Sacrifice of the Cross, which (as Cornelius à Lapide points out) is continued after one manner in Heaven, and in another manner on earth. He is the High Priest Who is ever standing before his Father, that He may obtain for us the good things to come: " Christ being come an High Priest of the good things to come . . . entered once into the Holies, having obtained eternal redemption" (Heb. ix. 11, 12). What confidence ought not so consoling a thought to awake in us! We Priests make our voice daily heard at the Right Hand of the Father, whence we cause Jesus to descend into our hands. How ardently should not we desire to see, with face revealed, the glory which the Father has given Him!

2. *To sit at the Right Hand of the Father* signifies (says St. Thomas) both the eternal rest of Jesus in the blessedness of the Father, and the royal and judicial power which He has received from the Father. Clothed with this glory, He exercises full and absolute power in Heaven and on earth—a power which, as Man, He merited by humbling Himself and submitting to the power of an earthly judge. "All power is given to Me in heaven and in earth" (St. Matt. xxviii. 18). Now, this power (as Cornelius à Lapide shows) exceeds all created power by its origin, which is Divine; by its stability which is insuperable

c

and eternal; by its extension, which embraces Heaven and earth. And worthy was the Lamb to receive this power, because " He has redeemed with His Blood " those over whom He exercises it (Apoc. v. 9). Meanwhile He says to us, "Without Me you can do nothing," (St. John xv. 5); and (as St. Augustin observes) He says not ' Perform,' but simply ' Do.' Therefore, in all the offices for which we prepare ourselves in the fulfilment of our Ministry, let us remember our Saviour, Who can bless, prosper, sanctify them; for the Father "hath subjected all things under His feet, and hath made Him head over all the Church . . . Who is filled all in all" (Eph. i. 22, 23). Let us pray to Him to sanctify us, and to prosper the works of our hands, so that, as His faithful Ministers, we may merit that throne which He, sitting at the Right Hand of the Father, has taken possession of in our name.

3. *Our Divine Redeemer, sitting at the Right Hand of the Father,* ceases not to intercede for us—ceases not to offer Himself for the human race—in order, says St. Thomas, that God, having so highly exalted human nature in Christ, may also have compassion on men, for whom the Son of God assumed that same nature—nay (continues St. Thomas), preferred to that sublime throne as God and Lord. He ceases not to dispense Divine gifts to men, whence each one has " grace given, according to the measure of the giving of Christ " (Eph. iv. 7). It was the fruit of His eternal Pontificate to bring with Himself into Heaven the holy Fathers who were in Limbo, and successively to lead thither, and establish in the "many mansions," each one of the elect. He does this by reuniting them to Himself as members to the Head, and so are the words verified, " No man hath ascended into Heaven but He that descended from Heaven " (St. John iii. 13). He alone hath ascended into Heaven, since all the elect may be considered as one sole Body with Him, incorporated with Him, glorified in Him. Nor will He cease from this operation until He shall have saved all those whose names are written in the " Book of Life " (Apoc. v. 5). Then will His Priestly Heart have full content, when He shall have sanctified His Body—that is, even the flesh of His Church—

and so shall offer to His Father a Sacrifice of praise for endless ages of ages. .Meanwhile He waits until His enemies are made His footstool : " He for ever sitteth on the Right Hand of God, from henceforth expecting until His enemies be made His footstool" (Heb. x. 12, 13). Where will be our place in eternity ? Shall we be among His Members or His enemies ?

"The Lord is in His holy temple, the Lord's throne is in Heaven."—*Ps.* x. 4.

" O great High Priest, Who, as our forerunner, hast entered even within the veil, have mercy on us."—From *Heb.* vi. 20.

SATURDAY.

—◆—

IN THE ASCENSION, MARY IS AN EXAMPLE TO HER SON'S PRIESTS.

I. IN SORROW.
II. IN JOY.
III. IN OBEDIENCE.

—◆—

" And it came to pass, whilst He blessed them, He departed from them, and was carried up to Heaven, and they adoring went back into Jerusalem with great joy."—*St. Luke* xxiv. 51, 52.

1. *He departed from them.* St. Bernardin of Sienna, contemplating the tender and secret colloquies which the Mother held with Her Son in His Ascension, says that no human tongue is capable of expressing them. We may, however, easily imagine how the heart of the Mother was affected by this separation, and how Jesus sought to console Her with loving words. Who can say how great was the ardour with which the Mother longed

to accompany Her Son to heavenly glory? Could She ever forget Her Son, or stay Her longing desire to unite Herself with Him? "Can a woman forget her infant?" (Is. xlix. 15.) Justly could the Psalmist say, speaking in Her person, "My life is wasted with grief, and my years in sighs" (Ps. xxx. 11). In this, then, She is a great example to Priests. Well did that Priest imitate Her who spoke of "having a desire to be dissolved, and to be with Christ" (Phil. i. 23)—and who regarded it as an affliction that the time of his pilgrimage was prolonged: "Unhappy man that I am, who shall deliver me from the body of this death?" (Rom. vii. 24.) When this happy disposition is found in the Priest's heart, with what fervour will he celebrate Mass, recite his Office, and perform the other duties of his ministry!

2. "*With great joy.*" Great was the conflict between sorrow and joy in Mary's heart. It was like that which She experienced in the hour of Her Divine delivery, when, as St. Augustin remarks, She was typified by Sarah, who at the birth of Isaac rejoiced in her pain. Who, indeed, had so much reason to rejoice as Mary, when She beheld Jesus, at the head of heavenly hosts, entering into the Heavens, that He might sit at the Right Hand of the Father? The Apostles might rejoice that the flesh of Jesus, Who had vouchsafed to call them brethren, ascended to so great glory; and they might justly say, " for He is our brother, and our flesh " (Gen. xxxvii. 27); but the Blessed Virgin, in a stricter and more exact sense, could regard as her own the glorified Flesh of Her true and natural Son. Of Her joy, therefore (says St. Cyprian), no one can describe the intensity: it surpasses human thought. She, above all others, could comprehend the glorious mystery of the Ascension. Let us rejoice with Her in her exceeding joy, and let us endeavour to imitate Her during the course of this solemnity. Let us call to mind that we also have God for our Father, Christ for our Brother; and, as this was a source of joy for the first Priests, so likewise let it tend to the increase of our joy. Let us ever look up to Jesus at the Right Hand of the Father, inviting us to take our part in His Kingdom, and, if we are eager for glory, let us hasten to follow Him thither. How great are the opportunities which the Priest

enjoys for the attainment of this glory! Let us ascend after our Lord, in compunction, in good-will, in concord, in charity.

3. *And they went back into Jerusalem.* Neither grief nor joy kept Mary back from executing Her Son's commands. He had said, "Stay you in the city" (St. Luke xxiv. 49); and She returned to Jerusalem with the disciples, who, as St. Bernard says, were at once sorrowful and rejoicing, frightened and astonished, at the spectacle which they had beheld. They looked upon themselves as orphans, and as infants deprived of the shelter and protection of their nursing-mother. It was Mary's office, however, to be the Mother of this blessed company, and, as She abounds in all grace, She encouraged and illuminated the Apostles themselves; so that She has been rightly called the "Apostle of the Apostles." It was the will of Jesus (says St. Antoninus) that after His Ascension She should remain upon earth, in order to be the teacher and enlightener of the Apostles. Let us then pray to Her to enlighten us also, for we are far more destitute of light than the Apostles were; let us pray to Her to obtain for us obedience to God's commands, and resignation to His will; let us pray to Her to obtain for us that we may live upon earth in the faithful and exact fulfilment of all the duties of our ministry.

"Rejoice, Queen of Heaven, because thy Son is exalted exceedingly above all gods." —From *Ps.* xcvi. 9.

"O Mother in Israel, leave us not orphans." From *Judges* v. 7; *St. John* xiv. 18.

SUNDAY WITHIN THE OCTAVE OF THE ASCENSION.

THE GRATITUDE OF PRIESTS TO THE HOLY SPIRIT.

I. It is justly due.

II. It is readily shewn.

III. It is fruitful in results.

" When the Paraclete cometh."—*St. John* xvi. 26.

1. The Holy Ghost, the Paraclete, came to us when we were baptised "in the Holy Ghost and fire" (St. Matt. iii. 2). Then, for the first time, "God sent the Spirit of His Son into our hearts, crying, Abba, Father" (Gal. iv. 6). Then He favoured us above many infidels: afterwards, in Confirmation, He favoured us above many Christians, who neither "tasted the heavenly gift" nor "were made partakers of the Holy Ghost" (Heb. vi. 4). For the hands of the Bishop were imposed on us, and "the Holy Ghost came upon us" (Acts xix. 6). Not content with this, in our Diaconate and in our Priesthood He "anointed us . . . and sealed us "(2 Cor. i. 21, 22). Let us consider the honour which He has conferred upon us, the predilection which He has shewn us, the reward which He has prepared for us. The Holy Spirit (says St. Chrysostom) is the origin of all the multitudes of Priests—of all the array of Doctors—of all those glorious ranks which adorn the Church of God: all are His gift. Moreover, He has consigned to our hands the Letter which He

Himself has written, that is to say, the Holy Scripture: for "the holy men of God spoke, inspired by the Holy Ghost" (2 Pet. i. 21). He has given us this Book, called "the Book of the Priest," in order that we might, in reading it, be kindled with His light and fire. Again, who can tell the many visits He has made us in the other Sacraments—what light He has given us—with what aids, with what means of salvation, He has enriched us? Of the things which concern our salvation, what is there (asks St. Chrysostom) which is not dispensed to us by the Spirit? Let us recall with gratitude the inspiration received from Him for our vocation—the right intention, the firmness, the help which He has given us in order to arrive at the Priesthood. Let us reflect on the light which He gave to us—to our superiors—to our Bishop—for the removal of all impediments: for "the Spirit . . . . worketh all in all" (1 Cor. xii. 6). Who would not be moved by such considerations? Who would not be grateful to such a Benefactor? Ingratitude in us would be indeed a special sin, meriting the withdrawal of these benefits.

2. If the Paraclete has come to us, and has heaped so many gifts upon us, we can profit by the means which He Himself gives us to shew our gratitude. In the first place, let us teach the Faithful to know, love, and honour the Father and the Son from whom He proceeds, and of whom He is the Love an the Bond; so shall we please Him and imitate those blessed disciples who, so soon as they had received Him, spoke "the wonderful works of God" (Acts ii. 11). Let us relate to the Faithful how this sevenfold Spirit formed the Body of Jesus in the womb of the Blessed Virgin, and anointed Her holy soul before all others which have partaken of the same Spirit (Acts x. 38). Let us tell them how "the Spirit of God descended as a dove" upon the Incarnate Son (St. Matt. iii. 16),—how "by the Holy Ghost" the immaculate Victim was offered for the expiation of our sins (Heb. ix. 14). Lastly, let us diligently instruct the Faithful as to the properties of this third Divine Person, Who is neither honoured, nor loved, nor known by the world. This will be a good proof that we have received Him, and that we desire to shew Him our gratitude. The Holy Spir··

(says St. Gregory) sat upon the first Pastors in the form of tongues, because He caused those whom He filled to speak of Himself. Above all, let us be enkindled with His fire, let us be inflamed with holy love, let us aspire to the heavenly country; for the Holy Spirit will remove from us all our torpor and coldness and negligence, and cause us to burn with the fire of Divine love. Let us at the same time strive earnestly to subdue all sin within us, especially all sins against the Holy Spirit. Lastly, let us diligently prepare the Faithful for the Holy Sacraments; for in them, and especially in Confirmation He pours Himself upon them. How happy is the Minister of the Sanctuary who adopts every means of showing himself grateful for the benefits received from the Holy Spirit! Are we of this number?

3. *The Holy Ghost, the Paraclete,* comes into our hearts willingly, because He is benevolent (Wisd. i. 6). All that we do for Him, all the gratitude that we shew Him, will not be without magnificent recompense. He will "help our weakness." With His infinite goodness He will plead for us. If we are in sin, He will convince us of it. If we are the slaves of some passion, He will set us free; for "where the Spirit of the Lord is, there is liberty" (2 Cor. iii. 17). So St. Thomas of Villanova. He is as a bright lamp, given to us (says St. Chrysostom) to guide our steps in the darkness of this world. And these are the five signs by which His presence within us may be discovered (as Cardinal Hugo says), viz., (1) He makes penance appear sweet to us; (2) He makes us abhor all that is displeasing to Him; (3) He kindles in us vehement sorrow for the sins of others; (4) He causes us to grieve for the injuries done to good men, and (5) for the little good which we ourselves can do for God. Who will not desire to gain these blessings from this Divine Person? Who will not show gratitude for all such benefits, and dispose himself for the reception of still greater gifts?

"I will cry to God the Most High, to God Who hath done good to me."— *Ps.* lvi. 3.

"From above He hath sent fire into my bones, and hath chastised me."— *Lam.* i. 13.

MONDAY.

———◆———

*THE CLERGY HAVE ESPECIAL NEED OF THE
PARACLETE.*

I. As an Advocate.
II. As a Counsellor.
III. As a Comforter.

———◆———

" When the Paraclete cometh."—*St. John* xvi, 26.

1. The word "Paraclete" signifies, in the first place,"Advocate."
The Holy Ghost bears this title because He bestows on devout
souls the grace of prayer, and so causes them to obtain for us
the blessings of which we stand in need. Moreover, inasmuch
as the Third Person in the Trinity is the Goodness of God,
and it is through the Divine Goodness that we receive graces
from God, He is thus the interpreter of our desires, and the
principle from which we derive all heavenly benefits. Thus He
is said to intercede for us with the Father. He is called the
"Advocate" (says St. Gregory) because He mediates between
sinners and the Justice of the Father. St. Bernard thus expresses
this doctrine. The Holy Spirit (he says) "intercedes for the
Saints with unspeakable groaning " (Rom. viii. 26), and He does
this in our own heart. As He thus intercedes for us within our
own heart, so, being in the Father, He forgives our sins together
with the Father. So far as He is in us, He is our Advocate: as He
is in the Father, He is also our Lord and God. Now, Priests
above all men have need of the Paraclete in this sense, for they

have special cause for pleading for indulgence. That which is a venial sin in the laity often becomes a grave matter in the case of Priests (as St. Peter of Blois says). They have need of Him, also, in order that He may inspire others to pray for them; for they especially require the prayer of the Faithful to enable them to fulfil their important duties worthily. Thus, the Apostle wrote, " I beseech you that you help me in your prayers for me to God " (Rom. xv. 30);—" you helping withal in prayer for us" (2 Cor. i. 11). They have need of Him in order to become men of prayer, masters of prayer, and advocates with God for the people, so that (according to Innocent III.) the Priests may be better able to stand between God and man. Meditating on these things, shall we not pray for fresh visitations of the Paraclete, and implore His special favour?

2. The word Paraclete signifies also "Exhorter," it being His office to exhort us to do good. He has been called the Minister and Teacher in the struggles of virtue. Now, the Clergy have especial need of the exhortations of the Holy Spirit in order to produce His fruits, so that they may live, not after the flesh, but after the Spirit, and may become an example to the laity. Those, assuredly, whom He fills are made to be fervent in the Spirit, and to know the truth (says St. Bernard). The Priest must make himself all things to all men; and this, which is impossible to natural strength, becomes possible—nay, easy—by the grace of this Spirit (adds the same Father). The Priest must be able to "exhort in sound doctrine " (Titus i. 9). " These things speak and exhort" (ii. 15); and, as he cannot be exhorted by the laity, he must seek the direct exhortations of the Holy Spirit: " by the exhortations wherewith we also are exhorted by God " (2 Cor. i. 4). Shall we not, then, prepare ourselves to receive so beneficent a guest in this His own solemnity?

3. The third meaning of the word Paraclete is "Comforter;" and such He truly is, for (St. Gregory says) He comforts sorrowful sinners with the hope of pardon. He is God, and therefore He is able to console fully the heart of His creatures; He is "the pledge of our inheritance " (Eph. i. 14); He is " the Spirit of adoption of the sons of God " (Rom. viii. 15); and therefore we

have especial need of His visits, in order that we may be able to say, with the Prophet, before the people, " The Spirit of the Lord is upon me . . . to comfort all that mourn " (Is. lxi. 1, 2). As Moses, when he was destined to free the people from slavery, was filled with the Spirit of God, so, when a Priest is called to free many sinners from the chains of the Devil, Almighty God fills him with this same Spirit, to enable Him to succeed. The Spirit consoles him, in order that he may be able to console others by invoking on them the same Holy Spirit, Whose " fruits are joy, peace " (Gal. v. 22). Again, it is the Priest's office to console the just in their tribulations, for "many are the afflictions of the just " (Ps. xxxiii. 20); and therefore we ourselves have need first to be consoled by that Spirit, " Who comforteth us in all our tribulation, that we also may be able to comfort them who are in all distress " (2 Cor. i. 4). Therefore, let us invoke His presence, opening with ardent desire the mouth of our heart; and let us look for His blessed visit, that He may render us worthy Ministers of the New Testament.

" I opened my mouth, and panted for the Spirit."—*Ps.* cxviii. 131.
" Arise, O north wind, and come, O south wind, blow through my garden."—*Cant.* iv. 16.

TUESDAY.

THE SOURCE FROM WHENCE TO SEEK THE PRESENCE OT THE HOLY SPIRIT.

I. FROM THE SPIRIT HIMSELF, WHO COMES TO US.
II. FROM THE SON, WHO SENDS HIM TO US.
III. FROM THE FATHER, WHO GIVES HIM TO US.

"When the Paraclete cometh, whom I will send you from the Father, the Spirit of truth, Who proceedeth from the Father, He shall give testimony of Me."—*St. John* xv. 26.

1. *When the Paraclete cometh.* In speaking thus, Jesus Christ desired to express the sweetness of the Holy Spirit, calling Him the consoler of the Church; for we know that the Church was "filled with the consolation of the Holy Ghost" (Acts. ix. 31). He desired also to point out the freedom of this third Person of the Trinity by saying "When He cometh;" for, if He comes of Himself, He comes freely and of His own authority, says St. Thomas. "I called," said Solomon, "and the Spirit of wisdom came upon me" (Wisd. vii. 7); and our Saviour Himself said to Nicodemus, "The Spirit breatheth when He will" (St. John iii. 8). Therefore, let us pray to Him that He would vouchsafe to visit us, regarding, not our merits, but that goodness which He is of Himself, and which of its own nature is diffusive. Let us say to Him, *Mentes tuorum visita;* for we are His, not only as creatures and as Christians, but also as Priests. Let us say to Him, *Imple uperná gratiá quæ Tu creásti pectora;* for it is He Who make us

Priests, anointing and consecrating us in our holy Ordination. He sat upon the head of the first Priests, in order (says Theophylact) to represent their Ordination, which is now effected by the imposition of hands upon the head. This too (says St. Bernard) was a sign of the superiority of the Priesthood over the Christian people. He has made us to be as streams which fertilise the field of the Church: as it is said, "Out of his belly shall flow rivers of living water" (St. John vii. 38), and, again, "the floods have lifted up their voice" (Ps. xcii. 3); for St. Augustin explains both these passages as signifying the voice of Priests. But how shall we have this everliving water—how shall we dispense it to the people—if it come not to us from Him who is the Fount of life? Therefore, let us say to Him with St. Augustin, "Come, Thou sole grace of all the living, Thou only hope of all the dying."

2. *Whom I will send you.* Our Lord here brings forward Himself as sending (says St. Thomas), and adds, "the Spirit of truth," in order to show that the Holy Spirit pertains to the Son; for He is "the Truth." He thus shows the procession of the Paraclete from the Son (St. Thomas continues), as He derives from Him from Whom He proceeds the property of sanctifying the rational creature in which He dwells. Let, us therefore, instructed as we have been in this great doctrine—knowing also how strenuously the Church has maintained it in vindication of the honour of her Divine Spouse, that He might not be robbed of His prerogative of breathing forth the Holy Spirit—let us, during these solemn days of preparation for the Feast of Pentecost, recall to our minds this all-important truth; let us renew our acts of faith in the doctrine, in order to honour our Great High Priest, the immaculate Lamb, from Whose throne proceeds the river of life—that is, the Holy Spirit, Whom we are now expecting (Apoc. xxii. 1). Jesus Christ prayed to the Father that He would "sanctify us in the truth" (St. John xvii. 17); and how can we be truly holy without the "Spirit of truth and of sanctification" (Rom. i. 4)? According to the purpose of our Divine Master, we should be "the light of the world" (St. Matt. v. 14); and how can this be if we be not kindled by this heavenly fire? Jesus

Christ would have us preach the truth publicly (St. Matt. x. 27), and how can we do this without tongues—that is to say, without that Spirit Who appeared in the form of tongues? Therefore, in our thanksgiving after Holy Mass, let us pray to our Lord Jesus Christ to send us this Spirit, Who proceeds from Him, and let us frequently and fervently repeat this prayer.

3. *From the Father.* St. Thomas says, that our Lord Jesus Christ, in order to point out to us that the Holy Spirit is sent with equal power, and with the same power, by the Father and by Himself, refers at one time to the Father as sending Him, yet not without the Son—at another time to Himself as sending Him, yet not without the Father. Therefore let us turn to the Eternal Father, and implore Him to send us His Spirit, this being the only gift which can be put in comparison with the infinite merits of His Son, through which we ask it. He desires to multiply His family by increasing the number of His adopted children ; therefore let Him send us the " Spirit of His Son (Gal. iv. 6), the Spirit of the " First-born amongst many brethren" (Rom. viii. 29). He would have His Priests to be as fruitful mothers—" none of them barren" (Cant. iv. 2). May He, therefore, send down upon us that Dove which descended upon our First-born Brother ; so that, as the dove is the symbol of fruitfulness, we may become fruitful, and cause others to participate in the gifts of His Spirit. He would have us to be "faithful ministers" of His Son, and such we shall never be unless "that which is His Spirit resteth upon us" (1 Pet. iv. 14). Let us ask of Him the good Spirit, confiding in His Son's most sacred promise, "Your Father from Heaven will give the good Spirit to them that ask Him" (St. Luke xi. 13).

" Thy good Spirit shall lead me into the right land."—*Ps.* cxlii. 10.

" O, how good and sweet is Thy Spirit, O Lord, in all things."—*Wisdom* xii. 1.

WEDNESDAY.

THE HOLY SPIRIT GIVETH TESTIMONY TO THE CLERGY. `

I. HE GIVES US HIS TESTIMONY.
II. HE CAUSES US TO GIVE TESTIMONY.
III. HE ENABLES US TO FORM PUPILS CAPABLE OF GIVING TESTIMONY.

"He shall give testimony of Me, and you shall give testimony, because you are with Me from the beginning."—*St. John* xv. 26, 27.

1. *He shall give testimony of Me.* By these words (says St. Thomas) our Saviour explains the operation of the Spirit; and, in truth, the Holy Spirit gave His testimony to the Apostles by instructing them and supplying them with courage to preach the truth. Nay, He accompanied their preaching with signs and wonders—"bearing them witness by signs and wonders, and divers miracles, and distributions of His grace" (Heb. ii. 4). The Church no longer possesses this public open testimony; but the Clergy still proclaim that faith which is at once the virtue and the gift of the Holy Spirit, and the effect of their preaching is sustained by His testimony. St. Augustin therefore explains these words of our Lord thus: "The Paraclete giveth testimony of Me by causing those to believe in Me who see Me not." Further, this Spirit renders us at peace in regard to our Vocation, our Ordination, our Mission; for He has given us sufficient assurance of the legitimacy of the first, of the validity of the second, of the regularity of the third; and

these three things stimulate us to "war in them a good warfare" (1 Tim. i. 18). He has furnished us with strong weapons for this warfare; and those are (says St. Chrysostom) sobriety, temperance, and perpetual watchfulness. Lastly, He gives us—not, indeed, full certainty of being in a state of grace, as Protestants pretend—but a conjectural certainty, which ought to make us run with fervour in the way of God's commandments; and that is impossible (says St. Bernard) "for him who is oppressed with the weight of sin. Let us thank the Divine Spirit for so many favours, and let us pray to Him to enable us to walk in the ways of the Lord in a manner worthy of such gifts.

2. *And you shall give testimony of Me.* Our Saviour had commanded the Apostles to become His witnesses (Acts. i. 8), and they, filled with the Holy Spirit, proclaimed with loud voice, "We are witnesses of these things, and the Holy Ghost, Whom God hath given to all that obey Him" (Acts v. 32). It was, then, the Holy Spirit Who gave them words and power and success in the testimony which they rendered to Christ. On us also does He freely bestow His gifts, which will cause us never to be ashamed of the testimony of Jesus; for to each one of us also is it said, "Be not thou ashamed of the testimony of our Lord . . . . but labour with the gospel according to the power of God" (2 Tim. i. 8). Let us, then, give this testimony by our words, by our example, by our labours. Our words will be most "faithful and true" (Apoc. xxi. 5) if they come from the Spirit of Truth; they will be "words of salvation" (Acts xiii. 26) if they are pronounced in "shewing of the Spirit and power" (1 Cor. ii. 4). He will give testimony by inspiring us (says St. Augustin), and we shall give testimony by our words. Our example will confirm this testimony, if it spring not from the flesh but from the Spirit, and if it be the fruit of the Spirit; for "that which is born of the flesh is flesh, and that which is born of the Spirit is spirit." Our labours will not overpower us if only we are strengthened by the grace of His Spirit: "Thou, therefore, my son, be strong in grace" (2 Tim. ii. 1). "Be ye filled with the Holy Spirit" (Eph. v. 18). For "no man can say" even the Name of "the Lord Jesus, but by the Holy Ghost" (1 Cor. xii. 3). Let

us, then, have confidence in the goodness of God, Who will vouch-safe to aid our weakness.

3. *Because you are with Me from the beginning.* We have been allowed to be for a long time with Jesus, and this renders us fit to be His witnesses ; but our words will not gain fresh witnesses for Jesus unless (according to St. Thomas) the Spirit softens the heart of our hearers, "A new creature" (2 Cor. v. 17) has to be formed in them, and this is the work of the Holy Spirit : "Thou shalt send forth Thy Spirit, and they shall be created" (Ps. ciii. 30). The dead must be raised again ; and who can do this "but the Spirit that quickeneth?" (St. John vi. 64.) Do we desire to form disciples who shall one day take our place—nay, who may surpass us in giving testimony of Jesus to the Faithful ? We must say to them, as Ananias said to Saul : " The Lord Jesus hath sent me . . . . that thou mayst receive thy sight, and be filled with the Holy Ghost" (Acts ix. 17); and they must say to us " I beseech thee that in me may be thy double spirit" (2 Kings ii. 9). What a precious inheritance shall we then leave them (says St. Ambrose) ! Let us pray to this Spirit to fill the souls who are under our charge, and especially our pupils who are destined for the Priesthood.

"O Jesus, Who hast ascended on high . . give gifts to men."—From *Ps.* lxvii. 19.
"The Spirit of God made me, and the breath of the Almighty gave me life."—*Job* xxxiii. 4.

THURSDAY.

SPECIAL OPERATIONS OF THE HOLY SPIRIT IN THE PRIEST'S SOUL.

 I. He preserves it from scandals.
 II. He causes it to abhor blasphemy against Himself.
 III. He shews it the cause of so great an evil.

"These things have I spoken to you that you may not be scandalized. They will put you out of the synagogues ; yea, the hour cometh that whosoever killeth you will think that he doeth a service to God. And these things will they do to you, because they have not known the Father, nor Me."—*St. John* xvi. 1-3.

1. *That you may not be scandalized.* After the promise of the Holy Spirit, Christ added a prediction of future persecutions ; but assured His disciples that, through the charity shed abroad in their hearts by the Holy Spirit, they would be kept in peace, so that (as St. Augustin observes) the words of the Psalm would thus be verified, "Much peace have they that love Thy law, O Lord, and to them there is no stumblingblock" (Ps. cxviii. 165). To us also, in our sacred Ordination, was the Holy Spirit given, in order that we might become men of God—nay, perfect men of God : "that the man of God may be perfect" (2 Tim. iii. 17). Let us, therefore, as having attained to this perfection, avoid the corruptions of the world. Priests must of necessity find hemselves surrounded by the scandals of the world in which they live for—"the whole world is seated in wickedness"—and therefore they are required to surpass the laity in perfection, so as not to be drawn away by these scandals. Those (says St. Thomas)

who are advanced in perfection adhere to God alone, and they
are not affected by any scandals. The examples of others, whom
they see walking disorderly, in word or deed, do not cause them
to swerve from their own rectitude. And if it be not so with us—
if our feet are easily removed from the right path—if our steps
wander from it—let us attribute this great evil to our own imperfection, to our neglect of prayer and watchfulness, and to our
failure in corresponding to the light of the Holy Spirit. Let us
weep with the Prophet, repeating this lamentation—" My feet
were almost moved, my steps had wellnigh slipt " (Ps. lxxii. 2).

2. *They will put you out of the Synagogues.* Our Lord has assured
us that sin or blasphemy against the Holy Ghost " shall not be
forgiven " (St. Matt. xii. 32); that is to say, it will be forgiven
with the utmost difficulty. This blasphemy, according to St.
Augustin (whose opinions on the subject have been collected
by St. Thomas), may be committed either in word or deed ; and
it consists in contending against known truth, envy of the
graces received by others, obstinacy in sin, and final impeni-
tence. In the case of many who are guilty of this sin (says St.
Augustin), the very sin itself hinders the humiliation necessary
for obtaining pardon. The Priest will feel his heart stirred both
with horror and compassion in all such cases ; he will not cease
to implore the mercy of God, which sometimes, through the
prayers of the Saints, is moved to work (as by a miracle) the
conversion of such a miserable sinner and to remit so grave a
sin. At the same time he will fear for himself, knowing that he
is but a man and may himself fall into the same sin. For, though
such cases be rare, still they are possible through the malice of
the Evil one ; and the history of the Church is not without instances of Priests who, like Judas, after having begun well, ended
with a most miserable death. Let us pray to the Holy Spirit
that He abandon us not, either in life or in death.

3. *Because they have not known the Father nor Me.* Behold the
fatal cause of the persecutions of the Apostles, and of other
Ecclesiastics ! behold the source of the damnation of innumerable
souls—viz., ignorance, wilful and deliberate ! " Because no one
understandeth, they shall perish for ever " (Job. iv. 20). If G

people are, in great part, slaves of the devil, it is from want of knowledge: "Therefore is My people led away captive, because they had not knowledge" (Is. v. 13). "Where there is no knowledge of the soul there is no good" (Prov. xix. 2). And we must acknowledge with grief that this ignorance, which is the mother of all vices, springs from the carelessness of Priests, because they neglect to preach the Word of God, which is "living and effectual" (Heb. iv. 12). Justly, therefore, does St. Gregory declare against such Priests as render themselves guilty of the ruin of innumerable souls, who are thus lost for want of instruction. We who are called Priests, he says, are guilty of murdering men's souls, for we are the cause of the death of all those whom by our tepidity and silence we allow to go to destruction. Let us remember what the devil one day said to a French Priest, who was preparing to make a speech at the opening of a synod: "The Rulers of the infernal darkness salute the Rectors of Parish Churches, and thank them for their negligence in teaching the people; because sin is born of ignorance, and damnation is born of sin." Let us implore the Holy Spirit to bestow on us a little of that light and zeal which he gave to St. Paul, so that we may be able to say with him, "I am clear from the blood of all men, for I have not spared to declare unto you all the counsel of God" (Acts xx. 26, 27).

"By the Word of the Lord the heavens were established, and all the power of them by the Spirit of His mouth."—*Ps.* xxxii. 6.

"I will pour out My Spirit upon thy seed, and My blessing upon thy stock." *Is* xliv. 3.

FRIDAY.

THE HOLY SPIRIT THE SPIRIT OF ECCLESIASTICS.

I. He is the Spirit of the Eternal Priest.
II. He is the Spirit of the Priesthood.
III. He is the Spirit of Priestly functions.

"These things have I told you that, when the hour shall come, you may remember that I told you of them."—*St. John* xvi. 4.

1. *These things have I told you.* Our Lord Jesus Christ had spoken of the Holy Ghost, of His operations, and especially of the strength which He would communicate to the Disciples in persecutions. He had also taught them that this Spirit is His Spirit, and is rightly called "the Spirit of Christ" (1 Pet. i. 11), as proceeding from Him. Moreover, according to the doctrine of "circuminsession," the Holy Spirit is in Christ as Christ is in the Holy Spirit, so that he who sees Christ sees the Holy Spirit ; as is also true in respect of the Father, according to our Lord's words, "He that seeth Me seeth the Father also . . . for I am in the Father, and the Father in Me" (St. John xiv. 9, 10). Lastly, all the fulness of the Divinity dwells in Christ, and therefore is the Holy Spirit the Spirit of Christ, for "in Him dwelleth all the fulness of the Godhead corporally" (Col. ii. 9). St. Thomas observes, with reference to this passage, that, as the body has three dimensions, so in three ways does the Divinity dwell in Christ's Body—viz., first, by "essence, presence, and power," as in other creatures ; secondly, *per gratiam gratum facientem*, as in the Saints ; thirdly, and after a peculiar manner, by the hypo-

static union, which is proper only to Christ. Hence our Saviour justly applied to Himself the words of the prophet Isaias, "The Spirit of the Lord is upon Me" (St. Luke iv. 18); and He had just cause to exult in the fulness of the Holy Spirit. "He rejoiced in the Holy Ghost" (St. Luke x. 21). Let us, then, continually look up to this our Great High Priest, and let us pray to Him that "of His fulness we may all receive" the Spirit (St. John i. 16). Without this Spirit we can neither know, nor love, nor follow, nor enjoy the High Priest "of the good things to come" (Heb. ix. 11).

2. *You may remember them.* St. Augustin says that our Saviour desired that the Apostles should remember the assistance of the Holy Spirit in their persecutions ; and therefore He promised it to them in order that they might not be troubled. In like manner does He desire that Priests should remember the Holy Spirit amidst the labours of their Ministry, and that they should look upon Him as the Spirit of their Priesthood. For, if they have to judge men's consciences, they must be spiritual men ; for "the sensual man perceives not the things which are of the Spirit of God . . . . but the spiritual man judgeth all things" (1 Cor. ii. 14, 15). They must be spiritual, in order to instruct the ignorant: "You, who are spiritual, instruct such a one" (Gal. vi. 1). But how can they be spiritual men without the Spirit of God? Moreover, they are Heads of the people— "great men, heads of the people" (Amos. vi. 1) ; and (says St. Thomas) the spirit and the senses are most vigorous in the head. Hence we, by right of our Priesthood, have been united in a new and special manner to Christ, the Supreme Head of the Church, in order that, through this union with Him, we may have one sole Spirit with Him ; for "he who is joined to the Lord is one spirit" (1 Cor. vi. 17). Woe, then, to the Priest who has not the Spirit of Christ ! Let him remember that tremendous sentence, "If any have not the Spirit of Christ, he is none of His" (Rom. viii. 9). Such a Priest is a corpse, a dead member, and not (as he ought to be) a member fair and sound, and adhering to the Body ; living to God through God (as St. Augustin says).

3. *That I told you.* Let us remember what our Lord Jesus Christ has said in regard to Priestly functions. He would have us exercise them, not in the spirit of this world, but in the Spirit of God : "we have received not the spirit of this world, but the Spirit that is of God, that we may know the things that are given us from God" (1 Cor. ii. 12). Now, we exercise these functions in the spirit of this world if some worldly end per vert us from the right intention. Priests who labour in the spirit of vanity, pride, ambition, interest, or caprice, are not of the number of those who are " led by the Spirit of God" (Rom. viii. 14). Our ministration is called "the ministration of the Spirit" (2 Cor. iii. 8). We are the ministers of grace, which is communicated by the Holy Spirit: "this grace which is administered by us " (2 Cor. viii. 19). Let us, then, cast away from our heart all those hidden worldly motives which are so great a reproach to us, and let us strive to administer the heavenly treasures from the sole motive of charity. " We have this ministration, according as we have obtained mercy, we faint not, but we renounce the hidden things of dishonesty" (2 Cor. iv. 1, 2). Thus we shall, indeed, work by the Spirit ; for He is Charity, and through Him charity is diffused in our hearts : "The charity of God is poured forth in our hearts by the Holy Ghost, Who is given to us" (Rom. v. 5).

"Create a clean heart in me, O God ; and renew a right spirit within my bowels."—*Ps.* l. 12.

"The Spirit shall be poured upon us from on high, and the desert shall be as a Charmel."—*Is.* xxxii. 15.

WHITSUN EVE.

MARY OBTAINED FOR THE FIRST PRIESTS GRACE TO PREPARE FOR THE COMING OF THE HOLY SPIRIT.

I. BY HUMBLE PRAYER.

II. BY UNITED PRAYER.

III. BY PERSEVERING PRAYER.

"All these were persevering with one mind in prayer, with the women, and Mary, the Mother of Jesus.—*Acts* i. 14.

1. *In prayer with Mary.* St. Bernard is amazed that, in the company of the Apostles, Mary is named last by St. Luke, and takes the last place; and the reason he gives for it is, Her profound humility. The higher She was, he says, the more did She humble Herself, not only in all respects, but before all. Her joy at the coming of the Holy Spirit was even more intense than that of all the Apostles, and She received His gifts and His graces *gratis data* in greater abundance than they all: so that (as St. John Damascene says) all Her words issued forth from a treasure of wisdom, and were dictated by the Holy Spirit. These gifts were especially necessary for Her after our Lord's Ascension, because then (according to Suarez) She became, as it were, the oracle of all the Faithful who resorted to Her for counsel, as appears from the writings of St. Ignatius, and of other early Fathers. "Who can tell how much was effected by Her prayers, offered as they were with such great humility?" "The prayer of him that humbleth himself shall pierce the clouds,

and will not depart till the Most High behold." (Eccl. xxxv. 21). She prayed, not for Herself alone, but for the new-born Church, whose Mother She was. She prayed (as Albertus Magnus says) for Her children, for whom She solicited both human and divine goods. Through Her merits and Her prayers Almighty God poured forth the Holy Spirit in greater abundance in the Cænaculum; and, in like manner, as the Word descended from Heaven at Her humble consent, so did the Holy Spirit descend from Heaven at Her humble prayer; according to Her own words, "He hath regarded the humility of His handmaid" (St. Luke i. 48). The Disciples followed Her example, and humbly asked for the sevenfold Spirit; and their prayer was heard speedily. Let us also imitate Her in the approaching Feast of the Holy Ghost; for (says St. Thomas of Villanova) She is the pattern for all ages.

2. *Of one mind.* Mary was the Mother of the living, says St. Epiphanius; She gathered about Her the Disciples, who were already living in grace, and who were shortly to receive new gifts of the vivifying Spirit; and She gathered them "as the hen doth gather her chickens under her wings" (St. Matt. xxiii. 37). She caused them to dwell in the Cænaculum with entire concord. She made them to be "men of one manner, dwelling in a house" (Ps. lxvii. 7.) Let us also prepare for the coming of the Holy Spirit by uniting with one another in prayer, and by calling upon the people to pray with us; for (says St. John Chrysostom) God has respect to the multitude who are of one mind and one heart in prayer. The best disposition for receiving this Divine Guest (says St. Bernardin of Sienna) is peace with our neighbour, union with our brethren, together with earnest prayer to God. The Holy Spirit descends on those who are of one mind (says St. Laurence Justinian), because He loves unity, peace, and concord. Let us seek peace with our neighbours, under Mary's auspices, and let us look to God to strengthen and confirm our concord.

3. *Persevering.* The Blessed Virgin ceases not to pray for us until Her Son sends us His Holy Spirit; for, says St. John Damascene, "She is our advocate with God, and Her impetration

procures for us this Gift above all other gifts. In the Cænacu-lum She prayed to Her Divine Spouse, Who had rendered Her fruitful without taking away her virginity, and with Whom her soul was perfectly united; and her sighs and prayers supplied all that was wanting in the prayers of the Disciples. As Diony-sius of Carthage says, the Apostles were filled with the Holy Spirit through the sighs and tears of Mary. They persevered with Her in prayer, and so pointed out to us that the Holy Spirit is given abundantly to such as pray with devotion and perseve-rance. Jesus Christ has promised the Holy Spirit to them that ask (St. Luke xi. 13), but He would have us ask with impor-tunity. He would have us take Heaven, as it were, by violence ; for this violence is grateful to God, says Tertullian. Therefore, let us not fear; let us ask through the merits and intercession of the Blessed Virgin, and God will not delay to hear us : " The Lord delayeth not His promise " (2 Pet. iii. 9).

" For Thee my soul hath thirsted, for Thee my flesh, O how many ways !"—*Ps.* lxii. 2.

" The voice of the bridegroom, and the voice of the bride, the voice of them that shall say, Give ye glory to the Lord of Hosts, for the Lord is good."—*Jer.* xxxlii. 2.

WHITSUN DAY.

THE HEART OF THE GOOD PRIEST PRECIOUS THROUGH THE OPERATION OF THE HOLY SPIRIT.

I. IT INSPIRES HIM WITH THE LOVE OF GOD.

II. IT RENDERS HIM ACCEPTABLE TO GOD.

III. IT PROCURES FOR HIM THE PRESENCE OF GOD.

"If any one love Me he will keep My word, and My Father will love him, and We will come to him, and will make Our abode with him."—*St. John* xiv. 23.

1. *If any one love Me.* To all Priests the Holy Spirit imparts those graces which are called *gratis datæ*, by which they are sup-. ported in discharging the functions of their ministry; but in good Priests He works after yet another manner—that is to say, He diffuses in their hearts the love of God. For (as St. Thomas says) we are made partakers of love, which is the Holy Spirit ; and by that participation in Him we are rendered lovers of God. He draws us near to God ; He raises our soul to God, and causes our heart to be where our treasure is ; He detaches us from all affection for earthly goods. Moreover, charity is poured forth by Him through the works of the Priest ; and this charity is the proof of His love, says St. Gregory. Doubtless (as St. Thomas says) the love of God is never idle : if it exists, it works great things : if it work them not, it is not love. And, if this be true of all good Christians, what will not the Holy Spirit work in the Priest's heart who burns with charity ? As he must be holy, must he not have charity for the guardian of his sanctity?—charity.

without which all virtues are nought (says St. Isidore.) The Holy Spirit is the substantial fire of Divine love, and ever nourishes that fire in the Priest's heart. During these days let us frequently make acts of love, for (as St. Alphonsus tells us) such acts are as the fuel which feeds the heavenly flame.

2. *And My Father will love him.* These words shew how exceeding precious in the sight of God is the man who loves Him and keeps His commandments. And who can tell how acceptable to God are those Ministers of the Sanctuary who honour Him and love Him, and who use all their efforts to make Him known and loved by others? God (says St. Ambrose) has skilful ministers for the performance of all His works; they are fishermen for Him; they are hunters, they are reapers, in His service. In proportion to the earnestness with which each devotes himself to promote the glory of God, so do they become acceptable in His eyes. As Moses, who also was "among the Priests of the Lord, beloved of God and men " (Eccl. xlv. 1), so is the Priest who, "in the goodness and readiness of his soul, appeaseth God " (v. 29), and who does that which is "good and acceptable in the sight of God our Saviour " (1 Tim. ii. 3). But how can we obtain the love of God but through the goodness of the Holy Spirit? Unless He prevent, accompany, and follow us, in all our actions, can they be pleasing to God? Well is it for us that He has loved us from all eternity! Let us love this good Spirit, Who is the source of all good things.

3. *We will come to Him.* The Father and the Son come to us, and dwell with us, if we have sanctifying grace. There was no need to mention the Holy Spirit; for He is the mutual Love of both, and, therefore, He comes to us together with the other Divine Persons (as St. Thomas shows). It is, then (as St. Augustin says), the Most Holy Trinity that comes into our heart, to aid us, to enlighten us, to fill us with Itself. What a great treasure is this, which we carry "in earthen vessels " (2 Cor. iv. 7)—that is, in our body, which is dust and will return to dust! The more diligently we seek for so great a good as is this presence of God in the soul, the sweeter shall we find it: the more frequently we find it, the more eagerly shall we seek for it (as St. Augustin says).

Let, then, the Priest reflect that the Blessed Trinity dwells in his heart, that in it the Father generates the Son, and that from the Father and the Son is breathed forth the Holy Spirit. If we would live according to this Spirit, let us remember St. Augustin's words—Keep charity, love unity. Let us meditate upon these truths, let us examine ourselves, and let this be our prayer—

" Confirm, O God, what Thou hast wrought in us."—*Ps.* lxvii. 29.
" May our fellowship be with the Father, and with His Son Jesus Christ."—*1 John* i. 3.

WHITSUN MONDAY.

THE OUTRAGE DONE TO THE HOLY SPIRIT BY A PRIEST WHO COMMITS SIN.

I. HE GRIEVES THE SPIRIT.
II. HE RESISTS THE SPIRIT.
III. HE PROFANES THE TEMPLE OF THE SPIRIT.

" He that loveth Me not, keepeth not My words, and the word which you hav heard is not Mine, but the Father's who sent Me. These things have I spoken to you, abiding with you."—*St. John* xiv. 24, 25.

1. *He that loveth Me not, keepeth not My words.* They who love not Jesus Christ through the operation of the Holy Spirit, and who transgress His law, grieve the Spirit; and therefore the Apostle said, " Grieve not the Holy Spirit of God, whereby you are sealed " (Eph. iv. 30). St. Bonaventure preached three Pentecostal Sermons on these words, and in the third he points out that the evil spirit impresses four seals on the sinner's soul, which grieve the Holy Spirit—viz., the seals of infidelity, of

carnality, of covetousness, and of deceit. Now, if it be so displeasing to the Holy Spirit to see the character which He has imprinted on every Christian soul defaced by such stains, what must be His grief and anger at beholding in the Ministers of the Sanctuary the Priestly character defiled by sin? " But they provoked to wrath, and afflicted the Spirit of the Holy One" (Is. lxiii. 10). Doubtless God is incapable of anger or of grief; but so great is the hatred which His infinite goodness has for sin, that no sooner is it committed, even in thought, than He departs from that soul in which He had dwelt by sanctifying grace. The Holy Spirit " will withdraw himself from thoughts that are without understanding, and He shall not abide when iniquity cometh in " (Wisdom i. 5). What will be the magnitude of this guilt in a Priest who has received from Him, not only the Priestly character, but so many other benefits—so many lights—so many means for conquering sin? Can it be that a Priest, in whom the Holy Spirit had placed His confidence, and whom He had destined to dispense His gifts to others, should thus offend Him? Such an one has given Him, as it were, a blow, and has driven Him from the soul which was once His own. "The man of My peace, in whom I trusted, hath greatly supplanted Me" (Ps. lx. 10).

2. *The word which you have heard is not Mine.* Jesus Christ is the Word of the Father, and therefore His words come to us from the Father, and he who resists these words resists the Father Himself. But it is by means of the Holy Spirit that such words penetrate our soul; and, therefore, he who despises them resists also the Holy Spirit: " You always resist the Holy Ghost " (Acts vii. 51). Now, this is precisely the crime of the wicked Priest. He reads the sacred Scriptures continually; he recites, chants, preaches the Divine word; nor can he exclude the voice of the Spirit from his heart, for " it is not in man's power to stop the Spirit " (Eccles. viii. 8). Yet he deadens his conscience against the reproof of that voice, disregarding the Apostle's warning, " Extinguish not the Spirit " (1 Thess. v. 19). The Spirit does, indeed, continually cry in his ears, warning him (as St. Lawrence Justinian says) that it is no slight crime

for the servants and ministers of God to be conquered by sin. His is no sin of frailty, which might find its excuse in the weakness of the flesh—no sin of ignorance, which might find its excuse in want of light; his is the sin of positive malice, and is without excuse; and, as by sins of frailty we offend the Power of the Father, and by sins of ignorance the Wisdom of the Word, so by sins of malice we offend the Goodness of the Holy Spirit. Let us weep bitterly for our sins, and let us pray to the same Spirit that we may avoid them in future; for (says St. Thomas) all which hinders the choice of sin is the effect of the Holy Spirit in us.

3. *Abiding with you.* When our Lord Jesus Christ abides with us, we are living members of His mystical Body, and then are our members "the temple of the Holy Ghost, Who is in us, Whom we have from God; and we are not our own" (1 Cor. vi. 19). This is especially true of Priests, who received the Holy Ghost in Ordination, and have consecrated their body to God by the vow of chastity; and, therefore, if they are guilty of the sin of lust, they do especial outrage to the Holy Spirit, and commit sacrilege, taking away (as Cornelius à Lapide says) the body which had been dedicated to Him, and transferring it to the demon of lasciviousness. They, indeed, sin "against their own body" (1 Cor. vi. 18); and who is ignorant of the manner in which God will punish those who profane His temple? "If any man violate the temple of God, him shall God destroy" (1 Cor. iii. 17). Let us weep over our sins in this, which is indeed no slight matter; for is it not a great crime to take away from the Holy Spirit His own temple, and give it to the spirit of fornication? Is it not violating the temple of God, asks St. Peter Damian, to introduce into it the spirit of licentiousness in place of His Spirit? Let us call to mind the words of the Apostle "Glorify and bear God in your body" (1 Cor. vi. 20).

"For Thy Name's sake, O Lord, Thou wilt pardon my sin, for it is great."—*Ps.* xxiv. 11.

"Give us a new heart, and a new spirit, O Lord."—From *Ezechiel* xviii. 31.

WHITSUN TUESDAY.

THE IMPORTANCE OF INVOKING THE HOLY SPIRIT BEFORE OUR PRIESTLY MINISTRATIONS.

I. To obtain His inspirations.

II. For a right guidance.

III. For the elevation of our thoughts to spiritual subjects.

"But the Paraclete, the Holy Ghost, Whom the Father will send in My Name, He will teach you all things, and bring all things to your mind, whatsoever I have said to you."—*St. John* xiv. 26.

1. *Whom the Father will send in My Name.* If we ask the Eternal Father for the Holy Spirit, in the Name—that is, through the merits—of His Son, we shall have the benefit of His holy inspirations ; for (says St. Thomas) He aids us by inspiring us inwardly. Hence the Church, in her most sublime functions, prescribes, in the first place, the solemn invocation of the Holy Spirit by the ministers of the Sanctuary, and so also in her various liturgical offices there are petitions for the light and inspirations of the Holy Spirit. And, truly, this Spirit is *one*, but *manifold* (Wisd. vii. 22) ; for, as the spirit of man is one, but performs diverse operations in different members of his body, so is the Holy Spirit *one*, but accomplishes His various purposes as it seems good to Him, through the different members of the Church, each member having his own special office. From His inspirations (says St. Leo) proceed good prayers, lively faith, knowledge, charity, chastity, and every other virtue ; and if we wish that our

words should move sinners to compunction we must implore
His inspirations. If only we invoked Him, with how great
fervour should we not recite our office, and celebrate holy mass!
If we had recourse to Him before entering the pulpit, or the
confessional, how many conversions should we not effect!

2. *He will teach you all things.* The Holy Spirit not only aids
us by His inspirations, but also by His direction; inasmuch (says
St. Thomas) as He supplies us from a hidden source with power
to know the truth. The direction of this Spirit is worthy of His
omnipotence and of His goodness; for (says St. Leo) where
God is the Master that which is taught is quickly learnt. Let us
call to mind the wonders which this Divine Spirit worked in
former generations, because they had confidence in Him, and invoked Him fervently. He filled David the shepherd-boy, and made
him the Psalmist; He filled the young man Daniel, and made
him judge of the elders; He filled Peter, the fisherman, and
made him a preacher; He filled Paul, the persecutor, and made
him the doctor of the Gentiles; He filled Matthew, the publican,
and made him an evangelist. Hence St. Gregory remarks, "He
teaches whom He touches. His very touch imparts instruction."
We do not indeed say, with the heretics, that we may trust each
to his own private judgment for the interpretation of Holy Scripture, and for deciding questions of faith; for they who utter such
profanity have the "spirit of error," and not the Spirit of truth.
On the contrary, we maintain that the Holy Spirit directs us
through the Church, and also by means of pious books and of
preaching; for (says St. Gregory) without Him we can neither
understand, believe, nor love supernatural truths. What high
grade of sanctity might not we have maintained had we duly profited by the directions with which He has so generously supplied
us! How ungrateful have we shown ourselves to His goodness!
What loss have we thus caused to our own souls!

3. *And bring all things to our mind.* The Holy Spirit aids us by
elevating us to spiritual things (says St. Thomas). He does this
when He impels us to do good works, and when He recalls to
memory the truths of faith. How useful is it to bring to mind
the things which concern our salvation! Sometimes the recol-

lection carries conversion in its train : " They shall remember, and shall be converted to the Lord " (Ps. xxi. 28). Sometimes it serves as a shield against the darts of the enemy ; it is as "the shield of faith, wherewith we may be able to extinguish the fiery darts of the most wicked one" (Eph. vi. 16). It is the special effect of the grace of the Holy Spirit (says St. Augustin) that we remember at the right moment any salutary counsels we may have received. Let us, therefore, invoke His assistance in all the works of our ministry, and let us be well assured that it is He Who admonishes, teaches, and moves (as St. Bernard says)— that is to say, He admonishes the memory; He teaches the intellect; He moves the will ; and He does this by suggestion, by instruction, and by influence.

"Cast me not away from Thy face, and take not Thy Holy Spirit from me."— *Ps.* l. 13.

"Send, O Father, the Holy Ghost, the Paraclete, in the Name of Thy Son."— From *St. John* xiv. 26.

WEDNESDAY.

CONTRAST BETWEEN THE PEACE PROMISED BY THE WORLD AND THE PEACE GIVEN BY CHRIST.

I. THE PEACE OF CHRIST.
II. THE PEACE OF THE WORLD.
III. THE PEACE WHICH THE WORLD EXPECTS OF THE CLERGY.

"Peace I leave with you, My peace I give you : not as the world giveth, do I give unto you."—*St. John* xiv. 27.

1. *Peace I leave with you.* Our Saviour, in promising the Holy Spirit, promised also that fruit of the Spirit which is Peace ; and, in order to teach us that the Holy Spirit proceeds from Himself, He says that He Himself bestows this peace, as though it were His own: "*My* peace I give you." This was, as it were, His dying bequest, left to His first Priests, and enjoyed by them immediately ; but it is also an inheritance reverting to all His Priests in successive ages. For it is their office to diffuse peace among the people, and to present to God the prayer of peace. By that peace (says St. Thomas) three of our faculties are regulated, viz., the intellect, the will, and the sensitive appetite ; for the intellect reposes in the eternal truths thus presented to it, the will is directed by the intellect, and the sensitive appetite is controlled by both. This present peace is, however, but an earnest of that which is to come. In the former we are enabled to conquer the world, in the latter we shall reign without an enemy. Our Lord left us (says St. Augustin) peace in this pre

sent world, in which we have to subdue our enemies ; and in the world to come, when we shall reign secure from all enemies, He will impart to us of His own peace.   The former peace renders the Priest tranquil in the midst of the most grievous persecution and temporal calamities ; as it is said : " We have peace with God, through our Lord Jesus Christ " (Rom. v. 1).   Priests may thus be true followers of the Apostles, to whom our Lord, when He foretold the enmities and conflicts which they should endure, promised at the same time the gift of peace.   When (says St. Chrysostom) their thoughts were troubled with the prospect of the hatred and strife awaiting them at His departure, He consoled them by saying, " Peace I leave you."   How great the consolation which those words suggest to the Priest who confides in the promise of the Eternal High Priest ! Let us beseech our Divine Lord to bestow on us this glorious heritage.

  2. *Not as the world giveth.*   The peace which the world gives is distinguished from this Divine peace in three respects (according to St. Thomas) ; viz., in its aim, in its false pretence, in its imperfection.   For the world's peace has regard to temporal goods and the tranquil enjoyment of them, although accompanied by the war of the passions and the supreme evils of ignorance and sin : " They lived in a great war of ignorance : they call so many and so great evils peace " (Wisdom xiv. 22). Again, this peace is also a false pretence ; for worldly men conceal the vexation of their heart, and even their hatred against those with whom they speak peaceably ; they "speak peace with their neighbour, but evils are within their heart."   Lastly, this peace of the world is most imperfect, inasmuch as it fails to tranquillise the heart, and it endures only for the short space of this life.   " There is no peace for all flesh " (Jerem. xii. 12).   Let us examine ourselves, then, on this point, and inquire whether the peace we possess be that of Christ or of the world.   It will be Christ's peace if our minds be directed to that heavenly country from whence God makes to flow the river of peace, according to the words of the prophet—" I will bring upon him, as it were, a river of peace " (Is. lxii. 12).   It will be the world's peace if the remembrance of death is bitter to us.   " O death, how bitter is

the remembrance of thee to a man who has peace in his possessions" (Eccles. xli. 1)! It will be Christ's peace if we are delighted with solitude, with meditation, with the duties of our ministry, and with the sanctification of souls. It will be the world's peace if we find our enjoyment in worldly society and frivolous amusements, and if we deceive our neighbours under a false pretence of friendship.

3. *Let not your heart be troubled.* The world cannot endure the zealous Priest, because it is he who disturbs its false peace, according to the Psalmist's words, "I had a zeal on occasion of the wicked, seing the peace of sinners" (Ps. lxii. 3). It is, however, the duty of a good Priest to show how the specious peace of worldlings leads to eternal ruin. It is the duty of a good Priest to disturb the false security of erroneous or hardened consciences, and to obey the summons, "Blow ye the trumpet in Sion, and sound an alarm in My holy mountain; let all the inhabitants of the earth tremble" (Joel ii. 1); and such a sound does not convey pleasure, but terror, to those who hear it (as St. Augustin observes). It is impossible, therefore, for the world to love us; and, though it may not openly persecute us, yet it can never have any real peace with us. For (as St. Augustin says again) there can be no true peace where there is no concord, and there can be no concord between us and the world if our heart be altogether severed from the world.

THURSDAY.

OF THE IMPOSITION OF HANDS..

I. THAT WHICH WE HAVE RECEIVED.
II. THAT WHICH WE HAVE TO PERFORM.
III. THAT WHICH WE HAVE TO PROCURE FOR OTHERS.

"You have heard that I said to you, I go away and I come unto you. If you loved Me, you would indeed be glad because I go to the Father; for the Father is greater than I. And now I have told you before it come to pass, that when it shall come to pass you may believe."—*St. John* xiv. 28, 29.

1. *I go to the Father.* Christ, when He went to His Father, to sit on the throne of His glory, left upon earth His Ministers, as representatives of His love; and they were made fit for the right fulfilment of their office by means of the imposition of hands. In Holy Scripture, in the definitions of Councils, and in the Fathers, Ordination is frequently called "the imposition of hands." This rite signifies that Priests are, as it were, victims consecrated to God and separated from the people (Exodus xxix. 10; Numbers viii. 14). It signifies further that the newly-ordained Minister is confided to the government, direction, and protection of the Holy Spirit. Finally, it signifies the fulness of grace and power which God bestows upon him. In conferring the Diaconate, the Bishop alone lays his hand on the head of the person ordained; in conferring the Priesthood, the Bishop is followed in the imposition of hands by the other Priests who are present; and in conferring the Episcopate, not only the consecrating Bishop, but the two other assisting Bishops, lay their hands on the Bishop conse-

crated, and invoke and impart the fulness of the Holy Spirit. Let us, then, call to mind this holy rite which has been performed over us ; let us call to mind its mysterious significance ; let us call to mind the Apostle's words : " Neglect not the grace that is in thee, which was given thee by prophecy, with imposition of the hands of the Priesthood " (1 Tim. iv. 14). If this grace is stifled in us through timidity, dissipation of mind, or torpor, let us remember the Apostolical admonition, " I admonish thee that thou stir up the grace of God, which is in thee by the imposition of my hands " (2 Tim. i. 6). Let us invoke the Holy Spirit, Who then came down upon us ; and pray Him to kindle afresh—to nourish and increase in us—the flame of charity, and to cause us to abound in all good works.

2. *You would indeed be glad.* Good reason have we to be glad when we consider that Jesus Christ, after having reconciled Heaven and earth, not only carried gifts from earth to Heaven— that is to say, His sacred humanity, and the souls He had freed from Limbo—in token of the peace which He had concluded, but also sent down from Heaven the Holy Spirit, and conferred upon us His gifts. And, in like manner, as He, when He was upon earth, laid His hands upon children to bless them (St. Matt. xix. 15), and upon the sick to heal them (St. Luke iv. 40), —so, when He was about to depart out of this world, He told His disciples that they should " lay their hands upon the sick, and they should recover " (St. Mark xvi. 18). Moreover, the Church, instructed by Christ's example, enjoins the imposition of hands in the administration of the Sacraments of Baptism, Penance, and Extreme Unction ; also in the reconciliation of heretics to the Church, and in the exorcism of those who are possessed by evil spirits ; and again in the sacred Liturgy, shortly before the consecration of the Bread and Wine. Woe to the Priest who, when summoned to lay his hands upon the Faithful in their spiritual necessities, fails to discharge this duty aright ! Woe to him who performs it negligently, or with evil disposition of heart !

3. *I have told you before it come to pass.* Our Lord Jesus Christ had desired the Apostles to wait for the Holy Spirit during the

forty days which preceded His Ascension, and He had Himself instructed them in regard to the imposition of hands in the Sacrament of Confirmation: "Speaking of the kingdom of God" (Acts i. 3). Accordingly, as soon as they had received the Holy Spirit, they were prepared to administer this great Sacrament (Acts viii. 17 ; xix. 16). It is for Priests in the present day to instruct the Faithful concerning this Sacrament—to make them understand that it is a mortal sin to neglect to receive it. If Priests did but thoroughly explain the rites of the Church, point out their excellence, declare their effects, and show their importance, we should not see, as we do, this Sacrament neglected by some, received with bad dispositions and from worldly motives by others—its grace quickly lost by many. Let us, then, endeavour to instruct children in it carefully : " Instruct them, and bow down their neck from their childhood " (Eccl. vii. 25). Let us be well assured that the Holy Spirit will fill us with all good things in reward for our labours in this respect. " By the fruit of his own mouth shall a man be filled with good things " (Prov. xii. 14). Great will be our consolation at beholding those who have worthily received this Sacrament defending Christ's cause with great courage, and fulfilling the words of St. Augustin, " Be thou bold-faced when thou hearest a reproach concerning Christ—yea, be bold-faced. Why fearest thou for thy forehead, which thou hast armed with the sign of the Cross ?"

" Restore unto me the joy of Thy salvation, and strengthen me with a perfect spirit."—*Ps.* l. 14.

" I am filled with the strength of the Spirit of the Lord, with judgment, and power."—*Micheas* iii. 8.

FRIDAY.

THE CHASTITY OF PRIESTS SUSTAINED BY THE HOLY SPIRIT.

I. THE HOLY SPIRIT DICTATED THIS OBLIGATION.

II. HE INSPIRES PRIESTS WITH THE LOVE OF IT.

III. HE FURNISHES THEM WITH ABUNDANT AIDS TO PRE-SERVE IT.

"I will not now speak many things with you ; for the prince of this world cometh, and in Me he hath not anything. But that the world may know that I love the Father, and as the Father hath given Me commandment, so do I."—*St. John* xiv. 30, 31.

1. *In Me he hath not anything.* The Church desires that her Ministers should belong wholly to God, and that the prince of this world should have no power over them ; and, as a powerful means to attain this noble end, she has obliged us to perpetual chastity, and required of us a solemn vow of chastity in receiving the Subdiaconate. In this she was guided by the Holy Spirit ; for when the Apostle gave only the simple counsel of celibacy he declared that it had been suggested to him by the Holy Ghost: "and (he added) I think, also, that I have the Spirit of God" (1 Cor. vii. 40). This word, "*I think,*" says St. Augustin, does not imply doubt, but a modest affirmation. The Holy Spirit, then, has taught the Church (as St. Chrysostom and St. Isidore point out) that, though matrimony is a great Sacrament, chastity is as superior to marriage as Heaven to earth, as the soul to the body. The Holy Spirit directed the Church to declare, as a definition of faith, " If any one shall say that the married state is to be preferred before

virginity or celibacy, or that it is not better and more blessed to remain in virginity or celibacy than to be joined in matrimony, let him be anathema." The Holy Spirit decreed that this obligation should be specially imposed on Priests, in order that they might not be hindered from prayer, and from the daily celebration of the holy mysteries ; as St. Jerome and St. Peter Damian declare. In this state, also (as St. Ambrose says), Priests have a better title to speak in praise of chastity, and to urge the practice of it, since they give example of it in their own person. It enables them also to gain greater respect from the laity (as St. Augustin explains). Moreover, in a state of chastity, Priests can consecrate themselves wholly to the service of the Church and the sanctification of souls, and are able to bestow their ecclesiastical revenues on the poor. Let us, then, give thanks to the Holy Spirit for having made us Priests of the Latin Church, and for having given us so many brilliant examples of chastity among her clergy.

2. *That the world may know that I love the Father.* The love of chastity is a great proof of the love of God, and the love of God and of chastity can come from no other than the Holy Spirit. Through His influence did St. Athanasius, St. Basil, St. Gregory of Nyssa, St. John Chrysostom, St. Jerome, St. Augustin, and many others write precious treatises in praise of virginity, and show forth to all ages how highly they valued this great virtue. He it is Who has caused so many preachers to inspire their hearers, and the souls under their direction, with the love of chastity. He it is Who has led them to show themselves patterns of this angelic virtue. It is desired and loved when its sweetness is felt ; and this blessing, says St. Augustin, is the effect of the operation of the Holy Spirit. Therefore, let the Priest pray that he may be filled with the Holy Spirit, so that he may experience so precious a delight. By the sweetness inspired by the Divine Spirit (continues St. Augustin), all obstacles which oppose themselves to the fulfilment of the vow of chastity are overcome. The flesh may indeed struggle and resist, but the will of the Spirit will overcome in us the will of the flesh. Therefore, let us pray to Him to pour out upon us His sweetness, and to inspire us with this

love of chastity, so as to make dear to us a virtue which enables us to become like the angels in the tenor of our life, even as we are like them in our ministry.

3. *As the Father hath given Me commandment, so do I.* Let us consider that, whenever Almighty God has set apart some individual for the fulfilment of great designs, He has filled him first of all with the Holy Spirit. Joseph, in order to provide for the necessities of Egypt, was " full of the Spirit of God " (Gen. xli. 38). God said of Beseleel who was to build the Tabernacle, that He had " filled him with the Spirit of God " (Ex. xxxi. 3). When the seventy Ancients were chosen to judge the people, " the Spirit rested on them " (Num. xi. 25). When Josue was appointed to lead the people into the Promised Land, he " was filled with the Spirit of wisdom " (Deut. xxxi. 9). In like manner, the Judges whom God raised up to deliver His people were full of the same Spirit, as we read of Othoniel, Gedeon, Jephta, Samson (Judges iii. 10; vi. 34; xi. 29; xiii. 25). Moreover, the Spirit is said to have come upon Saul, David, and the other Kings whom God called to rule over His people (1 Kings ix. 6; xvi. 13). Under the new dispensation, in which grace is more abundant, not only the Apostles, but the seven Deacons also, and all Priests who are rightly disposed, have received, and continue to receive, the fulness of the Holy Spirit. Now, this fulness carries with it strength to preserve the precious treasure of chastity, and therefore did the Holy Spirit appear upon Mount Tabor under the figure of a cloud, in order to show us that He defends us from the heat of concupiscence ; for (says St. Gregory of Nyssa) the fire of sensuality is as a scorching sun when its heat is not tempered by the cloud of the Spirit. Let us, then, have recourse to the Holy Spirit, Who has also likened Himself to a fountain, to assure us (as St. Chrysostom says) that He mitigates the fire kindled by the spirit of impurity.

" He shall rule us for evermore."—*Ps.* xlvii. 15.

" Deliver me . . . from the oppression of the flame which surrounds me, and in the midst of the fire let me not be burnt."—From *Eccl.* li. 6.

SATURDAY.

MARY, AS THE COMPLEMENT OF THE MOST HOLY TRINITY, IS THE SUPPORT OF PRIESTS.

I. In relation to the Father.
II. To the Son.
III. To the Holy Spirit.

" The Holy Ghost shall come upon thee, and the power of the Most High shall overshadow thee; and therefore also the Holy which shall be born of thee shall be called the Son of God."—*St. Luke* i. 35.

1. *Shall be called the Son of God.* Mary has been termed the "complement of the Trinity, and also the resting-place of the Trinity;" and well does this glorious title befit her, because of her intimate and indissoluble relations with the three Divine Persons. She is, indeed, as St. Lawrence Justinian calls her, " the beloved Daughter of the Eternal Father." With the Eternal Father she has one common Son, to whom the Father in respect of His eternal generation, and Mary in respect of His birth, in time, can say, "Thou art my Son, this day have I begotten Thee" (Ps. ii. 7); the same "Only-begotten Son, who is in the bosom of the Father" (St. John i. 18), is called also "the only-begotten Son of Mary." Through Mary the Eternal Father received infinite honour, when the Son—Who, being in the form of God, is co-equal with the Father—in the Virgin's womb took the form of a servant; so that He could then address the Father as His Lord and His God, according to the words of the Prophet, " From my mother's womb Thou art My God "

(Ps. xxi. 11). Further, from His Mother's womb He began to offer that great Sacrifice which alone is worthy of God and renders infinite honour to the Father (Ps. xxxix. 7 ; Heb. x. 5). Who, after her Son Himself, is better able than this Blessed Virgin to obtain for us access to-the Father ? After Thine only-begotten Son (says St. Bernard), by Whom we have access to the Father, Thou art the anchor of salvation to mortals. We need the power of the Father that we may sustain the weight of our Ministry, and be able to say with the Apostle, "When I am weak, them am I powerful" (2 Cor. xii. 10). Let us have recourse to Mary, and she will cause the Father to assist us in our necessities, and to incline a gracious ear to our prayers. Through Mary's protection, how readily will a Priest obtain for the Faithful, not only the grace of the Saviour, and the communication of the Holy Spirit, but also the charity of the Father, from which our Redemption had its beginning ! With what effect will he say, with St. Paul, " The grace of our Lord Jesus Christ, and the charity of God, and the communication of the Holy Ghost, be with you all " (2 Cor. xiii. 13) !

2. *The Holy which shall be born of thee.* The Blessed Virgin has that strict relation with the Eternal Word which a true mother has with a true son (as St. Augustin says). She, indeed, brought forth the Man-God. She is the Mother of the Lord (says St. Jerome), who for us bore Him Who is God and Man— neither Man without God, nor God without Man, but God and Man, the one true Jesus Christ. In this respect was the Word subject to Her as a son to his mother, and by Her He chose to begin the great work of Redemption, so that (as St. Ambrose says) She who was the means through which salvation was procured for the human race was the first to taste its fruit. And, because in the generation of Christ She knew not man, St. Antoninus even calls Her the Father of Christ ; for, says he, Christ had no other father upon earth. Moreover (says St. Germanus) She was associated with Her only-begotten Son, by constant union, during His whole life. Now, we Priests have continual need of the grace of Christ, Whose Person we represent, and without Whom we can do nothing. We have need of a Media-

trix with the great Mediator (says St. Bernard), nor can any be
more useful to us than Mary. Let us, then, implore Her intercession with Her Son, and in the most difficult circumstances of
our Ministry our prayers will be heard and granted.

3. *The Holy Ghost shall come upon thee.* Mary is fitly called by
St. Ildefonsus the "spouse of the Holy Spirit." From Him
(says St. Bernard) She received a double dower; that is to say,
immense grace and immense glory. He guarded Her virginity, so
that, according to St. Anselm, she was the Virgin Spouse by whom
a fallen world was lifted up. Moreover, She received a threefold
beauty from the Holy Spirit (says St. Bonaventure); that is to say,
She was fair in justice and judgment in regard to Herself—fair in
compassion and mercy towards men—fair in faith towards God.
To whom, then, rather than to Her, can we have recourse, in order
to obtain for ourselves and for the souls committed to our charge
the gifts of the Holy Spirit? She (says St. Bridget) is the channel of His grace. Let us remember that, from the very moment
of Her conception (as St. Peter Damian says), the Holy Spirit took
Her wholly for His own; and He made Her a furnace of love, and
the theatre of the greatest of His works—that is, of the Incarnation (says St. Bernardin of Sienna). Obtain for me also, O blessed
Virgin, that I may so ravish the heart of Thy Spouse that He may
inflame my heart with Divine love, and render it the scene of
His merciful operations.

"Understand my cry; hearken to the voice of my prayer."—*Ps.* v. 2, 3.
"Blessed be the Lord, Who made heaven and earth, Who hath directed thee."—
Judith xiii. 24.

TRINITY SUNDAY.

————•————

THE HONOUR DUE FROM PRIESTS TO THE HOLY TRINITY.

I. They have the Trinity ever before their eyes.
II. They cause the people to adore the Trinity.
III. They work in the name of the Trinity.

————•————

" Going therefore, teach ye all nations, baptising them in the Name of the Father, and of the Son, and of the Holy Ghost ; teaching them to observe all things, whatsoever I have commanded you."—*St. Matt.* xxviii. 19.

1. *In the Name of the Father, &c.* Priests should have a deeper knowledge of the mystery of the Trinity than the rest of the Faithful, in consequence of their study of dogmatic treatises, in which all the truths relating to this sublime subject are so carefully set forth. Profiting by such instruction, they will discover traces of the Trinity in all creation ; for " of Him, and by Him, and in Him are all things " (Rom. xi. 36). Even in their own souls, the memory, the understanding, and the will may serve to remind them of the Trinity of Persons in unity of essence ; whilst all their actions should be directed (as St. Augustin enjoins), to the remembrance, the contemplation, and the love of the Most High Trinity. Further, Priests offer the Sacrifice of the Mass to the Holy Trinity, as they assert so frequently in the sacred Liturgy ; they chant the Trisagium in profound adoration of the Blessed Trinity, thus fulfilling upon earth the office of the Seraphim, and of the four mystical living creatures, who sing the same hymn continually in Heaven (Is. vi. 3 ; Apoc. iv. 8). In this Trisagium the

distinction of Persons and unity of substance are clearly set forth (says St. John Damascene); for when we say thrice, "Holy, Holy, Holy," we praise and adore the glory of the Triune God. Again, when we say "Lord God of Hosts, the Heavens and earth are full of Thy glory!" the three Divine Persons are worshipped with equal homage. Lastly, Priests are bound to the frequent repetition of the "*Gloria Patri*," by which they are invited to profound adoration of the Trinity ; and in repeating those words let them call to mind St. Bernard's remarks. There is (says he) the Creative Trinity—the Father, the Son, and the Holy Ghost. From this Trinity the created trinity fell away—that is to say, the memory, the reason, and the will ; and that by means of another trinity—viz., suggestion, delight, consent; and this trinity into which it fell consists of weakness, blindness, and uncleanness. What important subject of examination is this! What motives does it not suggest for adoring, loving, invoking the Divine Trinity!

2. *Teach ye.* St. Jerome admires the order indicated by the Saviour's command, which was, that the Apostles should first teach all nations, and afterwards baptise them. Let us, too, in teaching these sublime truths to the unlearned and ignorant, follow (as St. Gregory Nazianzen bids us) the Prophets and Apostles; nay, let us tread in the footsteps of our Redeemer, Who, before He left this world, said to His Father, "I have manifested Thy Name to men" (St. John xvii. 6); by which words (says St. Chrysostom) He indicated the Mystery of the Trinity to men. How many are there, even amongst Catholics, Who are ignorant of this Mystery, and, therefore, incapable of receiving the Sacraments! Perhaps we might say more truly now than St. Philip Neri said in his day, "We have Indians in Italy." And may not this possibly be due to the negligence of the Priesthood ? Priests, however, are bound to defend this august Mystery from the attacks of all those who oppose it, whether Jews, Unitarians, or unbelievers. They should look to the example of those who devote their tongue and pen to its defence, as well as of those who have undergone bitter persecutions and cruel martyrdom in support of this great truth. St. Augustin teaches Priests how they should defend this Mystery :

" First we show that our faith is consistent with the teaching of Holy Scripture. Then we shall, perhaps, satisfy the demands of those contentious babblers who are puffed up with their own conceit rather than possessed of any real capacity for comprehending the truth : thus, I say, we may leave even such persons no room for doubt. Let us, then, do our utmost to promote the direct worship of the Trinity, so that it may not happen that, while the Saints receive their due homage, there should be any neglect in the adoration of the Three Divine Persons—the Triune God—the uncreated Sanctity—the sole Author and source of all sanctity." Let us strive to realise the desire thus expressed by St. Augustin:—"When we shall have reached Thee, Thou alone shalt be in us, all in all. Then we shall be ever praising Thee; then we shall be made one in Thee, O Triune God."

3. *Baptising them in the Name of the Father, &c.* Baptism is the door of entrance to all the Sacraments ; and, as our Saviour, by the words "Teach ye," gave the Gospel trumpet into the Apostles' hands (says St. Leo), so, when He commanded them to baptise in the Name of the Trinity, He shewed by what authority they were to act in dispensing the heavenly treasures. As the three Persons have one and the same Divinity, so is the gift of grace one (says St. Jerome) which They bestow through one agency. And, as all men were created by God, Who is one in essence and three in Persons, so by the same Triune God have they been created anew to salvation. Hence it has been said that the whole dispensation of the Church is perfected in the Trinity. What confidence, therefore, in the Trinity ought not we to have in the discharge of the duties of the ministry ! And how great blessings will not that Priest procure for himself who invokes the Most Holy Trinity in all trials and dangers ! How many Priests, thus filled with the Spirit of God, have experienced in a sensible manner the protection of the Blessed Trinity !

" May God, our God, bless us : may God bless us."—*Ps.* lxvi. 7.
" Holy, Holy, Holy, the Lord God of hosts."—*Is.* vi. 3.

MONDAY.

——◆——

*THE ETERNAL FATHER IMPARTS TO THE PRIEST
A SHARE IN HIS OWN DIGNITY.*

I. HE HONOURS HIM WITH THE TITLE OF "FATHER."
II. HE INVESTS HIM WITH SUPREME POWER.
III. HE CONFERS ON HIM AUTHORITY OVER HIS SON.

——◆——

"In the Name of the Father."—*St. Matt.* xxviii. 19.

1. The High Priest, under the old dispensation, bore upon his forehead a plate of gold, on which were engraved the words, "Holy to the Lord" (Exodus xxviii. 36). These words, which far more justly might be inscribed on the forehead of Priests of the New Testament, remind them that they are consecrated to the Eternal Father, to Whom, as the source of the whole Godhead, is ascribed in the sacred Scriptures the name Jehovah. The First Person, indeed, as the beginning without beginning— nay, as the beginning of all beginning—is He Who has introduced the title of Father into heaven and earth, and, according to the riches of His goodness, communicates it to whom He will: "Of Whom all paternity in heaven and earth is named" (Eph. iii. 15). By Him is the Priest called spiritual Father— "Father of spirits" (Heb. xii. 9), as St. Thomas points out. For he, by means of preaching, and by means of the administration of those Sacraments called 'Sacraments of the dead,' begets men to a new life, and, from children of wrath, makes them children of light, children of the kingdom, children of God. Accordingly St. Paul refers to Onesimus as his "son,

whom he had begotten in his bonds" (Philemon 10); and to the Corinthians he wrote, "By the Gospel I have begotten you" (1 Cor. iv. 15). Then, by means of the other Sacraments, called "Sacraments of the living," and by other spiritual aids, the Priest brings forth the Faithful anew, until Christ be perfectly formed in them, so that he is able to say with the Apostle, "My little children, of whom I am in labour again, until Christ be formed in you" (Gal. iv. 19). Observe, also, that Priests, being Fathers of Christians, who are members of Christ, become united to Christ by ties of special relationship, Let us, then, strive to imitate the Eternal Father by shewing compassion and tenderness to our spiritual children, and by affording them all the consolation in our power, mindful of Him Who is "the Father of mercies, and the God of all comfort" (2 Cor. i. 3).

2. The Father is Power; and hence the working of miracles, and the creation of heaven and earth, are ascribed to Him. Now, the Father invests Priests with a far greater gift of power than that which He bestowed on the most famous amongst the ancient workers of miracles. For those miracles were, indeed, but figures of the wonders worked by the hands of Priests. Moses—who led the people through the Red Sea, quenched their thirst with water from the rock, and fed them with manna— prefigured baptism, preaching, and the holy Eucharist. Josue —who made the sun obey his word, overthrew the walls of Jericho, and led the people into the promised land—symbolized the Priest, whom the Sun of Justice obeys, who overthrows the edifice of sin, and who by his counsels, his persuasions, and his assistance, leads the elect to Paradise. Elias—who multiplied the oil, raised a dead child to life, and brought down fire from heaven—represented the Priest, who multiplies the oil of grace and peace for the Faithful, calls sinners to a new life, and causes the Holy Spirit to come down upon them. Let us pause at the holy Eucharist, remembering that St. John, in recording its institution, said that Christ worked this greatest of all miracles, "knowing that the Father hath given Him all things into His hands" (St. John xiii. 3). Let us remember that St. Bernardin

of Sienna said, that the transubstantiation of bread is as great
an act of power as the creation of the world. Let us consider,
also, that the absolution of a sinner (as we have already seen) is
a greater work than the creation of the universe. Hence, Cardinal Hugo represents the Eternal Father as thus addressing the
Priest :—"I made heaven and earth, but truly a greater and a
nobler work of creation do I assign to thee : do thou make
anew that soul which is in sin. I made the earth bring forth
its fruits : to thee I appoint a still better task—in causing souls
to bring forth fruit."   What, then, ought to be our love and our
gratitude to our heavenly Father, Who has given us such power !
What should be our fidelity, our prudence, in exercising this
power ! What a rigorous account shall we not have to render
if we abuse it or keep it idle !

3. The *ideal Act* of the First Person of the Blessed Trinity is,
properly, the generation of the Word, to Whom, through all eternity, He communicates His essence amidst the splendour of
His sanctity.   Now, He bestows upon the Priest the power of
giving sacramental existence to the same incarnate Word ; for
by the words of consecration he causes Christ to be present
sacramentally under the appearances of bread and wine, and by
those words he produces Him as a victim to be offered to the
Divine Majesty.   Hence St. Laurence Justinian exclaimed, " O
wonderful power of the Priest, at whose will the Body of Christ is
present under the appearance of bread, and the Word made Flesh
descends from heaven, and is found on the table of the altar ! "
Nay, more : the Priest blesses Christ Himself upon the altar as
the Victim, whilst Christ, as the principal offerer, blesses the
Priest.   Let us consider further that Christ made Himself obedient to the Father, even unto death, and said to His Father, " I
come to do Thy will " (Philip. ii. 8 ; Ps. xxxix. 8); and He Himself, every day, makes Himself obedient to the Priest in order
to carry on the sacrifice of His death.   He comes when the
Priest calls ; He abandons Himself in the Priest's hands ; He
allows Himself to be exposed, to be carried about, to be shut up,
to be dispensed as food.   He gives no sign of life ; He moves
not but when moved by the Priest's hands : " I am become . . .

free among the dead " (Ps. lxxxvii. 6). What dignity, then, can be greater than this ? St. Ignatius, the martyr, was right in saying, "The Priesthood is the apex of all things." But does our life correspond to this our dignity? Has the Eternal Father no cause of complaint against us ? Let us cast ourselves at His feet with humble and contrite heart to ask pardon for our sins.

"As a father hath compassion on his children, so hath the Lord compassion on them that fear Him ; for He knoweth our frame."—*Ps.* cii. 13, 14.

" O Lord, Thou art our Father, and we are clay."—*Is.* lxiv. 8.

· TUESDAY.

THE PRIEST ASSOCIATED WITH THE PRIESTHOOD OF THE WORD MADE FLESH.

I. The Priesthood of the Word made flesh.

II. Priests are associated with this Priesthood.

III. Effects of this association.

" And of the Son."—*St. Matt.* xxviii. 19.

1. St. Cyril of Jerusalem teaches that Christ was Priest before all ages, anointed by the Father in His eternal generation, so that His Priesthood had not its beginning in time, but is immutable. This Priesthood consisted not in humiliations, in sufferings, in prayers, but in knowing the Father, in acknowledging Him as the source of the Godhead, and Himself as true God of true God. It consisted (according to St. Thomas) in saying to Him, " Thou art my Father," " I am in Thee, and Thou in Me;

I love Thee and honour Thee with an infinite love and infinite glory; for infinite is the love which Thou bearest Me, and infinite the glory which Thou hast communicated to Me." He united this Priesthood with His temporal Priesthood when He assumed human nature; taking from us (as St. Augustin says) that which He would offer for us. The Word (says St. Ambrose) appeared clothed with flesh, in His dignity of King and of Judge, and full of sacerdotal justice. Our guilt could not be cancelled without a sacrifice, and therein a sacrifice was sought. The Son (says St. Gregory) took our nature, but not our sin, and offered Himself a sinless Victim. His Incarnation was itself a Sacrifice which lasted His whole mortal life, was consummated upon the Cross, and is continued in glory at the Right Hand of the Father, and on our altars on earth. In the womb of Mary (says Dionysius of Alexandria) the King of Glory was made a High Priest; and He continueth such for ever, now that He has entered once into the Holies, having obtained eternal redemption. Let us adore our great High Priest, in Whose hands is our salvation.

2. Aaron and his sons represented typically this Priesthood; and all that was prescribed in regard to vestments, ceremonies, and actions was but symbolical of the great High Priest Who was to come. We belong to this Priesthood, being associated with it by virtue of the indelible character received at our Ordination. As God is one, as the Faith is one, as the Church is one, so is the Priesthood one; the sacramental Character being, as it were, a participation of the Priesthood of Christ (says St. Thomas). When we received Holy Baptism we were united to Christ as "members of member" (1 Cor. xii. 27). In our sacred Ordination we were associated with Him (as St. Cyril says) in such a manner as to be bound for ever to Divine and sacred ministrations. Hence, when the Priest consecrates, he says not, "This is Christ's Body, this is Christ's Blood," but "This is My Body, This is My Blood." Therefore our Lord can justly say to us, "I have chosen you, and I have separated you from other people, that you should be Mine" (Levit. xxiv. 26). Justly, too, may the Church declare that she has united us with her Divine Spouse, and say to

us. "It is a small thing unto you that the God of Israel hath separated you from the people, and joined you to Himself" (Numb. xvi. 9). Let us, therefore, reflect on the blessed privilege which we thus enjoy, and let us endeavour to clothe ourselves with our Lord Jesus Christ ; for it would be a monstrous deformity to be associated with Christ and to live in a manner opposed to Him, doing dishonour to Him. Let us obey the injunction, "Put ye on the Lord Jesus" (Rom. xiii. 14).

3. The consequence and effect of this association is that of which our Lord Jesus Christ spoke when He said to His Eternal Father, concerning Priests, "As Thou hast sent Me into the world, I also have sent them into the world" (St. John xvii. 18); for (says St. Augustin) they are His members. Moreover, the consequence and effect is also found in those other words, which He Himself spoke to the first Priests, "He that heareth you heareth Me; he that despiseth you despiseth Me" (St. Luke x. 16). As Venerable Bede points out, when Christ's Minister in preaching the Gospel is heard and despised, it is not a mere creature who is thus treated, but our Saviour Himself. Again, we find the consequence and effect of this association in that sentence, "He that receiveth you receiveth Me" (St. Matt. x. 40); and, again, in the words of St. Ignatius, the martyr, who says, that he who despises the Priesthood despises God and the First-begotten, our Lord Jesus Christ, Who alone by nature is Priest of the Father. Let us, then, thank our Lord Jesus Christ for having conferred on us so distinguished an office in spite of our sins; let us pray to Him to enable us to sustain it worthily, even till death. Let us have firm hope in His goodness, that, as He has attached us to Himself on earth, so He will unite us with Himself in heaven, and cause us to experience the power of His prayer to the Father—"I in them, and Thou in Me, that they may be made perfect in one " (St. John xvii. 23).

"My soul hath stuck close to Thee: Thy right hand hath received Me."—*Ps.* lxii. 9.

"I live ; now, not I, but Christ liveth in me."—*Gal.* ii. 20.

WEDNESDAY.

----◆----

THE DIFFUSION OF THE HOLY SPIRIT BY THE PRIESTHOOD.

I. The Holy Spirit loves to diffuse Himself.

II. He destined the Apostles to diffuse Him abroad.

III. It is our office to assist in this diffusion.

----◆----

" And of the Holy Ghost."—*St. Matt.* xxviii. 19.

1. If the Father and the Son exalt the sacerdotal dignity, the Holy Ghost likewise ennobles it by destining it to the diffusion of Himself. In the first place, let us remember that goodness is, of its very nature, diffusive of itself; and it is said to be diffusive (says St. Thomas) in the same way as the end is said to be the motive power. Now, the Holy Spirit is the uncreated Goodness, and therefore He loves to diffuse Himself; nay, He calls Himself the Gift, precisely because He gives Himself freely. As the gift of God He is given, yet in such a manner that, as God, He gives Himself (says St. Augustin). He is kind—that is, according to the Greek text, He is a lover of men: the spirit of wisdom is benevolent. And (as St. Gregory Nazianzen points out), being most wise and most loving towards men, He renders them no less virtuous than He had found them vicious. Let us, then, love so great Goodness; let us learn how to profit by it, and let us endeavour that through our aid the Faithful may also profit by the same.

2. It had been foretold that the dry land should of a sudden be fertilised by the water of grace: " that which was dry land shall become a pool, and the thirsty land springs of water" (Is. xxxv. 7); and this came to pass at the descent of the Holy Spirit, Who through the labours of the Apostles irrigated all the dry and barren earth. From the day of Pentecost (says St. Leo) streams of graces and blessings watered the desert and the whole of the dry land. Nor was the Holy Spirit merely a living fountain, but also a great river, filling many other rivers (says St. Augustin)—that is to say, the Apostles and the first disciples. And St. Ambrose says, that, whilst the Spirit is compared to water because of His tendency to diffuse Himself, He is also compared to a river because of the abundance of this diffusion. This was manifested in the case of the Apostles on the day of Pentecost ; for by their labours charity was diffused throughout the whole world, and it is by the Holy Ghost that " the charity of God is poured forth" (Rom. v. 5). St. Chrysostom observes, that, because of the abundance of grace, it is not said that charity is " given," but that it is " poured forth." The Holy Spirit (he adds) pours forth a fount of good things, fully, and with abundance. Let us pray to those great Priests who have gone before us to obtain for us from God the imitation of their zeal and the continual diffusion of the Holy Spirit.

3. It is our office to carry on the work of the Apostles in that part of the Ministry which has been confided to us ; and, therefore, by our means also should the Holy Ghost be poured forth amongst the Faithful. He descends upon Priests in their Ordination, in order (says Theophylact) that they may become dispensers of Divine gifts, and that grace may operate through them again. The Priest (says St. Ambrose) discharges the functions of the Holy Spirit, and therefore (says St. Paulinus) the Priest is brought into most intimate relations with the Holy Spirit. Let us remember that prayer is absolutely necessary for the diffusion of the Holy Spirit, and on this account that we must be ministers of prayer. The Priest (says St. Lawrence Justinian) prays for the salvation of all, in order that they may be transferred from darkness to light, and that, having been raised from the death

of sin, they may continue in life. Let us remember, also, that the Holy Spirit is diffused by the preaching of the Word; for He it is Who speaks by the mouth of His Ministers, pouring forth light in the understanding and charity in the heart. Nay, more: were there no Holy Spirit (says St. Chrysostom) there would be no preaching, no word of wisdom or knowledge in the Church, no pastors and teachers. Lastly, let us remember that by means of the Sacraments, in which grace is so abundantly diffused, the Holy Ghost is poured forth in the hearts of the Faithful, and therefore (says St. Chrysostom again) He is likened to water, which both washes and gives refreshment. Let us, then, faithfully dispense the Divine Word and the Holy Sacraments to the Faithful; so shall we be acceptable to that God Who will recompense us abundantly in this life and in the life to come.

" He brought forth water out of the rock, and made streams to run down as rivers."—*Ps.* lxxvii. 16.

" The Spirit of the Lord hath filled the whole world."—*Wisd.* i. 7.

FEAST OF CORPUS CHRISTI.

THE PRIEST COMMUNICATES HIMSELF.

I. Jesus Christ communicated Himself.
II. The Priest does the same.
III. The greatness of this privilege.

—◆—

" My Flesh is meat indeed, and My Blood is drink indeed: he that eateth My Flesh, and drinketh My Blood, abideth in Me, and I in him."—*St. John* vi. 56, 57.

1. *My Flesh is meat indeed.* In instituting the Sacrament of the Eucharist, our Lord Jesus Christ first communicated Himself. He fed Himself with the food which was Himself (says St. Thomas). He it was (says St. Jerome) Who ate and Who was eaten. He was alike the guest of the feast and the feast itself. Who, indeed, would have dared to receive this Sacrament (asks St. Chrysostom) knowing that in It are contained the Body and Blood of God—who with a quiet mind could have eaten this food—had not He Himself first given us the example ? But as, for our example, He would be baptised, in order to induce us to receive Baptism, which is the door of the Sacraments, so, for our example, would He communicate Himself, in order to encourage us to receive the Eucharist, which is the end of all the Sacraments. In so doing (says St. Thomas) grace was not augmented in Him, but He had in it a certain spiritual delectation. Who, indeed, can understand the immensity of this spiritual joy ? He considered this Communion as the one entirely worthy Communion, and then only was His most precious Flesh received into an abode

adequately fitted to it. He considered this Communion as the beginning, the pledge, the model, of all the Communions which His living members would make, even to the consummation of the world, and which were so ardently desired by His loving Heart. Let us bless our Lord Jesus Christ, and let us love Him Who has loved us so greatly.

2. *He that eateth My Flesh.* The Priest, by Divine institution, after having consecrated, communicates Himself; following Christ's command, Who, after He had consecrated, and after He had communicated Himself, said, " This do for the commemoration of Me " (1 Cor. xi. 24). Hence it is defined by the Church, " If any one shall say that it is not lawful for the celebrating Priest to communicate himself, let him be anathema." For, as he offers the Sacrifice, he ought to be the first to partake of it, in order to show that he participates in the interior sacrifice of which the exterior is a sign. So does he become the first partaker of the Altar : " They that eat of the sacrifices are partakers of the altar " (1 Cor. x. 10). In dispensing the Sacrifice to the people, he shows himself to be a dispenser of divine things ; and, therefore, he ought to be the first to profit by them. What a mystery is this ! What an office ! What a prerogative ! By our words we make God descend from Heaven upon earth, and with our hands we introduce Him into our body—we, who are but dust and ashes !

3. *Abideth in Me, and I in him.* Christ enters into us in order to become our spiritual nourishment. When we utter the words of the centurion, " Lord, I am not worthy " (St. Matt. viii. 8), we should reflect deeply on our unworthiness ; but when, in the words of the Psalmist, we say, " I will take the bread of Heaven .. . I will take the chalice of salvation " (Ps. cxv. 13), we should reflect on our great dignity. When we pronounce those other words, " I will call on the Name of the Lord," we should beg of Jesus grace to receive Him well, in order that there be not found in us wicked presumption (Eccl. xxxvii. 3). When we add, " Preserve my soul to life eternal," we ought to remember the salutary effects of this Sacrament ; reflecting, with St. Cyril, that the Word, united to His own Flesh, rendered that Flesh the source

of life. Let us consider that a day will come when we shall receive Him no longer from our own hands, but from the hands of another Priest, as our Viaticum, as the companion of our journey from this world to the Heavenly Jerusalem (as St. Thomas says). O my God, touch my heart, I pray Thee, that it may be softened by the consideration of these truths!

"I will take the chalice of salvation, and I will call upon the Name of the Lord."—*Ps.* cxv. 13.

"I will eat the bread of consecration, as the Lord commanded me."—From *Levit.* viii. 31.

FRIDAY.

———◆———

THE DISPOSITION REQUIRED BY THE PRIEST WHO COMMUNICATES EVERY DAY.

I. The disposition required of the Faithful in respect of daily Communion.

II. Still more is required of Priests who celebrate daily.

III. Frivolous excuses of tepid Priests.

———◆———

"As the living Father hath sent Me, and I live by the Father; so he that eateth Me, the same also shall live by Me. This is the Bread that came down from Heaven. Not as your fathers did eat manna, and are dead."—*St. John* vi. 58, 59.

1. *I live by the Father.* The life of our Divine Lord is the model of the life of every Christian who is nourished by this Bread of Life, but especially of one who partakes frequently or daily of that heavenly food. By partaking of Him (says St. Augustin) we live by Him. And yet the practice of daily Com-

munion requires such conditions that St. Augustin declared that
he could neither praise nor blame it. Doubtless, this is the daily
Bread which, when received daily, causes us to experience day
by day its salutary effects, if only our life be so ordered as to
render us worthy of this great privilege. The daily reception of
of this Blessed Sacrament is to be commended (says St. Thomas)
if he who communicates thus frequently approach the Altar with
great devotion and reverence. There must be an absence of all
affection towards venial sins, evil inclinations must be to a great
extent subdued, and there must be an ardent desire to communicate, in him who is a daily communicant (as St. Francis of Sales
says). These are the conditions which directors of souls justly
expect in the laity, and without such conditions they admit them
not to frequent Communion. But what do they require in their
own case? In refusing this privilege to others the Priest pro-
nounces his own condemnation, so long as he is himself in a
similar condition. "Wherein thou judgest another, thou con-
demnest thyself" (Rom. ii. 1).

2. *This is the Bread that came down from Heaven.* If so great
purity is required for the daily participation of this Sacrament, how
much more in the case of Him who is the Minister of the same,
and who causes this Divine Bread to descend from Heaven! The
fragrance of our sanctity should be such that our Divine Lord on
the Altar might say, in the words of Isaac, "Behold, the smell of
my son is as the smell of a plentiful field which the Lord hath
blessed" (Gen. xxvii. 27). We should be like frankincense,
which is composed of many choice perfumes, when we approach
the Altar (says St. Gregory); that is to say, our soul should be
fragrant with the manifold virtues of our good works. Let us
call to mind, with St. Chrysostom, that when our Divine Lord
descends into our hands we are surrounded with innumerable
multitudes of Angels—nay (continues the same holy Father), the
Angels, seized with holy fear, dare not freely gaze on the splendour of that heavenly Victim. As St. Chrysostom also says, surely
the hands which divide this sacred Flesh—the mouth which is
filled with this spiritual fire—the tongue which is empurpled with
the Blood of this tremendous Sacrifice—should shine with the

purity of the very sunbeams. The Priest (continues the same Father) should be pure as though he were in the midst of the Angels in Heaven. Is this truly the state of our conscience when we prepare to celebrate holy Mass? Are we not made unworthy of daily Communion, and much more unworthy of celebrating daily, by some attachment to vanity, ambition, self-interest, gluttony—by our careless freedom in the use of our eyes and tongues —by our readiness to take offence, to treat our neighbour sharply, to let our attention wander in prayer? Let us, at any rate, make some effort to amend.

3. *This is the Bread that came down from Heaven.* Our Lord Jesus Christ descends from Heaven (says St. Augustin) in order to increase and preserve our spiritual life. But, if in some Priests the spiritual life is neither preserved nor increased, how can they excuse themselves in their daily approach to the Altar? They say that they are bound to celebrate : by what law, it may be asked, is this obligation imposed on them? In any case, let them remember that they are at least equally bound to observe holiness of life. Let them follow the good advice of St. Cyril—" Meditate devoutly ; live a zealous and holy life ; and thus partake of the Bread of Life." They say, perhaps, that the Church supplies their imperfections. Let them, however, bear in mind that she enjoins them to celebrate the divine mysteries with the utmost possible inward sanctity and purity of heart. Let us conclude with the words of St. Chrysostom, " Think well, man, what is that Host thou art to touch—what is that table to which thou art to approach." Let us draw near to these tremendous mysteries with fear and trembling, with a pure conscience, and with prayer.

SATURDAY.

———◆———

———◆———

"He that eateth this Bread shall live for ever."—*St. John* vi. 59.

1. *He that eateth this Bread.* In the primitive Church (says St. Thomas) when the fervour of Christians was great, daily Communion was prescribed. Then were the Faithful not only persevering in the reception of the Apostles' doctrine and in prayer, but also in Communion—"in the communication of the breaking of bread" (Acts ii. 42.) They were well assured that by means of Holy Communion they were united in one mass with Christ's Body (as St. Chrysostom says)—that, as wax mingles with wax already liquefied, and as fire insinuates itself into red-hot iron, so by means of the Eucharist (as St. Cyril says) we are joined in one Body and one Blood with Christ. No one has ever doubted that the Blessed Virgin communicated, in order that She might be the chief imitator of Christ, Her Son, who communicated Himself in instituting the Holy Eucharist; and She communicated daily, in order to become the pattern for all future ages (says St. Thomas of Villanova). She desired to do this because of the love which She bore Her Son, with Whom She longed to be ever more and more united. Above all, She desired it (as St. Thomas

points out) in order to enjoy the admirable effects of this Sacrament—that is to say, augmentation of grace, and the delight which this heavenly food carries with it. Let us learn from Her, not to neglect the celebration of Holy Mass without grave reason, but to imitate those Priests who, at their daily celebration, dispense the Holy Communion to the Faithful, saying to them, "Taste and see how sweet is the Lord."

2. *He that eateth this Bread.* Who, among all creatures, was ever so well prepared for Holy Communion as Mary? Who could ever attain to Her fervour? She (says St. Bernard) was the *Bread* which fed on the Divine Bread. She is called by Origen "the fulness of sanctity," and by St. Anselm "the brightness of sanctity;" and therefore worthily might She approach to receive the Holy of Holies. She was the "ardour of divine Love," says St. Bernardin, and thus with immense fervour did She receive Her Son. Let us, then, learn from Her to prepare ourselves worthily; let us learn from Her to be fervent in celebrating, and to guard ourselves from tepidity. As St. Bonaventure warns us, we should indeed be unworthy did we not draw near reverently, circumspectly, and with due consideration. Let us imitate Mary, and let us also imitate all those holy Priests who so carefully prepared their souls for this sublime function, and who, when the hour of offering the Holy Sacrifice arrived, offered themselves also in sacrifice with tears and with the utmost contrition of heart.

3. *Shall live for ever.* The spiritual life was most perfect in Mary, and this life (as St. Thomas shows) is obtained by means of grace! If, then, She lived, as is commonly supposed, twenty-four years and some months after Christ's Ascension, She must have communicated more than eight thousand eight hundred and fifty times. And if, in the Sacrament of the Altar, grace is distributed in proportion to the disposition of the soul, who can comprehend what treasures of grace must have been continually poured into the bosom of the Mother from the inexhaustible mine of Her Son's most precious Blood? Rightly is She called by St. John Damascene "an immense abyss of grace;" and who could ever fathom the depth of this abyss? (Eccl. i. 2.) Let us

pray to our blessed Lady to obtain for us from Almighty God the dispositions for celebrating worthily, and also greater fervour in celebrating, so that we may receive in full abundance the fruit of so great a Mystery. Above all, may She preserve us from approaching the Altar with a conscience stained with mortal sin! Let us constantly meditate on the awful statement of St. Peter Damian, that no greater injury is ever done to Almighty God—no more grievous sin is ever committed—than by the Priest who offers sacrifice unworthily.

"O Queen of Angels, make haste to help me, that I may worthily eat the Bread of Angels."—From *Ps.* lxix. 2, and *Ps.* lxxvii. 25.

"Make me a follower of Thee, and an observer of them who walk so as they have Saints for their model."—From *Philip.* iii. 17.

SECOND SUNDAY AFTER PENTECOST

(WITHIN THE OCTAVE OF CORPUS CHRISTI).

———◆———

THE LITTLE PROFIT WHICH SOME PRIESTS DERIVE FROM THE HOLY EUCHARIST.

I. The admirable effects of the Eucharist.

II. The failure of Priests in regard to these benefits.

III. The cause of this failure.

———◆———

" Jesus spoke to the Pharisees this parable: A certain man made a great supper, and invited many: and he sent his servant at the hour of supper to say to them that were invited, that they should come, for now all things are ready."—*St. Luke* xiv. 16, 17.

1. *Made a great supper.* This great supper (says St. Cyril) reminds us of our Lord's Last Supper, in which He instituted the holy Eucharist. This Supper was prefigured by the banquet of Assuerus; and it is truly great, whether we consider Him Who serves it, the food which is offered, the number of those invited, or the time of its duration. In the first place, Priests partake of this Supper; for "they that serve the altar partake with the altar" (1 Cor. ix. 13), and so great is our Lord's goodness that, whilst, on the one hand, they are represented by the servants who summon the guests, they are, on the other hand, the guests who partake of the banquet, for they receive this heavenly food before others, and sometimes alone. They, therefore, ought to be before others in experiencing its wonde

ful effects. Now, these effects of the holy Eucharist are described by St. Cyril of Alexandria, who says that it drives away, not death alone, but all maladies; for the passions are thereby quieted, piety is strengthened, trouble of soul extinguished, the sick are healed, and the fallen are restored. This great Sacrament produces in the soul the same effects which material food produces in the body; that is to say, it nourishes spiritual strength, it increases the life of grace, and it is a safeguard against our infirmities; for it keeps us from relapsing into sin, it causes us to atone for past sins, and makes us taste spiritual sweetness in its very source. In short (as expressed in a single Latin verse), "it nourishes, preserves, repairs, delights, and increases." What a banquet is this! What a sign of the vast love of our Divine Lord! What folly is theirs who refuse to profit by it!

2. *Invited many.* Numerous are the Priests invited to this banquet, but all do not profit by it. St. Bernard complains that the world is overrun with Priests, and yet that good Priests are few; and another writer, bearing the same name, says that there is abundance of Priests, but a want of Priestly men. What is required is an increase of merit, not of mere numbers. Is not this true at the present time? · Are there not many in regard to whom the promise fails of its fulfilment, "He shall live by Me" —many, that is to say, who do not make Christ the principle of their whole life? Christ lives not in them, but the old man is still predominant; for, if Christ lived in them, wisdom, strength, peace, joy, and every other virtue would be conspicuous in them; as St. Jerome points out. Few there are who can say, with St. Bernard (as those who communicate daily ought to say), "I am dead to all other things, I taste them not, I attend to them not, I care not for them; the things of Christ alone occupy my care, for them I live, and to them I devote my whole life." Let us examine ourselves at the foot of the Cross, and let us see what profit we have hitherto derived from holy Mass. If one of our penitents shewed that he profited so little, should we admit him to daily Communion? May it not be that we readily perceive the mote in the eye of others, whilst we discern not the beam which is in our own eye?

3. *All things are ready.* It happens, perhaps, because the heavenly Banquet is always ready for us, that we celebrate out of custom. The hour for Mass comes, just as the hour for dinner, for sleep, or for recreation, recurs; and we go to the Church in order to satisfy the obligations of our cure, without considering whether we have fit dispositions. St. Chrysostom says that he observed many partaking of Christ's Body lightly and heedlessly, and rather from custom and form than with consideration and reflection. This is the first cause why so little profit is derived from frequent celebration. Another cause is tepidity. Those who are wanting in fervour (for I speak not of such as are in mortal sin) lose in a great measure the effects of the holy Eucharist. They make void the Passion of Christ (says Peter of Blois) who consider not with what reverence the Body and Blood of Christ should be offered—with what devotion it is to be handled—with what sanctity it is to be received—with what diligence dispensed. Next, although past venial sins do not necessarily in themselves destroy the effect of the Blessed Sacrament if it be received devoutly, yet, if such sins be committed in the very act of approaching the Altar, they hinder us from receiving the actual grace which is its fruit, and there remains only habitual grace. In other words (says St. Thomas), there will be an augmentation of grace in the case of those who are distracted by venial sins, but they lose that spiritual sweetness with which their souls would otherwise be refreshed. Is it possible that we are of the number of those Priests who celebrate with so many distractions and such neglect of the sacred ceremonies as not to taste the delights of this divine food? What anguish shall we feel when we come to die at having profited so little by so many Masses! O Jesus, Who art the Way, the Truth, and the Life, by Thee may I come, to Thee may I come, in Thee may I rest!

"I will go in to the Altar of God, to Christ, Who giveth joy to my youth."—*Ps.* xlii. 4.

"That we may in all things grow up in Him, Who is the head, even Christ."—*Eph.* iv. 15.

MONDAY.

PRIESTS SHOULD EXTOL THE HOLY EUCHARIST BEFORE THE PEOPLE.

I. To promote frequent visits to the Blessed Sacrament.

II. To procure increased devotion at Mass.

III. To increase the frequency of Communions.

"And they began all at once to make excuse. The first said to him, I have bought a farm, and I must needs go and see it : I pray thee hold me excused. And another said, I have bought five yoke of oxen, and I go to try them : I pray thee, hold me excused. And another said, I have married a wife, and therefore I cannot come."
—*St. Luke* xiv. 18—20.

1. *I must needs go and see it.* The servant charged with this invitation is a figure of the whole body of Preachers, who are sent by God (says St. Gregory) to give men this invitation ; and it is a most noble charge, for it was exercised by Christ Himself. This servant who was sent is Christ (says St. Cyril). If Ecclesiastics would exercise their zeal in pointing out the advantages which the Faithful would derive from visiting the Blessed Sacrament, we should not see immense multitudes of Christians neglect this duty on the plea of business, or even idle pleasure and amusement, which, for want of proper religious instruction, they look upon as more necessary, saying, "I must needs go and see it." If pride is humbled through preaching, and man is taught by it his own indigence and the need he has of visiting Jesus Christ, he will not allege this excuse, which properly signifies pride.   In the

farm which was bought (says St. Augustin) is represented dominion; therefore, let pride be the first vice to be chastised.
Let us tell the Faithful that, if they seek comfort in their tribulations, they should visit Jesus, Who has given the invitation and
the promise, " Come to Me, all you that labour and are burdened, and I will refresh you" (St. Matt. xi. 28). Let us make
them understand that, whilst conversation with men often gives
rise to innumerable troubles, conversation with Christ, on the
contrary, "hath no bitterness .... but joy and gladness"
(Wisd. viii. 16). Let us show them Jesus, Who, in order to pour
out His benefits upon us, ardently desires our visit, "looking
through the windows, looking through the lattices " (Cant. ii. 9);
and let us set them a good example by passing much time in
visiting Jesus in the Blessed Sacrament.

2. *I go to prove them.* The spirit of avarice often hinders men
from assisting at the Sacrifice of the Altar for those who are
wholly absorbed in worldly affairs and in the acquisition of riches
readily excuse themselves from this duty, and neglect the pursuit of heavenly treasures. The second excuse comes from the
solicitude of avarice (says St. Bonaventure), which causes a man
to regard only the things of earth. Let us show such persons
the immense store of spiritual riches which the soul may derive
from the Sacrifice of the Mass, in comparison of which "all
gold is as a little sand, and silver .... shall be counted as
clay " (Wisd. vii. 9). Were the Faithful carefully instructed in
regard to the utility of holy Mass, they would form the habit of
never neglecting it, but would look upon it as the most sublime
and fruitful of pious exercises. Woe to the Priest who omits
this duty! especially if his dissipation, if his avaricious or irreligious spirit, keep the Faithful away from the holy Sacrifice.
Let us remember what is written of two Priests—Ophni and
Phinees—that "their sin was exceeding great before the Lord,
because they withdrew men from the sacrifice of the Lord"
(1 Kings ii. 17). But, if it is a great sin thus to withdraw men
from the Holy Sacrifice, great is the merit, and great will be the
reward, of those who attract them to it, and teach them how to
assist at it with recollection, fervour, and profit.

3. *I have married a wife, and therefore I cannot come.* The pleasures of the flesh keep many away from approaching the Eucharistic feast (as St. Augustin observes), for those who find their delight in such pleasures are ready to excuse themselves and die of inward hunger. Let Priests make such unhappy men comprehend that the soul also has its pleasures. While the senses of the body have their pleasures, is the soul to be deprived of its delight? (asks St. Augustin.) The pleasure which the soul tastes in Holy Communion is supreme and ineffable. Nothing suffices to express the delight of this Sacrament (says St. Thomas), in which spiritual sweetness is tasted in its proper source. Let us urge sensual men to vanquish their carnal passions, that they may taste the hidden manna; for it is written, " To him that overcometh I will give the hidden manna " (Apoc. ii. 17). Let us continually exhort them to make good Confessions, in order that they may taste that Bread which has in it " all that is delicious " (Wisd. xvi. 20), and that they may not imitate the carnal Jews who loathed the manna, and were severely punished by God (Numb. xxi. 5). What great benefits may be procured for the Faithful by the Priest who loves Jesus in the Sacrament of the Altar! Has this been our case? If not, let us resolve to amend.

" With the voice of joy and praise, the noise of one feasting."—*Ps.* xli. 5.

" Neither is there any other nation so great, that hath gods so nigh them, as our God is present to all our petitions."—*Deut.* iv. 7.

TUESDAY.

———◆———

THE CARE WHICH PRIESTS SHOULD BESTOW IN FREQUENT COMMUNION.

I. The Eucharist the end of all the labours of our Ministry.

II. Frequency of Communion the means of spiritual advancement.

III. The Faithful to be invited to a participation in this privilege.

———◆———

" And the servant returning told these things to his lord. Then the master of the house, being angry, said to his servant, Go out quickly into the streets and lanes of the city, and bring in hither the poor and the feeble, and the blind and the lame."
—*St. Luke* xiv. 21.

1. *Go out quickly.* Behold the command which God gives to the good Priest, His obedient servant, to go forth and summon all (even the least worthy of such honour) to the heavenly banquet. And what, it may be asked, is the aim of all preaching, if not to induce those who are sinners to confess their sins and communicate aright, and to incite those who are in a state of grace to derive fresh increase of grace from the same source ? The Eucharist, then, is the term of all preaching, as it is the term of all the Sacraments. Baptism is, indeed, ordained to make us capable of receiving the Eucharist; Confirmation serves to drive away that human respect which might be a hindrance to approaching the Altar; by means of Penance and Extreme Unction men are prepared to eat the Body of Christ worthily; the Sacrament of

Order was ordained for the consecration of the Eucharist; and, lastly, the Sacrament of Matrimony has this relation to the Eucharist—that it signifies the union of Christ with His Church, of which union the Eucharist is a figure. So St. Thomas. Therefore ought we to look upon Holy Communion as the aim and end of all Ministerial labours, for (says St. Dionysius) the Eucharist is, as it were, the consummation of all the Sacraments.

2. *Into the streets and lanes of the city.* There is no more efficacious means for raising the standard of morality in any community than promoting frequent Communion. For, as by Christ's Passion the face of the world was changed, so by means of this Sacrament, which represents the same Passion, are men changed (says St. Thomas). By this means, indeed, is union established with God, and concord among men, inasmuch as they are invited to one table, and eat of that one Bread—under the species of bread composed of many grains of wheat—which is an apt representation of fraternal charity, and a safeguard against strife and dissension. Hence the Eucharist is called by St. Augustin the seal of unity, the bond of charity. A zealous Priest who multiplies Communions confers far more advantage on society, hinders far more sin, than philosophers by their moral teaching, or civil authority with all its power. For the Eucharist strengthens man's weakness against his spiritual enemies, and so preserves him from sin: it is the "Bread that strengthens man's heart" (Ps. ciii. 15). It enables us to resist the assaults of the devil when he tempts us to return to sin. We retire from that table (says St. Chrysostom) like lions breathing out spiritual fire—made terrible to the devils. Frequency of Communion is thus the great means of sanctification to the Faithful. But what have we done hitherto for this important object? What is our intention for the future?

3. *The poor and the feeble, and the blind and the lame.* The order given by the master of the house to his servant shows us how great is the desire of Almighty God to receive penitent sinners to His table. Be it that the Faithful are *poor* in grace, *feeble* in virtue, *blind* for want of prudence, *lame* for want of firmness; yet Jesus, Who came not to call the just, but sinners, desires

only that they be converted, and so partake of His Flesh. And, if the Master of the house is so liberal, it is not fitting that the servant be miserly; it is not fitting that Priests put impediments in the way of frequent Communion, especially in the case of those who avoid not only mortal sin, but also habitual venial sin. Let us remember that for some centuries daily Communion was prescribed, and that frequent—nay, daily—Communion, was always approved by the Church. Let us remember St. Thomas's sentence, that, if any one finds by experience that daily Communion increases the fervour of his love, and does not diminish his reverence, he should communicate every day. Some Confessors, however, are sufficiently indulgent to themselves in the matter of daily celebrating, and apply to themselves with perfect ease the teaching of St. Ambrose, that he who is always sinning must be always taking the remedy—as well as St. Augustin's words, "Your sins, though they be daily, at least let them not be deadly, before ye approach the Altar;"—and yet at the same time they show severity to others whose defects are less obvious, and who endeavour to hate even venial sins and desire to procure their pardon in this Sacrament. According to the proverb, "the doves are harassed, while the crows escape their censures." But let us rather follow the rules of St. Alphonsus, who, under the guidance of the Holy Spirit, has discussed this subject with great learning and perspicuity.

"By the fruit of their corn and wine the Faithful are multiplied."—From *Ps.* iv. 8.

"With the bread of life and understanding feed Thy people, O Lord,"—*Eccl.* xv. 3.

WEDNESDAY.

THE SPECIAL FRUIT OF THE HOLY MASS.

I. IT SPRINGS FROM THE OBLATION OF THE SACRIFICE.
II. IT IS INCREASED THROUGH THE PRAYERS OF THE CHURCH.
III. IT IS COMPLETED BY HOLY COMMUNION.

"And the servant said, Lord, it is done as Thou hast commanded, and yet there is room."—*St. Luke* xiv. 22.

1. *It is done as Thou hast commanded.* When the Priest honours Almighty God with the tribute of Sacrifice he may say, "Lord, it is done as Thou hast commanded;" for, according to St. Alphonsus, it is the common opinion of the Doctors of the Church that Priests are guilty of mortal sin who either absolutely neglect the celebration of holy Mass or omit to celebrate on the great Festivals. Every time Priests offer the holy Sacrifice they offer it for themselves ; that is, that they may reap from it that fruit which is called by theologians *specialissimus*, and thus also they may say, "Lord, it is done as Thou hast commanded." · For the Apostle teaches us that the Priest should offer sacrifice, first for himself or for his own sins, and afterwards for others : "Jesus . . needed not daily, as the other Priests to offer sacrifice, first for His own sins, and then for the people's" (Heb. vii. 27). Accordingly the Church directs the Priest to declare to Almighty God that he offers the Host "for his own innumerable sins, offences, and negligences ;" and this fruit, being by these words applied to the Priest who is offering the Sacrifice, cannot (as Cardinal Bona points out) be applied to others. Now, St. Thomas says that the

first effect of such application is the gift of grace to detest venial sins, and also the pardon of such sins; another effect is the remission of the punishment due to past sins (as Suarez shows); the third effect is the augmentation of grace, and those helps by which grace is increased; the last effect is the obtaining of temporal blessings in so far as they may profit the soul. What a treasure is this, which Almighty God opens to us every day! What gratitude do we show for so great mercy? What love for so great goodness?

2. *It is done as Thou hast commanded.* At the Altar the Priest prays for the Church, and consequently for himself, inasmuch as he is the public Minister of the Church. Moreover, he prays several times for himself particularly, for the Church prescribes various prayers to be said by the Priest for himself. And in this respect, as following the directions of the Church, by whose voice Jesus commands, he may say to Jesus, " It is done as Thou hast commanded." By this means (as Origen shows) he will be able to purge himself from his defects; and these holy prayers produce the effect divinely promised to prayer—"Ask, and it shall be given you . . for every one that asketh receiveth" (St. Matt. vii. 7, 8). Moreover, they have a greater effect in that the Priest prays for himself, for St. Augustin tells us that all the saints are heard for themselves, but they are not heard for all. Again, he prays to Jesus in the name of the Church, His beloved Spouse; for the Priest's prayers at the Altar are made in the Church's name (says St. Thomas). Further, these prayers are commanded, and so have greater value than if made of his own accord. Behold the care of holy Church to sanctify her Ministers, and her anxiety to see them worthy dispensers of the divine Mysteries. She knows and requires (according to the words of Pope Hormisdas) that he who has to pray for the people should be more perfect than the people. As St. Isidore says, there ought to be as great difference between a Priest and a layman as there is between Heaven and earth.

3. *And yet there is room.* The Priest occupies the first place at the Sacred Table, as being the first guest, and then he gives place to others. To him and to his colleagues our Lord says

literally, "Eat My bread, and drink the wine which I have mingled for you" (Prov. ix. 5). The Priest receives Holy Communion under both species, and, therefore, not only receives grace at the moment of reception, but also can enjoy the real presence of Jesus Christ within him for a longer time than others, and can thus render the acts of virtue which he then makes more meritorious. This is the "Bread which strengthens our heart" (Ps. ciii. 15). This is the Wine which was created for our spiritual joy (Eccl. xxxi. 36). In a word, this Victim delivers us from eternal death (as St. Gregory says). Meanwhile, what thanksgiving do we make for so great a benefit ? Let us call to mind the advice of St. Charles Borromeo, that after the celebrating of Mass Priests should give thanks to God for His immense benefits.

"Be mindful, O Lord, of our sacrifices, and make fat our whole burnt offering."— From *Ps.* xix. 4.

"In the spirit of humility, and in a contrite mind, may we be received by Thee, O Lord, and so may our sacrifice be made."—From *Dan.* iii. 39.

THURSDAY.

THE SACERDOTAL POWER OF APPLYING THE SPECIAL FRUIT OF HOLY MASS.

I. THE VALUE OF THIS POWER.

II. THE USE TO BE MADE OF IT.

III. THE DANGERS TO WHICH WE ARE EXPOSED IN THIS RESPECT.

" And the lord said to the servant, Go out into the highways and hedges, and compel them to come in, that my house may be filled. But I say unto you, that none of those men that were invited shall taste of my supper."—*St. Luke* xiv. 23, 24.

1. *Compel them to come in.* In celebrating Holy Mass, Priests obtain the grace which urges men to enter Heaven ; and they obtain it for those especially who are in the "highway"—that is, of good will (says St. Ambrose) ; and also for those who are in the "hedges"—that is, who distinguish not between good and evil. In short, they obtain it for the just and for sinners ; they obtain it for the living and for the dead ; and, through the power which Christ has given them, they apply freely, and to whom they will, a notable part of the fruit of the Sacrifice ; which part is called by Theologians its "special fruit" (says Cardinal Bona). Such a power was conferred upon Priests in their sacred Ordination, and, belonging as it does to the power of Order, is subject to their will. Let us consider, with Hugo of St. Victor, the value and importance of such a power, as extending over the Blood of Christ, His merits, and His mediation. Of old, Priests received the oblations of the people, presented and offered them to God,

and prayed for those who had given them the material of the
Sacrifice. But we receive from Heaven itself that Victim Who
has caused shadows to disappear and figures to cease (says St.
Leo); we give great part of the fruit of this offering to whom we
will ; nor (says St. Lawrence Justinian) can we offer to God the
Father an offering more acceptable to Him and more available
for the reconciliation of sinners, for the expiation of crimes, or
for the redemption of the Faithful in captivity. How has Jesus
Christ ennobled His ministers in giving them this authority
over His merits ! Have we hitherto sufficiently considered these
great favours ? What feelings have they excited in our heart ?

2. *That my house may be filled.* By means of holy Mass we
fill Heaven with souls set free from Purgatory—with the just who
have persevered—with sinners who have been converted. For
(says St. Bonaventure) the heavenly mansion is filled by the salvation of the whole body of the elect. This is the aim which
Jesus Christ has determined for us, in giving us power over the
special fruit of holy Mass ; this is the will of our heavenly Father,
and this should be also our will—namely, that the Faithful who
have reposed their confidence in the Sacrifice of the Son of God
should have life eternal: " This is the will of My Father that sent
Me, that every one who seeth the Son, and believeth in Him,
may have life everlasting" (St. John vi. 40). We must also
observe fidelity towards those to whom we have promised to
apply that fruit, for it is a grave sin to break a promise, especially
in so important a matter; and he who commits this sin is a man
of whom it may be said, "As clouds and wind when no rain
followeth, so is the man that boasteth and doth not fulfil his
promises" (Prov. xxv. 14). Moreover, as St. Chrysostom sets
forth, Jesus Christ, in conferring this power, intended also to
provide for the support of His Priests, giving them the right to
take alms from those who desire the application of this fruit,
and binding them, by obligation of justice, to pay it. The
Apostle makes use of many arguments to prove the right of
Priests who serve the Altar to live by the Altar " (1 Cor. ix. 18).
Let us admire the goodness of our Saviour, in providing thus
lovingly, not only for our spiritual, but also for our temporal

needs. He would not have money the price of the consecration, but He would have it be the stipend for our support (as St. Thomas says). Let us, then, consecrate to our Lord both our soul and body, since in holy Mass He has provided for the nourishment of both.

3. *None of those men . . . shall taste of my supper.* Exceedingly tremendous is this sentence (says St. Gregory), affecting, as it does, not so much those who refuse the Eucharistic Supper as those sacrilegious Priests who, in eating the Flesh of Jesus, are far more guilty than those who keep away, and who, therefore, deserve far more to be excluded from the heavenly banquet. One of the motives which usually tempt them to commit this sacrilege is excessive covetousness of the stipend to be obtained by celebrating holy Mass. How many times have not the Supreme Pontiffs been obliged to prohibit the abuses which are committed from such motives! How many propositions in regard to such stipend were condemned by Alexander VII. as of too great laxity! How many Priests have stained their conscience by deferring the celebration of Masses, and by neglecting to follow the teaching of accredited theologians on this subject! How many others sin by making illicit trade of these alms! How many others run risk of eternal damnation by not satisfying the obligations with which they have charged themselves, by violating promises, or by neglecting the conditions of legacies, or circumstances of place and time, to which they were bound! Let us remember that the sons of Heli were called "children of Belial, not knowing the Lord, nor the office of. the priests" (1 Kings ii. 12, 13), precisely because of their unlawful usurpation of a portion of the Sacrifices. Let us meditate on St. Augustin's words, that he who celebrates, or preaches, or baptizes, in order to gain money, by so doing deprives himself of heavenly goods. Let us guard against such sordid sacrilegious avarice, which (according to the teaching of Innocent III.) offends Almighty God, our neighbour, and ourselves; for it is ingratitude towards God, impiety towards our neighbour, cruelty to ourselves.

"I will offer up to Thee holocausts full of marrow, in order that Thou mayest deliver those who call upon Thee in the day of trouble."—From *Ps.* lxv. 15, and *Ps.* xlix. 15.

"In the simplicity of my heart I have joyfully offered all these things, and I have seen with great joy Thy people which are here present offer Thee their offering . . . keep for ever this will."—1 *Paralip.* xxix. 17, 18.

FRIDAY.

THE HEART OF JESUS THE TRUE MODEL OF THE PRIEST'S HEART.

I. IN HUMILITY.

II. IN CHARITY.

III. IN USEFULNESS.

"One of the soldiers with a spear opened His side, and immediately there came out blood and water."—*St. John* xix. 34.

1. *Opened His side.* St. Augustin admires the use of the word "opened" by the Evangelist in this passage. Our Lord's sacred side being opened, we are invited to behold His most holy Heart, already set before us as a pattern of humility: "Learn of Me, because I am meek and humble of heart" (St. Matt. xi. 29). Jesus was truly humble of heart, humble in the affection of His Heart—that is, in will; for He loved and chose humiliations, preferring them before worldly glory—"His heart expected reproach and misery;" whereas, if we suffer humiliations, it is either through the condition of our nature, through the depravity of our life, or through the injuries which we have received from the hands of men against our will. Let Priests, however, learn from this pat-

tern to be likewise humble of heart, in order to render themselves
worthy to bless God in the sacred mysteries; for it is written,
"O ye holy and humble of heart, bless the Lord" (Dan. iii. 87).
God desires to be honoured and served by humble Priests:
"Great is the power of God alone, and He is honoured by the
humble" (Eccl. iii. 21). Now, they will become pleasing both
to God and man (as St. Jerome declares) if, whilst deserving to
be honoured for their virtues, out of humility they yet esteem
themselves the last of all. Let us examine our hearts to see if
humility be there. The signs by which we may recognise it (says
St. Augustin) are as follows, viz.,—to be proud of nothing, to
murmur at nothing, to be neither ungrateful nor querulous, and
to give thanks to God in all His judgments. Can these signs
of humility be discerned in us?

3. *Opened His side.* The wound in the Heart of Jesus, which
otherwise had remained hidden, was rendered visible by the
thrust of the lance; and for this end was His Heart wounded
(says St. Bernard). Who would not love a Heart which has loved
us so much, and which out of love surrendered itself to the executioners? With the lance He has inscribed our name in letters
of blood in His Heart, and has He not therefore the right to
oblige us to write His Name in our heart by works of love? Has
He not the right to say to us, as the Spouse in the Canticles,
"Put me as a seal upon thy heart" (Cant. viii. 6)? When, in
vesting for the Mass, we put on the chasuble, let us remember
that it signifies charity, and therefore was it said to us by the
Bishop at our Ordination, "Receive the sacerdotal garment,
which represents charity." Hence an ancient author, speaking
of the sacred vestments, said that a Priest without charity, although
he may possess every other virtue, is not a Priest. Let us throw
ourselves into the Heart of Jesus, as into a glowing furnace of
love, that so the ice of our heart may be dissolved; let us draw
near with love, in order that He may vouchsafe to bind our hard
impenitent heart with the bond of a stronger love, and may
wound it with the burning arrow of His love (says St. Bernard).

3. *And immediately there came out blood and water.* The holy
Fathers have frequently extolled the utility of this opening of

the Divine Heart. Then, in truth, was opened the door of life, prefigured (as St. Augustin points out) by the door which Noe set in the side of the Ark. From thence was formed the Church (says St. Chrysostom), already foreshadowed by the first woman, who was formed from Adam's side. Then (says St. Cyril) did two Sacraments—the first of Sacraments and the chief of Sacraments—that is to say, Baptism and the Holy Eucharist— issue from that sacred Heart. Then (says St. Bonaventure) did a salutary drink, and a fountain springing up to eternal life, over- flow from that Heart. Therefore (says St. Bernard) let us love God and our neighbour ; manifesting our love, not only in words and with our lips, but by the labours of our ministry. Let us endeavour to be useful to our brethren by leading them into the Ark of salvation ; let us serve the Church, the Spouse of Christ, with fervour ; let us faithfully administer the Sacraments, which took their power from the Blood of Jesus ; and let us dispense to the people the water of salutary wisdom, which has its inexhaustible spring in the Heart of Jesus.

"My heart hath been inflamed, and my reins have been changed; I am brought to nothing, and I knew it not."—*Ps.* lxxii. 21.

"Open ye the gates, and let the just nation, that keepeth the truth, enter in."— *Is.* xxvi. 2.

SATURDAY.

———◆———

THE HEART OF MARY IN THE EYES OF PRIESTS.

I. As a temple.
II. As an altar.
III. As a victim.

———◆———

"Blessed are they who hear the word of God, and keep it."—*St. Luke* xi, 28.

1. *Keep it.* The Blessed Virgin kept the Word, and therefore was She "the sole keeper of the Lord;" and, being the keeper of Her Lord, She kept in Her heart the Altar and Temple of God (says St. Anselm). If the heart of every one of the Faithful should be "the temple of the living God" (2 Cor. vi. 16), far more was Mary's heart a Temple of the living God, for in Her womb He took flesh and made His abode, in Whom "dwelleth all the fulness of the Godhead corporally" (Col. ii. 9). Her heart was filled with that sanctity which becomes the Temple of God: "holiness becometh Thy house, O Lord" (Ps. xcii. 5) Like the Temple of Solomon, no sound of hammer was heard in building it; for there was no concupiscence therein to curb, no defects to correct, no disordered affections to cut off (3 Kings vi. 7). The very stones of which it was composed were all heavenly and divine (as St. John Damascene says). And while the two Temples of the former Covenant, and many Temples of the new Covenant, have been destroyed and violated, the heart of Mary (says St. Cyril) is a Temple ever intact and inviolable. With St. Antoninus, let us pause to meditate how it is a Temple

which it merits. Whether as just or as sinners, let us seek refuge in this Temple (says Albertus Magnus), and we shall be secure.

2. If the heart of Mary "kept the Word," it was also the Altar on which "always burnt the fire" of love towards the Word Himself; it was an altar of gold because of the fire of charity which burnt therein, because of its union with God. This heart may justly be considered as an "altar" because it was "high" in contemplation and "deep" in humility, and at the same time an "altar" on account of the fire of divine love. In this altar Almighty God united all the various kinds of altars which He had prescribed in the Old Law. It was made an altar of incense (says St. Albertus Magnus) by the sweet odour of Her devotion; an altar of bread (says St. Methodius), because by Her was given us the Bread of eternal life; an altar of holocaust (says St. Proclus), because of Her continual martyrdom. Therefore, let us present ourselves before this altar, in order to appease our Eternal Father; for Mary (says St. Albertus Magnus) is an altar of propitiation, on which will be offered all the Faithful who are presented by the great High-Priest to the Eternal Father.

3. The Faithful, who "keep the divine word in their heart," offer to God "spiritual sacrifices" (1 Peter ii. 5); they offer "the sacrifice of a contrite and humble heart" (Ps. l. 19); they offer the "sacrifice of praise" (Ps. xlix. 14); they offer the "wholesome sacrifice of obedience to the divine law" (Eccl. xxxv. 2); but the heart of the Blessed Virgin was a holocaust ever consecrated to Her Creator. It was a Victim most acceptable to God, and worthy of all veneration, as dedicated to Him · (says St. Andrew of Crete). Let us go, then, to this Altar as to our refuge, for we shall find there a heart melting with charity; we shall find there a heart most like to Her Son's Heart—nay (says St. Bridget), a heart which is one with His Heart. We Priests, who pass our days in the Temple, who ascend the Altar, who offer the divine Victim—we surely ought to have great confidence in the love and tenderness of this heart of Mary.

"Here will I dwell, for I have chosen it."—*Ps.* cxxxi. 14.

THIRD SUNDAY AFTER PENTECOST.

WORLDLY SOCIETY TO BE AVOIDED.

I. IT IS A LOSS OF TIME.

II. IT INJURES OUR REPUTATION.

III. IT DESTROYS SANCTITY.

. " Now the publicans and sinners drew near unto Him to hear Him : and the Pharisees and the Scribes murmured, saying, This man receiveth sinners, and eateth with them."—*St. Luke* xv. 1, 2.

1. *To hear Him.* When worldly men draw near to a Priest to listen to his teaching, his time is not lost, but is employed in a praiseworthy manner for them. For He shows himself a follower of Jesus, Who allowed sinners to approach Him that he might instruct them, according to the invitation of the Wise Man, " Draw near to Me, ye unlearned, and gather yourselves together into the house of discipline " (Eccl. li. 31). The Priest says to the sinner, " Draw nigh to hear " (Eccl. iv. 17); and the sinner " who approaches to his feet shall receive of his doctrine " (Deut. xxxiii. 3), and depart instructed and contrite. But, on the contrary, when a Priest seeks the company of worldly men, to listen to conversation which, to say the least, is idle talking, or to pass his time in vain amusements, he loses that time which he ought to spend usefully in the service of God and His Church; he forgets the warning, " Son, observe the time " (Eccl. iv. 23). We have, indeed, no time to lose; for the Apostle's words are

ever sounding in our ears—" In doing good let us not fail; for in due time we shall reap, not failing; therefore, whilst we have time, let us work good to all men" (Gal. vi. 9, 10). St. Bernard declares it is no slight loss to spend an hour in idle talking; for (says he) "in that hour thou mightest pray, labour, repent, awake thyself to heavenly desires, weep over thy sins, and induce others to follow thy example."

2. *They murmured.* The murmurs of the Pharisees were most unjust, for (as St. Gregory says) they kept their own heart dry, and yet sought to repress the very Fountain of Mercy which would pour the water of divine grace into the heart of sinners. But the laity are not equally unjust in censuring an Ecclesiastic who forgets the teaching given by St. Paul—"Withdraw yourselves from every brother walking disorderly" (2 Thess. iii. 6). St. Ephrem, commenting on this passage, says that the Apostle uttered this warning in order that we might not give occasion to those who see us to think ill of us. Hence St. Chrysostom enjoins Priests to fly such company as would give people occasion to form a bad opinion of them, since their duty is to avoid every- thing likely to bring them into disrepute. They who incur public reproach "fall into the snare of the devil" (1 Tim. iii. 7), who thus renders them unprofitable servants and hinders them from doing good. Granted that thou art as thou sayest (wrote St. Bernard), still I may form suspicions of thee: thou art to me cause of scandal, thou scandalisest the Church. Therefore, let us avoid promiscuous company if we would disarm suspicion and preserve our good name. What remorse will they who have not observed this rule feel when they come to die! What an account will they have to give to their great High-Priest!

3. *This man receiveth sinners.* Jesus Christ, being the Holy of Holies, had no cause to fear injury from contact with sinners; but it is not so with us. By conversing with the proud (that is, with sinners, pride being the beginning of all sin) the contagion of pride may easily attack us: "He that hath fellowship with the proud shall put on pride" (Eccl. xiii. 1). In such company (says St. Basil) incentives to sin enter by the eyes and by the ears, and are secretly admitted; and thus, unconsciously perhaps

to ourselves, we lose our horror of sin. As waters make the grass grow, so (says St. Ephrem) does the company of worldly people make pride at the least grow in us; and all other vices take their growth from pride. It is very difficult to quit the society of worldly men as we entered it; it is very difficult (says St. Gregory) not to have our conscience stained by contact with the tongue of such persons. In promiscuous company, the appearance, conversation, neighbourhood, of women is always dangerous, especially for those who ought to give example of chastity, and who have made a solemn vow of chastity to God. Thus does St. Isidore, in writing to a Priest, exhort him to flee the company of women as far as possible. Let us repent if we have hitherto frequented such company: let us redeem the time which we have thus misused: so shall we free our consciences from all stain, and recover our lost reputation.

" The innocent and the upright have adhered to me, because I have waited on Thee."—*Ps.* xxiv. 21.

" Because Thy name is called upon me, O Lord God of Hosts, I sat not in the assembly of jesters."—*Jer.* xv. 16, 17.

MONDAY.

———◆———

VOCATION TO MISSIONS AMONG THE INFIDELS.

I. The sublime character of this vocation.
II. The difficulty of fulfilling it.
III. The danger of resisting it.

———◆———

"And He spoke to them this parable, saying, What man of you that hath an hundred sheep, and if he shall lose one of them, doth he not leave the ninety-nine in the desert, and go after that which was lost till he find it ? And when he hath found it, lay it upon his shoulders, rejoicing."—*St. Luke* xv. 3—5.

1. *Go after that which was lost.* In this Parable Jesus Christ indicates Himself, Who (says St. Gregory) left the choirs of Angels in Heaven, and, in order to fill up the number of His flock in Heaven, sought lost man upon earth. And the Priest who leaves the charge of devout souls in order to visit the land of infidels, and to seek the salvation of those lost souls towards whom Jesus has such compassion, is a follower of this Good Shepherd, Who came down upon earth to seek the lost sheep. Most necessary is it to have pity on those who are perishing (says St. Cyril). This is a most noble vocation, for it is similar to that of the Son of God ; most glorious is this destiny, which renders the Missionary a partaker of the Apostolate. The Apostles were to "sit upon thrones " (St. Luke xxii. 30)—to be " the salt of the earth," " the light of the world," " the light put upon a candle-stick " (St. Matt. v. 13, 14, 15) ; and the rewards promised to them—" the hundredfold " of that which they had left, and the "thrones" on which they should "judge the twelve tribes of Israel"

(St. Matt. xix. 28)—represent the infinite value of the recompense reserved for them, and for all those who are partakers of the Apostolical ministry. Happy those who "are numbered with them and have part in this ministry" (Acts i. 17)! whereas to many others God says, "Thou hast no part nor lot in this matter, for thy heart is not right in the sight of God" (Acts viii. 21). What worldly glory can be put in comparison with that of a man thus truly Apostolical? How many good works, what great virtue, what abundant merits, are his! How sweet will death become to him! How superabundant his happiness in Heaven!

2. *When he hath found it.* Jesus Christ, in order to find the lost sheep, became as "a sign which should be contradicted" (St. Luke ii. 34). He led a life of humility, sorrow, and labour. He made Himself obedient to death, even to the death of the Cross. Similar to the mission which He had received from His Father was that which He gave to His Apostles, and which He still gives to Apostolical men. He loves those whom He thus sends amidst the scandals of persecution (says St. Gregory), as the Father loved Him, Whom He sent to endure His bitter Passion. But he who would embark in this career must first "sit down and reckon the charges necessary, and whether he have means to finish it" (St. Luke xiv. 30). Let him seriously reflect on the troubles, the watchings, the fasts, the mortifications, the fatigues, the journeys, the privations which he will have to endure. Let him strive to render himself like St. Francis of Sales, whom the Church celebrates as a man "ripened for the Apostolic office by the austerity and sanctity of his life." Let him prepare himself for troubles and anguish of mind, for perplexities, vexations, fears, humiliations, contradictions. Let him meditate on the words of the Apostle, "Our flesh had no rest, but we suffered all tribulations" (2 Cor. vii. 5); and on those other words, "We were pressed out of measure above our strength, so that we were weary even of life; but we had in ourselves the answer of death" (2 Cor. i. 8, 9). For the rest, he must trust in the all-powerful efficacy of Divine grace, with which our Lord never fails to succour those whom He calls to labour in any field of His ministry.

The world, indeed, discerns only the trials and difficulties to be
endured in these cases : it fails to perceive the consolations and
encouragement afforded to all who thus labour. Let us remember
the words of the great Apostle, bearing witness to the support
which he received in like circumstances : " In all things we suffer
tribulation, but are not distressed ; we are straitened, but are not
destitute ; we suffer persecution, but are not forsaken ; we are cast
down, but we perish not " (2 Cor. iv. 8, 9).

3. *Lay it upon his shoulders.* When Jesus Christ has found
the lost sheep, He carries it back to the fold, carefully supporting it on His own shoulders, and restoring it to His flock. In
this work He deserves to have associates and followers ; and for
this purpose He called the Apostles, saying to them, "Come ye
after Me " (St. Matt. iv. 19). Woe to such as refuse to follow
Him ! Woe to those who, in attachment to their kindred, resemble the man who refused to follow Jesus until he buried his
father (St. Luke ix. 59) ! Woe to those who, " having put their
hand to the plough, look back ;" that is to say, who, having begun
to follow their vocation, allow themselves to be diverted from it
by sloth, love of pleasure, vanity, human respect, or the like ! Woe
to those who, from dissipation of mind, neglect of prayer and of
counsel, either do not hear or feign not to hear the voice of
their Lord saying to them, " Go thou and preach the kingdom
of God " (St. Luke ix. 60) ! They will lose not only the merits
which they would have acquired in the Apostolical life, but even
the grace which they require for sanctity of life, and which
Almighty God had prepared for them in another state. God has
reserved to Himself the right to direct the lot of His Ministers :
" With the Lord shall the steps of a man be directed, and he shall
like well his way " (Ps. xxxvi, 23). Therefore, if God say to
thee, " Go forth out of thy country " (Gen. xii. 1) ; if He say to
thee, " Go, and I will be in thy mouth " (Exod. iv. 12) ; if He
say to thee, " As I have been with Moses, so will I be with thee,
I will not leave thee nor forsake thee " (Jos. i. 5)—then imitate
the Apostle, and say with him, " Immediately I condescended
not to flesh and blood . . . but I went " (Gal. i. 16, 17). Otherwise, if thou presume to disobey a manifest vocation, thou wilt

have no contentment in thy life; thy labours will have no happy success; thou wilt be tormented by remorse of conscience; and unless thou repent of thy disobedience thy death will be evil. The usual means for recognising a Divine vocation have been manifested to us by our instructors, even from our earliest years; let us make use of them with attention; let us profit by them with docility and promptitude.

"I am become as a beast before Thee, and I am always with Thee."—Ps. lxxii. 23.
"Thou shalt call me, and I will answer Thee."—*Job* xiv. 15.

TUESDAY.

THE WORK OF THE PROPAGATION OF THE FAITH.

 I. THE IMPORTANCE OF THIS WORK.
 II. ITS GREAT UTILITY.
 III. PRIESTS SHOULD CO-OPERATE WITH IT.

"And coming home call together his friends and neighbours, saying to them, Rejoice with me, because I have found my sheep that was lost."—*St. Luke* xv. 6.

1. *Call together his friends and neighbours.* Our Saviour manifests the joy which the Supreme Pastor shows His friends and neighbours for the recovery of His lost sheep, as it were by an oath, " Amen, I say to you, he rejoiceth more for that than for the ninety-nine that went not astray" (St. Matt. xviii. 13). Now, those who belong to the work entitled "the Propagation of the Faith" seek to give Him this joy continually and in abundance; for (says St. Jerome) in "one fold" a number of sinners is to be under-

stood. This work was founded at Lyons in 1823, and obtained the approbation, praise, and encouragement of Pius VII. on the 15th March of the same year; of Leo XII. on the 11th of May, 1824; of Pius VIII. on the 29th of September, 1830; and of Gregory XVI. on the 15th of August, 1840. This authority suffices those who recognise in the Sovereign Pontiff the voice of St. Peter, saying, " God made choice among us, that by my mouth the Gentiles should hear the word of the gospel " (Acts xv. 7). And, in truth, it is a work which tends to the fulfilment of our Lord's prediction, that before His second coming "the gospel of the kingdom shall be preached in the whole world " (St. Matt, xxiv. 14). Its object is the enlightenment of those " that sit in darkness and in the shadow of death," in order to lead them to the life of grace and of glory (St. Luke i. 79); the deliverance of barbarians and infidels, who were created in the image of God, and redeemed by the Blood of His Son from the condition of the beasts that perish (for without Christianity man is "compared to senseless beasts, and made like to them") (Ps. xlviii. 21); the restoration to the true faith of heretics who, deceived by the frauds of the devil, " have erred from the faith, and have entangled themselves in many sorrows" (1 Tim. vi. 10); the instruction of many millions of Catholics who, for want of Priests, are deprived of the Divine word and of the Sacraments, in which state it may be that " they will faint in the way " and be lost (St. Mark viii. 3). It is a work which is connected not only with the advancement of science, arts, commerce, but also with the improvement of the bodily condition of those idolators whose misery is as described by St. Paul (Rom. i. 28). In fine, its object is to convey to a large portion of the human race all the inestimable benefits which follow in the train of faith and grace : " All good things come together with her" (Wisd. vii. 11). " Doth the charity of God abide in him" (1 John iii. 17) who can meditate on these things without being moved to aid so noble a work ?

2. *Rejoice with me.*   St. Gregory points out that our Lord Jesus Christ does not say "Rejoice with the sheep," but "Rejoice with *Me;*" showing us that His joy is in our salvation. Therefore, if we love Jesus, if we desire to give Him this great joy,

we must not be backward in co-operating in the propagation of the Faith. This co-operation consists in daily prayers; that is, in one " Our Father," and one " Hail Mary," with the ejaculation, "St. Francis Xavier, pray for us." By these prayers we implore of God the spread of this work, the sending of Labourers into the Harvest, and the good success of their labours, as St. Paul also sought the aid of the prayers of the Faithful in his labours: "praying withal for us also, that God may open unto us a door of speech to speak the mystery of Christ " (Col. iv. 3). Further, this co-operation consists in the weekly contribution of a small sum towards the support of the Apostolic labourers, the exercise of Christian charity towards the neophytes, and the deliverance of the Faithful from the violence of persecutions; as the Encyclical of Gregory XVI. sets forth. Great is the reward which members of this Association may expect from Almighty God; for it is written, "Do good to the just, and thou shalt find great recompense; and, if not of him, assuredly of the Lord" (Eccl. xii. 2). If Almighty God bestows a Prophet's reward on him who receives a Prophet in the name of a Prophet, may not the same be expected in regard to those who assist in the support of the Missionaries of His Church? "He that receiveth a Prophet in the name of a Prophet shall receive the reward of a Prophet " (St. Matt. x. 41). The reason of this (as pointed out by St. Gregory) is, that the bodily wants of a Prophet must be supplied, or his voice is silenced ; so that they who contribute to his support help also in furnishing him with the requisite strength for speaking. Justly, then, have the Supreme Pontiffs opened the treasure of holy Church to the associates of this pious work; the Indulgences attached to the Association being a Plenary Indulgence on the usual conditions of Confession and Communion, with fervent prayer for the extension of the Church and for the intentions of the Supreme Pontiff, on the Feasts of the Finding of the Holy Cross and of St. Francis Xavier, as well as on one day of each month at choice; with the condition also of visiting a church or oratory of the association, if possible; and, if not, the parochial church. Moreover, an Indulgence of 100 days is granted each time the prescribed prayers are said with a contrite heart, or a donation made to the Missions, or any other pious or charitable work performed. Let us not neglect, then, to participate in so great a good, lest a day come in which we shall have bitterly to lament our fatal negligence.

3. *I have found my sheep.* Whose duty is it to assist in recovering the lost sheep? Surely it is that of Priests especially, who are set apart in order to have care of the sheep. Hence it is for them to "sound with the trumpet in the land, to cry aloud" (Jerem. iv. 5), to "call a solemn assembly, to gather together the people" (Joel ii. 15, 16), and stir them up to assist in this work. "Behold and see the countries white already to harvest" (St. John iv. 35); and those countries ready for the harvest are such souls as are now found in many infidel lands, well disposed to receive the Faith, the true sickle being (according to St. Cyril) Apostolical preaching, which will transfer them into the barn—that is, into the Church; and then shall they who have contributed to the sowing and to the reaping "rejoice together with great joy and glory" (St. John iv. 36). We know how zealously the authors of falsehood, the apostles of Satan, labour in disseminating their heresies in heathen lands. How many missionaries, or rather emissaries of sects, are to be found even in the isles of the Pacific! How many pestilential books! How many false versions of the Sacred Scriptures do they not freely dispense! Is it not, therefore, time for us to redouble our efforts, and to unite our powers to oppose the armies of Satan? Let us use all our efforts to persuade the Faithful to join this Association; let us give them the example of so doing, and thus shall we gain great merit before God.

"Let all the earth adore Thee, and sing to Thee."—*Ps.* lxv. 4.

"The Gentiles shall see Thy just one, and all the kings Thy glorious one."—*Is.* lxii. 2.

WEDNESDAY.

JUBILEES, AND MISSIONS IN CATHOLIC COUNTRIES.

I. THE WORK OF GRACE.
II. THE CO-OPERATION OF PRIESTS.
III. DEFECTS OF THE LABOURERS.

"I say unto you, that even so there shall be joy in heaven, upon one sinner that doth penance, more than upon ninety-nine just, who need not penance."—*St. Luke*, xv. 7.

1. *There shall be joy in Heaven.* Those who cavil at Jubilees and Missions in Catholic countries, as only tending to disquiet men's consciences, show that they would have sinners continue for ever in the slumber of a false peace—a peace which will be the occasion of their eternal distress and despair. They do not imitate the good Shepherd, Who says, "I had a zeal on occasion of the wicked, seeing the prosperity of sinners" (Ps. lxxii. 3). And, if they speak ill of Missions because people fall back into their former vices after having repented of them, they forget that such is human misery, through which many lose the grace which they had recovered; they regard not the Apostle's awful words, "He that thinketh himself to stand, let him take heed lest he fall" (1 Cor. x. 12). Indeed, it is difficult to understand how it is that Catholics, and even Priests, can be found to speak in this way, when holy Church has approved so many religious institutions, founded expressly for Missions—has conferred so many graces and privileges upon Priests who devote

I

themselves to such works, besides opening her treasures to the Faithful during the time in which Missions are held. Surely the teaching of the great Pontiff Benedict XIV. ought to suffice to silence such cavillers. There is (he says) nothing which tends so much to the correction of scandals and abuses—whether they be just creeping in, or whether they have already become inveterate —nothing which so helps to raise the standard of morality, however low it may have fallen, in any diocese—as the establishment of sacred Missions. It is the most ancient, the most suitable, if not the only, remedy for such evils. St. Alphonsus Liguori, who employed the greater part of his life in this Apostleship, wrote the following words, which deserve to be carefully pondered: "Those who give Missions," he says, "well know how many long-standing quarrels are closed, how many evil practices are eradicated, how many restitutions made, how many lawsuits (those hotbeds of hatred) adjusted; above all, how many bad Confessions are repaired, especially in rural parishes and small places, where Missions are not only useful, as they are in great cities, but may be said to be even necessary for this very reason; for in such parishes, where all are so well known to each other, many are kept back through false shame from confessing their sins to the local Confessor." And he adds, "Were there nothing else, it is certain that an infinity of sins are hindered during the time of the Mission; by means of the Mission many souls return to God, and persevere till death in a state of grace; many maintain themselves in a state of grace for many months; and, even if they fall afterwards, at least during the time of the Mission they acquire a greater horror of sin, greater knowledge of God and of the importance of eternal salvation." What joy must there then be in Heaven for one successful Mission, when so great is the rejoicing for the conversion of one sinner!

2. *Than upon ninety-nine.* The Missionary should present himself to the people as one of the ninety-nine just—nay, as a pattern of holiness. Six virtues especially ought to shine forth in him; that is to say, obedience, humility, mortification, devotion, modesty, and gentleness. If he obey not his Superior exactly, all will be trouble, confusion, and disorder; nor will the

victory be gained over hell, for "an obedient man shall speak of victory " (Prov. xxi. 28). If, through pride, he seek the applause of the world, the labours of the Confessional will be thrown away, and the Missionary in securing worldly fame "will have received his reward " (St. Matt. vi. 2). Father Segneri said well that he who has not courage to bear some contempt and bitterness ought not to pretend to be a Missionary. Again, he must mortify all his bodily senses ; for people look upon Missionaries as men dead to the things of this world, and therefore they should consider the Apostle's words as addressed to them, "Mortify your members which are upon the earth " (Col. iii. 5). Further, if he be wanting in devotion, especially in celebrating Holy Mass, he gives grave scandal to the people, who lose their good opinion of the Missionary, and make small account of his words; and therefore he ought to appear such an one as offers "victims, and praises, and holocausts with a devout mind " (2 Paralip. xxix. 31). His modesty in looks and words ought to be such as to give edification; and be well assured of this (says St. Alphonsus)—that people are particularly careful in observing whether any Missionary looks at women. This modesty and gravity ought to be joined to courtesy, which is the daughter of charity, and attracts the heart of the lower orders especially : " Make thyself affable to the congregation of the poor, and humble thy soul to the ancient, and bow thy head to a great man " (Eccl. iv. 7).

3. *Who need not penance.* Missionaries ought to be holy men, having no need of penance (St. Alphonsus says), for any action of theirs which does not savour of sanctity causes wonder and scandal in those who witness it. The fruit of a Mission is some-times lost through the fault of the labourers. As St. Gregory says, the ruin of many may be traced to the sin of a few. Again, a preacher who, through vanity or ignorance, corrupts God's Word—who remembers not that he has to announce the truth to the learned and to the ignorant, according to the words of the Apostle, "to the wise and to the unwise I am a debtor " (Rom. i. 14)—is a hindrance to the fruit of the Mission. Above all, it is essential that in Missions the preaching be like that of

the Apostles: "My speech and my preaching was not in the persuasive words of human wisdom, but in shewing of the Spirit and power" (1 Cor. ii. 4). Lastly, the method in which the Mission is given may be so defective as to produce harm rather than profit. For example, when the Missionaries are few in number, it may happen that, in certain places, a Mission may tend rather to the loss of souls than to their salvation. Therefore, let the rules of the sacred Congregations, and the directions given by those who have most excelled in these ministrations, be observed. Let the teaching of the Apostle be followed faithfully—"Let all things be done decently, and according to order" (1 Cor. xiv. 40). Let us pray to our Lord Jesus Christ—the Supreme Master of all Missionaries, Himself first Missionary sent by the Eternal Father—to give His Spirit to His Missionaries, and to bless their labours, so that they may be followers of Him.

"Who went about all the cities and towns, teaching in their synagogues, and preaching the Gospel of the kingdom, and healing every disease and every infirmity."
—*St. Matt.* ix. 35.

"Going they went and wept, casting their seeds; but coming they shall come with joyfulness, carrying their sheaves."—*Ps.* cxxv. 6.

"The Lord will send them many hunters, and they shall hunt them from every mountain, and from every hill, and out of the holes of the rocks."—*Jerem.* xvi. 16.

THURSDAY.

---

*OUR LORD JESUS CHRIST ENCOURAGES PRIESTS
IN THEIR APOSTOLICAL LABOURS BY A
PARABLE.*

   I. HE POINTS OUT HOW MUCH HE HAS DONE FOR
     THEM.

  II. HE REMINDS THEM HOW MUCH HE HAS DONE IN
     THEM.

 III. HE SHEWS HOW MUCH HE WILL DO BY THEIR
     MEANS.

" Or what woman having ten groats, if she lose one groat, doth not light a candle
and sweep the house, and seek diligently until she find it ? "—*St. Luke* xv. 8.

1. *A woman . . . light a candle.* Jesus Christ, in describing
the work of redemption, represents Himself under the character
of a woman, to show the honour in which He holds the devout
female sex, and also to express His maternal affection ; for
He Who is represented by the Shepherd is also signified
by the woman in the parable (says St. Gregory). He, indeed, is
the " Wisdom of God " (1 Cor. i. 24). He is our "mother," recommending "His children to keep His law " (Prov. i. 8; Eccl.
xxiv. 24). This mother sought our soul, represented by a piece of
money, on which was stamped the image of the King ; for (says
St. Cyril) we are set forth as made after the image and likeness
of God, as a piece of money is engraved with the image of the
king. In order to find this piece of money which was lost, He
lighted a candle; that is, He became incarnate, putting the light

of His Divinity into the clay of the flesh which He assumed ; for, (says St. Gregory) as a candle is light in a vessel, so the true light is the Divinity in the vessel of flesh. Let us call to mind the humiliations, the labours, the persecutions, the torments, the death, which Jesus suffered for each one of us. Let us say to Him, "What is a man that Thou shouldst magnify him ? or why dost Thou set Thy heart upon him ?" (Job vii. 17.) Let us say to Him, If Thou hast done such great things for me, what can I do for Thee to show my gratitude? But I know what Thou desirest from me— I know the new commandment which Thou hast given me : "A new commandment I give unto you, that you love one another " (St. John xiii. 34). I am ready to give my life for my brethren, mindful of the teaching of Thy beloved disciple—" He hath laid down His life for us, and we ought to lay down our lives for the brethren," (1 John iii. 16).

2. *And sweep the house.* The groat of our soul was found by our Saviour, Who purchased it with His Blood ; but it was lost many times afterwards—as often, that is to say, as we committed grave sin, supposing this fatal misfortune to have befallen us. And, as money cannot itself return to its owner, but must be sought and recovered by him, so we could never have returned to to God had not He himself sought us. And, in truth, He " enlightened us " by the words of His Ministers, and by inward illuminations; He "swept" our conscience by representing to us in a lively manner the unworthiness and hideousness of sin, in order to inspire us with a horror of it, and thus (as St. Gregory says) to restore in man the image of his Creator. Then did we begin to weep and blush for our youthful transgressions, saying with Jeremias, "After thou didst convert me I did penance . . I am confounded and ashamed, because I have borne the reproach of my youth" (xxxii. 19). Let us hope that the prayer has been granted which we then made to our Saviour—"The sins of my youth, and my ignorances, do not remember" (Ps. xxiv. 7); and let us encourage ourselves to do now for our brethren what other Priests have done for us, and what we should desire to have done for us again should we have the misfortune to lose the favour of Almighty God. What more powerful spur can we have

than this to excite in us efficacious zeal ? What more exact
measure can we have than this, to which, as our Saviour assures
us, all the Law and all the teaching of the Prophets is reduced ?
" For this is the Law and the Prophets " (St. Matt. vii. 12.)
3. *And seek diligently.* In this parable we have the rule which
we ought to follow for the conversion of sinners. We must "light
the candle" under their eyes; that is to say, we must shew
them the light of the Divine Law, the torch of His word: "The
commandment is a lamp" (Prov. vi. 23). " Thy word is a lamp
to my feet " (Ps. cxviii. 105). We must sweep their conscience;
that is, we must disturb it ; we must bring to light their hidden
vices, remove from them all affection for sin, cause them to cut
off all occasions of sin, to repair scandals, to make restitution,
and to be reconciled to their enemies. We must "use all diligence;" that is, we must seek out sinners in their lurking-places
and in their obstinacy. We must do this sometimes with affability,
sometimes with severity, sometimes with other wiles of charity, in
imitation of Him Who came " to seek and to save that which
was lost " (St. Luke xix, 10). Let us remember what St. Dionysius says—that the most divine of all divine things is to co-
operate with Almighty God in the conversion of sinners and in
the salvation of souls. No sacrifice is more acceptable to God
(says St. Gregory) than zeal for souls.

" Save us, O Lord our God, and gather us from among the nations, that we may
give thanks to Thy holy Name."—*Ps.* cv. 47.

" Thou, O God, wilt not have a soul to perish, but recallest, meaning that he that
is cast off should not altogether perish."—From 2 *Kings* xiv. 14.

FRIDAY.

EVANGELICAL LABOURERS DEAR TO THE ANGELS.

I. By the similarity of their office.
II. By their co-operation.
III. By increasing the joy of the Angels.

"And when she hath found it, call together her friends and neighbours, saying, Rejoice with me, because I have found the groat which I had lost. So I say to you, there shall be joy before the Angels of God upon one sinner doing penance."— *St. Luke* xv. 9, 10.

1. *Call together her friends and neighbours.* In holy Scripture Priests are called Angels, for the Angels are called God's "Ministers" (Ps. cii. 21; Ps. ciii. 4), and often Priests receive the same title (Rom. xv. 16; 1 Thess. iii. 2). Jesus Christ (says St. Gregory) in this passage calls the Angels His "friends and neighbours," because they do His will, and because they see Him face to face. Now, Jesus Christ gave to Priests also this title of "friends" (St. John xv. 15), and it is well known that it is they who stand nearest to Him: "whom He shall choose, they shall approach to Him" (Numb. xvi. 5). Moreover, as they have a common name, so have they also a common mission; for Priests also are sent for the salvation of the people, and to announce "the gospel of salvation" (Eph. i. 13). The very name of Angels implies that they announce good tidings, and they are all sent by God as "ministering spirits . . . to minister

for them who shall receive the inheritance of salvation " (Heb. i. 14). Even the seven most noble Spirits who stand before God's throne are the eyes and horns of the Lamb, "sent forth into all the earth " (Apoc. v. 6). Nay (says St. Thomas), the nine Choirs of Angels co-operate in our salvation, some in one way, some in another. How dear, therefore, to these heavenly intelligences must be those Priests who execute their ministry faithfully, and so become like them, not only in chastity and in union with God, but also in their zeal for souls !

2. *Rejoice with me.* Almighty God invites the Angels to rejoice at the conversion of a sinner, knowing that they have desired it and sought to effect it. Those whom He has made ministers of His dispensations He causes to participate in His joy (says St. Gregory). Now, in the conversion of sinners, Angels co-operate with Him in one way, Priests in another; and in like manner, as St. Paul loved those that had "laboured with him in the Gospel" (Philipp. iv. 3), so do the Angels love their fellow-labourers, the Ministers of the Sanctuary. The Angels aid sinners by their prayers, by persuading them to good, by curbing the fierceness of the devil. As St. Augustin says, they help them when they labour, they protect them when they rest, they exhort them when they fight, they crown them when they conquer. But the protection they afford pertains to things secret and invisible (says St. Thòmas) ; and hence Priests are needed to aid men after a visible manner, for men must receive salutary aid by means of the senses. For this reason the guardian Angel of Macedonia invited St. Paul to come into that country, saying, " Pass over into Macedonia and help us " (Acts xvi. 9). Therefore, when we preach, hear Confessions, or do any other things for the salvation of men, let us often call to mind that their Angel guardian, who always " sees the face of their Father who is in heaven" (St. Matt. xviii. 10), who prays for them to God face to face, is helping us. Let us call to mind, that God's Angel often speaks in us : "the Angel that spoke in me " (Zach. ii. 3). Let us call to mind that the Angel guards us, and stands round about us, to deliver us from many perils : for " My angel is with you" (Baruch vi. 6). In the doubts, and trials, and sor-

rows of our Ministry, let us often invoke (as St. Bernard enjoins us) our guardian, our leader, our helper.

3. *There shall be joy before the Angels of God.* Who could imagine that festival should be held in Paradise for the conversion of a sinner, in which the Angels rejoice, sharing the Saviour's joy? Who could have supposed that God would invite the Angels to rejoice with Him for the recovery of the lost groat, as though He had found His own salvation, His own treasure, His own God? As though man were the God of God (says St. Thomas), as if Divine salvation depended wholly on finding him, and as if God without him could not be blessed! And yet the only-begotten Son, Who is in the bosom of the Father, assures us of it, Who said to Nicodemus, "We speak what we know, and we testify what we have seen" (St. John iii. 11). The Angels do indeed rejoice when Priests convert sinners; for it is thus that sin is destroyed, justice restored, the pride of the devil weakened, the guardianship of Angels rendered efficacious, the wounds of the Church healed, and the losses of the heavenly Jerusalem repaired (says St. Bonaventure). And how dear will that Priest be to the Angels who has procured them this joy, not once only, but times without number! They love us already, because Christ has loved us (says St. Bernard); but how much more will they love us, bless us, and pray for us, if we strive to multiply the festivals of Paradise! Here, then, is a continual incentive to our zeal for the conversion of sinners; and therefore (as St. Ambrose says) let us make that our aim, in order that we may obtain the patronage of the Angels; and let us never cause them displeasure by our slothfulness.

"Bless the Lord, all ye his hosts, you ministers of His that do His will."—*Ps.* cii. 21.

"Send now also, O Lord of Heaven, Thy good angel before us."—2 *Mach.* xv. 23.

SATURDAY.

THE VISITATION OF THE BLESSED VIRGIN MARY A SPECIAL SUBJECT OF MEDITATION FOR MISSIONARIES.

I. MARY EXERCISES THE FIRST MISSION
II. SHE IS THEIR ADVOCATE.
III. SHE IS THE PATTERN OF MISSIONARIES.

" And Mary rising up in those days, went into the hill country with haste, into a city of Juda, and she entered into the house of Zachariah."—*St. Luke* i. 39, 40.

1. *Mary rising up in those days, went into the hill country.* The Blessed Virgin was to hold the first place in every class of Christians: " In every nation I have had the chief rule " (Eccl. xxiv. 19): and it is no matter of surprise that She should be the first to exercise an Apostolical Mission, and so to merit the title of Queen of Apostles. If (as St. Augustin says) Missionaries are compared in Holy Scripture to " clouds," carrying showers of grace to the places over which they rest, Mary was the first among these clouds, giving the showers of the Holy Spirit to fertilize the barren earth and cause it to bring forth the fruits of faith (as St. Epiphanius says). She began Her mission in the house of Zachary, whither She was sent by the Word incarnate in Her, Who hastened (says Origen) to sanctify His precursor in his mother's womb. Now, Missionaries make it their object to convert sinners, to animate the tepid to fervour, to sanctify the just. In like manner Mary converted the Baptist; that is, She obtained for him the pardon of original sin. She animated to fervour the Priest Zachary, who had grown tepid through want

of faith ; She increased the sanctity of Elizabeth, who was filled with the Holy Ghost. Missionaries are sent for the benefit of Priests and laymen, of men and women, of great and small ; and they strive to make God's voice to be heard by all. Mary also was an example to them, in all these points, in Her holy Visitation. Her voice, indeed, was the voice of sanctification to all, for all were represented in that family which She visited, and the voice of the Word spoke (as St. Jerome says) by Her mouth. The voice of the Missionary ought also to be the voice of Christ, "that speaketh in him" (2 Cor. xiii. 3), as the voice of Mary was the voice of God incarnate in Her. O Mary, thou art truly an Apostle; thou didst possess the Apostolate in a supreme degree, and that which thou didst in the house of Elizabeth is but an example of what thou hast done, and art still doing, in the whole world ! So Albertus Magnus.

2. *With haste.* Mary is a pattern to Evangelical Missionaries, and especially in zeal; for She hastened to impart Her spiritual benefits to the house of Elizabeth. They who have true zeal for the salvation of souls delay not their undertaking, for the grace of the Holy Spirit knows no lingering, no delay (says St. Ambrose). They regard not difficulties, they do not calculate labours, they weary not of trouble; in short, they imitate Her whose zeal (as St. Ambrose again remarks) overcame even her virginal modesty, and to whom the ruggedness of the mountains and the length of the journey presented no obstacle. Let, then, the Priest undertake this ministry, when he is disposed for it, like Mary, who was (according to the same Father) "full of God;" let him undertake it when he has Jesus within him, when he carries Him in his heart, when he glorifies and bears God in his body, when he is a "vessel of election to carry the name of Jesus before the children of Israel." Let him carefully meditate on those words, "Glorify and bear God in your body" (1 Cor. vi. 20); and on those other words, "This man is to Me a vessel of election to carry My Name before . . . the children of Israel" (Acts ix. 15). Let him imitate Mary in faith, in humility, in modesty, in all those virtues which can make His presence an advantage to

so beneficial to the house of Zachary. But let him be careful to be first of all a man of prayer; for (as it has been observed) Mary did not undertake Her missionary journey until She had first, for some days, contemplated the mystery of the Incarnation. Afterwards, when he sees the good success of his labours let him refer all the glory to God, like Her, who, "magnifying the Lord," was wont to say, "I will devote all the powers of my soul to give thanks and praise." So Venerable Bede.

3. *She entered into the house of Zachary.* As Mary entered into the house of Zachary, a Priest of the course of Aaron, to bless it, so should She enter into the heart of the Christian Priest when he prepares himself for holy Missions. St. Thomas says that the Faithful, in invoking a Saint who has fulfilled some ministry, are more readily heard of the Saint when they are in the exercise, and amidst the perils, of the same ministry. Therefore, let Missionaries invoke Mary, who so well fulfilled Her mission, coming, as She did, over rugged and dangerous mountain-tracks to perform Her friendly offices (as St. Ildephonsus points out). In Missions we have especial need of grace to enrich us with light, and to furnish us with strength to fulfil our Ministry. We must also pour grace abroad in the Faithful, for without it our words will be useless; and for this purpose to whom should we have recourse if not to Mary, who (as St. Bonaventure says) was, in a certain sense, grace itself, because of the abundance of grace with which She was adorned? Grace comes to us from our Head—that is, from Jesus; but it passes into His mystical Body by means of the neck—that is, Mary. The fulness of grace is in Christ, as in the Heart from which it is poured; and it is said to be in the Blessed Virgin as in the neck through which it is transferred into the Body. Let us carefully meditate on this sentence of St. Thomas, "In every work of virtue thou canst have Her aid, and therefore She Herself declares, "In me is all hope of life and of virtue" (Eccl. xxiv. 26). Let us then invoke Her, and let us confide in Her protection.

"What is man that Thou art mindful of him? or the son of man that thou visitest him?"—*Ps.* viii. 5.

"How beautiful are thy steps in shoes, O prince's daughter!"—*Cant.* vii. 1.

FOURTH SUNDAY AFTER PENTECOST.

THE PREACHER'S AUDIENCE.

I. Thoughts awakened by a numerous audience.
II. Virtues to be exercised when it is scanty.
III. Means by which it may be increased.

" When the multitudes pressed upon Him to hear the word of God, He stood by
the lake of Genesareth . . . and sitting He taught the multitudes out of the ship."—
St. Luke v. i. 3.

1. *When the multitudes pressed upon Jesus.* The multitudes who
pressed upon our Saviour were numerous. They were eager to
hear Him, full of love and admiration (says St. Chrysostom), and
they did not interrupt the course of His instruction. Sometimes
a preacher sees himself surrounded by an audience remarkable
for its number and quality, and then the devil fails not to suggest
vain thoughts, and to awaken in him some motion of self-complacency, so that he can hardly escape soiling his feet with
either external or internal vanity (as St. Augustin says). Thus (as
the same Father remarks), the condition of hearers is more
secure than that of preachers, for the former can more easily
preserve humility than the latter. Sometimes pride, ostentation,
vanity, are so visible to the eyes of the hearers as to disgust
them. Unhappy preacher! puffed up externally (as St. Augustin
says again), he is wasting away inwardly. Now, to avoid this
fault and its fatal consequences, the affection to be excited at

the sight of a numerous audience (St. Chrysostom tells us) is that of joy at beholding the Church adorned with so many children, joy at beholding them thus eager to hear the Divine word. Let the preacher rejoice in God's glory, when many come together to hear the sacred word, and not in his own glory. Woe to such as convert to their own vainglory that which should be employed for God's glory (says St. Bernard)! Let them rather reflect on the account, which they will have to give to Almighty God, of the many hearers for whose failure in profiting by their discourses they may perhaps be themselves responsible ; for had they been truly Apostolical preachers the case might have been different. Let them reflect (with St. Chrysostom) that a great part of their hearers will leave the church without reaping any fruit from their words, and that, therefore, on this account they should rather weep and lament.

2. *To hear the word of God.* Sometimes it happens that few desire to hear the word of 'God, and then the preacher naturally feels the want of excitement. But he who has the Spirit of God will call to mind (with St. Charles Borromeo) that our Saviour once preached to a single Samaritan woman, and that He constantly preached to the Apostles without other hearers. On such an occasion let him (as St. Chrysostom enjoins) console himself with the reflection that, although he may have but one hearer, it is no small conquest to gain one lost sheep, since for that one the Son of God was made Man. Let him imitate St. Francis of Assisi, who spoke with the same constancy to the many as to the few. Let him imitate St. Francis of Sales, who rejoiced at preaching even to a very few hearers. This is, indeed, a great protection to humility, and a safeguard against pride and vainglory, which are ever followed by avidity and trouble of mind (as St. Augustin points out). God may perchance be pleased thus to humble the pride of the preacher, and it is good to be humbled by God: "Thou hast humbled the proud one, as one that is slain" (Ps. lxxx. viii. 11).

3. *Sitting He taught the multitudes out of the ship.* Our Saviour, being on the sea (says St. Chrysostom), fished for souls among the multitudes who were upon the land. We, too, should fish

for hearers, and endeavour to gain many to come and listen to us; and this is effected (says St. Jerome) by such preaching as is seasoned by the Holy Spirit. Let us be convinced that, if we preach thus, and with a view only to the fruit of our preaching, we shall merit true praise; for all who have within them the habit of faith—the Christian instinct to desire to draw profit from preaching—will say with St. Bernard, "I gladly listen to the voice of this preacher, who moves me, not to applaud him, but to bewail my own soul." If we preach with unction, if we speak to the heart, we shall attract and instruct our hearers: "His unction teacheth you" (1 John ii. 27). Then will Almighty God console His faithful and laborious Ministers, not by the mere multitude of their hearers, but by proofs of the profit derived from their preaching. Let them only (as St. Charles Borromeo enjoins) set before themselves, as their one great object, the glory of Almighty God and the salvation of souls. Let us carefully examine our conscience in this respect. What errors have we committed by reason of our numerous hearers? Have we, in any way, by our own fault diminished the fruit of the Divine word? Let us repair the evil we have done; let us bewail it before God.

"Bless Thy word to our hearers, and multiply them exceedingly."—From *Ps.* cvi. 38.

"Thou hast multiplied the nation, and hast not increased the joy."—*Isaias* ix. 3.

MONDAY.

RENEWAL OF SPIRIT.

I. Its importance.

II. Means of attaining it.

III. Bad effects of neglecting it.

"But the fishermen were gone out of them, and were washing their nets . . . and their net broke.—*St. Luke v.* 2—6.

1. *But the fishermen were gone out of them.* The circumstance related by the Evangelist in these words is not without a mystical significance, for it shows us (says St. Chrysostom) that this was a time of leisure for the fishermen. It shows, also, that those who are fishermen in a spiritual sense—that is, preachers of the Gospel—must not spend all their time in instructing others, but must reserve a portion of it (as Venerable Bede points out) for descending, as it were, into themselves and taking care of the state of their own soul. St. Paul recommended this practice to Timothy, and, in the person of Timothy, to all Ecclesiastics: "Carefully study to present thyself approved unto God, a workman that needeth not to be ashamed" (2 Tim. ii. 15). But how can a Priest be said to act thus who gives no time for that renovation of spirit by which (as St. Ambrose points out) fervour is rekindled, and the Priest begins his course, as it were, afresh. However pure and well-regulated his life may be, still (says St. Augustin) it ever needs to be polished afresh; and without this renewal (says St. Leo) the spirit grows rusty, as it were, and makes no progress in virtue. Wisely, therefore, has

K

this practice been instituted in all congregations of Priests, and is earnestly recommended. Have we, however, reaped the full benefit of it ?

2. *Washing their nets.* These fishermen were washing their nets, and mending them at the same time (St. Matt. iv. 21). Too easily does the Evangelical labourer soil his feet with the dust of this world ; and therefore we ought to detect these stains and wash them away; and to do so is a holy pursuit, an Apostolic practice. It may be that the net of the soul is broken—that is to say, our virtues are impaired by many defects ; but by penance this net is repaired; for (says St. Gregory) when the soul inquires into itself, and examines itself carefully with penitence, it is renewed afresh by tears and compunction. If we would, in short, understand the effects of this pious exercise, let us meditate on the words of St. Lawrence Justinian. It cuts off (he says) superfluities, drives away what is hurtful, strengthens what is crooked, exposes all deceit, disperses darkness, and removes all inordinate affections. Therefore, after the example of Moses and Jeremias, it is good to take a little rest from external cares, in order that in retirement we may attend to ourselves, and afterwards execute the Divine commands (as St. Gregory Nazianzen says). In such retirement (says St. Basil) the soul recovers the likeness of the Creator, and returns to its original purity. By this means the " new man " which is within us " is renewed unto knowledge, according to the image of Him who created him ;" that is to say, a clearer knowledge of God is attained as we make it our study to reflect His image in ourselves. Let us imitate the eagle, who renews its youth (Ps. cii. 5); that is (as St. Augustin explains), it sharpens its beak against a rock so as to render it more capable of taking its food. In like manner, we ought to approach the Rock, which is Christ, by retirement, meditation, and penance, that our youth may be, as it were, restored ; for (continues the same Father) we have " grown old among our enemies" (according to the words of the Psalm); and how have we grown old ? In our mortal flesh, that flesh of grass.

3. *Their net broke.* This is the danger to which those who neglect renovation of spirit expose themselves ; their net will easily

break; that is to say, they will easily fall into grave sin. Unless (says St. Chrysostom) we take time to set up within ourselves a severe tribunal, and to judge ourselves, we shall not have a sufficiently strong incentive to avoid sin. Moreover (as St. Augustin warns us), unless we have chosen a time to judge and amend ourselves, we shall find ourselves discouraged and perplexed when death approaches and we have to present ourselves at the judgment-seat of God. But (as St. Basil tells us) if we judged ourselves carefully we should not fear the approach of God's judgment. The last evil which results from the neglect of this renovation (and it is no light one) is the loss of a powerful means for attaining the perfection proper to our state; for (says St. Chrysostom) a great help for attaining perfection is to be found in retirement. Therefore, let us resolve to find a time for retirement, in which we may examine our conscience and strive after greater perfection; let us remember that St. Bernard inculcated its necessity on a great Pontiff, and that, to another Priest who had care of souls he wrote thus :—Avoid all external cares, in order that, with Samuel, thou mayst say with more readiness from thy heart, " Speak, Lord, for Thy servant heareth."

"I have watched, and am become a sparrow, all alone on the house top."—
Ps. ci. 8.
" Renew me, O Lord, in the spirit of my mind, and put on me the new man."—
From Eph. iv. 23, 24.

TUESDAY.

ANALOGY BETWEEN PREACHING AND FISHING.

I. Sinners compared to fish.
II. Preachers compared to fishermen.
III. Distinction between the two kinds of fishing.

" At the draught of fishes which they had taken . . . And Jesus saith to Simon, Fear not : from henceforth thou shall catch men."—*St. Luke* v. 9, 10.

1. *At the draught of fishes.* In the holy Scriptures mankind are often compared to fish. Thus, it is said in Habacuc (i. 14), " Thou wilt make men as the fishes of the sea, and as the creeping things that have no ruler ;" and Cornelius à Lapide, commenting on this passage, finds twenty different analogies between men and fish, especially when through vice man has degenerated from his original dignity. However, it is sufficient for us to observe (with St. Basil) that among wicked men, as among fish, the greater devour the less ; or (with St. Gregory Nazanzen) that sinners are men swimming in the troubled waters, and amidst the bitter storms of life ; or (with St. Augustin) that the sea is a figure of this world, salt and bitter, troubled with storms, and where men of perverse and depraved appetites become like fishes devouring one another. St. Bernard further distinguishes three kinds of sea, in which sinners are found, viz., the sea of vices, the sea of the tribulations of this world, and the sea of hell. O my God, have compassion on these fish, whom Thou didst create in Thy own image, as stars made for Heaven, and whom Thou didst redeem with the Blood of Thy Son ; suffer not the Leviathan, the whale

of hell, to devour them, and to make them to be as fish in the pool of fire and brimstone, which is prepared for them (Apoc. xxi. 8).

2. *Thou shall catch men.* Almighty God had promised by Jeremias (xvi. 16) that He would "send many fishers into the world, and that they should fish" the people; and this was verified in the Apostles, to whom our Saviour said, "I will make you to be fishers of men" (St. Matt. iv. 19). As the fisher takes the fish that least expect to be taken, so did the Apostles take in their nets idolaters who seemed little disposed for so great a favour, and of whom Almighty God might justly say, "I was found by them that did not seek me" (Rom. x. 20). In like manner, also, as he who fishes knows not what fish will come into the net, so the Apostles and other preachers cannot foresee who will profit by their words. Let us admire the ways of Providence and the omnipotence of our Lord Jesus Christ, Who (says St. Augustin), designing to break the necks of the proud, did not seek a fisherman by means of an orator, but through a fisherman gained an emperor. In other words, He chose not orators and senators for the Evangelical fishing, but fishermen; and in their nets He took not only orators but emperors. Moreover, He chose a small number of fishermen to take innumerable and rare fish—that is to say, the very philosophers themselves. Who, then, can tell the power of our Lord, or who can grow weary of praising Him? Let us also fish, and let us bless the Author of our fishing.

3. *Fear not.* Why should we fear to undertake this fishing so long as Jesus is with us, to Whom all "power is given in heaven and in earth?" Not only at the calling of the Apostles, but also after His Resurrection, He animated their faith by two miraculously abundant fishings. The second of these was still more marvellous than the first; for on the first occasion the nets were thrown only on the right side, whereas on the latter they were thrown indifferently on the right or left. In the latter case the net was not broken; whereas it was broken in the former, and there came mingled together innumerable fish, both bad and good; but, on the second occasion, the fish were choice and

xxi. 6, 11). St. Augustin observes that these two fishings represent the Church in two diverse conditions; that is, as she is in
this present time, and as she shall be in the end of the world.
In the first fishing is described the Church militant, which is
likened by our Saviour to "a net cast into the sea, and gathering
together of all kind of fishes" (St. Matt. xiii. 47); but in the
fishing after His Resurrection our Saviour points to the predestinate, who after the resurrection of the body shall be carried
to the shore; that is, to the land of the living. Now, God has
ordained the ministry of Priests as an indispensable condition to
both these fishings; and to all eternity Priests are destined to be
"fishers of men;" that is to say, they are to lead men, by the net
of the Divine Word, to live for God in time and in eternity.
Upon them is laid the injunction to take men by the net of God's
word out of the stormy and dangerous sea of this world, in order
to translate them into the land of the living. But, alas! how
little and how negligently have we fulfilled this duty! How
many are the souls whom we have led to faith, to grace, and to
glory?

"Gather into Thy net, O Lord, the fishes of the sea, that pass through the paths
of the sea."—From *Habac.* i. 15, and *Ps.* viii. 9. "Send, O Lord, many fishers."—
From *Jerem.* xvi. 16.

WEDNESDAY.

———◆———

EVANGELICAL FISHERMEN TO BE IN ENTIRE
DEPENDENCE ON THE SUPREME PONTIFF.

I. JESUS CHRIST TAUGHT THIS TRUTH.
II. IT IS PROVED BY EXPERIENCE.
III. THE NATURE OF THIS DEPENDENCE.

———◆———

" And going up into one of the ships, that was Simon's, He desired him to draw
back a little from the land. Now, when he had ceased to speak, He said to Simon,
Launch out into the deep, and let down your nets for a draught."—*St. Luke* v. 3, 4.

1. *Into one of the ships, that was Simon's.* Our fishing is by
means of the word of God, and this word comes but from one
sole ship—from the ship of Peter ; that is, from the Catholic
Church, of which Peter is head. Rightly is it said, " one of the
ships," because (as Venerable Bede observes) by depending on
this one pilot the Faithful have but one heart and one soul; and
(as St. Augustin points out) our Saviour, by teaching the multitude from Peter's ship, shews us that all nations were to be
instructed by means of the authority of the Church, which is
governed by Peter. This ship (says St. Ambrose) is not troubled,
because Peter is at its helm, on whom the Church is founded.
Moreover, our Saviour in this same ship gave to Peter especially the charge of fishing. To him (says St. Bonaventure) was
this charge especially committed. Therefore, let us consider
that the Roman Pontiff was by Christ constituted the interpreter
of the voice of St. Peter, and (as the Council of Chalcedon declares) for the benefit of the whole human race. Hence, in

order that the laity may hear the voice of St. Peter from the lips of Priests, these latter must depend on him as the Interpreter; and in order that their fishing may be successful they must be firmly attached to the Supreme Pontiff, whom St. Jerome calls "the Disciple of the Cross, the Successor of the Fisherman." If they would build on a solid foundation—if they would instruct the world— if they would draw their net to shore—if they would have a counsellor who is indispensable to them—if they would speak the language of Heaven—let them depend on him, who is justly called by St. Chrysostom "the immoveable Foundation, the Teacher of the whole world, the Harbour of Faith, the necessary Counsellor of Christians;" and by St. Peter Damian, "the Tongue of Heaven."

2. *Launch out into the deep.* By these words our Saviour charged St. Peter to convey the Divine word to the most remote nations of the earth ; and experience has shewn that all fishers who depend not on Peter's Successor will, according to the words of the Prophet, "mourn and lament, and languish away; for in vain will they spread nets upon the waters" (Is. xix. 8). We see, in point of fact, that missionaries sent by the Supreme Pontiff, whether to heathen lands or to Catholic countries, make immense conquests of souls. For (as St. Cyprian says) they are like rays issuing from one sole light, like branches springing from one sole root ; nor is there a Christian Church, however heretical or schismatical it may have now become, which does not acknowledge as its first Apostle some missionary sent forth by St. Peter or his successors. Churches, on the contrary, who have divorced themselves from their true Spouse, have lost all fruitfulness, and have become as barren women, suffering not the fruitful mother to rejoice in Her holy joy (Ps. cxii. 9). Innovators, whose zeal is ever in accordance with their passions and interests, know not how to abandon all things for the preaching of the gospel. Such men have no success in making new Christians, but rather pervert weak Christians, and so become evil fishers, sent by the devil, of whom the Prophet says, "he lifted up all of them with his hook, he drew them in his drag, he gathered them into his net . . . and will not spare continu-

ally to slay the nations" (Habac. i. 15, 17). Let us bless God for having placed us among the labourers of the Gospel; let us strive to reunite all nations to the Church, to bring back those who have unfortunately forsaken her, to guard those who are found in this blessed net.

3. *Let down your nets.* The Prophet inculcates upon Bishops immediate dependence on the Supreme Pontiff; "Look unto the rock whence you are hewn, and to the hole of the pit from which you are dug out" (Is. li. 1); but let all Ecclesiastics remember that from Peter, as from the head, all gifts are shed abroad throughout the whole body (as St. Leo teaches). Let them courageously cast their nets for the draught, under the guidance of St. Peter's successor, in such wise that Peter himself may cast them by their means: "Let down your nets for a draught . . . . Simon said to him . . . I will let down the net." Let them shew dependence on the Chief Pontiff by receiving his teaching with filial affection and obedience, as from St. Peter; let them shew it by regulating their life by the books which bear the august seal of this authority. Let them fly from all teachers of error and lies condemned by him, however brilliant their maxims, however sublime their sentiments, however affectionate their language. Such teachers seek only to poison and corrupt us; and therefore let us call to mind the words of St. Ambrose to Pope Siricius—"That which thy Holiness has condemned, be assured that my own judgment also has condemned, because it is condemned by thee." Let us shew this dependence by obeying all Constitutions and regulations which emanate from the Holy See and from its Congregations; let us promulgate the Indulgences which it grants; let us inculcate upon all exact obedience to its Constitutions, reminding them of the terrible menace—"He that will be proud, and refuse to obey the commandment of the priest who ministereth at that time to the Lord thy God, and the decree of the judge, that man shall die . . and let no one afterwards swell with pride" (Deut. xvii. 12). Let us pray, and let us make others pray, for the Holy Father and for his See, for on his and its prosperity the prosperity of the whole Priesthood depends; and therefore does St. Chrysostom, in his interpretation of the

47th Psalm, say, " Surround this new Sion, and encompass her ;" that is to say, guard her, fortify her, strengthen her by your prayers.

" Let them exalt him in the Church of the people, and praise him in the chair of the ancients."—*Ps.* cvi. 32.

" O Lord, Aaron shall invoke Thy name upon the children of Israel, and Thou wilt bless them."—From *Num.* vi. 27.

THURSDAY.

—-◆—

AN ABUNDANT DRAUGHT OF SOULS.

I. It is taken in the full day.
II. With confidence in God.
III. With concord amongst the fishermen.

—◆—

" And Simon answering said to Him, Master, we have laboured all the night, and have taken nothing; but at Thy word I will let down the net. And when they had done this they enclosed a very great multitude of fishes . . . And they beckoned to their partners that were in the other ship, that they should come and help them. And they came and filled both the ships, so that they were almost sinking."—*St. Luke* v. 5—7.

1. *We have laboured all the night and have taken nothing.* The fishing of the Gospel succeeds not by night; it must be done in full day. Evangelical fishermen must be " children of the light" (Eph. v. 8); they must " walk honestly, as in the day" (Rom xiii. 13); they must preach " in the light" what they have heard as it were " in the dark" (St. Matt. x. 27); that is to say, by the reading of the sacred Scriptures, the Traditions of the Church, by

internal inspirations. They must present the Christian religion to their hearers, as it is in itself, without duplicity, without artifice, without dissimulation. Thus they will set the sublimity of its dogma against the pride of the world, the severity of its morals against human corruption, the unity of its worship against superstition, the stability of the Faith against persecution ; and thus they can say to the world, " Whilst you have the light, believe in light, that you may be the children of light" (St. John xii. 36). For us Priests especially "the night is past, the day is at hand; therefore, let us cast off the works of darkness, and put on the armour of light " (Rom. xiii. 12). So shall we not fish in vain, but (as St. Cyril says), spreading our nets, we shall gather in a great multitude of people.

2. *At Thy word I will lay down the net.* St. Peter meant to say (as St. Bonaventure points out) that they had laboured in vain the whole night, because they had depended on their own efforts; but now their trust was not in their own strength, but in His. Here, then, is the pattern for the Evangelical fisherman to follow, if he would not have to say with the prophet, "I have laboured in vain " (Is. xlix. 4). If, on the contrary, he place all his confidence in the efficacy of Christ's word and Christ's omnipotence; he may apply to himself this saying, " My word, which shall go forth from my mouth, shall not return to me void, but it shall do whatsoever I please, and shall prosper in the things for which I sent it" (Is. lv. 11). Therefore, let us trust in Him Who sends us to fish, and say to the people, " He Who is hath sent me to you " (Exod. iii. 14); let us trust in Him Who, in sending us, worketh in us and in our hearers, by His omnipotent grace, "both to will and to accomplish " (Phil. ii. 13); let us trust in Him Who sends us, because "He loves souls" and died on the Cross to save them (Wisd. xi. 27 ; 1 Cor. viii. 11). Let us consider the lawfulness of our Mission, and have regard to its faithful fulfilment, for " how shall they preach unless they be sent ?" (Rom. x. 15.)

3. *And they beckoned to their partners.* A sign sufficed to make these fishermen hasten to help their partners. Neither self-love nor jealousy nor slothfulness held them back ; and this is the pattern (says St. Cyril) which the Gospel sets before the fishers of

souls, and which they must follow if they would draw to shore a net full of fish. Far otherwise will it be if jealousy enters the hearts of God's Ministers; if they are displeased should Almighty God prosper the labours of another rather than their own; if they are unwilling to stretch out the hand of fellowship to him because the honour is his, and not theirs; if they begin to speak of him contemptuously, to censure his actions, to put a bad interpretation on his intentions, to throw discredit on his good fame, to rob him of the respect which is so necessary for the success of such fishing. Our Saviour gave another proof of this truth when He sent the seventy-two Disciples "two and two before His face" (St. Luke x. 1); for He sent them thus in order (says St. Bonaventure) that they might mutually guard and aid one another. This concord and mutual co-operation in our Evangelical labours is frequently recommended to us by the Holy Spirit. Let us call to mind that great sentence of the Preacher, "It is better that two should be together than one, for they have the advantage of their society" (Eccls. iv. 9); and again, "A brother that is helped by his brother is like a strong city" (Prov. xviii. 19); and "A man amiable in society shall be more friendly than a brother" (ver. 24); that is to say, an Apostolic labourer derives more help from one who shews him true friendship than from a brother according to the flesh. If Priests are animated solely by motives of charity in their labours, they will not allow themselves to be overcome by the base affections of jealousy, envy, emulation; for "charity envieth not, dealeth not perversely, is not puffed up, is not ambitious, seeketh not her own, is not provoked to anger" (1 Cor. xiii. 4, 5). Let us pray to Almighty God to shed abroad this charity in our heart, and in the heart of all holy fishers of souls.

"The Lord hath done great things for us: we are become joyful."—*Ps.* cxxv. 3.
"In Thy name I will let down the net."—*St. Luke* v. 5.

FRIDAY.

THE SENTIMENTS CALLED FORTH BY SUCCESS IN EVANGELICAL FISHING.

I. Admiration of God's work.
II. Self-humiliation.
III. Affection for following Jesus.

" Which when Simon Peter saw, he fell down at Jesus' knees, saying, Depart from me, for I am a sinful man, O Lord. For he was wholly astonished, and all that were with him . . . and so were also James and John the sons of Zebedee, who were Simon's partners . . . And having brought their ships to land, they followed Him."—*St. Luke* v. 8—11.

1. *For he was wholly astonished.* The spectacle of the conversion of the Gentile world ought to fill us with wonder, for this is the miracle of miracles, by which Almighty God has awakened the admiration of all ages : " Behold I will proceed to cause an admiration in this people, by a great and wonderful miracle " (Is. xxix. 14). A slight net (says St. Ambrose)—that is to say, a composition of words—made by poor fishermen, has taken an immense multitude of fish ; and this net, these fishing implements, have not killed the fish caught by them, but have taken them in order to their preservation, freeing them from bitter and stormy waters, and landing them in eternal bliss. And is not the sight of so many converted sinners an object of admiration to us ? Is not this the most wonderful of the works of the Creator of the universe ? Are not the operations of grace carried on in the depths of the heart more wonderful than all the works of nature ?

"These have seen the works of the Lord, and His wonders in the deep" (Ps. cvi. 24).

2. *I am a sinful man.* St. Peter, on beholding this abundant and unexpected draught of fishes, marvelled at the Divine gifts ; and the more he feared the less did he presume on himself (says Venerable Bede). Calling to mind his sins (says St. Cyprian), he trembled and feared, thinking himself unworthy to entertain in his ship, and to stand in such nearness to, so holy a Master. He drove his Saviour away from him, esteeming himself unworthy of His company; but by his humility he did not repel Him, but attracted Him (says St. Bonaventure). Let us also humble ourselves when we perceive that Jesus has made use of us for the conversion of sinners, employing us as the unworthy instruments of His mercies. Let us remember that we also have been, and still are, sinners, and that by self-abasement and compunction of heart we may draw down upon ourselves a pitiful look from our Saviour : "To whom shall I have respect, but to him that is poor and little, and of a contrite spirit, and that trembleth at My words ?" (Is. lxvi. 2.) Let us consider, with St. Augustin, that our Saviour did not leave Peter when he prayed Him to depart from him, in order to teach those Ecclesiastics who lead spiritual lives that the sins of the people ought not to cause them to shrink from the work of their Ministry, or to desert it for the sake of peace and tranquillity of mind. Let us admire the wisdom and goodness of our Lord Jesus Christ, Who instructed His Apostles, and through them all His Priests, by so many lessons. Let us meditate on those lessons carefully, let us pray to Him that we may profit by them.

3. *They followed Him.* When we perceive that Jesus, in His immense condescension, deigns to make use of us as instruments for working the wonders of His mercy, let us attach ourselves more and more to Him and to His Church, in the hope that He will continue to bless us in the work of our Ministry. Let us imitate the faith and obedience of these Disciples, who, without delay, abandoned all things in order to follow the Redeemer ; and let us convince ourselves (as St. Chrysostom teaches) that He requires a similar obedience from us. This following of Jesus

(says St. Bonaventure) consists in that perfect imitation of our Master which is the way to attain to the perfection of justice, and is the means of our highest glory. We have a model of this perfect following in the words of Elias to Eliseus, " As the Lord liveth, and as thy soul liveth, I will not leave thee" (2 Kings ii. 4). What a consolation will it be to us at the point of death to remember that we have faithfully followed Him, and to be able then to repeat the words of holy Job, " My foot hath followed His steps ; I have kept His way, and have not declined from it " (Job. xxiii. 11).

" Blessed be the Lord, the God of Israel, Who alone doth wonderful things."—Ps. lxxi. 18.

" Depart from me, for I am a sinful man, O Lord.—St. Luke v. 8.

SATURDAY.

—◆—

THE VISITATION OF THE BLESSED VIRGIN MARY.—II.

In Her Canticle, Mary teaches Priests how to thank God for their elevation to the Priesthood—

I. WITH DUE AFFECTION.
II. WITH DUE CAUSE.
III. IN A FITTING MANNER.

" My soul doth magnify the Lord."—St. Luke i. 45.

1. *My soul doth magnify the Lord.* In this Canticle (says St. Bonaventure) three things are to be observed ; viz., first, the affection of Her who praises ; secondly, the reason of Her praise ; thirdly.

the enlargement of the Divine praise; for no praise is perfect unless it be accompanied by a due affection and reason, and performed in due method . . . The Blessed Virgin listened to the praise which St. Elizabeth bestowed on Her, and immediately referred all the praise to God. When Elizabeth told Her that her son rejoiced in her womb with joy at the voice of Her salutation, Mary replied that Her spirit rejoiced in God. "Thou magnifiest the Mother of thy Lord, but my soul doth magnify the Lord. Thy son exulteth at my voice, but my spirit rejoiceth in God my Saviour." Thus does St. Bernard explain Her words. Or (according to St. Athanasius) "the greater is the miracle of Divine goodness of which I am the instrument, the more am I constrained to glorify Him Who works wonders in me." Now, let us enter into ourselves, and consider what the Priesthood is which God has conferred upon us. Is it not a great miracle of Divine omnipotence by reason of its Divine dignity, and because of the means with which it furnishes us for exercising it aright? Do not we work miracles at the Altar, in the Confessional, in administering the other Sacraments? What, then, is the affection with which we "magnify the Lord," and "rejoice in Him?" St. Basil says that, in Holy Scripture, by this term is signified the lively, joyful, affection of a soul which is rightly disposed! Oh that in each one of us were the soul of Mary to magnify the Lord! Oh that each one of us had Mary's spirit to rejoice in God! And yet how few are the Priests who thank God with sincere affection for their vocation! Might they not at least take pattern by the gratitude of Nebuchadnezer, and say, "I praise and magnify and glorify the King of Heaven?" (Dan. iv. 34.)

2. *Because 'He hath regarded the humility of His hand-maid.*
Here (says St. Bonaventure) Mary adds the reason of Her praise. The Blessed Virgin shows forth the beneficence of grace, which had made Her amiable before God, and worthy of the praises of men; and She shows forth also the great and merciful miracle of His power which He had worked in Her (says the same St. Bonaventure). We, too, ought to acknowledge that stream of grace by which Almighty God has united us to Himself, and caused us to be called blessed by the Faithful; we, too,

ought to acknowledge that truly great and merciful miracle by which "God hath chosen the weak and base things of the world to confound the strong" (1 Cor. i. 27, 28); and this should be our reason for praising God, Who hath "looked upon us for good, and hath lifted us up from our low estate" (Eccl. xi. 13). What merit had we that we should be preferred before so many millions of men? The whole reason of this act consists in the power of the doer (says St. Augustin). Who, among men, can ask of God why He should have preferred us before them? for He will do all that pleaseth Him, and His word is full of power; neither can any man say to Him, "Why dost thou so?" (Eccl. viii. 3, 4.) Let us speak continually the words of Azarias—"Blessed is the Holy Name of Thy glory" (Dan. iii. 52).

3. *And His mercy is from generation unto generations.* The third part of the Canticle enlarges the Divine praises, by celebrating God's mercy, His power, His liberality, and the truth of His promises (as St. Bonaventure points out). Are not we Priests bound to praise the mercy of the Lord, Who by His special providence has freed us from innumerable dangers of soul and body, in order to lead us to the Altar, and to make us what we are—so that each one of us might say with the Apostle, "By the grace of God I am what I am, and His grace in me hath not been void . . . . yet not I, but the grace of God with me?" (1 Cor. xv. 10.) We also have experienced God's power, Who "hath showed might in His arm;" "Who hath raised up the needy from the dust, and lifted up the poor from the dung-hill; that he might sit with princes, and hold the throne of glory?" (1 Kings ii. 8.) Again, ought we not to praise God's liberality in that He hath "poured forth upon us abundantly" the Holy Spirit (Tit. iii. 6), and thus "hath filled the hungry with good things, but the rich He hath sent empty away?" Lastly, the truth of the Divine promises was magnified by the Blessed Virgin in these words—"As He spoke, &c.;" and ought not we, too, to call to mind the innumerable promises, made by Almighty God in Holy Scripture, that He would "raise up among His people a faithful priest, who should do according to His heart" (1 Kings ii. 35), and give to His flocks "pastors according

to His own heart" (Jer. iii. 15); "to fill the soul of the Priests with fatness" (xxxi. 14); and "to give glory, joy, and power to the Priests of the new covenant?" (Is. lvi. 4.) Therefore, let us bless the Lord, and, in the daily recital of this magnificent Canticle, let us join ourselves in spirit with Mary in blessing Him, praying to Her to offer Him our benedictions in such wise as to obtain for us a blessing, which shall enrich us with all "good things."

"I will praise the Name of God with a canticle, and I will magnify Him with praise."—*Ps.* lxviii. 31.

"My soul doth magnify the Lord."—*St. Luke* i. 46.

FIFTH SUNDAY AFTER PENTECOST.

THE JUSTICE WHICH GOD EXPECTS IN PRIESTS.

I. Its attainment is not difficult.

II. It was required even in Priests of the Old Law.

III. It is founded on the justice of Jesus Christ.

"Unless your justice abound . . . you shall not enter into the kingdom of Heaven."—*St. Matt.* v. 20.

1. *Your justice.* Our Saviour rightly expects perfect justice from His disciples, for His law extends not only to outward actions, but also to the sanctification of the soul; and yet (as St. Thomas explains) being, as it is, the law of love, it is light; for love renders all things light. We Priests have special commandments given us in our quality of sacred Ministers, but

" His commandments are not heavy" (1 John v. 3). Almighty God is content if Priests love Him from the heart ; for if they so love Him they will easily cause Him to be loved by others, and will perfectly fulfil their duties. How can a Priest possibly say (asks St. Jerome), " I cannot love?" Is not charity itself diffused in His heart ? The gift of charity, and the power to exercise it, are from the Holy Spirit Himself, but require also our co-operation. For this end has the Holy Ghost been so often shed abroad in us, and therefore (as St. Ambrose says) the Priest's life should abound even as grace abounds. Our co-operation is easy through the many occasions which we have of doing good— through the numerous examples of heroic Priests which the Church puts before our eyes—through the many virtuous habits which our ecclesiastical education has supplied. It is easy through the word of God, which constantly sounds in our ears ; it is easy through prayer, of which we are ministers; it is easy through the abundance of grace with which we are supplied in our daily Communion. Rightly, therefore, did the Council of Trent prescribe that the Clergy, in whatever Order they might be, should be pre-eminent among the people of God in the sanctity of their lives and conversation, as well as in knowledge ; for it is written, " Be ye holy, because I am holy." The very honour, the very dignity of the Priesthood, obliges Priests to clothe themselves with justice ; for the higher the degree of honour and dignity, the more should they excel in all kinds of virtue. Truly (as St. Jerome says), it would be a great injury to the Church of God if Ecclesiastics were surpassed in sanctity by the laity.

2. *Unless it shall abound.* St. Thomas observes that the Aaronic liturgy and all the ceremonial precepts imposed upon the Priests of the Old Law, by implication, that "abundant justice" which is clearly prescribed to Priests of the New Law. Of the sons of Aaron, indeed, God said plainly, " They shall be holy to their God, and shall not profane His Name, for they offer the burnt offering of the Lord, and the bread of their God, and therefore they shall be holy " (Levit. xxi. 6). And Bellarmin justly remarks that, if so great sanctity was required for offering mere sheep and

the Lamb of God ? Many of these Priests were praised for their sanctity, as Aaron, Samuel, Zacharias and his father Barachias, Jeremias, Nehemias, Onias, Simon, and Zacharias the father of the Baptist. They bore upon their shoulders that burden, called by St. Peter "a yoke, which neither our fathers nor we have been able to bear" (Acts xv. 10); and what shall we say in the great Day of Judgment—how shall we excuse our vileness—if we have been unable to bear the easy yoke of our Divine Master ?

3. *You shall not enter into the kingdom of Heaven.* Our Saviour looks for "abundant justice" from us—that is to say, great virtue, —if we would enter into the kingdom of Heaven: "In abundant justice there is the greatest strength" (Prov. xv. 5), and justice (as St. Chrysostom says) comprises the whole aggregate of Christian virtues. To make the attainment of it easy to us, He was Himself "made unto us wisdom and justice, and sanctification and redemption" (1 Cor. i. 30); that is (according to St. Bernard) wisdom in preaching, justice in the absolution of sinners, sanctification in the intercourse which He had with sinners, and redemption in the suffering which He bore for sinners. We have, then, the support of Jesus Christ, Who is with us, Who is in us, Who has ingrafted us into His Priesthood, Who nourishes us with Himself. If He commands us to sow seed in His field, He feeds us also with the bread which gives us strength for the work ; and, whilst He Himself causes the seed to grow, He multiplies the harvest of our justice. "He that ministereth seed to the sower will both give you bread to eat, and will multiply your seed, and increase the growth of the fruits of your justice" (2 Cor. xi. 10). Let us strive, therefore, as Priests, to become a congregation of Saints ; for who should be holy if not Priests ? Let us remember that Jesus Christ came into the world to sanctify Priests especially, and to render them fit to offer sacrifices in abundant justice: "He shall purify the sons of Levi, and shall refine them as gold and as silver, and they shall offer sacrifices to the Lord in justice" (Malachias iii. 3).

"Conduct me, O Lord, in Thy justice, because of my enemies."—*Ps.* v. 9.

"O Lord Jesus Christ, to know Thee is perfect justice, and to know Thy justice and Thy power is the root of immortality."—From *Prov.* xv. 3.

MONDAY.

------◆------

PRIESTS MAY EASILY FALL INTO THE SINS OF THE SCRIBES AND PHARISEES.

I. THE EVIL DISPOSITION OF THE HEART OF THESE MEN.
II. THEIR ERRONEOUS CONSCIENCE.
III. THE CORRUPTION OF THEIR LIFE.

------◆------

"More than that of the Scribes and Pharisees."—*St. Matt.* v. 20.

1. The Scribes and Pharisees, whose defective justice is here by pointed out by our Saviour, were most severely rebuked Him on another occasion, as we read in the twenty-third chapter of St. Matthew. He first of all (says St. Thomas) set forth their dignity, in that they occupied the chair of Moses; and then shewed their perverse intention in the use of their authority. Cornelius à Lapide observes that, although many among them were Priests, He did not address them as Priests, out of regard for the honour of the Priesthood. He denounced the Scribes and Pharisees—and in that designation included Priests—for their negligence, cruelty, and vainglory (as St. Chrysostom says). He declared, indeed, that they sat on the chair of Moses, and explained the Law, but did not obey it; "for they say, and do not" (St. Matt. xxiii. 3); and by these words He warned Priests, that if they fulfil not that which they teach others, they will receive condemnation, not honour, from their Priesthood. He added, that they bound heavy and insupportable burdens on other men's consciences, whilst they would not move them with even a finger; and in that respect they were a figure of those Priests who oblige

sinners to heavy penances, but will do no penance themselves.
Lastly, our Lord denounced their vainglory as the cause of all
their evils, whereby their intention was corrupted at its source ;
for they did all their good works through vainglory, in order to
be seen of men ; they wore garments which betokened sanctity ;
they sought the chief honours, the first places, the most honourable titles. From this passage the Angelical Doctor, following the
authority of St. Chrysostom, lays down this great maxim—Take
away vain glory from the Clergy, and every other vice will be
easily cut off. Let us examine the state of our conscience ; let
us scrutinize the dispositions of our heart ; and let us strive to
be in the number of those good Priests who, by despising the
praise of men, have merited the highest honour in the kingdom
of Heaven.

2. *The Scribes and Pharisees.* Our Saviour launched eight
Anathemas against these Scribes and Pharisees, in contrast to the
eight Beatitudes which He had uttered on a former occasion.
He uses the word "Wo" eight times. This word (as St. Basil
says) was directed against those who, in a short time, would be
thrust down into the place of eternal punishment. Some of
these Anathemas regard the abuse of knowledge, by which they
shut the kingdom of Heaven against themselves and against
others (St. Matt. xxiii. 13). Here let us remember that by the
kingdom of Heaven is represented heavenly bliss, of which Christ
is the door ; while the key of it is the knowledge of the Scriptures.
Now, this key is entrusted to Priests, to whom it is given to teach
and interpret Holy Scripture. O my God, suffer me not to become as those Priests who, through negligence or false doctrine,
close the gate of Paradise against themselves and others ! Further, the Pharisees instructed Proselytes, and then, taking no care
of their lives, rendered them " twofold more the children of hell"
than themselves (St. Matt. xxiii. 15.) In this they resembled those
Priests who instruct their pupils in Christian doctrine, but neglect
to cultivate a Christian spirit in them—nay, who often injure them
by wicked example. They bring forth children in the faith (says
St. Gregory), but they cannot nourish them by good living ; they
carelessly suffer those whom they have begotten to devote them-

selves to earthly objects. The Scribes, in short, taught false morality, and so contributed to the damnation of their hearers ; and this may be well applied to some Confessors, who are also "blind guides . . . foolish and blind," calling that which is sin lawful, and *vice versâ.* "Wo to you that call evil good, and good evil, that put darkness for light, and light for darkness" (Is. v. 20). Deliver me, O God, from being myself deceived in this respect, and from deceiving others.

3. *The Scribes and Pharisees,* under the cloak of piety, "devoured widows' houses" (St. Matt. xxiii. 14); they scrupulously offered the tithe of their herbs to God, whilst they transgressed the weighty commandments of the law (v. 24); they were careful in regard to outward cleanliness, but neglected that which was internal (v. 25); they were whited sepulchres, cunningly hiding, under the mantle of hypocrisy, the corruptions of vice (v. 27); they built sumptuous sepulchres to dead prophets, and persecuted living prophets (v. 29). In their whole conduct, in short, there was a simulation of religion, purity, and piety; and it is this which our Saviour rebukes. How easy is it for the Clergy to fall into this simulation, which (says Venerable Bede) no sooner infects the soul than it robs it of all true and real virtue! Therefore let us engrave on our heart, and carefully meditate on, our Saviour's warning—"Beware ye of the leaven of the Pharisees, which is hypocrisy" (St. Luke xii. 1). Thus may our lives be acceptable, not to men only, but to God; and thus shall we find true happiness both on earth and in heaven.

"God hath scattered the bones of them that please men : they have been confounded, because God hath despised them."—*Ps.* lii. 6.

"If I yet pleased men, I should not be the servant of Christ."—*Gal.* i. 10.

TUESDAY.

—◆—

ON SCANDAL.

I. HE WHO GIVES SCANDAL IS A MURDERER.
II. THE SPECIAL GUILT OF SCANDAL IN PRIESTS.
III. IT IS DIRECTLY OPPOSED TO THE INSTITUTION OF THE PRIESTHOOD.

—◆—

"You have heard that it was said to them of old : Thou shalt not kill, and whosoever shall kill shall be in danger of the judgment."—*St. Matt.* v. 21.

1. *Thou shalt not kill.* If it be a grave sin to kill man's body, what will it be to kill the soul ? Rather (says St. Thomas of Villanova) would I have caused the death of a thousand men than have been the means of eternal death to one single soul. To speak a word deficient in goodness, to perform an action deficient in rectitude, so as to bring occasion of spiritual ruin to others— this (says St. Thomas) is scandal. And this ruin of others is no other than their spiritual death ; that is, mortal sin. He, then, who gives scandal is the devil's huntsman, who surprises his incautious brother and kills him : " Every one hunteth his brother to death " (Mich. vii. 2). His sword (says St. Gregory) easily forces its way into the defences of man's inward uprightness, and thus does the weak Christian perish " for whom Christ died " (1 Cor. viii. 11). The devil is called " a murderer " in holy Scripture, although he has never attacked men with the sword. In like manner, those who give occasion of sin to their brethren are murderers. If thou persuadest thy brother to evil thou murderest thy brother (says St. Augustin). How terrible are these truths, but how little do we consider them !

2. *Thou shalt be in danger of the judgment.* The crime of the Priest who gives scandal is greater because of his greater dignity; for (says St. Gregory) the laity easily persuade themselves that anything which they see done by their Pastors must be lawful in their own case. Such Priests become as a snare and a net in the hands of the enemy of souls, and against them shall a terrible judgment be pronounced (Osee v. 1). In fact (St. Chrysostom says), the corruption of the Priesthood is sufficient to cause the spiritual death of the whole people; and it is most difficult to raise up those who are thus spiritually dead, because the Priest's evil example takes away shame, lessens remorse, and banishes from their minds the thought of conversion. Our Lord Himself revealed to St. Bridget that the example of wicked Priests makes sinners sin boldly, so that they begin to glory in what they formerly looked upon as a cause of shame. Daily experience too surely proves this truth, as all Confessors must know. What, then, has our life been? what the example we have given? what the words which the laity have heard from our lips? Let us carefully examine ourselves on this head, and remember that, "when we sin thus against the brethren, and wound their weak conscience, we sin against Christ" (1 Cor. viii. 2); we take from Him the soul which He purchased with His Blood. And, inasmuch as He regarded the salvation of souls more than His own life, He is more grievously injured by such as give scandal than by those who crucified Him (as St. Bernard observes).

3. *Thou shalt be in danger of the judgment.* The crime of Priests who give scandal is the greater because of the obligation they are under to be "the salt of the earth;" that is, to preserve the Faithful from corruption. They ought to be the root giving vital sap to the plant, whereas they furnish it with a juice which causes death. We know that when we see a tree with sickly and fading foliage there is something faulty at the root. In like manner, when we see a people without religion we may be sure that the fault lies in the Priesthood. Instead of leading Christians to eternal life, they lead them to eternal perdition (says St. Gregory). Justly are such Priests, being "salt without savour," despised and trodden under foot by the laity. But, if they have "lain in

wait as fowlers, setting snares and traps to catch men " (Jerem. v. 26) in the service of the devil, what answer will they make before the tribunal of Christ ?   How will they excuse themselves before Him who chose them out of all men to offer Sacrifice to Him, and to bring forth fruits of eternal life ?   Often, doubtless, have we preached upon scandal : let us take heed lest such preaching be our condemnation, for to us more than to the laity is it said, " Woe to that man by whom the scandal cometh" (St. Matt. xviii. 7).

" They have slain the widow and the stranger, and they have murdered the fatherless, and they have said, The Lord shall not see."—*Ps.* xciii. 6, 7.
 " O Lord, father, let ... not my offences be multiplied and my sins abound."— *Eccl.* xxiii. 1—3.

WEDNESDAY.

—◆—

DUTIES OF PRIESTS IN REGARD TO ANGER.

I. To REPRESS ANGER IN THEMSELVES.
II. To REPRESS IT IN THE FAITHFUL.
III. To APPEASE THE ANGER OF GOD.

—◆—

" But I say to you, that whosoever is angry with his brother shall be in danger of the judgment."—*St. Matt.* v. 22.

1. *But I say to you.* Our Saviour desires to show the superiority of the Gospel over the Law of Moses, and He begins with a condemnation of anger. He condemns it with the authority of a lawgiver, for He uses language which had never been employed by the Prophets of old (as St. Chrysostom observes), since they

spoke not thus, but said, "Thus saith the Lord." Now, this passion is not in itself necessarily and entirely a deformity, because reason has some share in it; it is often but a venial sin, because of circumstances which extenuate its guilt; it infects even spiritual persons who are scrupulous in regard to other faults. Nay, it is most difficult to restrain the motions of anger, because of their sudden violence; just as the motions of concupiscence are difficult to vanquish because of their longer continuance. But the Priest must show himself to be "not subject to anger" (Tit. i. 7); for truly anger and fury, which are both of them abominable, are unbecoming Ecclesiastics, on whom they impress the character of sinners; for "the sinful man shall be subject to them" (Eccl. xxvii. 33). Anger is a passion which renders men capable of committing any crimes (as St. Bonaventure says). As St. Antoninus says, it hinders the use of reason, and blinds the eye of the understanding. Let us pray to God to give us patience, that we may restrain a passion which deprives us of dominion over our soul, ever remembering that "the patient man is better than the valiant, and he that ruleth his spirit than he that taketh cities" (Prov. xvi. 32).

2. *Whosoever is angry with his brother.* Amongst the duties of Priests is that of removing those hatreds which, if they do not spring from anger, are far worse and more serious than anger. In order to destroy the root of the evil, they must enjoin Christians to lay aside anger in its three different forms; that is to say (according to St. Gregory), anger without speech, anger in the tone of the voice, anger expressed in words. They must point out how the Christian should be known (as St. Chrysostom says) by his meekness rather than by the name given him in Baptism. They must show how those who are subject to anger are not acting according to justice, but tread the laws of justice under foot, "for the anger of man worketh not the justice of God" (St. James i. 20). They must teach them that Christians should not harbour this serpent in their bosom to the going down of the sun—"Let not the sun go down upon your anger" (Eph. iv. 26); and that the passionate man is his own enemy, killing soul and body—"Anger, indeed, killeth the foolish" (Job

v. 2). So shall we imitate our Lord Jesus Christ, Who began His teaching by condemning anger, and made meekness the fourth Beatitude : " Blessed are the meek, for they shall possess the land" (St. Matt. v. 4). Above all, let us strive to give an example of meekness, in imitation of our Divine Lord, Who said of Himself, " Learn of Me, because I am meek, and humble of heart " (St. Matt. xi. 29).

3. *Shall be in danger of the judgment.* How terrible is the judgment of God when He condemns sinners in His just anger! Therefore said the Psalmist, " Rebuke me not, O Lord, in Thy indignation, nor chastise me in Thy wrath" (Ps. xxxvii. 2). God, indeed, is not unjust when He is angry and when He punishes —"Is God unjust, Who executeth wrath?" (Rom. iii. 5 ;) but His justice must be satisfied, for (as St. Thomas says) anger in God signifies the act of His will towards vengeance. Now, it is the duty of Priests to appease this Divine anger. Moses was among His Priests, and "appeased the Lord" (Exod. xxxii. 14); so also did Aaron (Numb. xvi. 46). Why should not we do the same ? In the ancient Temple "sacrifices and atonements were offered " (1 Mach. i. 47); Priests were destined to appease God's indignation against men—"they shall make atonement upon it in your generations" (Exod. xxx. 10). They were to appease God, Whom the sinner had offended: "that he may appease the Lord for him" (Lev. xiv. 29). Yet those ceremonies of the old law— those sacrifices—were but weak figures, shadows, of the good things to come which are in our hands. How, then, should we be unable to effect that which the Priests of Aaron effected ? We have in our hands the Sacrifice of propitiation, which is more than sufficient to cancel the sins of ten thousand worlds. We have our Lord's own promise to hear and grant our prayers ; but perchance we are wanting in that faith which renders prayer omnipotent. "Let him ask in faith, nothing wavering, for he that wavereth is like a wave of the sea, which is moved and carried about by the wind: therefore, let not that man think that he shall receive anything of the Lord" (St. James i. 6, 7). Our prayers, perchance, are not armed with tears and fasting, like those of Daniel, which obtained for the people the graces

he desired (Dan. ix. 3); yet how great consolation shall we experience in calling to mind the many prayers we have made to avert God's anger from sinners, so as to be able to say to Almighty God with Jeremias, who was also a Priest, " Remember that I stood in Thy sight, to speak good for them, and to turn away Thy indignation from them !" (Jerem. xviii. 20.)

"I did eat ashes like bread, and mingled my drink with weeping, because of Thy anger and indignation."—*Ps.* ci. 10, 11.

"O Lord, hear: O Lord be appeased: hearken and do: delay not for Thy own sake, O my God."—*Dan.* ix. 19.

THURSDAY.

THE ANGER SUITABLE TO A PRIEST.

I. ANGER AGAINST VICE.
II. ANGER WHICH DOES NOT IMPAIR MEEKNESS.
III. ANGER WHICH FOLLOWS JUST RULES.

" And whosoever shall say to his brother, Raca, shall be in danger of the council ; and whosoever shall say, Thou fool, shall be in danger of hell fire."—*St. Matt.* v. 22.

1. *And whosoever shall say to his brother, Raca.* Our Lord Jesus Christ forbade that anger should be manifested by the accent of the voice expressing it (says St. Augustin), but yet He tells us by His Apostle, " Be angry, and sin not " (Eph. iv. 26). The Stoics declared that all passions of the mind, and especially anger, should have no place in the wise man; while the Peripatetics taught that anger might exist even in the wise, but that the wise would know how to regulate it. To regulate this passion (says

St. Augustin) signifies, to be angry, and to manifest anger, not against our brother, but against his sin. It is the proper office of a zealous Priest to be moved to anger against sin—nay, against his brother insomuch as he is a sinner, in order to amend him ; for then this passion is kindled by the love of good, and by a holy charity. Wo to the Priest who (as St. Augustin says) takes languor for charity, and who burns not with zeal for the correction of offenders. Let the Priest raise his voice, let him apply remedies with fitting vigour to the wounds which he shall heal. The sick man may cry out and exclaim (as St. Cyprian says), but when he shall see himself cured he will render thanks. Pursue the plague in order to cure the sick : hate the one because you love the other. Have we done so hitherto ?

2. *And whosoever shall say, Thou fool.* It is sometimes necessary for Priests to make use of harsh words for the correction of those who are ignorant and in error. Our Saviour Himself called two of His disciples "foolish" (St. Luke xxiv. 25). St. Paul called the Galatians "senseless" and "foolish" (Gal. iii. 1—3); he reproached Elymas the sorcerer (Acts xiii. 10); he wrote to Titus, "Rebuke them sharply" (Tit. i. 13). But in so doing and so speaking meekness must never be lost sight of, but must precede severity; for this is the great means for calling back the lost sheep to the fold, and for keeping within it those who have not wandered (says St. Chrysostom). Let us remember that Moses ruled the people by meekness, and that by meekness the Apostles made themselves masters of the world, according to our Lord's promise (St. Matt. v. 4). To suffer injuries peaceably ; not to seek vengeance ; to render good for evil ; to show humility before the proud ;—these (says St. Basil) are the marks of a good Prelate, who ought to fulfil the Apostle's teaching "Pursue . . . mildness" (1 Tim. vi. 11). The Minister of Christ should be clearly distinguished by his meekness (as St. Chrysostom says). This virtue is called by St. John Climacus the door—nay, the mother—of charity, the minister of pardon, the conductor of brotherly love, the imitation of Christ. It is said by St. Basil to be the greatest of all the virtues, and as such inserted among the Beatitudes. Without it (says St. Gregory)

the Priest stains his own soul, discredits his own judgment, destroys the souls whom he ought to rescue, and ruins the work of the Ministry committed to him. Let us ask of the Holy Spirit the grace of meekness, which is at once a virtue, a beatitude, and the fruit of the Holy Spirit. Let us meditate on St. Augustin's statement, that the first and greatest gift of the Spirit is that of humility and meekness.

3. *Shall be in danger of hell fire.* The Ecclesiastic must follow certain salutary rules if he would avoid that eternal fire which our Lord declares to be the punishment due to such as sin through anger. In the first place, anger must be directed against sin, and especially our own sins, since (as St. Bernard says) they alone can injure us. This indignation is just and necessary (says Venerable Bede). In the next place, we must see clearly whether, in rebuking our neighbour, we are moved by self-love or by love of our brother. As St. Augustin says, if thou dost this out of self-love thou dost nothing : if thou dost it from love towards him thou dost excellently. In the third place, we must take care (as St. Jerome warns us) that our anger be not so excessive as to make us lose self-control. In the fourth place, let us suffer patiently any persecution which God may permit to come upon us : " give place unto wrath " (Rom. xii. 19). Let us, however, not provoke it nor irritate it, so as to add fire to fire ; nor let us break out into bitter complaints. Lastly, let us never lose sight of that noble mode of vengeance, and of victory over our enemies, which the Apostle suggests to us : " Be not overcome by evil, but overcome evil by good " (Rom. xii. 21).

" O Lord, afflict not my eye, my soul, and my belly in wrath."—From *Ps.* xxx. 10.
"Give me not over to a shameless and foolish mind."—*Eccl.* xxiii. 6.

FRIDAY.

EXAMINATION OF CONSCIENCE SHOULD PRECEDE THE CELEBRATION OF HOLY MASS.

I. Because of the intrinsic usefulness of such examination.

II. That we may be reconciled to our First-born Brother.

III. To strengthen our concord with the rest of our brethren.

" If, therefore, thou offer thy gift at the altar, and there thou remember that thy brother hath anything against thee ; leave there thy offering before the altar, and go first to be reconciled to thy brother, and then coming thou shalt offer thy gift.—*S. Matt.* v. 23, 24.

1. *If . . . thou remember.* We have to offer to God the gift of all gifts ; we have to offer Him on the holy Altar a Victim worthy of Himself, and we must treat holily that which is thus supremely holy. But we shall never do this well if we examine not our own conscience—if (as St. Gregory says) our mind does not make a daily inquiry as to the position in which we stand before God, and the light in which God regards us, weighing well the good things we have received from Him, and the ill return we have made for his goodness, according to the constant practice of the Saints. It is needful to do this every day, and to sit in judgment on our life; and (as St. Bernard says), just as we set apart a time for prayer and for reading, so ought we to give a special time to the examination of our conscience. It is needful

to make this examination in a special manner, that we may not expose ourselves to the danger of celebrating a sacrilegious Mass, and in order that we may use that circumspection, consideration, and reverence without which (as St. Bonaventure warns us) we should be unworthy to perform so sublime an act. Let us, then (according to St. Bernard's advice), take away the girdle we have inherited from Adam; let us break the veil of leaves, which covers our shame but does not heal our wounds; and let us carefully examine our conscience in all its nakedness.

2. *Thy brother hath anything against thee.* Jesus is, indeed, our Brother, for He " is not ashamed to call us brethren" (Heb. ii. 11). He is "the first-born amongst many brethren" (Rom. viii. 29), and if He have anything against us we must reconcile ourselves to Him. But we must practice self-examination in order to know our guilt. The Apostle's words should never be forgotten by us—" Let a man prove himself, and so let him eat of the Bread and drink of the Chalice" (1 Cor. xi. 28). If we find that we have committed grave sins, we must make our confession before Mass, and submit to our Confessor's judgment in regard to celebrating. If our faults are venial, let us follow the teaching of the great Pontiff, St. Gregory, and immolate ourselves, as it were, before God with contrition of heart. We must wash our soul, after the example of the Priests of the Old Law, who washed themselves before putting on the sacred vestments (Levit. xvi. 4), and who "washed their hands and feet when they were going to the altar" (xxx. 19, 20). To them it was said, before they received in their hands the sacred vessels, "Be ye clean that carry the vessels of the Lord" (Is. lii. 11). Let us call to mind that the Lord Jesus would wash His disciples feet before giving them the Holy Eucharist, and by this action would point out to us (says St. Cyprian) the spiritual purification which ought to precede the reception of Holy Communion. So shall we be purified from the stains and defects which cling to the soul through our earthly conversation, even as dust sticks to the feet in walking. For (says St. Augustin) our human affections, without which in this mortal state we cannot live, are as the feet brought into continual contact with the things of earth, and in such a manner

M

that "if we say we have no sin we deceive ourselves." For this end does the Church put the confession of our own sins in our mouth at the beginning of Mass—most rightly so, for the Holy Spirit declares, "The just is first accuser of himself" (Prov. xviii. 17).

3. *Go first to be reconciled to thy brother.* The matter of the Eucharist—that is, bread and wine—signifies (says St. Augustin) that concord which Jesus Christ especially recommends to those who approach to receive Him. Thus does He enjoin us to be reconciled to our brethren before we offer sacrifice to God, for He will receive no offering (says St. Gregory) from those who are living in enmity with their brethren. Dearer to God is the concord of the Faithful than their gifts. Hence, St. John the Alms-giver (as we read in his life), remembering when he was at the Altar that a cleric had offended him, interrupted the sacred function, in order to reconcile himself to him, and then completed the sacrifice. Let us remember this especially whenever in solemn Masses, according to ancient rite, "the kiss of peace" is given. Let us endeavour to advance from charity with our neighbour to charity with God, for (as St. Hilary says) when we have established peace with men we return to the peace of God. Wo to us if, without examining our conscience, without caring for all that has been laid upon us, we hasten to celebrate Mass as we would perform any profane act ! But how have we acted hitherto in this respect ? Let us repair, as best we may, the evil we have done.

"I have thought on my ways, and turned my feet unto Thy testimonies.—*Ps.* cxviii. 59.

"Let us search our way, and seek, and return to the Lord."—*Lam.* iii. 40.

SATURDAY.

——◆——

THE DEVOTION OF THE SCAPULAR OF MOUNT CARMEL.

I. AS A MARK OF HONOUR.
II. AS A PLEDGE OF PROTECTION.
III. AS AN OBLIGATION TO SANCTITY.

——◆——

"Blessed is the womb that bore Thee, and the paps that gave Thee suck."—*St. Luke* xi. 27.

1. We may say to the Carmelite Order, "Blessed is the womb that bore thee, and the paps that gave thee suck;" for the Supreme Pontiff Gregory XIII. spoke of the Order of Mount Carmel as spiritually begotten from Mary's womb, and nourished from Her breasts. Now, all who wear the Scapular belong to this Order, and therefore should they look upon themselves as Mary's children, whom She has adopted by a special grace; for (as St. Thomas points out, adoption is not a matter of debt, but of indulgence. Now, this great title of honour is signified by the Scapular; for the Queen of Heaven calls those who are so enrolled Her brethren, and ever adopts them as Her children. Is not, then, this distinction, which causes us to be recognised as children of the Mother of God, a mark of glory? Surely we should look upon it as incomparably more glorious than "the chain of gold" which Pharao gave to Joseph (Gen. xli. 42), or than that which Baltassar gave to Daniel (Dan. v. 29). Far more glorious is it than the "coat of divers colours" which Jacob made for Joseph, or than

"the little coat" which Anna gave to Samuel (1 Kings ii. 19). Further, whilst we are honoured by it, we honour at the same time our august Mother, the Queen of Heaven; for whosoever puts on the livery of the Prince does him honour, and it is written, "He that honoureth his mother is as one that layeth up a treasure" (Eccl. xii. 5). Therefore, let us exhort the Faithful to put on the Scapular, saying to each one of them, in the words of the Prophet, "Put on beauty and honour" (Bar. v. 1).

2. Blessed also is the breast which bears this emblem, for it is a pledge of the protection which the Blessed Virgin accords to Her children. Mary was symbolized by "the little cloud" which Elias saw upon Carmel, and which brought the desired rain (says Albertus Magnus); for She indeed sheds the dew of Her graces upon Her children, and protects them from the burning heats of the sun. Mary, indeed, is that cloud of which it is written, "He spread a cloud for their protection;" for She has been made and ordained by God to be a defence and protection to sinners. She leads them to Carmel, in order that they may eat the fruit of that blessed country: "I brought you into the land of Carmel, to eat the fruit thereof" (Jerem. ii. 7). Let us meditate on the magnificent promise made by Mary to St. Simon Stock when She gave him the Scapular, that all who wore this badge of the Order and of Her Confraternity should be delivered from eternal fire; that it should be a sign of salvation, a safety in danger, an eternal covenant of peace. See, then, what powerful protection we shall have procured for the Faithful when we have inscribed them among the children of Mary; for Mary is the protection of Her servants (says St. John Damascene). See what powerful protection we shall have if we honour Her by wearing Her Scapular and inducing others to wear it, for (says the same Saint) Mary is the strong protection of those who honour Her.

3. Blessed are they who are raised to true sanctity through this symbol; for they who wear the Scapular have in it a curb to keep them from sin, and to make them ashamed of sin. As Tertullian says of the Pall, reflection on it must cause one to blush for any irregularity of life. The sinner will more easily repent (as St. Jerome says) when he sees how by sin he has defiled such an

ornament. The Faithful, too, who fulfil the engagements which the Scapular lays upon them—that is, who preserve chastity according to their state, recite the prescribed prayers, and observe abstinence every Wednesday—will have constant occasion for the exercise of virtues, so that it may be well said of this Devotion, "All good things came to me together with her, and innumerable riches through her hands" (Wisd. vii. 11). The Blessed Virgin has conducted innumerable souls to sanctity by this means, for (says St. Chrysostom) She was born to be a means of sanctification to us, and through Her aid we are rendered worthy of the kingdom of Heaven. How many sinners have been delivered from eternal death through this Devotion! As Albertus Magnus says, Mary is the Propitiatory upon which Almighty God is propitious to sinners. From how many temporal dangers has She not delivered those who are inscribed in this Order, showing Herself their Patroness in their necessities and adversities (says St. John Damascene)! Therefore, if we have zeal for the salvation of souls—if we desire to convert sinners—if we have compassion on those who suffer either in body or in mind—let us propagate this Devotion. So shall we accomplish the will of holy Church, whose Ministers we are, and who for this end has ordained a solemn Festival, causing Mass to be celebrated and the Divine Office recited in honour of Our Lady of Mount Carmel. Let us say to the Faithful, "Put you on the armour of God" (Eph. vi. 11).

"O Mary, let me put on thy blessing like a garment, and let it come like water into my entrails, and like oil into my bones."—From *Ps.* cviii. 18.

"The glory of Libanus is given to it, the beauty of Carmel and Saron."—*Is.* xxxv. 2.

SIXTH SUNDAY AFTER PENTECOST.

THE BENEFIT OF ENCOURAGING THE FAITHFUL TO TRUST IN OUR LORD'S MERCY.

I. FOR THE CONVERSION OF SINNERS.
II. FOR THE CONSOLATION OF THE FAINT-HEARTED.
III. FOR A CHECK TO THE PRESUMPTUOUS.

" When there was a great multitude with Jesus, and had nothing to eat, calling His disciples together, He saith to them, I have compassion on the multitude, for behold they have now been with Me three days, and have nothing to eat."—*St. Mark* viii. 1, 2.

1. *I have compassion on the multitude.* Jesus took pity on the hunger of the multitudes who surrounded Him, and He uttered these compassionate words both as God and as Man. As God, He is "merciful and gracious, patient, and of much compassion" (Exod. xxxiv. 6). As man, He compassionates our miseries with immense tenderness, for " we have not a High Priest who cannot have compassion on our infirmities" (Heb. iv. 15). And, if He have compassion on our temporal afflictions, much more will He have compassion on those which are spiritual, and, above all, on the miserable condition of sinners. It is the duty of Priests to make known to those unhappy men the mercy of Jesus, in inviting them to penance, and in receiving them when they repent. St. Vincent Ferrer was commanded by God to preach on this subject, as the most powerful incentive to the conversion of sinners. The Church celebrates the Conversion of St. Paul in order

that we may derive profit from its commemoration, for (as St. Bernard says) it suggests the hope of pardon, and is an incentive to penance. We must encourage sinners by telling them, with that great Priest St. Cyril, that their sins are not greater than the multitude of God's mercies, and that their wounds do not surpass the experience of the Physician. We may make of our very sins (says St. Augustin) a ladder to ascend to heaven, if we do but know how to tread them under foot, to turn our face to God, and to implore his pardon. Let us urge sinners to repentance, assuring them that when they are penitent the power of Divine love (as St. Peter Chrysologus says) no longer regards their sins ; and that, if sin have abounded in them, grace shall still more abound (Rom. v. 20).

2. *They have now been with me three days.* These multitudes were a figure of those who, in the faith of the Most Holy Trinity (as Venerable Bede says), persevere in imploring pardon of their sins, and who are converted to God in deed, in word, and in thought. These, with firm hope, should wait for God's mercy, and say with the Psalmist, " Our soul waiteth for the Lord, for He is our helper and protector" (Ps. xxxii. 20). Nevertheless, many, and perhaps even Priests, allow themselves to be cast down by an unworthy fear, which renders them faint-hearted. This faint-heartedness is sometimes a mortal sin, sometimes only venial, but it ever produces fatal consequences (says St. Thomas); and therefore a Confessor and Director of souls should make men understand that such a feeling springs from secret pride, which seeks the support of its hope and the strength of its fear in itself, and not in God. Let us, then, cry to the Lord in the words of the royal Prophet, " None of them that wait on Thee shall be confounded " (Ps. xxiv. 3); let us ever hope in the mercy of the Lord ; let us cast ourselves into the arms of His infinite goodness, saying, "I have trusted in Thy mercy, my heart shall rejoice in Thy salvation " (Ps. xii. 6.).

3. *And have nothing to eat.* A soul that presumes on God's mercy, and remembers not His justice, is, indeed, in grievous error ; for (as St. Basil points out) in Holy Scripture God's mercy and justice are ever joined together, nor must we consider one of

these attributes without the other. Sinners presume on God's mercy when they abuse it so as to sin the more, thinking themselves safe (as St. Leo says) because they are not promptly punished, and forgetting that time is granted them only in order to their conversion. This presumption on God's mercy is called by St. Bernard "a well of pitch," into which the devil is wont to cast sinners; and Priests must use every effort to draw souls out of this well, encouraging in them both the love and the fear of God. How sweet is love, how just is fear (says St. Augustin)! May Almighty God preserve us from falling into this miserable state! Let us take care of ourselves; let us learn (as St. Bernard warns us) from the greatest of God's mercy to recognise the greatness of His vengeance; for His justice, as well as His mercy, is infinite; and, if He is great in pardoning, great also is He in taking vengeance.

"Mercy and judgment will I sing to Thee, O Lord."—*Ps.* c. i.

"Forasmuch as the Lord is patient, let us be penitent for this same thing, and with many tears let us beg His pardon."—*Judith* viii. 14.

MONDAY.

THE FAITHFUL TO BE ENCOURAGED TO FREQUENT COMMUNION.

I. LEST THEY SUFFER HUNGER.

II. LEST THEY FAINT BY THE WAY.

III. AS A COMPENSATION FOR THEIR LONG ABSENCE FROM THEIR LORD.

"And if I shall send them away fasting to their home, they will faint in the way; for some of them come from afar off."—*St. Mark* viii. 3.·

1. *If I shall send them away fasting.* The soul, deprived of the living Bread which came down from Heaven, is left fasting, and suffers hunger. This divine Bread (says St. Basil) is the food of the heart, the strength of the soul. The Flesh and Blood of Christ (says St. Chrysostom) not only give beauty and nobility to the soul, but are its food and refreshment, so that it may not languish away. The Faithful, therefore, should be instructed in this truth, and encouraged to frequent Communion—taught to dispose themselves to receive it worthily by sincere faith, confident hope, ardent charity, and purity of soul. It is thus the duty of Parish Priests, Preachers, and Confessors to exhort their people to frequent Communion, and to due reverence towards so great a Sacrament. Therefore (as St. Laurence Justinian enjoins) let Priests use all diligence in impressing on the minds of the Faithful, and in producing in them, the right dispositions for receiving the Bread of Life.

2. *They will faint in the way.* As food must be given to the

body, so the soul must not be left fasting, lest it faint in the toil-
some journey of life—that is to say, lest it fall into sin ; and on
this account the Church has impressed upon Pastors the duty of
inculcating frequent Communion on their people. Jesus (says
St. Ignatius the Martyr) has left Himself in the Eucharist as the
medicine of immortality, and as an antidote against death. The
soul loses fervour, and faints in the struggle against temptations,
if it be not invigorated and inflamed by the holy Eucharist (says
St. Cyprian). How (asks St. Bernard) can you subdue the fierce im-
pulses of passion—how can you be secure—unless strengthened
by the precious Body and Blood of the Lord ? On the other
hand, how shall he die (says St. Ambrose) who has Life itself for
his food ? Priests who are persuaded of this truth, who sincerely
desire to diminish offences against God and to see souls freed
from the corruption of sin, will readily imitate St. Francis of Sales,
St. Philip Neri, and many other patterns of zeal, who so earnestly
promoted the frequent use of the Sacraments.

3. *Came from afar off.* Who are those that come to Jesus from
afar off, if not they who (as Venerable Bede says) are habituated
in sin, and who at length approach Him by penance ? For the
longer a sinner has wandered in wicked ways the farther has he
withdrawn himself from Almighty God. But our good Lord (says
St. Ambrose) would not have these left fasting and without
strength, lest from faintness they should return to their former
state. The good Director of souls will, therefore, clothe himself
with the bowels of Jesus Christ, will take diligent care of these
weak souls, and persuade them that the Eucharist is not only the
food of the strong, but also the medicine of the sick, for whose
sake our Lord Jesus Christ comes, saying, " I will come and heal
him " (St. Matt. viii. 7). Let us call to mind those "other seven
more wicked spirits " whom the devil, after he has been once
driven out of a man, takes to himself in order to conquer him
anew (St. Matt. xii. 45). How can those who are fasting sustain
so obstinate a struggle ? They will be as warriors "fainting
through poverty" (Eccl. xxvi. 26). Let us, then, examine ourselves
on this part of our duty, and let us see whether we bring many to
frequent the Sacraments, and whether, by this means, we guard

them from falling again. But, alas! how few are the Priests who duly fulfil this charge! The world (says St. Gregory) is filled with Priests, but how few show themselves true Priests! We seek the Priestly office, but we fulfil not the work of our office.

"They were hungry and thirsty : their soul fainted in them."—*Ps.* cvi. 5.

"That we might be satisfied with bread . . . Convert us, O Lord, to Thee, and we shall be converted."—*Lam.* v. 6, 21.

TUESDAY.

THE SEVEN LOAVES.

I. What these seven loaves represent.
II. How they are found in the hands of Priests.
III. Why some are ignorant of their sufficiency.

"And His disciples answered Him, From whence can any one fill them here with bread in the wilderness? And He asked them, How many loaves have ye? Who said, Seven."—*St. Mark* viii. 4, 5.

1. *Who said, Seven.* St. Bernard considers the seven loaves as a figure of the seven gifts of God, with which the Christian soul is nourished. The first loaf is the Word of God, for man lives "in every word that proceedeth from the mouth of God" (St. Matt. iv. 4). The second is obedience to the will of God; for our Saviour said, "My meat is to do the will of Him that sent Me" (St. John iv. 34). The third is meditation on the eternal truths, called by the Wise Man "the bread of life and understanding" (Eccl. xv. 3). The fourth consists in the tears of a supplicating heart: "My tears have been my bread day and

night" (Ps. xli. 4): "Thou feedest us with the bread of tears" (Ps. lxxix. 6). The fifth is the labour of penance: "I did eat ashes like bread" (Ps. ci. 10). The sixth is that happy unanimity whereby various minds are, as it were, leavened into one loaf of divine wisdom : "Eat thy bread with joy" (Eccl. ix. 7): "A secure mind is like a continual feast" (Prov. xv. 15). The seventh is the Eucharist: "the Bread that I will give is My Flesh for the life of the world" (St. John vi. 52). How munificent is Jesus in dispensing His gifts, and in nourishing and enriching His people !

2. *How many loaves have ye?* Let us meditate on each one of these loaves, and we shall find that good Priests have them in abundance, and that the Lord "fills them with the bread of heaven" (Ps. civ. 40). By them is each one of these loaves offered to the people; it is sent by their hands from God, Who "sent them provisions in abundance" (Ps. lxxvii. 25). The proper office of those who have care of souls is to distribute to the people spiritual nourishment in due season : "Who, thinkest thou, is a faithful and wise servant, whom his lord hath appointed over his family, to give them meat in season ?" (St. Matt. xxiv. 45). And again : "Who, thinkest thou, is the faithful and wise steward whom his lord setteth over his family, to give them their measure of wheat in due season ?" (St. Luke xii. 42). What does our Saviour intend to express by this question? Our Lord asks it (says St. Chrysostom), not as though He knew not the faithful and wise steward, but to show us how rare it is to find one wise and faithful in dispensing the food which the Father of the family has confided to him. Let us look into ourselves; let us inquire what use we have made of the seven loaves which Jesus has confided to us. Let us carefully weigh His question, which (as St. Ambrose says) is directed to Priests alone.

3. *Whence can any one fill them here with bread in the wilderness ?* St. Chrysostom admires the sincerity of the Apostles in handing down their defects to posterity, exposing even so great a fault as this want of confidence in the power of Jesus Christ. We, too, may not conceal the serious fault of many Priests who, while they have in their hands the spiritual food of the people, hide it, and

do not dispense it abroad, thus meriting the curse threatened against him who " hideth up corn " from a famishing people (Prov. xi. 26). Such Priests understand not the deep meaning of the words which our Saviour spoke to the Apostles, and, in their person, to all Priests : " Give you them to eat " (St. Matt. xiv. 16). They hear not those other words, " Labour not for the meat which perisheth, but for that which endureth unto life everlasting " (St. John vi. 27). Let us be moved to compassion for so many who are fainting in spiritual hunger, and let us remember that, if it be a work pleasing to Christ to give corruptible bread to the hungry, far more acceptable to Him is it to give the Bread which confers eternal life. Therefore, let us make due resolve, let us anticipate the just reproofs of our Lord ; let us repent of the past, and let us change our practice in the future.

" The eyes of all hope in Thee, O Lord, and Thou givest them meat in due season."—*Ps.* cxliv. 15.

" Lord, give us always this bread."—*St. John* vi. 34.

WEDNESDAY.

———•———

CHRIST'S MINISTERS MULTIPLYING THE MYSTICAL BREAD

I. They must consult the convenience of their people.

II. They must disregard their own convenience.

III. They must imitate the action of Jesus Christ.

———•———

"And He commanded the multitude to sit down upon the ground, and, taking the seven loaves, giving thanks He broke and gave to His disciples for to set before them, and they set them before the people."—*St. Matt.* xv. 35; *St. Mark* viii. 6.

1. *He commanded the multitude to sit down.* Our Saviour would have the multitude eat at their ease, and provided for their accommodation; so that, whether they sat down or stretched themselves upon the ground (according to ancient custom), they certainly adopted a convenient and accustomed posture for their meal. Thus did He teach the Apostles that in dealing with the Faithful they should seek their convenience, and adapt themselves to circumstances of time and place. So also did He fulfil the type of Assuerus, who, in his great banquet, accommodated all the guests, and "set over every table one of his nobles to see that every man was well served" (Esther i. 8). For the Faithful are tempted by the devil not to partake of divine benefits; nay, they suffer two kinds of temptation—one through inclination to evil and backwardness to do good, which is the sad inheritance of original sin; the other (as St. Augustin says) through the weariness of good itself, even after its sweetness has been tasted.

Now, we should be careful not to add to these a further temptation, by placing obstacles and difficulties in their way, so as to
retard them from doing good. Neither must we be like that
Pastor who (as St. Gregory says) seeks not the profit of souls,
but the good things of earth—who regards only external advantages, and makes no account of the internal ruin of the flock.
But, alas! how many Preachers are there who seek their own
convenience, and not that of their people! Many (says St.
Augustin) follow earthly goods whilst they preach Christ in the
Church. Blessed is that servant (says St. Hilary) whom his Lord
shall find careful of the convenience and benefit of the people
committed to him.

2. *And gave to His disciples for to set before them.* No slight labour
was that of the Apostles in distributing the loaves and fishes
which multiplied in their hands. For they had to traverse this
vast solitude, and give food to four thousand persons, besides
women and children; which multitude (says St. Hilary) was a
figure of the inhabitants of the four parts of the world, who were
to receive spiritual nourishment from the hands of the Apostles
and their successors. Thus did our Lord teach Priests to renounce their own conscience for the good of others, and gave
them to understand that they were to be the servants of Christians.
He pointed this out also in the parable of the Supper, when He
likened them to the servant who invited the guests (St. Luke xiv.
16); and, the better to instruct them in regard to this most important
subject, He left them a most solemn charge before His death;
"He that is the greater among you," said He, "let him become
as the younger; and he that is the leader, as he that serveth"
(St. Luke xxii. 26). He also set before them His own example in
the words which follow: "Which is greater, he that sitteth at
table, or he that serveth? Is not he that sitteth at table? But
I am in the midst of you as he that serveth" (v. 27). St. Paul,
instructed in this truth, not only called himself "the servant of
the servants of God," but declared himself ready to "endure all
things for the sake of the elect, that they might obtain salvation"
(2 Tim. ii. 10). But, alas! how many Ecclesiastics are there who
aspire to Holy Orders for the sake of an easy life, instead of

devoting themselves to Apostolical labour! St. Gregory says that our Lord detests those who seek to draw near to Him through Holy Orders and use that privilege with a view to temporal sustenance rather than as a means of advancement in virtue. What was our intention in seeking Holy Orders? What is our intention now in exercising our Ministry?

3. *And they set them before the people.* The heavenly Bread (says St. Ambrose) is multiplied when broken, but, in order to its being multiplied, let us call to mind what Jesus did. He raised His eyes to heaven, blessed the loaves, broke them, and distributed them to the Apostles, in order that they might distribute them to the multitude. All this is a mystery, signifying that the abundance of heavenly nourishment is multiplied by means of the prayer with which we look up to heaven, by means of the devotion with which it is blessed, by means of the meditation by which it is broken, by means of the preaching by which it is distributed. So St. Bonaventure. Acting after Christ's example, we shall not see the Faithful solicitous for the nourishment only of the servant—that is, the body—whilst they neglect the nourishment of the nobler substance—that is, the soul. We shall not see them thinking of a corruptible food, whilst they make but little account of that which confers on them immortal life. For (says St. Chrysostom) the food of our life is twofold, the one kind inferior, the other more excellent. Our chief object must be to nourish the soul and to preserve it from hunger. In this way men will no longer be guilty of that great injustice which St. Augustin deplored; that is to say, whilst careful to give food to the body several times during the day, leaving the soul, which is the image of God, languishing and fasting. Let us, then, do our duty, and remember that (as St. Bonaventure observes) in the Court of our Lord Jesus Christ, the more noble minister to others.

" Hear me : Thou shalt multiply strength in my soul."—*Ps.* cxxxvii. 3.

" O Lord, multiply the seed of David thy servant, and the Levites thy ministers."
—From *Jerem.* xxxiii. 22.

THURSDAY.

THE HOLY SCRIPTURES IN THE HANDS OF PRIESTS.

I. PRIESTS HAVE THEM IN THEIR HANDS.

II. THEY HAVE THE DIVINE BLESSING FOR UNDERSTANDING THEM.

III. THEY OUGHT TO EXPLAIN THEM TO THE PEOPLE.

"And they had a few little fishes, and He blessed them, and commanded them to be set before them."—*St. Mark* viii. 7.

1. *And they had a few little fishes.* St. Jerome says that the little fishes signified the books of the New Testament, just as the seven loaves signified the gifts of the Holy Spirit. Now, the books of both the Old and New Testament are in the hands of Priests, as those fishes were in the hands of the Disciples, and therefore are those Scriptures called by St. Ambrose the Book of the Priest. St. Isidore says that Almighty God has consigned them to Priests as the "viaticum of salvation." St. Gregory says that the mind of a good Priest is the ark which guards them; and St. Augustin says that they are the delight of the heart, furnishing abundant nourishment for Priests and people. They are called by St. Bernard the "mirror of Pastors," flattering none, but shewing man as he is. Therefore, a Priest who gives not the first place in his library to the Bible—who does not seek to obtain a good interpretation of its obscure passages—offends God. Can such an one have understood the value and necessity of this Book? He certainly cannot remember the injunction of

the Council of Toledo, that Priests should know the Holy Scriptures.

2. *And He blessed them.* Many passages of the Holy Scriptures are obscure, and Protestants vainly impugn this truth. The key to the understanding of these passages is in the hand of our Lord Jesus Christ. He only Who has the key of David (says St. Jerome)—He Who opens and no man shuts, Who shuts and no man opens—He, and none else, can unfold those sacred truths. None but Christ (says St. Ambrose) was found worthy to open this book, and to loosen the seals thereof. And He gives His blessing to Priests who read the Sacred Scriptures with submission to the decisions of Holy Church and to the interpretations which She approves, with a sincere humility and desire to find the truth, and with the intention of conforming their own life to the teaching of those Divine oracles. Nay (says St. Cyprian), He renders those who do this invincible; no enemy shall be able to overcome them. Therefore, in reading this letter which God has sent to man, let us follow the counsel of St. Ephrem ; that is, let us pray to our Lord Jesus Christ to give His blessing to our reading, opening the eyes and ears of our heart, so that we may understand and follow these saving truths.

3. *Commanded them to be set before them.* The study of Holy Scripture should not be neglected, but should be applied to our own benefit and that of others. St. Chrysostom urges Priests to pursue this study in order that they may become interpreters of the Divine law to those who contemplate them. St. Prosper bids the preacher draw from this source the materials of his discourses, rather than from his own imagination. Let the Priest, then, apply to himself the words spoken by God to His Prophet, "Eat this book, and go, speak to the children of Israel" (Ezech. iii. 1). It is, indeed, proved by constant experience (as Hugh of St. Victor points out) that Priests who are much occupied in this precious study preach with emotion and courage, and to the delight and profit of their hearers.

" Thy word is exceedingly refined, and Thy servant hath loved it."—*Ps.* cxviii. 140.

" To Him that giveth me wisdom will I give glory."—*Eccl.* li. 23.

FRIDAY.

———◆———

PRIESTS WHO HAVE CARE OF CHILDREN ARE DEAR TO OUR LORD JESUS CHRIST—

I. IN INSTRUCTING THEM.
II. IN HEARING THEIR CONFSSIONS.
III. IN DRAWING THEM TO HOLY COMMUNION.

——◆——

"And they did eat and were filled; and they took up that which was left of the fragments, seven baskets. And they that had eaten were about four thousand, and He sent them away."—*St. Mark* viii. 8, 9.

1. *Of the fragments.* In gathering up the fragments the disciples executed the command given them by our Saviour on the occasion of the first miracle of the multiplication of the loaves—"Gather up the fragments that remain, lest they be lost" (St. John vi. 12). Now, these fragments may be looked upon as a figure of children, of whom He would have us take diligent care. The zealous Priest should gather children together for instruction, saying to them, "Draw near to me, ye unlearned, and gather yourselves together into the house of discipline" (Eccl. li. 31). The explanation of holy doctrine will give them heavenly light, and make them understand eternal truths: "The declaration of Thy words giveth light, and giveth understanding to little ones" (Ps. cxviii. 130). We must begin to instruct them early, in order that salutary maxims may be the first impressed on their soul, and that this impression may remain indelible, as it was with Tobias, whose father "from his infancy taught him to fear God, and to abstain from all sin" (Tob. i. 10).

How dear to Jesus is he who disdains not this exercise of charity and humility! how dear to Jesus is he who adapts himself to the capacity of children, and makes known to them this divine Master! Such a Priest imitates the Apostl*, who said, " We became little ones in the midst of you, as if a nurse should cherish her children" (1 Thess. ii. 7). "As unto little ones in Christ, I gave you milk to drink, not meat" (1 Cor. iii. 2). Such a Priest imitates St. Joseph Calasanctius, St. Jerome Emilian, and many others who impressed Christ crucified on the hearts of these little ones. The less glorious he may seem in the eyes of men, the more pleasing will he be to God.

2. *They took up . . . seven baskets.* The labour of the Apostles, and their joy, in taking up as many baskets of fragments as there had been loaves, is a lively image of the labour and joy of Priests, who, having the care of children, receive as it were a full basket (says St. Bernard) for each single loaf. Great patience is required for hearing the Confessions of children, and the Confessor must imitate Elias and Eliseus ; that is to say, he must (as it were) warm them with sacred fire, so as to raise them from the death of sin (3 Kings xvii. 21 ; 4 Kings iv. 34). But (as St. Augustin teaches us) this exercise of patience will be full of consolation if we consider what that death is from which we free souls redeemed with the Blood of Jesus Christ. Great circumspection, great prudence, and no light labour are required, in order so to question them as not to teach them any evil of which they are as yet ignorant, and at the same time to induce them to manifest sins which shame would tempt them to conceal; and still greater efforts are required to move them to detest sin as an offence against God. But let us remember our Lord's words, "Whosoever shall receive this child in My name receiveth Me" (St. Luke ix. 48). Let us remember (with St. Chrysostom) that every child, from the first moment of his existence, has been the subject of an Angel's care ; that the Word became incarnate for him ; and that it is the will of the Eternal Father that he be converted and live. Let us reflect that often, through the Confessor's care, by the help of Divine grace, a child preserves his baptismal innocence—conceives the love of God, the horror of sin, and the

desire of salvation; thus, like Tobias, who, "when younger than any . . . did no childish thing in his work" (Tob. i. 4), showing the wisdom and bearing of age even in childhood. And, if we sometimes appear to derive small profit from our labours, let us not be discouraged, but consider St. Bernard's words, "Be not disheartened: *care* is required of thee, not *cure*. The words spoken to thee were, 'Take care of him,' and not 'Cure or heal him.' Do thine own duty. It is God (and not thou thyself) Who will give the increase, as it shall please Him : if it please Him not, thou hast lost nothing."

3. *They did eat and were filled.* St. Matthew says clearly that children ate also: "And they that did eat were four thousand men, besides children and women" (St. Matt. xv. 38). Jesus delights to give the living Bread—that is, Himself—even to children ; and He says to us, "Suffer the little children to come unto Me, and forbid them not" (St. Mark x. 14). We must make them understand what the Holy Eucharist is, and we must dispose them for its reception. The Synod of Toulouse complained that children came too late to make their first Communion, and enjoined that, so soon as their Parish Priest or Confessor judged that they had sufficient discernment of this great Mystery, they should be admitted, and even urged, to the reception of Holy Communion. Let us, then, endeavour to put them in the right road, and to instruct them, and to lead them to holiness and virtues; and (as the Council of Narbonne enjoins) let those only be admitted who show signs of sanctity and modesty of life, and who are able to comprehend with the understanding what it is which they receive with the mouth. We may learn the practical method of confessing children, and of preparing them for Holy Communion, from St. Alphonsus Liguori, who treats of it at great length. In this work we may be assured that we are doing that which is most acceptable to Jesus Christ, Who has said to us, "As long as you did it to one of these My least brethren, you did it to Me" (St. Matt. xxv. 40).

"Come, children, hearken to me : I will teach you the fear of the Lord."—*Ps.* xxxiii. 12.

"Behold, I and my children, whom the Lord hath given me."—*Is.* viii. 18.

SATURDAY.

---◆---

---◆---

" The Angel Gabriel was sent from God into a city of Galilee called Nazareth, to a virgin espoused to a man whose name was Joseph, of the house of David ; and the virgin's name was Mary . . . Behold the handmaid of the Lord."—*St. Luke* i. 26, 27, 38.

1. *Into a city of Galilee called Nazareth.* In the despised region of Galilee—in the mean city of Nazareth—dwelt the Blessed among women, the seat of Wisdom, the most prudent Virgin, at the time when it was a saying of the Jews, " Can anything of good come from Nazareth ?" (St. John i. 46.) In this does Mary's humility commend itself to us—that She was not elated by Her perfect knowledge, which was incomparably superior to the teaching of the Apostles; for, although they (says St. Anselm) were taught all truths by the revelation of the Holy Spirit, She, in a still more manifest and eminent degree, understood these profound truths through this same Spirit of Truth. She (says St. Augustin) had the knowledge of the Holy Scriptures, for She brought forth the fulness of truth. More perfectly than Adam in his deep sleep, than John on the Lord's breast, than Paul in his heavenly rapture, did She know all supernatural mysteries (says Albertus Magnus). And yet, with this knowledge, She descended lower into the abyss of humility than any other crea-

ture (says St. Bernardin). Hence, St. Augustin exclaims, O true humility, which has given birth to God, which has given life to mortals, which has renovated Heaven, quickened the world, opened Paradise, and freed the souls of men ! Let us, then, pray to Her, that we may not be puffed up because of knowledge, but rather by means of knowledge may advance in the way of salvation. As Peter of Blois says, we should reject such knowledge as leads to our ruin, but lay hold of that knowledge which edifies to salvation.

2. *To a virgin espoused to a man.* St. Bernard admires the beautiful union of sanctity and humility in the Blessed Virgin ; for, whilst she is reverently saluted by the Angel because of Her sanctity, She is, because of Her humility, found to be the spouse of a carpenter. Jesus, the Holy of Holies and most perfect pattern of humility, would have a Mother humble in Her immense sanctity. From Heaven He "regarded the humility of His hand-maid" (St. Luke i. 48), as She Herself attested ; for (as St. Augustin observes) the grace which man had lost through pride was recovered in Her through humility. Let us learn, then, from Her to preserve humility, which St. Cyprian calls the foundation of sanctity ; let us take care that other virtues do not give us occasion of self-complacency and vain-glory, and so cause us to lose this virtue, which is (according to St. Ambrose) the throne of wisdom, the ornament of grace, the prelude of glory; and which St. Laurence Justinian calls the jewel of Priests and Bishops.

3. *Behold the hand-maid of the Lord.* The infinite dignity of Mother of God kindled no pride in Mary; rather did it produce in Her a fresh act of humility. Mary's humility was so sublime that it was proof against temptation caused by the honours and glory thrust upon her. As St. Bernard says, when chosen to be Mother of God She calls Herself His hand-maid. Priests likewise receive great honour in the Church ; their dignity is of a high order, and their functions august. Let them, therefore, be careful not to lose humility, which is not so rare in a lowly station, but is seldom found amidst honours. Let us remember that our Ministry is called by St. Isidore a Ministry of humility. Our humility ought to be in proportion to our dignity, for the

danger of pride is so much the greater in our case in proportion to our greatness (says St. Augustin). Let us recommend ourselves to Mary, whose humility is commemorated in many places by a special festival on the 17th July, and let us frequently use the prayer which the Church recites on the occasion of that solemnity—" O God, Who regardest the humble, and beholdest the proud afar off, grant to Thy servants that with pure hearts they may follow the humility of the Blessed Mary ever Virgin, which rendered Her worthy to become the Mother of our Lord Jesus Christ, Thy Son, &c."

" Thou will save the humble people, but will bring down the eyes of the proud."— *Ps.* xvii. 28.

" Thou receivest the spirit of the humble, and revivest the heart of the contrite."—From *Is.* lvii. 15.

SEVENTH SUNDAY AFTER PENTECOST.

—◆—

THE CLERGY SHOULD ATTEND TO THOSE WHO ARE TRUE PROPHETS—

    I. BY LISTENING TO THEIR PREACHING.
    II. BY STUDYING THEIR WORKS.
    III. BY READING THEIR LIVES.

—◆—

" Beware of false Prophets."—*St. Matt.* vi. 15.

1. *Beware of false Prophets.* When our Saviour commanded His disciples to beware of false Prophets, He taught them by implication to attend to the teaching of true Prophets—that is to say, of preachers, the Doctors of the Church—who are the interpreters of ancient prophecies. These are they who proclaim the Divine

Word in the Church, and Priests should assist at their preaching, so as to edify the people and to "be an example of the Faithful" (1 Tim. iv. 12). Although they themselves may be masters in Israel, they will yet derive profit from listening to salutary admonitions; for innumerable are the benefits which the Word of God bestows on the soul (says St. Thomas of Villanova)—keeping it back from sin, vivifying, enlightening, inflaming, cleansing, nourishing, strengthening, healing, fertilising, softening, and rendering it capable of all good. Nay, more : St. Bernardin of Sienna says, that to listen willingly to God's Word is a sign of actual sanctity, and of the presence of the Holy Spirit ; and St. Anthony of Padua calls it a mark of predestination. Though Priests may be as Angels, let them remember that the Angels were supported by the exhortation of St. Michael, so as to remain faithful to God and not to follow the rebellion of Lucifer (Apoc. xii. 7). Though they be in a position of honour, as David, let them remember that David was converted by the preaching of Nathan (2 Kings xii. 1); though they be holy, as Cephas, let them remember that Cephas was admonished by St. Paul (Gal. ii. 11). That venerable servant of God, Mariano Arcieri, often listened to preaching, and used to say that it was a grace of which we should make great account, and never think that we have had enough of it.

2. The Holy Fathers may be called "true Prophets" of the Lord in the above sense. Almighty God has placed them in the Church for the sure administration of His Word, and for the edification of the Body of Christ ; and their teaching is drawn (as St. Augustin shows) either from the Canonical books or from theological reasonings, so that they are safe guides to the truth. In studying the writings of the holy Doctors (says St. Gregory), our minds are refreshed, our faith intensified, the fruit of good works is multiplied, and the soul is illumined with interior light. Therefore does the Church make us daily read some homily of the Fathers in order to kindle in us a love of their teaching. If, then, we would know the will of God in the various circumstances of life—if we would have practical rules for the guidance of souls—if we would acquire ample materials

for preaching—let us "ask our father, and he will declare to us; let us ask our elders, and they will tell us" (Deut. xxxii. 7). If Priests did not waste their time in useless, profane, dangerous reading, but took delight in studying the Fathers and Doctors of the Church, how greatly would they profit in spirit! "Search diligently into the memory of the fathers . . . . and they shall teach thee; they shall speak to thee, and utter words out of their hearts" (Job viii. 8, 10).

3. The Saints in their lives manifested the dignity of "true Prophets:" "Let us praise men of renown, and our fathers in their generation . . . . shewing forth in the prophets the dignity of prophets" (Eccl. xliv. 1, 3). St. Basil bids us imitate painters, who when they are copying from an original work constantly turn their eyes to it. We must, in like manner, if we would acquire perfection, look continually to the lives of holy men ; for (as he also says) their history is as a light which points out the path of life to those who are in the way of salvation. Let us be assured that the glorious virtues of the Saints are (as Origen says) shining perpetually, and ever setting forth a pattern of good works, as the luminaries and stars of heaven are continually shedding light upon the earth. Hence, in the Divine Office, the Church obliges us to read the lives of the Saints, in order that we may be led to study them more fully, and that our spiritual life may be nourished by such study. "Remember your Prelates, who have spoken the Word of God to you; whose faith follow, considering the end of their conversation" (Heb. xiii. 7). Let us read especially the lives of those Saints who have exercised the works of the Ministry committed to us, and who have filled the same rank in the Church as that in which we find ourselves. By so doing we shall obtain guidance in doubtful matters, increase of fervour, and an abundant supply of material for the edification of our people. Have we adopted this practice? What is our intention for the future?

"We have heard, O God, with our ears: our fathers have declared to us."—*Ps.* xliii. 2.

"Remember, O Lord, these men who have gained glory in their generations, and who were praised in their days."—From *Eccl.* xliv. 7.

MONDAY.

------◆------

ON PROHIBITED BOOKS.

I. PRIESTS SHOULD AVOID READING THEM.

II. THEY SHOULD POINT OUT THE JUSTICE OF THE PRO-
HIBITION.

III. THEY SHOULD ENDEAVOUR TO REMOVE THEM FROM THE
FAITHFUL.

------◆------

"Beware of false prophets, who come to you in the clothing of sheep, but inwardly they are ravening wolves : by their fruits you shall know them.—*S. Matt.* vii. 15, 16.

1. *Beware of false prophets.* The authors of condemned books are undoubtedly false prophets ; for under this name our Saviour referred to the teachers of various heresies. He referred, also, to those writers who are corrupt in their life, and, indeed (says St. Chrysostom), to all who publish irreligious, lascivious, ribald, or seditious books. And this warning of our Saviour was addressed to the Apostles, who were to be the model of Priests. Hence St. Paul gave this injunction to a bishop—"A man that is a heretic . . . . avoid" (Tit. iii. 10); and to another bishop he wrote, "Shun profane and vain babbling; for they grow much towards ungodliness, and their speech spreadeth like a cancer" (2 Tim. ii. 10). Priests, most assuredly, are exposed to special danger in this respect: Bardesanes of Mesopotamia was a Confessor of the Faith, yet by reading heretical works he became (as St. Epiphanius tells us) an apostate and heresiarch. Avitus was a Priest, yet by reading a poisonous

book he deceived himself, and excited terrible disturbances in Spain. Eutyches was a Monk, yet by reading a Manichean author he was himself perverted from the truth, and was followed in his error by immense multitudes. And, as for obscene books, let us remember that we are but flesh, and that one single impure thought to which we consent suffices to rob us of the chastity we have vowed. Hence (says St. Isidore), fly the reading of that which is base and obscene. Let us resolve never to take such books in our hands without clear necessity, without the required Pontifical Indulgence, and without recommending ourselves to God, if we would not expose our souls to peril.

2. *Who come to you in the clothing of sheep, but inwardly they are ravening wolves.* Wicked writers frequently hide their poison under sweet words : "his words are smoother than oil, and the same are darts" (Ps. liv. 22): they mix and conceal their poison with honey (says St. Basil). And whose duty is it to warn the Faithful of such hidden danger—to make known to the sheep that the wolf has put on their clothing in order to devour them more easily? Surely, it is his duty to whom it was said, "Feed My lambs . . . feed My sheep" (St. John xxi. 15, 16); and they who despise his word despise God Himself: "he that heareth you heareth Me, and he that despiseth you despiseth Me" (St. Luke x. 16). He who refuses to hear St. Peter in the person of his successor, the Head of the Church, refuses to hear Christ Himself, and consequently is not a Christian: "if he will not hear the Church, let him be to thee as the heathen and publican" (St. Matt. xviii. 17). Let us, then, make the Faithful understand the authority which the Supreme Pontiff has over their consciences—the authority of binding and loosing (St. Matt. xvi. 19); let us show them how the Church has in all ages prohibited the reading of pernicious books ; let us read the Dissertation of St. Alphonsus on the first prohibition and abolition of the reading of such books. Let us impress upon all the duty of obedience and respect to the Pontifical decisions, and also instil in them a wholesome fear of the excommunication launched against all who transgress the commands given on this head. Let us remember St. Paul's words—" Having in readiness to revenge all

disobedience, when your obedience shall be fulfilled" (2 Cor. x. 6).

3. *By their fruits you shall know them.* The evil fruits of these books are known not less by the wicked lives of their authors than by the ruin which they bring upon the Faithful. It is enough to remember that the Popes Paul IV., Julius III., Gregory XV., and Urban VIII., found themselves under the necessity of revoking the licences which they had given to certain persons to read prohibited books, because of the harm which was found by experience to have resulted from them. See also the opinion of St. Alphonsus, in the treatise above mentioned. It is enough to remember the injury to the Priesthood and the Empire—to the Altar and the Throne—which such Books have occasioned in recent times; for through them has it come to pass, that the people have "transgressed the laws, and have changed the ordinance, and have broken the everlasting covenant: therefore shall a curse devour the earth, and the inhabitants thereof shall sin, and therefore they that dwell therein shall be mad" (Is. xxiv. 5, 6). Let us snatch them from the hands of all, and especially from the hands of the young; warning them, with St. Cyprian, not to be ready to assent to deceitful words, lest they mistake darkness for light, night for day, hunger for food, thirst for drink, poison for remedy, death for health. And, should any answer that they desire to read such books in order to learn something from them, let us remind them that (as St. Jerome puts it) ignorance with security is in some cases better than knowledge with danger. We shall merit well of the Church and society if we induce the Faithful of the present day to imitate those of whom it is written, "Many of them who had followed curious arts brought together their books, and burnt them before all; and, counting the price of them, they found the money to be fifty thousand pieces of silver" (Acts xix. 19).

"Depart from me, ye malignant; and I will reach the commandments of my God."
—*Ps.* cxix. 115.

"O Lord, the wicked that denied to know Thee were scourged by the strength of Thy arm."—*Wisd.* xvi. 16.

TUESDAY.

THE FRUITS OF A GOOD PRIEST.

I. Fruits unworthy of the name.
II. Evil fruits.
III. Good fruits.

"By their fruits you shall know them. Do men gather grapes of thorns, or figs of thistles?"—*St. Matt.* vii. 16.

1. *By their fruits you shall know them.* Our Saviour repeated this maxim a little time after to His disciples, and elsewhere to the multitudes, when he compared Himself to a tree, and his works to fruit, saying, "Either make the tree good and its fruit good, or make the tree evil and its fruit evil; for by the fruit the tree is known" (St. Matt. xii. 33). No marvel, therefore, is it if, in another place, Almighty God likens Priests to trees, and declares they shall be known by their fruits. And, in truth, by the mouth of the Prophet He complains of the sinful Priest in these words—"What is the meaning that My beloved hath wrought much wickedness in My house?" (Jerem. xi. 15); and then adds, "the Lord called thy name a plentiful olive-tree, fair, fruitful, and beautiful" (ver. 16). But we must not deceive ourselves on this point; we must not suppose *that* to be fruit which is not—such as fasts, alms, prayers. These things often form the clothing of sheep, and deceive other sheep—nay, sometimes deceive the very shepherds themselves (as St. Augustin points out). It is true that Priests must not abandon this clothing because they see it on the backs of wolves; but neither must

they think themselves just, holy, or sincere, because of such Christian practices. Let them examine themselves more thoroughly; let them observe their conduct under spiritual trials, tribulations, and adversities ; for these (says St. Thomas) are the most certain indications of the state of the heart. How many unhappy Priests have been satisfied with the outward clothing of the sheep, without regarding the inward malignity of the tree, and have been miserably lost through such illusions !

2. *Gather of thorns . . . . of thistles.* The earth brings forth thorns and thistles because of God's curse : "Thorns and thistles shall it bring forth to thee " (Gen. iii. 8). Such thorns and thistles are an image of sinners who are " born of blood," and not of God—who have the " wisdom of the world," and who " live after the flesh," which is earth, and will return to earth. Their fruits are none other than those called by the Apostle "works of the flesh," and they shew that the tree is evil (says St. Augustin). Let us meditate carefully on the following words of the Apostle, and see whether any of these fruits are manifest in us—" The works of the flesh are manifest; which are, fornication, unclean-ness, immodesty, luxury, idolatry, witchcraft, enmities, conten-tions, emulations, wraths, quarrels, dissensions, sects, envies, murders, drunkenness, revellings, and such like " (Gal. v. 19, 21). They who commit such works as these and amend not will not inherit the Kingdom of Heaven ; and the Priestly character, so far from removing the penalty, does but increase the guilt. Therefore, let us fight against our flesh (as St. Augustin enjoins us), for it is our nearest and most implacable enemy, and is ever in league with our other enemies to destroy us.

3. *Gather . . . grapes . . . figs.* The fig expresses charity by its sweetness, and unity by its many seeds compressed together ; while the grape signifies patience in that it is squeezed in the wine-press—joy because wine makes glad the heart of man— sincerity because it has no mixture of water—sweetness because it is pleasant to the palate ; and all these are fruits of the eccle-siastical spirit. So St. Chrysostom. For the rest, when we would more carefully examine the fruits of our tree, let us follow St. Augustin's counsel ; that is, let us see if it produces those

fruits which St. Paul calls "fruits of the Spirit." Now, St. Thomas says that these are effected by the operation of the reasoning faculty, and, so far as that is moved by God, they are called the fruits of the Holy Ghost: "The fruit of the Spirit is charity, joy, peace, patience, benignity, goodness, longanimity, mildness, faith, modesty, continency, chastity" (Gal. v. 22, 23). These (says St. Thomas) are the latest product of the tree, and therefore do they give ineffable sweetness to such as taste them. Let us beg of the Holy Spirit that He would come to us, and produce in us these most sweet fruits, which are the foretaste of eternal happiness.

"May Thy good Spirit give the earth His fruit."—*Ps.* cxlii. 10, and *Ps.* lxvi. 7.

"Let Thy children, O Lord, whom Thou lovedst, know that it is not the growing of fruits that nourisheth men, but that Thy Word preserveth them that believe in Thee."—*Wisd.* xvi. 26.

WEDNESDAY.

————◆————

THE PRIEST WHO BECOMES AS AN EVIL TREE.

I. THE DANGER OF SUCH A CALAMITY.

II. THE DISGRACE TO THE PRIESTLY CHARACTER.

III. THE REMEDY.

————◆————

" So every good tree bringeth forth good fruit, and the evil tree bringeth forth evil fruit. A good tree cannot bring forth evil fruit, neither can an evil tree bring forth good fruit."—*St. Matt.* vii. 17, 18.

1. *A good tree bringeth forth good fruit.* If our Saviour compares false Prophets to evil trees, let us consider how easy it is for an Ecclesiastic, by placing himself in the class of false Prophets, to become an evil tree. St. Thomas says that those are to be called false Prophets who have not been sent, or who teach lies. Let us, then, inquire of ourselves whether we are preachers without mission, taking upon ourselves to perform ministerial work without the will of our lawful Superiors, so as to give room for that complaint of Almighty God, "I did not send prophets, yet they ran: I have not spoken to them, yet they prophesied" (Jerem. xxiii. 21). Let us also inquire of ourselves whether, out of ignorance or malice, we teach false doctrine, so as to merit that still more fatal reproach, "They prophesy falsely to you" (Jerem. xxix. 9). In that case we should reveal only our own foolish thoughts, and not God's will; we should be both deceivers and deceived: "They prophecy to you and deceive you; they speak a vision of their own heart, and not out of the

o

mouth of the Lord" (Jerem. xxiii. 16). We should produce a
false peace—a peace which must end in the whirlwind of God's
indignation. We should say to the Faithful, " No evil shall
come upon you;" whereas it will come to pass that "the whirlwind of the Lord's indignation shall come forth" (17, 19).
Lastly, St. Chrysostom says, that by false prophets are meant
such Ecclesiastics as lead a corrupt life whilst covering themselves with the appearance of piety. Of such it is written,
" The prophet and the priest are defiled, and in My house have
I found their wickedness, saith the Lord" (Jerem. xxiii. 11).
Let us reflect on the misery of such a state, and let us pray to
God for our unhappy brethren who have fallen into it.

2. *An evil tree bringeth forth evil fruit.* The tree is the soul—
that is, man himself; the fruits are man's works; and, therefore,
if man would bring forth good fruit, let him first make himself
good. So St. Augustin. The will of man is properly the tree
(says St. Augustin again); so that, when man's will is changed
from good to evil, in like manner will his works be changed.
Now, who but Priests are charged with the duty of changing
men's wills—that is, of converting them? It is the Priest's
office to preserve good trees, and to change the bad into good.
Let us call to mind the parable of the unfruitful fig-tree, which
the lord of the vineyard would cut down, while the compassionate
dresser of the vineyard asked him to cultivate it, saying, " Lord,
let it alone this year also, until I dig about it, and dung it"
(St. Luke xiii. 8). St. Gregory says that Priests are represented
in this dresser of the vineyard, for to them is committed the
care of the Lord's vineyard." What an awful spectacle does the
Priest become who should have been the dresser of the vineyard, but is as an evil tree—who, instead of multiplying good
trees and good fruit, dishonours his Lord's vineyard by his
perversity and by the scandal of his evil works ! O my God,
through the merits of Thy Son, Who planted this vineyard with
His Blood, let me rather die than bring myself to such a state.

3. *An evil tree cannot bring forth good fruit.* If the will is evil,
evil also will be its operations; but (says St. Augustin) the evil
tree can become good, and then will it bring forth good things.

But how can a tree become good? By means of conversion; and whilst there is life there is always time and opportunity, with the help of grace, for conversion. " May not this conversion, if thou wilt, be effected to-day?" (says St. Augustin). "Can it not, if thou wilt, be completed now? No specifics, no voyages, no ships are needed for this end. But observe that, although God promises pardon on thy conversion, He does not promise thee a day for thy delay. Observe that to-day thou mayest, though unworthy, touch this visible altar, and God suffers thee to do so ; but no one embraceth the heavenly altar, to which we aspire after death, but those who have washed their hands in innocency. No one will draw near to the heavenly altar but he who draws near the earthly altar with a tranquil conscience, without cause of fear." What great truths are these ! What subject for serious consideration !

" O Lord, make me like a tree planted near the running waters, which shall bring forth its fruit in due season."—From *Ps.* i. 3.

" Let the priest be like a tree, great and strong . . . . let his fruit be exceeding much, and in it food for all."—From *Dan.* iv. 8, 9.

THURSDAY.

THE CONDEMNATION OF PRIESTS.

I. The Priests who are threatened by our Lord.
II. The threat of the pain of loss.
III. The threat of the pain of sense.

"Every tree that bringeth not forth good fruit shall be cut down, and shall be cast into the fire. Wherefore by their fruits you shall know them."—*St. Matt.* vii. 19, 20.

1. *Every tree that bringeth not forth good fruit.* Our Saviour had spoken of false Prophets, and in their person had signified wicked Priests: He had enjoined His disciples to avoid them, but He had not enjoined them to punish them. He fills them with fear, threatening them with the punishment of God (says St. Chrysostom). A wicked Priest has, indeed, need of threats rather than of promises, and for his amendment he has need to think of the former rather than of the latter. And, did he but reflect on the tremendous truth which is here inculcated—that is to say, that a Priest may be condemned for failing to produce good fruit—then surely he would never bring forth those many evil fruits which may be traced to him. He would shrink from incurring that dreadful curse, "You shall bear the iniquity of the sanctuary . . . you shall bear the sins of your priesthood" (Numb. xviii. 1). If we are branches of that great Vine, which is Jesus Christ, we ought to remember His word, "Every branch in Me that beareth not fruit He will take away;" and again, "If any one abide not in Me, he shall be cast forth as a branch, and shall wither,

and they shall gather him up, and cast him into the fire, and he burneth " (St. John xv. 2, 6). Let us, then, fear the fulfilment of so terrible a menace ; let us fear the teeth of the dragon (says St. Bernard); let us fear the belly of hell, the roaring of fierce beasts that stand ready to devour, the worm that ever gnaws, the fire that always burns, the smoke, the brimstone, the whirlwind, and the exterior darkness. It may be that our death is near, and that " the axe is already laid to the root of the tree " (St. Matt. iii. 10); it may be the Watcher and the Holy One has already cried aloud from heaven, " Cut down the tree " (Dan. iv. 11). Whither shall we then flee from the wrath of the Lamb ? Why do we not now by penance forestall this fatal stroke ?"

2. *Shall be cut down.* What terrible words are these I They point to *separation* from the heavenly kingdom, which separation is incomparably more terrible than eternal fire; although (as St. Chrysostom says) many fear hell more than they fear the loss of heaven. But the loss of a kingdom, and *that* the kingdom of God, will be most terrible for Priests, who have held the keys of it, who have opened it to others, and who will hear from the lips of devils that they have lost it, as the devils have lost it, without hope of recovery : " Thou also art wounded as well as we, thou art become like unto us " (Is. xiv. 10).—" *Shall be cut down.*" They shall be separated from the Eternal Father Who had communicated to them immense power, Who had confided to them His Son, Who had made them Ministers of His mercies, but Who now says, " I will hide My face from them, and they shall be devoured " (Deut. xxxi. 17).—" *Shall be cut down.*" What an awful punishment is that of Priests—to be separated from Christ, to become the object of His hatred, and to hate Him and curse Him, through all eternity, after having been so familiarly associated with Him —after having called Him down so many times from heaven, held Him in their hands, taken Him for food, dispensed Him to the Faithful I The punishment of ten thousand hells could not equal this (says St. Chrysostom).—" *Shall be cut down.*" How terrible for Priests to be separated for all eternity from the Holy Spirit, by Whom they were anointed, illuminated, sanctified, and made the instruments of diffusing Him on Whom the Angels,

whose name and office they have borne, "desire to look!" (1 Pet. i. 12).—"*Shall be cut down.*" Surely, nothing ought to be so terrible to Priests who still retain their faith as the thought of losing for all eternity the sight, the possession, the enjoyment of the Blessed Trinity, with Whom they have been so closely associated on earth.

3. *Shall be cast into the fire.* The fire which is kindled by God's wrath is "a fire full of wisdom;" that is, it punishes each one according to the number and heinousness of his sins. Hence the sins of Priests, which are most heinous—because of their contempt of Divine light, their ingratitude for the Divine benefits, and because of the fatal consequences of such sins— will bring upon them a more severe and intense suffering than those of any others. Supreme is God's indignation against His reprobate Ministers, and therefore against them in an especial manner is "a fire kindled in His wrath, which shall burn even to the lower hell" (Deut. xxxii. 22). The breath of Almighty God, which, when breathed upon them, gave His Priests power to remit sins, will then be "as a torrent of brimstone" to punish their iniquity (Is. xxx. 33). Let us consider that the devils have already prepared a dwelling for us, and desire to see us precipitated into that furnace of fire; "for Topheth is prepared from yesterday, deep and wide; the nourishment thereof is fire and much wood." (*Ibid.*) What anguish for Priests to see themselves changed from shining stars into fire-brands of hell! O Jesus, Author of our Priesthood, and Supreme High Priest, abandon not Thy unworthy Minister. Convert me and save me.

"Deliver, O God, my soul from the sword, my only one from the hand of the dog."—*Ps.* xxi. 21.

"Which of you can dwell with devouring fire? Which of you shall dwell with everlasting burnings?"—*Is.* xxxiii. 14.

FRIDAY.

———◆———

THE FALSE CONFIDENCE OF PRIESTS IN REGARD TO THEIR SALVATION.

I. CONFIDENCE IN THEIR MINISTERIAL FUNCTIONS.

II. CONFIDENCE IN THEIR LABOURS.

III. CONFIDENCE IN THEIR CHASTITY.

———◆———

"Not every one that saith to Me, Lord, Lord, shall enter into the Kingdom of Heaven, but he that doth the will of My Father Who is in Heaven, he shall enter into the Kingdom of Heaven."—*St. Matt.* vii. 21.

1. *Saith to Me, Lord, Lord.* Faith is not sufficient for salvation; neither is integrity of doctrine sufficient, if it be spoilt by wicked actions. As St. Jerome says, in commenting on these words of our Lord, they (that is, the Prophets of God) must confirm their works by their preaching, and their preaching by their works. Hence, the sacred functions of their office are not in themselves sufficient to distinguish good from bad Priests, or to ensure them the Kingdom of Heaven, without the fruits of a holy life; as our Lord manifestly teaches in this place. For the functions of our Ministry may be reduced to words—that is, to words of teaching, words of prayer, and the form of the Sacraments; and St. Hilary warns us that the Kingdom of Heaven is not obtained through words alone. If charity be not dominant in our heart —if it be not the soul of our actions—if it have not the marks pointed out by the Apostle—we are nothing; we are "as sounding brass, or a tinkling cymbal (1 Cor. xiii. 1). Nay, more:

our preaching becomes our condemnation; prayer is changed into sin; the Holy Sacrifice and the Sacraments are a series of sacrileges. All these things will Almighty God cast in our face at the point of death, as unclean: "I will scatter upon your face the dung of your solemnities" (Malach. ii. 3). Therefore, let us not delude ourselves because of the applause which we receive in the exercise of our functions; let us watch over our hearts, and let us fear the deep judgments of God.

2. *Shall enter into the Kingdom of Heaven.* There are two points to be considered by those who have too great confidence in their Ecclesiastical labours as a means of entering into the Kingdom of Heaven. The first is, that if we are guilty before God of mortal sin all our works are dead works; so that it may easily happen to many Ecclesiastics that, after having preached in the name of the Lord—even after having driven out devils from men's souls in His name—after having performed many other virtuous actions—they may in the Day of Judgment be disowned and driven away by their Lord. Therefore did our Saviour add to the words which form the subject of our meditation, "Many will say to Me in that day, Lord, Lord, have we not prophesied in Thy name, and cast out devils in Thy name, and done many miracles in Thy name? And then will I profess unto them, I never knew you; depart from Me, you that work iniquity" (St. Matt. vii. 22, 23). Our Lord may have dissembled long (says St. Jerome), but then will He raise His voice; and those words, "I never knew you," will be far more formidable than hell itself to those miserable Priests (as St. Chrysostom declares). The second consideration is that suggested by St. Bernard, who says, "There are some who bring forth no fruit at all; there are some who bring forth fruit, but it is not their own; there are some, again, who bring forth fruit which is their own, but not in due season." Let us inquire of ourselves to which class we belong, and if we find ourselves in error let us reform our life.

3. *He that doth the will of My Father.* Some trust in their chastity, without considering that (as St. Gregory says) chastity is not of great merit without good works. They forget that out

of ten virgins five were foolish, and heard the fatal words, "I know you not"(St. Matt. xxv. 12). Justly were they called "foolish," because (as St. Chrysostom says), after having sustained the fiercer combat in guarding their chastity, they lost all their labour by disregarding that which was comparatively easy to accomplish. St. Bernard points out with great force the folly of those who abandon themselves to a vain confidence in their virginity, and who strive not to acquire other virtues, especially that of humility. In such cases pride will rob chastity of its brightest lustre. O my God, suffer not that Priestly wisdom should in me be changed into folly; and, since thou givest me these lights, give me grace to use them aright. I trust in Thy mercy; I will strive to fulfil Thy will.

"Lead me into the path of Thy commandments, for this same have I desired."—*Ps.* cxviii. 35.

"Lord, do with me what is good and right in Thy eyes."—From *Jerem.* xxvi. 14.

SATURDAY.

THE CONFIDENCE OF PRIESTS IN THE SUCCOUR OF MARY.

I. BECAUSE THEY REPRESENT HER SON.
II. BECAUSE THEY INVOKE HER IN THE NAME OF THE CHURCH.
III. BECAUSE THEY PROMOTE HER WORSHIP.

" He saith to His Mother, Woman, behold thy Son. After that, He saith to the disciple, Behold thy mother. And from that hour the disciple took her to his own."—*St. John* xix. 26, 27.

1. *Behold thy Son.* If the Blessed Virgin looks upon all the Faithful as Her children because of the charge given Her by Jesus, much more does She regard Priests in this light, since they are (as St. Ambrose calls them) leaders and rulers of Christ's flock. They represent the Church's divine Spouse; they stand in His place; nay, they may be even called (as St. Bernard calls them) spouses of the Church, vicars of Christ. And, again, because of the intimate union with Christ proceeding from the Priestly character, they are called by St. Gregory Nazianzen " Christopheri "—bearers of Christ. Hence (as St. Chrysostom points out), he who loves Christ loves His Priests, whosoever they may be—nay, whoever insults Priests insults Christ, Whose vicars they are. Now, we know that, of all creatures, none has ever loved Jesus so much as Mary loved Him; and this love was in the first place a natural love (as St. Anselm shows), because Jesus was Her Son—Her own Son,

wholly and entirely—that is, without an earthly father—Her Son Whom She had conceived without shame and brought forth without pain—Her only Son, supremely desired by Her, and loved by Her above all creatures. But to this natural love was also added a supernatural love, not only infused but acquired by means of perpetual acts of charity. Hence (as St. Bonaventure says), the Blessed Virgin loved Jesus more perfectly than all other Saints united together; and how is it possible, then, that She should not love Priests, who form one sole Priesthood with Jesus? How is it possible that She should despise their prayers? How is it possible that She should deny them the succour they implore?

2. *Behold thy Mother.* The Faithful invoke Mary as their Mother, but they invoke Her as private individuals: Priests, on the contrary, invoke Mary, not only as private individuals, but also in the capacity of public ministers of the Church, and in the name of the Church. It is certain that in celebrating Mass, in reciting their Office, and in other functions they shine with a splendour which the laity cannot possess, because (as St. Ignatius the Martyr says) they are nearer to the light—they are, as it were, clothed with the light. Now, the Church continually charges Priests to invoke Mary; and, however much faith may sometimes languish, Mary has ever been held in honour and special veneration. How great, then, will be Her liberality to Priests who strive to honour Her, not only in the Church's name, but in the Church's spirit! Therefore, let us invoke Her as our tender Mother, and be assured that She will protect those who labour for the Church under Her shadow (as Blessed Amadeus says), and that She will, at the least, obtain for us strength to bear our tribulations. Let us be assured that She has a special right over us, because Her Son has communicated His rights to Her. Let us, then, call upon Her for succour with the greatest confidence, and She will fill us with grace, and will not refuse us help in fit time.

3. *The disciple took her to his own.* If we look upon the Blessed Virgin as our Mother—if we promote Her honour and worship —we shall acquire a special title to be protected and succoured

by Her in our necessities. Let us remember that She is truly
the "most venerable Virgin," being the place where Jesus
dwelt : "We will adore in the place where His feet stood" (Ps.
cxxxi. 7). Let us exhort the Faithful to venerate Her, saying
to them, "Adore His foot-stool, for it is holy" (Ps. xcviii. 5).
Let us extol Her to the utmost of our power, and we shall ever
say far less than She merits ; for (says St. Anselm) no heavenly
nor earthly tongue suffices for the praises of Mary. She will be
grateful for our service, and we shall find in Her an impregnable
tower : " As the tower of David, which is built with bulwarks,"
from which "a thousand bucklers hang, all the armour of valiant
men " (Cant. iv. 4). Let us strive that all may honour this great
Tower, which (as St. Thomas of Villanova says) is founded upon
the most solid Rock—even Jesus ; and let us instruct all our
people to seek refuge in it. In all tribulations, whether they
arise from sin or from persecution or from temptations, let us
incite every man to seek refuge in this Tower. The Church has
approved the Feast of our Lady of Succour, which is celebrated
on the 16th June. Let us lean upon this "pillar and ground
of the truth," imploring and causing others to implore Her
succour.

"Bow down Thy ear to me ; make haste to deliver me."—*Ps.* xxx. 3.

"In this hour look on the works of Thy hands, that . . . . what I believe
might be done by Thee may be brought to pass."—From *Judith* xiii. 7.

EIGHTH SUNDAY AFTER PENTECOST.

——◆——

THE UNJUST STEWARD A FIGURE OF BAD PRIESTS.

I. His ADMINISTRATION.

II. His DISGRACE.

III. His WASTEFULNESS.

——◆——

"Jesus said also to His disciples, There was a certain rich man who had a steward, and the same was accused unto him, that he had wasted his goods."— *St. Luke* xvi. 1.

1. *Had a steward.* In a general sense, under the term "steward" may be understood all men who have received gifts from God, whether in the order of nature or of grace; for such are not owners, but simply administrators. In a more particular sense, however, the word represents Priests, and especially those who have the care of souls (as St. Anselm says), for they have committed to them the care and direction of the carnal. The Greek word, indeed, is "*œconomus*," which St. Jerome translates "dispenser," as he likewise uses the word to "dispense" and "dispensation" of the office of a steward. Now, who are the stewards and dispensers of the house of God if not Priests? Let us meditate on the Apostle's words, in which we are called "dispensers of the mysteries of God" (1 Cor. iv. 1); let us meditate on those other words in which he calls the Bishop and the Priest "the steward of God" (Tit. i. 7); let us profit by the exhor-

tation of the Prince of the Apostles, "As every man hath received grace, ministering the same one to another, as good stewards of the manifold grace of God" (1 Pet. iv. 10). All the power which our Lord Jesus Christ, "the rich man," rich in Divine treasures, has conferred upon us, is but an administration and stewardship (says St. Bonaventure) with which He entrusts us for a time determined by Himself. Holy Mass, the Sacraments, the Ministry of the Word, are treasures of which we have the administration. What treasures are these! what a dignity! how surpassing human reason and understanding! (says St. Charles Borromeo.)

2. *Was accused unto him.* It was not a simple accusation, but public defamation, which induced his lord to take away from the unfaithful steward the administration of his goods. This signifies that, even if God were to suffer for a time the irregular lives of Priests, He would be provoked to punish them by the accusations of others. For, first, the devil is their accuser, called, as he is, "the accuser of our brethren" (Apoc. xii. 10). Next, the good Angels are their accusers, who see their care for the salvation of souls made of no avail through the wickedness and slothfulness of Priests. Again, the damned souls are their accusers, laying the blame of their ruin on the Confessor, the Preacher, the parish Priest, whose lack of zeal has caused their eternal ruin; for it is the wont of impenitent sinners (says St. Augustin) to seek to accuse others of their own sins. The just also are their accusers, who would have been still more justified, and have avoided the pains of purgatory, had they been better instructed, exhorted, encouraged, and purified; for it is written, "He that is just, let him be justified still" (Apoc. xxii. 11). Finally, inanimate things are their accusers; for God's temples squalid, profaned, and without worshippers—the sacred vestments torn, dirty, and ill-kept—ecclesiastical functions performed without the requisite ceremonies, without recollection, without modesty—the people ignorant, corrupt, and irreligious—all these things cry aloud to Heaven against the Clergy. "Their cry went up unto God" (Exod. ii. 23). "I will deliver My flock from their mouth" (Ezech. xxxiv. 10). Our Saviour speaks,

then, of this defamation in order that Priests, having (as St. Bonaventure says) a natural horror of infamy, should not abuse the treasures committed to them. Let us examine ourselves as to the impression which these terrible truths produce upon our heart, and if we are not made to tremble we may be assured that we are in danger.

3. *That he had wasted his goods.* It is not said that the steward injured his lord, for the latter was so rich that he could sustain no loss; nor is it said that he was a thief, for he gained nothing for himself. It is simply said that he "wasted," as the prodigal son wasted; that is to say, he lost that which belonged to his master and others, because he distributed not the goods as he ought. "He doth not distribute with right understanding that which was to be had, in like manner also that which was not to be had" (Eccl. xx. 19). When goods, health, talents, eloquence, supernatural lights, graces "*gratis datæ,*" are not employed in the way which God has prescribed, they are "wasted;" and, therefore, when we dispense not these goods according to our Lord's will, but only so as to satisfy our passions, we are "wasteful" stewards. Woe to us if we find ourselves in this state, and seek not to remedy it!

" O Lord, my heart was not right with Thee, nor was my counsel faithful in Thy covenant : be merciful, and forgive my sins."—From *Ps.* lxxvii. 37.

" A dispensation is committed to me . . . I will not abuse my power."—From 1 *Cor.* ix. 17, 18.

MONDAY.

CAUSES OF THE CORRUPTION OF ECCLESIASTICS.

I. They do not remember the past.
II. They do not reflect on the present.
III. They do not foresee the future.

"And he called him, and said to him, How is it that I hear this of thee? Give an account of thy stewardship, for now thou canst be steward no longer."—*St. Luke* xvi. 2.

1. *He called him.* We should remember how many of our friends have been called by their Lord, and called when they least expected it. How many have there been within our own recollection who in the morning seemed in good health and in the evening had entered on eternity! Some have been called to their account when they were at table, some when they were walking, some when they were conversing with friends; and in calling these stewards our Lord called us also, shewing us in their case (as St. Chrysostom reminds us) what may happen to us. God called us when we were suffering that sickness during which we felt ourselves incited to good resolutions, which (says St. Anselm) the Angels offered to our Lord, that He might defer our judgment. Finally, God called us (says St. Bonaventure) when He raised in our hearts a fear of the Divine judgments and of eternal damnation. It is through forgetfulness of these calls that we waste heavenly treasure, and live like the unfaithful steward. This steward had in truth some excuse for his wicked conduct, for he knew not that he had to give an

account to his lord—he did not suspect that he was accused before his lord—he had no warning of his lord's indignation. We, on the other hand, who have heard these truths so often, who have meditated on them so often—what excuse can we allege ? What shall we say to our Lord when He shall ask of us an account of the souls committed to us ? "Where is the flock that is given thee—thy beautiful cattle ? What wilt thou say when He shall visit thee ? . . Shall not sorrows lay hold on thee, as a woman in labour ?" (Jerem. xiii. 20, 21.)

2. *Give an account of thy stewardship.* Our wastefulness proceeds, also, from want of reflection on our present state, We ought to consider, with St. Ambrose, that we are not masters of the treasures entrusted to us, but simply administrators, bound to dispense them carefully. To look upon ourselves as masters is an error (says St. Chrysostom), which does but increase our guilt and diminish our merit. Let us consider that the time of our stewardship will be brief—that we shall be compelled to appear, against our will, and at a time when we least expect it, before the tribunal of God; and then will our stewardship be taken from us, and if we have not been good administrators we shall be left beggars. Let us, then, divest ourselves of all pride, and remember that we are stewards only, and not lords, and that this is a state which obliges us to humility and modesty: so shall we not be "lording it over the clergy," but looking for the day "when the Prince of pastors shall appear" (1 Pet. v. 3, 4).

3. *For now thou canst be steward no longer.* Let us think of the future if we would not have "sudden calamity fall upon us, and destruction as a tempest come upon us" (Prov. i. 27). Let us think of the judgment to which all our actions will be subjected; "for a most severe judgment shall be for them that bear rule" (Wisd. vi. 6). How will our life be improved if we remember that "we must all be manifested before the judgment-seat of Christ, that every one may receive the proper things of the body, according as he hath done, whether it be good or evil" (2 Cor. v. 10). And, if (says St. Bernard) we have to give account of that which we have done in our own body, what account shall we give of that which we have done in the Body of Christ,

which is the Church ?   Almighty God has given into our hands
" corn, and wine, and oil, and silver, and gold, and wool, and
flax "—that is, all kinds of riches—for our own profit and the
profit of others ; and if we waste them He will take them out of
our hands : " I will return and take away My corn in its season,
and My wine in its season ; and I will set at liberty My wool,
and My flax which covered her disgrace " (Osee ii. 8, 9); and
we shall be left to everlasting ignominy.   With our stewardship
taken out of our hands, what can we do ?   " Neither work, nor
reason, nor wisdom, nor knowledge shall be in hell, whither
thou art hastening" (Eccl. ix. 10).

" I will go into the sanctuary of God, and will understand concerning my last
end."—From *Ps.* lxii. 17.

" O that they would be wise, and would understand, and would provide for their
last end."—*Deut.* xxxii. 29.

TUESDAY.

———◆———

MEANS OF CONVERSION FOR BAD PRIESTS.

I. THE THOUGHT OF DEATH.
II. THE KNOWLEDGE OF THEIR OWN MISERY.
III. EARNEST RESOLUTION OF AMENDMENT.

———◆———

" And the steward said within himself, What shall I do, because my lord taketh
away from me the stewardship ?   To dig I am not able, to beg I am ashamed.   I
know what I will do, that when I shall be removed from the stewardship they may
receive me into their houses."—*St. Luke* xvi. 3, 4.

1. *What shall I do ?*   The holy Doctors affirm that the conversion of Ecclesiastics is slow and difficult.   Our blessed Lord

in His mercy, out of regard for their salvation, has set before them this parable of the Steward in order to facilitate their conversion. Whoever the sinful Cleric may be, it is necessary for his amendment and virtuous living that he should say from his heart, " What shall I do ?"—that is, that he think of death and of its consequences. Hence, St. Ambrose made it his prayer to Almighty God that he might ever remember the day of his death, the Day of Judgment, the punishment of eternal damnation, and the blessedness of the future kingdom. All sin comes from forgetfulness of death, and conversion springs from the thought of death. Commenting on the words, " What shall I do ?" St. Peter Chrysologus says that the steward spoke with himself as with another. The Priest must commune thus with himself, and avoid imitating the rich man in the Gospel, who said to himself, " Soul, thou hast much goods laid up for many years : take thy rest, eat, drink, make good cheer" (St. Luke xii. 19). Let us meditate on the answer God made to that rich man—" Thou fool, this night do they require thy soul of thee" (v. 20).

2. *To dig I am not able, to beg I am ashamed.* A Priest who knows what he owes to God's justice knows likewise that he ought to lead the hard and humble life which constitutes the perfection of penance (says St. Bonaventure), but because of the weakness of man's soul he refuses the labour and the humiliation which are signified by "digging" and by "begging." He ought to give himself to a mortified and austere life like that of the Cistercians, to fasts and vigils, to hair shirts and disciplines; he ought to expiate his pride and his delicacy of living by poverty; but (continues St. Bonaventure) he refuses labour out of weakness, and flies from poverty out of shame. This delicacy is a great obstacle to his conversion, as St. Bernard points out, who says, that when such a Priest tries to scrape away the rust which is engrained into his soul he will not endure the touch of a finger : according to the words of Scripture, " He has grown fat and kicked." He has not courage to resolve on a mode of life so different from that which he has led, and, from being unaccustomed to penance, he finds that which he ought

to do most difficult. Let us examine ourselves in order to see what courage we have for undertaking a life of penance. Perhaps we shall find that our body, having been delicately nurtured from childhood, is already become rebellious : " He that nourisheth his servant delicately from his childhood, afterwards shall find him stubborn " (Prov. xxix. 21). What cowardice, what misery, what humiliation ! Well is it for us that God has compassion on us, and has opened for us another way of salvation—that is, almsgiving.

3. *I know what I will do.*   A Priest has every reason to say, " I know what I will do." He knows well that the mercy of God is infinite—that sincere repentance, a confession well made, a return to God, suffices to obtain his pardon. He can say with St. Ambrose, "The more we have sinned the more may we gain ; for Thy grace enriches us more than our innocence." He fears no reproof from God if he but avert His anger by repentance. St. Peter Chrysologus points out that in the case of the Prodigal son the father said nothing harsh—he said not, " Whence cometh thou ? Where hast thou been ? Where is that which thou didst take away ? How is it thou hast changed so great glory into misery ?"   But he at once put on him the first robe, and put a ring on his hand. Let us, then, return to our God, Who will not only repair our lost innocence, but will also restore to us our Priestly robe, and our honour ; and more readily will He pardon us, and will cast our sins behind His back, if we give ourselves to the practice of works of mercy. Let us imitate the steward, who knew how to make friends in order to implore their help, and who, seeing (as St. Anselm says) that time was granted him for penance, took salutary counsel. Let us make use of the same means to expiate our faults, whether they be grave or light, and let us not fear that we shall be deceived.

" Why art thou cast down, O my soul, and why dost thou disquiet me ? Hope thou in God."—*Ps.* xli. 12.

"I know what I will do, that when I shall be removed from the stewardship they may receive me into their houses.—*St. Luke* xvi. 4.

WEDNESDAY.

OUR LORD INSTRUCTS THE CLERGY ON ALMS-GIVING.

I. Almsgiving in general.

II. Spiritual almsgiving.

III. Corporal almsgiving.

" Therefore calling together every one of his lord's debtors, he said to the first, How much dost thou owe my lord ? But he said, An hundred barrels of oil. And he said to him, Take thy bill, and sit down quickly, and write fifty. Then he said to another, And how much dost thou owe? Who said, An hundred quarters of wheat. He said to him, Take thy bill, and write eighty."—*St. Luke* xvi. 5—7.

1. *Therefore calling together every one of his lord's debtors.* The steward is a debtor to his lord through his unfaithfulness, but he finds a remedy for his own evils in giving relief to other debtors with the very goods of his lord. Here is the true, the most sublime idea of spiritual and corporal almsgiving, and it is set forth in this parable only, causing the parable to appear as a paradox. The truth is, that he who has need of help of any kind is God's debtor, not only because poverty of body and soul is usually the effect of sin, but because even the just man owes debt to God, and must join in the prayer, " Forgive us our debts." All, however, which is given to the needy is our Lord's (says St. Chrysostom); and he who gives gives nothing of his own—nay, the very goodwill to give is God's gift. Let us take, for example, the principal works of mercy, both spiritual and corporal. Does not the bread which we give to the hungry

come from God ? In like manner, in instructing the ignorant, from whom do we receive the talents, the strength, the time, the will for doing it ? " What hast thou that thou hast not received?" (1 Cor. iv. 7.) And the Lord is well pleased with the liberality and mercy of His steward—nay, He sets him before us as a pattern for us to follow (says St. Bonaventure), in order that we may attain eternal happiness. This idea of almsgiving seems to remove all vain-glory from the soul of the almsgiver; for alms are thus shown to be as it were a pious fraud, which we practice upon our Lord in order to repair our own unfaithfulness, for thereby we employ His goods for the welfare of our neighbour and to our own advantage. " If thou hast received it, why dost thou glory as if thou hadst not received it ?" (1 Cor. iv. 7.)

2. *Write fifty.* Oil is a figure of grace and of those spiritual goods which are communicated by the spiritual works of mercy (says St. Augustin). Now, the spiritual works of mercy belong especially to Priests, and chiefly that of humbling the sinner and bringing him to penance, after he has confessed the amount of his debts. The Priest is thus as the steward of the Church (as St. Anselm says). He makes the sinner take the "bill" of his debt ; he makes him sit down—that is, he brings before him the sins which he has committed—in order to humble him. The number of fifty designates the amount of penance and the remission of sins. And all good Confessors, and, in general, all Priests, whilst doing good to sinners by exercising the works of mercy proper to their state, promote also their own benefit. Hence St. Polycarp wrote, "Let Priests be ever tenderly affected and merciful, bringing back those who have erred." Let us therefore willingly employ our time, our talents, our strength, in works which are so pleasing to God ; let us recognize them as becoming our Ministry, and as means of obtaining pardon for our evil stewardship. Thus may we blot out by good works the evil of our past lives.

3. *Write eighty.* The debtor who owed a hundred quarters of wheat is a figure of him who needs bread and expects it from us : " Deal thy bread to the hungry " (Is. lviii. 7): and the

abatement of twenty on the hundred signifies the assistance given to the indigent by the corporal works of mercy. But in such cases means are more limited, and therefore fifty cannot be given on the hundred, but an amount proportioned to the condition of the almsgiver: "According to thy ability be merciful; if thou have much, give abundantly; if thou have little, take care even so to bestow willingly a little. For thus thou storest up to thyself a good reward for the day of necessity" (Tobias iv. 8—10). This steward is our model, for he gives relief not only liberally, but in due measure (says St. Bonaventure). Let us remember that the Ministers of the Altar should take to themselves bowels of mercy, and say with St. Ambrose, "Let us have compassion on the infirmities and necessities of others; let us help them to the utmost of our means, and sometimes even beyond our means." Let our hands be ever open to succour the poor, for otherwise (says St. Gregory) we bear the name of Bishop or Priest in vain. Let us pray to our Lord Jesus Christ to give us tenderness and mercy, infusing into us the spirit of charity, that our heart be not hardened in regard to the miseries of our brethren.

"Blessed is he that understandeth concerning the needy and the poor : the Lord will deliver him in the evil day.—*Ps.* xl. 2.
"I was an eye to the blind, and a foot to the lame. I was the father of the poor."
—Job. xxix. 15.

THURSDAY.

A CHARITABLE PRIEST DEAR TO GOD.

I. He is praised by God.
II. He is prudent according to God.
III. He is a child of the light.

———————

"And the lord commended the unjust steward, forasmuch as he had done wisely; for the children of this world are wiser in their generation than the children of light."—*St. Luke* xvi. 8.

1. *The lord commended the unjust steward.* The lord represented in the parable praised his steward (says Origen), not with true praise, but, as it were, unfitly; for he praised only his craftiness and cunning. How much more (says St. Augustin) does God praise that steward who performs the works of mercy which He Himself has prescribed, and which are so pleasing to Him! Hence, a charitable Priest is truly praised by God; and that is the greatest consolation and the greatest glory which he can have in life or in death: "He is approved whom God commendeth" (2 Cor. x. 18). Let us, then, strive to obtain this praise of God, and to be approved by Him for our almsgiving; for it was to a Priest that the Apostle wrote, "Carefully study to present thyself approved unto God" (2 Tim. ii. 15). The Eternal Father will certainly approve those who are conformed to the image of His Son, in Whom He is always well pleased; and we know that this Son "went about doing good" (Acts x. 38)—nay, that, although our Lord Jesus was poor and "had

not where to lay his head," He found means to give alms, "that he should give something to the poor" (St. John xiii. 29). From our Saviour's conduct in this matter we may see the use which should be made of Ecclesiastical revenues. God, then, praises the charitable Ecclesiastic: let us, therefore, following the judgment of God (as St. Augustin says), both praise and imitate him.

2. *Forasmuch as he had done wisely.* As the prudence of the flesh, which teaches men the art of amassing treasures, is death, so the prudence of the Spirit, which teaches them to give alms, is life and peace: "The wisdom of the flesh is death; the wisdom of the Spirit is life and peace" (Rom. viii. 6). Almsgiving makes us prudent according to God—"wise in Christ" (1 Cor. iv. 10); for (as St. Thomas teaches) prudence is that virtue which chooses the right means towards the end in view, and almsgiving is a most fit means for attaining our last end: "Alms delivereth from death, and the same is that which purgeth away sins, and maketh to find mercy and life everlasting" (Tobias xii. 9). We frequently inculcate upon the people the fulfilment of this great duty, so often insisted on by Almighty God; but if we do not set an example of it ourselves it is useless for us to attempt to persuade others to practise it. Our preaching produces little or no fruit in our hearers, because (as St. Gregory says) the preacher's life is a contradiction to his words. Moreover, in the conversion of the poor the hand prepares the way for the tongue; that is to say, our acts of mercy must dispose their hearts for the reception of our doctrine. They will even hold the Word of God in contempt if we seek to correct their sins without supplying them with the means of subsistence. We may be sure that a charitable Priest hinders a great number of sins committed through poverty. He is regarded as a holy man, he conciliates public benevolence, and is well spoken of even by unbelievers; and this is a protection, both to the Priest himself and to his ministrations, against that "reproach" which is "the snare of the devil" (1 Tim. iii. 7). Let us be careful to meditate on these important truths.

3. *The children of light.* God is light, and in Him is no

darkness. They who have the light of God are children of this light, and therefore children of God. Guided by this light, they will readily open their hands to the poor, whilst the children of this world think only of gain and temporal convenience. Guided by this light, the Priest need not fear being left through almsgiving without support in old age and sickness; for the Lord has promised to " help him on his bed of sorrow, to turn all his couch in his sickness " (Ps. xl. 4). He knows that Jesus Christ has put Himself in the person of the poor, and looks upon alms as money given to Him at usury: " He that hath mercy on the poor lendeth to the Lord, and He will repay him " (Prov. xix. 17). Hence (as St. Chrysostom says), almsgiving is the most profitable of all acts, recompensing us a hundred-fold; by it we build for ourselves, not houses of clay, but an eternal habitation. Let us remember that " alms shut up in the heart of the poor obtain help against all evil; better than the child of the mighty, better than the spear, it shall fight for thee against thy enemy" (Eccl. xxix. 15—17). Let us remember, too, that " God loveth a cheerful giver" (2 Cor. ix. 7). Surely it were a shame to know and preach these truths, and yet to act niggardly towards the poor for the sake of amassing money. What are our alms? What privations do we undergo for the sake of the poor? What proof of love do we give our Lord in the person of the needy?

" He hath distributed, he hath given to the poor, his justice remaineth for ever." —*Ps.* cxi. 9.

" If I have denied to the poor what they desired, and have made the eyes of the widow wail : if I have eaten my morsel alone, and the fatherless hath not eaten thereof.—*Job* xxxi. 16, 17.

FRIDAY.

———◆———

ECCLESIASTICAL BENEFICES.

I. THE DANGER OF POSSESSING THEM.
II. THE EVIL OF ABUSING THEM.
III. THE MERIT OF A RIGHT EMPLOYMENT OF THEM.

———◆———

"And I say unto you, Make unto you friends of the mammon of iniquity, that when you shall fail they may receive you into everlasting dwellings."—*St. Luke* xvi. 9.

1. *Of the mammon of iniquity.* Riches are called "iniquity" because they are often unjustly acquired, because they often furnish matter and incentive to sin, and because they are the sole object of the desires of the wicked. Ecclesiastical benefices are God's property; they are (as declared by the Fourth Council of Carthage) consecrated to God. But they are also called the "price of sins," and as such the expression of "mammon of iniquity" may be applied to them. Hence, they who hold these benefices, of which they must give strict account to the Eternal Spouse of the Church, are in great danger; and, in fact, Priests should look upon themselves as simple stewards of these goods, for they hold them, not for themselves, but for others. Therefore, it is folly to desire them without necessity, seeing that they are not our own property, and that we run the risk of misusing them. Priests (as St. Augustin says) are not possessors, but dispensers, of Ecclesiastical goods. How many have lost their souls through the misuse of such property, who otherwise might have been rich eternally in Paradise! Wise,

therefore, was the Apostle, who, whilst he exhorted the Faithful to give of their substance to the Church and to her Ministers, would himself have none of these things, but preached the Gospel without charge, so as not to lessen his eternal reward (1 Cor. ix. 7, 19); and who at his departure from Miletus could say, "I have not coveted any man's silver, gold, or apparel," having before his eyes our Lord's words, "It is a more blessed thing to give rather than to receive" (Acts xx. 33—35). Blessed, then, are Priests who labour for the Church gratuitously, and even spent the fruits of their patrimony and of their labour in alms. Why do we not aspire to this blessedness? Why do not we imitate their wisdom?

2. *Make unto you friends.* They who hold Ecclesiastical benefices might with them make friends of the poor, for (as St. Thomas says) they have received them, not for themselves, but for the poor. They who appropriate to themselves anything beyond necessary food and simple clothing are guilty of robbery and sacrilege (says St. Bernard). Moreover, Almighty God will not entrust such Priests with spiritual goods; that is, He will not give them grace to administer His Sacraments and His Word, and to exercise their jurisdiction worthily; for they will find themselves entangled in innumerable snares, binding their conscience, and dragging them to hell. Certain it is that to him who has not been faithful in administering false and "unjust mammon," God will not entrust "true riches." If he has not been "faithful in that which is another's"—that is, in temporal goods—"who will give him that which is his own?" that is to say, those riches of Divine grace, those heavenly gifts and supernatural virtues, which are eternal goods. If we do not dispense well those carnal riches which we brought not into the world and cannot carry away from this world to the next, and which escape from our hands, who will entrust us with the true and eternal riches of the doctrine of God? So St. Jerome.

3. *That when you shall fail they may receive you into everlasting dwellings.* He is truly happy (says St. Jerome) who reserves nothing to himself of the Church's goods. He is happy who makes use of Ecclesiastical property for the worship of God and

His Saints, who possess the eternal tabernacles; for who are they (asks St. Augustin) who possess the eternal tabernacles if not the Saints of God? Blessed, also, is he who makes use of them in suffrages for the holy souls, so as to hasten their entrance into the heavenly country, through God's promise and by God's permission, Who has exhorted us thus to make to ourselves friends in heaven. Blessed, too, is he who with these goods succours the poor, and who by careful charity makes such alms serve for the good of souls; for so will he procure advocates for himself in the sight of God. Fish are taken with the bait, and souls are gained by temporal succour. Let us consider that Jesus Christ suffered His Apostles to expect that His dominion would be a temporal one until the Holy Spirit had taken possession of their heart; and, indeed, all the others who believed in Him (except Mary Magdalene and the good thief) asked and obtained temporal benefits, and so were led on to heavenly desires. Therefore, let zealous Priests adopt this pious craft in drawing souls into the Lord's net, so as to bring them to the shore of salvation, and thus be able to say to them, "Being crafty, I caught you by guile" (2 Cor. xii. 16). What abundant reward is reserved for them in heaven! But how many are there of this number?

"O Lord, make me spare the poor and needy, that I may save the souls of the poor."—From *Ps.* lxxi. 13.

"Lord, shew me not judgment without mercy, because I have not done mercy."—From *St. James* ii. 13.

SATURDAY.

———◆———

THE FEAST OF THE BLESSED VIRGIN MARY "AD NIVES."

I. WHY THE BLESSED VIRGIN CHOSE THE SYMBOL OF SNOW.
II. WHY SHE WOULD HAVE TEMPLES IN HER HONOUR.
III. WHY HER PRAISES SHOULD BE SPECIALLY PREACHED IN THEM.

———◆———

"Blessed is the womb that bore Thee."—*St. Luke* xi. 27.

1. Truly *blessed was the womb* which bore the Saviour of the world; for His Mother was purer than the purest snow, and therefore did She wisely choose this beautiful symbol in the present solemnity: "He scattereth snow . . the eye admireth at the beauty of the whiteness thereof" (Eccl. xliii. 19). Thus did Mary show forth Her purity, according to those mysterious words, "If I be washed as it were with snow water, and my hands shall shine ever so clean" (Job. ix. 30). And we Priests ought to proclaim Her more blessed for Her pure virtue, of which the snow which on this day fell in such prodigious quantity was an emblem, than for Her dignity as Mother of God (as St. Justin declares). Under the same emblem She points out in another place how greatly She loves purity in us— how She protects it, and defends it from enemies: "Hast thou entered into the storehouses of the snow . . which I have prepared for the time of the enemy, against the day of battle and war?" (Job xxxviii. 22). She, indeed, it is who obtains for us

suffers us not to be consumed: "Snow and ice endured the force of fire, and melted not" (Wisd. xvi. 22): and, as the "cold of snow" refreshes man in the summer, "in the time of harvest," so does Mary, as "a faithful messenger of grace," give great refreshment to the soul amid the flames of concupiscence (Prov. xxv. 13). Let us pray to the Blessed Virgin to preserve our chastity, of which we have made a solemn vow; and let us trust in her that she will preserve us "whiter than snow" (Lam. iv. 7), for snow is the emblem of purity.

2. *Blessed is the womb*—which is called by the holy Fathers the Temple of the Word. In the present solemnity our Blessed Lady manifested to the Supreme Pontiff Liberius, and to a Roman patrician named John, and his wife (to whom She appeared in a dream), Her desire that a temple should be built in Her honour in the place designated by the snow. No wonder, then, is it that there should have been so many churches, chapels, oratories, and altars erected in Her honour through the efforts of so many zealous Priests; and vainly have heretics impugned this devotion of the Church. God ordained that His Temple should be destined, not only for offering sacrifices, but also for preserving the Ark (1 Paralip. xxviii. 2; 2 Paralip. v. 7); and this Ark was a type of Mary, in Whom was contained, not the Law merely, but the Lawgiver Himself. She was the living Ark of the Lawgiver of God (says St. Methodius). Mary exceeded in splendour the Ark, which was covered with most pure gold. She was illumined by the Holy Spirit Himself (says St. Germanus). She was the Ark over which were the Propitiatory and the Cherubim (says St. Ildephonsus), and in which the true manna was kept. Most fitting, therefore, is it that the Mother of God should be honoured in the temples of the Lord; and happy is the Priest who can contribute to the raising of these buildings in which Mary is venerated. She says of him, "He shall build a house to my name" (2 Kings vii. 13). Let us endeavour to maintain the splendour, beauty, and sanctity of such shrines, so as to be able to say to Her, "I have loved the beauty of Thy house" (Ps. xxv. 8). Let us in these Churches perform the sacred functions in honour of the Blessed Virgin

with due magnificence, in order that the Faithful may flock thither, and that their spiritual joy may be increased : " He chose priests without blemish, whose will was set upon the law of God, and they cleansed the holy places . . . and there was exceeding great joy among the people" (1 Mach. iv. 42, 43).

3. Priests should repeat continually the words, " Blessed is the womb which bore Thee." Exalt Mary, O ye Ministers of the Lord, to the utmost of your power, for She is greater than all praise (Eccl. xliii. 33). Remember that She has been praised by Angels, by Patriarchs, by Prophets, by Evangelists, by the holy Fathers and Doctors of the Church ; and that not one of them thought himself sufficient to praise Her. What tongue, even of Angels (says St. Bernard), can worthily extol the praises of the Virgin Mother ? To speak of Her kindles holy love in the soul ; to think of Her gives consolation (says St. Bonaventure). To each of us She promises to obtain for us grace to avoid sin, as a reward for our praise : " For My praise I will bridle thee, lest thou shouldst perish" (Is. xlviii. 9). Praise Her, then, frequently and gladly, and especially in the temples erected in Her honour ; and " She will meet thee" at the hour of thy death "as an honourable Mother" (Eccl. xv. 2), and will show thee Her Son.

" Sing to Her, yea, sing praises to Her, relate all Her wondrous works."—From *Ps.* civ. 2.

" I praise Thee, because Thou hast shewn me what we desired of Thee."—From *Dan.* ii 23.

———————

NINTH SUNDAY AFTER PENTECOST.

—◆—

COMPASSION THE FIRST CHARACTERISTIC OF ZEAL, AS TAUGHT BY OUR LORD—

> I. BY TEARS BECOMING HIS DIGNITY.
> II. BY TEARS SHED AT THE RIGHT SEASON.
> III. BY TEARS WORTHY OF HIS CHARITY.

—◆—

1. *He wept.* St. Basil, St. Augustin, and St. Bernard observe that our Lord Jesus Christ, in the days of His flesh, is never said to have laughed; for laughter became not His wisdom, inasmuch as it is written, " Laughter I counted error" (Eccl. ii. 2). We know also that of Him is interpreted the passage in which the Wise Man speaks of the period of his infancy—" The first voice which I uttered was crying, as all others do" (Wisd. vii. 3). We know, again, that when He raised Lazarus " Jesus wept" (St. John xi. 35). Lastly, we know that in the garden of Gethsemani and on Mount Calvary He offered up prayers and supplications to His Father, "with a strong cry and tears" (Heb. v. 7). In truth, tears became Him Who made Himself a " Man of sorrows" (Is. liii. 3), and " Whose sorrow was continually before Him" (Ps. xxxvii. 18). Sorrow became Him because (as Origen observes) He would in such wise participate in all the Beatitudes as to be Prince of the Blessed, and therefore would He participate in this one—" Blessed are they that mourn" (St. Matt. v. 5). Tears became Him because He was the

Wisdom of the wise—the Incarnate Wisdom; and it is written, "The heart of the wise is where there is mourning" (Eccl. vii. 5). Tears became Him because He is the Head of the elect, and to them He Himself hath said, "You shall lament and weep" (St. John xvi. 20). Tears became Him because He is the great High Priest, and Priests are enjoined to weep: "The Priests . . . shall weep" (Joel ii. 17). Let us, then, learn from Him to weep: let us not abandon ourselves to dissolute laughter, which is unbecoming our dignity; remembering that "a fool lifteth up his voice in laughter: a wise man will scarce laugh low to himself" (Eccl. xxi. 23). St. Ephrem wrote a treatise entitled "Laugh not," and St. Chrysostom observes that we never read of St. Paul or of any other Saints that they laughed. Let us, at least, guard against that excessive laughter in which worldly persons delight, and which prevents us from being an example to the Faithful "in gravity" (Tit. ii. 7); and let us remember St. Augustin's words, "Why did Christ weep, but to teach man how to weep?"

2. *When He drew near to Jerusalem.* Our Saviour chose for His triumphal entrance a moment in which Jerusalem presented her most magnificent aspect. He beheld her, and wept over her (says St. Bonaventure) in pitiful affection and loving compassion. As man He chose the moment and point of view which were most opportune: as God He fulfilled the words, "I have seen the affliction of My people . . . I am come down to deliver them" (Exod. iii. 7, 8). He chose, moreover, the time when Jerusalem was most joyful, to deplore the joy of the sacerdotal city, which was an idle and a foolish joy (says St. Bonaventure). He chose the occasion, too, in which He could best show Himself to be both King and Priest; for, whilst He was acknowledged and saluted "King of Israel," He united Priestly compassion with Kingly dignity. And, as in His Transfiguration He spoke of His Passion—"They spoke of His decease that He should accomplish in Jerusalem" (St. Luke ix. 31)—so in the glory of His triumph He wept, and spoke of the ruin which was to come upon Jerusalem. In this manner did He fitly teach us that in the midst of joy we should not

forget the evils which will one day come upon us: according to the saying of the Wise Man, "In the day of good things be not unmindful of evils" (Eccl. xi. 27). Let us, then, learn of our Lord Jesus Christ to remember in our joys the sorrows which may follow them, and for which we should be ever prepared: so shall we be neither puffed up by the praise of men nor elated by prosperity in the things of this world. Happy shall we be if we duly meditate upon this lesson.

3. *Seeing the city.* At the sight of the city the charity of Jesus moved Him to weep over her approaching ruin. He wept (says St. Gregory) over that ruin of which the guilty city herself had no knowledge. His tears were sincere and bitter, for His most tender Heart loved the people whom He was sent by His Father to save: "I was not sent but to the sheep that are lost of the house of Israel" (St. Matt. xv. 24). He wept not so much over the temporal misfortunes of Jerusalem as for the eternal misery to which the greater part of her citizens would be condemned. He beheld in Jerusalem a figure of every obstinate reprobate soul, and thus gave sensible token that He would "have all men to be saved," and that He desires not that one should perish. So St. Cyril. As we meditate on these things let us observe what impression the immense number of sinners—the eternal death of so many—makes upon us. And, if we weep not at such a spectacle, where is our zeal? where is the Spirit of our Lord Jesus Christ in us? It may be that we weep more readily for the loss of temporal goods, whereas they who weep for such things (says St. Augustin) weep foolishly.

"Hear my prayer, O Lord, and my supplication: give ear to my tears."—*Ps.* xxxviii. 13.

"Who will give . . . . a fountain of tears to my eyes, and I will weep day and night for the slain."—*Jerem.* ix. 1.

MONDAY.

———◆———

*PRUDENCE THE SECOND CHARACTERISTIC OF
ZEAL AS TAUGHT BY OUR LORD—*

I. BY THE TENDERNESS OF HIS ADMONITIONS.
II. BY SPEECH IN DUE SEASON.
III. BY THE BREVITY OF HIS SPEECH.

———◆———

"If thou also hadst known, and that in this thy day, the things that are to thy
peace."—*St. Luke* xix. 42.

1. *If thou also hadst known.* We observe in these words of
our Saviour (says St. Gregory) an interrupted and incomplete discourse. By such language He indicated the vehemence of His
sorrow, which hindered Him, amidst tears and sighs, from fully
expressing His thoughts. In admonishing Jerusalem He showed,
indeed, the tenderness of His Heart; and this was the surest
means of rendering His admonition efficacious. The Apostle
St. Paul, following this example, not only "served the Lord
with all humility and with tears," but also "ceased not with tears
to admonish each one" (Acts xx. 19, 31). St. Francis of Sales,
hearing the Confession of a person who narrated his sins almost
as though he gloried in them, broke out into bitter weeping,
and when his penitent asked the cause of his tears he replied,
" I weep because you do not weep." In like manner St. Ambrose
moved his penitents to tears and compunction by his own tears,
and so absolved them. St. Chrysostom says that admonition
without tenderness is envy and rage rather than zeal. But how
many of our admonitions may have been made void because

they wanted the tenderness suggested by Priestly prudence! He who loves souls (says St. Augustin) weeps for the ruin of souls, and has zeal to save them: he who has not zeal loves them not.

2. *In this thy day.* This was a suitable time for warning Jerusalem, for she was on this day well disposed to listen to the Heavenly Master, Whom she had received with joy and saluted with acclamations. Then the Divine Light pierced the darkness, and kindled even in the minds of children lively sentiments of reverence and love. The tears, lamentations, and admonitions of our Lord might seem inopportune, just as " music is out of tune in mourning " (Eccl. xxii. 6); but in this way He gave an example to all who have the charge of souls to " preach the Word," and to " be instant in season, out of season " (2 Tim. iv. 2). It is necessary, indeed, to find the seasonable moment in an unseasonable time, and not to judge of it from a worldly point of view, but by the light of true prudence, which must be sought from above, so that the Divine Word may not be despised. Let us carefully ponder the words of the Wise Man, " There is a time and opportunity for every business " (Eccl. viii. 6). How much good might we have done had we been silent in certain circumstances! " Who will set a guard before my mouth, and a sure seal upon my lips, that I fall not by them, and that my tongue destroy me not " (Eccl. xxii. 33). What advantage might have accrued both to the Faithful and to ourselves had we been of the number of those who know when they ought to speak! So St. Jerome.

3. *That are to thy peace.* Jesus was as " the wise man, who holdeth his peace, knowing the proper time: a wise man will hold his peace till he see opportunity " (Eccl. xx. 6, 7). But He would also show Himself the pattern of moderation in speaking, for " he that useth many words shall hurt his own soul " (*v.* 8). Hence, few were the words which He spake to Jerusalem, compassionating her in that she failed to seize the moment for securing her own peace by acknowledging Him as her Saviour. How many other things might He not have added! But He

that in admonishing, in exhorting, in reproving, and in teaching, we should avoid all unnecessary words and all that feeds our own vanity. Let us reflect on the maxim of St. Ambrose, "Restrain thy discourse from all superfluity of words. If not kept within bounds, it will become an occasion of sin; just as the river, when it overflows its banks, deposits mire." Let us choose the most effective and most seasonable mode of teaching (as St. Basil enjoins), so as to move the souls of our hearers; let us ponder the teaching of Solomon, "To speak a word in due time is like apples of gold on beds of silver" (Prov. xxv. 11). Let our words be "fruits" of the tree of Divine wisdom—"golden," because they kindle charity in our hearers—and so arranged as to furnish a "bed" of chaste repose for those who profit by them.

"My mouth shall speak wisdom, and the meditation of my heart understanding."—*Ps.* xlviii. 4.

"Remove from me, O Lord, the lying rebuke in the anger of an injurious man."—*Eccl.* xix. 28.

TUESDAY.

"For the days shall come upon thee, and thy enemies shall cast a trench about thee, and compass thee round, and straiten thee on every side, and beat thee flat to the ground, and thy children who are in thee, and they shall not leave in thee a stone upon a stone."—*St. Luke* xix. 43, 44.

1. *The days shall come upon thee.* Jesus Christ was that Prophet Whom the Eternal Father promised by the mouth of Moses with the express condition that "every soul which will not hear that Prophet shall be destroyed from among the people" (Acts iii. 23). As a Prophet He announced the destruction of Jerusalem, and the fulfilment of His prophecy was manifested to the whole world. The particular circumstances of the assault and destruction of the city were described by our Saviour, and were fulfilled to the letter; and He threatened this punishment for that execrable Deicide which she was about to perpetrate, through her unbelief, obstinacy, and ingratitude (as Cornelius à Lapide points out). Thus did the knowledge of our Master excite, accompany, and justify His zeal. Through this knowledge He discovered the crime, foretold the punishment, and deplored both the punishment and the crime. In this our Lord was prefigured by Ezechiel, Jeremias, and other Prophets, who spoke

in like manner to the Jewish people. Let us adore our Divine Master, and let us fear lest, knowing our sins, He should predict a like ruin for us. He is "the Lamb, Who has opened the book of life" (Apoc. v. 3), and, if our name is not found inscribed therein the prediction will apply to us. O God, how terrible art Thou in Thy judgments against the children of men !

2. *Thy enemies shall compass thee round.* The Ministers of God's Word are Prophets, who ought to preach to sinners, in God's name, the wrath which is coming upon the mystical city of their soul ; and wo to those Ministers who fulfil not such mission with exactness ! "If, when I say to the wicked, Thou shalt surely die, thou declare it not to him, nor speak to him, that he may be converted from his wicked way and live, the same wicked man shall die in his iniquity ; but I will require his blood at thy hand" (Ezech. iii. 18). Therefore we must make known to sinners that at their death will happen that which our Lord announced to Jerusalem—that is (as St. Gregory declares), the devils will "cast a trench about them," and their conscience will "straiten them on every side ;" for then will all their sins be brought to their mind, harassing them with anguish. They will be "beaten flat to the ground" when their flesh, in which they trusted, is brought to dust. Then will "their children who are in them" fall in death, when the evil imaginations which they had harboured are scattered to the ground. We should make sinners understand that this prediction of our Lord Jesus Christ will be fulfilled in the particular judgment ; for then will they see themselves "surrounded" by accusers, "straitened" by the rigour of Divine justice, "cast down" by the going forth of the sentence, "scattered" with their crimes (which are their children) far from God, without being able to set up one single "stone" in their defence. So St. Bonaventure. If Priests would clearly and effectually put the Faithful in mind of the last things, how profitably would they enter the pulpit and the confessional ! Then would men readily make their peace with God ; for it is written, "Remember thy last things, and let enmity cease" (Eccl. xxviii. 6).

3. *They shall not leave in thee a stone upon a stone.* When preaching courageously and clearly to sinners of their ultimate ruin, Priests should, as it were, put " stone upon stone ;" that is, "Wisdom should build for herself a house," from which she may speak to " the universe" (Prov. ix. 1, 4). If they have only zeal without knowledge, the greater the vehemence with which they launch out against vice, the more severely will they be dashed against the rock of stumbling, and will be driven back ; but if, on the contrary, they couple understanding with charity, and knowledge with devotion, their course will be safe and direct, and it will reach even to eternity. Let us endeavour to " grow up in the knowledge of God" (Eph. iv. 15); let us increase our treasure of that knowledge which is called " the knowledge of the holy " (Prov. ix. 10), and as this increases so will the desire of working for God increase ; so that in this sense it may be said, " He that addeth knowledge addeth also labour" (Eccl. i. 18). Zeal will consume us, and it will be zeal proceeding from an enlightened charity. That zeal is wholesome (says St. Augustin) which proceeds from love, and not from envy.

" My zeal hath made me pine away, because my enemies forgot Thy words."— —*Ps.* cxviii. 139.
" I have had a zeal for good, and shall not be confounded."—*Eccl.* li. 24.

WEDNESDAY.

———◆———

BOLDNESS THE FOURTH CHARACTERISTIC OF
ZEAL AS TAUGHT BY OUR LORD—

I. BY HIS OWN EXAMPLE AND THE EXAMPLE OF HIS SAINTS.
II. AS BEFITTING THE PRIESTLY OFFICE.
III. AS WELL-PLEASING TO GOD.

———◆———

"But now they are hidden from thy eyes . . . . because thou hast not known
the time of thy visitation."—*St. Luke* xix. 42, 44.

1. *But now they are hidden from thy eyes.* Here, as ever, our
Saviour speaks to the Jews with great boldness. The Pharisees
were present, and Jesus knew their malice would abuse His loving
words to foment the hatred of the people, and make them solicit
His death ; but He would exercise His zeal, even though it exposed Him to the peril of His life. From this St. Ambrose draws
the conclusion that Priests should have ardent zeal to preserve
the purity of the Church incorrupt ; and therefore (says he) did
the Prince of Priests declare, "The zeal of Thy house consumed
me." Let the example of the Saints move us ; let us consider
the Angels, whose name we bear, and who in the war with Lucifer
manifested their zeal for God's glory with great boldness. They
are indeed "flames of fire ;" but without zeal—that is, unless
zeal sustained their ardour (says St. Ambrose)—they would be
nothing. Let us call to mind the Apostles, who carried the name of
Jesus before rulers and kings, who contended against the enemies
of Christianity with the fire of zeal and inflamed them, as hay is

kindled by fire. Let us call to mind St. Paul, who spoke with such boldness in the Areopagus, and the cause of whose boldness was zeal: "His spirit was stirred within him, seeing the city wholly given to idolatry" (Acts xvii. 16). But what has our boldness been hitherto? How often have we been ashamed of the Gospel, and have shrunk from defending religion!

2. *Because thou hast not known.* The Priest knows that which is not known to the people. The eternal truths which he reads and meditates upon so constantly impart to him a fulness of light, which he ought to communicate to the Faithful (says St. Chrysostom) by a bold confession of these same truths. Now, this boldness of zeal (says St. Augustin) is good and useful in Priests in order that they may not allow their knowledge to remain idle, but may impart it to the people. If zeal be compared to fire, and fire cannot hide itself, so also should zeal become manifest. Sometimes one single man, inflamed with bold zeal, suffices to reform an entire population (says St. Chrysostom). What praise does he merit who manifests true paternal—nay, maternal—solicitude for souls! How greatly will he profit the Faithful! Let us engrave St. Jerome's maxim on our heart—that, if we would exercise the office of Priests, we should regard the salvation of others as a gain derived to our own souls. How rich in merits should we be before God if zeal had directed all our steps! How much have we lost through human respect!

3. *The time of thy visitation.* Almighty God, in His mercy, visits souls as often as He sends them a zealous Priest. In the work of Creation (says Peter of Blois) the Spirit of the Lord had no helper nor counsellor, but in applying to men the mystery of Redemption, wrought in the fulness of time, He would have Priests to aid him; He would employ them as His coadjutors and counsellors. If, then, the Priest would be dear to Christ, let him teach boldly the doctrines of the Faith, let him devote all his care to the salvation of the flock. And (as St. Chrysostom enjoins), if he would make his works acceptable to Christ, let him look to the advantage of the people, let him labour for the salvation of his brethren; for no other employment is dearer to our Lord. He (says St. Gregory) is sure to be the richest in

Divine love who has drawn the greatest number of souls to this love. Let us, then, make fitting resolutions to dedicate ourselves to this work, the importance and excellency of which God has thus made known to us; and let us, especially in Holy Mass, beg of Him that we may be zealous with great boldness for the glory of God and the salvation of souls.

"I will say to the wicked, Do not act wickedly; and to the sinners, Lift not up the horn."—From *Ps.* lxxiv. 5.

"I will not be ashamed of the testimony of our Lord . . . . but will labour with the Gospel according to the power of God."—From 2 *Tim.* i. 8.

THURSDAY.

ACTIVITY (ESPECIALLY IN THE TEMPLE) THE FIFTH CHARACTERISTIC OF ZEAL AS TAUGHT BY OUR LORD.

I. The zealous priest labours in the temple.

II. He hinders the profanation of the temple.

III. He promotes the spirit of prayer.

"And entering into the Temple He began to cast out them that sold therein and them that bought, saying to them, It is written, My house is the house of prayer; but you have made it a den of thieves."—*St. Luke* xix. 45, 46.

1. *And entering into the Temple.* Our Saviour immediately after His lamentation over Jerusalem, directed His steps to the

Temple, in order to show (says St. Gregory) that the Priests were the cause of all the evils which threatened Jerusalem, and that those evils could not be remedied without the amendment of those who served the Temple. He would teach the Priests of all ages that they ought to make their abode in the Temple, not as merchants engaged in traffic (says St. Ambrose), but as Ministers of God, freely dispensing that which they have freely received. Therefore, when He was acknowledged King of Israel, He went not to take possession of His kingdom in the citadel, or in the royal palace ; but He went to the Temple, to teach us that His Kingdom is the Kingdom of God. He entered the Temple in order to teach men to render to God a perfect service, and to accomplish that act of zeal of which He gave a sample at the commencement of His public life, as St. John relates (ii. 13). Let us, then, examine ourselves as to our mode of life. Do we love to dwell in the churches and to serve them well ? Do we serve them with affection—*"ex animo"*— or, on the contrary, out of self-interest, like the Jewish Priests —"for filthy lucre's sake" ? Let us strive to imitate Nepozianus, whom St. Jerome eulogized in these terms—viz., that his anxiety was to see the Altar in due order, the walls free from dirt, the floor cleansed ; to find the doorkeeper constantly at his post, the sanctuary clean, the sacred vessels bright, and the ceremonies of the Church carefully performed—that he neglected neither great nor small matters, and that whenever he was sought he was found in the church. Certainly (as St. Ambrose points out) it is the duty of Priests to promote the adornment of their churches and the splendour of Divine worship.

2. *He began to cast out them that sold therein.* The Divine Lamb, "Who opened not His mouth before His shearers," was inflamed with fiery zeal and drove from the Temple those who profaned it; and He did this on more than one occasion. Thus did He teach His Ministers how they also ought to be devoured by the zeal of His house—that is to say (says St. Augustin), that they should correct the abuses which profane it, and, if they cannot succeed in this, that they should at least groan over them and

show their affliction.   Look then, O Priest, upon your Master,
and, if you are His disciple, kindle your zeal, set forth your
authority, to hinder all profanation (as St. Bernard enjoins).
Call to mind what zealous Priests have said and done in this
particular.   Surely (as St. Chrysostom says) the profanations
which take place in churches are sufficient to bring down
thunderbolts from heaven.   But what hitherto has been our
zeal in removing all scandal from God's house ?   May not we
ourselves be of the number of those who have caused these
scandals ?   May we not be reckoned among the traffickers in the
Temple—that is to say, among those Priests who labour in the
Church for lucre's sake, and therefore merit to be driven out ?
Traffickers (says St. Augustin) are those who seek their own in
the Church, and not the things which are Jesus Christ's: all
their thoughts are set on merchandise and traffic.

3. *My house is the house of prayer.*   The office of zealous
Priests is to promote prayer in the Church, and to remove all
that hinders prayer.   As the Council of Turin enjoins, they
should admonish the Faithful to enter the church without noise
or tumult, and, when they are there to pray, not to indulge in
foolish talking; they should not tolerate the profane talking
which is carried on there, for it is the house of prayer.   Surely
all which can raise the mind to God—such as the sacred ceremonies, ecclesiastical music, images, ornaments, furniture—
should be directed by those who serve the Temple to this end.
What displeasure do they give to our Lord who take no pains
to make prayer easy to the people !   But what can be said of
those Priests who are themselves a cause of scandal to the
Faithful, by distracting them in their prayers through their
irreverence ?   What of those who perform the sacred functions
with negligence, slovenliness, and haste ?   And yet, unhappily
for themselves and for the Faithful, such Priests are not rare.
Through them is the sanctuary profaned—the holy Name of
God despised !   " You, O Priests, that despise My name, and
have said, Wherein have we despised Thy name ?" (Malach.
i. 7.)   Suffer me not to imitate them, O my God, either by my
words or my example; let me invite the Faithful to pray in

Thy house, in order that Thou mayest not say to me in the Day of Judgment, "Thou hast despised My sanctuaries" (Ezech. xxii. 8).

"The zeal of Thy house hath eaten me up."—*Ps.* lxviii. 10.

"Thou, O Lord, hath chosen this house for Thy name to be called upon therein that it might be a house of prayer and supplication for Thy people."—1 *Mach.* vii. 37.

FRIDAY.

PERSEVERANCE THE SIXTH CHARACTERISTIC OF ZEAL AS TAUGHT BY OUR LORD.

I. HE IS NOT WEARY OF LABOUR.
II. HE CEASES NOT TO DO GOOD.
III. HE IS NOT OVERCOME BY TRIALS.

"And He was teaching daily in the temple."—*St. Luke* xix. 47.

1. *He was teaching daily.* When our Lord entered the Temple He began to fulfil the Sacerdotal office—that is to say, He instructed the people; nor did He grow weary of preaching daily to His unworthy and ungrateful hearers. Here, then, is our Model; here is our Head; and who (as St. Augustin says) will be able to persevere in the exercise of zeal but he who shall have learnt from Jesus the lesson of perseverance, and who strives to imitate Him? Many undertake the work of the Ministry—nay, sometimes ambitiously aspire to it—and make

show of zeal; but they soon weary of it, or prosecute it for their own advantage, and at last abandon it almost in despair. Whence comes this weariness? It comes from the lack of true zeal—that is, of the zeal which springs from charity, for (as St. Ambrose says) zeal is charity. Had their zeal been true zeal it would have been lasting; it would not have suffered itself to be overcome by weariness; for "charity is patient . . beareth all things . . endureth all things . . charity never falleth away" (1 Cor. xiii. 4): Ambition or self-love moved them to undertake the office of the Priesthood, and therefore they lacked the strength which true zeal alone communicates; for nothing is so strong as zeal (says St. Chrysostom). Let us, then, examine ourselves in regard to our perseverance, and let us pray to God to kindle in us such a zeal that we may never lose firmness and constancy, for then only shall we labour in the Lord's vineyard with a willing mind.

2. *He was teaching daily.* Our Lord Jesus Christ not only bestowed the benefit of His teaching on the ungrateful Jews, but also healed the blind and the lame, who came to Him in the Temple (St. Matt. xxi. 14); and by these miracles (as Origen points out) He prefigured those supernatural works which, by means of His Ministers, He Himself was to fulfil in the Church. For (as Origen says) all who are in the Church do not see, all do not walk aright, but by approaching the Word of God they are healed. It is for us to enlighten the blindness of worldly men with the light of Faith; it is for us to direct their steps aright, in order that they may run in the way of God's commandments; and (as St. Isidore warns us) if we neglect to do this we expose ourselves to the peril of damnation. How many Priests have been lost for their negligence, and because, discouraged by men's ingratitude, they desisted from labour! It often happens (says St. Chrysostom) that Priests are lost, not for their own sins, but because they have not restrained the sins of other men. What matter is it to us if our people are ungrateful? That God for Whose glory we have been zealous will be grateful to us; and, although if we sow in a barren and stony soil the fruit may be little, yet (as St. Bonaventure says) it will

be of so much greater value. Let us, then, make fitting resolutions, trusting in God's grace for their fulfilment.

3. *He was . . in the temple.* When Jesus was preaching in the Temple He was continually tempted by the Chief Priests and Pharisees, by the Sadducees and Herodians; but He did not therefore cease to teach. Whilst His enemies, maddened with envy, broke out in reproaches against Him, He devoted Himself with all constancy to the fulfilment of the work which His Father had committed to Him. So did He teach us, by His example, not to be overcome by trials or difficulties if we would be zealous for God's glory and the salvation of souls. Look at thy great Mediator (says St. Laurence Justinian), and thou wilt find that, in spite of persecutions, He was firm in the exercise of zeal for His Father's honour and the salvation of souls. Put on the armour of love ; for love (says St. Peter Chrysologus) is an impenetrable breastplate, repelling darts, driving away the sword, defying danger, despising death : love conquers all things; that is, it suffers not itself to be overcome by any difficulties. Remember that zeal (as St. Chrysostom tells us) is the most powerful proof of our friendship with Christ; remember (as St. Chrysostom says again) that nothing is more pleasing to God than imperturbable constancy in employing our life for the benefit of our neighbour. And (as Venerable Bede declares) the goodness of God has provided that the time of combat and of labour is short, whilst the reward shall never have an end.

"Evening and morning, and at noon, I will speak and declare."—*Ps.* liv. 18.

"O Lord, set Thy jealousy in me, that it may execute with me in fury."—From *Ezech.* xxiii. 25.

SATURDAY.

THE ASSUMPTION OF THE BLESSED VIRGIN MARY.

I. HER DEATH WAS NOT A PUNISHMENT.

II. IT WAS A PURE OFFERING.

III. IT WAS FREE FROM BITTERNESS.

"Mary hath chosen the best part."—*St. Luke* x. 42.

1. *The best part.* Mary's death was indeed excellent, for because of its privileges it was "a new death" (Wisd. xix. 5) Death is for all men the punishment of original sin; it is man's just penalty. Having lost the Author of life by sin, by death he loses the life of the soul and of the body: "Death came by sin" (Rom. v. 12). Hence, Christ died chiefly in order to expiate Adam's sin; for this was the first, the general, the gravest sin, and was the cause of all other sins. So St. Thomas. But Mary died although conceived without original sin, and having therefore no obligation to pay that debt of fallen nature. Therefore was Her death a new and singular death. Moreover, men die in punishment of actual sins, which accelerate the execution of the Divine judgments: "The years of the wicked shall be shortened" (Prov. x. 27): "The sting of death is sin" (1 Cor. xv. 56). Yet the Blessed Virgin was sinless; She never committed the least, the most involuntary fault, both because the sanctity of the Mother was "the glory

of her Divine Son ;" and because Christ, Who had "no fellowship with Belial," had a singular consanguinity with His Mother;
and likewise because in Her dwelt, after a singular manner, that
wisdom which "will not enter into a malicious soul, nor dwell
in a body subject to sins." Lastly, men die sometimes in a
state of immaturity, when God would preserve them from future
sin: "He was taken away lest wickedness should alter his
understanding" (Wisd. iv. 11). But the Blessed Virgin was
confirmed in grace, and hence She could be in no danger of
sin. She was indeed free from the *fomes* of sin; moreover,
the abundance of grace inclined Her to good; and, again,
by a special providence, God would preserve Her from it.
If, therefore, She died neither in consequence of having contracted the debt of original sin, nor by reason of actual sin
committed, nor yet in order to Her preservation from future
sin, Her death was thus a new and excellent death, and was no
punishment. Let this great privilege of our Mother comfort
us; and let us have recourse to Her, that She may obtain for us
grace not to hasten our death by our sins, and also forgiveness
of those sins at the hands of God. Our great Priestess will
obtain this favour for Priests who love Her, who invoke Her,
and honour Her.

2. *Hath chosen.* Every man's death is a punishment, and at
the same time a sacrifice; for, whilst it is the penalty of sin, it
gives us occasion to offer ourselves in sacrifice to God. Our
Saviour, whilst He died to offer an oblation and sacrifice to
God, "was delivered up for our sins" (Rom. iv. 25). But
Mary's death, being no punishment, was a new sacrifice—
"a new sacrifice to the Lord" (Levit. xxiii. 16). She, indeed,
with all the ardent affection of Her heart offered this new
sacrifice—a sacrifice becoming Her dignity, required by Her
humility, produced by Her charity. For She had the dignity
of Mother of God, and therefore it became Her to be made like
unto Her Son, Who died. She had the dignity of being the
type of the Church militant, which by means of death passes to
triumph. She had the dignity of being the pattern and comforter of Christians in every circumstance of life, and therefore

also in the close of life. Thus, by embracing death She would
seem to say, "I might exempt myself from death, but I will not
so exempt myself, for God would have me show my dignity in
dying: 'by departing manfully out of this life . . . I suffer an
honourable death . . . . whereas I might be delivered from
death'" (2 Mach. vi. 27, 28, 30). The humility of the Blessed
Virgin—as in Her life, so in Her death—made Her refuse a
privilege which otherwise became Her. Humility moved Her
to annihilate Herself before God: dying in recognition of His
supreme dominion, glorifying Him in this act of Her humiliation, and causing Him to be acknowledged as "only having
immortality" (1 Tim. vi. 16). Again, Mary—the second Eve—
surrendered Herself to the Supreme Good through Divine charity.
She presumed not to think Herself like God, and desired to
offer Him an acceptable sacrifice of obedience; whereas the
first Eve died because she had extinguished charity, because
she had turned away from God, because she wished to be as
God, and because she had disobeyed Him. Give me, O Virgin
Mother, resignation in death; cause me to offer the sacrifice of
myself to God as becomes the Priestly dignity, as becomes
Christian humility, and the charity diffused in our heart by the
Holy Spirit. Suffer not that, "for a little time of a corruptible
life . . . I should bring a stain and a curse upon my old age"
(2 Mach. vi. 25)—that I should fail to conform myself to my
Lord's will, stain my conscience, and give scandal to the
Faithful.

3. *Mary hath chosen the best part.* The death of all men has
its bitterness, and most bitter was the death of the Son of Man.
But the death of Mary had a new and most sweet delight:
"Thou gavest them their desire of delicious food of a new
taste" (Wisd. xvi. 2). It was without disease, without pain,
without fear. She died, not from sickness, but through Divine
love, which is no less violent (says St. Ambrose) than the heat of
fever. She truly knew by experience that "love is strong as death"
(Cant. viii. 6). In Her were the words fulfilled, "I languish
with love" (Cant. ii. 5). She had none of the pains of sickness;
She suffered no agony of body or soul, for She had no attach-

ment to earth ; it gave Her no displeasure to separate Herself from perishing goods. Most truly could she say, with all God's Saints, "I rejoiced at the things that were said to me; we shall go into the house of the Lord" (Ps. cxxi. 1). She had no fear of losing eternal felicity, because She had no remorse, because Her Judge was Her Son, and because She was in a special manner established in hope. " Thou singularly hast settled me in hope" (Ps. iv. 10). I rejoice with Thee, my Queen, and during these days I will speak to the people of Thy glorious death. I will exhort them all to dispose themselves aright for the celebration of the glorious festival of Thy Assumption ; so that Thou mayest remember us at the hour of our death, and inspire us with courage and with confidence in Thy assistance.

" O Mary, though I should walk in the midst of the shadow of death, I will fear no evils, for Thou art with me."—From *Ps.* xxii. 4.

" His left hand is under my head, and His right hand shall embrace me."—*Cant.* ii. 6.

TENTH SUNDAY AFTER PENTECOST.

THE DANGER OF PRIESTS IN REGARD TO THE SIN OF THE PHARISEE—

I. Through self-confidence.
II. Through assurance of their own justice.
III. Through contempt of others.

" Jesus spoke to some, who trusted in themselves as just, and despised others, this parable."—*St. Luke* xviii. 9.

1. *Who trusted in themselves.* It is said by the Prophet, " Cursed be the man that trusteth in man" (Jerem. xvii. 5); for he rests on a fragile stay, instead of placing his confidence in the power and infinite goodness of God: " Who maketh flesh his arm, and whose heart departeth from the Lord . . he shall dwell in dryness in the desert" (*v.* 6). Yet such a man is only foolish and unadvised; he is not proud. On the other hand, he who trusts in himself is not only foolish and unadvised, because he trusts in man, but he is also proud, and thus merits a twofold curse from Almighty God. Now, this self-confidence easily insinuates itself into the Priest's heart, both in regard to recollection of the past and presumption as to the future. Such confidence (says St. Bonaventure) is the enemy of true justice. The presumptuous Priest, indeed, too readily forgets his past feelings, and remembers only his labours and other good works. He no longer says with Job, " I feared all my

works " (Job ix. 28); nor are those words of Almighty God impressed on his heart, "All your justices are as a menstruous rag" (Is. lxiv. 6). Moreover, in regard to the future, he considers not his own weakness and natural propensity to evil, but makes himself like the fool "who leapeth over and is confident" (Prov. xiv. 6). He rashly puts himself in the way of danger, and trusts in his own strength. Unhappy Priest! Relying on his own good works, he falls headlong into sin: "He that trusteth in his riches shall fall" (Prov. xi. 28). For, on account of his foolish and proud self-confidence, God will permit him to be overtaken by mortal sin: "Because thou hast trusted in thy bulwarks, and in thy treasures, thou also shalt be taken" (Jerem. xlviii. 7). Let us put our trust in God, that He will "turn away His face from our sins;" that He will "blot out all our iniquities;" that, for the future, He will give us "to be able, to will, and to perform;" and that He will bestow upon us the free gift of final perseverance. Trusting in Him, we shall be firm as a rock: "They that trust in the Lord shall be as Mount Sion" (Ps. cxxiv. 1).

2. *As just.* A Priest may easily believe himself just without suspecting himself to be guilty of sins which may have already rendered him the object of God's hatred. For "man knoweth not whether he be worthy of love or hatred, but all things are kept uncertain for the time to come" (Eccl. ix. 1, 2); and therefore the Apostle said, "I am not conscious to myself of anything, yet am I not hereby justified" (1 Cor. iv. 4). Every one should be ready to exclaim, with that servant of God, St. Augustin, "Wo to me, miserable man, who am in the region of the shadow of death! I know not if I be worthy of love or of hatred!" Many things concur to produce self-deception in Priests—viz., the habit of preaching, of administering the Sacraments, and celebrating Mass; the position of sanctity which they occupy in the Church; the honour which the Faithful render them, believing them to be holy; and, more than all, that knowledge which puffs up, and which easily finds false reasons for smothering remorse of conscience and justifying their own faults. How many Priests have deceived themselves, and their deception

has been dissipated only after death, when the eyes of the blind shall be opened! And yet to each one of them, who was a master in Israel, is addressed the reproof of the Apostle, "Thou approvest the more profitable things; being instructed by the law, art confident that thou thyself art a guide of the blind, a light of them that are in darkness, an instructor of the foolish, a teacher of infants, having the form of knowledge, and of truth in the law" (Rom. ii. 18—20). Let us, then, avoid this confidence, so hurtful to ourselves, so displeasing to God; for His will is that we should be in a state of uncertainty as to our condition, lest we lose humility, and that we should ever have recourse to Him, Who (according to the words of the Council of Trent) is "the source and origin of all justice." Hence, the Church continually puts these words in our mouth in prayer—"We have no confidence in our own justice." Consider, O Priest, that God sees the corruption of thy inmost heart; and then (as St. Chrysostom declares) all desire of praise, and vain self-complacency, will be extinguished in thee.

3. *And despised others.* Contempt of others is the effect of the little knowledge we have of ourselves, for if we knew ourselves thoroughly we should recognise the great number of our sins—our failure in profiting by the lights given to us from above—our abuse of Divine gifts, as well as the evils we have brought upon the people. Should we not, indeed, hide ourselves with shame, as those proud Priests who withdrew from the presence of Jesus when He said to them, before the adulteress, "He that is without sin among you, let him first cast a stone at her?" (St. John viii. 7.) How great would be our humiliation if our Lord, at the present moment, were to make manifest the whole series of our defects! And the day will come when He will do this: "I will shew thy nakedness to the nations" (Nahum iii. 5). Think that to-day thou despisest some man, and to-morrow thou shalt thyself be despised: "Woe . . to thee that despisest! Shall not thyself also be despised?" (Is. xxxiii. 1.) Let us take heed lest, by our pride and contempt of others, we fall into the condemnation of God, Who will say to us, "Depart from Me; come not near Me, because thou art

unclean: there shall be smoke in My anger, a fire burning all the day" (Is. lxv. 5). And, for the rest, even supposing we were now holy, are we not ever in danger of falling into grievous sin? Might we not have sinned more deeply than the sinner we despise but for the mercy of God, Who has loaded us with His grace? Who can tell whether our places may not be reversed in the end, and that, while we perish, the sinner may be saved, and become the object of our envy through all eternity? "Despise not a man for his look" (Eccl. xi. 2). Grow not proud because thou art clothed with the Priestly garment; be not puffed up because of the honour which is now rendered thee; despise thyself, and work out thy salvation in fear and trembling. "Glory not in apparel at any time, and be not exalted in the day of thy honour" (Eccl. xi. 4).

"Have mercy on me, O God, have mercy on me; for my soul trusteth in Thee."—*Ps.* lvi. 2.

"O Lord, I will converse in fear during the time of my sojourning."—From 1 *Pet.* i. 17.

MONDAY.

DEFECTS WHICH OFTEN BLEMISH THE PRAYERS OF THE CLERGY.

I. IGNORANCE OF THAT WHICH THEY RECITE.
II. DISTRACTION OF MIND.
III. NEGLECT OF THE RUBRICS.

"Two men went up into the temple to pray: the one a Pharisee, and the other a publican."—*St. Luke* xviii. 19.

1. *To pray.* The Clergy ought to consider that their special occupation (as St. Jerome points out) is the recital of the Divine Office, and the exercise of mental and vocal prayer. The Priest should be always praying for the people, but how can he fulfil this obligation perfectly if he understand not what he is reciting? He surely, in such a case, cannot fulfil the Psalmist's injunction, "Sing ye wisely" (Ps. xlvi. 8). St. Augustin, commenting on those words, observes that we must use our understanding, regarding not the sound of the ear, but the light of the heart, in our Psalmody. If the Priest were, as he ought to be, "a Priest learned and perfect" (1 Esdr. ii. 63), he would endeavour to understand what he says; and he would find in the various parts of Holy Scripture which he recites that which is useful for every condition of man. Thus the very exercise of prayer would serve to increase his knowledge, and to improve the condition of his heart. For (says St. Augustin) Holy Scripture by its sublimity mocks our pride, by its deep significance arrests our attention; by the truths which it contains it feeds the

great, by its gentleness it nourishes Christ's little ones. Let us resolve, then, never to abandon the study of Holy Scripture, and especially of the Psalms; in order that our prayers may not be rendered defective through ignorance, and that we may not be surpassed by the laity in our knowledge of these sacred books.

2. *Went up into the temple.* The Temple stood on a height, and it was necessary to mount up to it by many steps. This signified (says St. Bonaventure) that he who prays must elevate his mind and heart above the things of this earth; and thus the Lord said to Moses, "Come up to Me into the mount" (Exod. xxiv. 12). Hence follows the obligation of attending to what we say in prayer, and especially in public prayer, and of putting away from our mind all carnal and worldly thoughts, so as to think only of that which is the subject of our prayer. Almighty God would be adored "in spirit and in truth;" that is to say, not with the lips only, but with the mind also (St. John iv. 24). Nevertheless, it is true that we are not always masters of our attention, and that involuntary distraction is one of the fruits of original sin; so that even the Psalmist, complaining to God of the wandering of his mind in prayer, said, "My heart hath forsaken me" (Ps. xxxix. 13). But, in order to avoid the defect of wandering thoughts, we should keep St. Augustin's rule before our eyes—viz., to consider in the heart what we utter with the lips when we pray to God in psalms and hymns: although distraction of mind, contrary to this intention, takes not away the fruit of our prayer. Let us pray to our Lord to give us the spirit of prayer, and let us strive to be as recollected as possible. In that case Almighty God will not impute our distractions to us as sin, but (as St. Basil says) will regard them as the effect of human weakness.

3. *Men.* Ecclesiastics are not all alike when they recite the Divine Office or celebrate the sacred Mysteries. The Church has given us many Rubrics for our entrance into choir, for the due recital of our Office, for the worthy celebration of Holy Mass. The Synods held by St. Charles Borromeo show the importance and wisdom of these Rubrics. One rule, at least,

we must observe; that is, we must remember that our object in prayer is the honour of God, the salvation of our souls, the obtaining of spiritual and temporal goods for the people, and the relief of the souls in Purgatory. Hence we must place ourselves in the presence of the Almighty, and recollect that we are associated with the heavenly choirs in His worship. Let us observe with exactness the rites and ceremonies prescribed by Holy Church with the authority which She has received from God, remembering these words—" If thou wilt not hear the voice of the Lord thy God to keep and to do all His commandments and ceremonies . . . . all these curses shall come upon thee, and overtake thee " (Deut. xxxviii. 15). Let us be especially careful in regard to the ecclesiastical chant; let us learn it thoroughly, and execute it to the best of our ability; so that (as St. Gregory Nazianzen enjoins) the Priest's tongue may be as an instrument of music in singing the praises of God. Many (as St. Isidore says) are moved to compunction and tears, and are converted to God, by means of the sweet harmony of ecclesiastical singing. St. Augustin tells us in his Confessions that he experienced the most lively and salutary emotions in his heart at the singing of the Psalms. Blessed is the Priest who meditates on these truths, and who puts them in practice; cursed, on the contrary, is he who does the work of God negligently. How full of defects are the prayers of such an one before the most holy eyes of our God !

" I will sing to the Lord as long as I live ; I will sing praise to my God while I have my being."—*Ps.* ciii. 33.

" O Lord, save me, and we will sing our Psalms all the days of our life in the house of the Lord.—*Is.* xxxviii. 20.

TUESDAY.

THE DANGER OF PRIDE IN THE CASE OF PRIESTS.

I. THE DISGUISES WHICH IT WEARS.
II. THE OCCASIONS WHICH GIVE RISE TO IT.
III. THE FOOD WHICH NOURISHES IT.

"The Pharisee standing prayed thus with himself: O God, I give Thee thanks that I am not as the rest of men, extortioners, unjust, adulterers, as also is this publican. I fast twice in a week; I give tithes of all that I possess."—*St. Luke* xviii. 11, 12.

1. *O God, I give Thee thanks.* St. Bonaventure points out three defects in these words of the Pharisee—viz., that he gives thanks proudly, he censures others presumptuously, and commends himself vaingloriously. His pride was disguised by the religious act in which he was engaged—viz., prayer and thanksgiving; but (as St. Gregory says) whilst he directed his attention to thanksgiving he paid no heed to humility, and what avails it to guard all the city if one approach be left open whereby the enemy may obtain an entrance? Now, in how many Priests (unconscious as they may be of the evil) does pride insinuate itself? As St. Basil says, in their very prayers, and whilst they are praising God, they fall back upon themselves through pride, as did the Pharisee. Nay (says St. Bonaventure), if they give God thanks, if they thank Him after celebrating Holy Mass, they do it in a proud manner. Thanksgiving is a part of prayer; it is the duty of the creature who has received benefits; but in order that it

may not be stained by pride five conditions are requisite—
(i.) It must be based on the knowledge of our own unworthiness;
(ii.) It must be accompanied by feelings of shame and sorrow
that we have profited so little by the benefits we have received;
(iii.) It should excite in our heart fear of the account we shall
have to render of all heavenly favours; (iv.) It should be
directed wholly to the praise of Almighty God, and not to our
own praise, and have for its aim the love of God and our neighbour—not self-love and contempt of others; (v.) It must conclude with prayer, to obtain perseverance, and the increase of
all graces. If pride so far blinds Priests as to make them forget
that all their goods are alms bestowed upon them by God, we
must judge them worse than the Pharisee, and exclaim, with
St. Augustin, "Thou art worse and more detestable than the
Pharisee! He did indeed call himself just, but yet gave thanks
to God for it." May God deliver us from so miserable a disposition!

2. *As also is this publican.* This is what St. Bonaventure calls
presumptuous censure of others. St. Augustin says that the
Pharisee takes occasion of greater pride from the neighbourhood
of the Publican. Occasions of pride to Priests are sinners who
throw themselves at their feet and say with the Prophet, "My
iniquities are gone over my head, and as a heavy burden are
become heavy upon me. My sores are putrified and corrupted"
(Ps. xxxvii. 5, 6). Let us be careful to rebut this temptation
with the thought that, if God had not preserved us with His
grace, we might have been guilty of the same, and worse sins;
for it is through the grace of God that we have escaped occasions of evil, or that we have resisted temptation when the
occasion offered itself. Almighty God says to us, "Thou didst
not sin, because there was no one to entice thee. No: for I
had removed the tempter from thee." Or—"The time and
place for the sin were unsuitable. I had put these occasions
out of thy way." Again: "There was a tempter at hand; the
time and the place favoured the sin; but thou didst not consent,
because I deterred thee. Acknowledge the grace of Him to
whom thou owest thy escape from the sin." So St. Augustin.

Let us often say to Him, with the same Saint, "To Thy grace I ascribe whatsoever I have not done of evil." Let us consider that many sinners, if they had received the lights, the means, the aids, which God in His mercy has given us, would have corresponded to such grace better than we have done: "If in Tyre and Sidon had been wrought the mighty works that have been wrought in you, they would have done penance long ago, sitting in sackcloth and ashes" (St. Luke x. 13). Let us consider that one sole act of pride suffices to cause us to fall, abandoned by God, into greater sins: "Pride goeth before destruction, and the spirit is lifted up before a fall" (Prov. xvi. 18). Let us consider how many Christians there are who are better than ourselves; let us not fix our eyes only on those who are worse; for to consider those who are inferior to us is an incentive to pride (says St. Bernard), whilst it is an incentive to humility to consider those who are our superiors.

3. *I fast twice in a week.* Good works—such as Holy Mass, the Divine Office, preaching, innocence of life, fasting, almsgiving—furnish food for pride, and hence are produced vainglory and self-commendation. In fact, pride is the only evil which springs from good; all other evils spring from evil. What shall we do, then, in order to avoid pride, which deprives us of all merits, and changes good works into bad? Let us arm ourselves with the following thoughts, which will be as a shield sheltering us from the darts of our infernal enemy, who is the Prince of pride. Let us fear lest perhaps our good works are not done in a state of grace, and are therefore lost; and that even otherwise they may be defective in God's sight either in regard to their aim, their order, or their manner (as St. Bernard testifies). Let us consider that perhaps mortal sin, which is compared in Holy Scripture to the vintage, to shipwreck, to a conflagration, may come upon us; and then all will be lost for us: "If the just man turn himself away from his justice, and do iniquity . . . all his justices which he had done shall not be remembered" (Ezech. xviii. 24). Let us be on our guard lest we imitate the Pharisee, who destroyed by pride the edifice which he had raised by his justice (as St. Paulinus says). Pride is that enemy

which, with rapacious hand, robs us of all our treasures : " The enemy hath put out his hand to all her desirable things " (Lam. i. 10).

" Let not the foot of pride come to me, and let not the hand of the sinner move me."—*Ps.* xxxv. 12.

"If I would justify myself, my own mouth shall condemn me : if I would sh myself innocent, he shall prove me wicked."—*Job* ix. 20.

WEDNESDAY.

PRIESTS MAY IMITATE THE PUBLICAN WITHOUT PREJUDICE TO THEIR DIGNITY—

I. IN THE POSITION WHICH HE ASSUMED.

II. IN HIS OUTWARD TOKENS OF PENITENCE.

III. IN THE WORDS OF HIS PRAYER.

" And the publican standing afar off would not so much as lift up his eyes towards heaven ; but struck his breast, saying, O God, be merciful to me a sinner."— *St. Luke* xviii. 13.

1. *Standing afar off.* Doubtless the Priest's position in God's temple is close to the altar. The Priesthood (as St. Peter Damian says) is associated to the services of the Divine household ; and to Priests, then, belongs what St. Gregory calls the place of holiness. Yet there is required of them a sincere inward humility, by which they should regard themselves as unworthy to draw near to God, in order (as Venerable Bede says) that God may draw near to them. There is required of them that remorse of nscience which causes them to shrink from the Altar, whilst

piety draws them near to the Altar. Consciousness of his heart kept the Publican away (says St. Augustin), piety brought him close. More than this: he suffered the contumely of the Pharisee, and so removed from himself the reproach of sin (as St. Chrysostom points out); and thus, without toil, without labour, without lengthened penance, but only by endurance of this injury, he merited the crown of justice. In like manner, if we suffer patiently the affronts which the wicked, or sometimes persons of good repute, inflict upon us, we shall participate in the reward of the Publican, and our enemy, unknown to himself, will become our benefactor. Let us ponder these truths and resolve to profit by them.

2. *Would not so much as lift up his eyes towards heaven, but struck his breast.* In the sacred Liturgy we are often obliged to lift up our eyes to heaven, but, if our conscience reproach us with our sins, let us, filled with salutary confusion, lower them again to earth, so that God, in Whose mercy we place all our hopes, may deign to look upon us with an eye of compassion. The Publican looked not (says St. Augustin), that he might be looked upon; he did not dare to look upwards; his conscience pressed him down, but hope lifted him up. God would have us pray to Him with humble shame, and nothing in a penitent is more pleasing to Him than such humiliation (says St. Bernard). Therefore does Holy Church prescribe that we bow down profoundly when we recite the "Confiteor" and other prayers. Let us accompany these acts with the sentiments of Esdras—"My God, I am confounded and ashamed to lift up my face to Thee; for our iniquities are multiplied over our heads, and our sins are grown up even unto heaven" (1 Esdr. ix. 6). Let us fulfil this ceremony with exactness, and with inward recollection; let us thus fulfil the prophecy—"They shall worship Thee with their face towards the earth, and they shall lick up the dust of Thy feet" (Is. xlix. 23). Moreover, the sacred Rubrics frequently enjoin that we strike our breast, as the Publican did; who thus, as it were, punished himself in indignation against his own sins (as St. Augustin says). Therefore, to obtain remission of our venial sins, let us not neglect this act, regarding it as a "Sacramental;"

and let us accompany it with lively contrition; for (as St. Augustin says again) to strike the breast is to reprove what is hidden in the breast, and by outward blows to chastise secret sin. By this holy ceremony (St. Isidore says) the Priest may be said to praise God as with timbrel and choir; and most pleasing to God (says St. Peter Chrysologus) is such a sound, if only it be a real reproof of the conscience, and not an act of hypocrisy.

3. *O God, be merciful to me a sinner.* The Publican imitated David, of whom we read that " David's heart struck him . . . . and he said to the Lord, I have sinned very much in what I have done; but I pray Thee, O Lord, to take away the iniquity of Thy servant" (2 Kings xxiv. 10). He imitated him in that contrition which is so manifest in the Penitential Psalms. Now, when we recite these Psalms, we ought on those occasions to excite in ourselves contrition of heart. Nay, we should consider that, if God sometimes mortifies and humbles us, it is infinitely less than we have deserved: " I have sinned, and indeed I have offended; and I have not received what I have deserved" (Job. xxxiii. 27). If we are unable to feel compunction of heart in the recital of these Psalms and of other like prayers of the Church, let us at least humble ourselves for this inability, and so supply our want of fervour (as St. Bernard enjoins). How many Priests would be in heaven, in spite of their grievous sins, if they had humbled themselves before God, and if they had offered Him a truly contrite heart! They have been lost through pride rather than through other sins. How many, again, have repented solely because of the loss of worldly honour, and not for the offence done to God, which should, indeed, have humbled them! Let us, then, humble ourselves at the feet of our Lord, Who uses mercy to all who are penitent : " Thou hast mercy upon all, because Thou canst do all things ; and overlookest the sins of men for the sake of repentence" (Wisd. xi. 24).

"I have acknowledged my sin to Thee, and my injustice I have not concealed."— *Ps.* xxxi. 5.

"O God, be merciful to me a sinner."—*St. Luke* xviii. 13.

THURSDAY.

—————◆—————

PRESUMPTUOUS PRIESTS SHOULD REFLECT ON OUR LORD'S SENTENCE—

I. ON THE PHARISEE AND ON THE PUBLICAN.
II. ON THOSE WHO MAKE GOOD CONFESSIONS.
III. ON THE PRIEST WHO ABSOLVES THEM.

—————◆—————

" Amen, I say to you, this man went down into his house justified rather than the other."—*St. Luke* xviii. 14.

1. *This man went down . . . justified rather than the other.* We have heard the Pharisee, the proud accuser of the Publican : we have also heard the humble self-accuser. Now let us hear that sentence of the Judge which is without appeal. St. Chrysostom, reflecting on the known sentence of the Judge, develops the following thought at length :—There were two drivers (he says), each of whom drove two horses ; the Pharisee held the reins of Justice and of Pride ; the Publican held the reins of Sin and of Humility. The chariot of Sin outstripped that of Justice, not by its own power, but by the power of Humility, which was joined with it, whilst the chariot of Justice was overtaken because it was retarded by Pride. And he draws thence this conclusion—that, though we may have innumerable good works, yet, if we presume on ourselves, we shall wholly lose the fruit of our prayers ; and, on the contrary, that, though we may have our conscience burdened with sins, yet if we humble ourselves before God we have much ground for hope in the Divine clemency. For humility procured the salvation of the Publican before that of the Pharisee, whereas pride caused the spiritual powers to fall from heaven. Hence we may infer (with St.

Optatus) that sins followed by humility are sometimes better than innocence with pride. Further, the Pharisee was a type of the Jews, whilst the Publican was a type of the Gentiles; for the Jews (as Venerable Bede points out) estranged themselves from God through pride, and were humbled, while the Gentiles, lamenting their sins, were exalted. We are Ministers of the Church of the Gentiles, not of the Synagogue of the Jews. Shall we, then, imitate the Pharisee, and have part in the humiliation of the Synagogue ?

2. *Amen, I say to you.* Jesus Christ, by a species of oath, assures us of a truth which would seem to be scarcely credible (says St. Bonaventure)—viz., that He sets more value on one humble supplication of the penitent sinner than on innumerable good actions of the just man who presumes on himself. He observes further, that, while many enter the church sinners, throw themselves at our feet, confess their sins, and go away justified according to the truth, the Priest who has confessed them often goes away justified only according to his own opinion. Almighty God " hath regard to the prayer of the humble, and He hath not despised their petition " (Ps. ci. 18). In proportion as men set less value on their own justice, and the more they humble themselves, the more will they see the justice of God come upon them, and it shall exalt them. Let a man take away altogether his own justice, and be humbled (says St. Augustin), the justice of God shall come, and he shall be exalted. That sinner came to us with his head bent down, oppressed by the weight of his crimes, and God has bowed down His ear to listen to his confession and his prayer, and has exalted him to be His own friend; but such would not have been the result had the sinner exalted himself. God bows down His ear to thee (says St. Augustin) if thou dost not lift up thy neck; for unto the humble He draweth near, but from him that is exalted He removes afar off. And why should not we do the same ? Why, when we enter the church, should not we humble ourselves in the presence of God and at the feet of our Confessor ? Why should we esteem ourselves more holy than the rest of men ? Why should we assert a claim to pre-eminence in

sanctity? This is, indeed, to imitate our first parent in listening to the voice of the tempter, saying, "You shall be as gods" (Gen. iii. 5). Why should we lament the wickedness of mankind, and suppose ourselves to be the only exceptions to the general corruption of the human race? Let us remember that, when Elias declared "I alone am left," God answered him, "I will leave me seven thousand men in Israel whose knees have not been bowed before Baal" (3 Kings xix. 18).

3. *Than the other.* The Publican was justified before the Pharisee, or (as St. Augustin explains it) was justified more than the Pharisee. How often does it happen that the Priest returns to his house from the church laden with sins committed during his ministrations! He has sinned in the holy place, either from pride, or negligence, or from some other passion, and has rendered himself unworthy to behold the glory of the Lord: "In the land of the Saints he hath done wicked things, and he shall not see the glory of the Lord" (Is. xxvi. 10). Let the Clergy, let the Ministers of the Church, fear (says St. Bernard) lest they fail, through want of humility, in obtaining pardon for the sins they have committed in the church, which is "the land of the Saints." Their iniquity will become so hateful to God that its forgiveness will be most difficult. Let us conclude with two reflections. If our pride is coupled with some sin—perhaps with many sins—what will be our condemnation, since the pride of the Pharisee, though coupled with justice, sufficed to plunge him into hell? Again, if the humility of the Publican, coupled with his sins, quickly obtained for him pardon, how much more will our humility, if joined to justice, procure acceptance for us at God's hands? Let us, then, pray to our Lord Jesus Christ to make us truly humble of heart; and let us offer Him this prayer by means of the most humble and most exalted of creatures—that is, by means of Mary.

"There is no health in my flesh: I am afflicted and humbled exceedingly: I roared with the groaning of my heart."—*Ps.* xxxvii. 8, 9.

"The soul that is sorrowful for the greatness of evil she hath done, and goeth bowed down and feeble, and the eyes that fail, and the hungry soul, giveth glory to Thee."—*Baruch* ii. 18.

FRIDAY.

GOD FREQUENTLY HUMBLES PROUD PRIESTS.

I. HE BLESSES NOT THEIR LABOURS.
II. HE SUBJECTS THEM TO VARIOUS TEMPTATIONS.
III. HE SUFFERS THEM TO FALL INTO SHAMEFUL SINS.

" Because every one that exalteth himself shall be humbled; and he that humbleth himself shall be exalted."—*St. Luke* xviii. 14.

1. *He that exalteth himself shall be humbled.* It gives supreme displeasure to Almighty God when Priests, who should be teachers of humility, become by their example teachers of pride. In such cases He resists and thwarts their undertakings : " God resisteth the proud " (St. James iv. 6). To humble them, He sets before them Priests inferior to themselves in knowledge, in age, in birth, who undertake great things and succeed in them; He sets before them those who are ignorant and despised by the world, but who work marvels for His glory, and render their name immortal : " I will vex them with a foolish nation " (Deut. xxxii. 21). He chooses for the execution of His magnificent designs " the foolish things of the world that may confound the wise, and the weak things of the world . . that may confound the strong, and the base things of the world, and the things that are contemptible . . that no flesh should glory in His sight " (1 Cor. i. 27—29). There are some Priests who if they only had humility would find nothing difficult—neither the conversion of sinners, nor the perseverance of the just com-

mitted to their care, nor the good instruction of youth, nor the magnificence of the Church's worship, nor the establishment of works of mercy. Nothing is hard to the humble (says St. Leo). If, instead of presuming on their own strength, they confided in God, they would work with the arm of the Almighty, and they would feel sufficient strength supplied to them: "They that hope in the Lord shall renew their strength" (Is. xl. 31). How much good might we have done had we adhered to the counsel of St. Joseph Calasanctius, that he who would have God make use of him for great ends must strive to be the most humble of all!

2. *He that humbleth himself shall be exalted.* God often allows His servants to be tempted, in order to preserve their humility, and especially by temptations of impurity. Such was St. Paul's case, who says, "Lest the greatness of the revelations should exalt me, there was given me a sting of my flesh, an angel of Satan to buffet me: for which thing thrice I besought the Lord, that it might depart from me: and He said to me, My grace is sufficient for thee; for power is made perfect in infirmity" (2 Cor. xii. 7—9). This sting was given to St. Paul (says St. Jerome) to admonish him to preserve humility. In like manner our Lord is wont to allow His Priests to suffer temptations in order to keep them humble. For humility (as St. Laurence Justinian says) renders a man self-possessed, acceptable to God, dear to men, worthy of heaven, a companion of the Angels, a mirror of religion, a temple of the Paraclete, a despiser of the world, a conqueror of the devil. Other temptations sometimes come upon Priests, such as persecutions, calamities, contumely, calumny, corporal infirmities, which hinder them from working; in order to destroy the vice of pride, and together with it all other vices. Take away pride (says an ancient writer) and the desire of pleasing the world, and you will easily eradicate all other faults from the Clergy. Humble thyself, then, O Minister of God, before the Divine Majesty, and then thou mayest expect from His hands whatever grace thou canst desire; for He closes His hand for the proud, but opens it for the humble: "Humble thyself to God, and wait for His hand" (Eccl. xiii. 9).

3. *Every one that exalteth himself shall be humbled.* The greatest of all humiliations is to fall into sin, which renders the soul truly ignominious and vile: "See, O Lord, for I am become vile" (Lam. i. 11). It is the want of humility which causes men to fall into this humiliation. Thus Montanus had advanced so far in sanctity as to work miracles, but through ambition he became a heresiarch. Tatian had written much and well against idolators, and yet through pride he fell into heresy. Justin, a Franciscan, attained to the highest grade of contemplation, but through haughtiness he died an apostate. Not to mention other examples, which might be found almost without number, let us remember and meditate attentively on the teaching of the Wise Man: "The beginning of the pride of man is to fall off from God . . for pride is the beginning of all sin" (Eccl. x. 14, 15). Almighty God often suffers the proud to fall into some sin of the flesh, and therefore is pride called by St. Gregory the hotbed of lasciviousness, and they whose mind is lifted up on high are thus cast down by the flesh into hell. Thus it is that, when men highly esteem themselves, God punishes them by "giving them up to the desires of their heart unto uncleanness, to dishonour their own bodies among themselves" (Rom. i. 24). Sometimes such permission on God's part is remedial; that is to say, in order to cure the graver malady, pride, He permits that which is by comparison the lesser evil of impurity. Then, by God's mercy (as St. Augustin teaches), the proud often rise from their fall more humble and distrustful of themselves. Let us pray to God to preserve us from pride, and let us profit by all the humiliations which He has permitted or willed that we should suffer.

"It is good for me that Thou hast humbled me, that I may learn Thy justifications."—*Ps.* cxviii. 71.

"Let us ask the Lord with tears, that according to His will so He would shew His mercy to us . . . let us humbly wait for His consolation."—*Judith* viii. 17, 18.

SATURDAY.

THE ASSUMPTION OF THE BLESSED VIRGIN MARY.—II.

I. HER FREEDOM FROM CORRUPTION.
II. HER ANTICIPATION OF THE GENERAL RESURRECTION.
III. HER ENTRANCE INTO HEAVEN.

"Mary hath chosen the best part."—*St. Luke* x. 42.

1. *Hath chosen the best part.* The Flesh which our Lord Jesus Christ carried to the tomb was lacerated and drained of blood; but He would not have it see corruption. It is, indeed, His will that man's flesh should become corrupt in the grave; but Mary's flesh, which was so closely allied to His own Flesh, was exempt from this law: "Thou wilt not give Thy holy one to see corruption" (Ps. xv. 10). And truly it was not fitting that that flesh should see corruption which (i.) served not a sinful spirit; (ii.) incited not to sin; (iii.) bore not the curse of sin. For, first, it is evident that Almighty God manifests His hatred of sin by punishing even the instruments of sin, as He did in the universal Deluge and in the destruction of the cities of Canaan. Hence, He punishes man's flesh because it is the habitation of a sinful spirit, and the instrument of a sinful soul. For the soul sins through the body, abusing its members for sinful purposes; and thus those sins which materially belong to the body are formally sins of the soul. But Mary was endowed with a soul (as St. Bernardin says) the perfection of all creatures. Her body was never the instrument of sin, but was (as Hesychius calls it) the instrument of the Incarnation of Him Who produced all thing

No vice defiled Her members, which (says St. Peter Damian) were all of virginal purity. Secondly, Mary had not the *fomes* of concupiscence; and hence Her flesh never suggested to Her an impure fancy, a carnal motion, an impulse to any sin whatsoever, but was rather (says St. Bonaventure) the *fomes* of piety. Lastly, the curse of sin never touched Her flesh; for it was not conceived in sin, nor did it conceive with shame, or bring forth in pain, or return to the earth from whence it was taken. Let us make people understand these privileges which Mary enjoyed, and let us urge them to prize and guard that purity for which the world has no regard.

2. History tells us that Mary's body was not found in the tomb, where for three days it had been honoured by the melodies of angels. Hence the disciples justly concluded that it had risen before the general resurrection, and had passed to the life of glory. And this was truly befitting it; (i.) because the Word had taken a new life in that body; (ii.) because through Her His life had been preserved; (iii.) because through Him She had given life to all mankind. First, the Word had taken a mortal, passible, temporal life from the Virgin's flesh; and thus the Apostle speaks of Him as "made of a woman, made under the law" (Gal. iv. 4). In this way He, who had ennobled the male sex by being made Man, ennobled the female sex by taking flesh from it. Men receive life from man and from woman: Adam had it from the earth, Eve from man alone: Christ took His temporal life only from woman. So St. Augustin. In the second place, Mary nourished Her Son in Her womb with Her most chaste blood; then She fed Him with Her milk, and afterwards maintained Him in Her house; for in all these things He would not be distinguished from other mortal men (Wisd. vii. 1). Lastly, by means of Mary the human race has received "the Author of life" (Acts iii. 15); it has received Him who is "the Resurrection and the Life" (St. John xi. 25). What marvel, then, if Christ Himself should have honoured Her with a new life, and reanimated that flesh before the resurrection of all the human race? Let us call to mind these truths, and especially when we celebrate Holy Mass; and let us remember that the

flesh of Jesus, on which we feed, is the seed of immortality, which shall confer on us a glorious life.

3. It was not fitting that the Ark of the living God—that is, the risen body of Mary—should remain upon earth; but it was to be taken up into Heaven in a singular manner, and, as it were, upon a new car (2 Kings vi. 3). Elias was transported into Heaven on a chariot of fire; Jesus ascended to Heaven on a cloud; Mary was assumed "leaning on her beloved" (Cant. viii. 5). It was fitting that She should take possession of Heaven (i.) because She had caused God to descend from Heaven; (ii.) because the Angels desired it; (iii.) because men had need of Her patronage in Heaven. First, Her humility, Her prayers, and Her merits had (as St. Thomas of Villanova observes) hastened the Incarnation of the Word; or had, as it were, attracted God from Heaven, that He might unite Himself with our humanity. Secondly, the Angels all desired that that immaculate Vessel which had contained God (as St. Athanasius says) should be placed in Heaven; they desired that Mary, who was (as St. Epiphanius calls Her) the heavenly abode of the Godhead, and who surpasses the cherubim in splendour, should be established in Heaven; they desired that their Queen, by whom (as Albertus· Magnus says) the vials of grace and mercy are poured forth upon them all, should reign in Heaven. Lastly, men had need not only to see their Head, our Lord Jesus Christ, in possession of Heaven, but also the representative of the Mystical Body—that is, Mary, who shows forth in Herself the figure of Holy Church (says St. Augustin). There She intercedes for all Her members, and is (as St. Bernardin of Sienna calls Her) the rainbow of peace surrounding the Throne of God). Let us, then, have recourse to Her, imploring Her to represent to Her Son in our behalf the womb which bore Him, the breasts which gave Him milk. Let us teach the Faithful to honour the triumph of this great Mother, and to have confidence in Her patronage.

"Arise, O Lord, into Thy resting-place, Thou, and the ark which Thou hast sanctified."—*Ps.* cxxxi. 8.

"Who is this that cometh up from the desert, flowing with delights, leaning upon her beloved?"—*Cant.* viii. 5.

ELEVENTH SUNDAY AFTER PENTECOST.

THE PATTERN OF A LABORIOUS PRIEST.

I. HE COMES FROM EXERCISES OF PENANCE.
II. HE GOES IN PURSUIT OF SOULS.
III. HE DEPARTS NOT FROM THE LAW.

"Jesus, going out of the coasts of Tyre, came by Sidon to the Sea of Galilee, through the midst of the coast of Decapolis."—*St. Mark* vii. 31.

1. *Going out of the coasts of Tyre.* Jesus came out of the coasts of Tyre when He would cure him who was deaf and dumb, and who was thus the type of sinners ; nor does the Evangelist relate this and the following circumstances without mystery. The mystical interpretation of Tyre (says St. Jerome) is "distress." Distress expresses the tribulations and mortifications which come to us from God : "Trouble and anguish have found me" (Ps. cxviii. 143). It signifies also mortification practised in the spirit of penance : "They shall eat bread by weight and with care, and they shall drink water by measure and in distress" (Ezech. iv. 16). Let us learn, then, that if we would prepare ourselves to preach penance we must first of all practise it, and much more must we suffer with resignation the crosses which God sends us. A Priest should prepare himself by passing his days (as St. Augustin tells us) in equanimity, neither elated by abundance nor depressed by poverty. He who preaches penance

should give an example of penance (says St. Chrysostom); and (as St. Gregory of Nazianzen says) no one is worthy of God, of the Sacrifice, and of the Priesthood, unless he mortifies himself, and makes of his body a living sacrifice to God. His life must be like the pomegranate, which is bitter and hard without, but sweet within; that is to say, his delights must be all spiritual, and not derived from the pleasures of sense. How profitable would be our exhortations and our preaching did we but shew forth in ourselves the pattern of a life of penance !

2. *Came by Sidon.* Sidon signifies, according to the interpretation of St. Jerome, "the chase," and a sea boisterous and inconstant. The sinner becomes like a beast—nay, even like a wild beast: "God would prove them, and shew them to be like beasts" (Eccl. iii. 18). And God promised that He would "send them many hunters, and they shall hunt them" (Jerem. xvi. 16). Let us imitate the action of the hunter (as St. Augustin bids us)— that is, in beating the woods and thickets, and drawing the prey into our nets. Our life is our net if only it be influenced by charity. Let us be careful not to let the prey escape us; let us tame these wild beasts and offer them to our Saviour (as St. Basil enjoins us). The Lord promises us His blessing when we shall set before Him our spoils: "When thou hast taken something by hunting . . . . my soul may bless thee" (Gen. xxvii. 3, 4). Why should not we give our Lord this pleasure? Why should we not obtain His blessing?

3. *Through the midst of the coasts of Decapolis.* The name of Decapolis (says St. Jerome) represents the Decalogue, from the bounds of which the Priest who labours in the Lord's vineyard should never depart. Let us, then, never be inclined to "do evil that there may come good" (Rom. iii. 8). The Apostle, in reference to those words, says, that they who do evil in order to obtain good, or those who induce others to do so, merit damnation: "Whose damnation is just." Cajeta, commenting on this passage, says, that even the most venial sin must not be committed for the sake of hindering the gravest sins. How, then, can some Priests venture to speak falsehoods under pretence of a good end? To such we should say, "Hath God any need of

your lie, that you should speak deceitfully for Him" (Job xiii. 7). When we choose unlawful means, when we neglect God's commandments, when we tread under foot the canons of the Church, in order to succeed in some work of God, it is not charity which is the motive of our labour—it is self-love; it is vainglory; it is self-interest. He who acts thus may be reckoned among those who are called by our Lord "workers of iniquity" (St. Luke xiii. 27), and by the Apostle "deceitful workmen" (2 Cor. xi. 13). Let us meditate on these truths ; and let each one of us "fly from sin as one flies from the face of a serpent," so as to render ourselves in very-truth "workmen that need not to be ashamed" (2 Tim. ii. 15).

"Blessed is the man whom Thou shalt instruct, O Lord, and shalt teach him out of Thy law."—*Ps.* xciii. 12.

"The care of discipline is love : and love is the keeping of Thy laws : and the keeping of Thy laws is the firm foundation of incorruption."—From *Wisd.* vi. 19.

MONDAY.

—◆—

THE UNHAPPY CONDITION OF A BAD PRIEST.

I. HE IS DEAF.

II. HE IS DUMB.

III. HE GRIEVES THE CHURCH.

—◆—

"And they bring to Him one deaf and dumb; and they beseech Him that He would lay His hand upon him."—*St. Mark* vii. 32.

1. *Deaf.* This deaf man is a figure of one who has not ears to hear the Word of God (says Venerable Bede). In this unhappy condition are obstinate sinners, and especially those

Priests who will not awake even at the sound of God's menaces, which are so often repeated in their ears in the lessons of Holy Scripture. Almighty God speaks to them by means of remorse of conscience, by means of the Sacred Books which are in their hands, by means of their Superiors, by means of their colleagues in the Ministry, and by means of many examples, many benefits, many chastisements; but their ears are and ever "shall be deaf" (Mich. vii. 16). They are the servants of God, and therefore should they more promptly listen to their Lord's voice, and yet they abandon themselves to blindness and deafness: "Who is blind but My servant? or deaf but he to whom I have sent My messengers?" (Is. xlii. 19). Their deafness is voluntary, and therefore is it the more incurable: "He would not understand that he might do well" (Ps. xxxv. 4). Nay, deafness itself is a heavy punishment which God inflicts upon the sinner: "Make their ears heavy" (Is. vi. 10). And (as St. Basil says) this punishment is well deserved by Priests against whom God's wrath is justly excited because of the heinousness of the sin they have committed. How many Priests have already become deaf, and who knows whether our many sins have not merited the same misfortune? O my God, punish me not in this manner, but deal with me according to Thy mercy!

2. *And dumb.* The tongue must be loosed in order to utter a good word, but this is precisely what sinners will not do whose mouth (says Venerable Bede) opens not to speak. Sometimes they who are adorned with the Priestly character have a pernicious shame in confessing their iniquities—they seem to be possessed by "a dumb devil." But they should follow the rule necessary for every Christian: "When by human frailty thou fallest into sin," says St. Thomas of Villanova, "rise immediately, and straightway make confession of thy sin." And surely there is great cause! When we see that a house has caught fire, we immediately raise a cry and call out for help (says St. Bernardin of Sienna): so when thou hast sinned have recourse to the cry of penitence, that the fire in thy soul may be extinguished. Why should we be ashamed to confess that

which we have not been ashamed to commit? Shall we be backward (says St. Chrysostom) in relating to our Lord that which we have done without shame in His presence? But the sinful Priest will not speak, and therefore sins grow old in his soul: "Because I was silent my bones grew old" (Ps. xxxi. 3) —that is (as St. Augustin explains), because I was silent in confessing my sins. May God deliver us from this fatal dumbness! How many have been lost through their silence!

3. *And they besought Him.* This deaf and dumb man was doubtless a burden to his family, and therefore they had recourse to Jesus, and made fervent entreaty to Him to cure him. This may represent to us the Church's desire to see her Priests converted and sanctified. If confession be not made, if God do not call back His Minister, the Church receives no profit from him, but rather suffers serious injury: "The prophet is become a snare of ruin upon all his ways" (Osee ix. 8). He becomes like a wild beast that cannot be tamed without a miracle, for no beast in the world (says St. Jerome) is so cruel as a wicked Priest who suffers not himself to be corrected. He omits that good which he ought to do, and, moreover, sinning through ignorance or through malice, he involves the people in his sins (says St. Peter Damian); those whom he ought to raise up by his teaching he weighs down by his ignorance. If such a Priest had his ears open to hear God's voice and the confessions of sinners—if his tongue were loosed to confess his sins and to preach God's Word—what good would he bring upon the Church! But, unfortunately (says St. Peter Damian), not only does he confer no benefit on the Church—not only does he plunge himself into the abyss of sins—but he involves others in his ruin. He who neglects his own salvation has no regard for that of others. He who ruins himself destroys his people also. How terrible a calamity is this! What a subject for meditation and prayer!

"O Lord, Thou wilt open my lips; and my mouth shall declare Thy praise."— *Ps.* l. 17.

"O Lord, give me a learned tongue . . . . awaken my ear in the morning, that I may hear Thee as a master."—From *L.* l. 4.

TUESDAY.

THE PRIEST MUST IMITATE OUR LORD IN THE CONVERSION OF SINNERS—

I. BY REMOVING IMPEDIMENTS TO THEIR CONVERSION.
II. BY HAVING RECOURSE TO THE SOURCE OF CONVERSION.
III. BY DILIGENT USE OF THE RIGHT MEANS.

" And, taking him from the multitude apart, He put His fingers into his ears, and spitting He touched his tongue : and looking up to heaven He groaned, and said to him, Ephpheta, which is, Be thou opened."—*St. Mark*, vii. 33.

1. *And taking him from the multitude apart.* It would, without doubt, have sufficed for the cure of the deaf and dumb if our Lord had put His hands on him. as they prayed Him to do. But this would not have availed for the instruction of His Ministers, who were to learn of Him the method to be followed in the conversion of sinners. He therefore took the sufferer apart from the multitude, in order to teach us that the first step to be taken for curing the spiritually sick is to remove all impediments to their conversion—that is, to separate them as far as possible from the world, from turbulent thoughts, from inordinate actions, from irregular conversation (as St. Jerome explains). We must take out of the hands of sinners those worldly books in which is found nothing profitable for eternal life, but, on the contrary, the poison of perverse maxims and disordered passions. We must separate them from evil asso · ciates, for they are snares and fetters for those who would be converted and who aspire to salvation. We must also, as far as circumstances will permit, separate them from the

world, for (says S. Ambrose) he who would be saved must rise
above the world, must seek to speak with God, must fly the
world, must relinquish earth. Happy the Priest who can persuade the sinner to retire into solitude for a few days and there
listen to God's voice, Who "in solitude speaks to him in his
heart!" St. Basil calls such retirement a golden path, a sure
and expeditious way by which men are conducted to their
heavenly country, a bath for the soul. How many have been
saved by such means! But, above all, we must remove sinners
from occasions of sin, and say to them, "Flee from sins . . . .
for if thou comest near them they will take hold of thee" (Eccl.
xxi. 2). Let us not use indulgence with those who flatter themselves that they will be converted and yet expose themselves to
proximate voluntary occasions of sin.

2. *Looking up to heaven He groaned.* Our Saviour would show
us that the cure of sinners is a gift coming from Heaven—a
gift purchased by His tears and Blood. He would also (says
Venerable Bede) give us an example of the prayers and groans
which we should offer for our own conversion and for that of
others. Let us, then, learn to turn the eyes of our heart to
Heaven, whence comes every good, and especially the beginning
and the perfection of a good will (says St. Fulgentius). Let us
groan for the unhappy state in which sinners find themselves,
for the intrinsic difficulty of their conversion, for our unworthiness
to obtain this grace, for the many offences committed by them
against God, for the victories obtained over them by the devil.
"Her Priests sigh" (Lam. i. 4). Happy the Priest who, in
respect of his penitents, can say with the Prophet, "I am
wearied with my groans, and I find no rest" (Jerem. xlv. 3).
Meanwhile let us confide in our Lord Jesus Christ, for He
(says St. Chrysostom) has groaned over sinners, and His groans
are of infinite value. The Priest who trusts in the omnipotence, the mercy, the Blood of Jesus, will work marvels of
conversion. This has been the great secret of Apostolical
men. Why should not we stir up our hearts to imitate them?

3. *He put His fingers, &c.* Whilst we confide in Jesus, we
must neglect no means of moving sinners to conversion; for

(according to the maxim of St. Ignatius) we must confide in God as though all depended on Him, and use at the same time all available means as diligently as though they were alone effectual for the purpose. We must, then, put our fingers in the ears of sinners—that is, stop them against those maxims of the world which St. Gregory the Great calls pestiferous counsels, and St. Bernard poisonous suggestions; we must put spittle on the tongue of sinners—that is, the word of Divine Wisdom (says St. Jerome); we must make them taste the savour of the doctrine instilled into us from the mouth of our Redeemer (says St. Gregory). Lastly, we must say to them, " *Ephpheta*—that is, Be thou opened." Let us induce sinners, with the help of grace, to be docile to our exhortations, to open their mouth, to confess their sins, and " to speak right." " Be not ashamed to confess thy sins" (Eccl. iv. 31). What joy, both for heaven and for ourselves ! How truly great a work is this !

" O Lord God of Hosts, convert us."—*Ps.* lxxix. 20.

" The ears of the deaf shall be unstopped . . . . the tongue of the dumb shall be free."—From *Is.* xxxv. 5, 6.

WEDNESDAY.

SACRED CEREMONIES.

I. THE REVERENCE DUE TO THEM.
II. THE EXACTNESS WITH WHICH THEY SHOULD BE OBSERVED.
III. THE EXPLANATION TO BE GIVEN OF THEM.

"And taking him from the multitude apart He put His fingers into his ears, and spitting He touched his tongue: and looking up to heaven He groaned, and said to him, Ephpheta, which is, Be thou opened. And immediately his ears were opened, and the string of his tongue was loosed, and he spoke right."—*St. Mark* vii. 33—35.

1. *And taking him.* If we reflect attentively on this sacred narrative, we shall observe that our Saviour makes use of seven ceremonies in the cure of the deaf and dumb man. He thus taught the Church by His example (as Cardinal Bellarmine says) to employ ceremonies in the solemn administration of the Sacraments, in the Holy Sacrifice, and in other sacred functions. Ceremonies, then, are to be held in reverence, because some are inculcated by Nature itself; others are taught by God; others, again, are prescribed by the Apostles or their successors. Some have spiritual efficacy, such as the sign of the Cross, which (as St. Augustin tells us) is reverenced even by the devils, who dare not despise it, and tremble for fear whenever they see it. These and other ceremonies are useful, meritorious, and part of Divine worship; and therefore Clerics are bound to learn them accurately. God gave this express commandment—" Hear, O Israel, the ceremonies and judgments which I speak in your ears this day: learn them, and fulfil them in work" (Deut. v. 1).

And even Priests advanced in age ought to learn them afresh if they have forgotten them, for (as St. Augustin says) no age is too great for learning, and, though it is for the old to teach rather than to learn, it is better for them to learn than to be ignorant of what they profess to teach. But, alas! what ignorance, what little reverence, in regard to these sacred rites, is exhibited by many Priests!

2. *And immediately his ears were opened.* The wonderful effect produced by the sacred ceremonies justifies the anxiety which the Church displays for their exact performance. God Himself has said, "Keep the ceremonies and judgments which I command thee this day to do" (Deut. vii. 11, viii. 11). Moreover, the nature of man is such (as the Council of Trent teaches us) that it cannot easily be brought to the meditation of Divine things without external aids. These ceremonies are established by the authority conferred by God on the Church·herself, who, under heavy penalties, has enforced their observance; and " he that resisteth the power resisteth the ordinance of God; and they that resist purchase to themselves damnation" (Rom. xiii. 2). Let those Priests, therefore, who despise, or think that they can neglect at their pleasure, the prescribed rites, remember this Canon of the Council of Trent—" If any one shall say that the rites received and approved by the Catholic Church, and used in the solemn administration of the Sacraments, may be despised or omitted by the Ministers of the Sacraments at their pleasure . . let him be anathema." Let them remember that in the Bull prefixed to the Roman Missal the Pontiff, in virtue of his supreme authority, rigorously commands, under holy obedience, that Mass be celebrated according to the prescribed rites; so that any notable abuse of ceremonies is mortal sin. Further, what great good is done to the Faithful when Priests perform them with exactness! They incite the people to raise their heart to God; they edify, they revive their faith, they awaken their attention, they excite their devotion; they cause the Priesthood and Priestly functions to be reverenced. Have we been thus careful hitherto? If we feel ourselves guilty, let us ask pardon of our Lord Jesus Christ.

3. *And the string of his tongue was loosed.*   If our Saviour would loose our tongue, we should explain the meaning of the sacred ceremonies to the people.   In that case they would not assist at the sacred functions as mere gazers and hearers, understanding nothing of what is said and done—like the Jews, who, gazing at the ceremonies without understanding their meaning, and not as "children of the light," beheld "the shadow," and knew not "the good things to come" (Heb. x. 1).   Therefore, we ought ourselves, first of all, diligently to investigate the mystical significance of these ceremonies, for otherwise we shall never attain to an exact performance of them (says St. Laurence Justinian).   We should consult those numerous works which have been published in explanation of the Ecclesiastical ceremonies ; and thus, by our eyes, by the movements of our body, by our tone of voice (as St. Cyprian says), we shall please Almighty God.   Finally, after having gathered the oil of these explanations, let us pour it into empty vessels—that is, into persons who need to be instructed—for (as St. Augustin tells us) the more we pour into others the more shall we ourselves possess.

" I cried unto Thee, Save me, that I may keep Thy commandments."—*Ps.* cxviii. 146.

" I will shew the people the ceremonies, and the manner of worshipping, and the way wherein they ought to walk."—From *Exod.* xviii. 20.

THURSDAY.

THE CONDUCT OF PRIESTS IN REGARD TO WORLDLY FAME.

I. THEY SHOULD NOT SEEK IT.
II. THEY FIND IT BY NOT SEEKING IT.
III. THE USE TO BE MADE OF IT.

" And He charged them that they should tell no man ; but the more He charged them, so much the more a great deal did they publish it, and so much the more did they wonder."—*St. Mark* viii. 36, 37.

1. *And He charged them that they should tell no man.* Our Saviour charged the people not to make known His good deeds, in order to teach us not to seek after worldly fame ; and therefore we ought to know that such honour is vain—that it vanishes like smoke, and depends on the idle caprice of a few individuals. In the efforts we make to gain it we imitate the spider, who disembowels herself in order to catch a vile fly ; for what is vain glory (asks Peter Blosius) but a vile, buzzing, sordid, stinging fly ? We ought to convince ourselves that this glory is injurious to us—that (as St. Chrysostom says) it is like a wind troubling the tranquil sea, and mixing sand with the waves. We ought to convince ourselves that it is opposed to the servitude which the Priest has vowed to Almighty God. In fact (says St. Gregory), he who seeks his own glory ministers to himself, and not to God.

2. *But the more He charged them so much the more a great deal did they publish it.* These men did not think themselves bound to obey this command of our Saviour, looking upon it rather as

the expression of His modesty than as a command; and thus all the more did they exalt His power and goodness, which, as a city set upon a hill, could not be hid. A city placed upon a hill is visible on all sides, and cannot be hid (says St. Jerome); and humility ever precedes glory. So it is with humble modest Priests, who receive the more glory in proportion as they shrink from it. St. Paul said, "Only to God be honour and glory" (1 Tim. i. 17); he ever sought God's glory, not his own; and in how great honour was he held by the Faithful! Let us remember their conduct when he departed from them: "There was much weeping among them all; and falling on the neck of Paul they kissed him . . . . and they brought him on his way to the ship" (Acts xx. 37, 38). Let us remember how he was received when he visited the Christians whom he had converted: they received him, he says, "as an angel of God, even as Jesus Christ: . . . if it could be done," they "would have plucked out their own eyes, and given them" to him (Gal. iv. 14, 15). Let us call to mind other holy Priests who have received innumerable proofs of esteem from Christians, so that of them it might be said, "All these have gained glory in their generation, and were praised in their days" (Eccl. xliv. 7). If we had avoided vain-glory—if we had not manifested our mad desire of it—we should not have received so many humiliations with so great dishonour to our sacred character! In our case has the Divine oracle been too truly fulfilled—"By what things a man sinneth, by the same also he is tormented" (Wisd. xi. 17).

3. *And so much the more did they wonder.* The admiration of the multitude increased in proportion as our Saviour showed that He sought not their applause. In like manner, those Priests who labour in the Lord's vineyard with the greatest humility are the most esteemed amongst men, being (as St. Jerome says) fore-most in work, but last in the position which they assume. But we must not allow the admiration and esteem we may have gained to lie idle, but must use it for the good of our people, in whose service a good Priest willingly spends all things, even himself: "I most gladly will spend, and be spent myself, for your souls" (2 Cor. xii. 15). How great benefits did Moses,

Samuel, Esdras, Nehemias, and many others of the Old Testament, confer on their nation through the esteem they so justly acquired! In our days, likewise, many ministers of the Sanctuary, in consequence of the high esteem in which they are held, have the supreme consolation of witnessing the marvellous effects produced by their exhortations—effects similar to those wrought by the preaching of St. Barnabas on the people of Antioch: "He exhorted them all with purpose of heart to continue in the Lord ; for he was a good man, and full of the Holy Ghost, and of faith; and a great multitude was added to the Lord" (Acts xi. 24). Let us follow such examples ; and let us strive to employ for God's honour the honour which He Himself has given us. Let us employ all things in the service of God, Whose servants we are ; and let us remember that if we thus serve Him we shall reign with Him for ever and ever : " Let all Thy creatures serve Thee" (Judith xvi. 17).

" Bring to the Lord glory and honour ; bring to the Lord glory to His name."— *Ps.* xxviii. 2.

" I will give glory to the Lord my God before it be dark, and before my feet stumble upon the dark mountains."—From *Jerem.* xiii 16.

FRIDAY.

PORTRAIT OF A GOOD PRIEST.

I. He does all things well.
II. He makes the deaf to hear.
III. He makes the dumb to speak.

"He hath done all things well; He hath made the deaf to hear, and the dumb
to speak."—*St. Mark* vii. 37.

1. *He hath done all things well.* Cornelius à Lapide interprets
the word "well" as "blamelessly," and reminds us that St. Paul,
in God's name, requires a blameless life in a Bishop, or (according to the more common interpretation of the passage) in a
Priest : "It behoveth a bishop to be blameless" (1 Tim. iii. 2):
"The sound word that cannot be blamed" (Titus ii. 8). And in
this word the Apostle has comprised all virtues (says St. Jerome).
It corresponds with the word "holy," used by the same Apostle :
"A bishop must be without crime, as the steward of God . .
holy" (Titus i. 7, 8). Sanctity comprises two things (according
to St. Thomas), viz., purity and stedfastness. Now, what is the
care with which we study to preserve such sanctity? Is our life
consistent? Do we never give the Faithful any occasion for
censuring us? Do we use all diligence in subduing our inordinate
affections and in correcting any sinful habits that we may have
formed? Let us remember that our aim must be to so conduct
ourselves that even the enemies of the Priestly name may be
constrained to say, "He has done all things well." So far
ought we to carry our circumspection (says St. Ambrose) as to

take from the mouth of our adversaries any word of censure. Thus will Priests acquire that reputation for sanctity which honours the Church, edifies the Faithful, and is in itself a motive to increased sanctity.

2. *He hath made the deaf to hear.* The sinner is a deaf man, and especially when he joins hardness of heart to ignorance; for then, "like the deaf asp," he stops his ears (Ps. lvii. 5). For the asp (as St. Augustin tells us) presses one ear upon the rock, which is the figure of hardness, and with its tail, the symbol of ignorance, it closes up the other. Many such deaf sinners are still to be found, and we must bear with them patiently. Grace is necessary to enable them to hear, and grace is obtained by means of prayer. Good Priests will therefore pray for these unhappy men, remembering that the Priests of the Old Law—whose Priesthood was but a figure of ours, "a shadow only, and not the very image," of the "High Priest of the good things to come"—entered into the holy place, and offered victims for the Jewish people, who were "uncircumcised in heart and ears." Having implored the Divine grace, let Priests so speak as to break the heart of the most hardened of the deaf, "as a hammer that breaketh the rock in pieces" (Jerem. xxxiii. 29). Let their voice be the voice of the entire Church; that is, let them teach in Her spirit, with Her doctrine, with Her efficacy; for then shall their voice be as the voice of "an immense multitude" (Dan. x. 6), which shall make even the deaf hear. Let them add example, which speaks to the eyes, and which supplies the defects of the ears—nay, which has a voice clearer than a trumpet (as St. Chrysostom says). How great a work is it before God to make these deaf to hear! How rich shall we be for eternity if we have accomplished it!

3. *And the dumb to speak.* The dumb speak (says St. Jerome) when they pronounce the praises of God in hymns, and psalms, and canticles; and this is effected by zealous and laborious Priests, who take profane songs out of men's mouth, and substitute pious canticles. As St. Augustin says, he is dumb before God who is forgetful of Jerusalem, who sings not the Lord's song. We shall do great good by teaching these spiritual

canticles, and thus shall we execute the charge laid upon us by the Apostle—" Teaching, and speaking to yourselves in psalms, and hymns, and spiritual canticles" (Col. iii. 16; Eph. v. 19). It is the Priest's duty, also, to teach the young to recite their prayers, and to sing God's praises with heartfelt devotion, so as to please God; for (as St. Augustin says) we sing with the voice to incite our own devotion, we sing with the heart to please God.   Moreover, let us induce the Faithful to frequent the Sacrament of Penance, in order that they may be cured of that fatal dumbness which is the cause of eternal death. Some from unbelief, some from shame, some from sloth, neglect to approach this Sacrament; some come to the Confessional, not to accuse, but to excuse, themselves. They do not sincerely manifest their sins in contrition of heart, and being thus dumb they cannot use the Psalmist's words—" I said, I will confess against myself my injustice to the Lord" (Ps. xxxi. 5). These unhappy persons we must exhort, admonish, rebuke—open to them the bowels of mercy, so that (as Venerable Bede says) the dumb devil being driven out, the mute tongue may speak, and speak well.   Lastly, the Priest is the agent by whom Divine Wisdom teaches children to speak of God: "Wisdom opened the mouth of the dumb, and made the tongues of infants eloquent" (Wisd. x. 21).   Blessed are they who do these things, and persevere in them till death!

" Direct my steps according to Thy word, and let no iniquity have dominion over me."—*Ps.* cxviii. 133.

" O Lord, open my dumb mouth."—From *Prov.* xxxi. 8.

SATURDAY.

THE ASSUMPTION OF THE BLESSED VIRGIN MARY.—III.

I. A DAUGHTER OF ADAM IS CROWNED QUEEN OF ANGELS.
II. A VIRGIN IS CROWNED MOTHER OF ALL MEN.
III. HER RELATION TO US BOTH AS QUEEN AND MOTHER.

"Mary hath chosen the best part."—*St. Luke* x. 42.

Although all the Saints reign with God—although all the citizens of Heaven are of royal dignity—yet God has willed that Mary should be Queen in a special sense. She, indeed, has taken from God's hands a robe new and singular: "She took a new robe" (Judith xvi. 10), and by it does She bear rule over all the Saints and Angels of Heaven. She is superior to the Angels (i.) by Her merits; (ii.) by Her dignity; (iii.) by Her authority. In the first place, Mary is declared purer than the Angels. What angelical purity (asks St. Bernard) can be compared with the virginity of Her who was worthy to be the Sanctuary of the Holy Spirit, and the dwelling-place of the Son of God? She added to Her purity merits which the Angels could not acquire, and by which She has surpassed all creatures taken together: "Thou hast surpassed them all" (Prov. xxxi. 29). Secondly, the dignity of Mother of God attains the infinite (says St. Thomas), and for this is She called by St. Ephrem Queen of the supernal City, and Ruler of the Angels; for, because of the intimate relationship which the Blessed Virgin has contracted with God, there is an infinite distance between Her and all

God's servants and ministers, such as are the Angels (says St. John Damascene). Thirdly, Her authority is such that it contributes to the glory of the Angels themselves (says St. Antoninus), and of them She may be called the Mother. The Angels, in fact, assist with fear and trembling before God's throne, but Mary (as says St. Chrysostom) with supreme confidence presents the human race to Her Son. What a stupendous spectacle is this! A daughter of Adam thus gloriously crowned! What a consolation for us Priests, who are also the Angels of the Lord, to salute Her with the title of Queen!

2. Let us meditate on this other truth—viz., that the name of Mother of the whole human race was given by God to this Virgin: "Thou shalt be called by a new name, which the mouth of the Lord shall name" (Is. lxii. 2). This name was (i.) justly merited; (ii.) gloriously conferred; (iii.) faithfully fulfilled. Who, in truth, merited to be Mother of the whole Body, if not the true worthy Mother of the Head? From the moment in which Mary conceived Her Divine Son She became the Second Eve, for (as St. Bernardin of Sienna teaches) by means of Mary is the invisible life of grace infused into all who love Christ, even as by means of Eve is transfused into us the life of nature. And (as Cornelius à Lapide says) She brought us forth with most bitter pains when, in the person of St. John, we were committed to Her as Her children. Again, Almighty God has not taken from Mary in Heaven the dignity of our Mother, which He gave Her on earth; rather He desires that She should exercise it there. Hence St. Anselm says to Her, "O happy Mary, Thou art the Mother of God; Thou art the Mother of the Judge: since Thou art Mother of both, Thou canst never suffer discord between Thy children." Indeed, "the gifts of God are without repentance;" that is, God never withdraws them from His creatures without demerit, and therefore does Mary retain Her Maternal office in heaven. Nay, more: as Her Son in His glory is ever our Advocate with the Eternal Father, so Mary also in Her glory continues to be our Advocate with Her Divine Son. Thus, also, does She faithfully fulfil this office of Mother; for, being Mother of Omnipotence and Mother of Mercy, She

employs both for our profit; She both can and will have pity on us. When can the Mother of Omnipotence fail to pity us? (asks St. Bonaventure.) When will the Queen of Mercy refuse to pity us? Therefore let us never cease to thank God for having given us a Mother who reigns in Heaven.

3. The power of a Queen and the tenderness of a Mother are united in Mary, whereas among men it usually happens that they who have it in their power to succour the miserable are not inclined to pity, while they who are inclined to pity often have not the power to succour. Meditating on the marvellous union of these two qualities in our Blessed Lady, let us pour forth a new song to Almighty God: "Sing ye to the Lord a new canticle, because He hath done wonderful things" (Ps. xcvii. 1). In fact, so just is Mary's power that nothing can resist it; all depends on Her commands. Thou hast insuperable strength, invincible force (says St. Gregory of Nicomedia): nothing resists Thy power, nothing opposes Thy force: all things fall before Thy commands, all things obey Thy rule, all things serve Thy power. The reason of this is that the Creator esteems the glory of His Mother as His own glory, and grants Her petitions almost as though discharging a debt. Again, Her clemency far surpasses the tenderness of the most tender mother (as St. Bernard says). Lastly, Her power and tenderness combined render Her patronage most profitable to us; of it we may truly say that it "is an infinite treasure to men" (Wisd. vii. 14). Let us, then, have recourse to Her with confidence; let us honour Her; let us promote Her worship. Let us show ourselves faithful Ministers both of the Son and of the Mother.

"The Queen stood on Thy right hand, in gilded clothing, surrounded by variety." —*Ps.* xliv. 10.

"O Mary, in Thee God maketh peace in His high places."—From *Job* xxv. 2.

END OF VOL. III.

MEDITATIONS.

MEDITATIONS

FOR THE USE OF THE CLERGY,

For Every Day in the Year.

ON THE GOSPELS FOR THE SUNDAYS.

FROM THE ITALIAN OF MGR. SCOTTI, ARCHBISHOP OF THESSALONICA.

REVISED AND EDITED BY THE OBLATES OF ST. CHARLES.

VOL. IV.

FROM THE TWELFTH TO THE LAST SUNDAY AFTER PENTECOST.

LONDON: BURNS AND OATES,
PORTMAN STREET AND PATERNOSTER ROW.
MDCCCLXXV.

TWELFTH SUNDAY AFTER PENTECOST.

OF THE BLESSEDNESS OF THE PRIESTS OF THE NEW LAW.

I. IT SURPASSES THAT OF THE PRIESTS OF THE OLD LAW.
II. IT SURPASSES THAT OF THE PROPHETS.
III. IT SURPASSES THAT OF THE KINGS.

"Jesus said to His disciples, Blessed are the eyes that see the things which you see. For I say to you that many prophets and kings have desired to see the things that you see and have not seen them, and to hear the things which you hear and have not heard them."—*St. Luke* x. 23.

1. *Blessed are the eyes that see the things which you see.* Our Lord called the eyes of the Apostles "blessed" because they saw the miracles which He wrought. Afterwards, however, He spoke of the blessedness of those who should believe without seeing (St. John xx. 29). Are we not, therefore, more blessed than the Priests of the Old Law? God, indeed, showed that He had conferred great dignity on those Priests and Levites in chosing them as His ministers: "Is it a small thing unto you that the God of Israel hath separated you from all the people . . . that you should serve Him in the service of the Tabernacle, and should stand before the congregation of the people and should minister to Him"? (Num. xvi. 9.) But yet those Priests, whose succession was by natural descent, inherited only a heavy burden of ceremonial ordinances, which were but as types, shadows,

and figures of the good things to come; which promised grace, but did not confer it. We, on the other hand, are bound to thank God for having called us to behold light and truth—for having called us to receive and dispense grace, and to hold in our hands Christ Himself, Who is the end of the whole Law : "The end of the Law is Christ" (Rom. x. 4). Those Priests could only offer to the people "weak and needy elements," which had no efficacy in themselves (Galat. iv. 9). We, on the contrary, administer Sacraments which, though fewer and simpler in form, are yet far more efficacious and precious than the former ordinances (as St. Augustin explains). The Priests of the Old Law stood in that part of the Temple which is called "the Holy Place," and they could not enter into the "Holy of Holies," because the sacrifices which they offered had no power to purify their consciences, and to render them fit for such a service: "Gifts and sacrifices were offered which could not, as to the conscience, make him perfect that served" (Heb. ix. 9). We, however, have within our reach that which cannot fail to render us fit ministers of the New Law, and therefore we ought to shew deep gratitude to God for such privileges. We should, indeed, be guilty of great sin if we refused to be content with our Divine vocation. The sons of Aaron were consumed by fire for a sin which is usually regarded as only venial : Oza was punished with sudden death for a venial sin : Moses, who was "amongst the Priests of the Lord," was not allowed to enter the promised land on account of a venial sin (Num. xxii. 11). Let us reflect on the warning of the Apostle as to the penalty which may be exacted for our negligence: "If every transgression and disobedience received a just recompense of reward, how shall we escape if we neglect so great salvation ?" (Heb. ii. 2.)

2. *Many Prophets . . . . have desired to see.* The Prophets of old desired to see that glorious characteristic of the Christian Church which they foretold—the "clean oblation," which was to be "offered in the name of the Lord throughout the world" Zach. ix. 17 ; Malach. i. 11). They desired to see those "waters" of Divine grace which were to "break out in the

desert and thirsty land " (Isa. xxxv. 6, 7). They desired to see the remission of sins and the conversion of the world. But none of these things were they allowed to see. They were enabled to strike terror into the hearts of sinners, and to warn them of the punishment due to their sins, but they were not chosen to convert the Gentiles (as St. Francis of Sales observes). While they foretold the coming of the Messias they were subject to the most cruel persecutions. " Which of the Prophets," said St. Stephen to the Jews, " have not your fathers persecuted ? And they have slain them who foretold of the coming of the Just One " (Acts vii. 52). The Priests of the New Law have been permitted to see all these things ; they have been chosen to perform great works, and to be in themselves the living representatives of Christ, Who has associated them with His own Divine Priesthood. The end, indeed, for which Priests are ordained is, to be like God, to represent God—to exercise the power of purifying others through their own superabundant purity, of illuminating others through their own superabundant light, of advancing others in perfection through their own virtue. The Faithful, therefore, ought to regard their Pastors in this light, and 'to obey them as they would obey Christ Himself (as St. Thomas says). If, then, we sin after being thus associated with Christ, and representing the very person of Christ, we make it appear as though Christ Himself were sinning ! My obstinacy and rebellion (says St. Gregory Nazianzen) Christ ascribes to Himself. When I am disobedient it is as though He were disobedient. What an awful thought is this ! Should it not intensify our horror of sin ?

3. *And Kings.*—David, Solomon, Ezechias, Josias, and many other Kings eagerly longed for the coming of the Messias ; and they recognised the value and dignity of that Priesthood which He, the Great High Priest, was to impart to His Ministers. We, too, have a clear insight into these truths, and we are invested with a power which does not belong to the Princes of this world. They are entrusted with the care of men's bodies only ; they have authority to remit bodily punishments ; but we have the charge of men's souls, and have to wash away their

spiritual stains. The King (says St. Chrysostom) can absolve from guilt so far as relates to the body; the Priest removes the stains of sin from the soul. Kings employ material weapons, and wage war with human beings ; whereas the weapons of our warfare are spiritual, and our conflict is with the spirits of evil in behalf of the Christian people. Our princely dignity is, therefore, far greater than that of kings, and thus the latter receive their crowns at the hand of the Priesthood. Greater (says St. Chrysostom) is this our royalty than that of the kings of this world, and therefore does the king submit his head to the hand of the Priest. The power of Princes is of the earth : the power of God's Priests reaches to the heavens (continues the same Father), so that the acts of the Priests on earth are ratified in heaven. Yet, alas ! although we are invested with such power— although we lift up our hands to heaven—although in the sacred writings we are even spoken of as the " heavens " in distinction to the rest of men, who are called the " earth "—yet we are far from being secure of our eternal salvation; we may still fall away through sin. Many (says St. Jerome) are changed from earth to heaven, many from heaven to earth. He who is as heaven ought not to feel secure; he who is as earth ought not to despair.

" Thou hast exalted me on a rock : Thou hast conducted me ; for Thou hast been my hope."—*Ps.* lx. 3.

" I remembered Thy mercy, O Lord, and Thy works which are from the beginning of the world."—*Eccl.* li. 11.

MONDAY.

THE THEOLOGIAN WHO HAS NOT CHARITY.

I. HE IS MALIGNANT.
II. HE IS PROUD.
III. HE IS OBSTINATE.

"And, behold, a certain lawyer stood up, tempting Him and saying, Master what must I do to possess eternal life? But He said to him, What is written in the Law, how readest thou? . . . . . . He, answering, said to Jesus, And who is my neighbour?"

1. *A lawyer rose up tempting Him.* This teacher of the Mosaic law was possessed of knowledge, but had not charity. Hence, he became malignant, and tempted our Lord craftily (as St. Cyril says). He hoped to entrap Him into some statement opposed to the Law, and therefore addressed Him as "Master" by way of flattery. He called Him "Master" (continues St. Cyril) without submitting to His teaching; and made use of the expression "eternal life," which had been so often on the lips of our Divine Lord, as a snare. Let us observe, then, the effects of knowledge without charity. It causes a man to resemble the devil, who abuses the knowledge which he possesses to the injury of others, and, therefore, he is called in Holy Scripture "the wicked one." Knowledge in such a case is often accompanied by ambition, and teachers of this sort are found "provoking one another, envying one another." Alas! how often have we found theologians, in their eagerness to exalt themselves above others, treating their brethren in the Priesthood

with scorn and contempt, to the great scandal of the Church. In their ambition, and in the display which they make of their learning, they are imitators of the fallen Angels, and follow in the steps of the first Adam, thus injuring, not only themselves, but others also. As St. Bernard says, a thirst for power deprived Angels of the happiness of heaven, and an inordinate desire of knowledge stripped man of the glory of inmortality. Let us bear in mind that (as St. Ambrose observes) it is a Priest's duty to do harm to none, and to wish to do good to all.

2. *He, answering, said.* The lawyer would have been prudent if he had made no answer, as he might have thus concealed his evil motive ; but his pride got the better of his cunning, and he shewed that he already knew the reply to the question which he had put. Through pride he had craftily pretended ignorance. We see, then, how knowledge without charity puffs a man up; that is to say, it renders him proud : " knowledge puffeth up, but charity edifieth " (1 Cor. viii. 1). Doubtless (as St. Augustine says), if knowledge outweighs charity it does not edify, but puffs up. Let us, therefore, pursue that knowledge only which is the handmaid of charity and the mistress of humility. Otherwise we shall be punished for our pride, as so many theologians have been punished, " whose foolish hearts have become darkened," and who, " professing themselves to be wise, became fools " (Rom. i. 21). This may happen only too easily, for (as St. Bernard says) knowledge is apt to swell into pride if it be not kept under by the fear of God. Let us, then, guard ourselves against such an evil ; and, if we have attained to any excellence in theological learning, let us humbly thank God for His goodness.

3. *But he, willing to justify himself.* Here we see the third fault of this lawyer. After having furnished the reply to his own question, he goes on to suggest another difficulty, in order to shew that he had a right to interrogate the Saviour as he had done. Such is the extent of his arrogance that he persists in regarding himself as in the right, and at the same time is proved to be devoid of charity (as St. Cyril shews). In like

manner proud theologians, when they fall into error, obstinately refuse to acknowledge themselves in the wrong, resist the truth if it contradicts their own theories, and thus abuse whatever talent and learning they may possess. They neglect the warning of inspired wisdom: " In no wise speak against the truth, but be ashamed of the lie of thy ignorance" (Eccl. iv. 30). It would be well for them if they could but learn that the shame which follows from the acknowledgment of one's own ignorance is good for the soul's health, and tends to sanctification. Far better is it to endure such a shame than to incur the risk of committing that sin against the Holy Ghost which, according to St. Thomas, consists in "impugning acknowledged truth." False shame, indeed! How many have thus been rendered obstinate and reprobate! False shame (exclaims St. Bernard), thou art void of reason; thou art the enemy of men's salvation, and a stranger to true honour and integrity! Deliver me, O my God, from that knowledge which is corrupted by pride, and which is wanting in charity, and obstinate in maintaining its errors.

" Teach me goodness and discipline and knowledge; for I have believed Thy commandments."—*Ps.* cxviii. 66.

" Thy wisdom and thy knowledge : this hath deceived thee."—*Is.* xlvii. 10.

TUESDAY.

THE BLESSEDNESS OF THE THEOLOGIAN WHO IS ANIMATED BY CHARITY.

I. HE GLORIFIES GOD.
II. HE SANCTIFIES HIMSELF.
III. HE BENEFITS HIS NEIGHBOUR.

"What is written in the law? How readest thou? He answering said, Thou shalt love the Lord thy God with thy whole heart, and with thy whole soul, and with all thy strength, and with all thy mind, and thy neighbour as thyself. And He said to him, Do this and thou shalt live."

1. *Thou shalt love the Lord thy God.* We see here the end of the whole law of Christ, viz., charity, which St. Gregory Nazianzen declares to be the "head of theology." Those who love charity doubtless find a more perfect idea of God through theology, as it unfolds to them the Divine attributes, mysteries, operations, and goodness; and the more God is known the more He will be loved and praised. If we always love God (says St. Augustin), we shall be always praising Him. Again, it is through theology that the Priest is instructed in his duties as a creature, as a Christian, and as a Minister of Christ; and if he follows the precepts contained in the Sacred Scriptures he will avoid offending God, and will glorify Him—planting in his heart every virtue, and rooting out of it every vice. For human nature (says St. Ephrem) is as the soil, the will being its husbandman, whose counsellors and attendants are the Sacred Scrip-

tures, pointing out the evil habits which it must root out, and the virtues which it must plant. Lastly, theology supplies the means of attaining to the perfection of charity; for, so far as may be, the Priest resembles the cherubim graven on the bases of the Temple, as representing the fulness of knowledge. In the annals of the Church we may find a long roll of Priests who, in proportion to their eminence in theological learning, were ardent in charity, and contributed to the glory of God. The charity of such Priests was worthy of honour, for "the love of God is honourable wisdom" (Eccl. i. 14). Let us strive to follow their example.

2. *As thyself.* Theology is a science which depends not on the intellect alone, but penetrates to the heart, and induces charity. As St. Isidore says, it instructs the understanding, and, after detaching a man from the vanities of the world, it leads him on to the love of God. The Priest who meditates on the Divine Law and applies it to himself with prayer will procure mercies from God and eternal life (as St. Ambrose says). In this study he must not have regard to worldly honour, fame, dignity, or profit, but must seek after God with sincerity, so as to sanctify himself and others. Thus will he follow the example of Esdras the Priest, of whom we read that "he had prepared his heart to seek the law of the Lord, and to do and to teach in Israel the command- ments and judgments" (1 Esdras vii. 10). Let us be well as- sured that it is not sufficient for a Priest to be ready at answer- ing questions, to have acquired knowledge, to be a skilful teacher, an elegant speaker, or a distinguished worker; but he must be a man of action, and in that respect must surpass the laity. He speaks the most who does the most (says St. Jerome). Therefore, O Priest, throw away your worldly literature, your tragedies and comedies, and all that kind of reading which is dangerous to faith and morals; have nothing to do with poli- tics; but make the study of theology your delight, that it may nourish in you the love of God, and confer on you true glory. Love and embrace this science (says St. Isidore), and it will exalt and glorify you.

3. *Thy neighbour.* The study of sacred things tends to in-

crease the usefulness of the Priest, for it does not suffice that he lead a good life, but he must also instruct and edify others; and this he cannot do unless he be both learned and full of charity. A doctor of the Church (says St. Isidore) must be distinguished both by his piety and his learning. Learning without piety will render him arrogant; piety without learning, useless. He must himself shine with that light which the Sacred Scriptures shed upon their readers, and he must impart the same to others. The Priests of old were equipped with shields and armour, to fight the battles of their people against visible foes. Thus it is said of Judas Machabeus that "he put on a breast-plate as a giant, and girt his warlike armour about him in battles, and protected his camp with his sword" (1 Mach. iii. 3). Those Priests were types of the Ministers of the New Law, who, inflamed with Divine love, put on the shield of faith, and gird themselves with weapons furnished by the Sacred Scriptures, to defend the Christian army against spiritual foes. The Divine Scriptures (says St. Cyprian) are a continual support to our faith, and their heavenly voice encourages the servants of God in their spiritual warfare. Let us, therefore, have recourse to the Eternal Priest, beseeching Him to inflame us with charity, and to lead us by His example to employ the learning we possess to the sanctification of the Faithful. "By his knowledge shall this my just servant justify many" (Is. liii. 11).

"Blessed is the man whom Thou shalt instruct, O Lord; and shalt teach him out of Thy law."—*Ps.* xciii. 12.

"God hath given to a good man in His sight wisdom, and knowledge, and joy."—*Eccles.* ii. 26.

WEDNESDAY.

———◆———

THE GUILT OF THE NEGLIGENT PRIEST.

I. The misery of the neglected sinner.
II. The cruelty of neglecting him.
III. The consequences of this negligence.

———◆———

" Jesus answering said, A certain man went down from Jerusalem to Jericho and fell among robbers, who also stripped him, and having wounded him went away, leaving him half dead. And it chanced that a certain Priest went down the same way, and, seeing him, passed by. In like manner also, a Levite, when he was near the place and saw him, passed by."—*St. Luke* x. 30, 32.

1. *Fell among robbers.* This unhappy man, having left Jerusalem, which represents *sanctity*, and going towards Jericho, which represents *sin*, " fell among robbers," by which term are signified all the transgressors of the Divine Law. Here, surely, is a spectacle which should excite compassion. An unarmed man in the hands of robbers! Those robbers are the demons—the implacable enemies of mankind. Who (says St. Ambrose) are those robbers but the angels of darkness? By them the sinner is surrounded on all sides so soon as he gives consent to their suggestions. By them he is stripped of sanctifying grace, and of all those gifts which grace confer upon the soul. By them he is wounded mortally; at their hands he receives stripes and blows in proportion to the number of his sins; for sins are as blows to the soul (says Venerable Bede), because they destroy the integrity of human nature. He is left half dead; for the sinner, so far as he has the knowledge of God may be said to be alive, and so far as he is corrupted by

sin he is dead (as St. Augustin explains). Who could gaze on
such a spectacle unmoved ? Yet such is the condition of every
sinner, and the less conscious he is of his state the greater is
his danger.

2. *A Priest* . . . . . *seeing him, passed by.* In these words our
Lord sets before us the hardship of heart which characterized
the Priests of the Old Law. He represents the Priest as so
destitute of all the feelings of humanity as to look without any
compassion upon a man who had been robbed, wounded, and
left half dead. This hardness of heart is the offspring of pride,
which will not stoop to lend a helping hand to others in their
misery; and also of avarice, which grudges them any means of
relief. Here, then, our Lord points to those who are to be
found, even amongst the Priests of the New Law, under the
influence of pride and covetousness. To these do the words
apply, "Thou shalt not harden thy heart nor close thy hand"
(Deut. xv. 17); for such Priests, being destitute of all charity,
refuse to hold out their hands to those many sinners who are, in
the eyes of God and man, as regards their faith and their works
of faith, stripped, wounded, and half dead. They neglect this
duty partly because they see that no worldly honour or gain will
result from it, and partly because they are without any "bowels
of commiseration" (Philipp. ii. 1). The charity of God is not
in them, and he who hath not charity "abideth in death"
(1 St. John iii. 14). Surely these words of the beloved disciple
apply still more fully to the spiritual than to the bodily wants of
our brethren: "He that shall see his brother hath need and
shall put up his bowels from him, how doth the charity of God
abide in him?" (*Ibid.* 17.) Our Lord gave to His Disciples and
Ministers "a new commandment," to love one another, in
imitation of His own love, Who laid down His life for sinners:
"A new commandment I give to you, that you love one another,
as I loved you" (St. John xiii. 34). From those words St. John
concludes, "He has laid down His life for us, and we ought to
lay down our lives for the brethren" (1 St. John iii. 16). Now,
it may be that both I who write and thou who readest were in
the mind of our Lord when He described the hardness of that

Priest's heart. Alas, how little have we hitherto done to deliver our brethren from eternal death! Do we not thus merit the hatred both of God and man?

3. *In like manner also a Levite.* Most wisely did our Lord add those words, because those in the inferior ranks of the ministry, as were the Levites, are wont to imitate the Priesthood in hardness of heart. In the present day it may generally be observed that the inferior clergy, in this respect, follow the example of their superiors. As is the Priest, so is the Levite; as is the Prelate, so is the Deacon; as is the Master, so is the Disciple (says Cornelius à Lapide commenting on this passage). Clerics who are in course of training for the Priesthood watch closely the conduct of their seniors in age and ecclesiastical rank and dignity. If they find them devoted to secular affairs and to the acquisition of riches, thinking only of the opportunities of gaining promotion or taking their pleasure, and not occupied in the conversion of sinners, they will be prepared to imitate them as soon as they arrive at the Priesthood. Priests who set such an example do not lay to heart the maxim of St. Leo, that the Priest who does not reclaim others from error shews that he himself is wandering from the right path. They desire to offer the most holy Sacrifice upon the Altar, and hasten to attain the Priesthood, but they have no regard for that sacrifice of the salvation of sinners which is most pleasing to God. St. Laurence Justinian says that there is no greater offering, nor one of sweeter savour to our Lord, than the gaining of souls. In leaving others to perish they disregard their own peril of eternal ruin, for we cannot perish alone (says St. Bernard), as it is our office to take the lead both in teaching and working. Do we keep these truths before our eyes? Do we study to impress upon young Clerics zeal for the conversion of sinners? When shall we learn to follow in this respect the example of the Saints?

"My heart hath been inflamed, and my veins have been changed."—*Ps.* lxxii. 21.

"Behold, O Lord, for . . my bowels are troubled, my heart is turned within me . . . abroad the sword destroyeth, and at home there is death alike."—*Lam.* i. 20.

THURSDAY.

JESUS CHRIST, BY HIS EXAMPLE, INCITES IN HIS PRIESTS A ZEAL FOR THE SALVATION OF SINNERS.

    I. He draws a portrait of Himself.
    II. He shews it as a pattern.
    III. He implores us to imitate it.

"But a certain Samaritan, being on his journey, came near him, and, seeing him, was moved with compassion, and, going up to him, bound up his wounds, pouring in oil and wine'. . . Which of these three, in thy opinion, was neighbour to him that fell among robbers ? But he said, He that showed mercy to him. And Jesus said to him, Go, and do thou in like manner."—*St. Luke* x. 33, 34, 36, 37.

1. *But a certain Samaritan, &c.* Our Lord has here given us a portrait of Himself, for the word "Samaritan" signifies a guardian. He is the true guardian of our souls (says St. Gregory). He it was Who looked with compassion upon Adam when he had been driven from Paradise and was lying half dead from the blows inflicted on him by the devil, and when neither the Law nor the Prophets were of avail to raise him up and heal him. As Origen points out, the man who "went down" is Adam ; Jerusalem is Paradise ; Jericho is the world ; the robbers, the powers of evil ; the Priest, the Law ; the Levite, the Prophets. The good Samaritan beheld us all (says St. Augustin) stripped of our supernatural goods, and wounded in our natural faculties. Struck with compassion for this our misery, He came to repair our loss (as St. Leo says), and our recovery was due to His mercy alone.

He came to us from afar; that is to say, He was removed from us by nature and condition, rather than by space (as St. Augustin says). He bound up our wounds; that is, He restrained our sins, and stayed the course of our troubles. He poured "wine" over them—that is, His Blood; and with the wine he poured in "oil"—that is, grace (as St. Chrysostom explains). Do we, however, meditate on this work of our Redemption? If we did but frequently reflect on our Lord's Passion, every labour in which we engage for the salvation of souls would seem light. But we neglect meditation, and therefore labour wearies us.

2. *Which of these three, in thy opinion, was neighbour?* Our Lord, when He drew this portrait of Himself, vouchsafed to call Himself our neighbour, and that in virtue of the help which He had thus afforded us when we were as the man lying half dead on the road. Now, in thus calling Himself our neighbour, and obliging us to love our neighbour as ourselves, He implied that He expects succour, and especially spiritual succour, from us. He expects it, not in His own person, but in the person of those poor sinners of whom he said, " As long as you did it to one of these, My least brethren, you did it to Me" (St. Matt. xxv. 40). He expects it from Priests, and especially from such as are well instructed; for useless will be the dignity of the Priesthood and the knowledge of the Law unless tested by works of mercy (says St. Cyril). It is a marvellous thought that, whilst Christ declared Himself our neighbour in order to inculcate upon us the duty of compassion, He also showed Himself a model of compassion in order that we might do for sinners who are thrown in our way that which He has done for all the race of men, and for ourselves among the rest. Let us, then, cure their wounds with oil and wine; that is (as St. Gregory explains), let us temper mildness and gentleness with salutary rigour. Let us do to sinners what we would have done to ourselves in that lamentable state, and when we have done it let us say, " Jesus, the true Samaritan, has done infinitely more for me than I can ever do for my brethren."

3. *Do thou in like manner.* Jesus commands us to imitate Himself, not only in regard to the bodily wants, but more espe-

cially in relieving the spiritual necessities of our neighbour. We know His will, but we are kept back by sloth : we pass our life desiring to obey Him, but are "killed with fruitless desires, for our hands have refused to work" (Prov. xxi. 25). We pass our life desiring to employ ourselves in dispensing heavenly medicine to souls, and seeing many zealous Priests incessantly engaged in this work : " He longeth and desireth all the day, but he that is just will give, and will not cease" (v. 26). The slothful man finds first one hindrance, then another, and so the most favourable occasions of benefiting the needy slip by. Experience shows us how the powers of the slothful are weakened and rendered useless,—how (as St. Bernard admirably expresses it) vigour flags, languor takes possession of the man, energy is diminished, grace withdrawn, life is dragged on, reason sleeps, the spirit is extinguished. Yet the slothful Priest knows full well that he is the minister of Jesus Christ; he knows in what abyss sinners are plunged ; he knows to what a height he ought to strive to raise them (as St. Gregory Nazianzen points out). Moreover, there is no need for him to go in search of difficult remedies to cure them ; it suffices that he make use of the doctrine of God's Word, which (as St. Chrysostom says) is as a sword, and as iron, and can be applied even to putrid and ulcerating wounds, whether they require caustic or the knife. Why do not we employ this remedy ? Why have we not made use of it hitherto ? How great evils have been caused by our slothfulness !

" As a neighbour, and as my own brother, so did I please."—*Ps.* xxxiv. 14.

" He hath sent me . . . to heal the contrite of heart, and to preach a release to the captives, and deliverance to them that are shut up."—*Is.* lxi. 1.

FRIDAY.

———◆———

THE CARE FOR MEN'S SOULS WHICH OUR LORD TEACHES HIS PRIESTS.

I. THE MEANS WHICH HE SUPPLIES.
II. THE COMMAND WHICH HE GIVES.
III. THE REWARD WHICH HE PROMISES.

———◆———

" And, setting him upon his own beast, brought him to an inn, and took care of him. And the next day he took out two pence, and gave to the host, and said, Take care of him, and, whatsoever thou shalt spend over and above, I at my return will repay thee."— *St. Luke* x. 34, 35.

1. *He took out two pence.* The host to whom the sick man was consigned signified (says St. Augustin) all Apostolical men, and all who explain holy Scripture to the people. Truly blessed is he who, as represented by the faithful host, receives charge (says St. Ambrose) to heal the wounds of others. What means had he at his disposal for curing him ? He had two pence—that is, the two Testaments, which are, as it were, two coins adorned with the impress of the eternal King, and by whose price our wounds are healed. Further, these two pence (says St. Augustin) are the two precepts of that charity which, by means of the Holy Spirit, was poured out upon the Apostles for the evangelization of the world. Lastly, these two pence are the promise of spiritual goods in this present life, and of eternal goods in the life to come. We, too, have received this money, and we have received it for the cure of the sick ; but what use have we

made of it ? how many have we cured up to this moment ? how
many might we not have cured had we not buried our money in
the cursed earth of slothfulness ?

2. *Take care of him.*   The Samaritan was the first to take care
of the man : " He took care of him;" and afterwards he enjoined the host to continue this care, saying, " Take care of
him." To cure us sinners our Lord Jesus Christ descended from
heaven, made Himself a wayfarer, subjected Himself to our
miseries, cured our wounds by taking them on Himself : " He
hath borne our infirmities and carried our sorrows " (Is. liii. 4).
It is the office of His Ministers to apply to the sick the remedies
that He has prepared for them in the Sacraments and by means
of preaching ; and without doubt (as St. Athanasius declares)
this charge was laid upon us from the moment of our ordination.
Thenceforth our life should be devoted, not to ourselves, but to
others. With what conscience, then (asks St. Leo), can we take
to ourselves the power due to the Priesthood, if we labour not
for the salvation of souls ?   We shew (says St. Gregory) that we
have no love for Jesus, if we have neither love nor care for the
sheep which cost Him His Blood. With just severity the Church
used to punish such negligence, by ordering that the Priest
who had no care for the people, and who did not teach them
piety, should be suspended, and if he continued negligent
should be deposed from his office.   How have we hitherto fulfilled the will of Jesus and of His Spouse ?   Is our Lord—is
the Church—content with our labours ?   What does our conscience tell us ?

3. *Whatsoever thou shalt spend over and above . . I will repay thee.*
In these words our Saviour promises to return, and He will return, to judge his Priests. He promises to pay as a debt all
that they shall have expended for the sick, and blessed are
they (says St. Ambrose) to whom He is a debtor.   They who
shall have abundantly provided all that is needful for the Faithful, considering them as the representatives of Jesus Christ
Himself, shall be rewarded by Almighty God with grace and
glory.   Hence St. Bonaventure, in explaining the passage we
have just quoted, makes use of the words of the Psalm, " For

God loveth mercy and truth, the Lord will give grace and glory." The more promptly will the sins of Priests be cancelled (says St. Gregory) in proportion as they have cancelled the sins of others, for it is impossible (says St. Laurence Justinian) that they should not receive an eternal reward for all the good which, for the love of God, they have done to their neighbour by labouring for the salvation of men. They prepare for themselves a golden crown adorned with precious jewels. Will not such splendid promises arouse us from our slothfulness ? It may be, alas ! that the hope of fleeting goods incapable of satisfying the soul—worthless and empty—would make more powerful impression upon us.

"If I shall give sleep to my eyes, or slumber to my eye-lids, or rest to my temples, until I find out a place for the Lord."—*Ps.* cxxxi. 4, 5.

"Wounds, and bruises, and swelling sores, they are not bound up, nor dressed, nor fomented with oil."—*Is.* i. 6.

THE NATIVITY OF
THE BLESSED VIRGIN MARY.

---

*HOW PRIESTS SHOULD PREPARE THE PEOPLE
FOR THIS SOLEMNITY.*

I. BY EXPLAINING THE GLORIES OF THIS NATIVITY.

II. BY PROMISING GRACE TO THOSE WHO CELEBRATE IT
WORTHILY.

III. BY INCULCATING THE RIGHT DISPOSITIONS FOR ITS
OBSERVANCE.

"Of whom was born Jesus."—*St. Matt.* i. 16.

1. *Of whom was born Jesus.* Justly, then, are the most magnificent things said of our Lady, Who is the city of God: "Glorious things are said of thee, O city of God" (Ps. lxxxvi. 3). All the glories of Mary are comprised in these words—She was the true and worthy Mother of God. All that we can know or understand of the Blessed Virgin (says St. Thomas of Villanova) is summed up in this brief sentence—"Of whom was born Jesus." Most fitting was it that She should surpass all others in virtues and in merits, even in her tender years. She says of Herself (for thus does the Church apply the words), "When I was a little one I pleased the Most High." Without doubt She was adorned with so perfect a sanctity as to be worthy of the dignity of Mother of Christ, to which "from all eternity" She was predestinated. So St. Thomas. By the most lively knowledge

of God, by most ardent charity, by the exercise of all other virtues, was this little Infant as a mountain placed upon the summit of the highest mountains. As St. Gregory declares, as a mountain upon the top of a mountain, so is the greatness of Mary above all Saints. Thus, the present solemnity should be one of general exultation, and Priests should make known the motive of this joy, saying with St. Augustin, "Let earth rejoice with supreme exultation, illumined by the Birth of so great a Virgin." Let us call to mind the Mystery of the Incarnation, which is to be accomplished in the womb of this Virgin. Let us (as St. Peter Damian says) rejoice and exult in the Nativity of Blessed Mary, Mother of God, which brought new joy to the world, and was the beginning of salvation to the whole human race.

2. If from Mary was born Jesus, by Whom came "grace and truth," then by means of His Mother, and especially in Her Nativity, should we expect grace and truth. Holy Church says, "Let us celebrate devoutly the Nativity of the Blessed Virgin Mary, in order that She may intercede for us with our Lord Jesus Christ," and thus gives us to understand that Mary especially intercedes for those who devoutly celebrate Her Nativity. She, indeed, was prefigured by the little cloud which appeared to the servant of Elias : "Behold, a little cloud arose out of the sea, like a man's foot" (3 Kings xviii. 44) : and by this vision the Lord foretold the appearance of a little Child who was destined to bring showers of grace upon the world (as St. John of Jerusalem explains). And, if it is customary for earthly kings and queens to dispense favours to their subjects on their birthdays, how great favours may we not expect Mary, the Queen of the whole world, to confer, who was born (as St. Germanus says) to dispense grace to the world, to bestow life, to take away the curse, and to draw down blessing upon us? On this day the just shall receive augmentation of grace, and sinners pardon (exclaims St. Bernard). How great benefit, then, shall not we confer on souls committed to our charge, if we shall excite in them due homage to Mary on this Festival that we are celebrating!

3. But it is for us to remind the people that the Church

invites them to celebrate the Nativity of Mary "most devoutly."
Now, devotion is defined by St. Thomas to be "a spiritual act of
the will promptly surrendering itself to the service of God."
Hence they deceive themselves who think they can worthily celebrate this Festival whilst they remain obstinate in sin, without
even the desire to return to God's service.   Mary is the Mother
of all sinners who wish to amend, as She herself revealed to St.
Bridget ; and therefore Priests should encourage such sinners to
come to Mary, Who loves them from Her heart, as the physician
loves the limbs which he heals, and as the artist loves the rough
trunk out of which he designs to carve a beautiful statue.   For
this cause is She called by St. Anselm the Restorer of the fallen,
the Restorer of sinners.   But, on the other hand, Priests should
take away from the minds of men the hope (which is not hope,
but culpable rashness) which leads many sinners to practise
little devotions to Mary, that they may sin more boldly and
continue in sin with impunity.   Let them say to each one of
these sinners, with St. Gregory, "Put an end to the will to sin,
and thou wilt find Mary more prompt than a mother in loving
thee."   Such exhortations, however, must be made with prudence, so that obstinate sinners may be induced to cease from
their sins rather than from their devotions to Mary.   For it may
happen that in time the Blessed Virgin will obtain for them a
change of will.   Let us, then, conclude our discourse with words
which deserve to be carefully pondered by ourselves as well as by
others—"You that love the Lord, hate evil." (From Ps. xcvi. 10.)

" Hearken, O daughter, and see, and incline thy ear."—*Ps.* xliv. 11.
" Thy plants are a paradise of pomegranates, with the fruits of the orchard . . the
fountain of gardens, the well of living waters."—*Cant.* iv. 13, 14.

THIRTEENTH SUNDAY AFTER PENTECOST.

ECCLESIASTICAL CENSURES.

I. The Priest should fear them.

II. He should inspire others with dread of them.

III. He should endeavour to liberate those who have incurred them.

"As Jesus was going to Jerusalem, He passed through the midst of Samaria and Galilee, and as He entered into a certain town there met him ten men that were lepers."—*St. Luke* xvii. 11, 12.

1. *He passed through the midst of Samaria and Galilee.* In order to accomplish our journey to the heavenly Jerusalem, the Church of the first-born, the holy city, we must pass by Samaria—that is, the "keeping" of the Law imposed on us; and thence we must pass to Galilee—that is, to a happy "transmigration" towards our country. Not only the laws of God, but the laws of the Church also, must be kept by the Faithful, and especially by the Ministers of the Church, for (says St. Cyprian) none can have God for their Father who have not the Church for their Mother. Now, whoever has thoroughly studied the Treatise on Censures will have observed two things—viz., first, that they most frequently affect Ecclesiastics, and that the higher the dignity of the clergy the more easy is it for them to fall under these censures; and also that they are sometimes incurred in "vincible ignorance," as St. Alphonsus Liguori points out. Priests, therefore, should learn the

Canons of the Church, so as to escape these terrible chains, and
the peril of condemnation before the tribunal of Christ. Priests
(as St. Leo says) should certainly never be ignorant of what has
been ruled and defined by the Canons. Neither let them rashly
rely on their own judgment in interpreting doubtful cases in
matter of censures, either for themselves or for others: "Lean
not upon thy own prudence" (Prov. iii. 5). Let them meditate
carefully on St. Gregory the Great's maxim, that the sentence of
the Pastor, be it just or be it unjust, is to be feared. Let them
read repeatedly the dissertation of St. Thomas on this head.
Wo to those who do not keep themselves steadfast in the Communion of Saints! Wo to those who in so miserable a state will
have to present themselves at Christ's tribunal!

2. *As He entered into a certain town.* The lepers remained outside the town, and in like manner the excommunicated are
outside the Church, for (says St. Thomas) excommunication is
separation from the lawful communion of the Faithful. We
should, therefore, inspire the Faithful with a great dread of this,
and of all other Ecclesiastical penalties, more especially in these
days, when so many are indifferent to them, and even ridicule
them. Let us make such persons understand that the Church
has substituted excommunication (as St. Augustin shows) for the
extreme punishment decreed by the Synagogue against such as
were guilty of most heinous crimes. Let us tell them that if they
hear not the Church they are as the Heathen and Publican,
and that it is lighter pain to be wounded by the sword, to be
devoured by the flames, to be cast to wild beasts, than to despise
the Church, and to be separated from Her. They who are
excommunicated are members cut off from the body: "I would
that they were even cut off who trouble you" (Gal. v. 12).
They are delivered over to Satan, who, seeing them deprived of
spiritual aids, exercises a fierce rule over them: "I have
judged . . . to deliver such a one to Satan, for the destruction
of the flesh" (1 Cor. v. 3, 5). The Church imitates God's
judgment, Who chastises the sinner and leaves him alone, in
order that he may be humbled and return to Him; and therefore does She separate them from the communion of the Faith-

ful, and deprive them of their suffrages, and of other spiritual
benefits. So St. Thomas. Have we delivered this salutary
teaching to the people? Have we rebuked those who have
ridiculed Ecclesiastical Censures in our presence? Or have we
been silent through servile fear? Have we not even ourselves
used similar language in regard to these things?

3. *There met him ten men that were lepers.* These ten lepers
(says St. Ambrose) represented the great number of Christians
who lie under Ecclesiastical Censures, and especially such as are
inflicted for heresy. How many are there at this moment
bound by excommunication for heresy! How many lie under
the same penalty for other crimes, by which it is *ipso facto*
incurred through the decrees of the Universal Church, or else
through those of a particular Diocese. Now, these Censures
are a medicinal punishment, inflicted " that the spirit may be
saved " (1 Cor. v. 5); they are called by St. Gregory of Nyssa
a paternal law; for Prelates, who are spiritual Fathers of the
people, impose them "for edification, not for destruction."
Thus it is the duty of Priests to exert themselves in behalf of
these lepers, sending them to the waters of the mystical Jordan,
as Eliseus sent Naaman—that is to say, directing them to those
who have the faculty to absolve and cleanse them. Let us say,
in the words of God Himself, Whose ministers we are, "I will
seek that which was lost, and that which was driven away I will
bring again; and I will bind up that which was broken, and I
will strengthen that which was weak" (Ezech. xxxiv. 16). Charity
to our neighbour, which is "holy, just, and true," urges us to
this duty, says St. Augustin. It is "holy" because we practise it
to please Almighty God; it is "just" because it tends to great
good; it is "true" because it is not moved by self-interest. To
labour for such an end is to "labour not in vain in the Lord"
(1 Cor. xv. 58). And "God is not unjust, that He should forget
such work" (Heb. vi. 10).

"I am a partaker with all them that fear Thee and that keep Thy commandments."—*Ps.* cxviii. 63.

" Neither will God have a soul to perish, but recalleth, meaning that he that is
cast off should not altogether perish."—*2 Kings* xiv. 14.

MONDAY.

PRIESTS SHOULD AVOID VENIAL SINS.

I. BECAUSE OF THEIR KNOWLEDGE OF THE CONSEQUENCES.
II. BECAUSE OF THEIR NEARNESS TO GOD.
III. BECAUSE OF THE FACILITY OF AVOIDING SUCH SINS.

" There met him ten men that were lepers, who stood afar off, and lifted up their voice, saying, Jesus, master, have mercy on us."—*St. Luke* xvi. 12, 13.

1. *Ten men that were lepers.* Besides the leprosy that was mortal, there was another called "a flying and wandering leprosy" (Levit. xiii. 57). Under the figure of this leprosy may be understood venial sins, especially such as are committed with full knowledge and deliberation; and these eat like a canker (says Cardinal Hugo) into the whole spiritual life, and spoil the merit of our good works. Priests know better than other men that the devil seeks first to infect us with this leprosy, and afterwards to kill us with the other; for (as St. Chrysostom says) he generally begins his temptations in small matters. Therefore (as St. Ephrem teaches) we should watch with all care and diligence against his wiles even in regard to the smallest things, so as to be proof against his snares. It often happens that a great flame is kindled from a small spark; that is (as St. Gregory Nazianzen teaches), a venial sin may produce the most terrible and unexpected consequences. He that is "unjust in that which is little will be unjust also in that which is greater" (St. Luke xvi. 10). If we consult Ecclesiastical History—beginning with the traitor Judas, who from small thefts attained to the guilt of treason, sacrilege, and despair—we shall find that a great number of

Priests have thus advanced from small to great sins. A single hair given up to the devil (as St. Bonaventure says) will grow into a beam in his hands. Let us, then, watch and pray, lest, as a punishment for so many venial sins, we fall into mortal sin, and lest also the well-merited chastisements of God for our venial sins come upon us in this life, and in the life to come. Let us remember St. Bernard's warning, that after this life we shall have to pay a hundredfold in the pains of purgatory for that which we have neglected here. Let us give thanks to God that hitherto He has not given free course to His justice in our regard, as He has with so many others; that is to say, that He has neither punished us for our venial sins on this earth, nor sent us to purgatory, nor suffered us to fall into grave sins, from which possibly we should never have been delivered.

2. *Stood afar off.* These lepers dared not to approach Christ, because they were ashamed of their uncleanness (says Theophylact), and feared lest He should spurn them. But Priests, although covered with the leprosy of venial sin, continually in their ministrations approach Him who is " holy, innocent, undefiled, separated from sinners." They cause Him to descend from heaven into their hands; they offer Him to the Father; they feed on Him; they dispense Him to others; yet they are not ignorant of (nay, they have often preached to others) the exact obedience which God requires of His creatures : "Keep My law as the apple of thy eye " (Prov. vii 2). They are not ignorant (nay, they have often preached to others) that " he that feareth God neglecteth nothing " (Eccle. vii. 19). They are not ignorant (nay, they have often preached to others) that, although venial sin may be called light in comparison with mortal sin, still it is in itself a greater evil than all physical evils or sufferings, inasmuch as it is an injury and contempt offered to God; for, as the Apostle assures us, he who transgresses the law dishonours God. We must not consider in venial sin the action in itself (says St. Augustin), but rather the goodness, love, and tenderness of Him who is offended by it. And, if this be true in respect of all the Faithful, what shall we say of Ecclesiastics, who, because of the lights vouchsafed to them, the benefits they have received,

the functions they exercise, ought to be more perfect than other men: "Perfect and entire, failing in nothing" (James i. 4).

3. *Lifted up their voice, &c.* The lepers raised their voice, making known their uncleanness, expressing their misery, and imploring the Divine mercy (says St. Bonaventure). Here, then, we have, in regard to venial sins, both a remedy and a safeguard— a remedy for the past, a safeguard against the future. Let us acknowledge our guilt; let us pour out our misery before God and implore His mercy; let us have recourse to meditation and prayer. As St. Bernard says, meditation teaches us our own needs, and through prayer we obtain their supply ; meditation shows us the way, prayer leads us in it; meditation makes known to us our danger, prayer helps us to avoid it. Let us, then, never neglect meditation, in order that we may keeps God's law ever before our eyes: "the things that God hath commanded thee, tkink on them always" (Eccl. iii. 22). The Saints in heaven cannot sin, because they are in the continual enjoyment of the light of God, which shines on them as the sun in the meridian, so that they cannot be deceived by evil under the appearance of good. We, then, approach the more nearly to this blessed state in proportion to the steadfastness with which we contemplate the truth, which in this life shines as a lamp in the darkness. Meanwhile let us make the generous resolution inculcated by St. Alphonsus, viz., to suffer any torture rather than deliberately commit the slightest venial sin. Let us implore the mercy of our Lord Jesus Christ, Who expiated even our venial sins upon the Cross with His Blood and death, and merited for us grace to avoid them. Let us pray to Him to pardon those which we have already committed, and to give us strength to adhere closely to the commandments of God, and to shrink from any deliberate venial sin. Let us intreat Him daily to lessen the number of those sins into which we fall through human frailty, to increase our hatred of such sins, and to consume them in the fire of Divine love.

"I shall be spotless with them, and shall keep myself from my iniquity."— *Ps.* xvii. 24.

"Jesus, master, have mercy on us."—*St. Luke* xvii. 13.

TUESDAY.

THE PRIESTS' DUTY IN REGARD TO SPIRITUAL LEPROSY.

I. TO DISCERN IT.
II. TO CURE IT.
III. TO KEEP HIMSELF FREE FROM IT.

" Whom when He saw, He said, Go, shew yourselves to the Priests."—
St. Luke xvii. 14.

1. *Shew yourselves to the Priests.* Jesus Christ commanded the
lepers to shew themselves to the Priests, because His wish was
to cleanse them, and it was the office of the Priests to judge of
their cure. Almighty God had, in fact, given the Priests certain
marks by which they might know leprosy, distinguish its different forms, and satisfy themselves of its cure. (Levit. xiii.) Leprosy
was a figure of sin, just as the ten lepers signified the great
number of sinners who transgress the Decalogue ; and it is for
Priests (says St. Bonaventure) to judge of this spiritual leprosy.
How is it, then, that some Priests look upon the study of Moral
Theology as unworthy of their talents?   It is, indeed, not only a
vast and difficult subject, but absolutely necessary for the Ministers of Reconciliation, who have to discern "between leprosy and
leprosy." Let us meditate on God's words, " It is an everlasting
precept through your generations, and that you may have knowledge to discern between holy and unholy" (Lev. x. 9, 10).
What shall we say, then, of such as take their place in the Con-

fessional, having scarcely learnt the brief elements of this science, and who, from neglect in calculating it, have almost forgotten the little which they once knew? They ruin both themselves and their penitents. As St. Laurence Justinian declares, a Priest who knows not how to discern beween leprosy and leprosy cannot tell the quality of the sins confessed to him, or the gravity of the offences committed against God; and thus, without benefiting his penitent, he slays himself with his own weapon. Let us examine the state of our conscience, and let us resolve never to abandon the study of Moral Theology.

2. *Shew yourselves to the Priests.* The Priests to whom our Saviour sent the lepers could not but wonder at the sudden and miraculous cure which had been already wrought in them, but when our Lord sends sinners to Priests of the New Law He does so in order that they may obtain their cure. The Priest (says St. Laurence Justinian) absolves those whom Divine grace has directed to him. Accordingly (as St. Bonaventure teaches), Confessors must not abhor and drive away any who throw themselves at their feet, however heinous, vile, and odious their crimes may be. Let us seriously ponder the words of the Holy Spirit, "Thou shalt not abhor the Edomite, because he is thy brother, nor the Egyptian, because thou wast a stranger in his land" (Deut. xxiii. 7). For the sinner, represented by the Edomite and the Egyptian, is our brother, and we have been (or at any rate may one day find ourselves) in his miserable condition. Let us endeavour to cure these unhappy men, since, as it has been well said, the power of curing them is in our lips. By this means we shall save the souls of others and our own; we shall (as St. Bonaventure tells us) obtain the blotting out of our sins, and an increase of joy and glory in Paradise.

3. *Shew yourselves to the Priests.* The sons of Aaron, in judging leprosy, had to be careful not to touch the lepers, lest they should incur danger of infection, and contract legal uncleanness: "Whatever a person toucheth who is unclean, he shall make it unclean" (Numb. xix. 22). In like manner the Priests of the Catholic Church, unless they use great circumspection in listening to the recital of sins, may stain their own soul, and subject it to God's

terrible judgment. Let us observe that Jesus Christ says to them, " You are the light of the world " (St. Matt. v. 14). Now, light enters into the most sordid places, and lights up the most filthy objects, but in itself incurs no stain, and ever remains pure. It is not defiled by uncleanness, says St. Thomas. So should the Priest enter into the very sewers (according to the expression of St. Francis of Sales)—that is, into the most corrupt consciences— and come forth without defilement, and without losing his lustre or his purity. But how great viligance is required for this ! We must stand ever on our guard, keeping before our eyes the sins into which we might fall, and the eternal Judge from Whom nothing is hid (says St. Gregory). We must, moreover, recommend ourselves to Almighty God, imploring His help, and we must thank Him if He permit not our soul to contract any stain in the fulfilment of the trust committed to us by our Lord. "The Lord hath brought me back to you without pollution of sin, rejoicing for his victory, for my escape, and for your deliverance" (Judith xiii. 20).

"I have walked in my innocence, and I have put my trust in the Lord."— *Ps.* xxv. 1.

"I will say to God . . . if I be wicked, wo unto me; and if just, I shall not lift up my head."—*Job* x. 15.

WEDNESDAY.

FREQUENT CONFESSION PROFITABLE FOR PRIESTS.

I. As a means of purifying the soul.
II. As an occasion of practising many virtues.
III. As an opportunity of obtaining direction.

"And it came to pass, as they went, they were made clean. And one of them, when he saw that he was made clean, went back, with a loud voice, glorifying God, and he fell on his face before His feet."—*St. Luke* xvii. 14, 16.

1. *As they went, they were made clean.* Our Saviour enjoined on the lepers, when He cleansed them, an act of obedience and humiliation, by commanding them to show themselves to the Priests. In this way He pointed out how sinners must approach the Priest with all humility and confess their sins, as it is said, "Give honour to the Priests and purify thyself" (Eccl. viii. 33), for this honour (says St. Bonaventure) is self-accusation. From this precept the holy Fathers have inferred the efficacy of Sacramental Confession, which cures all sickness and languor of soul. Let us well understand that it is befitting us Priests to confess frequently, in order that (as the Constitutions of Benedict XIV. enjoin) we may bring to holy Mass a heart removed from all wickedness, and, so far as posssible, pure and clean. Hence the Rules of Religious Communities usually prescribe Confession twice a week; and, if we read the lives of holy Priests, such as St. Francis of Sales, St. Alphonsus, and others,

we shall find that they confessed almost daily. A Priest, therefore, is in fault if he does not frequently repair to his own Confessor. Indeed, we ought to fear even in regard to sins already confessed: "Be not without fear about sins forgiven" (Eccl. v. 5). Thou hast attained wisdom (says St. Bernard) if . thou weepest continually over the sins of thy past life. If our past sins cause us to fear, and if we frequently declare our detestation of them at the feet of our Confessor, this very fear (says the same Father) will become a firm and efficacious ground of hope. Moreover, daily venial sins are also washed away by a good Confession; and so, whilst the sinner is cleansed, the just becomes more just. In fine, the efficacy of the Sacrament increases grace, strength, joy, peace of soul; for after the announcement, "Thy sins are forgiven thee," there follows the command, "Go in peace" (St. Luke vii. 48, 50). Why, then, should we be deprived of so great a good? Why should we give it to others and not know how to enjoy it ourselves?

2. *Went back, with a loud voice, &c.* Here (says St. Bonaventure) is described the virtue of gratitude, which was exercised by the Samaritan and commended by God. But how many virtues does not the Priest exercise in the one single act of Confession! First, he exercises faith, which teaches that by means of this Sacrament the sinner is justified: "to him that believeth in Him that justifieth the ungodly, his faith is reputed to justice" (Rom. iv. 5). Next, hope is exercised, which promises pardon, but leaves a salutary fear in those who confess; for (says St. Bernardin of Sienna) we must not hope without fear of God, nor fear without hope in God. Again, charity is exercised, and that is, as it were, the soul of this Sacrament; and the greater that charity the more abundant is the pardon: "many sins are forgiven her because she hath loved much" (St. Luke vii. 47). Love of our neighbour is exercised, because we thus afford a good example to the Faithful, who are edified when they see Priests confessing their venial sins, and fulfilling the precept, "Confess your sins one to another" (James v. 16). Penance, too, is exercised, which is a special virtue, worthy fruits of which are usually

brought forth by means of Confession: "Bring forth fruits worthy of penance" (St. Luke iii. 8). And, not to mention other virtues, humility is exercised, because of the contrite and humble heart which is requisite, because of the manifestation of our weaknesses to God's Minister, and because of the due reproof and penance received from him. Let us remember also (as St. Ambrose teaches us) that humility sustains the whole body of our good works. Let us, then, rejoice in exercising by this one act so many virtues; considering that (as St. Peter Chrysologus tells us) Priests should be patterns of all virtues.

3. *He fell on his face before His feet.* Let us throw ourselves at our Confessor's feet, not only to receive absolution, but also to obtain spiritual direction from him. All men have need of a counsellor, even should they be like Moses in wisdom; for even he (as St. Chrysostom reminds us) took counsel of Jethro. Nor let us flatter ourselves that we are sufficient for ourselves and our own guidance, for we have need of some special direction from another in order to rule ourselves well and save our soul. Almighty God has decreed (says St. Bernard) that man should be instructed by man, and he who determines to be his own master becomes the disciple of a fool. To have no director, and not to follow the example of St. Paul when he went to Ananias in obedience to the Divine command, is a most dangerous temptation, against which St. Augustin warns us. How many instances, alas! are to be found of persons, both learned and holy, who make shipwreck of their faith for want of a good director to pilot them on their course! On the other hand, we read that even the most perfect Saints, with humble submission, governed themselves by the counsels of their directors. Let us resolve to imitate them, and let us pray to God to give us grace ever to keep this resolution.

"Wash me yet more from my iniquity, and cleanse me from my sin."—*Ps.* l. 4.

"My God, I am confounded, and ashamed to lift up my face to Thee, for our iniquities are multiplied over our heads."—1 *Esdras* ix. 6.

THURSDAY.

THE MISERABLE CONDITION OF UNGRATEFUL PRIESTS.

I. THEY ARE CONDEMNED BY THE GRATITUDE OF THE LAITY.

II. THEY ARE ABANDONED BY GOD.

III. THEY DEFRAUD GOD OF HIS GLORY.

"And Jesus, answering, said, Were not ten made clean? And where are the nine? There is no one found to return and give glory to God, but this stranger."
—*St. Luke* xvii. 17, 18.

1. *There is no one found . . but this stranger.* These words (says St. Ambrose) are a reproof to the ungrateful. Thus (says St. Bonaventure) does our Lord rebuke the vice of ingratitude. How justly does this condemnation apply to certain Priests, of whom it may be said, "You are now full, you are now become rich, you reign without us!" (1 Cor. iv. 8.) We might often see devout communicants with bended head, shedding tears of thanksgiving in the fervency of their joy, who thus imitate this stranger, and exhibit (as St. Bonaventure says) love, humility, gratitude, and filial fear. On the other hand, how many Priests, who have received still greater benefits—having caused our Lord to descend from heaven, having offered Him to the Father, having taken Him in food, and received that spiritual purification which is the effect of the Sacrament—leave the Church with distracted minds, and without thanksgiving; and thus resemble the nine lepers! This happens because they think they have a right to the Divine favours, and, as they are wanting in devotion, frequency of reception produces a habit of negligence and ingratitude. It would

seem as though they despised both the benefit and the Benefactor: "I have brought up children and exalted them, but they have despised Me" (Is. i. 2): and their conduct is the same in regard to the other innumerable benefits which they receive both in the order of nature and of grace, although they have a clearer knowledge than the laity both of their Benefactor and of the value of His gifts, as also of the duty of giving Him thanks: "When they knew God they have not glorified Him as God, or given thanks" (Rom. i. 21). Let us examine ourselves, and, if we find ourselves to be of this number, let us hasten to imitate the Samaritan.

2. *To return.* Thanksgiving is a return which the soul makes to her heavenly Benefactor, and therefore is it exhibited by the Samaritan, who "keeps" for the Giver the gifts received, and returns them to Him, according to the words of the Psalm, "I will keep my strength to Thee" (lviii. 10). Our Lord asks, "Where are the nine?" and by these words implies that the nine ungrateful lepers are, as it were, unknown to Him. Thus do ungrateful Priests deserve to be abandoned by God, and our Lord shews that He does not recognise them. Let us learn from St. Augustin how fatal this is to a Minister of God. Not to be known of the Lord is to perish, and to be known of Him is to stand fast. If we would still better understand the fatal effects of ingratitude, let us consider St. Bernard's description of it, who calls it "the enemy of the soul, the destroyer of merit, and the spoiler of all virtues." Ingratitude, he adds, is as a parching wind, which dries up the fountain of piety, the dew of mercy, the streams of grace. Nothing is so displeasing to Almighty God as to see that Priests neither thank Him for their vocation, nor for the exercise of their functions, nor for good success in the work of the Ministry, nor for the lights, aids, and means with which they are continually enriched. Justly, then, do we see these ungrateful men cast down from the height of sanctity and lost: "I cast thee out from the mountain of God, and destroyed thee" (Ezech. xxviii. 16). O my God, regard not my ingratitude, but the wounds of Thy Son, and deliver me from the chastisement that I have justly merited !

3. *And give glory to God.* He who is thankful gives glory to God, for he thereby increases His accidental glory, to which God's creatures contribute by the recognition of His benefits, by love, praise, and worship : "The sacrifice of praise shall glorify Me" (Ps. xlix. 23.) Moreover, thanksgiving gives glory to God, because it exalts His mercies and places the creature in its natural position as a poor and needy suppliant. Remember (says St. Augustin) that the good which thou hast is not of thyself, but from God. Let us, then, reflect that all the benefits we have received from God are His free gifts, nor have we first given Him anything by which we have constituted Him our debtor : "Who hath first given to Him, and recompense shall be made Him ?" (Rom. xi. 35.) "Who hath given Me before," says the Lord, " that I should repay him ?" (Job xli. 2.) The very fulfilment of His law, by which we merit the crown of justice, is as a rich treasure of His gifts, for (as St. Augustin reminds us) all that we do He does, because He aids us in our labours. Let us reflect on the mortal sins we may have committed, on hell which we have merited by them, and on the innumerable venial sins on account of which God might justly have suffered us to fall into mortal sin. Thus we shall find that God, in His infinite mercy, has caused " grace to superabound where sin abounded," and that in despite of our merits He has redoubled His gifts: " She hath received of the hand of the Lord double for all her sins" (Is. xl. 2). Influenced by such considerations, we shall strive to be ever grateful to God for His favours, and we shall repent of the ingratitude and injustice of which we have been guilty in offending Him after so many mercies received from Him. By this acknowledgment of our sins we shall escape the reproach which otherwise we should have merited—a reproach like that which David received from Nathan, and which the royal Prophet himself uttered against Achitophel, the type of the traitor Judas: "If my enemy had reviled me I would verily have borne with it " (Ps. liv. 13).

" I have acknowledged my sin to Thee, and my injustice I have not concealed."
—*Ps.* xxxi 5.

" Behold, we are before Thee in our sin, for there can be no standing before Thee

FRIDAY.

THE CHURCH INVITES HER MINISTERS TO PRACTICE THANKSGIVING.

I. IN THE PRAYERS OF THE LITURGY.
II. IN THE RECITAL OF THE DIVINE OFFICE.
III. IN THE OBLATION OF THE SACRIFICE.

" And He said to him, Arise, go thy way, for thy faith hath made thee whole."
—*St. Luke* xvii. 19.

1. *Arise.* The Church, in the sacred Liturgy, puts into the mouth of the Priests the words "*Sursum corda*—Lift up your hearts ; " and (as Cardinal Bona explains), while thus exhorting others to train their hearts to God, we should expand our own also, in thanksgiving for His benefits conferred upon all His creatures. Then, in the words of our Spiritual Mother, do we call thanksgiving "truly worthy and just, right and salutary." It is "worthy," for (as St. Augustin says) it is a great dignity in man to have received a mind capable of acknowledging and thanking its eternal Benefactor—capable of seeking after, of longing for, its Creator; of praising Him, and fixing itself upon Him. It is "just," for justice requires that we render to all their due, and the unjust refuses : "The sinner shall borrow and not pay again" (Ps. xxxvi. 21); that is to say, he does not thank his Benefactor, nor pay Him the tribute of praise which He expects from him. He receiveth and will not pay (says St. Augustin); and what is it that he will not repay?—Thanksgiving. Again, it is "right"—

that it is to say, it accords with equity—that the creature, being unable to render the Creator like for like, should at least shew its gratitude in words and in effect, so that God may rejoice in beholding this equity: "Let thy eyes behold the things that are equitable" (Ps. xvi. 2). Let us at least offer this service of thanksgiving, since (as St. Augustin says) we have nothing else to give in return for that which we have received. Lastly, it is "salutary," for, in proportion to the abundance of our thanksgiving, the more abundant will be the gifts which God will bestow upon us; and hence our Holy Mother the Church, among the many incentives which she give us to thanksgiving, makes us repeat this sentiment, "Grant that by our gratitude for the gifts which we have received we may procure still greater benefits." Had we but understood the meaning of these words and profited by them, how great a treasure of Divine gifts should we not have acquired !

2. *Go thy way.* What do these words signify ? They signify (says St. Bonaventure) to go "from God to God, according to God, and for the sake of God;" and this we do in recital of the Divine Office. The Church, in enjoining this duty, bids us go from God to God, and according to God, and for God. All the Psalmody is a continual sacrifice of praise, and especially that part which is called *Lauds,* and so called (says Hugh of St. Victor) because it consists in the utterance of the Divine praises. Here let us consider how the Psalmist and the Three Children invite even senseless creatures to praise God; for, in truth, they bless their Creator (as St. Jerome declares), not with their lips, but by their works, and move those who behold them to the praise and admiration of their Maker. Let us recite these Canticles with affection; of heart, so as not to be of the number of those ungrateful men of whom it is written, "They remembered not the multitude of Thy mercies" (Ps. cv. 7). Truly happy are they who, like the Samaritan, value God's benefits as free and unmerited, and never cease to bless Him for them.

3. *Thy faith hath made thee whole.* Venerable Bede says that, while faith saves those who give thanks, ingratitude causes the ruin of those who neglect to give glory to God for the benefits

which they have received. Now, faith supplies us with the method in which we may fully and worthily render thanks to God. God's benefits are truly infinite, not only because they are innumerable, but also because we are infinitely unworthy of them. Infinite also is the majesty of that God Who dispenses them; infinite is the value of the Blood of Jesus Christ, through which they are bestowed on us; infinite is that eternity from which Almighty God has prepared them for us; infinite is the glory for which they dispose us. So Lessius. Hence we ought to give Him infinite thanks (as Cornelius à Lapide says)—infinite in their duration, with infinite affection, with infinite humility, with infinite devotion, and with infinite joy of spirit. But, since we are incapable of doing this because of our frailty and misery, let us offer the Eucharistic Sacrifice, which is so called because one chief end for which it serves is thanksgiving to God. Let us unite ourselves with our great High Priest, Who comes into our hands that He may supply for the weakness of our thanksgivings: "Giving thanks to God and the Father by Him" (Col. iii. 17). So will the rivers of Divine grace return to that God Who sent them forth, in order (as St. Bernard says) that He may cause them to fall again in greater profusion upon the soil of our heart. Therefore, said the Apostle, "In all things give thanks" (1 Thess. v. 18).

"I will sing to the Lord, Who giveth me good things; yea, I will sing t the name of the Lord the most high."—*Ps.* xii. 6.

"O Adonai, Lord, great art Thou, and glorious in Thy power, and no one can overcome Thee: let all Thy creatures serve Thee."—*Judith* xvi. 16.

SATURDAY.

THE NATIVITY OF THE BLESSED VIRGIN MARY REMINDS US OF THE BENEFIT OF OUR VOCATION TO THE PRIESTHOOD.

I. BECAUSE OF ITS FITNESS.
II. BECAUSE OF ITS DIGNITY.
III. BECAUSE OF ITS UTILITY.

"Of whom was born Jesus."—*St. Matt.* i. 16.

1. Mary, in Her birth, surpassed all creatures in purity and sanctity of body and soul (says St. Anselm) because She was to be "the Mother of Jesus." Now, we, though called to the Priesthood, were born sinners, and nevertheless God prepared for us as much grace as was necessary to render us worthy Ministers. Every one (says St Thomas) receives grace according to his vocation, and it is a general rule (says St. Bernardin of Sienna) that, when God destines persons to a high calling, He gives them all the gifts necessary to themselves and to their office. Had we not, therefore, received the grace of God in vain—had we not resisted the Holy Spirit—to what perfection might we not have attained! what merits should we not have acquired! Nay, God, as the Author of nature, prepared even our body for the influence of grace, giving us such a temperament, strength, and physical constitution as should make the exercise of the Priestly

functions easy to us. Let us thank God if we can say, " From my infancy mercy grew up with me, and it came out with me from my mother's womb" (Job xxxi. 18). Let us thank Him if we can say, "I was a witty child" (Wisd. viii. 19). Let us thank Him if we were as "a young man of excellent disposition" (1 Paralip. xxi. 28), "a young man ingenious" (3 Kings xi. 28). Let us thank Him if He has given us memory, voice, action suitable to preaching: "Who separated me from my mother's womb, and called me by His grace to reveal His Son in me that I might preach Him" (Gal. i. 15, 16). We may observe that Priests who have not been called by God cannot even perform the sacred ceremonies so suitably as those who have had a true vocation. Let us, then, pray to the Blessed Virgin, that we may correspond to grace, and make profit of our bodily faculties, in imitation of Her who made perfect use of Her gifts, both of grace and nature.

2. We venerate the birth of Mary, considering the sublime dignity to which "from all eternity" she was predestined ; and justly do we say with St. Ildelphonsus, " O blessed nativity, delight of the Angels, and expectation of the Saints, necessity of the lost, restoration of the ruined!" She appeared to the world like the dawn, which heralds the rising of the sun (says St. Bonaventure), and, since She was destined to be the Mother of the Redeemer, immense should be the joy of Christians in Her nativity (says St. Peter Damian). Now, we were born into the world destined by God to the great dignity of the Priesthood ; and well may we exclaim with St. Epiphanius, " How tremendous and adorable the gift containing so great a dignity!" But how have we preserved this dignity ? How have we passed our childhood and youth ? What are we doing to glorify our Ministry ?

3. We celebrate the birth of Mary, also, because She surpasses all creatures in the benefits which She has procured for the world ; for She hastened the coming of the Saviour, gave Him the material for our ransom, devoted Her life to assist in the work of redemption, suffered immense sorrows for us, and in heaven is our most powerful and clement advocate. Who, then (asks St.

Augustin), can worthily thank Her and praise Her? Hence, universal is the joy at the coming of this light: "A new light seemed to rise—joy, honour, and dancing; and in all there was wonderful rejoicing" (Esther viii. 16, 17). Let us, then (as St. Bernard enjoins), preach on this Festival in honour of Her Who has deserved so much from the human race; let us preach of Her as reverenced by the angels, and the desire of nations; Who had Patriarchs and Prophets for Her ancestors; Who was chosen out of all, illustrious before all. Let us make known to the Faithful that She is born Who found grace with God, and Who is the great means of our salvation, and of the restoration of the world. But at the same time let us remember that we, too, were born for the public good; for Priests (says St. Eucherius) are pillars supporting the tottering world by their prayers; they are the foundations of the world (says St. Gregory Nazianzen), the example and pattern of all virtues (says St. Prosper). Let us, then, pray to the Blessed Virgin to obtain for us efficacious grace, that we may fulfil our duties worthily; and, as we shall have honoured Her Nativity on earth, so will She, at the hour of our death, obtain for us a new birth in our heavenly country, so that we may be of the number of those whom She brings forth in this present life for a happy eternity.

"All the rich among the people shall entreat Thy countenance."—*Ps.* xliv. 13.

"Who is she that cometh forth as the morning rising?"—*Cant.* vi. 9.

FOURTEENTH SUNDAY AFTER PENTECOST.

OUR LORD TEACHES HIS PRIESTS TO DESPISE WORLDLY RICHES.

I. By a general precept.
II. By the example of true Priests.
III. By shewing the condition of reprobate Priests.

"No man can serve two masters, for either he will hate the one and love the other, or he will sustain the one and despise the other. You cannot serve God and Mammon."—*St. Matt.* vi. 24.

1. *No man can serve two masters.* This is a general maxim, reminding us of the Master to Whose service we are bound. We are "the servants of the Lord, that stand in the house of the Lord," and are invited to praise and bless Him continually (Ps. cxxxi. 1, 2). We have one only Master, because God is one (says St. Ambrose); and hence (says St. Cyril) all our study should be to serve God and to renounce worldly riches. Let us be well assured that (according to St. Thomas) God and riches are two masters contrary the one to the other; for, while God's service elevates the soul, the things of this world draw it downwards. He is a slave to riches who keeps them laid by in a coffer, as a slave keeps his master's goods; but he who has shaken off the yoke of servitude distributes them to others, and so makes himself their master. So St. Jerome. Therefore, he who makes good use of riches, and receives from them fruit of

eternal life, is their master (says St. Thomas); but he who
derives not this fruit from them becomes their slave. Let us
examine our heart and our conduct. Whom do we serve? What
do we set before us as the end of our actions? Are we moved
by temporal or by eternal interests? What fruit of eternal-life
have we hitherto derived from riches?

2. *Either he will hate the one and love the other.* This has been
the conduct of the Apostles and of all Apostolical men, who
have despised riches, considering them as instruments of the
devil in deceiving men. The devil deceives mankind by means
of riches (says St. Jerome). In proportion as men love God they
despise the goods of this world. Such contempt is here called
"hatred;" and, indeed, riches well deserve to be "hated,"
because they furnish armour to those robbers who seek to spoil
us of our heavenly treasure. They darken our understanding,
and turn us away from God's service (as St. Chrysostom says).
True Priests have ever been distinguished for this hatred; and
rightly so, for they are called to rise superior to all that this
present world offers. Thus does St. Cyprian declare that he who
is above the world can desire nothing from the world. St. Gregory also laments over the case of Priests occupying the place of
holiness in the Church, who raise themselves up with earthly
things for the sake of gain. Let us, then, apply this test to ourselves—Do we love God, and devote ourselves to His service so
entirely as to despise, and even to abhor, worldly riches?

3. *Or he will sustain the one and despise the other.* Unhappy is
the condition of the Priest who subjects himself to the devil for
the sake of money. He began with a small affection for the idol,
and with this stain on his soul rashly approached the altar, re-
gardless of the prohibition, "He shall not offer bread to his God,
neither shall he approach to minister to Him . . . who hath a dry
scurf on his body" (Levit. xxi. 17, 18, 20). For the "dry scurf"
(as St. Gregory points out) is a figure of avarice, at first causing
neither pain nor annoyance, but afterwards destroying the whole
beauty of the body; just as avarice, in its beginning, causes man
neither dread nor displeasure, yet ends by reducing the soul to
a horrible deformity, and to a hard slavery. Shall he who is

destined by his ministry to overcome the devil in himself and in others become, through his own covetousness, the base slave of so hard a master? For he who serves Mammon serves a hard master (says St. Augustin); he despises God, and wastes Divine grace, in order to acquire gold; for he who amasses gold squanders grace (says St. Ambrose). How many sacrileges are committed through this vice! We make no account (says St. Bernard) of the sacrilege of those who love riches and follow after worldly gain. Deliver me, O my God, from this vice, through the merits of our Lord Jesus Christ, Who made Himself poor for my sake.

" I am Thy servant: give me understanding, that I may know Thy testimonies."
—*Ps.* cxviii. 125.

" Blessed are Thy servants who stand before Thee always." —3 *Kings* x. 8.

MONDAY.

JESUS CHRIST PROHIBITS THE CLERGY FROM ALL SOLICITUDE FOR EARTHLY THINGS.

I. He forbids such solicitude.
II. He restricts their wants.
III. The reason of His prohibition.

" Therefore I say to you, Be not solicitous for your life, what you shall eat, nor for your body, what you shall put on. Is not the life more than the meat, and the body more than raiment?"—*St. Matt.* vi. 25.

1. *I say to you, be not solicitous.* Solicitude (as St. Thomas teaches) is excessive care of temporal things; and it is sinful, if the end of our actions rests in them, if we bind ourselves to them

unnecessarily, or if our mind is agitated by fear of losing them. Our Lord forbade solicitude, but He did not forbid labour. Labour is to be exercised, solicitude is to be avoided (says St. Jerome). As St. Chrysostom declares, bread is gained by bodily labour, not by solicitude of mind, and therefore solicitude and anxiety of mind are not necessary in order to obtain it. This truth especially concerns Priests, who should have another kind of solicitude—that is to say, such as pertains to the good of souls: "he that ruleth, with carefulness" (Rom. xii. 8). And this was St. Paul's solicitude, when he wrote to the Faithful, "I would have you know what manner of care I have for you" (Coloss. ii. 1). He speaks of feeling . . . "solicitude for all the Churches" (2 Cor. xi. 28). Such solicitude finds no place in the heart of Priests who are anxious in regard to temporal goods, for they who are intent upon secular cares (says St. Gregory) become insensible to spiritual matters in proportion to their anxiety as to exterior things. Let us inquire of ourselves whether our anxiety has hitherto been concerned with the salvation of souls or the acquisition of worldly riches. What has been the real object of our labours and efforts?

2. *What you shall eat . . . what you shall put on.* Man's wants are few: food and raiment are sufficient for existence. Those natural wants which we have in common with all living creatures must indeed be cared for; but (says St. Jerome) our Lord limits the needs of Priests to these things. Now, the more closely they keep to this restriction the more nearly do they approach the happiness of Angels, whose name is often given them in Holy Scripture. Do not the Angels differ from us in this respect (asks St. Chrysostom)—that they do not share our wants? Therefore, the fewer our requirements, the nearer our approach to the condition of Angels. Hence, when the Apostle would point out to Timothy the maxims which were to form the rule of the clergy till the end of the world, he said, "Godliness with contentment is great gain"—that is, contentment with that which is sufficient to life; and this sufficiency consists in "having food, and wherewith to be covered; with these we are content" (1 Tim. xi. 6, 8). To satisfy these wants, it is not necessary to have a divided heart,

nor to devote excessive labour to the supply of them; and we need not thus attempt to serve two masters (as St. Augustin points out). How great the folly of the Priest who devotes himself to worldly goods, supposing them to be full of delights, whereas they are full of perils! (says St. Augustin again.) Let us consider that all superfluities will either be taken from us in this life or after our death will fall into the hands of others—and, it may be, of those whom we should not wish to possess them. O Holy Spirit, light of the heart, make me understand these truths, and impress them on my heart!

3. *Is not the life, &c.* Almighty God has given us a soul made in His image; He has anointed it with the Holy Spirit; impressed on it the character of an eternal Priesthood. He preserves it, aids it, sustains it. Almighty God has given us a body; He has made it His living temple; He preserves it by His unceasing support, and sanctifies it daily with the Flesh of His Son. He has done that which is greater, and will He not do that which is less? (asks St. Jerome;) that is, will He not give us wherewith to live until the term of our life which He Himself has appointed? Had He not willed to preserve us He would not have created us: had He not willed to maintain us in His Church He would not have chosen us to be His Priests. Why, then, do we not confide in His Providence? When has Jesus Christ allowed His labourers to want bread? Was not He Himself the first to illustrate His own maxim, "The labourer is worthy of his hire" (St. Luke x. 7). He might say to each one of us, as He said to the Apostles, "Did you want anything?" (St. Luke xxii. 35.) Have we ever wanted anything necessary to life ? Nay, if we read the lives of holy Priests, we shall find that, the more diligently they laboured in the Lord's Vineyard, the more abundantly did He provide for them—far better even than for rich worldlings; "The rich have wanted, and have suffered hunger; but they that seek the Lord shall not be deprived of any good" (Ps. xxxiii. 2). Let us conclude with the words of St. Chrysostom, which are calculated to give peace to all hearts, if carefully pondered: "We are fed by God; why, therefore, need we be solicitous?" Let the experience of the past tranquillize us

in regard to the future, and put far from us the desire of heaping up treasure on earth, since we have it in our power to lay up treasure in heaven.

"The Lord is careful for me : Thou art my helper and my protector."—*Ps. xxxix. 18.*

"Give me neither beggary nor riches : give me only the necessaries of life."—*Prov. xxx. 8.*

TUESDAY.

—◆—

HOW TO GAIN EXPERIENCE OF THE PROVIDENCE OF GOD.

I. By IMITATING THE BIRDS OF THE AIR.

II. By RESEMBLING THE LILIES OF THE FIELD.

III. By LIVING AS CHILDREN OF A HEAVENLY FATHER.

—◆—

" Behold the birds of the air, for they neither sow, nor do they reap, nor gather into barns ; and your Heavenly Father feedeth them. Are not you of much more value than they ? And which of you by taking thought can add to his stature one cubit ? And for raiment why are you solicitous ? Consider the lilies of the field."—*St. Matt. vi. 26, 28.*

1. *Behold the birds of the air.* Our Lord (says St. Chrysostom) might have spoken of Moses, Elias, John, and others like them, who, taking no thought for food, were nourished by God. But, that He might the more deeply touch the soul of these first Priests of the New Testament, He made mention of irrational creatures, and took His argument from the example of the lower

animals. Among animals, He chose birds, as being a figure
of devout souls, who direct their flight to God, and who, like
birds, love to dwell on high, and take from the earth only what
is sufficient for them. Birds represent spiritual hearts, which
enjoy the free air (says St. Augustin). Therefore, in regard to
ourselves, the more spiritual the life we lead, the more certain
shall we be that our Heavenly Father will take thought to feed
us ; and the dearer shall we be to Him, the more we exercise
ourselves in holy contemplation, which (as St. Gregory says)
raises us above ourselves, and lifts us, as it were, into the air.
If this be so, "who will give me wings like a dove, that I may
fly" to Thee, O my God, by contemplation, "and be at rest " in
the loving arms of Thy Providence ? (Ps. liv. 7.) Then shall I
fulfil the great precept which Thou Thyself givest me by Thy
Prophet, "Cast thy care upon the Lord, and He shall sustain
thee" (Ps. liv. 23).

2. *Consider the lilies of the field.* Our Saviour chose lilies
among all flowers, and desired His Apostles to fix their attention upon them, that they might observe the care with which
God had adorned them. Lilies, because of their whiteness, are
the symbol of purity, and therefore we read that Jesus calls
Himself "the lily of the valley" (Cant. ii. 1), and declares that
He " feedeth among the lilies " (Cant. vi. 2). Hence, the expression "the lily among thorns" (Cant. ii. 2) signifies (says St.
Gregory of Nyssa) that chastity receives continual wounds from
temptations and scandals, and that no one can gather its fruit
who does not approach cautiously. Now, if we are diligent in
guarding our chastity, surely we shall not care for those temporal
goods which are wont to corrupt this virtue; and our Lord, who
has such special love for virgin souls, will not deprive us of temporal succour, of which He knows our need better than we ourselves. Moreover, let the Minister of God consider, with St.
Bernard, that the world is full of thorns ; that they are on the
earth, in the air, in his own flesh ; and that he cannot preserve the
white lily, the tender and delicate flower of chastity, either in
soul or body, except by God's power. And will not He Who
'oes that which is greater in us do also that which is less ?

Will He Who bestows on us an Angelical virtue deny us the vile food which He gives even to "the young ravens," or a fitting clothing, which He grants even to "the grass of the field?" Let Priests resemble the lily: "Israel shall spring as the lily" (Osee xiv. 6): and it will be seen (as it always has been seen) that Almighty God will move the hearts of the Faithful to provide for their needs. Thus, St. Paul spoke of the Apostles as "having nothing and possessing all things" (2 Cor. vi. 10). Therefore, let us lay aside that vain fear which is the origin of solicitude, and, the more we confide in God with simplicity of heart, the better will our temporal affairs prosper.

3. *Your Heavenly Father.* Although all Christians are God's children, good Priests are so also in a special manner by imitation and by obedience; for (says St. Augustin) we prove ourselves sons inasmuch as we fulfil His commands. He Who called us to this called us also to His likeness. Now, our Heavenly Father "maketh His sun to rise upon the good and the bad, and raineth upon the just and the unjust" (St. Matt. v. 45); and good Priests, as His children, imitate Him in this respect when they exhibit the Sun of justice, Jesus Christ, to the just and to sinners, and when they cause the rain of heavenly doctrine to descend upon them. For (as St. Augustin explains) we may understand in this place, not only the visible sun, but that Sun of which it is said, "To you who fear the name of the Lord the Sun of Justice shall arise;" and by "rain" is signified the gift of heavenly doctrine which is manifested to good and bad when Christ is preached. Again, whilst they imitate their Heavenly Father, good Priests also fulfil His will, so as to correspond more exactly to the dignity of His children; for they labour for their own sanctification and that of others, and this is properly God's will: "This is the will of God, your sanctification" (1 Thess. iv. 3). Being, then, children of God, can they fear that this omnipotent and infinitely good Father should allow them to want the necessaries of life? What earthly father is there who will abandon his offspring to hunger and nakedness? And, if He be a father—and such a Father (says St. Chrysostom)—He surely will not overlook His children in their necessities, seeing that not even human

fathers can thus neglect their offspring. If sometimes He allows His Ministers to want the necessaries of life, He does it as a physician, who restricts his patients in their food (says St. Augustin), though not on account of poverty or avarice, but through his desire for their entire cure. Let us trust ourselves to His providence, and we shall experience the effects of His goodness.

"The eyes of all hope in Thee, O Lord, and Thou givest them meat in due season."—*Ps.* cxliv. 15.

" Thou hast remembered me, O God, and Thou hast not forsaken them that love Thee."—*Dan.* xiv. 37.

WEDNESDAY.

THE VANITY OF EARTHLY GOODS, AS SHEWN BY THE EXAMPLE OF SOLOMON.

I. SOLOMON ACKNOWLEDGES THEM TO BE VANITY.

II. HE WAS THE VICTIM OF THIS VANITY.

III. HE IS SURPASSED BY THOSE WHO DESPISE VANITIES.

"But I say to you, that not even Solomon in all his glory was arrayed as one of these. And, if the grass of the field, which is to-day, and to-morrow is cast into the oven, God doth so clothe, how much more you, O ye of little faith?"—*St. Matt.* vi. 29, 30.

1. *Not Solomon . . was arrayed as one of these.* Priests, who have the holy Scriptures in their hands, should never lose sight of that book of Solomon entitled *Ecclesiastes.* In it the Holy Spirit shews us (says St. Gregory Thaumaturgus) how vain and useless is all labour and study undertaken for mere human objects. In order that He might enforce this truth the more strongly,

He chose, both as a witness and a teacher of it, a man in whom were centred all natural gifts—viz., talents, knowledge, fame, sovereignty, wishes, delights, pleasures of every kind—but who confessed, as the result of his experience, "that all is vanity and vexation of spirit, . . . labour and vexation of spirit" (Eccle. i. 14, 17). Thus (as St. Augustin remarks) this great book of the wisest of men was written in order that we might be convinced that, even should we succeed in attaining the apparently happy condition of Solomon, earthly goods could never give rest to the heart; and that we might resolve to desire that life in which is found, not the vanity done under the sun, but the truth of Him who created this sun. With the maxims of this book in our hands, we shall easily persuade the Faithful to despise the world, as St. Jerome persuaded Blesilla, Paula, and Eustochium. But, before we begin to explain the teaching of Ecclesiastes to others, let us carefully meditate on it ourselves, in order that we may acquire that true and solid virtue which (as St. Chrysostom declares) consists in the contempt of those perishing goods which are but dreams and shadows, and in the continual desire of those which are eternal.

2. *In all his glory.* Solomon's glory consisted in the singular and incomparable abundance of means which he possessed for satisfying all his desires: "I surpassed in riches all that were before me in Jerusalem: my wisdom also remained with me" (Eccle. ii. 9). And he made full use of these means, as he himself declares: "Whatsoever my eyes desired, I refused them not; and I withheld not my heart from enjoying every pleasure" (10). But what fruit did he draw from all this? He grew weary of his very life: "I was weary of my life when I saw that all things under the sun are evil, and all vanity and vexation of spirit" (17). Not only so, but he loved vanity, and was the victim of vanity, and so provoked the anger of the Lord: "his heart was turned away by women to follow strange gods, . . . and the Lord was angry with Solomon" (III. Kings i. 4, 9). Many of the Fathers of the Church are even of opinion that he was lost eternally; and, if this be true, he, with other reprobates, is now saying in hell, "What hath pride profited us? or what

advantage hath the boasting of riches brought us? All things are passed away like a shadow" (Wisd. v. 8). And we, considering his renowned wisdom, might apply to him St. Augustin's words, who says of those philosophers who are enduring the torments of hell, "They burn where they are; they are praised where they are not." What folly! What misery! What blindness!

3. *How much more you, O ye of little faith?* The lily, which is clothed by God Himself, surpasses all the flowers embroidered on Solomon's garments. The difference (says St. Chrysostom) is as that which distinguishes truth from falsehood. Let us consider, too, that Solomon in all his glory was yet less glorious in the sight of God than the Priest clothed with that chastity of which the lily is the symbol. Whatever the splendour of those garments of Solomon, yet they could not cover the stain which was on Solomon's soul and body: "Thou hast stained thy glory" (Ecclus. xlvii. 22). And what was this stain? "Thou didst bow thyself to women, and by thy body thou wast brought under subjection" (21). However poor the garments of the Priest may be, yet will he be more highly esteemed than Solomon, whose yoke was odious to the people, and whose flagrant idolatry was a scandal to them (III. Kings xii. 4). A holy Ecclesiastic, on the contrary, is God's faithful minister, for he loves truth, and not vanity; he professes chastity, and is not the servant of lasciviousness. How beautiful is such an order of men in the sight of God and man! "Oh, how beautiful is the chaste generation with glory, for the memory thereof is immortal, because it is known both with God and with men!" (Wisd. iv. 1.) If raiment contributes to respect, who has more honour than an exemplary Priest when he is clad in the sacred vestments for the celebration of his august functions? Let us, then, thank God, Who has bestowed so great benefits upon us, and let us pray to Him to deliver us from sin.

"Blessed is the man whose trust is in the name of the Lord, and who hath not had regard to vanities."—*Ps.* xxxix. 5.

"We have been seduced by vanity, and have not kept Thy commandments and ceremonies."—2 *Esdr.* i. 7.

THURSDAY.

———

OUR LORD'S REASONS FOR TEACHING HIS FIRST
PRIESTS TO TRUST IN DIVINE PROVIDENCE.

I. For the promulgation of the Gospel.
II. For the sanctification of the Clergy.
III. For the preaching of His truth.

———

"Be not solicitous, therefore, saying, What shall we eat, or what shall we drink, or wherewith shall we be clothed ? For after all these things do the heathens seek. For your Father knoweth that you have need of all these things."—*St. Matt.* vi. 31, 32.

1. *Be not solicitous, therefore.* Jesus Christ, sometimes by a single word, sometimes by a sentence, sometimes by a parable, was accustomed to dictate His moral teaching to the first Priests; but when He sought to impress upon them trust in Divine Providence He spoke in an extraordinary and unusual manner. He brought forward, as we may observe, no less than seven arguments, so as to guard against solicitude in every possible way (as Cornelius à Lapide shews). This doctrine was truly of the highest importance, and also most difficult to penetrate men's hearts; and He sought to rid His Disciples of all distress, and fears, and anxieties (as St. Chrysostom says), in order that He might make them, as it were, men of steel and adamant, to enable them to preach the Gospel courageously. Accordingly,

when He sent them on a mission—which was a kind of prelude to their future labours, in order to accustom them to trust in Providence and to cast off earthly thoughts—He said to them, "Do not possess gold, nor silver, nor money in your purses" (St. Matt. x. 9). In like manner, when He appointed the seventy-two Disciples to prepare a way for Him in every city and place into which He was to enter, He gave them this command— "Carry neither purse, nor scrip, nor shoes" (St. Luke x. 4). In this manner did the Apostles give themselves wholly, and for their whole life, to the propagation of the Gospel, detaching themselves from the care even of such things as are necessary to life. Thus, also, did they give men an example without precedent, which excited admiration, conciliated esteem, and raised them above suspicion; so that (as St. Jerome says) they did not appear to be labouring for lucre's sake, but for the salvation of souls. Their life, detached from earthly goods, and a life of continued heroism, was looked upon by the heathen as a perpetual miracle; and thus they were easily distinguished from the idolatrous Priests, who were known to be "filled with iniquity, malice, fornication, avarice" (Rom. i. 29). Let us adore our Lord's wisdom in disposing the Apostles for the propagation of the Gospel, and let us also profit by His teaching.

2. *For after all these things do the heathens seek.* The Clergy, who recognise the Apostles as their pattern of holiness, should regard detachment from perishing goods the beginning of virtue. They should remember that they must not become like the Priests of Aaron, who, through their rights over tithes, first fruits, and sacrifices, acquired an attachment to such things, and through their avarice merited that bitter reproof, "Wo to the shepherds of Israel, that fed themselves, &c." (Ezech. xxxiv. 2.) These Priests merited also our Lord's censure for dispensing children from the duty of providing for their parents so often as they brought gifts to the Temple: "The gift whatsoever proceedeth from me shall profit thee" (St. Matt. xv. 5). Priests of the Gospel, on the contrary, must look upon themselves as "good soldiers of Jesus Christ" (2 Tim. ii. 3); and it is shameful in a soldier of God, fighting for a kingdom, and under the banner

of a King Who knows well how to provide for His servants' needs (as St. Ambrose says), to be anxious about his food. The more the Clergy confide in Divine Providence, the more sensible experience will they have of God's care. Peter did, indeed, resign the whole world, and he received the whole world (as St. Augustin says). Surely, then, it is a disgrace for a Priest to have enriched himself (as St. Peter Damian says); it is a disgrace for him to leave at his death a large inheritance of his own making. It is no honour for a soldier to brandish his sword in order to capture a fly (says Cardinal Hugo); and in the same way it is not fitting that a good soldier of Christ should devote his energies to the acquisition of transitory goods of this life. Enlighten me to understand this truth, O my God !

3. *For your Father knoweth that you have need of all these things.* When Priests are detached from earth, how profitably can they preach detachment ! and how earnestly can they speak of Divine providence when they daily experience its effects ! This was the case with the first Priests, who on the Day of Judgment will condemn the covetousness of their successors, and whose Head and Prince admonished all the Faithful in these words—"Casting all your care upon Him, for He hath care of you" (1 Pet. v. 7). Now, the effect of their preaching was, that "as many as were owners of lands or houses sold them, and brought the price of the things they sold" (Acts iv. 34). If we cannot do as much as this, let us at least, in preaching and in private exhortations, impress on the mind of the Faithful a true idea of Divine Providence, as of One who takes care of even the minutest of living creatures ; let us impress on their minds a high sense of that sonship which is received by means of Holy Baptism, as a ground of confidence in their Heavenly Father. Our Lord said not " God," but " Father " (says St. Chrysostom), in order to promote greater confidence in His loving care. Let us inspire our people with contempt of riches, reminding them (according to St. Augustin's wise reflection) that the sweetness of such possessions is fallacious, and the labour spent on them fruitless; that they are a source of constant fear and peril; that their beginning is without providence, and their end without re-

pentance. If we succeed in teaching them these truths, their hearts will be purified; they will attain the heroism of charity, and, bestowing all their labour, not on the things of earth, but on those of heaven, will save themselves with abundant merit.

"Thou openest Thy hand, and fillest with blessing every living creature."—From *Ps.* cxliv. 16.

"Help us, O Lord our God, for we have confidence in Thee and in Thy name.' —From II. *Paralip.* xiv. 11.

FRIDAY.

THE CONDUCT OF SECULAR PRIESTS TOWARDS REGULARS.

I. THEY SHOULD SHEW THEM CONSTANT VENERATION.

II. THEY SHOULD ACT IN CONCERT WITH THEM IN THEIR MINISTRY.

III. THEY SHOULD ENDEAVOUR TO INCREASE THEIR NUMBER.

"Seek ye, therefore, first the kingdom of God, and His justice, and all these things shall be added unto you."—*St. Matt.* vi. 33.

1. *Seek ye, therefore, &c.* This great promise of our Saviour (which has been ever magnificently fulfilled) has sustained the courage of holy Founders in instituting religious Orders with the patrimony of poverty, and that of their innumerable followers in professing their rules. Of these Divine words it may be said (as St. Bernard observes) that they have produced in men throughout the whole world both a contempt of the world and

also the love of voluntary poverty; they have filled the cloister
with Monks, and the desert with Anchorites. The secular Clergy,
therefore, should shew special veneration to Regulars, who,
trusting in this promise, make profession of the fulfilment of our
Lord's counsels, and by their vows offer to God the holocaust
of the whole man. For (says St. Gregory) that is a holocaust
when all that is possessed is offered. Religious, in fact, offer
to God all their goods—viz., external goods, by the vow of
poverty; bodily goods, by the vow of chastity; and goods per-
taining to the soul, by the vow of obedience. For this reason
are they called, in a special sense, "Religious." If we have not
the courage to embrace the practice of Evangelical perfection,
we ought at least to admire, respect, and praise those who
have done so. If, therefore, we should at any time hear reproaches, calumnies, idle tales, political arguments, uttered by
sacrilegious lips against the regular Orders, let us imitate St.
Chrysostom, who wrote in their defence; let us imitate St.
Jerome, St. Augustin—nay, all the Fathers of the Church—who
have eulogised the religious state. Yet some Priests have
adopted the language of Protestants and Atheists in speaking of
these venerable institutions. "They are resolute in wickedness"
(Ps. lxiii. 6). They have made no scruple of outraging the holy
Founders by such language, or even the Church herself (whether
assembled in Council or dispersed abroad), who has ever held
such men in great esteem. "They have taken a malicious
counsel against Thy people" (Ps. lxxxii. 4). The poisonous
words of such Ecclesiastics furnish a handle to the wicked in
persecuting the religious Orders, and when such persecution has
spent its fury upon them it will most probably be turned against
the Clergy themselves. When the bulwark is once destroyed
the wall will speedily fall away: "The bulwark hath mourned,
and the wall hath been destroyed together" (Lam. ii. 8). In
what position will these Priests find themselves at God's
tribunal? What condemnation will not they receive from
those holy Founders of religious Orders who, like the Apostles,
have renounced all worldly goods, and who will, like them,
judge even the Angels? Let us beg of our Lord to preserve us

2. *Seek ye, therefore, &c.* They who seek the kingdom of God and His justice consider only how to flee from evil and to do good, trusting in God, by Whose Providence they allow themselves to be governed. If Priests have not this trust and this detachment, they easily give occasion to divisions and quarrels with Regulars, which at times have been only too common : " I hear that there are schisms among you" (2 Cor. xi. 18). And yet they ought to reflect that Religious, who have given themselves to the contemplative life, have "chosen the best part" (St. Luke x. 42). They pray continually, in order to draw down upon earth heavenly blessings, and to appease the Divine wrath, offering their own penances in expiation of the sins of other men ; for, in the economy of grace, God gives nothing without prayer, and nothing is refused to those who pray with the requisite conditions. They stand upon the top of the mount, with outstretched arms, to obtain victory for us over our spiritual enemies, as Moses obtained it for Josue (Ex. xvii. 2). Regulars who dedicate themselves, according to the spirit of their institute, to study, to the defence of our holy religion, to the instruction of youth, to the care of the sick, to the assistance of the dying, to the lodging of pilgrims, to the promotion of worship, to the administration of the Sacraments, to the ministry of the word, to missions in Catholic countries, or to missions to the heathen, are ever (as St. Jerome calls them) flowers and most precious stones among ecclesiastical ornaments. If the spirit of self-interest or ambition did not excite us against them, we might truly say that in the house of God—that is, the Church —we "walked with consent " with them (Ps. liv. 14). If we had the Spirit of God we should compassionate the defects of some Religious, and abstain from bitter censures, which do not become us, both because we have not the authority to employ them and because we are not ourselves free from vice; nor should we censure with "a torn mind"—that is, with envy and wrath (says St. Dionysius). If hitherto we have not acted as we ought to do on this point, let us endeavour to repent and to remedy our error.

3. *Seek ye, therefore.* If we seek the kingdom of God and His justice, we shall willingly use all our efforts to promote the

enrichment, increase, and prosperity of religious houses, as good
Bishops and good Priests have ever done. Especially we shall
persuade the young who have a vocation to retire into the
cloister, because (as St. Augustin says) the world is full of
perils, full of snares; and we shall be careful that they do not
choose a Convent in which observance of the rule languishes,
for they would easily lose the little fervour that they have, and
would expose themselves to grave perils. So will souls under
our direction find, not only inward peace, but " a hundred times
as much " as they may have left, "now at this time, . . and in
the world to come life everlasting" (St. Mark x. 29, 30). They
will await with tranquillity their future life, for (as St. Bernard
says) to those who are accustomed to deprive themselves of
worldly delights it is no trial to leave this world. Lastly, they
will receive immense reward in heaven from Almighty God; for
a man who is bound by vows (says St. Thomas) gives to
Him the tree with its fruits, and not fruit alone. Should we
ourselves be called to such a life, let us correspond to our
vocation, mindful of that excellent maxim of St. Bernard, " Easy
is the way from the cell to heaven; seldom does one pass from
the cell to hell." In such cases, however, there is need of great
caution, for sometimes it is a temptation of the devil, and not
the will of God, which turns a man away from the duties of the
ministry to which he has been called in the first instance. The
venerable Mariano Ancieri answered a parish Priest who fulfilled
his duties with zeal, but proposed to retire into the cloister,
"We all desire the same retirement, but who then will act the part
of Jesus Christ? Make a cell in thy heart, retire into it and
dwell there." Let us call to mind also the saying of the Apostle,
" Walk worthy of the vocation in which you are called "
(Eph. iv. 1).

" O Lord, reprove me not in this thing : sitting thou didst speak against thy
brother, and didst lay a scandal against thy mother's son."—From *Ps.* xlix. 20.

" Give us in godliness love of brotherhood, and in love of brotherhood charity."
—From 2 *Pet.* i. 7.

SATURDAY.

FEAST OF THE NAME OF MARY.

DEVOUT PRIESTS SHOULD HONOUR THE HOLY. NAME OF MARY.

    I. By making it known.
    II. By causing it to be venerated.
    III. By causing it to be invoked.

1. *And the Virgin's name was Mary.* We read of three occasions on which Jesus Christ spoke to His Mother—that is to say, first, when He was found by Her in the Temple, afterwards at the marriage of Cana, and lastly on the Cross. On the second and third occasions He called Her " woman," in order to point out that She was the woman, and He the seed, promised from the beginning of the world for our redemption (Gen. iii. 15). He reserved to His Ministers, beginning with the Apostles and Evangelists, the charge of making known to all generations the august name of His Mother. As we must speak to men of the first and second Adam, so must we also speak of the first and second Eve (as St. Epiphanius says)—that is, of Mary. On all festivals of our Lord His Mother also shines forth, and furnishes us with occasions of commemorating Her: " On festival days she came forth with great glory" (Judith xiv. 27). Therefore, let us make known to men that this name was assigned to Her by Divine Providence, representing as it does many of Her glorious attributes. It signifies "Lady" (says St. Peter Chryso-

logus) inasmuch as She is exalted above all others; it signifies also "Lady of the Sea," for She was destined to govern us in the stormy ocean of the world; it signifies also "Illuminatrix" or Star of the Sea (says St. Jerome), because from Her was born "the Light of the world." O Mary, be Thou my Queen, my Mistress, my Directress; give me the light I ask ; guide me in my voyage over this stormy sea ; save me from the shipwreck of sin, and make me attain the harbour of a blessed eternity; for Thou art the refuge of sinners, through Thee we hope for pardon of our sins, on Thy aid do we depend for the heavenly reward to which we look.

2. *Mary*. In this Name the blessed in heaven recognise their Queen; the just, their Protectress ; sinners, their Advocate ; the devils, their ever victorious foe. How much have holy Priests done, how much will they ever do, to promote the glory of this Name ! She is blessed among women, because (as St. Augustin says) She has given life to men and to women. Blessed is Her Name because it reminds us of one who is greater than heaven, stronger than earth, greater than the world, and who (as St. Peter Chrysologus says) contained God, Whom the world cannot contain ; who carried in Her arms Him who upholds the world ; who gave birth to Him Who gave Her being ; who nourished Him Who feeds all living creatures. What love does not this Name merit! a Name desirable above measure—a Name redolent of sweetness ! If the High Priest Joachim, with all the Ancients, gave an example to the people in honouring Judith, and calling Her name "blessed for ever," shall not we Priests celebrate the Name of Her of whom Judith was but a type (Jud. xv. 10, 11)? Let us say to Her as Prince Ozias said to Judith, "Blessed be the Lord . . because He hath so magnified thy name this day, that thy praise shall not depart out of the mouth of man" (Judith xiii. 25); let us repeat the praises of Prince Achior—"In every nation which shall hear thy name, God shall be magnified on occasion of thee" (*Ibid*).

3. *Mary*. The great means to "obtain grace in seasonable aid" —a means which we should practise ourselves and suggest to the Faithful—is to invoke this most sweet Name. In dangers, in

trouble, in doubt, let us think of Mary; let us invoke Mary (says St. Bernard); let not this Name depart from our lips, let it not depart from our heart. St. Anselm says that sometimes men experience even more speedy help by invoking the Name of Mary than by invoking the Name of Jesus; for, in truth, the justice of Jesus often suffers us to be tempted in punishment of our sins, but these temptations cease when we invoke the Mother of Mercy, who (says St. Bernard) discusses not past merits. In like manner, in undertaking good works, which are the fruit of redemption, let us invoke Mary, from whom redemption began; for in Her (says St. Bernard) rested the redemption of the human race, the ransom of the universe. Again, let us invoke that Name in order to prosecute the works of the Ministry with perseverance, and as a means of confirming our good resolutions. This is, indeed, the name of our Advocate, who has received from God (as St. Anselm says) the charge of obtaining help for the guilty instead of condemnation, and instead of punishment eternal reward. Being at the same time Mother of the Judge and Mother of Mercy, She is (says St. Bernard) most efficacious in managing the affairs of our salvation. Let us hope that the last movement of our lips may be to utter Her holy Name, in order that with this Name on our lips, like the dove with the olive branch in her mouth, we may enter the Ark of eternal salvation. So St. Germanus.

"How admirable is Thy name in the whole earth!"—*Ps.* viii. 1.

"In every nation which shall hear thy name, the God of Israel shall be magnified on occasion of thee."—*Judith* xiii. 31.

FIFTEENTH SUNDAY AFTER PENTECOST.

THE MERIT TO BE GAINED BY PRIESTS IN THE PERFORMANCE OF FUNERAL RITES.

I. BY ASSISTING AT THEM IN THE SPIRIT OF THE CHURCH.
II. BY EXPLAINING THEM TO THE FAITHFUL.
III. BY EXCITING LOVE TOWARDS THE CHURCH.

"Jesus went into a city that is called Naim, and there went with Him His disciples, and a great multitude. And when He came nigh to the gate of the city, behold a dead man was carried out, the only son of his mother."—*St. Luke* vii. 11, 12.

1. *A dead man was carried out.* When Jesus Christ dissuaded the young man from burying his father, saying to him, "Let the dead bury their dead" (St. Matt. viii. 22), He desired to shew that this work of mercy must not be preferred before preaching, to which office this youth was destined; because (as St. Gregory says) the former consists in burying in the earth those who are dead in the flesh, the latter in raising to life those who are spiritually dead. But, when Priests are not occupied in preaching or in still more important affairs, they doubtless acquire great merit, and perform a great work of piety, in burying the dead—greater even (as St. Ambrose declares) than clothing the naked or conducting the wayfarer on his journey, because they are conducting those who have set out on their last journey to their eternal home. The Priest, then, as the

Minister of the Church, must perform these rites according to the spirit of the Church, who intends in them to benefit all her children, both the living and the dead : thus will he merit reward from God, as Tobias is said to have merited it, according to the testimony of the Angel Raphael (as St. Augustin shews). We benefit the dead when our devotion, animated by charity, moves us to pray for them, and our example incites the bystanders to join in these prayers; for (as St. Thomas says) in this way are men moved to compassion, and, as a consequence, to prayer. We may benefit the living, not only by inducing them to pray for the departed, but also by means of the consolation thus afforded to them in the funeral rites of their relatives and friends; for (as St. Thomas says) these things are rather a solace to the living than a help to the departed. We may further benefit the living by awakening in the spectators the salutary thought of death, and by reminding them that, as " the just shall be in everlasting remembrance," so shall the memory of the sinner "perish with great noise," and that, although "the wicked may be exalted above the cedars of Libanus," yet after a short duration " they shall be no more." Funeral obsequies, performed in a quiet, decorous, and solemn manner by exemplary Priests, have often served as an excellent sermon, which has opened the eyes of the blind, saying to them, " O ye sons of men, how long will you be dull of heart ? Why do you love vanity and seek after lying ?" (Ps. iv. 3.)

2. *A dead man was carried out.* St. Ambrose traces a mystical significance in the burial of this young man, in the circumstance of his being carried on a bier, as symbolising the wood of the cross on which our Lord was laid, and which was the means of salvation to mankind. Now, the rites which the Church employs for accompanying her children to the tomb represent many doctrines, which learned Priests can, with great benefit, unfold and explain to the Faithful. By such rites she invites them to pray for the departed, shews how they are still united with them through the Communion of Saints, and thus sweetens the bitterness of bereavement; as though saying to them, " We will not have you ignorant, brethren, concerning them that are asleep,

that you be not sorrowful even as others who have no hope "
(1 Thess. iv. 12). Hence, all funeral obsequies are directed to
revive faith in the resurrection of our bodies, by which those
who have gone before us will live with us in the very same flesh,
and so shall we be always with the Lord ; as we hope from the
Divine goodness. Accordingly, in the burial of the dead, we
are often reminded of "that day of wrath, calamity, and
misery" on which " we must all be manifested before the judgment-seat of Christ" (2 Cor. v. 10). Further, the honours which
holy Church pays to the corpse are directed to Christ and to His
Holy Spirit, for the bodies of Christians are "the members of
Christ," and "the temple of the Holy Ghost" (1 Cor. vi. 15, 19).
It is thus, we hope, that at the sound of the last trumpet this
body will rise again, "conformed to the glorious body of our
Lord Jesus Christ," if, at least, the soul have departed out of
this life with the light of faith and ardour of charity, as signified by the lighted tapers which accompany the corpse. Observe,
then, how many salutary instructions may be derived from funeral
obsequies, with vast advantage both to the living and the dead.
Such teaching has generally a happy effect, finding its way to
the heart of the Faithful, open as it then is to spiritual
impressions by the thought of death and by the sadness which
the loss of beloved friends occasions. From such teaching we
may also draw the comfort which the Apostle suggested in miti-
gation of the affliction of those who mourn—" Comfort ye one
another with these words" (1 Thess. iv. 17).

3. *A dead man was carried out, the only son of his mother.* The
care which this widow took for her son's burial excited the compassion of the multitude towards her in her bitter grief ; for (as
St. Cyril remarks) extreme suffering powerfully moves to compassion and to tears. Far more will the Church conciliate the
love of the Faithful when they see how much motherly care she
shows at the death of her children. She charges her Ministers
to pray for them; she puts fervent prayers in their mouth; she
authorises them to offer the Sacrifice of expiation, so that (as St.
Dionysius says) the stains which they may have contracted through
human frailty may be quickly cancelled. She makes known to

all that her suffrages are not offered for those who are already in heaven (who certainly have no need of them), nor for the damned (who can have no redemption in hell), but for suffering souls in purgatory, to whom they bring immense benefit. Suffrages (says St. Augustin) profit those who are moderately good or bad. Finally, she confides to her Ministers the charge of blessing the corpse, of accompanying it, and depositing it in consecrated ground, of registering the name, and of duly performing all the necessary rites. These offices, when fulfilled with exactness and devotion, render the Church dear to the living; for it is thus that she shews her maternal compassion and solicitude in behalf of her children. Would that these Priestly functions had never been stained by negligence, avarice, or vanity! Surely such vices should disappear at the sight of a corpse! In that case we should not see the power of the Priesthood, in regard to this part of their Ministry, restricted by law, as is now the case, so that we have reason to confess, in the words of St. Ambrose, "I grieve not because of the law; I grieve because we have deserved it." Let us, therefore, guard ourselves from taking any share in such abuses; let us thank God that He still suffers us to live, in preference to so many others who are daily carried to the tomb; and let us implore His mercy in their behalf, and a speedy deliverance from the flames of purgatory.

"Shall any one in the sepulchre declare Thy mercy, and Thy truth in destruction?" —*Ps.* lxxxvii. 12.

"After tears and weeping Thou pourest in joyfulness. Be Thy name, O God of Israel, blessed for ever."—*Job* iii. 22, 23.

MONDAY.

—◆—

HOW PRIESTS ARE TO SHEW THEIR ATTACHMENT TO THE CHURCH.

I. By HONOURING HER.

II. By LOVING HER.

III. By DEFENDING HER.

.

—◆—

"And she was a widow, and a great multitude of the city was with her."—
St Luke vii. 12.

1. *And a great multitude of the city was with her.* St. Ambrose recognises a figure of the Church in this matron, accompanied by the multitude, and meriting by her tears the restoration of her son to life—a figure of the Church, because, he says, the Church recalls her younger children to spiritual life by the spectacle of her tears of sorrow. She was a widow, and in this circumstance we see a sign of the death of the Church's spouse. Every soul (says Venerable Bede) who acknowledges herself to have been redeemed by her Lord's death proclaims the widowhood of the Church, for the Church is made up of individual souls. Now, all the Faithful, and Priests especially, are bound to render a true honour to this great Matron. Let us honour her who is the Matron of so great a Lord (says St. Augustin). She is the Spouse of the King of Kings, and the Queen typified by Saba; and therefore (says St. Ambrose) she is assuredly a Queen, whose kingdom is undivided, and formed of various peoples from all parts of the world all united into one body. She is

or (according to St. Ambrose) the temple and sanctuary of
the Trinity, and (in the words of St. Peter Damian) the throne
of God, the receptacle of all heavenly gifts.   She is the
Spouse of Christ, formed pure and immaculate from His side, at
once our mother and a virgin, fruitful in progeny, chaste in
body (as St. Augustin declares).   All the promises which God
makes to children who honour their mother, all his threats
against those who dishonour her, may be understood of the
Church.   Now, the honour which the Church expects from us
Priests especially is, that we adorn her with our own virtues and
with the virtues of others (as St. Chrysostom says).   It consists
in a willing and absolute submission to her authority (as St.
Bernard tells us), whether in defining the truth or in prescribing
matters of discipline.   It consists (as St. Augustin further
declares) in paying her, with humility and cheerfulness, all the
service which she requires of us.

   2. *She was a widow.*   The obligation which this young man
owed his mother after he had been raised from death is a figure of
our obligation to holy Church, by whose tears we have recovered
spiritual life (says St. Bonaventure).   Hence, we ought to love
and honour the Church, as the Jerusalem which is above, the
holy City of God, the Mother of us all (says St. Augustin).   He
who loves not the Church (says St. Bernard) shews that he does
not love God.   Let us consider that our great High Priest so
loved her as "to deliver Himself up" into the hands of His
enemies for her sake (Eph. v. 25); and that before He consigned her to St. Peter's care He drew from his lips three times
the assurance of his love, in order to teach both him and us how
much He loved her, how much we ought to love her, and with
what eagerness we ought to promote her well-being.   Let us,
then, imitate the Apostles and all holy Priests, who have ever
implored the blessing of Heaven upon the Church—who have rejoiced in her glory, wept for her wrongs, fed on her doctrine
and sacred books, promoted her institutions, delighted in her
functions, her music, and her temples ; repeating the beautiful
words of St. Augustin, " Let us love God, let us love the Church ;
let us love Him as our Father, her as our mother."

3. *And she was a widow.* This widow doubtless needed the support of her son, and it may be that one of the motives for her inconsolable weeping was that she had lost this support. He was the stock on which depended the continuance of her family, and he was the staff of her old age. In like manner, it is for us to maintain and defend our mother the Church (says St. Augustin), being well supported in this by the Divine testimonies. It is the duty of Priests jealously to guard this holy Matron, whom the great High Priest committed to their guardianship when He returned to His Father. Now, to defend her (says St. Augustin) means that we will not suffer her to be ill-treated, either by wicked children or by still more wicked servants. Espouse, then, the cause of your Mother, O sacred Ministers of God; suffer her not to be insulted by wicked servants; let not wolves devour her; crush the head of the serpent who would sting her. You are the sentinels who guard the city; therefore be ever on your guard night and day (says St. Bernard); watch and pray continually, in order to discover the enemy's craft, to anticipate the counsel of the wicked, to find out their snares, to elude their pit-falls, to break through their nets, to frustrate their evil machinations. Take the sword, to support the doctrines, the rights, the liberties of the Church; and if you suffer somewhat in the battle you will afford a grateful spectacle to the angels, and will experience the blessedness promised to those who endure persecution for the sake of justice. Let us, then, resolve to honour, to love, to defend the Church; particularly that portion of the whole Church to the service of which we were bound at our Ordination.

" Jerusalem . . . because of the house of the Lord our God, I have sought good things for thee."—*Ps.* cxxi. 9.

" Jerusalem . . blessed are all they that love thee, and that rejoice in thy peace."—*Tobias* xlii. 18.

TUESDAY.

THE DUTY OF ZEALOUS PRIESTS AT THE SIGHT OF SINNERS.

    I. To consider the state of sinners.
    II. To imitate the compassion of Jesus Christ
    III. To weep with the tears of a mother.

"Whom when the Lord had seen, being moved with mercy towards her, He said to her, Weep not."—*St. Luke* vii. 13.

1. *When the Lord had seen.* This dead youth (says St. Bonaventure) represented the condition of sinners, and of those in particular who, by acts of sin, openly manifest their state of death ; for sin is truly called mortal, not only because it hastens the death of the body, but also because it deprives the soul of God, Who is its life. Thy soul (says St. Augustin) is the life of thy body, and God is the life of thy soul ; as thy flesh dies when thy soul departs, which is its life, so does thy soul die when God departs, Who is its life. St. Antoninus shews how a soul dead in sin is like a corpse—frigid, putrid, horrible to behold, and destined to hell, as to its eternal tomb. If a zealous Priest looks at this spectacle with the eyes of faith, can he fail of being moved to compassion ? Yet we ourselves may possibly one day be in a like condition ; we may have been so once ; we may even be in such a state at this present moment. Did not our Lord say to a Bishop of His Church, " I know thy works, that thou hast the name of being alive, and thou art dead ?" (Apoc. iii. 1.) If God

withdraw His aid we shall fall into mortal sin, and unless God Himself raise us up we shall remain in mortal sin through all eternity. As St. Augustin says, "Unless He direct thee, thou fallest; unless He raise thee up, then, where thou hast fallen, there must thou lie." Let us reflect seriously on this.

2. *Being moved with mercy.* The Apostle exhorts us to "put on Jesus Christ" (Rom. xiii. 14), to "put on the new man" (Eph. iv. 24), to "put on bowels of mercy" (Col. iii. 12), to love "in the bowels of Jesus Christ" (Phil. i. 8). Shall we not, then, imitate our Lord, Who was moved at the sad spectacle of this corpse, and Who thus (as Venerable Bede observes) gave us an example of compassion which He commands us to imitate? If Priests are not moved at the sight of so many men spiritually dead, and make no effort to restore them to life, is it not evident that they have not the spirit of Christ, although they may be clad in the sacerdotal vestments? They resemble in this respect the dumb idol which "is laid over with gold and silver, and there is no spirit in the bowels thereof" (Habac. ii. 19). They have "the spirit of Egypt"—that is, the spirit of the world—"in their bowels" (Is. xix. 3). Let us examine ourselves as to the impression which the sight of so many sinners and evil livers makes upon us.

3. *Weep not.* This weeping woman, being a figure of the Church, should remind us (says St. Ambrose) that conversion is not the fruit of our merits, but of the tears of the Church; and we, being Ministers of the Church, ought to weep in her name. We ought (as St. Bernard tells us) to place ourselves like faithful attendants between the Church and her Divine Spouse, to offer Him her vows, carry back to her His gifts, awake the Bride, propitiate the Bridegroom. Faithful Priests (says St. Ambrose) look upon the perils of their neighbour as though they were their own; they weep over the sins of other men, and sympathise with the Faithful in their trouble, as though suffering them in their own person. The Church has been confided to Priests, and therefore they should regard her sentiments and her tears as their own. How efficacious will our prayers be for the Church, especially if they be strengthened by fasting and

accompanied by tears! The tears of Jeremias obtained the shortening of his nation's captivity, and knowledge of the length of its duration (Jerem. xxv. 11; xxix. 10). One prayer of Daniel, made with fasting, and sackcloth, and ashes, with true contrition, bore its fruit in ample promises of redemption for the human race (Dan. ix.); and another prayer was rewarded by special revelations in regard to the afflictions and consolations of his people (Dan. x. 1). The Israelites received pardon of their sins and change of life through Esdras "praying and beseeching, and weeping, and lying before the temple of God" (1 Esdr. x. 1). The rebuilding of the walls of Jerusalem, which is a figure of the conversion of souls, began when Nehemias "sat down and wept, and mourned for many days, and fasted and prayed before the God of heaven" (2 Esdr. i. 4). The tears of the Apostles resulted in an abundant harvest of souls: "Going they went and wept, casting their seeds; but coming they shall come with joyfulness, carrying their sheaves" (Ps. cxxv. 6, 7). Why have not we followed their example? If we had done so, then our Lord might have granted us the resurrection of many —that is, the conversion of many sinners. Let us resolve at least to act thus in future.

"The dead shall not praise Thee, O Lord, nor any of them that go down to hell."—*Ps.* cxiii. 17.

"O Lord my God, let the soul of this child, I beseech Thee, return into his body."—3 *Kings* xvii. 21.

WEDNESDAY.

THE DUTY OF PRIESTS IN RECALLING SINNERS TO THE LIFE OF GRACE.

I. To APPROACH THEM AND TO TOUCH THEIR CONSCIENCE.
II. To ARREST THE COURSE OF THEIR VICES.
III. To REVIVE THEM BY MEANS OF SANCTIFYING GRACE.

"And He came near, and touched the bier, and they that carried it stood still; and He said, Young man, I say to thee, Arise."—*St. Luke* viii. 14.

1. *And He came near and touched the bier.* Our Saviour desired to console this widow before being asked to do so, and, in order (as St. Bonaventure says) to shew His benignity to all, He drew near of His own accord to the corpse. Touching the bier with His hand, He shewed (says St. Cyprian) that His body was efficacious for human salvation, and that His flesh was the source of life. We then, who are members of Christ, ought to draw near to sinners, without waiting to be summoned, without looking for reward; imitating in this way St. Paul, who of himself "came to them" (Acts xviii. 2). How well did those first Priests follow the example of their Master, Who drew near to us, sought and raised us from death! "The Son of man is come to seek and to save that which was lost" (St. Luke xix. 10). Let us draw near to them by means of preaching, which opens a way into the soul; let us draw near to them also by means of Confession, in which judgment is made, and sins manifested: "I will come to you in judgment, and will be a speedy witness

against sorcerers, and adulterers, and false swearers " (Malach.
iii. 5). So shall we touch the conscience, which is the bier of
sinners, on which (says St. Ambrose) they lie dead. How
sublime a Ministry is this ! what a glorious imitation of Christ !
Happy the Priests who grow not weary of fulfilling it ! For this
end let us employ all means, both natural and supernatural, even
as our Saviour employed His Divinity to work the miracle, His
soul to compassionate the widow, His body to touch the bier.

2. *And they that carried it stood still.* Vices (says St. Ambrose)
carry a man to the eternal tomb; that is, to hell. Now, the first
good effect of the Priest's hand which touches the conscience
of the penitent, the first aim of his exhortations, the first means
of disposing the soul for justification, is to arrest the course of
disorders : " Take away the evil of your devices, cease to do
perversely " (Is. i. 16). This is the proof of change of will, and
of the heart being rightly disposed for Absolution ; for simple
Confession of sins is but the leaf of the tree, whilst good works,
resistance to temptation, interruption of evil habits, are the
fruits which attest that the quality of the tree is changed (says
St. Gregory). If we keep not this rule before our eyes, we run
great risk of transgressing our Lord's prohibition, " Give not
that which is holy to dogs, neither cast ye your pearls before
swine" (St. Matt. vii. 6). For by "that which is holy" is
meant Baptism, the Body of our Lord Jesus Christ, and the
other Sacraments ; by " pearls " are meant the mysteries of the
faith; "dogs" are the lapsed who return to their vomit; whilst
by " swine " are represented habitual sinners, wrapped up in
the mire of their iniquities. How many Priests will find themselves in an evil plight at the hour of death, through failing to
observe this holy rule, and giving Absolution to relapsed and
habitual sinners without either ordinary or extraordinary signs of
penitence ! Shall I be among that number ?

3. *Young man, I say to thee, Arise.* Thus did our Lord give
proof of His almighty power in calling to life whom He would
(says St. Bonaventure) ; and, indeed, with less ease does one
awake a sleeper than that with which Jesus calls the dead from
the grave (says St. Augustin). It is not given to us to raise the

spiritually dead with equal facility, but we must rather imitate Elias raising to life the son of the widow of Sarephta, Eliseus raising to life the son of the Sunamitess, St. Paul raising up Eutyches (Acts xx. 9). Their method was to bend themselves over the corpse, to touch the dead limbs, to breathe on the cold flesh, to exercise in fact all their powers, in order to dispose the dead for restoration to life. We are taught by these examples that good Confessors should not abandon the amendment of sinners entirely to God, but should diligently co-operate with Him ; that is, they should touch the sinner's heart with efficacious words, and remove every obstruction in the way of his conversion. We should also imitate St. Peter, who, in raising Tabitha, "kneeling down, prayed" (Acts ix. 40); for, in good truth, we ought to beg of God that our cowardice, our ignorance, our haste, our pride, our inconstancy, be not obstacles to the conversion of penitents ; and that they be not "rebellious against the light," but, by the help of grace, may return and live to God. If we had acted thus, how many souls might have received Absolution, and might now be in the state of salvation ! By saying, "I absolve thee," we should have imitated Jesus raising the dead to life. Grant, O my God, for Thy mercy's sake, that the absolutions given by me may never be without effect.

"Shew forth Thy wonderful mercies, Thou who savest them that trust in Thee." —*Ps.* xvi. 7.

"Breathe, O Lord, into the face of sinners, the breath of life, that man may become a living soul."—From *Gen.* ii. 7.

THURSDAY.

THE CONSOLATIONS EXPERIENCED BY PRIESTS IN THE CONVERSION OF SINNERS.

I. IN TRACING THE EFFECTS OF CONVERSION.
II. IN DELIVERING CONVERTED SINNERS TO THE CHURCH.
III. IN STIMULATING OTHERS TO CONVERSION.

" And he that was dead sat up, and began to speak. And He gave him to his mother. And there came a fear on them all."—*St. Luke* vii. 15.

1. *And he that was dead sat up.* As man's bodily life is known by motion and speech, so the spiritual life, when restored to penitents, may be recognised by the raising up of the penitent's head from the earth, and by the utterance of the Divine praises by the lips which had been hitherto mute. How great consolation do Priests experience when they see a man newly converted, drawn out of the abyss of sin, restored to the free air of heaven, bitterly lamenting his past sins in solitude! "I sat alone, because Thou hast filled me with threats" (Jerem. xv. 17). Such a penitent lifts up his head to heavenly desires: "Let us lift up our hearts with our hands to the Lord in the heavens" (Lam. iii. 41). "He sits in the beauty of peace, and in the tabernacles of confidence, and in wealthy rest" (Is. xxxii. 18). He recites prayers of true contrition: "I will not spare my mouth; I will speak in the affliction of my spirit; I will talk with the bitterness of my soul" (Job vii. 2). He praises God, Who has given him life: "We that live bless the Lord, from this

time now and for ever" (Ps. cxiii. 18). What an acceptable spectacle is this to God and to the angels! What a consolation for
those who have taken part in producing it! But let Priests be
careful not to glorify themselves as though this were their own
work, for they are but rough instruments in the hands of the
one omnipotent and merciful High Priest: "Shall the axe
boast itself against him that cutteth with it? Or shall the bow
exalt itself against him by whom it is drawn?" (Is. x. 15.)

2. *And He gave him to his mother.* If the Church is our Mother,
to her must we hand over repentant sinners, that she may
rejoice over them, welcome them, nourish them with all kinds of
spiritual food. As the weeping mother received her son raised
from the dead, so does holy Church receive with joy her penitent
children (says St. Bonaventure). Elias was a type of Jesus
Christ and His ministers when, having raised the child, he
"delivered him to his mother and said to her, Behold thy son
liveth" (III. Kings xvii. 23). In such cases holy Church
acknowledges the Priest as "a man of God, and that the word
of the Lord in his mouth is true" (*ibid.* 24). How great is the
consolation of Priests in observing the joy of the Church! As
good children, then, of this Mother, who heaps upon us spiritual
and corporal benefits, let us show in return our true love for her
(as St. Augustin bids us); let us console her by the resurrection
of her dead children. Again, let us consider that she desires to
bring forth sinners to a new life, and that it is on the assistance
of her Ministers that her fruitfulness depends. Had it not
been for the aid of zealous Priests we ourselves had not been
born of her, for they were concerned in obtaining for us
spiritual life. Let us, therefore (as St. Augustin warns us), not
prefer our own leisure to the necessities of the Church. Miserable
sloth! of how many children hast thou robbed the Church!
Indolence, thou cause of innumerable evils! of how much good
hast thou deprived me!

3. *And there came a fear on them all.* As the multitude of
sinners takes away the fear of God, so does the conversion of
even one sinner tend to excite this fear. Thus it often happens
that one such conversion helps to produce many others, and men

are thereby brought to praise God for instituting the Sacrament of Penance as a powerful remedy against eternal death. The wise in their own estimation are astounded at beholding simple Priests effect conversions which the most renowned philosophers would have been incapable of producing : " Men shall fear him, and all that seem to themselves to be wise shall not dare to behold him " (Job xxxvii. 24). Further, sinners take courage, and say to Priests, as some said to the Baptist, " Master, what shall we do ? . . . and what shall we do ?" (St. Luke iii. 12, 14.) They will say, as the Jews, when stricken with compunction of heart, said to St. Peter, " What shall we do, men and brethren?" (Acts ii. 37 ;) and the Priest will answer, "Do penance" (ver. 38). Thus shall we see the number of converted souls increase, just as the conversion of St. Matthew gave occasion to the other publicans and sinners to have recourse to Jesus and be converted (St. Luke v. 29). When they perceived that the publican had found a place for repentance, then they no longer despaired of salvation for themselves (as St. Jerome points out). Let us resolve to labour in this Divine work, and let us pray to our Lord to give us fervour and constancy.

" But I have hoped in the Lord, I will be glad and rejoice in Thy mercy."— Ps. xxx. 7.

" It is fit that I should make merry and be glad, for this my brother was dead, and is come to life again ; he was lost, and is found."—From *St. Luke* xv. 32.

FRIDAY.

THE PRIESTS DEVOTION TO THE PATRON SAINT OF HIS OWN PARTICULAR CHURCH.

I. The motives of this devotion.
II. The way to excite this devotion in ourselves.
III. The means of promoting it among the Faithful.

" And they glorified God, saying, A great Prophet is risen up among us, and God hath visited His people."—*St. Luke* vii. 16.

1. *A Great Prophet is risen up among us.* Christ is rightly called a "great Prophet" by virtue of His Mediatorial office (as St. Bonaventure points out). Now, heretics have impiously asserted that to implore the intercession of the Saints detracts from our Lord's Mediation; but they were condemned for thisblasphemy by the Council of Trent. In reward of their virtues and faithful service, God grants to the Saints who reign with Him the privilege of presiding over particular cities: "Thou shalt have power over ten cities . . . thou also over five cities" (St. Luke xix. 17, 19). He grants to them that they "rule over people" (Wisd. iii. 8); and, as it is His will that human acts should produce their effect, He designs that the prayers of these protectors should procure benefits for their respective nations (as St. Thomas points out). Hence, by the consent of the Faithful and by the wise constitutions of the Church, kingdoms, provinces, cities, and even the smallest towns, have their Patron Saints assigned to them, to whom special honour is paid. There

G

is not a country in the world which cannot gratefully com-
memorate many graces and favours obtained at different times
from Almighty God by means of such advocacy. A city in
making choice of its protector places its confidence in his
patronage, and says to him, "Our life is in thy hand; only let my
Lord look favourably upon us, and we will gladly serve the king"
(Gen. xlvii. 25). The Saints, on their side, are neither insensible
to the trust reposed in them, nor ungrateful for the service paid
them, nor deaf to the prayers offered to them; for in heaven
"charity never falleth away" (1 Cor. xiii. 8). Hence we ought
to regard the Patron Saint as "holding up his hands, praying
for all the people" (2 Machab. xv. 12). We ought to be certain
that of him it might be said, "This is he that prayeth much for
the people, and for all the holy city" (ver. 14). What motives for
sincere devotion are these—motives which the Clergy should
ever keep impressed upon their heart!

2. *God hath visited His people.* God visits His people as often
as He dispenses His favours, and especially when He sends His
word into our hearts (says Venerable Bede). Now, the intercession of the Patron Saint obtains these graces, for on hearing
our groans he intercedes for us (says St. Augustin). It seems,
indeed, as though he said to us, as Jacob said to his children,
"God will visit you after my death, and will make you go up out
of this land" (Gen. l. 23); and therefore it is for the Clergy to
practice great devotion towards their respective patrons. This
devotion consists principally in imitating their devotion, God
having constituted His Saints (says St. Leo) both as a protection and an example to His people. Let us, then, study the
lives of these Patrons, and endeavour to keep them in our
memory; and, if we delight in celebrating their Festivals, let it
not be irksome to us to follow their example (as St. Augustin
enjoins). We are frequently charged to deliver panegyrics in
their honour, but this praise will be our condemnation if it be
not accompanied by imitation, for (as St. Chrysostom says) they
are to be imitated, or else they are not to be praised. Let us
recommend ourselves to our Patrons daily; let us invoke them
especially in the works of our ministry, in order that, whilst we

labour upon earth, they may record our efforts in heaven and keep us under the shadow of their protection : " He shall lodge under her branches ; he shall be protected under her covering from the heat, and shall rest in her glory" (Eccle. xiv. 26, 27). Let us prepare ourselves for commemorating their Festivals by mortification and the Sacrament of Penance, so that we may celebrate it by a fervent Communion, being purified (as St. Leo says) both in body and soul.

3. *They glorified God.* Almighty God is magnified by the honour given to His Saints, in whom He is "wonderful" (Ps. lxvii. 36), and therefore the Clergy contribute to His glory by promoting devotion towards their holy Patrons. They also confer a great good upon the people, whose devotion to the Saints is never without reward, for (as St. Bernard says) it is for our own rather than for their benefit that we venerate their memory. Let us, then, set a good example by reverencing their images, their relics, and the temples in which they are specially honoured ; so that in this also we may be the pattern of the Faithful, and may say in effect, " Take us, my brethren, for an example" (James v. 10). If fervour languish in us, it will langush in our people ; if we join without due devotion in processions and other functions held in honour of the Patron Saint, the devotion of our people will languish also; for "what manner of man the ruler of a city is, such also are they that dwell therein " (Eccl. x. 2). In our sermons, in the Confessional, and in familiar discourse, let us make mention of favours received through the assistance of the Saint, so as to excite love and devotion to him; let us remember that, though he is secure himself, he is solicitous for us (as St. Bernard says). So shall we enjoy his special protection, and our labours will prosper and be blessed.

" For Thy servant David's sake, turn not away the face of Thy anointed."— *Ps.* cxxxi. 10.

" I will not let Thee go except Thou bless me."—*Gen.* xxxii. 26.

SATURDAY.

FEAST OF THE SEVEN DOLOURS OF THE BLESSED VIRGIN MARY.

THE MOTIVES FOR WHICH PRIESTS SHOULD SUFFER.

  I. For the glory of God.
  II. For their own sanctification.
  II. For the sins of others.

"He saith to the Disciple, Behold thy Mother."—*St. John* xix. 27.

1. *Behold thy Mother.* St. John, who represented all the Faithful, and Priests in particular, received from our Lord the charge to treat the Blessed Virgin as his own mother; and hence we are especially bound not to forget the Dolours which this great Mother suffered: "Forget not the groanings of thy mother" (Eccl. vii. 29). Tobias was a type of Jesus Christ when, in recommending the mother to her son, he said to him, "Thou must be mindful what and how great perils she suffered for thee in her womb" (Tob iv. 4). Now, we know that the whole life of the Blessed Virgin was full of sorrows, and that She might truly say, "My life is wasted with grief, and my years in sighs" (Ps. xxx. 11). But the present Festival was instituted in honour of those seven Dolours which are commemorated in the first seven Responsories of the Office of the day. We know also that they were suffered from the most perfect love of God:

"For Thy sake I have borne reproach" (Ps. lxviii. 8). Let us, then, imitate Her by suffering for the love of God all the mortifications that He may send us, so as to be able to say, "For Thy sake we are killed all the day long" (Ps. xliii. 22). May She guard us from the danger of losing the merit of patience—a loss which is incurred by those who suffer for human glory; for there are some in the Church who in their sufferings are influenced by notions of vainglory rather than of love (says St. Augustin). May She teach us the lesson addressed to Priests by the Apostle, "Follow . . . patience" (1 Tim. vi. 11): "In all things let us exhibit ourselves as the Ministers of God in much patience" (2 Cor. vi. 4). Patience must be our chief ornament (says St. Augustin) if we desire to be the Ministers of Christ.

2. *Behold thy Mother.* Our Mother is the Queen of Martyrs, and She obtained this title through Her most bitter sorrows, in which (says St. Laurence Justinian) Her heart became a clear mirror of Christ's Passion, and a perfect copy of His death. She suffered far beyond the ordinary strength of humanity; She suffered far greater torment than if She had Herself been tortured (says St. Amadeus), because She loved Him for whom She grieved incomparably more than Herself. Let us ever recollect that we, too, must suffer if we desire to be sanctified, for the entire perfection of Priests consists in fighting for the truth even to death, and bearing all evils for the supreme good. If we would be martyrs without the sword of the persecutor (says St. Bernard), let us truly keep our soul in patience; let us remember that tribulations (as St. Laurence Justinian teaches) produce the following good results :—They glorify the Creator; they compel the unwilling to draw near to God; they instruct the ignorant; they guard virtue; they protect the weak, excite the torpid, humble the proud, purify the penitent, associate with God those who are in trouble, weaken the enemy, crown the innocent. Let us remember (as St. Cyprian says) that patience conduces to our sanctification by tempering our anger, by bridling the tongue, by directing the understanding.

3. *Behold thy Mother.* Our Mother suffered for the sins of

those who were the children of Her own mother, the Synagogue: " The sons of my mother have fought against me " (Cant. i. 2). We Priests have often to suffer for the sins of other men, and at such times we must not turn upon those who cause our suffering, but have recourse to prayer, in order not to lose the treasure of charity. Let us be assured that the more we are ill-treated the greater will be our reward in heaven, and that (as St. Augustin says) the reproaches of our adversaries serve only to increase our eternal treasures. Much must we endure in order to succour our brethren in soul and body, and also through the ingratitude of those whom we have benefited or sought to benefit. We must also be prepared to endure calumny and injustice without shrinking, and, on the other hand, to maintain the truth at all costs (as St. Gregory says). In short, the Priest (as St. Ephrem says) must be like the anvil, which when beaten does not bend, but becomes the stronger. Moreover, patience is a gift of God, which (as St. Augustin says) is a help in battle, and a protection from the heat. It is God Who gives us strength to suffer; else who would endure so much ? (asks St. Augustin.) Could man—or, if man, could man alone—sustain the burden ? God Himself is the source of our patience. Let us implore this great gift through the Blessed Virgin, and She will certainly obtain it for us.

" The troubles of my heart are multiplied ; deliver me from my necessities."— *Ps.* xxiv. 17.

" Thou hast not spared thy life, by reason of the distress and tribulation of thy people."—*Judith* xiii. 25.

SIXTEENTH SUNDAY AFTER PENTECOST.

THE TEMPERANCE OF PRIESTS.

I. IT IS BECOMING THEIR STATE.
II. IT IS BENEFICIAL TO THEIR HEALTH.
III. IT GIVES EDIFICATION TO THEIR NEIGHBOURS.

"When Jesus went into the house of one of the chief of the Pharisees on the Sabbath day to eat bread . . they watched Him."—*St. Luke* xiv. 1.

1. *When Jesus went into the house, &c.* Here we may admire our Lord's poverty, in that He condescended to eat the bread of others, and, while infinitely rich, yet shewed Himself as poor among men (as St. Bonaventure says). Now, Priests should imitate Jesus Christ in this especially, as being one of the principal duties of their state, thus leading others to imitate Him ; for (as St. Bernard says) those who are leaders of the people should be foremost in the following of Christ, so as to shew the way to the weaker brethren, according to the words of St. Paul, "Be ye followers of me, as I also am of Christ" (1 Cor. iv. 16). But what kind of imitation of Christ will ours be if our table is luxurious and replete with delicacies ? The Council of Milan prescribed that Priests should be "content with a frugal and sparing table," and another Council prescribed that their table should be "frugal, of simple viands, neither exceedingly delicate nor exceedingly gross, but of such medium quality as is expedient for bodily health." What, indeed, would remain for

the poor should gluttony absorb the superfluity with which we might succour them? What will remain to enable us to give an example of alms-giving, to expiate our sins, to acquire Paradise? Let us observe St. Bernard's rule in regard to temperance—that is, to look for food which is eatable, and not for such as is palatable and agreeable. Especially let us be careful to be temperate in drinking, for the Apostle warns us against excess of wine, and in the Old Law wine was forbidden those who were destined to the service of the Altar (as St. Jerome points out); and hence (says St. Anselm) Priests should drink so little as to seem scarcely to have drunk at all.

2. *To eat bread.* It is true that this Hebrew form of speech may refer to every kind of food, but it seems also to shew our Lord's frugality when He assisted at meals. He had no need of temperance in order to guard the health of soul and body, but we greatly need it, for we know well how many sins spring from intemperance. St. Jerome says that an intemperate man can never be regarded as chaste. Moreover, too much eating renders a man indolent, dulls his intellect, and chills his devotion (as St. Bernard says). Let us reflect on the immense advantages which St. Prosper mentions as springing from temperance. He says that it makes us abstemious, sparing, sober, self-restrained, modest, silent, serious, bashful; it restrains sensuality, tempers affection, multiplies holy desires, chastises vice, defends the mind from all storms of vice, drives away wicked thoughts, instils holy thoughts, extinguishes the fire of voluptuousness, kindles warmth in the soul. Moreover (as St. Leo says), bodily sickness usually proceeds from excess in eating and drinking; and therefore, if we would prolong the days of our life in order to serve the Church for a longer period, and to acquire merits for eternity, let us love abstinence: "He that is temperate shall prolong life." Let us put in practice the teaching of the Holy Spirit, "Be not greedy in any feasting, and pour not out thyself upon any meat" (Eccl. xxxvii. 32).

3. *They watched Him.* As the Pharisees watched our Lord's conduct at the banquet, so do the laity watch Priests in regard to their temperance. They watched (says St. Cyril) to see

whether our Lord would shew respect to the Law, or do anything which was forbidden by it. The laity censure Priests, discredit them, ridicule them, whenever they see them intemperate in eating or drinking ; for intemperance is a grave cause of reproach (says St. Thomas). All excess renders vile the Ministry of the Priesthood; but especially drunkenness, which, while it is a sin in all men, becomes in Priests (as St. Peter Chrysologus says) a species of sacrilege, for it extinguishes the Holy Spirit in them. It is a disgrace to pamper our appetites while we preach Jesus Christ, Who was the Master of the poor, and suffered hunger; it is a disgrace for us (says St. Jerome) to preach the doctrine of fasting with red cheeks and lips swollen through intemperance. On the other hand, frugality gains us more praise than sumptuous living, and greater dishonour accrues to us from exquisite viands than from simplicity in our fare; for gravity and sobriety, not pomp and delicacies, form the commendation of a Priest's table.

" O Lord, let it not be so with us, that as yet their meat was in their mouth, and the wrath of God came upon them."—*Ps.* lxxvii. 29, 30.

" I chastise my body and bring it into subjection, lest perhaps, when I have preached to others, I myself should become a cast-away."—1 *Cor.* ix. 27.

MONDAY.

THE VICE OF INCONTINENCE.

I. ITS DEFORMITY IN PRIESTS.
II. THE DIFFICULTY OF ITS CURE.
III. THE REMEDIES.

"And behold there was a certain man before Him that had the dropsy . . But He, taking him, healed him, and sent him away."—*St. Luke* xiv. 2, 4.

1. *Behold there was a certain man that had the dropsy.* This rich man may be considered (says Venerable Bede) as a figure of the incontinent. As St. Basil says, the thirst of the dropsical expresses the insatiable character of concupiscence, which makes the sensual continually thirst after vile pleasures. Now, this vice, which in all men (as St. Prosper says) is as a hook by which Satan draws them to destruction, renders Priests especially hideous, since (says St. Isidore) it takes from them the source and dignity befitting their state. It renders them (says St. Peter Damian) unworthy to offer the most holy Sacrifice of the Altar, seeing that by impurity they have already devoted themselves to the service of the evil spirit. It casts discredit upon their teaching, which is ill received—nay, despised—by the people, who soon become aware of the lust of those who preach chastity. Are not you, who are constituted preachers of chastity, ashamed to be servants of sensuality? asks St. Peter Damian. Moreover, it is a grave stain upon the character of the whole Church, because, as she receives lustre from the purity of her Ministers,

so is she also defiled by their scandalous incontinence. Let us weep at the foot of the Cross for the persecution which the Church suffers from incontinent Priests—a persecution which never ceases (says St. Augustin)—a persecution which is most bitter (as St. Bernard declares).

2. *Was before Him.* This man was before Jesus, but he took no step to free himself from his mortal sickness; he did not utter a word to ask for cure (says St. Cyril). In like manner dissolute Priests stand before Jesus, approach close to Him in their Ministry, scruple not to present themselves at the Altar, but do nothing to help themselves, and do not even pray to Him to take them out of this miserable state. It is the penalty of this sin that those who give way to it are not aware of its horror, for among the daughters of lust enumerated by St. Gregory, and after him by St. Thomas, are " blindness of mind, hatred of God, love of this present world, horror of a future life." These men remain far off from God, and have no thought of returning to His feet, for, being inflamed by the spirit of fornication, "They will not set their thoughts to return to their God " (Osee v. 4). Indeed (as St. Chrysostom says), neither the admonitions of Superiors, nor the counsels of good friends, nor the fear of chastisement, nor the danger of being put to shame, suffice to enlighten them. And this is no wonder, because (as St. Thomas says) this vice extinguishes the judgment, and draws the whole soul to sensuality; moreover, this sin is highly pleasing to the devil, because it adheres to men so closely that they cannot free themselves from it without great difficulty. How many wretched Priests have been unable to escape eternal damnation from having, but once only, defiled themselves with this infernal pitch ! Who can assure me that I shall be kept free from it ? Thou, O my Jesus, canst alone preserve me from it, and from Thee do I look for this signal grace !

3. *He, taking him, healed him, and sent him away.* Our Saviour's beneficent hand healed this man in a moment, nor did He wait to be asked (as St. Cyril observes). He took him by the hand (says St. Bonaventure), to denote the infusion of grace which He bestows upon sinners; He healed him, to express the expia-

tion of his guilt ; He sent him away free, to signify the remission of his sin. Now, if Jesus did all this of His own accord, without any request being made, what will He not do for His Ministers if, with humble and contrite heart, they implore Him to deliver them from this cursed vice ? Let them pray to Him, then, to " put forth " His pitiful hand, and " take them out, and deliver them " from these putrid stifling "waters" (Ps. cxliii. 7). Let them pray to our Lord Jesus Christ to do it for His own glory—that is to say, that His holy Name may not be outraged, as it is, by the incontinence of His Ministers. Then will He answer them, " For My own sake, for My own sake will I do it, that I may not be blasphemed " (Is. xlviii. 9). Let them not say that they cannot overcome this vice, nor resist the incentives of the flesh, when the almighty power of their Lord will help them. "Say not," says St. Augustin, "I cannot hold and restrain my flesh, for thou art aided that thou mayest. The Lord helps thee on thy bed of pain. . . . Submit thyself to Him Who made thee, in order that that which is made for thee may serve thee: if thou serve God, thy flesh will serve thee."

" I am become miserable, and am bowed down even to the end . . . for my loins are filled with illusions, and there is no health in my flesh."—*Ps.* xxxvii. 7 8.

" Preserve my body from destruction, and from the snare of an unjust tongue, and from the lips of them that forge lies."—From *Eccle.* li. 3.

TUESDAY.

HOW PRIESTS SHOULD PROMOTE THE DUE OBSERVANCE OF HOLY DAYS.

I. BY INSTRUCTING THE FAITHFUL AS TO THIS OBLIGATION
II. BY CONTRIBUTING TO ITS FULFILMENT.
III. BY SILENCING THOSE WHO IMPUGN IT.

" And Jesus, answering, spoke to the lawyers and Pharisees, saying, Is it lawful to heal on the Sabbath day ? But they held their peace . . . And, answering them, He said, Which of you shall have an ass or an ox fall into a pit, and will not immediately draw him out on the Sabbath day ? And they could not answer Him to these things."—*St. Luke* xiv. 4, 6.

1. *Is it lawful to heal on the Sabbath day ?* Jesus Christ asked this question in order to teach His followers to inquire of His Priests respecting the sanctification of Holy days: "Ask the Priests the law" (Agg. ii. 12). At the same time He imposed on Priests the obligation of knowing perfectly the extent of this precept—partly divine and partly ecclesiastical, as it is—as well as of deciding, with the authority of teachers, all doubts which might be proposed to them. Let Priests know the law (says St. Jerome), for if they are ignorant of it it is a sign that they are not true Priests of the Lord. How profitable are the instructions of Priests for promoting the observance of Holy days, and especially in hindering the Faithful from spending them, as the Jews did, in mere bodily rest, or in dissipation and self-indulgence, or frivolity. But (as Venerable Bede says) the people must be taught that they should abstain from servile

works on Holy days for the purpose of employing themselves in works of piety and charity. As St. Chrysostom says, Almighty God has given these days to the Faithful in order that, by withdrawing from the care of temporal things, they may be wholly employed in those that are spiritual. For want of such instruction the Faithful render themselves deserving of the reproofs which Almighty God gave the Jews, who celebrated "lying Sabbaths"—that is to say (as St. Chrysostom explains), they were not intent on spiritual things, on sobriety, modesty, and hearing the word of God, but, on the contrary, became slaves to their bellies, and indulged in drunkenness, excess of food, and sensual delights. If instructions of this kind were given to children, and repeated frequently, we should not witness so great profanation of Holy days; or, at least, the number of sins would be diminished.

2. *Which of you shall have an ass or an ox, &c. ?* Our Saviour solved the question by shewing the Pharisees that they did not hesitate to violate the Sabbath for purposes of avarice, although they reproved Him for breaking it for a work of charity (says Venerable Bede). Our great High Priest did, indeed, work many miracles on the Sabbath, and chose to suffer many injuries for this pretended violation of it, in order to teach us, His Ministers, that by no means whatever must any works which tend to the salvation of our brethren (as St. Augustin says) be omitted on the Sabbath day. By enduring these humiliations He merited for us the grace to work the greatest spiritual cures on these days; and thus, on the old Sabbath day, and on the Lord's day, which is now its substitute, the greatest numbers of the Faithful are wont to approach the tribunal of Penance for the healing of their spiritual infirmities. A good Priest may therefore say with St. Chrysostom, "I keep the law of the Sabbath by healing the sick." Let us, then, endeavour to administer the Sacrament of Penance, to men especially, on Holy days, since women have greater facilities for receiving it on other days of the week. Thus (as St. Thomas inculcates) we shall enable men, with great benefit to themselves, to communicate on every Lord's day. Moreover, let us keep people engaged in the sacred

functions, inviting them (in St. Augustin's words) to come if possible to evening devotions, and to pray in the assembly of the Church for their sins. Lastly, let Parish Priests give sermons and catechisms, according to the wise directions of the Church, and let them be assisted in this work by other Priests. So shall the true rest of the Faithful be found in hearing the word of God. Let us be certain that the sanctification of Holy days depends in great measure on the zeal of Ecclesiastics.

3. *And they could not answer Him to these things.* If Jesus Christ closed the mouth of His enemies, let us also close the mouth of those who "have mocked at His Sabbaths" (Sam. i. 7). Let us close the mouth of those who seek the destruction and profanation of all Holy days : " They said in their hearts, the whole kindred of them together, let us abolish all the festival days of God from the land" (Ps. lxxiii. 8). Such men are the devil's instruments, who (as St. Jerome says) uses every effort to hinder the sanctification of Holy days, in order to deprive God of His honour, and men's souls of salvation. Let us proclaim God's threats against those who violate His festivals: " They grievously violated my Sabbaths ; I said, therefore, that I would pour out my indignation upon them " (Ezech. xx. 18). Let us point out how Almighty God prospers and blesses in body and soul those who keep Holy days in a becoming manner, " Then shalt thou be delighted in the Lord, and I will lift thee up above the high places of the earth, and will feed thee with the inheritance of Jacob" (Is. lviii. 14). Let us explain the antiquity, the reasonableness, and the justice, of the institution of Holy days, and how God Himself "sanctified them" (Gen. iii. 2). This is what good Preachers have always done, and we hy imitating them shall share their blessedness.

" They that hate Thee have made their boast in the midst of Thy solemnity."— *Ps* lxxiii. 4.

" Let me not defraud myself of a good day, O Lord, and let not the part of a good gift overpass me."—From *Eccles.* xiv. 14.

WEDNESDAY.

THE CLERGY AT SOCIAL ENTERTAINMENTS, AND IN THEIR INTERCOURSE WITH THE LAITY.

I. HOW THEY OUGHT TO REGARD SUCH FESTIVITIES.
II. THE END THEY SHOULD PROPOSE TO THEMSELVES.
III. THE SUBJECTS OF THEIR DISCOURSE.

" And He spoke a parable also to them that were invited, marking how they chose the first seats at the table, saying to them, When thou art invited to a wedding, sit not down in the first place, lest perhaps one more honourable than thou be invited by him, and he that invited thee and him come and say to thee, Give this man place ; and then thou begin with shame to take the lowest place."— *St. Luke* xiv. 7—9.

1. *Marking how they chose the first seats.* At this banquet our Lord found Himself in the midst of enemies, who watched His actions in order to censure them—in the midst of the sick in body, as was the man who had the dropsy—of the sick in soul, as were those proud ambitious men who were watching Him in order that they might convict Him, and who were choosing the chief seats to gratify their pride. Now, the position of Priests at worldly festivities, and in their intercourse with the laity, resembles that of our Lord on this occasion. For, first, they are surrounded by those who are watching them and seeking to find some blot in them, unmindful of the Divine command, "Lie not in wait, nor seek after wickedness in the house of the just" (Prov. xxiv. 15). It is better, therefore, not to be present at

such entertainments, so as to avoid calumnies, and to escape the danger of finding a bad construction put upon our words, however harmless they may be : " Eat not with an envious man, and desire not his meats, because, like a soothsayer and diviner, he thinketh that which he knoweth not. 'Eat and drink,' will he say to thee, and his mind is not with thee. The meats which thou hast eaten thou shalt vomit up, and shalt lose thy beautiful words" (Prov. xxiii. 6, 8). Again, Priests are there in the midst of the sick—that is to say, in the midst of vicious persons ; for vices are the maladies of the soul, and it is easy enough for us to be thereby infected, because (as St. Ambrose says) they cause us to lose our time in things extraneous to our Ministry, and induce in us a desire for feasting. Moreover, we cannot shut our ears to the worldly conversation usual on such occasions, nor can we hinder it without giving offence. Let us call to mind our own experience, and we shall acknowledge this to be too certain truth. Let us, then, ask ourselves whether we are altogether free from blame in these matters.

2. *When thou art invited to a wedding.* Jesus Christ did not forbid social entertainments, neither did He Himself avoid them ; but, on the contrary, for frequenting them He was even reproachfully called "a glutton and a wine-drinker" (St. Matt. xi. 19). Whilst He allowed the Baptist to take the way of fasting, He Himself chose a different path. As St. Chrysostom says, they were like two hunters coming on their prey from opposite directions ; St. John being conspicuous for his fasting, while our Lord, on the contrary, frequented the tables of publicans. The end which He proposed to Himself (says St. Cyril) was to benefit the guests by means of His teaching and miracles; and thus, in this banquet, while He cured the man who had the dropsy, He also taught humility. This, then, should be the object of Priests when they find themselves obliged to assist at banquets or assemblies : let them seek to cure some man who has the dropsy—that is (according to the mystical sense of the word, as understood by the Fathers), the proud, the avaricious, or the luxurious. But how often has the case been different ! How often have Priests, who should have cured others, fallen sick themselves, even to death !

Many (as St. Chrysostom says) have on such occasions been ensnared and set on fire by concupiscence.

3. *Sit not down in the first place.* Observe how our Lord commences His teaching. We never read in the Gospel of His being present at banquets without giving some salutary instruction to the guests ; thus teaching His Ministers (says St. Cyril) that, when present at worldly festivities, they should not waste the time, but occupy it in instilling heavenly doctrines into the hearts of those who entertain them. Thus did St. Francis Xavier act during his sea voyage, and in all places where he stayed. Such, too, was the practice of Blessed Peter Faber, the first disciple of St. Ignatius, who recommended Priests on entering a house to recite the Canonical hours, or to hold some pious discourse, in order to shew themselves to be spiritual men, to preserve themselves from temptations, and to benefit others by salutary teaching. So will Ecclesiastics, like the salt of the earth, season the minds of their hearers (says St. Gregory); otherwise they will readily expose themselves to contempt (as St. Jerome says). If we have neither the courage nor the aptness to behave in this manner, we shall do well to avoid accepting any hospitality from the laity—frequenting only the table of our Bishop. Let us examine ourselves in regard to our past conduct in this respect ; let us resolve to regulate our behaviour more wisely in future, that we may not have this subject of remorse at the hour of death.

" With men that work iniquity, and I will not communicate with the choicest of them."—*Ps.* cxl. 4.

" I will not go into the house of feasting, to sit with them, and to eat and drink."—From *Jerem.* xvi. 8.

THURSDAY.

———◆———

ON THE DESIRE OF PROMOTION TO THE EPISCOPATE.

I. The presumption of such a desire.
II. The danger to which it gives rise.
III. The disgrace attending it.

———◆———

"But when thou art invited go, sit down in the lowest place, that when he who inviteth thee cometh he may say to thee, Friend, go up higher. Then shalt thou have glory before them that sit at table with thee."—*St. Luke* xiv. 10.

1. *Sit down in the lowest place.* In these words our Lord not only forbids all ambitious desire of the rank of Bishop, but also commands His Priests to seek the lowest place (as St. Chrysostom explains). It is, then, presumption alone that can move Priests to seek this office. It is true that the Apostle said, "If a man desire the office of a bishop, he desireth a good work" (1 Tim. iii. 1); but in his time there was nothing to be desired in the Episcopate except a work which was indeed supremely good —that is to say, martyrdom. So St. Thomas. In those times, indeed (as St. Gregory declares), they who held rule over the Faithful were the first to meet the torments of martyrdom. Thus, the Apostle had no sooner praised this desire than he showed how much there was to be feared as regards the object in view, by enumerating all its obligations. Now, three things are to be considered in the Episcopate—viz., (i.) the labour for the souls of others which it implies, (ii.) the eminence of the rank, and (iii.) the temporal emoluments. The first is a laudable object of desire, but

the second and third are undoubtedly vanity; and, since these things are so intimately connected that one cannot be desired without the other, the desire must be always attended with presumption (as St. Thomas explains). Does not experience indeed show us that those Priests who desire the Episcopate are presumptuous? Has the devil ever tempted us with this presumption ? Have we resisted him ?

2. *Friend, go up higher.* Almighty God, Who calls the humble His friends, has often said to the worthiest Priests, "Go up higher"—that is, (as St. Bonaventure explains), to higher honour and dignity. Yet these Priests have greatly feared—some have earnestly refused—to undertake such a charge; others have obeyed with trembling and weeping, looking upon it, with St. Augustin, as a punishment for their sins. For they well understood that Bishops have to give account to God for the souls of others, and this renders their own salvation most difficult (as St. Chrysostom points out). Certainly (says St. Laurence Justinian) there is no employment more perilous than the cure of souls; in no other office (says St. Gregory) is there so great labour, in no other is there so great peril. Therefore, if we love our own salvation, let us put far from us so dangerous a desire, and let us not seek to be removed from humble posts, except in obedience to the will of God as manifested in the commands of our Superiors. How many unhappy men would have reigned eternally in heaven had they remained simple Priests, whereas they are now suffering the torments of hell for their presumption !

3. *Then shalt thou have glory, &c.* As it is glorious to attain promotion without having first desired it, so is it shameful to gain it by force of ambitious practices. The mere desire of it (says St. Cyril) is a sign of rashness in a Priest, and covers all his merit with disgrace. However great a Priest's merit may be, it is indecorous to desire the Episcopate (says St. Augustin). In fact, no sooner is such a desire manifested by a Priest than all look upon him as foolish ; for who that is wise would subject himself to such servitude and such peril ? All men look upon him as presumptuous, as though supposing himself to surpass others both in the active and contemplative life; for (as St. Thomas says) a

Bishop ought to excel in both. All men look upon him as condemned already, especially if he have asked for this post, for he who asks for himself is already judged (says St. Bernard). All men think him undeserving, precisely because he desires it, for, (as the same Saint says) those who hesitate and refuse are such as should be compelled to undertake the office. O my God, make me understand the weight of the Episcopate, that I may never desire it for myself, and may pray for those who sustain so great a burden !

" The Lord is the keeper of little ones ; I was humbled and He delivered me."— *Ps.* cxiv. 6.

" I will make myself meaner than I have done ; and I will be little in my own eyes."—2 *Kings* vi. 22.

FRIDAY.

—◆—

THE VANITY OF PRIESTS HUMBLED IN DEATH.

   I. BY THE MANNER OF THEIR DEATH.
   II. BY THE CIRCUMSTANCES OF THEIR DEATH.
   III. BY COMPARISON WITH THE DEATH OF OTHERS.

—◆—

" Because every one that exalteth himself shall be humbled, and he that humbleth himself shall be exalted."—*St. Luke* xiv. 11.

1. *Every one that exalteth himself shall be humbled.* It is a great evil and a frightful peril (says St. Bernard) for any man to exalt himself above the truth, and to prefer himself before another,

or even his superior. We have all to enter eternity by the gate of death, and therefore there will be no danger in finding ourselves lower than necessary; but there will be great peril if we are only a finger's breadth too high, so as to strike against the doorway and bruise our head. For, should a Priest be "exalted in honour as an eagle, and set his nest among the stars, thence will God bring him down," and humble him in death (Abdias i. 4). It often happens that for such a Priest Almighty God decrees a kind of death which truly humbles him; and thus many die wholly abandoned, "no one being able to help them" (2 Machab. iii. 28). Many are struck with sudden death, as were Heli and Oza; many others are devoured by horrible maladies, which attack them like a lion: "As a lion, so hath He broke my bones" (Is. xxxviii. 13). And thus they share the fate of the prophet who was killed by a lion for a sin commonly thought to be venial: "The Lord hath delivered him to the lion, and he hath torn him and killed him" (III. Kings xiii. 26). Let us also consider that, sometimes, God deals thus with such men in order to take away all occasion of pride to which they might be tempted were their death more serene. St. Bridget once asked our Lord why the just sometimes suffered an evil death: He replied that this mournful termination of their life frequently tends to their greater merit, for by means of a humiliating death they are exalted at once to heaven. Do thou, O my God, defend me in my last hour !

2. *Every one that exalteth himself shall be humbled.* St. Peter Damian relates that an Ecclesiastic, whose career had been a bold and prosperous one, on hearing this great maxim of our Lord Jesus Christ recited in the Mass, said insolently, "This saying is false in regard to me, for had I humbled myself I should never have obtained such greatness;" and shortly afterwards he met with a violent death. It has happened to other Ecclesiastics that their end has been accompanied by disgraceful circumstances. Death has often come quickly upon them after they had intrigued to obtain some promotion, and then all men might see that their greatness had vanished like a dream: "As the dream of them that awake, O Lord, so in Thy city shalt Thou

bring their image to nothing" (Ps. lxxii. 20). Or, again, it may be that at the close of their life they do not give such tokens of resignation, patience, recollection, favour, as become God's Ministers, so that there is just cause of fear lest the judgment of God at that hour may have been little favourable to them : " The time is that judgment should begin at the house of God " (1 Pet. iv. 17). Lastly, some memorials may be found among their books and papers which do them little honour, or a sum of money un-befitting their state discovered in their coffers, so that the words of the Psalmist come to pass—" The just shall see and fear, and shall laugh at him and say, Behold the man that made not God his helper, but trusted in the abundance of his riches, and pre-vailed in his vanity " (Ps. li. 8). If we would avoid such a shame-ful end, let us lay to heart those words of the prophet Isaias, "The lofty eyes of man are humbled, and the haughtiness of man shall be made to stoop" (Isa. ii. 11); or those of the Wise Man, "Extol not thyself in the the thoughts of thy soul like a bull, lest thy strength be quashed by folly . . and thou be left like a dry tree in the wilderness" (Eccl. vi. 2, 3). Awful, indeed, are these truths!

3. *And he that humbleth himself shall be exalted.* This promise, which our Lord repeated so often, cannot come to nought ; and we may be certain (as St. Hilary says) that God will bring down the haughty, and raise up the humble in glory. In reading the lives of Holy Priests when we celebrate their festivals, we see clearly that their humility was exalted in their death ; and thus God makes known to all men how He has humbled the proud and exalted the humble: "All the trees of the country shall know that I the Lord have brought down the high tree, and exalted the low tree " (Ezech. xvii. 24). Some of the Saints foretold their death, and prepared for it well; others met death with exemplary conformity to the Divine will, and even with joy. In other cases death has been accompanied and followed by miracles, and thus have been fulfilled the words, " Be you hum-bled under the mighty hand of God, that He may exalt you in the time of visitation " (1 Pet. v. 6). Their soul passed the days

and therefore their memory has remained in benediction and glory: "Because thou wast forsaken, and hated, and there was none that passed through thee, I will make thee to be an ever-lasting glory, a joy unto generation and generation" (Is. lx. 15). O Jesus, example of humility, do thou conquer the pride which I have inherited from the first Adam, and which was the cause of his death and of mine! Grant that at my death I may find the reward which Thou has promised to the poor in spirit, and to the humble of heart!

"Surely man passeth as an image; yea, and he is disquieted in vain."— *Ps.* xxxviii. 7.

"The day of the Lord of Hosts shall be upon every one that is proud and high minded, and upon every one that is arrogant, and he shall be humbled."—*Is.* ii. 12.

SATURDAY.

—◆—

FEAST OF OUR LADY OF MERCY.

I. THE IGNOMINY OF SPIRITUAL SLAVERY.
II. PRIESTS PRESERVED FROM IT BY MARY.
III. PRIESTS DELIVERED FROM IT BY MARY.

—◆—

"Blessed are they who hear the word of God and keep it."—*St. Luke* xi. 28.

1. *Blessed are they who hear, &c.* They are truly blessed who profit by our Lord's words—"words faithful and true"—for they enjoy the liberty which He has given them: "The truth shall make

spise His words remain the servants of sin : "Whosoever committeth sin is the servant of sin" (St. John viii. 34). If sins and vices are enormous, these miserable men groan under that which Jeremias calls "the greatness of the bondage" (Lam. i. 3). Nay, the slavery of sin is a slavery to the most cruel of tyrants—that is, to the devil, who looks upon man as his prey, chains him, and with the cords of hell seeks to draw him into that prison where he himself will burn for all eternity. The devil and his angels lead us captive (says St. Augustin): this is our captivity. How ignominious is it for Priests to be slaves of Lucifer—to be subject to this tyrant when they have received from Christ "power and authority over all devils" (St. Luke ix. 1), so that these evil spirits are subject to them! (St. Luke x. 20.) They groan in chains whilst in their preaching they seek to set loose the soul of their hearers, and say to them, "Loose the bonds from off thy neck, O captive daughter of Sion" (Is. lii. 2). To them does the command of our Lord to His Apostles apply, "Loose him, and let him go" (St. John xi. 44), for they loose consciences, and free them from the most miserable servitude. When the dead man comes forth (says St. Augustin) he is still bound ; while confessing, he is still guilty ; and our Lord gave this command to His ministers in order that they might loose him of his sins. Shall they not, then, be ashamed of bearing such heavy chains ? If we have ever at any time suffered this shameful slavery, let us humble ourselves before the High Priest of the good things to come, Whose Priesthood we have dishonoured; and let us repent bitterly of our sin.

2. *Blessed, &c.* The Blessed Virgin is the only daughter of Adam who, having ever "kept the Divine word," maintained perpetual enmities against the Serpent, while he in vain "lay in wait for Her heel" (Gen. iii. 15). She could truly say that the Prince of the wicked, "the Prince of this world, had not anything in Her" (St. John xiv. 30) ; and by Her powerful protection She preserves Her good children from this diabolical slavery, by making Her abode in them—that is, She constantly assists them : "My abode is in the full assembly of Saints" (Eccl. xxiv. 16). As St. Bonaventure says, She causes them to "abide

in fulness," taking care that their fulness does not diminish; She causes their virtues to "abide," so that they should not vanish away, and their merits, that they should not perish. She detains the devils in their abode; She stays the avenging arm of Her Son when He would strike the sinner. Who among Priests will not fear slavery, knowing that the devil made himself master even of an Apostle? "Satan entered into him" (St. John xiii. 27). Who among Ecclesiastics will not fear this calamity, knowing that the enemy assails Ecclesiastics with the utmost fury? To the Apostles and to all Priests was it said, "Satan hath desired to have you, that he may sift you as wheat" (St. Luke xxii. 31). Let us pray to Mary to have pity on us, and to keep us in the grace of God, and in the liberty of the children of God.

3. Meanwhile let all who find themselves slaves of the devil have recourse to the Blessed Virgin, Who says from heaven, " I have seen the captivity of my people, of my sons and of my daughters, which the Eternal hath brought upon them" (Baruch iv. 10). Nor let even a Priest who finds himself in a state of sin despair, for She will make him hear in the depth of his heart the consoling words, "I will break in pieces his rod with which he struck thy back, and I will burst thy bonds asunder" (Nahum i. 13); and in their place She will substitute other bonds, which are sweet, and worthy of man—that is to say, the bonds of charity: "I will draw them with the cords of Adam, with the bands of love "(Osee xi. 4). Jesus is indeed our true liberator, Who has paid the price of our ransom with His own most precious Blood. But He took that Blood from Mary, and deposited the whole price of the redemption of the human race (as St. Bernard says) in Mary's womb. And Mary, as a token of Her immense compassion for spiritual slavery, has shown Her maternal anxiety for the redemption of captives; in honour of which a special solemnity is celebrated throughout the whole Church. Of Her it may therefore be said with all truth (in the words of St. Bernard) that She opens the bosom of Her mercy to all, in order that all may receive of Her fulness—the captive, redemption; the sick, healing; the sad, consolation; sinners, pardon; the just,

grace. Let us remember (as St. Augustin warns us) that by our own power we can sell ourselves to the devil, but we cannot ransom ourselves; and, therefore, let us invoke the compassionate aid of Her who was the Mother of the Redeemer and was associated with Him in the redemption of the world. Let us invoke Her intercession for ourselves, and for all those sinners for whose conversion we are labouring.

"Let the sighing of the prisoners come in before Thee."—*Ps.* lxxvii. 11.

"If we sin we are Thine, knowing Thy greatness; and if we sin not, we know that we are counted with Thee."—*Wisdom* xv. 2.

SEVENTEENTH SUNDAY AFTER PENTECOST.

— ◆ —

PRIESTS SHOULD SURPASS THE LAITY IN LOVING GOD WITH THEIR WHOLE HEART.

I. THEIR HEART IS ESPECIALLY SANCTIFIED.

II. THEIR HEART IS PERPETUALLY UNDIVIDED.

III. THEIR HEART IS DESTINED TO INFLAME OTHERS WITH THIS LOVE.

— ◆ —

"The Pharisees came to Jesus; and one of them, a doctor of the law, asked Him, tempting Him, Master, which is the great commandment of the law? Jesus said to him, Thou shalt love the Lord thy God with thy whole heart."—*St. Matt.* xxii. 35—37.

1. *With thy whole heart.* The Priest's heart was sanctified in Baptism by means of the Holy Spirit, Who infused into him His

charity: "But you are washed, but you are sanctified" (1 Cor. vi. 11). In the Sacrament of Confirmation this Spirit descended into the same heart, in order to establish in it the kingdom of charity, which St. Augustin calls the bulwark of all virtues. In the Sacrament of Penance the same Spirit either rekindled the love of God, if it was extinguished through mortal sin, or increased it, if charity was still dominant, and so drew down the union of the soul with the Word. As St. Bernard says, charity espouses the soul to the Word, and a spiritual and holy union is indeed contracted; nay, it is not enough to call it a contract, for it is a close embrace. But the Holy Spirit was not content with giving us His charity, which is common to Priests and laity, but He came upon us again at our Ordination, in order that our heart might be a furnace of love, in which (as Peter of Blois says) the Priests of the Most High are raised to the dignity of friendship with Him. Further, the mystery of love which we daily celebrate, in which we ourselves participate, and which we administer to others, has for its proper effect (as St. Thomas says) the augmentation of charity. Our Saviour comes to us (says St. Chrysostom) in order that He may be more closely bound to us by charity; He comes in order that, as He is charity, so He may make us resemble Himself, for His Blood (continues St. Chrysostom) renews in us the image of the King. Let us inquire of ourselves what progress we are making in the love of God.

2. *With thy whole heart.* God is a jealous God: "His name is Jealous" (Exod. xxxiv. 14): and hence He would have our heart entirely His own, and threatens with death those who divide their heart: "Their heart is divided, now they shall perish" (Osee x. 2). The love of the heart is felt in the heart, for in a certain sense it has its seat in the flesh, so that we cannot love God with our whole heart unless we detach ourselves from the love of earthly things. When, therefore, God commands us to love Him with our whole heart, He forbids us to divide our thoughts and our life so as to bestow any portion on other objects; and thus (as St. Augustin says) the whole course of our affections should be directed towards that one object which is pro-

posed for our love. The married man is commanded to love his wife (Eph. v. 25), and therefore he is a "man divided" (1 Cor. vii. 33); but the Priest's heart is wholly God's, and wholly for God. He has nothing on earth which he ought to love except for the love of God : "You shall possess nothing in their land, neither shall you have a portion among them ; I am thy portion and inheritance in the midst of the children of Israel" (Numb. xviii. 20). Be careful, then, O Priest, to admit no other love into thy heart, lest (according to the expression of St. Augustin) vanity corrupt the fruit of charity.

3. *With thy whole heart.* The Son of God came down from heaven, and made known to us the object of His mission in these words—" I am come to cast fire on the earth, and what will I but that it be kindled ?" (St. Luke xii. 49.) By these words our Saviour seemed especially to refer to His Priests, who are destined by God (as St. Ambrose says) to be the representatives of His love. This divine fire is enkindled in the people when the heart of Priests is inflamed by it, for their preaching then sets on fire the coldest hearts, even such as are dead in sin (as St. Cyril says). Happy the Priest who can say, "Are not my words as a fire?" (Jerem. xxiii. 29.) Happy the Priest who, by the light of example, kindles flames of love: " The lamps thereof are fire and flames" (Cant. viii. 6). Happy the Priest who, in dispensing grace by means of the Sacraments, kindles a great fire in earthly hearts ! " On earth He shewed thee His exceeding great fire" (Deut. iv. 36). This will be the proof that the mission which the Father gave to the Son is given by the Son to His Priests, and by them is faithfully fulfilled.

"The God of my heart, and the God that is my portion for ever."— Ps. lxxii. 26.

"Thou, our God, art gracious and true, patient and ordering all things in mercy . . . let not my heart be ashes, and my hope vain earth."—From *Wisd.* xi. 1—10.

MONDAY.

———◆———

PRIESTS SHOULD SURPASS THE LAITY IN LOVING GOD WITH THEIR WHOLE SOUL.

I. By the perfection of their will.
II. By acts of the will.
III. By constancy of will.

———◆—·

" Thou shalt love the Lord thy God . . . with thy whole soul."—*St. Matt.* xxii. 37.

1. *With thy whole soul.* That which is here called the soul is to be interpreted as the will (says St. Thomas); and such should be the perfection of the Priest's will that he should be ready to lay down his life rather than offend God by the very least sin. It is thus that the will dies to itself in order that God alone may live in it : " I will die to myself, that Thou alone mayest live in me " says St. Augustin. Man no longer seeks his own pleasure, but the good pleasure of God: "I seek not My own will, but the will of Him that sent Me" (St. John v. 30). The will, being thus sanctified, suffers " the loss of all things, and counts them but as dung," in order that it may possess God (Philip. iii. 8). A soul that loves God abhors and avoids even venial sins, because they cause her to appear deformed and unsightly in the eyes of her divine Spouse, and (as St. Augustin says) either deprive her of His embraces or cause her to receive them with confusion. How full of defects is my soul !

How far from the perfection proper to my state ! "The man of God should be perfect" (1 Tim. iii. 17).

2. *With thy whole soul.* When the will is wholly God's (says St. Thomas) it cannot live without Him, but in all its actions it willingly seeks Him, willingly thinks of Him, willingly does all that pleases Him. How numerous are the good and meritorious acts of a will that seeks after God ! It rejoices in the essential glory of God; it exults continually in the blessedness of the three Divine Persons, and in their mutual relations ": Let us be glad and rejoice, and give glory to Him " (Apoc. xix. 7). It rejoices in the glory which Christ has contributed to the Holy Trinity; it rejoices in the glory which by Him, with Him, and in Him is given to it in heaven and on earth: "I will rejoice in the Lord, and I will joy in God my Jesus" (Habac. iii. 18). It is the beginning of the life of eternal blessedness (says St. Augustin) to rejoice in God and for God ; and this spiritual joy enables us, like the Apostles, to suffer willingly the afflictions and humiliations which God sends us, or which we encounter for His sake: "They went forth from the presence of the council rejoicing that they were accounted worthy to suffer reproach for the name of Jesus" (Acts v. 41). Then is contrition—or that sorrowful love which makes us "consider in God's presence all the years" which we have spent in not loving Him—felt more acutely and constantly ; then in all our works we seek none but God. But, alas ! how rare is it to find a will which seeks none other than God ! How rare (as St. Jerome says) to find a faithful soul which is not influenced by any motives of vainglory ! Let us, then, review the acts of our will, in order "to separate the precious from the vile." Alas ! how much that is vile and unworthy do I find in my soul !

3. *With thy whole soul.* In these words (says St. Augustin) God gives commandment to all men to subject their will throughout their whole life to Him. Surely (as St. Bernard says) if all we have is from God, if our very life comes to us from God, if our ransom cost God so much, it is just that our will should be wholly and always His. Hence, they who "halt between two sides," who "halt from their paths"—that is, who do not follow

Him with constancy—are most displeasing to God (III. Kings, xviii. 21 ; Ps. xvii. 46). And, if this displease Him in the laity, how much more must it offend Him in Priests, who (as St. Chrysostom declares) ought to be pure and holy above all men ! How shameful is it (says St. Peter Damian) that the reverence which the Levites exhibited for the Synagogue by their constant sanctity should be greater than that which many Ministers of Christ display for the Church ! Let us, then, adjure Priests to love God with their whole soul, as Christ has commanded : "I called the Priests and took an oath of them to do according to what I had said" (2 Esdr. v. 12). O Mary, "Mother of fair love," ever burning with this divine fire, obtain at least a spark of this heavenly flame for me !

"My soul hath stuck close to Thee ; Thy right hand hath received me."— Ps. lxii. 9.

"I found him whom my soul loveth, I held him, and I will not let him go."— Cant. iii. 4.

TUESDAY.

PRIESTS SHOULD SURPASS THE LAITY IN LOVING GOD WITH THEIR WHOLE MIND.

I. BECAUSE THEY UNDERSTAND MORE FULLY HIS CLAIMS TO THEIR LOVE.

II. BECAUSE THEY HAVE A CLEARER PERCEPTION OF THE DUTY OF LOVE.

III. BECAUSE THEY REALISE MORE PERFECTLY THE REWARD OF LOVE.

"Thou shalt love the Lord thy God . . . with thy whole mind: this is the greatest and the first commandment."—*St. Matt.* xxii. 37, 38.

1. *With thy whole mind.* This signifies that the whole intellect is to be consecrated to God (says St. Augustin). It signifies that all knowledge is to be referred to Him (says St. Thomas). Now, the Priest whose intellect is enlightened by the science of all sciences—that is, by theology—should have a fuller knowledge of God and His attributes than other men can obtain And, if (as St. Bernard says) he seeks this science, not only on its own account, but for the spiritual relish which it affords, he must be well acquainted with the goodness, the perfection, and the beauty of God. And the better, the more perfect, the more beautiful the object, so much the more worthy is it of love and praise. The Priest, then, should surpass other men in the love of God, because he is more instructed in the science of theology. Moreover, Priests know better than laymen that the human

heart is made to love, and that either it loves God or it loves creatures—that in loving God it loves the truth, and in loving creatures it loves vanity (as St. Chrysostom points out). They know also that God is Himself the source of blessedness to creatures endowed with intellect (as St. Augustin declares); and in pursuing theological studies they apply to their heart St. Augustin's words, "Hold fast to God, for His worth never decays; He alone is perfect beauty." Lastly, they have learnt that, though we are to make use of creatures, yet in God alone we can and ought to find enjoyment and happiness. Had we but made such use of our theological studies, what progress might we not have made in the love of God!

2. *This is the greatest.* To love God is called the "greatest" commandment because (says St. Thomas) it is supreme in dignity, supreme in importance, supreme in its obligation. Now, Priests understand better than laymen that Charity is (as St. Ephrem calls it) the head and sum of all virtues, and (as St. Gregory declares) the mother and guardian of all good; and therefore they know that (as Clement of Alexandria says) they must practise this virtue to the utmost of their power during their whole life. They are not ignorant that by means of this heavenly love they become dear to God and men, strong in virtue, despisers of the world, and followers of every good work (as St. Prosper shews). Moreover, they are so laden with the Divine benefits that to them may the words be applied, "Now therefore stand up, that I may plead in judgment against you before the Lord concerning all the kindness of the Lord which He hath shewn to you" (1 Kings xii. 7). It is not (says St. Augustin) lawful for them to love Him little, nor (says St. Ambrose) must their charity be of the same degree as that of other men. What can we say of ourselves in this respect? Have we a pre-eminent love of God? Are we at least striving to acquire it?

3. *And the first commandment.* Charity is the first commandment, from whence springs all the rest, because (to use St. Thomas's words) "the whole inclination of the appetitive virtue consists in love." Now, the mind of Priests is instructed in

this truth, nor are they ignorant of the immense gain which the love of God carries with it. From it, in fact, spring all our riches, our peace, our rest, which we vainly seek in earthly goods, for they are all inferior to us. Nothing is above thee (says St. Augustin) except thy Creator; raise thyself to Him alone. Love Him better than all others, and let not thy soul despair of attaining the Supreme Good, of possessing Him, of enjoying Him. It is far more difficult (continues St Augustin) to acquire gold than God, for, however ardently we may desire gold, we do not thereby gain it; but if we desire God we shall possess Him. Nothing but misery is to be found out of God, but, on the contrary, in finding God we find all blessedness. In proportion as we grow in the love of God will He look upon us with eyes of beneficence, and so shall we have the fulness of all good things: "The eyes of God are upon them that love Him" (Eccl. xxxiv. 15). Let us, then, resolve to exercise ourselves in frequent acts of the love of God and so shall we tread "a more excellent way" (1 Cor. xii. 31). Let us engrave on our heart the maxim which St. Charles Borromeo gave to his Priests, "Hold fast to charity above all things; for it is the source of all virtues."

"I will love Thee, O Lord, my strength."—*Ps.* xvii. 2.

"Let the best beloved of the Lord dwell confidently in Him; as in a bride-chamber shall he abide all the day long, and between His shoulders shall he rest."— From *Deut.* xxxiii. 12.

WEDNESDAY.

PRIESTS SHOULD SURPASS THE LAITY IN LOVE OF THEIR NEIGHBOUR.

I. THE STRENGTH OF THEIR MOTIVES.
II. THEIR OPPORTUNITIES OF EXERCISING THIS LOVE.
III. THEIR MEANS OF EXCITING IT IN OTHERS.

"And the second is like to this: Thou shalt love thy neighbour as thyself."—
St. Matt. xxii. 39.

1. *Is like to this.* The commandment to love our neighbour is said to be "like" the commandment to love God, because (as St. Thomas points out), man being created in the image and likeness of God, in loving man we love God in him. how, Priests, better than other men, understand the value of this "likeness," and the value which Almighty God assigns to the love of our neighbour, regarding Himself as honoured in this His likeness, in the same way that a king is honoured in the respect shewn to an image of himself. Again, Priests understand better than laymen how much God loves man—how much he has done, and how much he still does for man's happiness—with what earnestness He commands us to love our neighbour—what promises He often makes to those who fulfil this commandment—with what punishments He threatens those who transgress it. They understand, in short, that charity is "the fulfilling of the law" (Rom. xiii. 10), and that a Christian "that loveth not his brother that he seeth," certainly cannot love God, "Whom he

seeth not" (1 John iv. 20). Lastly, they understand that Jesus Christ, having raised men to the dignity of His brethren and members, regards what is done to men as done to Himself; and, therefore, He has declared the love of our neighbour to be His own commandment, and "a new commandment," setting before us Himself, in giving His life for man, as the model of this love (St. John xiii. 34; xv. 12). Nor can a Minister of God be ignorant that the way to render the love of men more certainly pleasing to our Lord, and more worthy of a Priest, is to love them (as St. Augustin points out) either because they are just or in order that they may become just. Were these truths ever before our eyes, we should not love our neighbour from mere inclination, or sympathy, or interest, or vanity, but only for God and in God. If, in loving our brethren, we regarded the love of the Holy Trinity—the Father Who created and adopted them, the Son Who redeemed them and nourishes them, the Holy Ghost Who sanctifies them, and is diffused in their hearts—great would be the merit which we should lay up for eternity. St. Leo's words have thus a special application to us Priests—"We have above all men a powerful motive for the love of our neighbour in the abundant grace which Christ has given us."

2. *Thou shalt love thy neighbour.* Our ministry ought to be a source of joy to us by reason of the occasions which it supplies of exercising charity towards our neighbour, and of giving proof (as St. Bernard says) that we are lovers of our brethren and of the whole Christian people. The Priestly office makes us look upon the Faithful as our children (says St. Jerome); it puts before us their necessities as our own, and moves us to regard their welfare as tending to our own glory, As St. Laurence Justinian says, we should look upon sinners as our own children, who have fallen into the pit of misery; and, inasmuch as they bear the image of God, by raising them out of this ignominious state we show our love and our reverence for Almighty God Himself. We have opportunities at every step we take for instructing, exhorting, correcting, admonishing, and imparting to souls a heavenly savour, for (as St. Gregory says) Priests ought to be as a condiment to men's souls. How despicable

are such Ministers of Christ as shew themselves insensible to the ruin of souls! They are not mothers (says St. Bernard); they are unworthy of the patrimony of the Crucified, for they think only of themselves. Let us reflect on the numerous occasions which we have of exercising the corporal works of mercy; for (as St. Augustin says) he has always wherewith to give whose bread is full of charity. Have we profited by these occasions hitherto? O my God, how great loss has my soul thus sustained!

3. *Thou shalt love thy neighbour.* The Gospel continually preaches charity; the Apostles never ceased to inculcate it; and it is "the end of the Commandments" (1 Tim. i. 5). Therefore, we are heralds of the Gospel if we carry on the preaching of the Apostles; and if we teach the Faithful the love of God we must incite men to the practice of fraternal charity. In all that we have to do (as St. Thomas points out) everything depends on the end; and, therefore, if our end be charity, all other things will depend on it. We ourselves (as St. Laurence Justinian says) must first be enkindled by this flame in order that we may impart the fire of love to others. But, if we ourselves are without this divine fire, how can we inflame others with it? Let us, then, imitate the beloved Disciple, who, burning with the heavenly flame which he drew from his Master's breast, never ceased to preach to men this doctrine—" Love one another;" adding (as St. Jerome tells us) this reason—It is our Lord's command; and, if we do this only, it is enough.

"As a neighbour, as an own brother, so did I please."—*Ps.* xxxiv. 14.

"I seek my brethren: tell me where they feed the flocks."—*Gen.* xxxvii. 16.

THURSDAY.

---

*THE PRIEST'S RECREATION SANCTIFIED BY
CHARITY.*

I. BY THE EXERCISE OF THE LOVE OF GOD.
II. BY CHARITY TOWARDS HIMSELF.
III. BY EXERCISING IT TOWARDS HIS NEIGHBOUR.

"On these two commandments dependeth the whole law, and the prophets."—
St. Matt. xxii. 40.

1. *On these two commandments.* Not without reason (says St.
Augustin) does Holy Scripture, instead of mentioning both
these commandments, refer in many places only to the first, as
necessarily implying the second also; for "we know that to them
that love God all things work together unto good" (Rom.
viii. 28). Now, if we love God truly, even our times of recreation will work together for our good, since this love can be
better felt and better exercised in repose, and tranquillity, and
solitude, than amidst the tumult of business, even when that
business is of an ecclesiastical kind. Then does the Priest
enjoy the familiar friendship of God (as St. Jerome says), for
surely by contemplating the works of God, by meditating on His
goodness towards us, by reflecting on the number of those of
our friends whom He has taken to Himself during the past year,
we may find in our retirement ample occasions of "rejoicing
in the Lord." As St. Bernard says, he who is with God is
never less alone than when alone, for then is he free to enjoy
God in Himself, and himself in God. Good Priests take this

repose as their Lord's gift, Who said to His disciples, "Come apart into a desert place, and rest awhile" (St. Mark vi. 31); for He said this in order to teach ecclesiastical Superiors that they who labour in the ministry are worthy of rest, and ought not to be incessantly working. Therefore let Priests take their recreation with a good intention; in order, that is, to recruit their strength for fresh labour. Let them take it as from the loving hand of Jesus; let them often make acts of love; let them make fervent ejaculations to God; let them repeat with St. Augustin, " For love of Thy love I do this."

2. *Dependeth the whole law.* The whole law (as St. Augustin says) refers to its end, and that is charity. We are bound, indeed, to practise charity towards ourselves, and, therefore, we should give our body moderate repose, and so imitate the practice of the Saints. St. John the Evangelist amused himself by playing with a partridge, and with his disciples (as Cassian relates); St. Gregory Nazianzen used to walk about on the sea-shore, and gave as his reason that the bow which is always bent either breaks or becomes useless. St. John Chrysostom recommended the enjoyment of picturesque scenery as a means of recreation. But, on the other hand, we must (as St. Ambrose warns us) avoid such pleasures and amusements as are not conformable to ecclesiastical rules and are not approved by the examples and teaching of Holy Scripture. We must avoid in our holidays all disturbance of the ecclesiastical life—that is, all omission of pious exercises, and, above all, of meditation—in order not to expose our soul to grave falls. We must recollect that the flesh is our enemy, and that the better it is fed the more will it rebel against the Spirit, so that in idleness is more frequently proved the truth of the Apostle's words, " I see another law in my members, fighting against the law of my mind, and captivating me in the law of sin" (Rom. vii. 23). Let us consider that Lot, who lived innocently in the city, fell into sin in the retirement of the country; let us reflect on the grave warning of St. Augustin, that David, Solomon, Samson, who were Saints when occupied, in idleness fell away; let us remember that (as St. Bernard says) luxury seriously inflames him whom it finds idle. Let us fear

lest death surprise us even in the midst of our amusements, and lest it be caused by that intemperance which is often thought almost allowable in times of recreation.

3. *And the prophets.* Holy men, who in the Scriptures are called Prophets, have often renounced all rest and relaxation in order not to interrupt those works of their ministry which might have suffered some loss from their absence; saying, "I am doing a great work, and I cannot come down, lest it be neglected whilst I come" (2 Esdr. vi. 3). And, when they have been induced to take their recreation, they have not forgotten their sacred character and office, but have been especially careful to avoid anything which might be a cause of scandal. Thus, they would never lay aside the clerical dress, which adds respect to the Priest both in his own eyes and in those of others; nor would they shew themselves addicted to pleasure, gluttony, and foolish talk, or wanting in modesty: "Giving no offence to any man, that our ministry be not blamed" (2 Cor. vi. 3). Moreover, they provided for the welfare of those souls whom they left for a short time, by praying for them: " I commend you to God, and to the word of His grace" (Acts xx. 32). They directed them to other Confessors, and would not suffer them to be left abandoned to themselves. Fear that our penitents should confess to others indicates either vanity, or self-interest, or bad direction, or something even worse; and therefore St. Alphonsus directed that the penitents of Missionary Priests should in their absence confess regularly to others. Lastly, these holy men strove to supply so far as possible the spiritual and corporal necessities of the country people among whom they spent their time of recreation. Listen, then, O Minister of God, to this teaching; for thus (says St. Bernard) wilt thou honour thy Ministry, and thy Ministry will honour thee. Resolve to imitate these holy men, and pray to God to confirm thee in thy good resolution. So wilt thou work for eternity even in thy leisure, and add lustre to thy crown of glory.

"In every place of His dominion, O my soul, bless thou the Lord."—*Ps.* cii. 32.

"Whether I eat or drink, or whatsoever else I do, I do all to the glory of God."—From 1 *Cor.* x. 31.

FRIDAY.

THE SPECIAL GLORY OF PRIESTS.

I. THEIR KNOWLEDGE OF JESUS CHRIST.
II. THEIR FERVENT LOVE OF HIM.
III. THEIR AWE OF HIM.

"And, the Pharisees being gathered together, Jesus asked them, saying, What think you of Christ? Whose son is He? They say to him, David's. He saith to them, How then doth David in spirit call Him Lord, saying, The Lord said to my Lord, Sit on My right hand until I make thy enemies thy footstool? If David, then, call Him Lord, how is He his Son? And no man was able to answer Him a word, neither durst any man from that day forth ask Him any more questions."— *St. Matt.* xxii. 41—46.

1. *What think you of Christ?* Their ignorance of the Messias was a great disgrace to the Scribes—that is (as St. Chrysostom points out), their ignorance of Him as the Lord of all things, as the only-begotten Son of the Eternal Father, and the heir of His glory. The glory of Priests, on the other hand, consists in their knowledge of Jesus Christ; for in this is "life eternal;" and (as St. Augustin declares) the more progress we make in the knowledge of Jesus Christ, the more shall we advance in eternal life. We have, indeed, not only the obligation, but the opportunity, the time, the means, of reading Holy Scripture in a greater degree than the laity, and we know well (as St. Augustin says) that all the Scriptures refer to Christ. Let us, then, dig deep into the mine of this Book, and we shall there find the precious treasure, the pearl of great price, which is Christ (says St.

Cyril). Let us consider how (as St. Bonaventure says) throughout the Old Testament Christ was prefigured in the types of the Law, represented in the historical narrative, foretold in the prophecies, and His doctrine anticipated in the moral writings—how in the New Testament His gospel is preached, and He Himself set before us both as the Crucified One and as exalted to the right hand of the Father. Thus may we exclaim with St. Augustin, "I seek Christ in Thine own books, O Lord."

2. *Whose son is he?* If Jesus Christ be the Son of God, and one God with the Father, He merits an infinite love. If this God has redeemed us, and has heaped infinite benefits upon us, at the cost of His own life, we ought to burn with love for Him: "If any man love not our Lord Jesus Christ, let him be anathema maran-atha" (1 Cor. xvi. 22). And who have been more richly loaded with His favours than Priests? Certainly (as St. Peter Damian says), in raising us to this sublime post, He has united us to His mystical Body by a closer union than any of His members. He has obtained a special dominion over us; He has made us, as it were, His senators (as Pope Alexander says); He has confided to us His treasures; nay, He has confided to us Himself, and daily comes to us that He may give us a continual increase of charity. How diligently should we strive to cherish in our hearts the love of Christ, and to become in our own persons a lively image of Christ! The image of our Lord reflected in us (says St. Cyril) is the glory of charity. If we would be reverenced by the Faithful and feared by our enemies, let us love Jesus Christ, Who loves, and cherishes, and protects us. For, if (as St. Chrysostom says) the love of those who are powerful causes men to be feared, how much more should the love of Christ have this effect in our case!

3. *I make thy enemies thy footstool.* Christ's enemies are infidels, and all those who (as St. Thomas says) neither fear Him, nor love Him, nor obey Him. To fear Christ and to love Christ is the wisdom of Christians (says Salvian), and Priests should surpass others in this holy fear: "He seemed . . one that feared God above the rest" (2 Esdr. vii. 2). If, in Holy Mass and the Divine Office, we constantly salute Him with the title

of "Lord," we have special reason for regarding Him with reverence and awe; "If I be a master, where is My fear?" (Malach. i. 6.) Let us consider that these words are addressed to Priests, for the Prophet adds immediately, "To you, O Priests, that despise My Name." The "ancients" in the Apocalypse were the first to fall down with their face to the earth to adore the immaculate Lamb, and they thus taught us that Priests should give example of reverence towards Jesus Christ, especially in the Eucharist (Apocal. v. 8). Let us consider that, whereas He now comes into our hands as the "Lamb slain," to offer Himself to the Father, He will one day come as "the Lion of Juda, and as a bear that is robbed of her whelps." Let us fear, therefore, the wrath of the Lamb, recollecting that Priests who fear Christ are not indeed subject to servile fear (as St. Ambrose says). Let us examine ourselves in regard to our reverence to Jesus Christ in the blessed Sacrament. How do we bear ourselves in the church? How do we celebrate the Divine mysteries? What example do we give the people? What dread do we feel of God's terrible judgments? When we stand in His presence, let us say, in the words of St. Anselm, "Thou art King of kings and Judge of judges, great and terrible, exalted on the throne of Thy majesty. Thine is the power, for Thou art the Lord of all power; Thou art the virtue of the eternal Father, and the source of all virtues."

"Thou, O Lord, art my protector, my glory, and the lifter up of my head."—*Ps.* iii. 4.

"The Lord shall be to me for an everlasting light, and my God for my glory."—From *Is.* lx. 19.

SATURDAY.

FEAST OF THE HOLY ROSARY OF THE BLESSED VIRGIN MARY.

THE CLERGY SHOULD ARDENTLY PROMOTE THE DEVOTION OF THE HOLY ROSARY.

   I. By their example.
   II. By shewing its advantages.
   III. By inculcating meditation on its mysteries.

"A certain woman from the crowd, lifting up her voice, said to Him, Blessed is the womb that bore Thee."—*St. Luke* xi. 27.

1. *A certain woman, lifting up her voice.* This woman in praising Mary was a type of the Church (says Venerable Bede); and, if Priests are Ministers of the Church, Her chief members and her representatives, they ought to be the first to honour Mary. Especially should they honour Her in the recital of the Rosary, for which the Church has set apart a special solemnity. We ought, indeed, to be moved to recite this prayer by the example of holy Priests who never neglected it. Such were not only St. Dominic and his children, but also St. Thomas of Villanova, St. Ignatius Loyola, St. Charles Borromeo, St. Francis of Sales, St. Alphonsus Liguori, &c. St. Philip Neri was wont to say that, if

for one single day he should neglect to recite the entire Rosary, he should not look upon that day as pleasing to God. We may observe, too, that all holy Founders of the Religious orders have inculcated this devotion upon their children, and also that innumerable Bishops, Archbishops, Cardinals, and even the Roman Pontiffs, have inscribed their names in Confraternities of the Rosary, in order to declare themselves (according to the words of St. Pius) beloved children of Mary, and specially dedicated to Her. Moreover, the immense number of Indulgences which the Church grants to those who recite it with devotion ought to move us to use it. Again, we must consider the obligation which we are under of being " in all things an example of good works " (Tit. ii. 7). Lastly, we must not forget that the Rosary possesses the advantages of both mental and vocal prayer, and that it is composed of those prayers which are most sublime, most efficacious, and most pleasing to Mary. Let us, then, pray to our Lady, with St. Ephrem, so to move our tongue and our lips that we may worthily recite Her Rosary, and that we may never for a single day neglect it. Thus, by reciting the Blessed Virgin's chaplet, we may trust that She will protect us "with a noble crown " (Prov. ix. 9).

2. *From the crowd.* The multitude remained silent whilst this woman spoke to her Saviour, but we, on the contrary, should strive to make the multitude unite in honouring Mary, and in praying to Her, in order the more easily to obtain grace. As St. Thomas says, it is impossible that the prayers of many should not be heard, if, as it were, they are united in one prayer. So shall we confer an immense benefit on Christians, procuring for them a blessing in life, and in death, and after death, with fulness of grace and immunity from all evils, according to the magnificent promise which our Blessed Lady is said to have made to a devout soul. She has taught us, too (as we are reminded by the Church in the Office of the day), that, as the Rosary is easy to learn and to recite, so is it most pleasing to Her, and well fitted to obtain the Divine mercy, the salvation of the Faithful, and help against adversities. It is a devotion which may be recited by the just and by sinners, by the learned and the ignorant, by nobles and

plebeians; and all will find in it a salutary water causing them
to "bud forth as the rose planted by the brooks of waters,
to send forth flowers as the lily, and yield a smell, and bring
forth leaves in grace" (Eccl. xxxix. 17—19). How many advantages both spiritual and corporal have not Christians derived
from this devotion! As St. Chrysostom declares, the Blessed
Virgin shews Her magnanimity by never rejecting the smallest
service, and in return for the poor offering of our prayers,
of which She has no need, She will give us a rich blessing.
Let us, then, urge the Faithful not to grow weary of reciting the
same prayers in the Rosary, reminding them that our Divine
Lord three times, with His face on the earth, repeated the self-
same prayer: "He prayed the third time, saying the self-same
word" (St. Matt. xxvi. 44). Let us remind them that Eliseus said
(with a mystical meaning) to King Joas, "If thou hadst smitten
five, or six, or seven times, thou hadst smitten Syria even to utter
destruction, but now three times shalt thou smite it" (4 Kings
xiii. 19). We should be ever knocking at the door of mercy,
for we know not when it may be opened to us.

3. *Blessed is the womb that bore Thee.* The Virgin was "blessed"
because she had a share in all the mysteries of our Redemption,
and to these mysteries ought we to turn our attention in reciting
the Rosary, in order to learn all virtues from Her. As St.
Thomas says, other Saints give example of particular virtues,
but the Blessed Virgin gives example of all virtues. Let us,
then, teach the Faithful to apply their mind to the mysteries
which are coupled with this devotion, in order that they may
honour God, not "with their lips only," but "in spirit and
in truth." In this way, offering to the Eternal Father the
merits of His Son and the intercession of the Mother, they
will obtain, if not what they themselves desire, at any rate
that which He knows to be advantageous for them (as St. Barnabas says). Meanwhile let us unfold these mysteries to our
people, so that they may receive them in their full sense, and
thereby avoid the danger of losing the full benefit of their
prayers through inattention of heart in the recital of the words.
How dear to Mary, how useful to the Faithful, is a Priest who

employs himself in promoting this beautiful devotion! Surely, if we join meditation to the recital of the Rosary, we weave a chaplet (as Albertus Magnus says) which will be not unworthy of the Queen of Heaven.

" Hearken, O daughter, and see, and incline thy ear, attend to my supplication."
—From *Ps.* xliv. 11 ; xvi. 1.
" Pray for thy servants to the Lord, thy Son, that we may not die."—From
1 Kings xii. 19.

EIGHTEENTH SUNDAY AFTER PENTECOST.

——◆——

JESUS CHRIST GIVES INSTRUCTION TO PRIESTS IN HIS JOURNEY.

I. HE DESCRIBES THEIR CONDITION.
II. HE POINTS OUT THEIR LABOURS.
III. HE SHEWS THEIR REWARD.

——◆——

" Jesus, entering into a boat, passed over the water and came into His own city."
—*S. Matt.* ix. 1.

1. *Jesus entering into a boat.* This boat (says St. Thomas) signified the Cross, and also the Church. Into this boat did our great High Priest enter, and into this same boat must His Ministers enter with Him and for Him. It may, perhaps, seem strange that our Saviour did not now walk upon the waves, as He once walked on them, or that He should not have opened the sea before His feet, as He opened it for the Israelites. The

reason (says St. Peter Chrysologus) is, that He chose to take upon Himself our infirmities in order to confer upon us His power. He would not always work miracles (says St. Chrysostom), but often, as on this occasion, made use of natural means. By this His humiliation He merited for His disciples the grace to ascend the Cross, to nail themselves to the Cross, and to make use of natural means for fulfilling many of the offices of their Ministry. He merited for them the grace " to go up"—that is, to enter into the Church, for the entrance into this ship is truly "a going up," as it raises us above the waves, and above the bitterness and the changeableness, of worldly things. It is truly "a going up," for this ship is for us "the house of the living God, the pillar and ground of the truth" (1 Tim. iii. 15); it is (as St. Peter Damian calls it) "the court of the heavenly kingdom," or (as St. Jerome calls it) "the crown of God." In the Church, Priests "go up" in the sense of being raised above the rest of the Faithful, as their heads and guardians—guardians of the Spouse of Christ (as Peter of Blois calls them). Hence is it necessary that they be strong spiritual men, and most faithful (says St. Bernard). Is this our case? When shall we begin to be as sublime in perfection as we are elevated in position?

2. *Passed over.* The Evangelist makes use of this expression (says St. Peter Chrysologus) in order to point out how short was the space to be passed over. During this short voyage the Apostles acted as rowers, whilst our Lord sat in the boat. He represented His mystical Body,—that is, the Church; for (says St. Augustin) Christ and the Church are one man; the Head and the Body constitute Christ Himself; the Head is the only-begotten Son of God, the Body is His Church. Let Priests remember that throughout the short, indispensable, and perilous voyage of this life they are conducting Christ in His members, and that all their good offices in behalf of those members Christ regards as done for Himself, since He Himself said to His Father, "I in them, and Thou in Me, that they may be made perfect in one" (St. John xvii. 23). Let them consider Christ as represented in the Faithful, and then the labour of this brief rowing will not seem grievous to them : " Christ is all and in all " (Coloss. iii. 2).

Moreover, as good rowers, they should be united in labour; each one should be at his post; they should make skilful use of the winds, and should not be discouraged in storms, until they have carried souls to the harbour of salvation, and to the eternal shore: "Hoisting up the mainsail to the wind, they made towards shore" (Acts xxvii. 40). Let us, then, inquire of ourselves whether we have hitherto kept these truths before our eyes? Should we have been so slothful, so careless in the Ministry, had we thought that we were conducting Christ Himself, and that we were toiling for Him?

3. *And came into His own city.* St. Jerome says that the city into which Christ came was Nazareth. St. Chrysostom thinks it was Capharnaum; St. Augustin, some other place in Galilee. It would seem as though the Holy Spirit had not named the city in order the better to point out the mystery of that "Holy City" seen and described by St. John (Apoc. xxi. 2). This is truly "His city," for He has created and formed it without man's work, so that it is called "a tabernacle not made with hands— that is, not of this creation" (Heb. ix. 11). He has purchased it for us at the price of His Blood; He is its sovereign, and over it He exercises all power. This is also the city of His mystical Body, which "has not here a lasting city, but seeks one that is to come" (Heb. xiii. 14), and this Body is in the ship, and is ever drawing near to the Holy City, "to mount Sion, and to the city of the living God" (Heb. xii. 22). Here let us consider how the blessedness of Priests will surpass that of the laity when each shall have reached their true country. The rower, the helmsman, the pilot, on reaching the port of their country, not only rejoice with those whom they have carried over, but also receive the special reward of their labour, which the others have not merited: "Under reward to Thy servants the prophets" (Apoc. xi. 18). In like manner Priests will be rewarded according to the number of souls, and in proportion to the burden, which they have carried: "Every man shall receive his own reward" (1 Cor. iii. 8). Let us remember that "he that shall do and teach, he shall be called great in the kingdom of heaven" (St. Matt. v. 19). If he who has saved a man from shipwreck

merits a great reward, how much greater reward (says St. Gregory) will not he merit who shall have delivered a soul from eternal death, and carried him safe to his heavenly country?

"The God of our salvation will make our journey prosperous to us."—*Ps.* lxvii. 20.

" Let us ask of the Lord our God a right way for us, and for our children, and for all our substance."—From 1 *Esdr.* viii. 2.

MONDAY.

THE VISITATION AND CARE OF THE SICK.

I. IT IS SUITABLE TO PRIESTS.
II. HOW IT MUST BE FULFILLED.
III. THE USE TO BE DERIVED FROM IT.

" And, behold, they brought to Him one sick of the palsy lying in a bed. And Jesus, seeing their faith, said to the man sick of the palsy, Be of good heart, son."—*St. Matt.* ix. 2.

1. *They brought to him one sick of the palsy.* Here we see the charity of these persons, who (as St. Thomas points out) must have assuredly visited the sick man, and, full of true devotion, let him down through the tiles into our Lord's presence. The care which they took of this unhappy man is the condemnation of indolent Priests, who have no thought for the sick. Let such remember that St. Jerome wrote to an Ecclesiastic, " It is thy office to visit the sick." Let them remember that the Roman Ritual speaks of this charge as by no means the least obligation of the office of Parish Priests, adding, that if they be lawfully hindered this duty must be performed by other Priests. Let them remember that St. Charles Borromeo prescribed that Parish Priests even when not summoned should visit the sick.

In this work they shew themselves lively images of Him Who came down from Heaven to visit the sick—that is, the human race —and said, "They that are in health need not a physician, but they that are ill" (St. Matt. ix. 12). So will they give the Faithful an example of following that which God has commanded : " Be not slow to visit the sick, for by these things thou shalt be confirmed in love" (Eccl. vii. 39). So will they have the consolation of hearing Christ say to them in the day of judgment, " I was sick, and you visited Me" (St. Matt. xxv. 36). Moreover, they will merit the praises which St. Gregory Nazianzen bestowed on St. Basil for this very thing, and they also will be Priests who "can have compassion on infirmities " (Heb. iv. 15).

2. *Jesus, seeing their faith.* Priests must visit the sick in the spirit of faith, in order, (as St. Chrysostom says) that our Saviour may shew his power and His mercy in their favour. And, in the same way as these pious Jews succoured the man sick of the palsy, who was unable to help himself, so does the Roman Ritual enjoin Priests to have special care of those who are destitute of human aid, and to seek them out with the charity and labour of kind and careful shepherds, and, should they be unable to relieve them from their own means, let them at least endeavour to procure alms from the charity of others. Let them (as St. Charles Borromeo commands) turn their chief attention to the soul, in order to direct it to the way of salvation ; and, above all, let them, as the Roman Ritual orders, shew such gravity and modesty as becomes the Priests of the Lord, in order that their visit may be useful to themselves, to the sick, and to their attendants. Let them avoid all that has the appearance of avarice, and let them abstain from such artifices as may excite suspicion of a perverse end in their visit; for Priests are bound to seek the salvation of souls, to the exclusion of all thought of worldly gain. Hence, should they deem it necessary for the sick man, through danger of death, to make his will, let them persuade him to do so, but let them carefully avoid any attempt at extorting from him any so-called pious legacies, the disposition of which ought to be left to the devotion and spiritual needs of the sick. In short, let Priests (as

St. Bonaventure enjoins) approach the sick bed with no other
thought than that they are visiting Jesus Christ—that He Himself lies there in suffering and distress ; and so will their every
word be holy and heavenly. Let them shew first (as St. Gregory
says) their tenderness and compassion, and then will their
Ministry be more acceptable and more efficacious. Have we
hitherto acted in this manner, or have we in any degree abandoned the sick ? Have we visited them in a worldly spirit ?
Let us carefully examine ourselves on this point.

3. *Be of good cheer, son.* What words of holy confidence and of
salutary admonition will not the Priest speak to the sick, if he
keeps before their mind the teaching of the Roman Ritual, and
of the above-mentioned Pontiff ! If he place before their eyes
some sacred image—if he put in their mouth short and suitable
prayers—if he relate the history of some Saint who may have
suffered a like sickness—if he prevent the use of some medicine
which might injure the soul—the sick will derive immense benefit,
and will exclaim, "What can we give to this holy man ?"
(Tobias xii. 1.) The visit of a holy Priest has often induced
the sick to make a good Confession, and to receive all the
Sacraments of the Church as prescribed by Pius V. and the
Lateran Council ; nay, it ordinarily happens that, returning
to God by means of the exhortations of the Priests, they either
receive from him the grace of their cure or are put in the right
dispositions for a holy death. Moreover, the Prayers which holy
Church directs Priests to recite over the sick are most efficacious, especially when they are said with faith and devotion :
"They shall lay their hands upon the sick, and they shall
recover" (St. Mark xvi. 18). In this way do Priests render
themselves dear and venerable in the eyes of the people, and
thus also do they acquire a vast store of merit for eternity.
Let us, then, resolve never to neglect such great opportunities of
doing good to ourselves and to others.

" May the Lord hear thee in the day of tribulation ; may the name of the God of
Jacob protect thee."—*Ps.* xix. 1.

" Thou scourgest and Thou savest ; Thou leadest down to hell and bringest up
again ; and there is none that can escape Thy hand."—*Tobias* xiii. 2.

TUESDAY.

———+———

THE ASSISTANCE GIVEN BY THE PRIEST TO THE DYING.

I. IN RESPECT OF THE DYING.
II. IN RESPECT OF THE BYSTANDERS.
III. IN RESPECT OF THE PRIEST.

———+———

" Son, thy sins are forgiven thee. And, behold, some of the Scribes said within themselves, He blasphemeth. And Jesus, seeing their thoughts, said, Why do you think evil in your hearts? Whether is easier to say, Thy sins are forgiven thee, or to say, Arise and walk?"—*St. Matt.* ix. 2—5.

1. *Son, thy sins are forgiven thee.* St. Jerome admires the humility of Jesus Christ in addressing the sick man as a son, whereas the Priests disdained even to approach him. But not only did He thus address him, but He imparted to him an immense benefit—that is, the remission of sins, the health of the soul. Now, if we considered our Lord's example, we should hasten to the bedside of the dying, looking upon them as our sons, often in need of the greatest of all benefits—that is, of the remission of sins. It is in our power to remit guilt even when, through violence of the temptation, it is incurred in the very last period of life; for (as St. Chrysostom says) to Priests is given a power which Almighty God has not been pleased to confer on Angels or Archangels. Further, we may suggest many good acts, to

which are annexed remission of venial sins and indulgences ; and if we have the requisite faculties we can impart the Plenary Indulgence by which the Kingdom of Heaven is immediately opened to the dying, if only they be contrite and offer to God the sacrifice of their life. We may suggest such holy thoughts as may drive away temptations, detach the soul from earth, and impart to it confidence in God's mercy and resignation to His will. We may exhort them to make, at least with the heart, short acts of Faith, Hope, Charity, and other virtues. The devil uses all his efforts to make the soul of the dying his prey; and, therefore, it is for us to endeavour to thwart him in this design. With the assistance of God and the holy Angels, who will suggest words to us (as happened to St. Philip Neri in similar circumstances), we shall succeed in this glorious undertaking. Moreover, the prayers which the Ministers of the Church offer to God for the dying have a particular efficacy in leading them to the harbour of salvation.

2. *They said within themselves, He blasphemeth.* Our Saviour not only conferred benefit on the man who was sick of the palsy, but also on the bystanders who were calumniating Him, by instructing them out of the superabundance of His wisdom (as St. Chrysostom observes). Now, Priests, when they are assisting the dying, may confer great benefit on the bystanders if they be pious and prudent, even as they may give scandal if they be wanting in these qualities. St. Alphonsus justly remarked that some Priests in fulfilling this office do more harm than good to the sick, to their own souls, and to the souls of the assistants, although they are bound to endeavour on these occasions to profit all who are present. For this purpose let us cause them to unite their prayers with the prayers of the Church; let us induce them to listen to all that we suggest to the dying as subjects for thought and pious exercise; for such words may be (says St. Chrysostom) both food and medicine, both fire and steel, to all who hear them. Nor is the profit less which the sight of the dying, worthily assisted by a Priest, confers on the assistants; for then "the living thinketh what is to come"

brought to conversion, and have resolved to make a good Confession. Perhaps even we, who are now making this meditation, may one day, by such means, "gain our brother" (St. Matt. xviii. 15).

3. *Whether is easier to say, &c.* It was easy for our Saviour to cure the soul and body of the sick man, but it is a laborious undertaking for Priests, in assisting the dying, to procure for them through the remission of sins the true healing of the soul. But, the greater the labour, so much the greater will be the merit; for (as St. Alphonsus says) no work of charity is more dear to God, or more beneficial for the salvation of souls, than that of helping men to die well, because at the hour of death (on which depends the eternal salvation of every one) the assaults of hell are wont to be more terrible, whilst the sick are less able to help themselves. Then have we sometimes to reap that which another hath sown : "I have sent you to reap that in which you did not labour; others have laboured, and you have entered into their labours" (St. John iv. 37, 38). The time of death is the time of harvest, when the Priest undertakes brief labour for infinite consolation (as St. Chrysostom says). The hours taken from sleep, the discomforts, the fœtid atmosphere, the weariness, are short; and, if (as St. Augustin says) they are compared with what worldly men will suffer for the sake of riches, or for the gratification of some passion, they are nothing. Sinners labour to commit iniquity : "Under his tongue are labour and sorrow, " (Ps. ix. 7): and (as St. Augustin says again) not only do they derive no fruit from their iniquity, but they receive the chastisement of it. But, on the contrary, Priests, in assisting the dying, have not only many incentives for sanctifying themselves, but also so many inward consolations, so many joyful hopes, that the labour seems not worth considering. Let us remember that we also must one day die, and that then we may hope for assistance and a good passage at God's hands in proportion as we shall have obtained these blessings for others : "Good measure, and pressed down, and shaken together, and running over, shall they give into your bosom; for with the same measure that you shall mete withal, it shall be measured

to you again" (St. Luke vi. 38). Therefore (as St. Camillus of Lellis advises), let us not suffer ourselves to be robbed by others of any opportunity of helping the dying, notwithstanding the inconvenience we thereby suffer, and the little credit we gain in the eyes of the world. Each soul, thus aided by us, on reaching Paradise will become our advocate, and, united with other beatified spirits, will plead for us to God, as the Israelites pleaded for the life of Jonathan, saying, "Shall Jonathan then die, who hath wrought this great salvation in Israel? for he hath wrought with God" (1 Kings xiv. 45).

"Into thy hands I commend my spirit. Thou hast redeemed me, O Lord, th God of truth."—*Ps.* xxx. 6.

"Lord Jesus, receive my spirit."—*Acts* vii. 58.

WEDNESDAY.

———◆———

THE BENEFITS WHICH PRIESTS CONFER ON THE FAITHFUL IN ADMINISTERING THE LAST SACRAMENTS.

I. PENANCE.
II. THE VIATICUM.
III. EXTREME UNCTION.

———◆———

" But, that you may know that the Son of Man hath power on earth to forgive sins (then said He to the man sick of the palsy), Arise, take up thy bed, and go into thy house."—*St. Matt.* ix. 6.

1. *The Son of Man hath power on earth to forgive sins.* The power to forgive sins is proper to our Lord Jesus Christ, nor does He need any human agency for the exercise of it (as St. Chrysostom points out). Yet He has communicated this power to His Ministers, and, by means of His Spouse, the Church, He has commanded them to exercise it, especially towards those who are in danger of death. Hence it is their office to dispose the sick by all charitable means to a good Confession, reminding them, with St. Augustin, that God, Who has promised pardon, has not promised another day to those who are inclined to put off this duty. The sick must be preferred before all other penitents, because their necessity is greater, and holy Church gives to all Priests whatsoever faculties to absolve them from all reserved cases and from all censures, provided the prescribed rules are observed. Sometimes they must be encouraged with the hope,

not only of pardon, but also of the cure of their sickness, which Almighty God not unfrequently bestows, and (as might be proved by many examples) so soon as Sacramental Absolution has been received. More often is it necessary to compassionate their sorrows, and almost always to help them in their examination of conscience, exciting them from various motives to true repentance, in order that we may with truth apply to ourselves the words, "To the weak I became weak, that I might gain the weak" (1 Cor. ix. 22). How great merit do those gain who perform all these duties well, and who, being furnished with moral teaching, prudence, and charity, provide for the needs of the conscience, and ward off all dangers from the soul! But, alas! in the Day of Judgment we shall see that many sick have been lost through the culpable delay, or ignorance, or deficient charity of Priests. Yet St. John tells us that "we ought to lay down our lives for the brethren" (1 John iii. 16).

2. *Then said He to the man sick of the palsy. . . Go into thy house.* Our Lord Jesus Christ, Who commanded the man sick of the palsy to go into his house, will, on the contrary, really and substantially come into the house of the sick, under the veil of the Eucharistic species, in order to lead them to Paradise, guarding them and preserving them from sin. On the other hand, we must exhort the sick to receive Him with a great faith and great desire, assuring them that Jesus Christ is the true Physician, and that the Holy Eucharist (as St. Cyril says) cures even corporal maladies if it be expedient for the soul. St. Gregory Nazianzen relates that his sick father no sooner received Holy Communion than he recovered. But, if our Lord chooses rather to call them to Himself in eternity, He comes first as a Father, and afterwards as a Judge. He comes to strengthen them against temptations, and to lead them to Paradise; and for that reason is He called our "Viaticum." How many holy sentiments may not Priests suggest to those who, from languor of soul and body, are not capable of helping themselves! Truly to each one of them may we say, with St. Augustin, "God made thy body, God made thy soul: He knows how to re-create

He has formed: do thou therefore place thyself in the hands of thy Physician." How great is the edification given to the bystanders when they hear words of peace and consolation from the Priest's lips! What confidence do they place in him! It would seem as though they said to him, "One that is a Priest of the seed of Aaron is come; he will not deceive us" (1 Maccab. vii. 14). A good effect also is produced on the people when the Viaticum is carried with pomp and devotion and is followed by a large number of the Faithful. Accordingly, the latter should be often admonished, from motives of charity and piety, to accompany the most august Sacrament—reverently to adore it, imploring help and defence for the sick—and, finally, to enter into the Church, and there attend upon our Divine Lord with awe and devotion. Let us not lose these occasions of doing good to ourselves and to others:. "Let not the part of a good gift overpass thee" (Eccl. xiv. 14). If we are not slothful, we shall gather abundant fruit, and we shall not groan in poverty: "If thou be diligent, thy harvest shall come as a fountain, and want shall flee far from thee" (Prov. vii. 11).

3. *Arise.* Our Lord Jesus Christ, who worked the cure of the man sick of the palsy, has constituted His Ministers in so great authority that they heal the sick in administering to them Extreme Unction. Cornelius à Lapide says, the proper effect of this Sacrament is to restore health, if it be expedient for the salvation of the soul; and many instances of this result have been related and witnessed even in our own days. But its principal effect regards the soul, which in the last moments of life is exposed to grave perils, and is thus furnished with a most powerful defence against them by our Divine Lord, Who instituted the Sacraments. Let Priests read with attention the teaching of the Council of Trent on this head, and let them especially consider the words which declare that the *res Sacramenti* is the grace of the Holy Spirit, Whose unction purges away those sins which have yet to be expiated, and frees the soul from the relics of sin—comforts and strengthens the sick man, exciting him to greater confidence in the Divine mercy—succours what is weak, and lightens the pains and inconvenience

of sickness; enabling the sick man easily to resist the temptations of the devil and to tread under foot his wiles; conferring bodily health, if it be expedient for the salvation of the soul. Yet many Faithful, deceived by the devil, who would deprive them of this great aid, fear to receive this Sacrament, as though it were a sentence of death, and defer it to the last moment, so that it often happens that they die without receiving it. Now, this is in great measure the fault of Priests, who neglect to instruct them from their early years in the teaching of St. James the Apostle in regard to this Sacrament (v. 14). Let us endeavour to excite in ourselves and others a lively desire of receiving it; let us resolve to make from time to time special prayer to Almighty God both for ourselves and our brethren, that He would not suffer us to depart out of this world without having first cancelled by means of Extreme Unction the remains of sin still adhering to us. Of this kind are venial sins, and even mortal sins, not known, or not absolved through involuntary nullity of Confession—the punishment still due to remitted sin—and languor in the powers of the soul. So may our souls be enabled to mount at once to heaven, or at least be detained but for a short time in Purgatory. Let us also pray to our Lord that He suffer us not to be of the number of those Priests who seem almost ashamed to confer this Sacrament, of which they are properly the Ministers.

" Thou considerest labour and sorrow."—*Ps.* ix. 14.

" In the time of their tribulation they cried to Thee, and Thou heardest from heaven, and, according to the multitude of Thy tender mercies, Thou gavest them saviours."—2 *Esdr.* ix. 27.

THURSDAY.

THE PRIEST IN SICKNESS.

I. The profit which the Priest may derive from sickness.

II. The edification he may give to the Faithful.

III. The benefit he may confer on the Church.

"And he arose, and went into his house."—*St. Matt.* ix. 7.

1. *He arose.* Our Saviour cured the man sick of the palsy, who lay on his bed, was carried by others, and could not walk alone (as St. Thomas points out), but whose condition was changed in a moment at the word of Christ. Now, our Lord might show the same grace to Ecclesiastics who ·would be useful to the Church, but who through some bodily infirmity cannot attend to the work of the Ministry. Let us reflect, however, that St. Paul, who worked such great miracles, did not cure his disciple Trophimus, whom "he left sick at Miletus" (2 Tim. iv. 7); and he counselled his disciple Timothy, Bishop of Ephesus, to "drink a little wine for his stomach's sake, and for his frequent infirmities" (1 Tim. v. 23). The Apostle cured neither of these, but it was not without important reasons that he refused to work a miracle in their favour. For these great Saints derived two advantages from their sickness, which zealous Priests may also gain in their own case. The first benefit is the patient endurance of the strokes of God's justice, Who mortifies His servants because of their defects (as St. Chrysostom points out); the second is, the occasion of self-humiliation

thereby afforded them, so that they may acknowledge their own misery. With regard to the faults which we have committed, let us remember when we are sick that "he that sinneth in the sight of his Maker shall fall into the hands of the physician" (Eccl. xxxviii. 15); let us remember the admonition given by St. Peter Damian to a Religious who was confined to his bed— "Dear brother," said he, "confess; do penance; and, if it be that thou art hindered through any fault of thy own from celebrating the tremendous mysteries, show thy readiness to submit thyself to the sacred Canons." Sickness is, in truth, the punishment of sin (as St. Basil says); and, as, according to the golden rule of charity, we must look upon the sickness of other men as sent by God for the exercise of their patience, so, according to the rule of humility, must we regard our own as the punishment of our sins, and, therefore, suffer it with resignation. Have we done so hitherto? Have we at least humbled ourselves in the knowledge that we are exposed to great perils of losing health and life, and that we endure pain with so little patience?

2. *He went into his house.* The man who was sick of the palsy went into his house, but (as St. Chrysostom points out) the bystanders did not profit by this miracle. Sick priests, on the contrary, do not move from their house, but it is there that they may edify their attendants. St. Chrysostom sets forth at great length the reasons for which Almighty God often suffers persons to languish in sickness whose health might be profitable to the well-being of the Church, although, as he says, this sickness may have the effect of rendering the Faithful tepid and slothful. One reason is, that those who attend upon Priests may be reminded that they are but men of the same nature as themselves, and may thus see that it is possible to imitate their virtues. Moreover, the exercise of patience edifies those who approach them, for they observe that they neither expect nor obtain temporal goods because of their merits, but that, by serving God, as they do, in tribulations, they aspire to an eternal reward. Again, those who are present at this spectacle are easily led to reflect on the doctrine of the resurrection; for when

they see a just man, and one abounding in virtue, suffering so many evils, and departing this present life in such circumstances, they are compelled to reflect on the future judgment. Lastly, should the bystanders at any time fall into adversity, they will find sufficient ground for consolation in considering the sufferings which have befallen those who have been called to such high privileges. Let us call to mind these truths, and profit by them, when God shall visit us with sickness, whereby he has tried, and still constantly tries, numerous ecclesiastics. So, by our example and by our words, shall we benefit our relations, our friends, and our servants.

3. *He went into his house.* The house, to which the man who was sick of the palsy went, may here signify the Church, which is "the house of the Living God" (1 Tim. iii. 15). Now, sick Priests may bring great profit to the Church, for by doing as much good as possible in their sickness they manifest the power of God, Whose word thereby takes effect through the instrumentality even of men bowed down by infirmity. Then, indeed, does Almighty God show that He has need of none, and that even when the leader is disabled He can cause his army to triumph; nay, that He chooses whom He will, and as long as He will, in order to the fulfilment of His magnificent designs. So St. Chrysostom. Moreover, it is profitable to the whole Church to observe, in the person of suffering Saints, that those are not truly blessed nor truly miserable whom the world accounts such; that true blessedness depends not on temporal goods, even as temporal evils do not constitute true misery. Lastly, conformity to the Divine will in tribulations is profitable to the whole Church, not only through the "Communion of Saints," but also by that force of example which made St. James the Apostle say, "Behold, we account them blessed that have endured. You have heard of the patience of Job, and you have seen the end of the Lord" (St. James, v. 11). For the rest, many zealous Priests imitate Timothy, who, in spite of his many infirmities, did the Lord's work even to the very day of his martyrdom: they imitate St. Jerome, who by continual reading and writing overcame the inconveniences of his weak health:

they imitate St. Gregory the Great, who in his very infirm health underwent immense labour for the Church. At least, let us in our sicknesses pray to God that He would deign by means of other Ministers to do that good to souls which we would fain do, but cannot; remembering, with St. Augustin, that "the prayer of the just is the key of heaven"—that prayer ascends thither, and that from thence the mercy of God descends.

"Have mercy upon me, O Lord, for I am weak ; heal me, O Lord, for my bones are troubled."—*Ps.* vi. 3.

"That this may be my comfort, that, afflicting me with sorrow, He spare not, nor I contradict the words of the Holy One."—*Job* vi. 10.

FRIDAY.

—◆—

HOW GOD KEEPS CONFESSORS IN HUMILITY.

I. THE GREATNESS OF THEIR POWER.
II. THE DANGER OF THEIR BEING LIFTED UP WITH PRIDE.
III. INCENTIVES TO THE PRESERVATION OF HUMILITY.

—◆—

"And the multitudes, seeing it, feared, and glorified God, that gave such power to men."—*St. Matt.* ix. 8.

1. *Glorified God.* The glory of remitting sins, and of having this great power given to men, must all be referred to God (says St. Hilary), and in very truth (as St. Thomas says) the Priesthood of the Man-God can alone cleanse consciences from sin. He, being God, can alone confer so great a benefit on sinners,

for (says St. Thomas again) the blotting out of sin belongs formally, and in effect, to God alone. For sin carries with it a triple injury—the stain on the soul, the corruption of natural good, and the liability to punishment. Now, this triple injury can only be repaired by God Himself, for the following reasons—viz., because the beauty of grace comes from the illustration of Divine light, and this beauty cannot be restored to the soul unless God give fresh light; and hence an habitual gift—that is, the light of grace—is required. In like manner, the order of nature cannot be repaired, so that the will of man should be subject to God, unless God draw the will of man to Himself. So also the debt of eternal punishment cannot be remitted except by God Himself, against Whom the offence is committed, and Who is the judge of men. So St. Thomas. Now, Christ, by the power of the keys given to His Ministers, has constituted them instruments of this Divine operation, but as Ministers only (says St. Thomas), because God alone of Himself can remit guilt. All the powers of nature, all the powers of humanity, can do nothing for those who, after mortal sin, desire to obtain Paradise. The great men of the world, beholding the Priest in the Confessional, may well exclaim, "Who is this that forgiveth sins also?" (St. Luke vii. 49.) Let us give thanks to God, Who has conferred on us so great power.

2. *That gave such power.* The power to remit and retain sins, and to rule the consciences of the Faithful—to see them kneeling at our feet, to hear their groans and miseries, to give directions for the guiding of their conscience, to impose penance, to have the right to enforce its execution—all these things may supply incentives to pride, and cause Confessors, should they be neophytes in virtue, to fall into the condemnation of the devil, according to St. Paul's words, "Not a neophyte, lest, being puffed up with pride, he fall into the judgment of the devil" (1 Tim. iii. 6). Pride, indeed, derives its strength from good works, and it is in them that we have most cause to fear its approach. St. Chrysostom warns us that we ought to fear the more in proportion to the amount of good works which we have performed, for so much the more fiercely does the devil then assail us. He

knows that, if he supplants and ruins one who is of little account and low in the scale of perfection, he brings no great injury to the common cause; whereas, when he causes one who is standing conspicuously, as it were, on an eminence of virtue, to fall into sin, and especially into pride, he brings great injury and destruction on the Church. Further, the greater authority we have over the Faithful, and the more we are their masters, so much the more guilty are we if we sin. Therefore, let us fear pride, which is the source of all sins; let us (as St. Augustin enjoins) humble ourselves before God, and, in spirit, even before those who cast themselves at our feet, remembering the strict account we shall have to give to Almighty God.

3. *To men.* In order to keep Confessors within the bounds of humility, Almighty God often reminds them that they are but men, and subject to human miseries, although they exercise a Divine Ministry. In the first place, He sometimes makes us feel that all our efforts are useless for the amendment of a penitent (perhaps in the case of one towards whom we have special regard) unless grace move him interiorly. He shows us that it is He who teaches (as St. Augustin says), He who admonishes, He who terrifies; that it is He who enlightens the understanding; and that, though we indeed labour, yet we labour as His workmen. Further, He causes us to learn by experience that all our zeal in guarding our penitents from sin produces no good result if He does not guard them. We labour in guarding them (says St. Augustin again), but vain is our labour unless God protect them. In this way Confessors recognise, and are practically convinced of, the great truth, that nothing good can come except from Him Who alone is good—the chief good, Nay, in many cases God leaves Confessors in doubt, in perplexity, in anguish, so that they must needs say, " My spirit is in anguish, my heart within me is troubled" (Ps. cxlii. 4). Often do they need to ask counsel; often do they need to consult authors; often do they confess that they have erred, saying to God, " Lest my ignorances increase " (Eccl. xxiii. 3). Sometimes God permits that serious disturbance should come upon them in their soul and in their body, and sometimes allows them to fall

into no light sins; and He deals thus with them (as St. Chrysostom explains) in order that their own failings may render
them gentle and patient in regard to the sins of others. If,
then, we would preserve ourselves from so great misfortune, let
us cherish humility, which (as St. Bernard declares) is the
foundation and guardian of all virtues.

"Having lifted me up, Thou hast thrown me down."—*Ps.* ci. 11.

"Thou art just in all things that have come upon us, because Thou hast done
truth, but we have done wickedly."—2 *Esdr.* ix. 33.

SATURDAY.

THE MATERNITY OF THE BLESSED VIRGIN MARY.

*IN HER MATERNITY, MARY TEACHES PRIESTS
HOW TO USE THE DIGNITY OF THEIR
OFFICE.*

 I. To promote the glory of God.
 II. To procure their own sanctification.
 III. To co-operate towards the salvation of their
   people

"His mother said to Him, Son, why hast Thou done so to us?"—*St. Luke* ii. 48.

1. *His mother said.* Mary, in the most proper and strict sense,
is the true Mother of God. For the Man-God is one sole

person, and this person is Divine, and therefore the Mother of this Divine person is the Mother of God. "If any one" says the Council of Ephesus, " does not confess Emmanuel to be true God, and, therefore, the Blessed Virgin to be the Mother of God (as having borne, according to the flesh, the incarnate Word of the Father), let him be anathema." And such She was from the first moment of the Incarnation, such She was in bringing forth Her Son, and such She will be in eternity. As St. Cyril says, if our Lord Jesus Christ be God, how can the Holy Virgin, who brought Him forth, not be Mother of God ? This maternity (says St. Thomas) has an infinite dignity, for Mary calls Him Her Son Whom the Angels adore as their God and their Lord. Now, the Blessed Virgin made use of this dignity to promote the glory of God, for She made the Divine attributes shine forth by means of the Incarnation, and of all the mysteries in which She ever had Her share. We also should remember that the Priesthood was instituted to promote God's glory, for, if " God has worked all things for His glory," much more has He directed the grand institution of so sublime a dignity to His glory ; and therefore did St. Peter Damian justly declare that the Clergy are constituted to preach the name, and praise, and glory of God. Therefore, let Priests remember, as the Council of Milan enjoins, that they have been anointed by God in order to preserve and propagate His glory.

2. *Son, why hast Thou done so to us ?* Mary makes use of Her dignity for Her own sanctification, for (as St. Thomas points out) from Her intimate union with Christ—from His example, from His words, from the very dolours which She suffered for His sake—She. derived a fulness of grace which incomparably surpassed that of all the Saints taken together. She was in fact " the worthy Mother of God," inasmuch as She merited to be preferred by God in His choice of a Mother (says St Augustin); further, She was also " the worthy Mother of God " inasmuch as, among all creatures, no other could have exercised this charge with so great perfection as She exercised it, and therefore was She rich in merits above all creatures: " Many daughters have gathered together riches: Thou hast sur-

passed them all" (Prov. xxxi. 29). Hence She surpassed the riches of all the Saints, being (as St. Bonaventure says) the chief of Virgins, the mirror of Confessors, the rose of Martyrs, the ruler of the Apostles, the teacher of the Prophets, the daughter of the Patriarchs, the queen of Angels. Truly (as St. Epiphanius declares) Mary had none superior to Her but God alone. Now, let us remember that the priestly dignity not only obliges us to sanctity, but also furnishes us with continual incentives and powerful means to be holy, so that it would be a disgrace to us (says St. Peter Damian) did our virtue only equal that of the laity. Let us, therefore, strive to be distinguished above the people, profiting by our dignity, and deriving thence, not only what is useful, but also, that which (as St. Gregory says) renders us in a certain way, singular. Let us implore our Lady's help, for She has ever looked upon the Clergy with the eyes of a mother, as associated with the Priesthood of Her Son. Let us pray to Her with St. Augustin, and with the Church, in St. Augustin's words, "Intercede for the Clergy."

3. *Son, why hast Thou done this?* Mary, in becoming the Mother of our Head—of our first-born Brother, became Mother of all the members—of all the brethren. Hence she has just cause to say to those who abandon Her, "Son, why hast thou done this?" If Esther knew that she had been raised by God to the throne for the good of her nation, and if she fulfilled this design of Divine Providence, how much more clearly does Mary know the reasons of her exaltation—how much more efficaciously has She ever made use of Her maternity for the benefit of mankind in general, and sinners in particular? She beholds our miseries (says St. Bonaventure), and hastens to implore mercy for us. She knew that She was chosen by God to co-operate with Him in the work of redemption, because (as St. Bernard says) it was expedient that both the male and female sex should take part in the restoration of fallen humanity. And, whereas the first Eve was a cruel mediatrix, by whose means man was poisoned by the venom of the old serpent, the second Eve has given us to drink the antidote of salvation. This great Mother is the "valiant woman," described by Solomon, who gives "a prey to her

household, and victuals to her maidens "—that is, to those who declare themselves her servants (Prov. xxxi. 15). She "opens Her hand to the needy," and the poor who have recourse to Her go not away discontented. Now, we also have been raised to the Priesthood for the salvation of the people, and we ought to employ all our efforts to improve their condition. It is our example which should tend to their sanctification, for (as St. Isidore says) if the Priests amend their life there is hope that the people will be followers of them. Our dignity places us in the position of reconciling God to the people (says St. Prosper), and leading back the people to God. Let us pray to the Blessed Virgin that this dignity be not for the fall, but for the resurrection, of many.

" With thy comeliness and thy beauty set out, proceed prosperously, and reign."
—*Ps.* xliv. 5.

" He that is mighty hath done great things to thee, and holy is His Name."—
From *St. Luke* i. 49.

NINETEENTH SUNDAY AFTER PENTECOST.

———◆———

AMUSEMENTS UNSUITABLE TO THE ECCLESIASTICAL STATE.

I. THEATRES.
II. THE CHASE.
III. CARDS.

———◆———

" Jesus spoke again to the chief priests and Pharisees in parables, saying, The kingdom of heaven is likened to a king who made a marriage for his son. And he sent his servants to call them that were invited to the marriage, and they would not come."—*St. Matt.* xxii, 1—3.

1. *Sent his servants.* Who are the servants sent by the King to invite men to the marriage feast—that is, to heavenly glory, in which the marriage of Christ with His Church, already begun upon earth, will be consummated ? They are (says St. Hilary) first of all the Apostles, after them Apostolical men. Now, when did the Apostles, when did Apostolical men, ever appear at profane plays ? And how can we aspire to their glory if we pursue a line of conduct different from that which they followed ? We know that they made use of every effort to draw Christians away from theatres, declaring them to be sinful, or at least dangerous ; calling them (as St. Cyprian did) "vain and light shows," the inventions of the devil. St. Chrysostom speaks of them as

"ridiculous and pernicious luxuries;" St. Augustin, as "miserable madness, miserable pleasure;" St. Maximin, as " vanity, madness, and false hood." Moreover, holy Fathers (as St. Cyril of Jerusalem, and St. Augustin) remind the Faithful that in their Baptism they renounced such amusements, classing them among the pomps of the devil. What, then, is the course which we should pursue? If we teach a contrary doctrine to this we shall depart from the teaching of the Fathers, but if we maintain their doctrine as we ought to do, and yet assist at these profane and dangerous amusements, shall we not destroy the effects of our words by our deeds? How many prohibitions have been issued forbidding clerics to appear at theatres! It will be sufficient to quote that of the Council of Aquilæa, which declares that it is unbecoming the Clergy, who are bound to be an example of soberness and prudence to others, to be present at dramatic performances or any such exhibitions. On the other hand, have we not (as St. Augustin reminds us) most delightful spectacles put before us by our holy Mother, the Church, in her sacred functions—spectacles which (as the same Saint says) serve not to the corruption, but to the protection, of virtue? How miserable is the condition of a Priest who grows weary of the sacred functions, and takes delight in profane plays! In what contempt will he be held by the Faithful!

2. *To call them that were invited.* Who are they whom we are bound to seek out? Those who are invited by our heavenly Father to the marriage of His Son—that is, to the Church militant and triumphant. We must invite them, and call them, and invite others; for these three kinds of service are to be considered in this parable (says St. Thomas). Priests, indeed, are "hunters" of souls, as the Prophet calls them (Jerem. xvi. 16); and they who prefer hunting brute beasts to hunting men—who go in chase of birds instead of seeking the lost sheep—will deserve to be placed among the goats at the Day of Judgment (as St. Peter of Blois says). If we turn to the lives of holy Prophets and Priests, we shall not find one who was occupied with the chase. If we turn to the holy Scriptures (says St. Ambrose), we shall not meet with any holy man who was a hunter. And surely it is not con-

sistent with the meekness and gentleness for which Ministers of the Altar should be distinguished that their hands, which touch the Immaculate Lamb, should handle murderous arms, and take pleasure in the death of animals; but they should rather find their refreshment and their weapons in prayers and tears. Let us, then, impress on our hearts the prohibition of the Fourth Council of Lateran, which strictly forbids Clerics to engage in hunting or hawking, or to keep dogs or birds for such a purpose. It is true that every kind of sport is not absolutely forbidden to Clerics, and we know what is allowed; still, let us pray to God to detach us wholly from it, and let us pray to Him to enlighten those Priests who lose both time and reputation through their passion for the chase.

3. *To the marriage.* The one great transaction, fraught with the most momentous consequences to the world, is the marriage of the Eternal Word with man. Now, this marriage may be explained in four senses, as St. Thomas sets forth, viz.—(1) by the Incarnation; (2) by the union of Christ with His Church; (3) by the espousals of the Word with the individual soul; and (4) by the resurrection of the body. Priests are charged, then, with the duty of assisting in this great business, and it is a duty which carries with it so many difficulties that time suffices not to overcome them all. What opinion, then, can we form of a Priest who, instead of attending to this business, wastes his precious time in play, as if he had nothing else to do? Justly, then, did St. Chrysostom observe that, if, when a grievous conflict is at hand and we have to wage fierce war against the powers unseen, we laugh and sport and take things easily, then by such levity we expose ourselves, even before the conflict, to the danger of being overthrown through our own remissness. Moreover (as St. Peter Damian says), the hand which offers Christ's Body—the tongue destined to mediate between God and the people—should not be contaminated by such profane and frivolous amusements as dice and cards, and by the idle conversation which usually accompanies them. Of the many Synods which have forbidden these games we need cite only one, viz., the Council of Aquilæa, which inhibits all Clerics

"from wasting their time in the miserable pleasures of dice and cards." It is true that some games of cards are permitted, but it is hard to see how Confessors can forbid those amusements to the people, on account of the sins which are connected with them, while they themselves take delight in them. People are thus led to say that Confessors are apt to do the things which they forbid their penitents. Happy is the Ecclesiastic who can say with St. Ambrose, "I am determined to decline, not only immoderate pleasures of this kind, but all such amusements." Happy he who can say with Tobias, "Never have I joined myself with them that play" (iii. 17).

"See if there be in me the way of iniquity, and lead me in the eternal way."— *Ps.* cxxxviii. 24.

"Let us search our ways, and seek, and return to the Lord."—*Lam.* iii. 40.

MONDAY.

WHAT CHRIST REQUIRES OF HIS MINISTERS.

I. THAT THEY BE GOOD SERVANTS.
II. THAT THEY BE FAITHFUL SERVANTS.
III. THAT THEY BE PRUDENT SERVANTS.

" Again he sent other servants, saying, Tell them that were invited, Behold, I have prepared my dinner, my beeves and fatlings are killed, and all things are ready: come ye to the marriage."—*St. Matt.* xxii. 4.

1. *He sent other servants.* These servants, of whom our Lord makes mention, are His prophets, His preachers, His ministers. Justly, then, did the Apostle frequently call himself "the servant of Christ," and every ecclesiastic "the servant of the Lord" (2 Tim. ii. 24). Every such servant will enter into the joy of his Lord when he shall hear from Him the words, "Well done, good servant" (St. Matt. xxv. 23). Now, we know that " One is good"—God alone (St. Matt. xix. 17); but, through that charity which He diffuses in our hearts, the good Spirit—that is, the Holy Ghost—comes and dwells within us, and renders us good ; for (as St. Augustin says) we cannot have love without having other good things by which man is made good. And St. Gregory points out that for this end has God anointed us Priests (for unction signifies the infusion of grace, and the

diffusion of charity), and so nourishes in us the fire of the Holy Spirit, so that we may enlighten others by our words. Meanwhile we must exercise caution over ourselves, that we be not too secure, too content, and even vainglorious, in regard to this our "goodness." If humility has made us "good," pride will make us "evil;" and if we praise ourselves as good (as St. Augustin warns us), we become evil. Therefore, let us be convinced that we are sinners, in order that we may become truly just; for (as St. Gregory declares) the greater sinners do Priests become in proportion to their trust in their own goodness. O good Spirit, make me truly good; "sanctify me in the truth!"

2. *Tell them that were invited.* The servants were instructed to carry a message to those who had been invited, and they carried it faithfully. It suffices not, indeed, to be good servants, but we must also be "faithful" servants, in order to deserve our Master's commendation, "Well done, good and faithful servant" (St. Matt. xxv. 23). To be "faithful" (as St. Chrysostom explains) is to avoid appropriating to ourselves anything that belongs to our Lord—not to squander His goods vainly or needlessly, but to advance His interests and promote His glory to the utmost of our power. Further, St. Thomas shews fidelity to be that virtue which causes us to fulfil the obligations we have contracted, and to keep the promises we have made, and which cannot certainly be violated without sin. "An unfaithful and foolish promise displeaseth God" (Eccle. v. 3). Let us, therefore, call to mind the promises we have made to God when we first received the tonsure, and in all the different steps by which we were promoted to Holy Orders. Nay, more: a kind of contract was entered into between our Superiors and ourselves as often as any charge has been laid upon us; for every charge has its obligations, and in accepting the charge we took upon us likewise the obligation. Let us remember that the Holy Spirit describes the various offices which were distributed by Esdras and Nehemias in Jerusalem, as types of the various charges distributed to the sacred Ministers in the Church. Some have to combat heretics, and these are "valiant men" (2 Esdr. xi. 6).

Others have to rule, or aid those who rule—"their ruler . . and second over the city" (*ibid.* 9). Others have to take care of the fabric, the beauty, the functions of the Temple—to "do the works of the Temple" (*ibid.* 12). Others have to make use of the advantages which birth, friendships, patronage, or riches place in their way, for maintaining the rights of the Church—"as sons of the mighty" (*ibid.* 14). Others have to watch over works of religion carried on outside the Temple—"over all the outward business of the house of God" (*ibid.* 16). Others have to be intent on praising God, and praying to Him—"to praise, and to give glory in prayer" (*ibid.* 17). Others have to attend to the education of youth, and especially of youths intended for the ecclesiastical state—"as overseers of the Levites in Jerusalem" (*ibid.* 22). Others have charge of the ecclesiastical music—"singing men in the ministry of the house of God." Others have to instruct the people and administer the Sacraments—"in all matters concerning the people" (*ibid.* 24). Others have to go forth on holy missions—"through all their countries" (*ibid.* 25). Let us pray to God that all Priests may fulfil their duties with perfect fidelity, "every one in his office" (2 Esdr. xii. 9).

3. *Come ye to the marriage.* These servants gave the intimation with prudence, making known its true character—that is to say, that it related to a marriage banquet, prepared by a king. In like manner, the servant of God must be not only faithful, but prudent also—"a faithful and wise servant" (St. Matt. xxiv. 45); not however, as the wise and prudent of this world, of whom our Saviour said, "Thou hast hid these things from the wise and prudent" (St. Matt. xi. 25). True prudence is the prudence of the serpent, who (as St. Hilary says) in all dangers protects its head, in which is its life, and cares not for its body ; and thus we should preach Christ, our Head, and expose ourselves to any kind of danger for His interests. True prudence, joined to fidelity, (says Origen) causes us to dispense the Sacraments to such only as are worthy of them, and to such as have greatest need of them, whatever be their condition. Prudence, again, makes us careful dispensers of the Church's goods. Let us reflect also that prudence, in Holy Scripture, is often identified

with wisdom, and is called also "the beginning and light of all virtues" (Prov. ix. 10). The house of the Lord—that is, the Church—"is built by wisdom, and by prudence shall be strengthened" (Prov. xxiv. 3). Let us remember, also, that our Lord Jesus Christ came upon earth to teach prudence to the ancients —that is, to Priests especially; and in this respect was Joseph a type of Him, as he was said to "instruct his princes as himself, and teach the ancients of Egypt wisdom" (Ps. civ. 22). Let us pray to God to give us true prudence, and to deliver us from "the wisdom of the flesh, which is death" (Rom. viii. 6).

"Make Thy face to shine upon Thy servant, and teach me Thy justifications."— Ps. cxviii. 135.

"Lord God, Who keepest covenant and mercy with Thy servants that have walked before Thee with all their heart."—3 Kings viii. 23.

TUESDAY.

———◆———

*THE PUNISHMENT OF THOSE WHO DISHONOUR
THE PRIESTHOOD.*

    I. HOW THE PRIESTHOOD IS DISHONOURED.
    II. THE DUTY OF THE CLERGY IN SUCH CASES.
    III. THE PENALTIES OF THIS SIN.

———◆———

" But they neglected, and went their ways, one to his farm, and another to his
merchandise ; and the rest laid hands on his servants, and, having treated them con-
tumeliously, put them to death. But when the king had heard of it he was angry,
and, sending his armies, he destroyed those murderers, and burnt their city."—
St. Matt. xxii. 5—7.

1. *But they neglected.* The Priesthood is dishonoured by disregard of the words which Priests utter in God's name : it is still
more dishonoured when they are despised or calumniated, for
God has said, "Give honour to the Priests" (Eccle. vii. 33). If
they be wicked, God would still have them honoured, for, even
as gold and precious stones, and pearls, however much they
may be soiled with mud, lose none of their intrinsic value (as
St. Ephrem says), so the Priesthood itself still' retains its worth
however unworthy the individual Priest may be. It is, indeed, a
great crime to persecute God's Priests, to ill-use them and to violate
their rights, according to our Lord's prediction, "If they have
persecuted Me, they will also persecute you" (St. John xv. 20).
Yet this is the way of the wicked, and the way of the world—
to hate those who are unspotted from the world : the world

at enmity with God hates the world reconciled to God : the condemned hate the saved (as St. Augustin says). And how common is this grave sin! How many wicked books, filled with ribaldry, slander, and calumnies, or with false theories of politics and morals, are launched against the Priesthood! "What things the enemy hath done wickedly in the sanctuary!" (Ps. lxxiii, 4.) Let us implore from God light for those who "know not what they do." "Lord, lay not this sin to their charge" (Acts vii. 59).

2. *The rest laid hands on his servants.* These words point to the meekness of the servants of God, who, like sheep before their shearers (in imitation of their Divine Master), open not their mouth. The profession of the Priesthood is a lamblike profession (says St. Ambrose), and (as St. Ignatius the Martyr says) the devil is conquered by this meekness. This ought to be the consolation of Priests if their virtue displeases the world and excites persecution—the reflection, namely, that in proportion to the misery of those who do such things is the blessedness of those who suffer them, if only this persecution is exercised for justice's sake, and for the Name of our Lord Jesus Christ (as St. Augustin says). This ought to be their consolation—the remembrance of our Saviour's great promise, "Be glad and rejoice, for your reward is very great in heaven" (Matt. v. 32). This ought to be their consolation—that they are treated as their Divine Master was treated, and as the Prophets were treated : "For so they persecuted the Prophets that were before you" (ver. 12). Meanwhile let them not cease to compassionate the unhappiness of their persecutors, who do this evil because they know not God : "All these things will they do to you" because they know not Him that sent Me" (St. John xv. 21). Let them not fear, let them not cease to fulfil their duties ; for, if the powerful now thunder upon them, these shall themselves in a little time feel the thunderbolt (as St. Augustin declares). Lastly, let them not exasperate their persecutors so as to give occasion to graver evils, but let them remember our Saviour's counsel, "When they shall persecute you in this city flee into another" (St. Mark x. 23). Blessed is the Priest who faithfully fulfils these maxims, even to death.

3. *But when the king had heard of it he was angry.* God is said to be angry when he avenges outrages against Himself. He (says St. Jerome) Who as man had invited the guests to the marriage, as King avenges the outrages committed against Himself and His Ministers. The punishment which God inflicted upon Dathan is but a shadow of that which awaits the persecutors of the Clergy (as St. Chrysostom points out). St. Cyril says that it suffices to despise the Priest in order to draw down God's vengeance. Just cause had a great Saint (St. Francis) for saying, "Woe to them who despise the Clergy; woe to them at the point of death!" Then, perchance, they may desire a Priest, and may be unable to find one: "You shall seek Me, and shall not find Me, and you shall die in your sin" (St. John xii. 34; viii. 21). Let us depart from these men, let us shake the dust of their cities from our feet, according to the command of Jesus Christ, and the practice of the Saints (Acts xiii. 51). On the other hand, how deep would be our guilt should we take part in the persecution of God's servants, as some unhappy Priests have done! Rather let us strive to console those who suffer; let us try to help them and to defend them, in imitation of that great Saint, St. Jerome, who is said to have always been a patron of pious and faithful Catholics.

"Thy enemies have made a noise, and they that hate Thee have lifted up the head. They have taken a malicious counsel against Thy people, and have consulted against Thy Saints."—*Ps.* lxxxii. 3, 4.

"Remember them, O Lord my God, that defile the Priesthood, and the law of the Priests and Levites."—2 *Esdr.* xiii. 29.

WEDNESDAY.

THE PARABLE OF THE MARRIAGE FEAST AN ENCOURAGEMENT IN ECCLESIASTICAL LABOURS.

I. BY ITS PROPHECIES.
II. BY ITS EXHORTATIONS.
III. BY ITS CONSOLATIONS.

" Then he saith to his servants, The marriage indeed is ready, but they that are invited were not worthy. Go ye, therefore, into the high-ways, and as many as you shall find call to the marriage. And his servants, going forth into the ways, gathered together all that they found, both bad and good, and the marriage was filled with guests."—*St. Matt.* xxii. 8—10.

1. *They that are invited were not worthy.* Our Saviour, thus showing Himself to be true God, speaks of the future as if already past, for all things are present in the mind of God. He foretells the mission of His servants to the Jews, the neglect of the latter to profit by the invitation, their ill-treatment of the former, and the consequent destruction of Jerusalem. He points out at once the incredible folly of those who, for frivolous pretexts, despised the King's invitation and preferred vile pleasures to the delights of a royal banquet, and also the awful crime of those who slew His innocent servants, and so aroused the anger of the King, and brought down upon themselves His wrath and vengeance. These are things at which the heavens are astonished (Jerem. ii. 12). "Who hath heard such horrible things?" (Jerem. xviii. 13.) Thence followed the calling of the Gentiles,

who (as St. Jerome points out) were not then in the way of salvation, but in the by-ways. The Apostles abandoned Judæa; they propagated the Gospel among idolaters; they brought together into the banqueting-chamber both bad and good; for (as St. Gregory says) in the Church the bad and good must exist together, and he is not good who knows not how to tolerate the bad. The fulfilment of such important prophecies should confirm us in the Faith, and we may also find encouragement in the remembrance of the labours of the Prophets and Apostles, and also of our brethren in the present day, who are engaged in the propagation of the Faith among the infidels. Let us acknowledge how far off we are from imitating their zeal and their sanctity.

2. *As many as you shall find call to the marriage.* The King of the heavenly mansion desires to fill its vacant seats, and if one refuses another is put in his place. Hence the warning, "Hold fast that which thou hast, that no man take thy crown" (Apoc. iii. 2). We are exhorted in this parable to avoid all "accepting of persons," and to turn ourselves alike to the poor and to the rich, rather than to say, "Perhaps these are poor and foolish, that know not the way of the Lord, the judgment of their God; I will go therefore to the great men" (Jerem. v. 45). Whatever be the condition of men, God wills not their death, but that they be converted and live; and therefore He commands us to invite them all to the Faith, and that faith must be, not dead, but living. Let us promise in God's name pardon of their sins to all men if they will but forsake the way of iniquity. Now, what have we done hitherto? Have we seconded the fatherly intentions of the King, Who invites all men without distinction to the banquet? Or have we imitated Saul, who, in the slaughter of the Amalekites, slew the common people, and everything that was vile, whilst he spared the best that was beautiful? (I. Kings xv. 8, 9.)

3. *And the marriage was filled with guests.* What a consolation is it for zealous Ecclesiastics to know the end of their calling! To people Paradise with souls, to fill the heavenly mansions with guests, to make them participate in the blessed nuptials con-

summated in heaven—this is the end of the Priesthood. The souls led by us to Paradise will have eternal life from Christ, and (says St. Augustin) in greater abundance than the life which they have lost : " I am come that they may have life, and may have it more abundantly " (St. John x. 10). First they will have the life of grace, then they will have the life of glory. How will these souls then bless us ! How will they bless Jesus Christ, Who shed His blood for them. But let us ever remember that our invitation will not lead men to Christ unless our heavenly Father draw them by His grace (St. John vi. 44), and that both we ourselves and the souls committed to us need the Divine aid, which we must continually invoke. Let us console ourselves with the thought that we are labouring under the eye of God, and in God's behalf, and therefore (as St. Thomas points out) does He show His anger against all who despise us and illtreat us. The day is not far off in which we shall see openly the triumph of Divine mercy and justice. Meanwhile let us adore the wisdom of our Lord, Who by this parable has so encouraged His Ministers.

" Thy hand shall help me, and Thy arm shall strengthen me."—From *Ps.* lxxxviii. 22.

" The hand of the Lord be with me strengthening me."—From *Ezech.* iii. 14.

THURSDAY.

THE GREAT SINFULNESS OF A SACRILEGIOUS MASS.

I. The multiplicity of sins.
II. Their enormity.
III. The aggravating circumstances attending them.

" And the king went in to see the guests, and he saw there a man who had not on a wedding garment, and he saith to him, Friend, how camest thou in hither, not having on a wedding garment? But he was silent."—*St. Matt.* xxii. 11, 12.

1. *Not having on a wedding garment.* St. Jerome, St. Hilary, St. Chrysostom, and innumerable other writers, understand by this wedding garment charity or sanctifying grace. It is sufficient to quote the words of St. Gregory the Great: " What must we understand by the wedding garment," says he, " but charity?" All, therefore, who draw near to the Eucharistic banquet should prove themselves, and make sure, so far as possible, that they have this wedding garment : otherwise they commit a grave sacrilege : " Let a man prove himself, and so let him eat of that bread, and drink of the chalice" (1 Cor. xi. 28). But the Priest who, unmindful of the maxim that holy things must be treated holily, celebrates Mass in mortal sin, commits not one sacrilege only, but four specifically distinct sacrileges (as St. Alphonsus declares), viz.,—first in consecrating unworthily ; secondly, in receiving unworthily ; thirdly, in administering unworthily ; fourthly, in administering to an unworthy recipient. For he

thus violates four distinct obligations of the virtue of Religion, binding under penalty of mortal sin ; and, therefore, according to the rules of sound theology, although the act be one, still the number of sins is multiplied, so that we may justly exclaim with St. Ambrose, " How many crimes are there in one wicked act ! " Each one of these sacrileges is a kind of violence done to the Body and the Blood of Christ (as St. Cyprian says). Moreover, in regard to each one of these sacrileges, we may consider with St. Augustin that there is no man so wicked that he would dare to touch Christ with hands defiled with mire ; and, in God's eyes, are not the hands of one in mortal sin infinitely more abominable than if they were besmeared with mire ?

2. *Friend, how camest thou in hither?* As our Lord Jesus Christ called Judas "friend" when he betrayed Him with a feigned kiss of peace, so does He call the sacrilegious Priest "friend" who feigns to be in the grace of God when he is the object of His hatred. He uses the word "friend" (says Origen) in reproach for his false pretence. Thou art indignant against the traitor and against the murderers of our Lord (says St. Chrysostom), yet dost thou not consider that by this sacrilege thou renderest thyself equally guilty of the Body and Blood of Christ. Nay, is not thy crime yet greater? for, while feigning to adore Him, thou slayest Him, so far as thou canst, in the very act of worship. And (as St. Augustin says) far greater is the crime of the Priest who unworthily offers Christ now that He is reigning in heaven than that of the Jews who crucified Him while on this earth. Moreover (as St. Thomas points out), in other sins God is offended indirectly, but the Holy Sacrifice offered unworthily is a direct offence against the very person of God Incarnate. Hence it is impossible for any one to sin more grievously against Almighty God than a sacrilegious Priest. Who, then, would not weep over the misery of Priests who celebrate Mass with the consciousness of mortal sin ? Again, who would not burn with love for Jesus Christ, who, for love of men, subjects Himself to such unworthy treatment ? Let us, at least, strive by acts of love to compensate Him for the many outrages which He receives from the sacrilegious.

3. *But he was silent.* This guest was silent because (says Origen) he had no excuse for his sin. And what excuse will sacrilegious Priests have, since their crime is so evident, and attended by so many aggravating circumstances? Can they allege ignorance? Do they not know that (as St. Thomas teaches) the gravest of all sacrileges is that which is committed against the Eucharist? Do they not know that (as St. Peter Damian teaches), so far as in them lies, they contaminate the saving Victim, and therefore commit the gravest sin? Moreover, the benefits which they have received from Jesus Christ render still more monstrous the ingratitude of sacrilegious Priests, to whom He might justly say, "Wherefore do you so ill repay your Benefactor? Why so great malice?" As St. Thomas of Villanova says, they impiously cast Jesus Christ Himself into the filthy sewer of their own impure hearts, even in the very Sacrifice in which He shows us the excess of His love and seeks to purify the souls of the Faithful. Shall a Minister of Religion, who is bound to guard and promote that virtue, offend against so many of its distinct obligations, and in its most sublime act? Oh, worst of all crimes! (exclaims St. Laurence Justinian.) Let us fear lest we may one day render ourselves guilty of so grave a sin; let us resolve always to confess our sins before Mass whenever our conscience shall reproach us with mortal sin; and let us pray to God to preserve us from this evil, the danger of which is daily present to us.

FRIDAY.

THE CHASTISEMENTS WITH WHICH ALMIGHTY GOD IS WONT TO PUNISH SACRILEGIOUS PRIESTS.

I. In life.
II. In death.
III. In eternity.

"Then the king said to the waiters, Bind his hands and feet and cast him into the exterior darkness; there shall be weeping and gnashing of teeth. For many are called, but few are chosen."—*St. Matt.* xxii. 13, 14.

1. *Cast him into the exterior darkness.* This is the sentence (says St. Augustin) which Almighty God is wont to fulminate against such as dare to ascend to the Altar without the wedding garment of grace. If he who seated himself at the table of an earthly king without the wedding garment was condemned to darkness, what (asks St. Peter Damian) can a Priest expect who dares to profane the table of the King of Heaven, to present himself before it, and to partake of it, whilst he is full of the filth of luxury, or the squalor of avarice? These miserable men are, in the first place, punished with blindness, in which the prince of darkness envelopes them, just as he blinded Judas, the first of sacrilegious Priests. For it was after he had received the Eucharist sacrilegiously that "Satan entered into him" (St. John xiii. 27); and he entered into that miserable Priest (as St. Augustin shows) to possess him for his own, and to conceal from

him the horror of the treason which he was about to consum-
mate. In like manner unworthy Priests are blinded by Satan;
they go from one excess to another, till the Eucharistic banquet
becomes a snare to them, and a punishment of their crimes, and
an occasion of sin: " Let their table become as a snare before
them, and a recompense, and a stumbling-block (Ps. lxviii. 23).
Let us pray to God to open our eyes, and to give us heavenly
light, which shall make us recognise their unhappy condition,
and the danger to which we are exposed of falling into it ourselves. Suffer not, O my Jesus, that the Holy Mass should be
to me "for judgment and condemnation."

2. *But few are chosen.* Among sacrilegious Priests few are
chosen ; that is, few of them are ever converted so as to die in
the Lord. They often go unpunished in this life, but nothing
is more miserable (as St. Augustin says) than such apparent
felicity; their impurity is in itself their punishment, for their evil
will is thereby strengthened. God seems, indeed, to have no
anger against them, but it is precisely because His indignation
is so great (says St. Jerome) that He does not show it, but reserves it for the day of their death. Jeremias, after having
asked of God, "Why doth the way of the wicked prosper ?"
adds, " Prepare them for the day of slaughter" (xii. 1—3). Some,
indeed, are carried off by sudden death, like that Priest mentioned in the life of St. Alphonsus, who died beginning the
Psalm, "Judica me, Deus." Others, although dying after long
sickness, neglect to reconcile themselves to God, and, as in
their lifetime they forgot Him, so, by His just judgment, in their
death they forget themselves. Sometimes sacrilegious Priests,
like Judas, die in despair ; and who is more miserable than such
as have no pity on themselves ? (asks St. Augustin.) They are
excluded from the number of God's people, and are not allowed
to reach their heavenly country: " He shall bear his iniquity
because he hath defiled the holy thing of the Lord, and that
soul shall perish from among his people" (Levit. xix. 8). Have
mercy on them, O my Jesus! Remember that no sooner was
Thy death for the sins of the whole world accomplished
than Thou gavest the grace of faith and the gift of repentance

to the centurion, and to Thine executioners, in order that they might obtain the pardon of their horrible sacrilege.

3. *There shall be weeping and gnashing of teeth.* In these words our Saviour pointed out the severity of the punishment which the sacrilegious will suffer, not only in their soul (says St. Thomas), but in their body also. If hell is prepared for every mortal sin, how much greater will be the punishment of those who have "trodden under foot the Son of God" and profaned the Blood of the Testament!" (Heb. x. 29.) For what is a sacrilegious Communion but the treading under foot of the Body of Christ? (says St. Ambrose.) Let us call to mind the rule defined by God Himself—"According to the measure of the sin shall the measure also of the stripes be" (Deut. xxv. 2) ; and, if yesterday we considered the heinousness of this sin, we may well meditate to-day on its punishment. As St. Thomas points out, it is one thing for a man to despise the edicts of a king, and another to wound a king with his own hand ; and the punishment is proportioned to the offence. A Priest who celebrates daily with devotion furnishes good proof of heroic humility : a Priest who celebrates sacrilegiously gives a sign of eternal reprobation. Let us reflect on the number of Priests who will weep in despair with Judas through all eternity, and let us pray to God that it may not be our lot to swell their number. Let us resolve that we will not imitate those wicked Ministers who think by hypocrisy to veil the corruption of their heart from God's eyes, and so approach the altar with impunity : "They think they can escape the justice of God, Who seeth all things" (Esther xvi. 4). How great is the devil's triumph over those whom he induces to commit sacrilege in order to destroy them !

"Let them not say . . . we have swallowed him up, let them blush and be ashamed together who rejoice at my evils."—*Ps.* xxxiv. 25, 26.

"Forsake us not, because Thou art a merciful and gracious God."—From 2 *Esdr.* ix. 31.

SATURDAY.

THE PURITY OF THE BLESSED VIRGIN MARY.

PRIESTS SHOULD IMPLORE THE AID OF THE BLESSED VIRGIN THAT THEY MAY PRESERVE PURITY.

        I. IN MIND.

        II. IN BODY.

        III. IN PROFESSION.

"The Holy Ghost shall come upon thee, and the power of the Most High shall overshadow thee, and therefore also the Holy which shall be born of thee shall be called the Son of God."—*St. Luke* i. 35.

1. *The Holy Ghost shall come upon thee.* The Archangel Gabriel was sent to Mary, who was a Virgin in mind, a Virgin in body, and a Virgin in profession (says St. Bernard). He found Her so pure that She merited to be chosen to be the Mother of the Lord (says St. Jerome). He found Her mind so separated from all sin that She merited to conceive and to bring forth the God of purity, Who is incapable of sin. He found Her so pure a Virgin in mind (says St. Ambrose) that Her affections had no corruption. Hence he assured Her that Her virginity would not suffer by the mystery of the Incarnation, and that by the operation of the Holy Spirit Her virginity, so far from being disturbed, would be perfected. Let us, then, have recourse to Her, in order that we may be pure from all vice, and fit also to purify our

people from vice. Above all, our purity ought to be in thought (as St. Gregory says). Modesty, with other virtues, is the ornament which the Clergy ought to cherish in their soul (as St. Clement teaches). Let us set the Blessed Virgin before us as our model, and employ all our efforts to imitate Her; for (as St. Bernard tells us) She loves those who imitate Her in chastity and in humility.

2. *And the power of the Most High shall overshadow thee.* The power of the Most High *overshadowed* Mary in order to preserve Her virginity, and therefore by these words 'the Angel declared to Her that She should be fruitful without corruption, that She should conceive without lust, and bring forth without pain. So says St. Bonaventure. It was by reason of the perfection of Mary's virginal purity that the Word assumed Her pure flesh (says St. Peter Damian). Her virginity (says St. Gregory of Nyssa) was like a vessel or a chariot, in which our God descended from heaven to earth. So perfect was this virginity (says St. Bernard) that in Her very flesh She surpassed the purity of all the Angels. And the particular value of this virginity was that it was to be most fruitful, and in its very fruitfulness to become more perfect. This was a miracle than which a greater could not be looked for from God (says St. Augustin)—a miracle the mode of which passes man's understanding—a miracle the like of which was never known, and the cause of which is the omnipotent will of the Creator. Surely we, as Priests, are bound to preserve chastity in our flesh, because (as St. Peter Damian tells us) we have to touch with our hands the Body of Christ, which was conceived in the Virgin's womb. A Priest (says St. Ignatius the Martyr) should be the house of God, the temple of Christ, the organ of the Holy Ghost; and therefore should he keep himself chaste and pure. And in order to attain to this purity we need against our spiritual foes the assistance of Her Who is "terrible as an army set in array" (Cant. vi. 3).

3. *The Holy which shall be born of thee.* Mary made profession of chastity because She had taken a vow of chastity, and had even renounced the dignity of mother in order to keep that vow. But Her very profession of purity (as St. Anselm shows)

rendered Her fit for so august a dignity. In fact (says St. Thomas), She indeed merited so high a rank in the profession of purity as to render Herself fit to be the Mother of God; and by this mystery (as St. Gregory of Nyssa points out) Almighty God would show us that He comes into pure souls, and that they alone are capable of receiving Him who are separated from all carnal affections. Now, all Priests likewise have made this profession, they are under this vow of chastity, and therefore their life must be in accordance with such a profession. We should, then, be the fathers of the Faithful; we should beget them to the life of grace and of glory, and thus, like Mary, couple virginity with fruitfulness. Let us, then, invoke Her holy name, and in this shall we find our shield against all temptations.

" After her shall virgins be brought to the king . . they shall be brought into the temple of the king."—*Ps.* xliv. 15, 16.

" My beloved to me, and I to him, who feedeth among the lilies."—*Cant.* ii. 16.

TWENTIETH SUNDAY AFTER PENTECOST.

THE RULER OF CAPHARNAUM A MODEL OF PRIESTLY ZEAL.

I. HE REPRESENTS THE PRIEST.
II. HE CONDEMNS THE SLOTHFUL PRIEST.
III. HE SHEWS THE FIRST EFFORT OF ZEAL.

"There was a certain ruler whose son was rich at Capharnaum. He, having heard that Jesus was come from Judea into Galilee, went to Him and prayed Him to come down and heal his son, for he was at the point of death." —*St. John* iv. 46, 47.

1. *There was a certain ruler.* The Evangelist is silent in regard to the name of this ruler, and we may thus consider him as representing zealous men in general, and the Priest in particular. St. Jerome speaks of him as one belonging to the emperor's court. St. Augustin interprets the word to mean a personage of the royal family, or one adorned with the dignity of prince; and Origen considers it to refer to a commander of the king's army. All these meanings well apply to the Priest, for he belongs to the king's palace, and is therefore (as St. Peter Damian calls him) a companion and fellow-servant of the Angels. Moreover, he has a "kingly priesthood" (I. Peter ii. 9); he is a prince among Christians, "prince of his brethren, the support of his family, the ruler of his brethren, the stay of the people" (Eccl. xlix. 17); and he leads that portion of the

Christian army which is confided to him in the war against spiritual enemies : " Captain of the army of the king " (2 Paralip. xxxii. 21). Further, he is the spiritual father of Christians, so that to Priests it may be justly said, amid the general corruption of morals, " Rule your houses, rule your children." So St. Augustin. O supreme Giver of light, enlighten my mind in regard to this truth ; make me understand how great is the dignity which Thou hast conferred upon me, how great the duties which Thou hast imposed upon me !

2. *Went to Him and prayed Him.* The ruler saw that his son's body was about to lose its life—that is to say, that the soul was about to depart from it. In like manner the zealous Priest observes that the soul of his spiritual children languishes, either because God has departed from them or is about to depart from them by reason of mortal sin. The ruler did not remain idle at this doleful spectacle, but asked information about Jesus Christ, and at once undertook a journey of fourteen leagues, without taking into account its inconvenience and danger, or his own dignity. Many Priests, on the contrary, behold the danger of their spiritual children, they know the means of helping them, but draw back from the work, and abandon it at the very least difficulty, saying, with the slothful and the coward, " There is a lion in the way, and a lioness in the roads " (Prov. xxvi. 13). As the door turneth upon its hinges, so does the slothful upon his bed " (ver. 14). Had the ruler been over careful of his own health, fearing to expose himself to any risk on account of his advanced age, he would not have acted as he did. Priests will undertake no laborious work for the good of souls if they are anxious or over careful in regard to their health, this being a hidden but powerful temptation of the devil. Nay (as St. Jerome says), they should understand that, with prudence, they can even in habitual sickness and in old age do great good to the Faithful by their counsels and teaching, and so compensate for what they cannot do by corporal labour. Lastly, the ruler asked no recompense of his son for his journey, and for the great service which he rendered him, all fatherly solicitude being gratuitous ; and so will the zealous Priest be father of the

Faithful if he cure them gratuitously, and if he do not render heavenly treasures vile by asking reward for them. It is, indeed, unworthy of an Ecclesiastic (as St. Chrysostom declares) to put a price upon his ministry. But, alas! many are but as hired pedagogues—few as fathers who have care of their spiritual children out of heart-felt affection : "If you have ten thousand instructors . . yet not many fathers" (1 Cor. iv. 15).

3. *And prayed Him.* The ruler took the best of all resolutions to see his son cured ; that is, he turned to the Author of health, though as yet he had not true faith in Him, and only directed His prayer to Him in a tentative manner. St. Chrysostom remarks that parents, in their great affliction, are wont to converse, not only with physicians in whom they have confidence, but even with those in whom they have no confidence, desiring to leave nothing untried in matters relating to their children's health. We know, on the contrary, that when we ask for spiritual cure Jesus Christ, the Son of God, prays for us as our Priest, prays in us as our Head, is prayed to by us as our God. So St. Augustin. Let us not be discouraged, but let us persevere in prayer, even if it be not quickly granted. Let us be assured that Jesus Christ will heal the sick in His own time, for (as St. Augustin says) He who cures knows what is the right moment for applying the remedy. Let us not desist from prayer, though He may defer to grant it ; let us trust in His promises, and let us remember that our very prayer is a gift of God, opening for us the way to further benefits. Let us not faint in prayer (says St. Augustin), for, though He put off what He intends to grant, He putteth it not away. Secure of His promise, let us not faint in praying, for even this gift of prayer is the effect of His goodness. Our zeal should, indeed, commence with ourselves, and, therefore, let us strive by fervent prayer to obtain from our Lord Jesus Christ the cure of our soul, which we should regard as our own son, sick with the fever of evil passions and desires, and in danger of death.

"Send Thy word and heal us, and deliver us from our destructions."—From *Ps. cvi.* 20.

"We all are the works of Thy hands : be not very angry, O Lord, and remember no longer our iniquity."—*Isaias* lxiv. 8, 9.

MONDAY.

THE BEARING OF PRIESTS TOWARDS THE GREAT MEN OF THE WORLD.

I. THEY SHOULD REGARD THEM WITH THE EYE OF FAITH.
II. THEY SHOULD TREAT THEM ACCORDING TO THE WORKS OF FAITH.
III. THEY SHOULD CONDUCT THEM INTO THE WAY OF FAITH.

"Jesus therefore said to him, Unless you see signs and wonders you believe not."
—*St. John* iv. 48.

1. *Jesus therefore said to him.* Our Lord Jesus Christ spoke to the ruler in order to lay bare the wound of his heart—namely, weakness of faith, for which He reproved him. He shewed him (says St. Augustin) to be a man lukewarm or cold in faith, or of no faith at all. Such are, for the most part, the great men of this world—tepid or cold in faith, or entirely without faith, even while they appear to possess it. Yet what avails all their greatness if they have not this Divine virtue, without which it is impossible to please God? Let the Priest, then, in his dealings with these men, recollect that all such as take advantage of their worldly position to despise those of humble rank are regarded by God "afar off" (Ps. cxxxvii. 6). In proportion as a man lifts himself up, so does God withdraw Himself from him, while the devil draws nearer to him in order to seize him as his prey. God will be raised above thee (says St. Augustin) in proportion as thou raisest thyself above others. Behold! "A king is to-

day, and to morrow he shall die; for when a man shall die he
shall inherit serpents, and beasts, and worms" (Eccl. x. 12, 13).
However great man's riches, "as the flower of the grass shall
he pass away . . . so also shall the rich man fade away in his
ways" (St. James i. 10, 11). He, then, who looks upon the rich
men of this world with the eye of faith will say to them with
the Apostle, "Go to now, ye rich men, weep and howl in your
miseries, which shall come upon you" (St. James v. 1). We
know what was our Lord's teaching in regard to the rich—how
He uttered the most terrible truths in reference to them—how
He declared the difficulty of their salvation—how He spoke of
the account which they will have to give to God. And shall the
Priest who is instructed in these truths be deceived by the appearance of greatness? Shall he forget his own supernatural
dignity? Shall he debase his august character by paying homage
to the rich and despising the poor? "You have respect to him
that is clothed with the fine apparel, and say to him, Sit thou
here well; but say to the poor man, Stand thou there, or sit
under my footstool" (St. James ii. 3). Let us rather learn by
faith to venerate those who are "rich in faith" (ver. 5), for
(as St. Ambrose teaches) God regards those only as rich who
are rich to eternity.

2. *Unless you see signs and wonders you believe not.* We, in treating
with the rich, cannot work signs and wonders as our Lord did,
but by another kind of miracle ought we to keep our conscience
pure, and not suffer ourselves to be corrupted; for it is a general
rule that "He that hath fellowship with the proud shall put on
pride" (Eccl. xiii. 1). In order not to expose ourselves to danger,
the first rule is to imitate Jesus, Who (as St. Thomas points out)
refused to go to the house of this prince, and so checked our
pride, which causes us to offer ourselves to serve great men.
We have before our eyes the teaching which God has given us
on this head—namely, that "he shall take a burden upon him
that hath fellowship with one more honourable than himself;"
and that it is good counsel to "have no fellowship with one
that is richer than thyself" (Eccl. xiii. 2). He has inculcated
upon us that, even when "invited by one that is mightier," we

should withdraw ourselves, "and believe not his many words," which are often only directed to tempt us and make sport of us (Eccl. xiii. 12, 14). Another most important rule is, that, having to treat with the great men of the world, we hide not true wisdom out of a false humility—that we suppress not the truth, nor omit correction, if necessary: "Be not lowly in thy wisdom, lest, being humbled, thou be deceived into folly" (Eccl. xiii. 11). How many Priests are there who, out of human respect, have neglected to correct those whose language wounded purity, charity, or religion, and have had to repeat with tears, "Wo is me, because I have held my peace!" (Isaias vi. 5.) How many are there who, in order to please the great, lay aside the clerical dress, frequent worldly society, appear at theatres, and thus (as St. Peter Damian declares), becoming servants of the world, and feeling the solicitations of concupiscence, bring ruin upon their soul! But let us remember that "God alone is great, and that all men are as though they were not, before Him."

3. *You believe not.* Our Lord Jesus Christ (as St. Chrysostom points out), by not going to the ruler's house, and showing that he could cure his servant even at a distance, led him to the Faith. On the other hand, many Priests have gained over the great men of this world by affability, gentleness, and courtesy. Doubtless great prudence, great suavity of manners, combined with firmness of purpose, are requisite in order to lead such men to that lively "faith which worketh by charity." In all services which Priests render to the great they should purify their intention ; all their dealings with them should be actuated by that charity which moves them to consider the sick before the healthy ; for (as St. Ambrose says) a king's court is, as it were, filled with men afflicted with dropsy—men swollen and inflated with pride. We ought to compassionate such men, because they are in great dangers, and (as St. Augustin declares) through many perils arrive at a greater peril. But if we shall succeed in gaining over a great man we shall bring much profit to the Church, for he will no longer make his servants the servants of iniquity, but his example will improve the morals of his inferiors, and his protection will great service to the Church in many matters of importance.

Let us, then, implore God's help that, if He sends us to treat with such men, He may say to us (as He said to His Prophet of old), " Thou shalt go to all that I send thee, and whatsoever I shall command thee thou shalt speak. Be not afraid at their presence, for I am with thee " (Jerem. i. 7, 8). Meanwhile let us examine our conscience on this point, and we may perhaps find that we owe much to God's justice, and have abundant matter for tears.

" Let not the oil of the sinner fatten my head."—*Ps.* cxl. 5.

" O Lord, say to me, Thou art my servant, I have chosen thee, and have not cast thee away ; fear not, for I am with thee."—From *Isaias* xli. 9, 10.

TUESDAY.

THE DUTY OF PRIESTS TOWARDS THEIR RELA-TIONS AND DOMESTICS.

I. To INSTRUCT THEM IN THE TRUTH.

II. To PRESERVE THEM IN CHARITY.

III. To RESTRAIN THEIR COVETOUSNESS.

" The ruler saith to Him, Lord, come down before that my son die. Jesus saith to him, Go thy way; thy son liveth."—*St. John* iv. 49, 50.

1. *Lord, come down.* At that time (as St. Chrysostom points out) the ruler gave no great heed to our Saviour's words, being wholly absorbed with the thought of his dying son. Priests should regard their immediate relatives as their children, in the care which they bestow upon them ; and so also should they watch

over all those connected with them, whether as kindred or servants; mindful of the Apostle's teaching, "If any man have not care of his own, and especially of those of his house, he hath denied the Faith, and is worse than an infidel" (1 Tim. v. 8). For charity ought to be well ordered, and therefore to begin with those who are nearest to us; and who can be nearer than our relations and our servants? Have not even the heathen a natural instinct of pity for those belonging to them? Justly, then, is it said to the Priest, "Despise not thy own flesh" (Isaias lviii. 7). This care should consist chiefly in instructing those belonging to his family, for it is indeed a shame to a Priest (as St. Chrysostom says) to neglect his own, and leave them in ignorance, whilst he is instructing others. Let the Priest's care, then, begin with instruction, for it is written, "Hast thou children? Instruct them, and bow down their neck from childhood" (Eccl. vii. 25). Sound doctrine—the four last things—the truths of our holy religion—should be explained, repeated, made the subject of daily meditation, in order that they may be impressed on their heart, and form the rule of all their actions. So shall the tongue of God's minister bring health to the understanding of those who belong to him: "The tongue of the wise is health" (Prov. xii. 18). There is no other beginning of cure for them and for all: "By wisdom they were healed; whosoever have pleased Thee, O Lord, from the beginning" (Wisd. ix. 19). The word of God, prudently administered, avails more than all medicines: "Neither herb nor mollifying plaster healed them, but Thy word, O Lord, which healeth all things" (Wisd. xvi. 12).

2. *Before that my son die.* The Priest's care for his family is in order to prevent spiritual death—that is, sin; and he who knows not how to do this is not fit to take charge of men's souls, and to fulfil the ecclesiastical ministry well: "It behoveth therefore a Bishop to be . . . one that ruleth well his own house, having his children in subjection with all chastity: but, if a man know not how to rule his own house, how shall he take care of the Church of God?" (1 Tim. iii. 4, 5.) As St. Jerome teaches, he who would inculcate the observance of God's law upon the people must first succeed in making his servants observe it, and

he who aspires to ecclesiastical dignities without having first put his family in the good order of charity is like a man who pretends to steer a ship without having first handled the oar. We must know how to row (says St. Ephraim) before we attempt to direct the boat. Doubtless (as St. Chrysostom points out), it is far more difficult to rule the Church than one's own house, and, therefore, he who cannot do the one will never succeed in the other. St. Bernard earnestly impresses upon a certain Pontiff to take care of his servants, to treat them well, and to procure their sanctification; and far more is this obligation binding on simple Priests, who, for this end, should make use of exhortations, admonitions, reproofs, good example, vigilance, and, above all, of prayer; saying to God, "Shew them the good way wherein they should walk" (3 Kings viii. 36). The fear of God once established in a family, "health, and life, and blessing" will be given to it (Eccl. xxxiv. 20). But, alas! how many Priests fail in this respect.

3. *My son liveth.* Our Saviour's words were a true prophecy, and, at the same time, a command over life (says the Abbot Rupert). But Priests' families ordinarily seek, not spiritual life from them, but riches. Yet (St. Jerome says) it is a Priest's duty to rule his house, but not with the view of increasing wealth. To us (as St. Augustin teaches) it pertains to give our kindred spiritual goods in place of carnal goods—things eternal instead of those which are temporal. It pertains not to us to place them in splendour, nor to enrich them; only, if they are poor, we should give them preference in the distribution of alms. Hence St. Vincent of Paul, the Blessed Sebastian Valfré, the Venerable Mariano Ancieri, and all other holy Priests, would never raise their relations from their lowly condition, but only help them in their indigence, well knowing that families enriched by the wealth of Priests soon fall back into poverty, and are ever poor in virtues. Let us, then, make our relations understand that we are destined by God to give them, not false, but "true riches," and that we do in fact further their temporal welfare by promoting their spiritual interests. For, if we free them from those vices which are often the cause of ruin in the things of this life, and if we cause

them to acquire that good name which is worth more than riches; if we accustom them to labour, which is the source of a good subsistence ; if we preserve them in that concord which multiplies strength—we shall provide indirectly for their temporal needs. Let us frequently repeat to them those Christian maxims which are found in the books both of the Old and New Testament: " I have been young, and now am old, and I have not seen the just forsaken, nor his seed seeking bread " (Ps. xxxvi. 25). " Better is a little to the just than the great riches of the wicked" (ver. 16). " Seek first the kingdom of God, and His justice, and all these things shall be added unto you" (St. Matt. vi. 33). " But godliness with contentment is great gain " (1 Tim. vi. 6). Let us ourselves meditate carefully on these truths, lest we incur the misfortunes of many Priests who, through the covetousness of relations, have changed their ministry into a means of gain, or who, by neglecting it for secular business, or by other unlawful actions, have stained their conscience and lost their soul.

"Glory and wealth shall be in his house, and his justice remaineth for ever and ever."—*Ps.* cxi. 3.

" Let not a Priest incur an uncleanness . . . for his kin, such as are near in blood,"—*Levit.* xxi. 1, 2.

WEDNESDAY.

THE DOCILITY WHICH MEN SHEW IN REGARD TO THE WORDS OF PRIESTS.

I. MANY BELIEVE WITHOUT SEEING MIRACLES.
II. OTHERS BELIEVE NOT, IN SPITE OF PROOFS.
III. THE PRIEST'S CONDUCT IN REGARD TO EACH CLASS.

" The man believed the word which Jesus said to him, and went his way. And as he was going down his servants met him, and they brought word saying that his son lived."—*St. John* iv. 50.

1. *The man believed.* The ruler's faith had its beginning when he sought his son's health ; it had its increase when he believed our Lord's word, its perfection when the servants related the miracle to him. So Venerable Bede. Now, the Priest beholds the Faithful receiving from him the doctrines of the Catholic religion in their earliest years, committing them to memory, and holding them with due certainty and veneration ; and thus he witnesses the fulfilment of that prophecy, " And they shall be all taught of God " (St. John vi. 45). He should remember, therefore, that the habit of faith was infused into his people by means of holy Baptism ; and that this habit disposes the heart to accept the truths of faith, in opposition to that penalty of original sin by which men are led to believe any doctrines, however absurd, rather than those which are revealed by God. He should admire the grace of the Holy Spirit manifested in the subduing of those human passions which harden the heart

and cause it to reject unpalatable truths (as St. Augustin teaches). He should remember that, while his words, in instructing the people, strike their ear, it is the Holy Spirit Who speaks to the heart. Without this Master our hearers would learn nothing; without His inspiration our words would be in vain. At this sight, therefore, let the Priest rejoice in the Lord, even as the Apostle rejoiced when he heard of the propagation of the Faith. Let this be his special consolation, and let him regard this docility as tending to the glory of God; for (as St. Bernardin of Sienna says) it bends the first power of man's mind—that is, the understanding—to the adoration of His Supreme Majesty.

2. *His servants met him.* If the ruler had not believed his servants' testimony, and if the miracle performed had made no impression upon his mind, he would have been truly obstinate and foolish; for (as St. Chrysostom points out) the miracle was evident, for in no ordinary way was the child freed from danger, but immediately and miraculously. Obstinate and foolish indeed are those who believe not the truths of our holy religion after so many proofs. Many in our days will not listen to the teaching of Priests, because they do not believe the words of Holy Scripture: "If you do not believe his writings, how will you believe My words? (St. John v. 47.) So great is their wickedness that, whatever a man may say or do, they are not moved to listen, but (as St. Chrysostom says) retain their peculiar venom. They have no desire to attain eternal life, and therefore they refuse to believe: "You will not come to me that you may have life (St. John v. 40). Either by irreligious discourse, or by impious books, or by sophisms suggested by the devil, their mind, already corrupted by vice, has made shipwreck of the faith. But, while Priests deplore the unhappy state of such men, they should adore the justice of God, Who, in punishment of their sins, has withdrawn His light, and has left these sinners in their natural darkness. For (as St. Augustin says) mercy teaches those who submit to be taught: justice teaches not those who refuse to be taught.

3. *They brought word.* The Gospel, in speaking of the ruler's

servants, points out his dignity (as Origen explains). Now, the dignity of men, if they are of the Faithful, is inestimable (says St. Thomas); but, even if they are unbelievers, we should remember that Christ died for them, and that in this respect their dignity is very great. A good Priest will look upon himself as "the servant of all" (1 Cor. ix. 19): "ourselves your servants through Jesus" (2 Cor. iv. 5): and thus he ought to serve the Faithful by strengthening them in the Faith, by making known to them a greater number of truths, and by preserving them from loss of the Faith; saying to them, "We are the children of saints, and look for that life which God will give to those that never change their faith from Him" (Tobias ii. 8). Further, let us make them comprehend that faith alone is not sufficient to save them, but that other virtues are likewise necessary. For these we must furnish them with all necessary means, for "the kingdom of God is not in speech, but in power" (1 Cor. iv. 20). With regard to those who do not believe, we must employ every mode of convincing them, and of leading them back to God. St. Cyprian says that there is no Priest so weak, so low and abject, so imbecile from human infirmity, as not to be upheld by God against His enemies and opposers; and St. Cyril says that Priests have in all ages been furnished with courage and strength to contend against the heresies of their own days. Let us pray to God that we may fulfil faithfully these important duties.

"Through God we shall do mightily, and will bring our enemies to nothing."—*Ps.* cvii. 14.

"That all the earth may know that Thou art the Lord our God, and that Thy name is called upon Israel."—*Baruch* ii. 15.

THURSDAY.

THE SIN OF FALSEHOOD IN PRIESTS.

I. THE SANCTITY OF THE PRIEST'S MOUTH.
II. THE HONOUR OF HIS MINISTRY.
III. THE EFFECTS OF THIS SIN ON THE PRIEST'S SOUL.

" He asked therefore of them the hour wherein he grew better. And they said to him, Yesterday, at the seventh hour, the fever left him."—*St. John* iv. 52.

1. *He asked therefore of them the hour.* St. Thomas says that the ruler inquired the time of the cure in order to be assured that the moment corresponded with Christ's word, and that it was not by a mere accident that his son was healed. Had he discovered falsehood in Christ, the precious effect of the miracle—that is, the increase of his faith and his conversion—would not have followed. Christ, being true God, could not lie; but Priests are not incapable of lying, for it is written, " God is true, and every man a liar" (Rom. iii. 4). Now, can it ever be fitting for a Minister of God to lie? Instead of bearing the image of God, he thereby assumes the likeness of the devil, who is the father of lies. The Priest's mouth is consecrated to God's word, and in uttering a lie he soils it with the word of the devil ; for he who lies (says St. Bonaventure) lies by persuasion of the devil, who is the author and instigator of lies. Albertus Magnus says that, if this be a sin in the mouth of any of the Faithful, in the mouth of the Priest, who should be the teacher of truth, it is a sacrilege. A tongue which (as St. Bernard

says) is reddened with the blood of Christ ought not to be stained with a lie. Let us weep bitterly if we have ever so defiled our tongue, and let us acknowledge that we have followed the way of the lying children of men: "I am a man of unclean lips, and I dwell in the midst of a people that hath unclean lips" (Isaias vi. 5).

2. *They said to Him.* Lying is a servile vice, and, therefore, in Holy Scripture the word "to lie" is used for "to serve" (Ps. xvii. 46, lxxx. 16). Yet the servants of the ruler lied not, and far less does it become "the man of God" to lie before the people: "Thou art a man of God, and the word of the Lord in thy mouth is true" (3 Kings xvii. 24). A lie is easily discovered, and, therefore, the Holy Spirit says, "Let not thy lips be a stumblingblock to thee" (Eccl. i. 37), which Cardinal Hugo explains as signifying, "Do not utter lies by which you may afterwards be confounded." By this vice Priests lower themselves before the multitude—"A lie is a foul blot in a man" (Eccl. xx. 26): they lose all authority (says St. Ephrem), and become odious to God and men: they will not be believed even when they speak the truth (says St. Jerome)—and that to the great loss of souls. Therefore was the prophet Jonas "exceedingly troubled, and was angry" (iv. 1), when he saw that his prediction against Ninive was not fulfilled. He feared (says St. Athanasius) to be looked upon as a liar, and (as St. Gregory Nazianzen says) he could not endure the reproach of a lying ministry. How great scandal may not we have given by this sin!

3. *At the seventh hour the fever left him.* The circumstance of the "seventh hour" signifies (says St. Bonaventure) the sevenfold Spirit whose coming cures us in all our ills. Now, the Holy Spirit is the "Spirit of truth," and, therefore, whoever lies offends Him; and especially does the Priest, who has so many times received the Holy Spirit, grieve Him by lying. As St. Isidore says, a lie destroys the truth; every lie is a sin, and all that departs from truth is iniquity. How foolish, therefore, is it in some Priests, under pretext of a good intention, and with a view to the profit of souls, to permit themselves to utter falsehoods!

As St. Augustin says, in proportion as a man departs from the truth he falls short of eternal happiness; and, therefore, if he who lies departs from the truth, it is absurd to say that he can thereby arrive at any real good. Let us be convinced that lying is wholly forbidden, chiefly because of its opposition to the Spirit of truth (as St. Thomas points out). Let us frequently meditate on the following passages of Holy Scripture :—" Thou wilt destroy all that speak a lie " (Ps. v. 7) . . . " The mouth that belieth killeth the soul" (Wisd. i. 11) . . . "Be not willing to make any manner of lie" (Eccl. vii. 14). When necessity arises let us resolve to conceal the truth by silence; for (as St. Bonaventure teaches) it is never lawful to tell a lie, but it is sometimes lawful and expedient to be silent. Let us firmly resolve rather to die than to utter a premeditated falsehood: " My lips shall not speak iniquity, neither shall my tongue continue lying " (Job. xxvii. 4).

" Take not Thou the word of truth utterly out of my mouth, for in Thy words I have hoped exceedingly."—*Ps.* cxviii. 43.

" O Lord, let my words be, Yea, yea ; No, no ; that I fall not under judgment."— From *St. James* v. 12.

FRIDAY.

—————

THE CLERGY AS INSTRUCTORS OF YOUTH.

I. The evil caused by wicked teachers.
II. The good resulting from pious masters.
III. The advantage of Clerical instructors.

—————

" The father therefore knew that it was at the same hour that Jesus said to him,
Thy son liveth, and himself believed, and his whole house."—*St. John* iv. 53.

1. *The father therefore knew.* The father, convinced by the
testimony of his servants, was converted, and through him his
whole family received from God the gift of faith. His family had
not at first believed, or only half believed (says St. Bonaventure) ;
and therefore was this testimony unalterable and demonstrative
of the truth. Now, masters are, as it were, the fathers of their
scholars ; and if they themselves are not sound in faith and
morals they cannot profit their hearers, but, on the contrary,
will lead astray the minds of the young. A wicked master is a
" lying teacher, who shall bring in sects of perdition, . . and
many shall follow their riotousness, through whom the way of
truth shall be evil spoken of" (2 Pet. ii. 1, 2). Their venom
leaves its trace on their school: "Their speech spreadeth like a
canker " (2 Tim. ii. 17). Sad, indeed, it is to find youths in
the hands of wicked teachers, who become their seducers rather
than instructors. They are as animals led to the shambles : " I
behold a foolish young man . . . immediately he followeth her as
an ox led to be a victim, and as a lamb playing the wanton, and

not knowing that he is drawn like a fool to bonds" (Prov. vii. 7, 22). St. Basil and Venerable Bede, commenting on this passage, teach that Solomon, under the figure of the harlot, describes heresy or impiety, which drags youths to perdition. Therefore, when Priests are aware of the corruption of such schools, let them raise their voice, and say to their disciples, " Separate yourselves from among this congregation " (Numbers' xvi. 21).

2. *Thy son liveth.* The life of grace is true life (says St. Augustin), and in order to the attainment of this life a good master, as well as a good father, is profitable. For if youths are early instructed and strengthened in the faith they will easily lead a good life, and, should they sometimes stray from the right path, they will soon return to it. Every day do we experience the truth of that great sentence of St. Augustin, that it is difficult for him who believes well to live ill; and hence the greatest treasure, the greatest advantage, is given to scholars by teaching them the right principles of religion. No riches, no treasures, no honours, no worldly substance (says St. Augustin) is comparable with the Catholic faith. A master can easily insinuate good doctrine, even when teaching of subjects which seem wholly extraneous—even when teaching the rudiments of grammar; and the less such words are expected by his disciples, the more are they wont to profit by them. By such words they become accustomed in their earliest years to think well and to live well, and these habits will easily accompany them to the tomb. St. Chrysostom says that, if from the very beginning and portals of life we lead youths away from iniquity, and guide them by the hand to the best road, we establish them for the time to come in a right habit and mode of life. In that case they will not easily change for the worse, since the force of custom will draw them to the performance of good actions. Disciples swear by their master's words, and can therefore readily learn virtue from his words, and carry it with them even to old age. Hence the wise man says, " My son, from thy youth up receive instruction, and even to thy grey hairs thou shalt find wisdom" (Eccl. vi. 18). Moreover, man is inclined to evil from his youth :

" The imagination and thought of man's heart are prone to evil from his youth " (Gen. viii. 21), and good instruction is the means of restraining this perverse tendency: " Folly is bound up in the heart of a child, and the rod of correction shall drive it away" (Prov. xxii. 15). Blessed, then, are those Priests who spend their days in forming the mind and heart of their pupils, and great is the benefit which they bestow upon the Church.

3. *Himself believed and his whole house.* The ruler became the apostle of his family, and in like manner an Ecclesiastic who undertakes the work of education, not from motives of interest, but with the holy aim of forming good Christians, is the apostle of his school. A good Priest will teach his pupils to observe God's law: " I know that he will command his children, and his household after him, to keep the way of the Lord, and do judgment and justice" (Gen. xviii. 19). Whether teaching letters or science, he will seize occasions for " uttering a good word," and he will watch over the ways of his pupils in order to lead them to works of piety. Thus will he save them from falling into the condition of those youths who are possessed by evil, made slaves of the devil, and led into all manner of disorders. He will obtain over their mind that influence which is proper for a master, and so (as St. Anselm says) will lead them wheresoever he will. He will have the consolation of seeing men leave his school who will do good to society, and who will readily (as St. Gregory says) give themselves to God's service. Let such a Priest take St. Augustin for his model, who relates how after his conversion he instructed his pupils in letters, in science, and in virtue.

" He commanded our fathers that they should make the same known to their children, that another generation might know them."—*Ps.* lxxvii. 5, 6.

" These shall lift up their voice and shall give praise, and shall glorify the Lord in instruction."—From *Isaias* xxiv. 14, 15.

SATURDAY.

FEAST OF OUR LADY, HELP OF THE DYING.

THE CLERGY SHOULD HONOUR THE BLESSED VIRGIN UNDER THIS TITLE.

I. THAT SHE MAY ASSIST THE DYING.
II. THAT SHE MAY INCITE US TO ASSIST THE DYING.
III. THAT SHE MAY ASSIST US AT OUR OWN DEATH.

"Blessed is the womb that bore Thee."—*St. Luke* xi. 27.

1. *Blessed is the womb that bore Thee.* Mary, in most bitter sorrow, assisted at the agony of Her firstborn Son ; and so great was Her anguish that, had it been divided among all creatures capable of suffering pain, they must all have died (says St. Bernardin of Sienna). Her heart (says St. Lawrence Justinian) was a mirror of Christ's Passion, so that She was crucified in soul whilst Her Son was crucified in body. Yet even then "blessed was the womb" that bore Jesus Christ, for by thus assisting at the death of the Head of the predestinate She acquired the right to assist at the death of all the members. She not only succours them, but places herself in their way (says St. Jerome). Though all the devils be set against the dying, Mary, the "seat of wisdom," will know how to turn their wiles to the good of the elect. The devils, against their will (says St. Chrysostom), become to us the means of obtaining crowns, and procure for us countless blessings, because God's wisdom turns their plots to our salvation and glory.

If this be so, shall we not, when assisting the dying, encourage them to raise their thoughts and their confidence to Her Whom St. Bonaventure calls "the Champion of the dying ?" Shall we not, in order that they may be victorious over all the spirits of evil, remind them that Mary is (as St. Antoninus calls Her) the "conqueror of the old serpent, and of the fiery dragon ?" But our words will avail them nothing in this last perilous conflict without the aid of Mary, whom Dionysius calls "the army of God, which, in the strength of the Creator, conquers all the powers of the air."

2. *Blessed is the womb that bore Jesus,* and gave Him birth : blessed also is the Priest who brings forth his brethren to life eternal. But, in order to obtain light, courage, and perseverance in this work, which is so burdensome to our weakness, we have need of Mary, whom St. John Damascene calls "the help of our weakness." On Calvary She became herself a Priestess, not only in offering Her Son to the Eternal Father, but also in assisting at His death. She ought, therefore, to be the model of Priests who devote themselves to this work of charity. She by Her example teaches them not to lose courage in the presence of those who languish and die, since She assisted with such fortitude at the awful spectacle of Her Son's death. For we read of Her as "standing" by the Cross, not as weeping (says St. Ambrose). Nay, She has obtained for many Priests the grace to meet death in assisting the plague-stricken, even as She desired to die for Her Son, offering Herself to the persecutors (says St. Ambrose) whilst Her Son hung on the Cross. Let us pray to Her to obtain for us grace not to fear death in the discharge of this great work of our ministry, and to imitate Her in accompanying the sacrifice which our spiritual children make of their life to God, looking ever upon Her (with St. Bernardin) as the "model of charity."

3. *Blessed is the womb that bore Jesus* because, in bearing the Head, it has borne also the members : the former Mary brought forth to this mortal life, the latter to life eternal. Let us consider that we, too, shall come to die, and let us hope that we shall then be by Her brought forth to Paradise ; let us hope

(with St. John Damascene) that She will be our help in the awful hour of our departure, and of the separation of our soul and body. Let us remember that She has promised Her devout children to come to them in death as their Queen and their Mother, to give them consolation and refreshment. Let us endeavour to serve Her with devotion and holiness, in order that She may assist us in our last moments, for (as She herself said to St. Matilda) She is willing to come as a compassionate Mother to all who have served Her holily, to console and protect them at the hour of death. Thus it was that the Blessed Virgin, appearing to St. John of God at his death, said to him, "It is not in me to forsake my own at this hour." The devil will assail us with the greater hatred in proportion to the prey which we have torn from him, and therefore have we need of Mary, Who is called by St. Antoninus the "strength of the religious." Let us, then, invoke Her, that She may pray for us sinners, "now, and at the hour of our death." Let us celebrate Holy Mass with great fervour, in order to obtain this grace, and let us recite more devoutly than heretofore the Office of this present solemnity.

"Though I should walk through the midst of the shadow of death, I will fear no evils, for Thou art with me; Thy rod and Thy staff, they have comforted me."
—*Ps.* xxii. 4.

"They that hope in Thee shall take wings as eagles, they shall fly and not faint."
—From *Isaias* xl. 31.

TWENTY-FIRST SUNDAY AFTER PENTECOST.

THE EMPLOYMENT OF THE ECCLESIASTICAL TALENT.

I. THE NATURE OF THE ECCLESIASTICAL TALENT.
II. THE HAPPINESS OF THOSE WHO USE IT ARIGHT.
III. THE PUNISHMENT OF THOSE WHO BURY IT IN THE EARTH.

" Jesus spake to His disciples this parable: Therefore is the kingdom of heaven likened to a king who would take an account of his servants."—*St. Matt.* xviii. 23.

1. *Of his servants.* Here the term "servants" includes all the Faithful, but it refers especially to Priests, for (as Origen points out) they are servants who are entrusted with the dispensation of God's Word. That is the talent which they must employ in the service of their Master. Hence this parable was addressed by our Lord Jesus Christ to St. Peter, the prince of Priests (says St. Jerome), after the question which this Apostle had put to Him concerning the number of times he should extend forgiveness to his brother. We may, therefore, in this place conveniently meditate on the Ecclesiastical talent which is given to Priests, and of which, according to the teaching of another parable (St. Matt. xxv. 14), a most strict account will be demanded. Some (as St. Jerome says) have more, some less, but every Ecclesiastic has his share according to his capacity. It is

the office of Priests, as the Roman Pontifical sets forth, to offer the Holy Sacrifice, to administer the Sacraments, to preach the Divine word, to bless the people, and to rule them well; and this power is their talent. This is a most precious talent (says St. Jerome), and great is the gain of those who trade with it. Almighty God has, in fact, ordained the Sacrament of Order in the Church (says St. Thomas) so that all they who receive it may, in a certain manner, be made like to God, co-operating with Him, and aiding, as more noble members, the other members. What wonder, therefore, is it that God should demand account of such a precious talent? How great folly on our part to disregard the account which we must thus render to Him!

2. *Would take an account.* Truly happy are those servants, who, in rendering an account of the talent which they have received, will bring with it great gain to their Lord. Peter (says St. Gregory) will bring Judæa converted by him; Paul, almost the whole world; Andrew, Achaia; John, Asia; Thomas, India. The fruits of their respective labours will be represented by the number of souls gained by each. One will say, "Behold, I have gained other five over and above" (St. Matt. xxv. 20); another will add, "Behold, I have gained other two" (23). Both these servants (says St. Gregory) represent those Ministers of Christ who feed the flock by their counsel, their wisdom and labours. By these expressions our Lord makes known that the good work is man's, who can justly say, "I have gained," whilst He afterwards makes use of different expressions to show that the same work is also God's, without Whose grace no good can be done, nor is done: "Lord, Thy pound hath gained ten pounds . . . Lord, Thy pound hath gained five pounds" (St. Luke xix. 16, 18). Let us, then, pray to our Lord to give us His grace to trade well with the talents we have received, in order that we may obtain the reward given to those faithful servants. That reward (as Venerable Bede says) denotes the abundant felicity and honour promised to zealous Priests who co-operate with Almighty God in the salvation of souls.

3. *A man, a king.* This man and king is the Man-God, Who by being made man united human nature to His Divine person ; for (as Origen says), when the Son of God was made in the likeness of sinful flesh, then was He made to resemble "a man, a king." He would take account with His servants, especially those who have care of souls. If, therefore, this King find a Priest who has suffered the talent which he received at his sacred Ordination to lie idle, He will treat him no otherwise than He treated the slothful servant of the parable : "Wicked and slothful servant," &c. (St. Matt. xxv. 26.) Hence the Apostle wrote to Timothy, "Neglect not the grace that is in thee, which was given thee by prophecy, with imposition of the hands of the Priesthood" (1 Tim. iv. 14); by which words he exhorted him not to suffer the talent confided to him to lie idle. As St. Augustin teaches, it is wicked and cruel not to benefit others when it is in our power to do so; it is, in fact, to imitate this miserable servant. Whenever, then, we are tempted to remain in idleness, let us say to ourselves (with St. Augustin), "Alas! dost not thou remember the fate of that servant who hid his talent, and would not lay it out?" Let us be careful lest we incur condemnation for the mere hiding of our talent. Let us multiply the gift which we received at Ordination; that is, let us make use of it for the benefit of many, as St. Basil enjoins in his explanation of this Parable. As St. Chrysostom also warns us, with reference to this same Parable, let us not persuade ourselves that any one can be saved without labouring to the utmost of his power for the salvation of his neighbour. In short, the power which we have received is a talent which (as St. Thomas says) we are bound to employ usefully. Let us frequently meditate on these truths, and let us reap profit from them.

" But I, as a faithful olive-tree in the house of God, have hoped in the mercy of God for ever."—*Ps.* li. 10.

" I will taste and see that my traffic is good."—From *Prov.* xxxi. 18.

MONDAY.

THE DEBT INCURRED BY WICKED PRIESTS.

I. Its great magnitude.

II. The impossibility of discharging it.

III. The punishment exacted by God.

"And, when he had begun to take the account, one was brought to him that owed him ten thousand talents. And, as he had not wherewith to pay it, his lord commanded that he should be sold, and his wife and children, and all that he had, and payment to be made."—*St. Matt.* xviii. 24.

1. *That owed him ten thousand talents.* In its literal sense this Parable represents to us what is impossible, for no master has ever entrusted so large a sum to a servant, nor has it ever been in the power of a servant to rob his master to so great an extent, the sum amounting to more than two millions of pounds. But, if we consider the scope of the Parable, and its true meaning, we shall understand that the debt originated in " damnification " (according to the scholastic expression), and Origen explains it thus :—The debtor (he says) had been the cause of his master sustaining severe losses. Trusts of great value had passed through his hands, and he had neglected to employ them aright. Now, the number of talents due to the master represents the number of men's souls that have been lost to God through negligence. Let us apply to ourselves this interpretation in detail. Much had been entrusted to him; that is to say, the Blood of Jesus Christ has been entrusted to us, in comparison of which all the treasures of earth are nothing : " You were not redeemed with corruptible things, as gold or silver . . . but with the precious blood " (1 Pet. i. 18, 19). The word of God, which is

called "a treasure to be desired" (Prov. xxi. 20)—the souls of men which are of infinite value—have been entrusted to us, and it has been said to us of each of those souls, "Thy life shall be for his life, or thou shalt pay a talent of silver (3 Kings xx. 39). Further, a Priest is the cause of much loss to his Master, because the scandal which he gives is like that of Lucifer, who drew after him "the third part of the stars" (Apoc. viii. 12), and because (as Innocent III. declares) the sin of Priests causes a whole multitude to sin. Lastly, the servant gained no profit. Thus, we ought to have hindered the sins of the souls entrusted to us, and we have not done so; and, therefore (as St. Thomas declares), their sins are a lack of due gain—are a real debt. How terrible is this teaching! How have even the saints trembled when meditating upon it!

2. *And, as he had not wherewith to pay it.* The wretched servant could not make satisfaction for so great a debt, and in like manner every sinner must acknowledge himself powerless to expiate his guilt. But if he be a Priest he has special need to say, "What shall I offer to the Lord that is worthy? . . . Shall I give my firstborn for my wickedness, the fruit of my body for the sin of my soul?" (Mich. vi. 6, 7.) Sin has an infinite malice, because it offends an infinite Majesty; and therefore does Almighty God justly punish it with an eternal punishment. Hence, in seeking a worthy satisfaction for it, He could find no more proper means than the Incarnation of the Word. So St. Thomas. No man, therefore, by his own power can free himself from the debt of even one single sin: it is Divine mercy alone which grants its pardon. We are all of us, indeed, powerless to pay the debt; but we are under obligation to conceive that loving sorrow by which, through Divine grace, we are disposed for pardon (as St. Bonaventure teaches). Further, in order to offer some satisfaction to Almighty God, we ought to resolve "to teach the unjust His ways, and to labour to convert the wicked to Him" (Ps. l. 15). How profitable (says St. Gregory) is the remission of sins in a Priest, who is not only himself set free from the bonds of sin, but draws others also from the way of iniquity, and kindles in them the flame of

charity. Almighty God often makes use of such sinners, as He made use of Peter and Paul, to whom the following passage of Job is applied—"He makes the rhinoceros willing to serve Him;" that is, He makes those who were once as wild beasts "stay in their crib; He makes them plough, and break the clods of the valleys in their great strength, and trusts them with seed which shall render an abundant harvest" (Job xxxix. 9, 12). Why do not we set before ourselves these blessed models of conversion ? We have imitated them as sinners; why, then, do we not imitate them as penitents ?

3. *His lord commanded that he should be sold.* The lord decreed the punishment of the debtor, and the sale of his wife and children, which St. Augustin explains as signifying the sinner's lust and wicked works—the price which he is condemned to pay. Let us note, however, that, though God threatens this condemnation, yet, of His unspeakable tenderness (as St. Chrysostom says), He does not forthwith execute it, but He chooses to terrify the sinner in order to bring him to repentance, so that the threatened punishment may be averted. Let us also note, that here it is not the manifest judgment that will take place after death, which is spoken of, but that hidden judgment which Almighty God is ever making in His observation of all our works, and in the inward remorse of conscience, whereby He warns us of the punishment of guilt. Judgment hath not yet been manifested (says St. Augustin), but it hath already taken place. This judgment begins with the Sanctuary—begins with Priests : "Begin ye at My sanctuary" (Ezech. ix. 6). So did God ordain, and so was it executed; for this judgment began, indeed, "at the ancient men, who were before the house." In very truth, Almighty God "shall not spare, nor will He have pity" on any who are obstinate, but He "will requite their way upon their head" (ver. 10). Let us tremble at these considerations, and let us make resolutions accordingly.

" My iniquities are gone over my head, and as a heavy burden are become heavy upon me."—*Ps.* xxxvii. 5.

"Our iniquities are multiplied before Thee, and our sins have testified against *'-nias* lix. 12.

TUESDAY.

INDULGENCES.

I. Priests should be the first to profit by them.

II. They should exhort the people not to neglect them.

III. They should teach the ignorant the mode of gaining them.

"But that servant, falling down, besought him, saying, Have patience with me, and I will pay thee all. And the lord of that servant, being moved with pity, forgave him the debt."—*St. Matt.* xviii. 26, 27.

1. *Forgave him the debt.* Who would not admire the surpassing benevolence of God, Who, under the figure of this master, gives more than is asked? The servant only asked for forbearance and delay (says St. Chrysostom), but the master gave him more than he asked—viz., remission and forgiveness of the entire debt. Such is the mercy which our Lord vouchsafes to exercise towards us, as often as He allows us to gain holy Indulgences. These (as St. Thomas teaches) are effectual for the remission of the penalties still due to sin after contrition, Confession, and Absolution, not only in the tribunal of the Church, but also before the judgment-seat of God. Now, let Priests consider the enormity of their debts, and let them recollect that God has ever exacted heavier penalties from persons of high dignity than from others, even after He has remitted the guilt of their sin; as was the case with Moses (Deut. xxxiv. 4) and with David (2 Kings xii. 9). Let them recollect that it was to the Priests that Judith

said, "Forasmuch as the Lord is patient, let us be penitent, and with many tears let us beg His pardon" (Judith viii. 14). Do we not understand that, as the holy Council of Trent declares, by means of Indulgences we gain "heavily treasures." And do we not fear to see fulfilled in our own case the terrible menace, "Thou shalt see with thy eyes, and shalt not eat thereof?" (4 Kings vii. 19.) Let us hasten, then, to stay God's avenging hand, beseeching Him to remit the penalties due to our sins, both in this present life and in the life to come : "Remember wrath, for it will not tarry long !" (Eccl. vii. 18.) Too late shall we repent of our negligence if we do not now resolve to profit by these Indulgences as much as we can. Above all, in time of solemn Indulgences let us give example to our people by fulfilling the works enjoined, so that they may rejoice and imitate us: "Juda was joyful in the Priests and Levites that assisted, and they kept the watch of their God, and the observance of expiation" (2 Esdr. xii. 43).

2. *Being moved with pity.* The Lord is moved with pity towards all who implore His mercy: "Thou, O Lord, art a God of compassion, and merciful, patient, and of much mercy, and true" (Ps. lxxxv. 15). It is the office of Priests "to preach a release to the captives" (Isaias lxi. 1); and, as they who publish false Indulgences out of interested motives incur the most terrible censures, so do they who preach true Indulgences please Almighty God. The Church has defined that the use of Indulgences is most salutary to the Christian people, and we by promoting their use confer great benefit on the Faithful ; for (as St. Clement VI. teaches) by this dispensation the devotion of the Faithful is increased, faith shines forth, hope flourishes, and the flame of charity is vehemently kindled. Confessors should, therefore, labour diligently on occasion of Indulgences; Confession and Communion being works enjoined for the gaining of all Plenary Indulgences. Do they fear that God does not see, and will not amply reward their labours ? Let them remember the promise, "Because his soul' hath laboured, he shall see and be filled". (Isaias liii. 11). Moreover, is it small consolation to Priests to consider that many Indulgences are applicable to the souls in

Purgatory? Let them remember that to these souls they may say, "Our mouth is open to you, our heart is enlarged" (2 Cor. vi. 11).

3. *Have patience with me.* St. Thomas says that in these words the humility of the servant, his discretion, and his readiness to satisfy justice, are commended. We should impress upon the Faithful the necessity of humbling themselves by a good Confession; for (as St. Thomas shews) they who are in the death of sin cannot receive the influence necessary to Indulgences, for this influence cannot penetrate from living members into those which are dead. Let us teach them to be "discreet"—that is, to be exact in performing the works enjoined. We may say to them, "Why are ye careless? Go ye down and buy necessaries" (Gen. xlii. 1, 2). Let us make them also understand that the justice of God in Indulgences is satisfied by the merits of Jesus Christ, of His Mother, and of all the Saints; whence is formed that treasure of Holy Church called "a never-failing treasure" (Eccl. xxx. 23). Our Lord Jesus Christ has assuredly given to the Supreme Pontiff the power of "loosing and binding" both in regard to the bonds of guilt and the bonds of punishment, and therefore it must be the greatest folly not to profit by this gift. Meanwhile let us recommend to all that they dispense not themselves from bringing forth "fruit worthy of penance," for St. Thomas says, that after having gained the Indulgences we must not abstain from joining thereto works of penance. Well would it be for us to instruct the Faithful to renew each morning their intention of gaining all the Indulgences possible during the day, as Blessed Leonard of Port Maurice desired. What great benefit should we procure for them! what great merit should we acquire for ourselves!

"Forgive us our sins for Thy name's sake."—*Ps.* lxviii. 9.
"Have patience with me, and I will pay thee all."—*St. Matt.* xviii. 26.

WEDNESDAY.

THE PRIVILEGES OF THE CLERGY.

I. Importance of the privileges of the Clergy.
II. Zeal of the Saints in maintaining them.
III. Duties imposed by these privileges.

"But, when that servant was gone out, he found one of his fellow-servants that owed him an hundred pence, and, laying hold on him, he throttled him, saying, Pay what thou owest. And his fellow-servant, falling down, besought him, saying, Have patience with me, and I will pay thee all. And he would not, but went and cast him into prison till he paid the debt. Now, his fellow-servants, seeing what was done, were very much grieved, and they came and told their lord all that was done."—*St. Matt.* xviii. 28—31.

1. *Laying hold of him, he throttled him.* This servant, in out-raging another servant of the same master, outraged the master himself, and shewed himself (as St. Augustin calls him) an evil, wicked, and ungrateful servant. Wicked also, and ungrateful to Almighty God, are those who violate Clerical privileges, because in injuring persons dedicated to God's service they injure God. One of these privileges is, that whoever, by persuasion of the devil, should strike a Cleric, is immediately deprived of the communion of the Church. Such a person is more grievously stricken in soul than was Jeroboam in body when "he stretched forth his hand against the man of God, saying, 'Lay hold on him :' and his hand which he stretched forth against him withered, and he was not able to draw it back again to him" (3 Kings xiii. 4). The other privileges consist in occupying the most dignified

place in the Temple, in having a right to Ecclesiastical dignities and to benefices, in order that thus they may "execute
the office of the Priesthood, and have praise, and glorify His
people in His name, . . . and have bread prepared them in the
first place unto fulness" (Eccl. xlv. 19, 26). Further, the piety of
Christian princes docile to the Church's influence has exempted
Clerics from lay tribunals, from public burdens, from military service, and from payment of taxes; and all this was in order that
"their good things might not be abolished, and that their glory
in their nation might be everlasting" (ver. 31). And, if all these
privileges are not now in their ancient and full vigour, we must
humbly adore God's justise, of Whom no one may ask account
of His acts: "Who is he that shall dare say, Why hath He done
so?" (2 Kings xvi. 10.) "He bringeth the searchers of secrets
to nothing" (Isaias xl. 23). We must, indeed, acknowledge that
the sins of many Priests have provoked God's wrath, and so obscured the splendour of their prerogatives: "Who hath given
Israel to robbers? Hath not the Lord Himself, against Whom we
have sinned?" (Isaias xlii. 24.)

2. *Now, his fellow-servants, seeing what was done, were very much
grieved.* By the fellow-servants who were grieved is to be understood the Church (says St. Augustin); and, in truth, the whole
Church is grieved, and the Saints, who are the most precious
part of it, are armed with zeal, when they see that the Priesthood
are oppressed, or deprived of some privilege. Then do they
lament that "her dishonour is increased according to her glory,
and her excellency turned into mourning" (1 Machab. i. 42).
We know with how much zeal St. Hilary endeavoured to prevent
Clerics from being judged by lay tribunals. We know how St.
Ambrose praised Valentinian, who would have Priests judged by
Priests. We know how other Saints have sought to maintain all
such privileges, and how the Church has confirmed them by her
laws. Most certain is it that they who love the Church and desire her glory love the Priesthood, and are zealous for the glory
of the Priesthood; and such are all those who have the Spirit
of God, for (as St. Augustin says), "in proportion as a man loves
the Church, so is he filled with the Holy Ghost." Priests, then,

who are lovers of the Church and full of the Holy Ghost, whilst they are undisturbed in other matters, are moved with zeal (as St. Ambrose says) when they behold this their Mother wronged in the person of Her ministers. Let us also meditate on this great truth—namely, that the honour which is given to Priests is given to God ; and, in like manner as they honour the king who honour his ministers, so do they who honour Priests honour God. Therefore let us always refer to God the privileges conferred on our ministry.

3. *They told their Lord.* The Lord is told the sin of those who outrage Priests, as well as the sins which Priests themselves commit in failing to correspond to the honour which they have received; and this "telling" (as Remigius points out) is the manifestation of an afflicted heart. Privileges are given to the Clergy (as St. Thomas shews) in recompense of their labours for the public good, according to the natural law of equity, so that they who, by ministering to God in spiritual things, labour for the peace of kingdoms, should receive recompense from kings. But they who look upon the Priesthood only as an honour, and not as a charge, merit not this privilege (says St. Jerome). To us (says St. Isidore) have been confided the dispensation of the mysteries of God, the instruction of the people, the ministry of the word, that in this way we may assist the Bishops in their labours. Let us, then, remember the warning which the Council of Trent gives to all Clerics, in whatever order of the ministry—that they should excel the laity in sanctity of life as well as in knowledge. May God preserve us from becoming as servants who serve not, from usurping privileges without deserving them, and from asserting rights without fulfilling the corresponding duties. May we rather follow the example of those holy Ministers of the Sanctuary who have gone before us.

"To me Thy friends, O God, are made exceedingly honourable."—*Ps.* cxxxviii. 17.

"Give to us, O Lord, in Thy house, and within Thy walls, a place, and a name better than sons and daughters."—From *Is.* lvi. 5.

THURSDAY.

———•———

THE CONDUCT OF ECCLESIASTICS TOWARDS THEIR ERRING BRETHREN.

I. They should conceal their defects.
II. They should endeavour to correct them.
III. They should pray for their amendment.

———•———

"Then his lord called him and said to him, Thou wicked servant, I forgave thee all the debt because thou besoughtest me. Shouldst not thou, then, also have had compassion on thy fellow-servant, even as I had compassion on thee ?"—*St. Matt.* xviii. 32, 33.

1. *Thou wicked servant.* St. Chrysostom remarks that the Lord called not the servant "wicked" as owing him ten thousand talents, and uttered no reproach against him on that account, but shewed mercy on him ; but, on the other hand, when he had become hard to his fellow-servant, then He said to him, " Thou wicked servant." Now, what servant is more "wicked" than he who has a " wicked tongue?" The Wise Man, speaking of de- tractors, says, " Hear not a wicked tongue, and make doors and bars to thy mouth " (Eccl. xxviii. 28). Surely there is no need for us to spend much time in meditating on the malice of de- traction after the numerous sermons which we have preached against it, and the countless warnings of Holy Scripture against this sin: " Keep yourselves from murmuring, which profiteth

nothing, and refrain your tongue from detraction" (Wisd. i. 11): "If a serpent bite in silence, he is nothing better that backbiteth secretly" (Eccl. x. 11): "Detractors, hateful to God" (Rom. i. 30). But to injure the good name of a Priest is an evil incomparably greater than speaking against a layman, for the ministry of the former is discredited, and cannot, in consequence, be exercised with success. Hence (as St. Bernardin of Sienna says) nothing is so injurious to the Church as the manifestation of the defects of her Ministers. Almighty God is jealous of the reputation of His Priests, and hence He said, even to Aaron, who had offended in this respect, "Why were you not afraid to speak ill of My servant?" (Numbers xii. 8.) The laity (as St. Bernardin says elsewhere) are always too ready to observe and speak of the defects, rather than the virtues, of Priests ; but, if Ecclesiastics themselves act in this way towards their colleagues, what honour will be left to them? Whether their defects be public, or natural, or even venial, to complain of them to others is always useless, idle, and (as St. Chrysostom says) a fault which deserves no pardon. Let evil-speaking Priests look into their own heart, and they will find that it is self-love, envy, jealousy, which makes them take pleasure in publishing the defects of others ; or, it may be, the fear of their colleagues being promoted above themselves. Thus (as St. Bernardin declares) they manifest their own malignity whilst they are seeking to expose the faults of their brethren. Let them imitate Constantine the Great, who declared that, if necessary, he would gladly cover the sins of Priests with his own robes! If they behold the shame of some Father of the Faithful, why should they imitate Cham rather than Sem?

2. *Shouldst not thou, then, have had compassion also on thy fellow-servant.* He who is merciful "teacheth" his brother with kindness : "He hath mercy and teacheth, and correcteth" (Eccl. xviii. 13). Fraternal correction is the means which the Gospel suggests to us for amending the erring: "If thy brother shall offend against thee, go and rebuke him between him and thee alone" (St. Matt. xviii. 15). When this correction is made with prudence, discretion, gentleness, and sagacity, it is wont to pro-

duce great fruit, and hence is most pleasing to God, for (as Albertus Magnus says) no work is more pleasing to God than fraternal admonition which springs from charity. St. Bernardin of Sienna points out how great things this saying, "Thou shalt gain thy brother," carries with it, and how many advantages are derived from brotherly correction. It is enough to remember that he who corrects a Priest is an imitator of Jesus Christ, Who corrected His Apostles; and it would seem as though He might say to Priests (according to the words of St. Chrysostom), that they who lead others from error to truth, or shew them the path from sin to virtue, are imitators of Him. And, if our correction profit not, let us give notice of it to our Ecclesiastical Superior, and woe to him should he follow the example of the High Priest Heli, of whom it is written, "I have foretold unto him that I will judge his house for ever for iniquity, because he knew that his sons did wickedly, and did not chastise them" (1 Kings iii. 13). Let each one of us ponder these truths, and strive earnestly to put them in practice.

3. *Even as I had compassion on thee.* We have received immense benefits from God (as St. Thomas declares), and shall we not confer on our erring fellow-servants the benefit of prayer in their behalf, which costs us so little? Truly (as St. Isidore shews) our corrections will avail nothing if Almighty God, moved by our prayers, dispose not the heart to profit by them. Hence the Church, in the canon of Holy Mass, enjoins us to pray for Priests, whether they be just or whether they be sinners, by prescribing the prayer, "Nobis quoque peccatoribus," &c.; and this prayer (as St. Thomas says) is offered to God in order to obtain special grace and pardon for Priests. Let us observe that we also pray to God that He "consider not our merits, but grant us forgiveness," when (as St. Benedict XIV. says) the word "merits" may be justly explained as "demerits or sins." St. Jerome alludes to the same expression when he addresses our Lord as "not regarding our merits, but pardoning our offences." Let us ever remember the words, "Pray one for another, that you may be saved" (St. James v. 16); being assured (as St. Gregory declares) that our prayers will be the more quickly heard in proportion to

the charity which moves us to pray for our sinful brethren : " Return, O Lord : how long ? And be entreated in favour of Thy servants " (Ps. lxxxix. 13).

" Return, O Lord : how long ? And be entreated in favour of Thy servants."— *Ps.* lxxxix. 13.

" Let Thy anger cease, and be appeased upon the wickedness of our brethren."— From *Exod.* xxxii. 12.

FRIDAY.

THE CONDUCT OF PRIESTS IN REGARD TO ENMITIES.

I. To PREVENT THEM FROM ARISING.

II. To REMOVE THEM WHEN THEY OCCUR.

III. To GUARD AGAINST THEM IN THEIR OWN CASE.

" And his lord, being angry, delivered him to the torturers until he paid all the debt. So also shall My Heavenly Father do to you if you forgive not every one his brother from your hearts."—*St. Matt.* xviii. 34, 35.

1. *His lord, being angry.* The lord in the parable rebuked this servant for his conduct to his fellow-servant, and in like manner God is angry with those who ill-treat their brethren : " As the roaring of a lion, so also is the anger of a king " (Prov. xix. 12). His wrath is kindled at every injury we do to our neighbour, because the latter is stamped with the Divine image. Priests, therefore, who desire to hinder offences against God, should strive to prevent men from offending their neighbours. They should look upon themselves as fathers of the family ; nay (as

St. Chrysostom says), they should excel even fathers in charity, and hence should strive to prevent all discord among their children. The Apostle enjoined Titus to teach the Faithful sound doctrine: "Speak thou the things that become sound doctrine" (Titus ii. 1): and it is sound doctrine (says St. Peter Damian) that Christ does not acknowledge those to be His living members who are divided amongst themselves by offences and discord. Hence, all our preaching should be reduced to the kindling of charity, which is called by St. Cyril the "recapitulation and complement of all virtues," But what have we done hitherto to prevent strife, discord, hatred? Have we not, perchance, been the cause of some offence, either by our word, our writings, or our acts? How many Priests (especially Parish Priests) have been guilty in this respect!

2. *Delivered him to the torturers.* Let us teach people that to each one who refuses to be reconciled with his enemy there remains (as St. Chrysostom says) a sentence of vengeance and punishment; for he will be delivered to devils, who (as St. Remigius says) hunger to make prey of lost souls, and to torment them eternally. He will have to pay the whole debt of his guilt in hell, but will never have fully discharged it, because he would not pardon those who had offended him. St. Peter Damian observes that the Cross of Christ inculcates on us two duties—viz., not to retaliate when injured, and also to do good to those who injure us. He is no disciple of the Cross, he is no disciple of Christ, who loves his friends only, for even the heathen and publicans do this (St. Matt. v. 46, 47). Hence, he is no good preacher of Jesus crucified who does not inculcate this duty, and who, in teaching it, does not imitate all the holy Fathers and sacred Orators who made it the special subject of their discourses. He, on the other hand, is a faithful dispenser of heavenly doctrine, who exerts himself to extinguish hatred and remove enmities, for (as St. Chrysostom declares) nothing is so hateful to God as a man eager for revenge. Let us recollect that, after the Apostle had said to Timothy, "We labour and are reviled," he adds, "These things command and teach" (1 Tim. 10, 11),—thereby admonishing Priests to inculcate mutual forgiveness.

Let us, then, teach the Faithful that the noblest way of avenging a wrong that they have sustained is by doing good to their enemies : " If thy enemy be hungry, give him to eat; if he thirst, give him to drink; for doing this thou shalt heap coals of fire upon his head " (Rom. xii. 20).

3. *If you forgive not.* We ought to give example of prompt pardon for all injuries whatsoever, confiding in our Lord Jesus Christ, Who, whilst He denies remission of sin to those who do not pardon injuries, promises, on the other hand, forgiveness of every sin to those who forgive others : " Forgive, and you shall be forgiven " (St. Luke vi. 37). In making this promise He neither deceives nor is deceived (says St. Chrysostom). Let us reflect that the Redeemer's words serve for the special instruction of Priests, and therefore were they addressed to St. Peter (as St. Jerome points out). Let us be convinced that, if we are not first in loving God and our neighbour, we shall not preach Charity with manifestation of the Spirit and power, and shall confer but little benefit on our hearers (as St. Laurence Justinian declares). Especially let us exercise ourselves in prayer to God for all who have offended us, for this is the most efficacious means of obtaining God's protection (says St. Ambrose), and, moreover, by such prayer shall we obtain mercy also for our enemies, to our own great consolation. Let us call to mind that Moses, Samuel, Elias, Stephen, prayed for their enemies and were heard ; such prayers being most grateful to God (says St. Bernardin of Sienna). In Holy Mass let us repress all desire of vengeance, and (as St. Gregory enjoins) let us pray expressly for our enemies.

" Instead of making a return of love they detracted me, but I gave myself to prayer."—*Ps.* cviii. 4.

" I beseech Thee . . . forgive them this trespass."—*Exod.* xxxii. 31.

SATURDAY.

FEAST OF OUR LADY OF SUFFRAGE.

THE BENEFIT OF PROPAGATING DEVOTION TO THE BLESSED VIRGIN UNDER THIS TITLE.

I. IT IS PROFITABLE TO THE HOLY SOULS.
II. IT IS PROFITABLE TO THE FAITHFUL.
III. IT IS PROFITABLE TO ZEALOUS PRIESTS.

"Blessed are they who hear the word of God and keep it."—*St. Luke* xi. 28.

1. *Blessed are they who hear, &c.* The holy souls in Purgatory are groaning in an abyss of suffering, yet are they in a manner "blessed," because, having "heard" the Divine word and having "kept it," they are certain of eternal blessedness. But more blessed still are those who, having often heard the praises of the Blessed Virgin, have practised constant devotion to Her; for (as St. Bernardin of Sienna says) She has dominion even in Purgatory, both in regard to lightening those pains and setting souls free from them. She says of Herself in Ecclesiasticus, "I have walked in the waves of the sea" (xxiv. 8); and is not Purgatory, indeed, a most bitter sea? of which St. Bernardin says the sufferings may be called waves, because they are transitory, in distinction from the pains of hell, which will never pass away. She continues, "I have penetrated to the bottom of the deep" (Eccl. xxiv. 8); and is not Purgatory an abyss of torment, which

exceeds (as Venerable Bede declares) the torments suffered by criminals, or by the holy Martyrs, or any that man can conceive? Now, St. Bonaventure applies the above passage of Ecclesiasticus to the Blessed Virgin, saying that She descends into this abyss of Purgatory in order to help the holy souls, and that by Her the souls therein detained obtain suffrage. Therefore shall we bring great benefit to these suffering souls if we engage the power and goodness of the Blessed Virgin in their favour, saying to Her (with St. Bridget), "Thou art the consolation of those who are in Purgatory." Hence Holy Church in many places celebrates the Sunday in the Octave of All Saints with a special Office, as the Feast of "Our Lady of Suffrage."

2. *Blessed are they who, having heard the word of God*, have hope and confidence in the Blessed Virgin (says St. Bonaventure). If they are condemned to Purgatory to expiate their sins, they will find even there a great protectress in Mary, who will diminish and shorten their pains. Hence St. Bernard says to Her, "Thy compassion obtains redemption for those who sit in darkness and in the shadow of death;" and he adds, that this is the consequence of that powerful and tender charity in which She abounds. It suffices to have true devotion in order to have, as it were, a right to a speedy deliverance from the bitter torments with which sin is there expiated; for (as St. Bernardin says) Mary chiefly delivers from these torments those who are devout to Her, and She is wont to make use of some one of Her Festivals, which they celebrated in their lifetime with especial devotion, to descend into Purgatory accompanied by the angels, and to draw them thence, as we learn from St. Peter Damian and from others. What an incentive is this to souls who care for their eternal salvation to implore the patronage of the Blessed Virgin, from Whom (as St. Joseph of Cupertinum said) we derive all good. Why, then, do we not strive to obtain this great benefit for the Faithful?

3. If they are "*blessed*" who "*hear the word of God and keep it*," far more blessed is the Priest who, in keeping it, proclaims it. If he promotes the benefit of the holy souls, and of the Faithful, most certainly will he at the same time promote his own benefit.

Let him, then, proclaim Mary as the liberator of those who are in Purgatory; let him fervently implore the help of the Blessed Virgin when he prays for the departed, remembering the words with which the Church addresses Almighty God at such time— "Grant them, through the intercession of Blessed Mary, ever Virgin, and of all Thy Saints, to attain the fellowship of perpetual bliss." Let them wear the scapular of our Lady of Mount Carmel, and induce others to wear it; the Blessed Virgin having promised to Pope John XXII. that all members of Her confraternity should be freed from Purgatory on the Saturday after their death, as he declared in his Bull, confirmed afterwards by Alexander V., by Clement VII., by Gregory XIII., and by Paul V. in the year 1612. Let us always remember that (as we read in the Office of this Festival), according to the pious belief of the Faithful, She consoles the suffering souls in Purgatory with all the affection of a mother, and conducts them as soon as possible to their heavenly country. It is certainly no small consolation to good Priests if (as St. Gregory says), in assisting the holy souls in Purgatory, they can rejoice in their deliverance from thence as though the happiness were their own. In this way, should we, by the just judgment of God, be thrust into the dark abode of Purgatory, we shall find Mary "fair as the morn" (Cant. vi. 9). She will cause Her rays to shine there to comfort us, for She has declared (as St. Bernardin says) that She will visit and supply the necessities and sufferings of Her devout children who may be detained there. Moreover, we may hope that in the day of judgment She will free us, Her servants (as St. Ephrem says) from condemnation and all tribulation. Let us, then, invoke Her aid, and let us never fear that we shall find Her deaf to our prayers.

"Put forth Thy hand from on high, take out the souls of the departed, and deliver them."—From *Ps.* cxliii. 7.

"Send forth Thy prisoners out of the pit, wherein is no water."—*Zachar.* ix. 11.

TWENTY-SECOND SUNDAY
AFTER PENTECOST.

THE COUNSELS OF THE WICKED AGAINST THE CLERGY.

I. THE NATURE OF THOSE COUNSELS.

II. THE PURPOSE TO WHICH THEY ARE DIRECTED.

III. THE MANNER IN WHICH THEY ARE EXECUTED.

"Then the Pharisees, going, consulted among themselves how to ensnare Him in His speech."—*St. Matt.* xxii. 15.

1. *Consulted among themselves.* The enemies of the Priesthood may be compared to running water, which is stopped by no obstacles, but, when they occur in its course, makes other channels for itself. However frequently the assailants of the Clergy may be refuted, they never cease to renew their attacks, and when foiled in one quarter they return to the charge in another direction. The counsels which they form are as malignant as their own hearts. Such counsellors are as "the gates of hell" (St. Matt. xvi. 18); for under the name of "gates" are represented the counsels which the ancients held in the "gates" of the city, and innumerable are the counsels which the powers of hell hold against the Clergy. They are followed by unbelievers, by heretics, by the vicious, by hypocrites; all of whom conspire to injure the Priesthood. The reason of this conspiracy is to be found in the vices and in the errors of such men, which St. Jerome rightly calls "the gates of hell;" for these are the means by which others are led into

evil. But what profit will the wicked derive from these miserable counsels ? The Priesthood will always triumph over them, sustained by the arm of its Omnipotent Author, against which such counsels will never prevail: "They have devised vain things" (Ps. ii. 1). Often, indeed, have they devised counsels against God and against His Christ ; but, whilst they were intent only on their own wickedness, they have unconsciously served our Saviour's designs (as St. Leo says). Now, they take counsel against His ministers and His people—"They have taken a malicious counsel against Thy people, and have consulted against Thy Saints" (Ps. lxxxii. 4); but they can do nothing to destroy the Priesthood—"He that dwelleth in heaven shall laugh at them" (Ps. ii. 4)—"They are caught in the counsels which they devise" (Ps. x. 2). Let us, then, trust in God, Who will give us the victory through our Lord Jesus Christ.

2. *How to ensnare Him.* The Pharisees sought to surprise Jesus, but foolish was their counsel (says St. Thomas), because He, being the Word of God, could not be ensnared. Priests, however, are all liable to be ensnared by men ; nay, they are often the victims of their frauds. They are " ignorant, and have been deceived by error" (Ezech. xlv. 20). The devices of the wicked tend to make a prey of them—that is, to corrupt their life, to stain their conscience. Evil men desire this in order that sin may raise its banner, so that the example of the Clergy may afford a sort of excuse for their own wickedness, and so that it may not be in the power of the former to reprove them, but that they may be able to say to the Priest, " Hold thy peace, and put thy finger on thy mouth, and come with us, that we may have thee for a father and a priest" (Judges xviii. 19). Moreover, these malicious counsels tend to compromise Priests in politics, so as to render the Clergy suspected by the civil authorities as instigators of the ignorant multitude. Such is the net which is spread before the feet of these unhappy men : " A man that speaketh to his friend with flattering and dissembling words spreadeth a net for his feet" (Prov. xxix. 5). This net will wound them in their own conscience, and in public opinion : " They spread their net over him, in their wounds he was

taken" (Ezech. xix. 8). The purport of these wicked counsels is also to make Priests lose their faith, so that they become like their seducers, who are "rebellious and incredulous" (Numb. xx. 10)—nay, to make them "the head of all unbelievers" (Judith xiv. 27). But, above all, they form these counsels with the view of depriving the Clergy of public esteem, of authority, of the free exercise of their ministry, and of ecclesiastical benefices. Thus are the words fulfilled in respect of the Church, "The enemy hath put his hand to all her desirable things" (Lam. i. 10). Let us, then, be careful of ourselves; let us strive ever to soar in thought to heaven, that we may not fall into the net of such evil counsellors: "A net is spread in vain before the eyes of them that have wings" (Prov. i. 17).

3. *In his speech.* The malicious carry out their evil designs by means of speech. Their tongue is as their armour and their net: "A flattering tongue deceiveth him" (Prov. xxviii. 23). They are wont to begin with flattering words, and thus endeavour to draw away the Priest from those who would correct him; but woe to him if he forget that saying of inspired wisdom, "It is better to be rebuked by a wise man than to be deceived by the flattery of fools" (Eccle. vii. 6). They hold irreligious, seditious, or perhaps obscene discourse in the presence of the Priest, and "their tongue is a fire, a world of iniquity" (St. James iii. 6), destroying all virtue, and kindling the flame of concupiscence. Hence St. Jerome, St. Bernard, and other Saints strongly urge upon Priests the duty of associating only with good and holy men, of employing their time in the works of their ministry, and of choosing the best amongst the Clergy for their companions. Let us pray for those who have neglected to follow these rules, and let us pray for ourselves that we may not imitate such men.

"O Lord, bring to nought the counsels of nations, and reject the devices of people, but let Thy counsel stand for ever."—From *Ps.* xxxii. 10, 11.

"Let not my soul go into their counsel, nor my glory be in their assembly."—*Gen.* xlix. 6.

MONDAY.

———◆———

THE IMITATION OF CHRIST THE CHIEF DUTY OF THE CLERGY.

I. Because Christ is their especial Master.

II. Because the true Priest must be formed after His example.

III. Because on this depends the sanctification of the people.

———◆———

"And they sent to Him their disciples with the Herodians, saying, Master, we know that Thou art a true speaker, and teachest the way of God in truth, neither carest Thou for any man, for Thou dost not regard the person of men."—*St. Matt.* xxii. 16.

1. *Master.* This title was given by these hypocrites to our Saviour deceitfully, and in order to ruin Him. They did not really recognise Him as their Master, and yet they called Him by that name in the hope that He would be flattered by such an honourable distinction, and be thereby induced to manifest the secrets of His heart to them. The Clergy, however, truly acknowledge Jesus Christ to be the Master of all men, especially of His Ministers, to whom He Himself has said, "You call Me Master and Lord, and you say well, for so I am" (St. John xiii. 13). And, because He taught by example as well as by words, He exacted from these disciples, not only the knowledge necessary to salvation, as contained in His words, but also the imitation of His example. As St. Augustin says, He would not be a Master, had He not disciples. Hence, they who aspire to the

Priesthood must propose to themselves the imitation of this great High Priest, and when anointed Priests they must strive to model themselves on this Divine original (as St. Cyril enjoins). St. Bernard says with truth that, if Priests are Christ's vicegerents, their conversation amongst men must resemble that of their Master; for, if all the Faithful are bound to walk as He walked, much more inexcusable are those who occupy His place on earth, and who are His representatives and ministers, if they follow Him not. Let us convince ourselves of the truth of this teaching, and let us impress it on our heart by serious meditation.

2. *Thou teachest the way of God in truth.* St. Thomas says that Jesus Christ, being the truth, knows what to teach; that He teaches things that are useful, and teaches them in the truth. Consequently (as St. Cyril says) His ministers must follow Him, and must imitate Him, if they desire to find the way of truth, and to be holy Priests; and thus the imitation of Christ is the priestly robe which constitutes our glory and honour. The same holy Father adds that, when the Psalmist says "I will clothe her Priests with salvation" (Ps. cxxxi. 16), he bade the Clergy be clothed with Christ—that is to say, to imitate Him; for (as St. Thomas says) he who imitates Christ manifests the works of Christ, and shews that Christ is in him, as the outer clothing of a man is a sign that the man himself is contained in it. Let us, then, study Christ's teaching and example, especially His humility, His charity, His patience, His modesty; let us strive to imitate Him; and let us apply to ourselves the words which He spoke to the Prince of all Priests—" Follow thou Me " (St. John xxi. 22); that is, Follow Me by imitation.

3. *Neither carest Thou for any man.* St. Thomas says that the tempters of our Lord by these words praised His constancy. Now, the Priest ought not, indeed, to " care for any man " in the sense of being influenced by human respect in the works of the Ministry; yet he ought, on the other hand, to care for the souls committed to him, in order to lead them into the way of salvation and perfection. But, if he would succeed in this arduous undertaking, he must follow the example of the Apostle, who said to his flock, " Be ye followers of me, as I also am of Christ"

(1 Cor. iv. 16). All his efforts should be directed to this one end—viz., to produce in the people of whom he has the charge the likeness of Christ. But the mere words of the preacher, if they are not confirmed by the example of his own life, will be of little avail. He must (as St. Bonaventure points out) represent in his life the doctrine of Christ which he preaches if he would impress that doctrine on men's hearts. If we would form Saints, we must put them in the "way," and this "way" is Christ. He who is out of this "way" runs in vain, and the more he runs the farther does he stray from the right way (as St. Augustin says). The office of Priests is to incite those who have stopped short to run in this way—to urge forward those who turn back—to recall those who have strayed from it. Most important are these duties, and happy are the Priests who fulfil them. Let us implore strength from our Lord Jesus Christ, Who is our pattern and our support.

"Shew, O Lord, Thy ways to me, and teach me Thy paths."—*Ps.* xxiv. 4.

"My Redeemer, O holy One of Israel, teach me profitable things; govern me in the way that I walk."—From *Is.* xlviii. 17.

TUESDAY.

PRIESTS MUST TEACH SUBMISSION TO CONSTITUTED AUTHORITY.

I. BY SHEWING THE DUTY OF CONSCIENCE.
II. BY DISCOVERING THE PERVERSITY OF THE SEDITIOUS.
III. BY AVOIDING ALL SUSPICION OF INSUBORDINATION.

"Tell us, therefore, what dost Thou think? Is it lawful to give tribute to Cæsar, or not? But Jesus, knowing their wickedness, said, Why do you tempt Me, ye hypocrites?"—*St. Matt.* xxii. 17, 18.

1. *Is it lawful to give tribute to Cæsar, or not?* The Jews considered themselves exempted from paying tribute to Cæsar, on the pretext that they were a nation subject to theocratical government alone, and therefore liable to no burthen except that of tithes. But we Christians have no pretext whatever for refusing submission to constituted authority, for the Apostle tells us clearly, " Render to all men their dues ; tribute to whom tribute is due, custom to whom custom, fear to whom fear, honour to whom honour" (Rom. xiii. 7). This obedience is a duty of conscience, and not merely to be performed through fear of punishment: "Be subject of necessity, not only for wrath, but also for conscience sake" (ver. 5). Faith, in fact, teaches us that "there is no power but from God," and that "those that

are ordained of God," and therefore "he that resisteth the power resisteth the ordinance of God, and they that resist purchase to themselves damnation" (Eph. vi. 5; Col. iii. 22; 1 Pet. ii. 13, 14, 17, 18). The teaching of the New Testament in this matter evidently agrees with the teaching of the Old, whereby princes are taught that "power is given" them "by the Lord, and strength by the Most High" (Wisd. vi. 4), so that it is said to an impious king, "God taketh away kingdoms and establisheth them ... the God of heaven hath given thee a kingdom, and strength, and power, and glory" (Dan. ii. 21, 37); and it is added, "God over every nation set a ruler" (Eccl. xvii. 14). Even a cruel tyrant, as Cyrus, is called by God "My anointed" (Isaias xlv. 1). In the case even of an unjust king, like Saul, no attempt must be made against "the anointed of the Lord" (1 Kings xxiv. 7, xxvi. 16). In reference even to a tyrant and persecutor, as was Nero, the Apostle wrote, "Let every soul be subject to higher powers" (Rom. xiii. 1). Let Priests ever keep these maxims before them, in order to oppose them to the false principles of rebels; and let them say to Christians, "My son, fear the Lord and the king, and have nothing to do with detractors" (Prov. xxiv. 21).

2. *But Jesus, knowing their wickedness.* Our Lord Jesus Christ knew the wickedness of these tempters, and it was on account of their malicious intention that He replied so severely. Great also is the malice of seditious men, who "despise dominion, and blaspheme majesty" (Jude 8). They are "murmurers, full of complaints, walking according to their own desires, and their mouth speaketh proud things" (ver. 16). They are described by the Apostle as "filled with all iniquity, malice, fornication, avarice, &c." (Rom. 1. 29); for they follow that philosophy which seduces, and is "vain deceit" (Coloss. ii. 8)—which is "an enemy to God" (Rom. viii. 7)—which is "knowledge falsely so called" (1 Tim. vi. 20). The followers of this philosophy promise men liberty in order to deceive them, and such liberty is but a "cloak" hiding their "malice" (1 Pet. ii. 16). But they promise not that true liberty which consists in being free from passions and sins, and which is given us by Jesus Christ: "For

if the Son shall make you free you shall be free indeed" (St. John viii. 36). They promise an equality which is absurd and impossible, and, even if it could be obtained, subversive of public order. Far different is this from the equality preached by the Apostle, which proceeds from almsgiving: "That their abundance may supply their want, that there may be an equality" (2 Cor. viii. 14). Let the ministers of truth, therefore, make people understand the deceptive nature of such promises; and let them preach the doctrines on this point which St. Augustin, St. Ambrose, and the other Fathers never ceased to inculcate. By such means they will relieve men from great troubles, and will conform themselves to the will of God.

3. *Why do you tempt Me, ye hypocrites ?* The Pharisees tempted our Saviour in order (says St. Jerome) that the Herodians might accuse Him of sedition should He answer that it was unlawful to pay the tribute. In like manner the devil tempts Priests to compromise themselves in political matters, to the serious injury of themselves and the rest of the Clergy. Formerly he caused the Apostles to be falsely accused of this crime, in order that they might suffer banishment, by inciting the wicked to utter the cries, "They that set the city in an uproar . . . and do contrary to the decrees of Cæsar, saying that there is another king, Jesus" (Acts xviii. 6, 7), and to declare that they "raise a tumult" (xxi. 38). "We have found this to be a pestilent man, and raising seditions" (xxiv. 5). What, however, if such reproach should have a foundation, in fact, through the language of some seditious Priest? In such a case the whole body of the Clergy becomes an object of suspicion to the authorities; and how can they, then, retain that influence over the people which is essential to good success in the works of the Ministry? Recent experience might supply many sad instances of this evil. Let us rather imitate our great High Priest, Who deigned even to be born in a stable, in order not to disobey the edict of Cæsar Augustus, and Who died upon the Cross without rebuking the unjust condemnation of a heathen magistrate, though He had said to him, "Thou shouldst not have any power against Me unless it were given thee from above" (St. John xix. 11). If

need be, let us suffer patiently unmerited troubles, in order to avoid the scandal of being called insubordinate, "for this is thanksworthy, if for conscience towards God a man endure sorrows, suffering wrongfully" (1 Pet. ii. 19). Let us avoid all murmuring against authority, for our words might be quickly carried to the ears of those in power, and thus we should be exposed to grave trials; "for their destruction shall rise suddenly, and who knoweth the ruin of both?" (Prov. xxiv. 22). Lastly, let us make our prayer, as the Apostle commanded Timothy, "for kings, and for all that are in high stations; that we may lead a quiet and a peaceful life, in all piety and chastity" (1 Tim. ii. 2). Priests who thus regulate their actions will be dear to God and men.

"O Lord, save the king, and hear us in the day that we call upon Thee."— Ps. xix. 10.

"Let Thy Priests, O Lord God, put on salvation, and Thy Saints rejoice in good things."—2 Paralip. vi. 41.

WEDNESDAY.

SECULAR CARES.

I. They distract the Priest in his duties.
II. They bring him into contempt.
III. They stain his conscience.

"Shew Me tne coin of the tribute. And they offered Him a penny."— *St. Matt. xxii. 19.*

1. *Show Me the coin of the tribute.* Our Lord Jesus Christ made this demand (says St. Thomas), not from ignorance, for He was well acquainted with the coin of the tribute, but from a wise economy, and in order to set forth some important truths. It would seem as though He desired to show that He was intent on other affairs than those of money and tribute—that is to say, that He had to finish the work committed to Him by the Father, to instruct men in the way of salvation, and to save the human race from eternal perdition—and, therefore, that He looked upon the questions which the world deems important as mere trifles. Let, then, the Priest be filled with the same sentiments, for (as St. Augustin says), inasmuch as we are Christians, we have to attend to our own souls, and, inasmuch as we are set over others, we have to watch over their spiritual welfare. We should never desist from bringing gain to Christ, for (as St. Augustin says) we are ourselves gained over by Him to Himself. Our office is to instruct men, and if we neglect study and preaching (as St. Basil says) we become murderers of souls. The time employed

in secular business (says St. Ambrose) is stolen from religion and from the duties of our Priestly office, and the more the mind is occupied with temporal matters (says St. Gregory) the less does it think of conferring eternal goods upon the people. How great loss have we incurred hitherto in this particular! how great loss has the Church suffered through our fault !

2. *And they offered Him a penny.* Wisdom ever acts wisely (says St. Jerome); and the incarnate Wisdom of God acted as became Him, and without detriment to His own dignity. But this is not the case with many Priests, who, when they mix themselves up with secular matters, fall in men's estimation and are looked upon as devoted to self-interest. Thus St. Paul's words apply to Ecclesiastics especially when he says, " No man, being a soldier to God, entangleth himself with secular business, that he may please Him to Whom he hath engaged himself" (2 Tim. ii. 4). St. Peter Damian says, that people look upon Priests when they act thus as Ecclesiastics who have quitted their own sphere and their proper duties, because they no longer see them intent solely on the salvation of souls and the discipline of their state. Such Priests become objects of contempt, because it is observed that the power which was given them over men's sins is exercised over earthly possessions. St. Gregory applies this passage of the Lamentations, " The finest colour is changed," to Priests who have given themselves up to worldly cares, and who thereby lose the respect and estimation in which they had once been held. If, however, it becomes necessary for the Priest to engage in matters of secular business, he should do so in such a manner as to shew that he is acting through necessity, or from motives of charity towards others, and not out of love for earthly goods, or through a taste for litigation. Let us reflect on these truths, that we may direct our steps like good Ecclesiastics.

3. *A penny.* How many souls are in hell through money— how many, even of Priests, are suffering with Judas, who betrayed his Master for money ! Now, what else but money is sought for in secular business ? and, thus, to how many and great spiritual dangers is the Priest's soul thereby exposed ! Such employments frequently leave the conscience torn by guilt and remorse. Let

us reflect that to Priests it was prescribed that "Not even for their father or their mother should they be defiled" (Levit. xxi. 11); and St. Peter Damian says that this prohibition refers to worldly business, by which the soul is so easily stained. Such stains redound to the injury of the whole Church, for (says St. Hilary) Priests are as the eyes of the mystical Body of Christ, and if their light be darkened the whole Body (according to the words of the Gospel) will be in darkness. Hence, the sacred Canons rigorously prohibit Clerics from trade, and from everything which might distract them from the service of God; and we frequently find it laid down as a general maxim, that they who have the care of souls should not frequent the market-place. Yet we have too good reason to lament (with St. Peter Damian) that many Priests are better informed about secular matters than the laity. Let us, then, seriously reflect on these truths; let us not suffer ourselves to be deluded by covetousness, by relations, by worldlings; let us detach ourselves from money, let us give ourselves wholly to the work of our ministry, and let us trust in God; for He will not abandon us, nor suffer us to want the necessaries of life.

"I will cast my care upon the Lord, and He shall sustain me."—From *Ps.* liv. 23.
"Blessed is the man that hath not gone after gold, nor put his trust in money, nor in treasures."—*Eccl.* xxxi. 8.

THURSDAY.

—•—

HOW THE IMAGE OF GOD IS SPECIALLY IMPRESSED UPON PRIESTS.

I. On their body.
II. On their soul.
III. On their will.

—•—

"And Jesus saith to them, Whose image and inscription is this? They say to Him, Cæsar's."—*St. Matt.* xxii. 20, 21.

1. *Whose image is this?* The image of the sovereign is impressed on all money, which is therefore to be rendered to the sovereign when he demands it. The image of God is impressed on every man, but especially on Priests, and hence arises in their case the obligation of giving up themselves absolutely to God. This image and this obligation may be referred in particular to the body, the soul, and the will (says St. Hilary). Although the body of man is not in a proper sense the image of God, still in a certain manner His glory is. reflected in it, says Cornelius à Lapide; and this is the teaching of St. Augustin and St. Bernard. Moreover, the Priest's body bears the image of God in a special way, because he is bound to chastity, which consists materially in the body. St. Thomas, in explaining the linen garments of the Priests of the Old Testament, says that they signify chastity and purity of life as necessary to all Priests. The Priest puts on daily the sacred vestments in order that he may recognise the dignity of his body (says St. Ambrose). Moreover, it is by means

of the body that the form of the Sacraments is expressed, the matter of them adapted to its purpose, and the ceremonies practised. The Priest's eyes are consecrated to the reading of holy books, his mouth to the recital of the praises of God and to the preaching of the Gospel, his ears to hearing confessions, his hands to touching the Body of Christ, his feet to the preparation of the Gospel of peace. Again (as St. Ambrose says), if he is conqueror of his passions, he covers even his own body with glory, subjects the flesh to the Spirit, restrains it with royal authority, and so, conforming himself to the likeness of God, is called by the name of God. What are the consequences of these truths? Let us meditate on the Apostle's words, "The body is not for fornication, but for the Lord" (1 Cor. vi. 13); "Yield your members to serve justice unto sanctification" (Rom. vi. 19).

2. *Whose image is this?* St. Thomas says that, besides the image of God, which is impressed on every rational soul, and which the Priest bears as a man and a Christian, he has also the Sacerdotal character, which consists in the image of the Trinity; and he goes on to say that this character is in the soul, and properly in the powers of the soul. By it the soul is made like to God, in Whom resides the authority of dispensing grace, of which Priests are deputed to be the instruments. Moreover, Priests being the masters of the people, and wisdom dwelling in the soul, even in this respect they represent God, the fountain and origin of wisdom : "Upon the person of the scribe He shall lay His honour" (Eccl. x. 5). Again, if they preserve the grace of Order and increase it, they will become a yet more lively image of God, and will be "partakers of the Divine nature (2 Pet. i. 4). Adorned with this grace and with this august character, they offer that great Sacrifice which is so wonderful in its efficacy ; for when a Priest celebrates Mass (says St. Thomas à Kempis) "he honours God, he rejoices the Angels, he edifies the Church, he helps the living, he obtains rest for the departed, and renders himself a partaker of all good things."

3. *Whose is this image?* The image of God is to be rendered back to God, and this image is found particularly in the will when it adheres to God. Whosoever willeth to be made like to God

(says St. Augustin) must not withdraw from Him, but must cleave to Him, so that His image may be stamped upon him, as the impression of a ring upon the wax to which it adheres. By separation from God, by the detachment of the will from the Divine will, this image becomes marred or effaced. Let us, then, examine ourselves, that we may see whether we preserve the impression of this precious image intact upon our wills, and whether we are of the number of those of whom it is written, " He chose Priests without blemish, whose will was set upon the law of God" (1 Machab. iv. 42). Our will ought certainly to be more raised up to God than that of the laity, and therefore do we read in the Gospel (as St. Ambrose points out) that our Lord caused His Disciples alone, as the first-fruits of the Priesthood, to go up with Him into the mountain. The great and lofty in perfection (continues St. Ambrose) are they who ascend the mountain : to them alone is it said, " Go up into the high mountain, thou that bringest glad tidings to Sion " (Isaias xl. 9). Let us pray to God to lift up our will from earth to heaven, and to conform it to His holy will, which is our sanctification.

"The light, O Lord, of Thy countenance is signed upon us ; Thou hast given gladness in my heart."—*Ps.* iv. 7.

"Thou hast anointed us, O God, and sealed us, and given us the pledge of the Spirit in our hearts."—From 2 *Cor.* i. 21, 22.

FRIDAY.

—◆—

THE ORIGIN OF EVIL COUNSELS CONCERNING THE RESPECTIVE LIMITS OF THE ECCLESIASTICAL AND CIVIL AUTHORITY.

I. DEFECT OF TEACHING.
II. DEFECT OF PRAYER.
III. DEFECT OF HOLINESS.

—◆—

" Then He saith to them, Render, therefore, to Cæsar the things that are Cæsar's, and to God the things that are God's."—*St. Matt.* xxii. 21.

1. *Render, therefore.* Priests often find themselves obliged to give counsel to magistrates, governors, ministers of state, and princes, either by word of mouth or writing, in regard to the respective limits of the Ecclesiastical and of the civil power. In such cases the general rule laid down by our Divine Lord in these words must be our guide. But those who thus take counsel of Priests are apt to regard only the first part of the maxim, and to forget the second; that is to say, they are solicitous to render to Cæsar even more than Cæsar's, but they withhold from God that which is God's; and thus they give tribute to Satan rather than to Cæsar, and rob Almighty God of that which is His due. Let us, however, bear in mind that (as St. Chrysostom points out) when Christ speaks of giving to Cæsar "the things which are Cæsar's," He is referring to those things only which do not interfere with the exercise of true religion, for all else is service paid to the devil rather than to Cæsar. Now, false answers in such matters often proceed from ignorance on the part of Priests who have neglected the study of dogmatic and moral theology,

and especially of the sacred Canons, the knowledge of which Pope Celestine declared that all Priests were bound to acquire. Is such ignorance, then, excusable before God? "If the blind lead the blind," shall he not fall with him into the pit? (St. Matt. xv. 14.) Nay, the more terrible will be the condemnation of such Priests, inasmuch as they may become (as St. Gregory declares) the cause of public disorders. They might at least have admitted their own insufficiency, and have had recourse to standard works, or consulted other Priests more enlightened than themselves. But, so far from this, it often happens that one who should be a learner acts the part of a master, and answers without thought or deliberation any inquiry that may be put to him. For such presumptuous ignorance the Priest will be justly punished by becoming a prey to the teeth of the lions of hell (as St. Peter Damian says). May Almighty God deliver us from so great a calamity, and give us grace to abandon a position which imperils our eternal salvation.

2. *Render, &c.* In doubtful cases it is no easy matter to define the limits of the Ecclesiastical and of the civil power—to choose in controversies authors who are above suspicion—to reconcile the civil with the Ecclesiastical laws, and to deliver a true judgment, so as to put the flatterers of Cæsar to silence and to maintain our position with firmness. These are the perils which (as St. Augustin declares) are wont to surround Priests in their prosperity, or whilst occupying the most important and responsible situations. Light to know the truth, and strength to defend it, are graces which God refuses not to those who pray to Him, especially when they have entered upon a course so beset with perils in obedience to His call: although the winds are boisterous (says St. Augustin), although the waves rage terribly, and though human frailty may have inspired thee with some doubt, yet thou hast it in thy power to cry for help; thou canst say, Lord, I perish. He who bids thee walk on the waters suffers thee not to perish. The Ecclesiastic who is truly wise "in his prayer will confess to the Lord, and He shall direct his counsel and his knowledge, and in His secrets shall he meditate; he shall shew forth the discipline he hath learned" (Eccl. xxxix. 9—11).

Doubtless (as it has been said by an ancient commentator on those words), God gives understanding to His faithful ambassador; He teaches him when, where, and how to speak; and He will direct his counsel aright. Such is the course which wise directors of souls always pursue (says St. Gregory); that is to say, when they find themselves in perilous circumstances, when they cannot settle doubtful points, they betake themselves to the secret recesses of their mind, as to a kind of tabernacle, and have recourse to prayer. How many errors might not we have avoided had we but implored Divine light and guidance!

3. *Render, therefore, &c.* We are both God's and Cæsar's (says St. Thomas), because we have for our use both the things of God and the things of Cæsar; and the justice of Priests consists in rendering their due both to God and to Cæsar. But how great virtue is required to do this! What sanctity of life is necessary in order to be able to say to the great of this world, " It is not lawful for thee!" (St. Mark vi. 19.) Sometimes, indeed, we are bound to say frankly, " It is not permitted you to break God's law; it is not permitted you to invade the rights of the Church; it is not permitted you to violate the sacred Canons." To deliver this testimony we need have the holiness of the Baptist, and of Elias and Eliseus, who spoke with like freedom to the princes of the earth. So great ought to be our detachment from the world (as St. Augustin teaches us) that we must not fear to lose our life, or to suffer any injustice, rather than to be silent in the cause of justice. · How difficult is it for those of slender virtue not to stain their own conscience in such circumstances! Hard, indeed, it is (as St. Ambrose has said) to maintain integrity in the courts of kings. Although it is lawful, in the interest of religion, to expose ourselves to such peril, yet we should do so always in fear for ourselves, remembering Peter, who (as St. Bernard observes) had no sooner entered the palace than he thrice denied his Lord.

" Even then, also, shall Thy hand lead me, and Thy right hand shall hold me."—*Ps.* cxxxviii. 10.

" Preserve me from the snare of an unjust tongue, and from the lips of them that forge lies, and be my helper in the sight of them that stand by."—From *Eccl.* li. 3.

SATURDAY.

● ──────

THE PATRONAGE OF THE BLESSED VIRGIN MARY.

THE GRACES TO BE ASKED OF ALMIGHTY GOD IN THE MASS AND OFFICE OF THIS FESTIVAL

I. THAT HE MAY GRANT US THIS PATRONAGE.
II. THAT HE MAY INSPIRE US WITH DUE CONFIDENCE IN IT.
III. THAT HE MAY GIVE US GRACE TO MERIT IT.

──────◆──────

" Blessed are they who hear the word of God and keep it."—*St. Luke* xi. 28.

1. *Blessed are they who hear.* He who hears the word of God, which is communicated to us by the Church, cannot hesitate to ask of Almighty God, through the merits of His Son, the intercession and protection of any Saint, as holy Church herself teaches in many of her prayers. Now, inasmuch as prayer and the protection of the Saints are a means of salvation, and every Christian is bound to seek from God, through the merits of Christ, the means of salvation, there is no just ground for the complaint of heretics that the Church so often asks of God this important grace. What shall we say, then, of the prayers and protection of Mary, Who in the sole act of consent to the Incarnation merited (as St. Bernardin declares) more than all the Saints in all their most meritorious acts? Does not Her power exceed that of all the Angels and all the Saints? Is She not more compassionate than any other of the blessed? Who is there upon whom the sun does not shine? In like manner, who

is there whom the rays of Mary's mercy cannot reach ? (asks St. Bonaventure.) Hence, if the protection of one Saint can contribute to the salvation of many, the protection of Mary (as St. Thomas declares) suffices for the salvation of all. Therefore, in holy Mass and in the recital of the Office, let us ask of God to place us under the protection of Her whom He Himself gave us for our mother, and in whom (as St. Antoninus says) He Himself implanted the most ineffable compassion. We, more than others, have need of this salutary patronage, for heavier are our duties, more terrible are our temptations ; therefore let us fervently ask it of God, in the name and in the spirit of holy Church.

2. *Blessed are they who hear the word of God and keep it :* blessed also are they who receive light from God—that light which illumines every man that cometh into this world. " Think not that thou art thyself light," says St Augustin, "for that is the true light which enlighteneth every man that cometh into this world : thou by thyself wast in darkness." Now, it is a great light from God to know Mary, and how much She loves us ; it is a great light from God which leads us to say, with St. Peter Damian, I know, O blessed Lady, that Thou art most kind, and that we are loved by Thee with an ineffable love, because Thy God loves us in Thee and through Thee. It is a great light from God to know how much Mary loves those who are devout to Her, and how She, being their mistress, makes Herself their servant (as has been said by an ancient commentator) in order to reconcile these Her servants with Her Son. It is a great light from God to know that She is (as St. Basil calls Her) the root of all good. Moreover, it is only through God's inspiration that we can have that confidence in Mary which the Saints have ever had, saying to Her (with St. Augustin), "By Thee the miserable inherit mercy ; sinners, pardon ; the abject, glory ; the earthly, heaven ; mortals, life ; and pilgrims, their true country." Without Divine inspiration we cannot flee to Mary as to a city of refuge—that City which is open to us (says St. Bernard) in all temptations, in all tribulations, in all necessities. In a word, without Divine inspiration we neither appreciate nor desire the patronage of the

Blessed Virgin, for (as St. Germanus says) it is a benefit which surpasses our understanding. Hence, let us on this festival implore our Lord to grant this light and this inspiration to all the Faithful, and especially to those of our charge, in order that our instructions and exhortations on this point may be successful.

3. *Blessed are they who hear the word of God and keep it*—who lay to heart that word especially which declares that every good gift comes from Him Who alone is good, and that they have no good in themselves. Now, devotion to the Blessed Virgin is a great good, for it is the source of innumerable good things. "All good things came to me together with her" (Wisd. vii. 11). A great treasure is it to honour this our Mother by various acts of devotion, to love Her, to invoke Her, to imitate Her: "He that honoureth his mother is as one that layeth up a treasure" (Eccl. iii. 5). Hence, this devotion, this worship, is a gift of God which we must ask of Him, in order so to obtain the patronage of His great Mother; for (as St. John Damascene says) God bestows this sign of predestination on those whom it is His will to save. Thus, whilst we inculcate on the Faithful devotion to the Blessed Virgin Mary, let us pray to God, especially on this day, to give efficacy to our words, so that those to whom we speak may practise all such good works as accompany true devotion to Her, and may obtain the patronage of so powerful an advocate. So will She shew Herself, both to us and to them, as the compassionate protector in our misery (as St. Antoninus calls Her) : She will show Herself our defender, to whom (as St. Thomas of Villanova says) we must all look : She will shew Herself, not only our protector, but (as St. Germanus says) a most powerful means of protection.

"Grace is found abroad in Thy lips, therefore hath God blessed thee for ever."— *Ps.* xliv. 3.

"Thy Priests are in mourning, and are brought low . . unless Thou help us."— 1 *Macbab.* iii. 51—53.

TWENTY-THIRD SUNDAY AFTER PENTECOST.

SPECIAL MOTIVES FOR PRIESTS TO PRESERVE MODESTY OF THE EYES.

I. BECAUSE OF THE MINISTRY WHICH THEY EXERCISE.
II. BECAUSE OF THE LIGHTS WITH WHICH THEY ARE FURNISHED.
III. BECAUSE OF THE FALL WHICH THEY SHOULD FEAR.

" As Jesus was speaking these things unto them, behold, a certain ruler came up and adored Him, saying, Lord, my daughter is even now dead ; but come, lay Thy hand upon her, and she shall live."—*St. Matt.* ix. 18.

1. *A certain ruler came up and adored Him.* This ruler is by St. Mark called Jairus—that is to say, " enlightened," and " one of the rulers of the synagogue " (St. Mark v. 22). Priests, therefore, who by reason of their Ministry are " full of light," and who are " rulers " of the Faithful, may consider themselves as typified by this ruler. But what if they fix their eyes on persons of the opposite sex ? An immodest eye betrays a sensual mind (says St. Bernard) ; and, therefore, if lay persons find that they are continually meeting the Priest's eyes, they will lose respect for him, for they know well that an unmortified eye does not serve to guard chastity, but rather to nourish curiosity. As St. Bernard also says, the undisciplined eye is a slave to curiosity. The Faithful are aware that the Clergy are required to have, not only chastity of minds but also modesty of eyes, and that Priests

ought to abstain from all allurements of sight. What opinion, then, will they form of Priests whose eyes are void of all modesty? The ruler in the Gospel drew near to adore Jesus: the Priest's eyes are fixed closely upon Him in the sacred Mysteries, and, therefore, should be kept from the sight of all such objects as might in any way impair their purity. His eyes represent the eyes of Christ (says St. Anselm), and therefore such eyes must never be turned to vanities.

2. *My daughter is even now dead.* This young damsel (says St. Chrysostom) was the ruler's only child, of the age of twelve years, in the very flower of her youth; yet death spared her not, but in a few short hours would have reduced her to a mass of corruption. What, then, is human beauty? "Dust and ashes" (Gen. xviii. 27) . . . "Who cometh forth like a flower, and is destroyed" (Job xiv. 2). Priests know this, and have often meditated upon it: how, then, can they suffer themselves to be fascinated by that which is thus destined to corruption? How can they allow the eyes which they have consecrated to God to be turned back from Him to gaze upon vanity? Moreover, they hope that one day their eyes will behold their Saviour in glory and gaze upon that beauty which fills the heavens; and therefore (says St. Jerome) they ought to despise earthly beauty. They know that, if material objects have a transitory beauty, "the Lord of them is more beautiful than they, for the first Author of beauty made all these things (Wisd. xii. 3); and that He will be seen, possessed, and enjoyed by the clean of heart. Again, they are bound to imitate Him, Whose eyes were downcast, so that He had to lift them up to behold His disciples: "He, lifting up his eyes on His disciples . . ." (St. Luke vi. 20). They know further that (as St. Isidore says) the modest bearing of the Clergy is a source of edification to the people, and contributes to the glory of the Church.

3. *She shall live.* If we desire to preserve true life—that is, the life of the soul—let us diligently guard the windows of the soul, by which "death cometh up" (Jerem. ix. 21). They who fear to fall into sin restrain their eyes, and observe the maxim of St. Gregory, viz., that it is not seemly to look at that which

one may not desire. The purity of Priests is stained by the mere sight of vain and lascivious objects (as the Council of Narbonne declares), and (as St. Bernard says) the custody of the eyes is the chief preservative of chastity. Let us remember that Samson, David, Solomon, by neglecting this precaution, lost the grace of God, their peace of conscience, and even temporal happiness ; and shall we suppose ourselves stronger than Samson, holier than David, wiser than Solomon ? Let us, then, resolve to follow the Divine teaching : " Gaze not upon a maiden, lest her beauty be a stumbling-block to thee " (Eccl. ix. 5). " Turn thy face away from a woman dressed up, and gaze not about upon another's beauty. For many have perished by the beauty of a woman, and hereby lust is enkindled as a fire " (ver. 8, 9). How many Priests would have escaped hell had they but observed these maxims ! How much do we owe to Divine justice for our violation of them ! Let us, then, imitate holy Job, who declares that he " made a covenant with his eyes," and " would not so much as think upon a virgin " (Job xxxi. 1).

" Turn away my eyes, that they may not behold vanity : quicken me in Thy way."—*Ps.* cxviii. 37.

" O Lord, I beseech Thee, let not beauty deceive me, nor lust pervert my heart." —From *Dan* xiii. 56.

MONDAY.

—◆—

THE SACRED VESTMENTS.

I. THE BENEDICTION OF THE SACRED VESTMENTS.

II. THE PRAYERS TO BE RECITED BY THE PRIEST IN VESTING.

III. THE VIRTUES OF WHICH THESE VESTMENTS ARE SIGNIFICANT.

—◆—

" And Jesus, rising up, followed him with His disciples. And, behold, a woman, who was troubled with an issue of blood twelve years, came behind Him and touched the hem of His garment."—*St. Matt.* ix. 19, 20.

1. *Touched the hem of his garment.* The Pharisees fastened thorns to the hem of their garments, lest any unclean thing should touch them ; but, on the other hand (as Remigius points out), the hem of Christ's garment was not the cause of wounds, but of healing. Now, in the Office for the blessing of the sacred vestments in the Roman Ritual, the Church implores heavenly grace upon those vestments, in order that they may be fitted to cure our infirmities and cause us to celebrate the Divine Mysteries worthily. The Church prays that Her sacred Ministers, in wearing them, " may be defended against the temptations of the devil, may serve God with devotion and praise, may receive the sevenfold gifts of the Spirit and the stole of chastity, in order that they may be afterwards clothed with the garment of immortality." Such prayers will doubtless be heard by Almighty God, and if Priests oppose no obstacles to them they will experience their salutary effects. On this account the Canons of the Church rigorously prescribe that this necessary blessing be given either bv

the Bishop or by a Priest who has received the faculties for that purpose. Let us, therefore, be careful to preserve those sacred vestments in due cleanliness and splendour, according to the decree of Innocent III. Priests who are negligent in these matters shew that they neglect to cleanse their own conscience. These are great truths, which have been too often confirmed by experience.

2. *Touched, &c.* It was not the mere touch of our Lord's most sacred garment which healed this woman, but the sentiment which accompanied that touch (says St. Chrysostom). Now, if we put on the sacred vestments without attention and without prayer, what advantage shall we derive from them? Can we suppose that the mere blessing of the Church will suffice? Certainly not: something is also necessary on our part (says St. Hilary); for the Church prescribes prayers adapted to each vestment—prayers suggested to her by Christ Himself and the Holy Ghost. For (as St. Thomas declares, in speaking of the Ceremonies of the Mass) that which the Church directs is ordained by Christ Himself. Such prayers, if duly recited, are a fit and needful preparation for the great Sacrifice. As St. Thomas says, it is written, "Keep thy foot when thou goest into the house of God" (Eccl. iv. 17); and therefore should we use due preparation for the celebration of these Mysteries, in order that the Sacrifice itself may be worthily performed. Should our distraction in reciting these prayers be involuntary, such is God's mercy that He will not despise our prayers, but even in that case He will accept them. St. Augustin says that the Psalmist speaks of God as " sweet and gentle," because He bears with so many who pray thus to Him with wandering thoughts. But, if (as is the case with some careless Priests) distractions are voluntary either in cause or in effect—if we converse with others when we ought only to be speaking to God alone—let us fear lest we provoke His just indignation by the outrage we are committing against Him. For (says St. Augustin again) to think of anything superfluous is a wrong done to Him with Whom you have begun to speak. Let us examine our conduct on this head; let us repent if we have failed; and let us resolve, with

God's help, to recite these holy prayers with attention and devotion.

3. *Touched, &c.* The vestments with which the Priests of the Old Law were adorned prefigured the future Messias—" the High Priest of good things to come, the Priest for ever;" and Almighty God attached so great importance to these sacred garments that He filled the makers of them "with the spirit of wisdom, that they might make Aaron's vestments, in which he, being consecrated, might minister" (Exod. xxviii. 3). These vestments expressed also the duties of Aaron and of his sons. In like manner the vestments of the Priests of the New Law are a token that in the sacred Ministry they represent Christ, and are associated with Him in His one Priesthood, for there is one Priest, one Mediator (says St. Augustin). Moreover, they remind us of the duties which were imposed upon us when we were first clad in those vestments at our Ordination, as set forth in the Pontifical. They remind us that the Ministers of the Church must be " perfect in faith and works," and of pure and sanctified life (as St. Ambrose says)—that the Priest is the "teacher of piety " (according to St. Gregory of Nyssa), and, as it were, "the common father of all men" (according to St. Chrysostom)—that (according to St. Peter Damian) he is "the teacher and standard-bearer of the Lord's army." How have we meditated on these sublime truths as signified by the sacred vestments ? What impression have they made on our heart ? What is our resolve for the future ? Let us reflect that our Lord Himself offered His great Sacrifice on the Altar of the Cross stripped of His garments, but left us to celebrate in an unbloody manner that same Sacrifice in these sacred vestments; and in this He was prefigured by the High Priest Judas Machabeus, who was slain before he had put on the sacred vestments, but left his brother Jonothan to succeed Him in the Priesthood, who "put on the holy vestment" (1 Machab. x. 21).

" O Lord, let the ointment of Thy grace run down to the skirt of my garments." —From *Ps.* cxxxii. 2.

" Clothe me, O Lord, with the garments of salvation, and with the robe of Thy justice cover me."—From *Isaias* lxi. 10,

TUESDAY.

———•———

———•———

"For she said within herself, If I shall touch only His garment I shall be healed."
—*St. Matt.* ix. 21.

1. *If I shall touch His garment.* The woman who had the issue
of blood deemed herself unworthy to touch our Saviour's feet,
or even His garments, but was content to touch only the hem of
His garment. Many Christians eagerly desire to behold Christ's
garments, and would consider themselves highly honoured indeed might they touch them ; but to Priests far more is granted,
for to them He giveth Himself (as St. Chrysostom says), not to
see only, but to touch, and to eat and receive within them. The
Bride, in the sacred Canticles, desiring to find her Spouse, exclaims, "Who shall give me . . . that I may find thee without,
and kiss thee, and now no man may despise me?" (Cant. viii. 1.)
Those words are applied by the Abbot Rupert to himself, because
when he shrunk from the Priesthood, to which his Superiors
desired to promote him, he was called to it by our Lord Himself,
Who, appearing to him on the Altar, drew him towards Him, and
allowed Himself to be embraced by him. Let us reflect that Almighty God forbade the Israelites, under pain of death, to touch
Mount Sinai, which was a figure of Christ: "Every one that
toucheth the mount, dying he shall die: no hands shall touch

him " (Ex. xix. 13, 14). The family of Caath were forbidden with the same severity to touch the vessels of the sanctuary, which were but a shadow of the sacred chalice : " They shall not touch the vessels of the sanctuary, lest they die " (Numb. iv. 15). In like manner they were forbidden to touch that part of the tabernacle which was called the holy of holies : " That they may not die by touching the holy of holies " (*ib.* 19). But our hands continually touch the true Holy of Holies, the Word of life . . . " Which our hands have handled of the Word of life " (1 John i. 1). What, then, is our gratitude to God for so great honour ?—what is our love to Jesus Christ, Who thus humbles Himself in His immense condescension to us ?

2. *If I shall touch His garment.* The hands of this woman were well disposed by faith to draw the desired grace from Christ, and therefore in touching the hem of His garment she obtained it. At the Crucifixion, however, the hands of the soldiers, contaminated by perfidy, whilst handling still more closely the same garments, derived no spiritual profit from them (as St. Chrysostom observes). Now, the Church, in order to prepare our hands for touching the most holy Flesh of Christ, consecrates them with holy oil, and with the prayer of the Pontifical, " Vouchsafe, O Lord, to bless and consecrate these hands, &c." Of the Priests of the Old Law it is written that " they were anointed, whose hands were filled and consecrated, to do the functions of Priesthood " (Numb. iii. 3) ; and with the blood of the ram that was immolated Moses " touched the thumb of the right hand, and in like manner also the great toe of his right foot " (Lev. viii. 24). The oil (says St. Cyprian) signified the unction, dignity, and grace of the Priests of the New Covenant ; the blood on the thumb of the right hand, firm accomplishment of the law of obedience. Let us bear in mind, then, that the eternal consecration of our hands by the Church was the symbol of the consecration of our actions ; for the hand is the symbol of action, and when we stretched out our hands to receive the holy unction we sig· nified the sanctification of all our actions. By the stretched-out hands (says St. Augustin) we may understand the continuation of good works throughout the whole day. But have we carried

out these good intentions? Are our hands really pure to touch the immaculate Flesh of God? Are our works holy? Alas! may we not be of the number of those "in whose hands is iniquity?"

3. *I shall be healed.* This woman was healed because, guided by the light of faith, she said within herself, "If I shall touch only the hem of His garment I shall be healed;" and, therefore, virtue went out from Jesus and healed her: "I know that virtue is gone out from Me" (St. Luke viii. 46). If, then, we recollected ourselves before celebrating Holy Mass, so as to be animated with the same sentiments of faith, virtue would go out from our Lord Jesus Christ, and would enter into us to heal our corruption, as signified by the disease of this woman. Jesus Christ is, indeed, ever of the same infinite power and goodness. On this occasion He communicated the power which was inherent in His Body, and extended its healing efficacy (says St. Hilary) even to the hem of His garment. How much more, therefore, would He transmit virtue to the Priest, who touches His very Body? But, alas! many Priests are as the crowd, pressing Jesus Christ and afflicting Him, while few touch Him efficaciously: "The multitudes throng and press Thee, and dost Thou say, Who touched Me?" (St. Luke viii. 45.) Truly (as St. Augustin says) do many visibly and carnally press with their teeth the Sacrament of the Body and Blood of Christ, but of few can He say, "Somebody hath touched Me" (St. Luke viii. 46); that is to say, few touch Him with the spirit of faith, with which they ought to be filled in handling this mystery of faith; few touch Him with that humility which springs from the knowledge of their own unworthiness, accompanied with the hope of pardon. For (as St. Ambrose remarks in commenting on this passage) faith urged this woman on, shame held her back; and faith combined with humility causes us to acknowledge our infirmity without despairing of pardon. Let us, then, excite in ourselves faith and hope and contrition, that we may obtain all the graces of the Sacrament.

"I stretched forth my hands to Thee : my soul is as earth without water unto Thee."—*Ps.* cxlii. 6.

"If I shall touch only His garment I shall be healed."—*St. Matt.* ix. 21.

WEDNESDAY.

MEANS OF PRESERVING CHASTITY.

I. To remember the presence of Jesus Christ.
II. To trust in the aid of Jesus Christ.
III. To live by faith in Jesus Christ

" But Jesus, turning and seeing her, said, Be of good heart, daughter; thy faith hath made thee whole. And the woman was made whole from that hour.

1. *Jesus, turning and seeing her.* No sooner had Jesus looked upon the woman than she, struck with fear, "trembling, came and fell down before Him, and told Him all the truth" (St. Mark v. 33). Now, if we remembered that the most pure eyes of our Lord Jesus Christ are ever turned upon us, as though we alone were before Him, should we not tremble with a holy fear? If the Priest do not preserve unspotted chastity, the reason is to be found in the words of the Psalmist, "God is not before his eyes: his ways are filthy at all times" (Ps. x. 6). To preserve continence, we must remember Him Who (says St. Bonaventure) is a Virgin, the Son of a Virgin, the Spouse of Virgins. As St. Peter Damian says, if He would be touched by pure hands in the manger, how far greater purity will He not require in the hands which touch Him on the Altar, now that He is raised to the glory of His Father in heaven? Therefore (says St. Paulinus), the more perfect the chastity of Priests in their senses and in their affections, the greater their capacity for receiving Christ. Let us, then, ever bear in mind that we are in the presence of

our Lord Jesus Christ; for who (asks St. Basil) would dare to offend his sovereign before his very eyes? He is the Judge at Whose tribunal we must one day appear, and therefore His eyes ought to instil into us fear and trembling. Surely (as St. Leo says), if it is a fearful thing to fall into the hands of the living God, it is madness to sin before His very eyes.

2. *Be of good heart, daughter.* The most powerful means of preserving chastity is to trust in Jesus Christ, and to cry to Him constantly, with St. Augustin, "Thou enjoinest us continency; give what Thou enjoinest, and enjoin what Thou wilt." By loving Jesus Christ, and trusting in Him, and not in our own strength, chastity is easily preserved. The guardian of virginity is charity, says (St. Augustin) and its abode is humility. Woe to those who trust in themselves, and who are without humility! for by losing humility (says St. Bernard) they merit not chastity. The wounds of Jesus must be our refuge in all assaults against this angelic virtue: "If my flesh presses me down," says St. Augustin, "the remembrance of my Lord's wounds lifts me up . . . in them I sleep safely and rest fearlessly." Had we but trusted in our Lord—had we not foolishly presumed on ourselves—had we avoided those occasions in which we had no right to trust in Jesus, and in which we ought not to have trusted ourselves—how well might we have preserved chastity! We should have followed the rule laid down by St. Augustin—viz., to escape the assaults of concupiscence by flight, since in such cases flight is victory.

3. *Thy faith hath made thee whole.* Christ (says Origen) bestowed on this woman first the healing of her soul, and afterwards the healing of her body, on account of her faith. And we, if we desire chastity of soul and body, shall obtain it from Jesus Christ by means of faith—that is, by living the life of faith. Let us consider that those who offend against this virtue of chastity are in the number of those of whom the Apostle said, "They shall not possess the kingdom of God" (1 Cor. vi. 10). Let us consider the obligation we contracted in the Sub-diaconate, and that "an unfaithful and foolish promise displeaseth God" (Eccle. v. 3). Let us consider that to each one of us it was said, "Keep

thyself chaste " (1 Tim. vi. 22) . . . " Be an example to the faithful
. . . in chastity " (iv. 12). Let us consider that by transgressing
this commandment we render ourselves unworthy to " follow
the Lamb whithersoever He goeth," and to sing in heaven that
canticle " which no man can say but those who were not defiled
with women " (Apoc. xiv. 3, 4). Now, what is the meaning of
" following the Lamb ?" It means (says St. Augustin) a joy exceeding that of all the other heavenly citizens—" a joy of the
virgins of Christ, in Christ, with Christ, after Christ, through
Christ, for Christ's sake." There are (he adds) various kinds of
joy in heaven, but there is none like this. Let us hope that we
may ourselves be admitted into the ranks of those who sing this
canticle in the heavenly Jerusalem, or at least may hear it sung;
for " the multitude of the Faithful," continues St. Augustin,
" though they will not be able to utter that new song, which
belongs to you alone, O Virgins, yet will be enabled to hear it,
and to rejoice in your great privilege."

" Draw me out of the mire, that I may not stick fast; deliver me from them
that hate me."—*Ps.* lxviii. 15.

" As I knew that I could not otherwise be continent except God gave it . . I
went to the Lord, and besought Him."—*Wisd.* viii. 21.

THURSDAY.

———•———

PRIESTS SHOULD LEARN FROM JESUS CHRIST TO DESPISE THE WORLD.

I. To DESPISE ITS ALLUREMENTS.

II. To REJECT ITS POMPS.

III. To DISREGARD ITS SCORN.

———•———

" And, when Jesus was come into the house of the ruler and saw the minstrels and the multitude making a rout, He said, Give place, for the girl is not dead, but sleepeth. And they laughed Him to scorn."—*St. Matt.* ix. 23, 24.

1. *When He saw the minstrels.* The delights of the world are like a melancholy song, with which men strive to alleviate the sorrows of our miserable mortal life; and those who promote such delights are justly called by St. Jerome "minstrels singing mournful songs." The Priest should fly from such diversions, attractive though they are to the mind of youth, which is given up to dissipation and frivolity. For to Priests has God said, "Flee from youthful desires" (2 Tim. ii. 22); and they should be old in wisdom, as their very name "presbyter" or "ancient" should remind them. They should be ever ready to say, with the aged Berzillai, "Are my senses quick to discern sweet and bitter? or can meat and drink delight thy servant? or can I hear any more the voice of singing men and singing women?" (2 Kings xix. 35.) Their senses are consecrated to God, and therefore ought they to be dead to all the pleasures of earth; and this (says St. Thomas) is what they shew forth in the celebration of Holy Mass,

wherein they should be conformed to Christ's death. This also is signified in the prayer which the Church directs us to use when we put on the maniple in vesting for Mass: " Merear, Domine, portare manipulum fletûs et doloris, &c." If, then, Priests desire to preserve chastity, let them guard their senses (as St. Augustin enjoins) as five virgins, to be protected against the assaults of the dragon of hell, lest by his allurements he corrupt them. The Apostle charged Timothy (and, in his person, all Ecclesiastics) to avoid " profane stories," and permitted him no other diversion than such as might be conducive to piety (as St. Ambrose observes). Let us ask ourselves how we have employed our senses. What have been our amusements? Let us examine ourselves seriously in order to amendment.

2. *He said, Give place.* In driving away the multitude before raising the damsel to life, our Lord teaches us (says St. Gregory) that the crowd of worldly cares must be first expelled from the inner recesses of the heart in order that the soul may rise to spiritual life. Now, these cares are inseparable from the pomps to which some Ecclesiastics are so foolishly addicted, and therefore all worldly pomps and display are especially forbidden them by the Council of Milan. How earnestly did St. Bernard protest against such a tendency in the Prelates of his day! and still more necessary is it for the inferior Clergy to avoid this snare. Let them gain the respect of their people by their virtues, and not by their ostentation ; for the latter, so far from conciliating esteem, causes men to speak evil of Priests. Let them be assured that by worldly vanities they can give no edification to the people, but on the contrary (as St. Bernard says) they cause them to love the world. Let them be assured that all superfluous ornaments and dress are a greater disgrace to them than squalor and filth. Let us, then, take care to preserve due modesty and simplicity in our attire, in our furniture, our household, and our table; and let us endeavour to make everything about us remind men of the modesty and simplicity of our Lord Jesus Christ, Whose Ministers we are.

3. *And they laughed Him to scorn.* Although our Lord Jesus Christ was thus laughed to scorn (says St. Chrysostom), He did not repress or rebuke such laughter. Let us follow His example,

and, if the world deride us, let us make no account of it ; for the world is blind and foolish, and therefore should its scorn be despised by those who see and are wise (as St. Bernard teaches). If Priests would please the world, of what avail is the Priesthood to them ? (asks the same St. Bernard.) If thou wouldst give true edification to the Faithful, despise the derision of worldlings ; for (as St. Laurence Justinian says) the Church of Christ is edified by our contempt of the world. St. Augustin calls the glory which we derive from the applause of the world " a glory of fools." How foolish, then, should we be, were we ambitious of this glory, —as much so as if we took account of the derision of the world! If we depend on the judgment of worldly men—if we seek their applause—if we fear their scorn—we shall never do any good. He who observes what men say of him (says St. Thomas) will never produce any good result, for, according to the words of Holy Scripture, " He that observeth the wind shall not sow, and he that considereth the clouds shall never reap" (Eccl. xi. 4). The scorn cast upon Jesus Christ passed away in a moment, and so will all the derision to which good Priests may be subject. But, if God despise and scorn us, what will become of us in eternity ? Let us call to mind (with St. Gregory) the transitory nature of all human judgments, while the Divine judgment is immutable ; and let us make it our rule to scorn the contempt of men.

" Let not our soul be humbled down to the dust, nor our belly cleave to the earth. Arise, O Lord, and help us."—From *Ps.* xliii. 25, 26.

" For Jesus Christ I have suffered the loss of all things, and count them but as dung, that I may gain Christ."—*Phil.* iii. 8.

FRIDAY.

———◆———

THE CONDITIONS UNDER WHICH PRIESTS SHOULD CONVERSE WITH FEMALES.

I. PUBLICITY.
II. INFREQUENCY.
III. EDIFICATION.

———◆———

" And, when the multitude was put forth, He went in and took her by the hand ; and the maid arose. And the fame hereof went abroad into all that country."— *St. Matt.* ix. 25, 26.

1. *He went in.* Our Lord Jesus Christ entered the room where the dead maiden lay, and " He suffered not any man to go in with Him but Peter, and James, and John, and the father and mother of the maiden" (St. Luke viii. 51). He was pleased (says St. Chrysostom) to have five witnesses of His Divine power, and He chose three of His Disciples and the father and mother of the maiden. Let us learn from this to avoid holding intercourse with women in secret and without witnesses, but when it is needful for us to converse with them let us be accompanied by Peter—that is, by the sacred Ministry ; let us be accompanied by James—that is, by courage, which is superior to human respect ; let us be accompanied by John—that is, by holy chastity. There is a well-known saying of St. Cyprian, that we should love women as present in the Church, but hate them in private intercourse. Intercourse with women ever generates suspicion, and the devil makes use of it in order to ruin the good fame of Priests (says

St. Laurence Justinian); and St. Augustin says that the suspicion created by Clerics sitting with women, talking to them, and frequenting their dwellings, is inevitable. Nor may we say that it suffices if our conscience is at ease, and that it matters not what others think or say of us; for the Apostle teaches us to provide " good things," not only in the sight of God, but also " in the sight of all men " (Rom. xii. 17); so that (as St. Chrysostom says) we must not only root up evil opinions when they arise, but also prevent them from arising. It may be true that our chastity suffers not from treating with women in private, but such conduct gives occasion for sins of suspicion and rash judgment in others, and casts discredit on ourselves; and thus (as St. Prosper declares) we are not, in such a case, free from guilt.

2. *The maid arose.* Our Lord Jesus Christ spoke to the maid in order to raise her up : " He saith to her, *Talitha, cumi*, which is, being interpreted, Damsel (I say to thee), arise " (St. Mark v. 41). This is one of the rare instances in which He is mentioned as speaking to women, and because of this rarity the Disciples were astonished when they found Him talking with the Samaritan woman : " They wondered that He talked with the woman " (St. John iv. 27). Yet this wonder arose from no suspicion dishonourable to our Lord, for the Disciples were marvelling at what was good, not suspecting an evil thing (says St. Augustin). But, if we are constantly talking with the same woman, how shall we escape malicious wonder, jests, and detractions? Vile, miserable, and weak are those Clerics reputed who frequently talk with women (says St. Augustin). Every one suspects that this habit causes the same injury to Clerics as to other men—that is, that frequent intercourse with women is the nourishment of incontinence (as St. Chrysostom declares). Men ordinarily suspect that, if at first chastity suffers no injury from these meetings, it will be impaired in course of time, just as the drops of water which fall upon the rock, by little and little, hollow out the stone (says St. Isidore). Let us, then, carefully observe St. Basil's rule—viz., to speak with females only when compelled by necessity, and even in such cases to withdraw from them as speedily as if we were escaping from danger of fire.

3. *And the fame hereof went abroad.* All that country celebrated the favour which Christ had conferred on the family of Jairus, and took occasion from it (as St. Hilary points out) to praise His other wonderful works. Now, we know that the raising up of this maiden was a type of the justification of a sinful soul. If, therefore, we have to converse with those of the opposite sex for the sake of saving or converting souls, our good intention will be acknowledged, and we shall suffer no loss of reputation. But let us reflect (with St. Thomas) that, the more holy women are, so much the more alluring are they, and that under pretext of soft words creeps the poison of sensuality. Spiritual writers, enlightened by the Holy Ghost, have shewn by examples how pious converse with holy women has become an instrument in the devil's hands whereby both parties have sustained serious injury, and scandal, rather than edification, has been the result. Let us, then, strive to follow St. Augustin's maxim, who says, "With women let your converse be brief and grave." Fatal experience has ever proved the truth of the same holy Father's words—viz., that "he will quickly fall into ruin who will not avoid suspicion of familiarity." Let us examine our conscience; let us cut off every attachment which might put our soul in peril or compromise our reputation; and let us bitterly repent of any failure in this respect.

"Turn away my reproach, which I have apprehended, for Thy judgments are delightful."—*Ps.* cxviii. 39.

"At two things my heart is grieved, and the third bringeth anger upon me : a man of war fainting through poverty, and a man of sense despised, and he that passeth over from justice to sin."—*Eccl.* xxvi. 25, 26, 27.

SATURDAY.

THE PRESENTATION OF THE BLESSED VIRGIN MARY.

SENTIMENTS WHICH THE FESTIVAL SHOULD INSPIRE IN ECCLESIASTICS.

I. GRATITUDE AS REGARDS THE PAST.
II. DEVOTION IN RESPECT OF THE PRESENT.
III. CONFIDENCE AS TO THE FUTURE.

"Blessed is the womb that bore Thee, and the paps that gave Thee suck."—
St. Luke xi. 27.

1. *Blessed is the womb.* The womb of the Blessed Virgin was the temple of the living God, and was the shrine of Him Who said, "Destroy this temple, and in three days I will raise it up" (St. John ii. 19). In Her childhood She was presented in the Temple, although (as it has been well said), on account of Her purity, She rather merited to be presented in the heaven of heavens. And, since (as St. Bernard declares) all good things come to us by Mary, and She may be looked upon as that overflowing channel whereby all grace is imparted to us, we ought to be grateful to Her Who, in our infancy, caused us to be presented in the Church to receive holy Baptism (as St. Cyril says). And, not content with this grace, which is common to all the Faithful, She also procured for us our presentation in the Temple for the reception of Holy Orders. She obtained our vocation for us, so that our entrance into the Temple might be (says St. Ambrose) a heavenly calling rather

than a voluntary offering or assumption of our own. She obtained for us the grace by which we were fitted for Ordination. She obtained for us a right intention for entering the Sanctuary, and preserved us from the sin of those vile mercenaries who (as St. Bernard says) purchase earthly goods at the expense of heavenly treasures. She obtained for us the spirit of prayer, and a holy indifference in asking counsel, and in subjecting ourselves to the direction of our Superiors as indicating the holy will of God, according to St. Bernard's rule. Finally, She removed any difficulties which stood in the way of the fulfilment of our vocation. In a word, if we are Priests, and if we are in any way distinguished among our colleagues, we owe it to this great Priestess. Let us, then, strive to shew our gratitude perpetually, and let us give special proofs of it in this solemnity.

2. *Blessed is the womb.* Almighty God called the Blessed Virgin to His Temple, whose womb was destined to be the chamber of the tremendous mystery of the Incarnation (says St. Andrew of Crete). He called Her to the Tabernacle, Himself, as it were, inviting Her, so that of Her it may be justly said, " The Lord came down in the pillar of the cloud, and stood in the entry of the Tabernacle calling, . . . Mary " (Numb. xii. 5). Thus was She introduced into the holy place, and planted in the house of the Lord (says St. John Damascene) as a fruitful olive-tree, and rendered the receptacle of all virtues. Then the Blessed Virgin renewed the consecration of Herself to God—a total consecration, a perpetual consecration ; offering Herself as an immaculate victim in the Temple—a victim most acceptable to God, and an object of veneration to angels and men (says St. Andrew of Crete). Now, we Priests are continually entering the Temple, and before doing so we ought to take from our feet— that is, from our affections—all earthly impurity, so as to fulfil the command, " Put off the shoes from thy feet, for the place whereon thou standest is holy ground " (Exod. iii. 5). Happy are we if we have recourse to Mary to obtain that purity of soul and body which is requisite for entering the Temple, and for the worthy exercise of our sacred functions. Happy are we if we implore Her patronage so as to profit by the treasures opened to us in

in the Sanctuary. Then would the Priest "grow up like the cedar of Libanus, planted in the house of the Lord, in the courts of the house of our God" (Ps. xci. 13, 14). He would become "as the lamp shining upon the holy candlestick" (Eccl. xxvi. 22); he would preserve holy chastity, in comparison of which all earthly riches, power, and dignity are worthless: "No price is worthy of a continent soul" (ver. 20).

3. *And the paps which Thou hast sucked.* The breasts of the Blessed Virgin are called "a tower" (Cant. viii. 10), and the meaning of this has been supposed to be that, whilst in Her maternal pity She nourishes us as children, She renders us impregnable against our enemies. Moreover, during the time that She was in the Temple of. the earthly Jerusalem, She made Herself more and more worthy to enter into the heavenly Jerusalem, and now, with maternal care, She disposes Priests who are devout to Her to be, like Herself, presented in the Temple not made with hands—that is, in Paradise. Truly over the gate of this Temple is it written, "Without are dogs and sorcerers, and unchaste, and murderers, and servers of idols, and every one that loveth and maketh a lie" (Apoc. xxii. 15); and it is the office of Mary to preserve us from those sins which would hinder our entrance into Paradise. It is Her office to appease our Judge, from Whom, at the hour of death, we look for our final sentence, and She can appease Him (says St. Bonaventure) by reminding Him of the womb that bore Him. If some have not courage to present themselves at the door of this Temple, which is Christ, let them enter by the window, which is Mary, for St. Bernardin calls Her "the window of Paradise;" Ernest of Prague, "the window of the ark;" Bartholomew of Pisa, "the window of those who despair." Let us, then, pray to Her, with holy Church, that at the hour of our death She would present us to Her Son—that She would open the doors of Paradise, and receive us therein.

"Blessed is he whom Thou hast chosen and taken up to Thee : he shall dwell in Thy courts."—*Ps.* lxiv. 5.

"How beautiful are thy steps in shoes, O prince's daughter ! "—*Cant.* vii. 1.

TWENTY-FOURTH SUNDAY AFTER PENTECOST.

THE WICKED PRIEST IN THE SANCTUARY.

I. He is an abomination in the sight of God.
II. He is the cause of the people's desolation.
III. He is subject to blindness.

"When, therefore, you shall see the abomination of desolation, which was spoken of by Daniel the prophet, standing in the holy place: he that readeth, let him understand."—*St. Matt.* xxiv. 15.

1. *Abomination . . . standing in the holy place.* The "abomination standing in the holy place" signifies, according to many interpreters, the sins committed by Priests in the Temple. Surely the sins of Priests must be abominable to God, since He abominates even the sins of the laity; nay, "Evil thoughts are an abomination to the Lord" (Prov. xv. 26). Under the Old Law Almighty God refused to accept a victim in which there was "any blemish, or any fault," and called it "an abomination to the Lord" (Deut. xvii. 1). Surely, then, He will abominate a Priest loathsome with the stains of sin, and infected with vices, who, as such, is rebellious, an enemy and traitor to Him—the object of His hatred and His malediction! Further, Almighty God has given the name of "abomination" to those who exhibit holiness externally while they possess it not inwardly: "Every mocker is an abomination to the Lord" (Prov. iii. 32): and such,

sacred offices in the Temple, whilst (as St. Augustin says) they
have not only destroyed the Temple of God in themselves, but
have made it the habitation of the evil one. Lastly, in Holy
Scripture idols are called "abominations" (Exod. viii. 26;
1 Mach. i. 57); and a depraved Pastor is, as it were, an idol, according to the Prophet's words, "O shepherd and idol" (Zach.
xi. 17). He is an idol because he has "the name of being alive,
and is dead" (Apoc. iii. 1). Such Priests are idols because
"they have mouths, and speak not" to confess their sin; "they
have eyes, and see not" their miserable condition; "they have
ears, and hear not" the voice of God (Ps. cxiii. 5, 6). Suffer
me not to become thus abominable to Thee, O my God!

2. *Of desolation.* The sins of the Priest may be called sins of
"desolation" because of the ruin which they bring upon the
Sanctuary and upon the people: "The sin of the desolation
which is made; and the Sanctuary, and the strength shall be
trodden under foot" (Dan. viii. 13). And truly (as St. Isidore
declares) sins committed by the Clergy may be regarded as the
crime of the city, the stain of the Church, the ruin and destruction of all who associate with them. As the sin of Heli the
Priest, and of his sons, caused the desolation of the Jewish people,
so is desolation brought upon the Christian people by the sins
and scandals of Priests. They are the pillars of the Temple, and
therefore (says St. Augustin), if they fall, their ruin must crush
the people who are placed beneath them. They are the keepers
of the rock of Sion, and therefore (says St. Bernard) their treason
causes the overthrow of the whole people. Ecclesiastical history confirms the truth of this teaching. Therefore, let us pray
to Almighty God to clothe His Clergy with holiness, so that His
people may be sanctified, and that the glory of the whole Church
may be increased.

3. *He that readeth, let him understand.* St. Jerome says that by
these words our Lord Jesus Christ intimates a mystical understanding of the words on which we have just meditated. Now,
this mystical understanding may remind us how wicked Priests
read but understand not; that is to say, they read Holy Scripture
as if they did not understand it, or, at least, they only understand

so much as suffices to render them inexcusable. It may be said to them, as it was said by Philip to the eunuch, "Thinkest thou that thou understandest what thou readest?" (Acts viii. 30.) For spiritual darkness falls upon them, and blinds them: "He is in darkness, and walketh in darkness, and knoweth not whither he goeth, because the darkness hath blinded his eyes" (1 St. John ii. 11). No sooner have they by sin departed from the true light, which is God, and turned their back on Him, than they become blind (says St. Augustin). The malice of their sin has blinded them, and their blindness is greater in proportion to the greater malice of their sin in comparison with that of the laity: "The Lord reward him that doeth evil, according to his wickedness" (2 Kings iii. 39). Who, then, is there who will not tremble at these considerations? Who does not see in this passage the portrait of many wicked Priests, who, after the manner of the Jews, read the Scriptures but do not understand them, whilst the elect among them have light to understand and profit by them: "The election hath obtained it, and the rest have been blinded" (Rom. xi. 7). If thou who now readest these words art not in this condition, take heed lest thou fall into it; and be not proud, but fear! "Thou standest by faith: be not high-minded, but fear" (ver. 20).

"He is my God and my Saviour: He is my protector: I shall be moved no more." *Ps.* lxi. 3.

"I beseech Thee, my Lord, lay not upon us this sin, which we have foolishly committed."—*Numb.* xii. 11.

MONDAY.

THE INTERIOR LIFE IN THE MIDST OF THE OCCUPATIONS OF THE ECCLESIASTICAL STATE.

I. THE FLIGHT ENJOINED US.
II. THE DETACHMENT REQUIRED OF US.
III. THE CARE OF SOULS BEFITTING US.

" Then they that are in Judea, let them flee to the mountains ; and he that is on the house-top, let him not come down to take anything out of his house; and he that is in the field, let him not go back to take his coat. And woe to them that are with child, and that give suck in those days."—*St. Matt.* xxiv. 16—19.

1. *Let them flee to the mountains.* Our Lord enjoined His Disciples to flee to the mountains when the destruction of Jerusalem should come, but He intended also to impress upon all Christians to flee from the world, and He here teaches them the manner of doing so. This flight is only to be obtained by means of prayer, by which we follow Jesus, Who " went up into a mountain alone to pray;" and this flight, sought and sustained by prayer, is the first means of forming interior men and the spiritual life. Hence the Apostle prayed to the Eternal Father for the Ephesians, " that He would grant them, according to the riches of His glory, to be strengthened by His Spirit, with might unto the inward man" (Eph. iii. 16). Now, prayer is made with fervour when we find time to withdraw ourselves, not indeed into the solitude of the desert, but into retirement (says St. Paulinus). Let Ecclesiastics, then, withdraw themselves to this mountain ; that is, let them raise

themselves up to God—let them raise themselves from the earth
—in order that they may afterwards return to their occupations
with greater alacrity (as St. Laurence Justinian exhorts them).
In prayer, by the light of truth, they gain a clear insight into
their own conscience, their understanding is illuminated, the
presence of God is manifested to them, their affections are raised
to Him, and they are led to bewail their frailty (as St. Bonaventure teaches). Without this aid they are as animal and "sensual
men," incapable of perceiving "those things that are of the
Spirit of God; for they are foolishness to them, and they cannot
understand them" nor judge of them (1 Cor. ii. 14). How
happy is the Priest who is intent upon his inner life, so as to be
able to repeat with truth St. Gregory Nazianzen's words, "It is
on the interior. life that we bestow the greater care and study!"

2. *Let him not take anything out of his house.* They who take
anything out of their house—even so much as their garment—
are such as are attached to temporal goods; for what are all
earthly things (asks St. Gregory) but the clothing of the body?
Now, this attachment is the chief obstacle to the formation of the
interior man, who lives by faith, and who says (with St. Paul),
" I am delighted with the law of God, according to the inward
man " (Rom. vii. 22). Freed from this attachment, our spiritual
life is easily strengthened, increased, and advances from virtue to
virtue, even whilst bodily goods, or our very health itself, may be
lost: "For which cause we faint not; but, though our outward man
is corrupted, yet the inward man is renewed day by day" (2 Cor.
iv. 16). But it is this attachment which robs so many Priests of
the inestimable gift of preferring the interior life to honours,
riches, and pleasures, and thus deprives them of the glory of
being patterns to the people, and of rendering themselves worthy
to occupy a glorious position in the Sanctuary (as St. Gregory
shews). And woe to those Priests (says St. Augustin) who, having
begun to lead an interior life, fall from the height of virtue into
vice, or who, instead of going forward, have gone back. Let us,
then, detach ourselves from earthly things by our own free will
before we are forcibly detached from them by death. If we are
shepherds, we ought not to walk like sheep with our face bent

upon the earth. Let us lift ourselves up in thought; let us look up to heaven; let us desire eternal goods. So St. Bernard. O my Jesus, who wast lifted up from the earth, draw me to Thee, and sever me from all earthly attachments.

3. *Woe to them that are with child, and that give suck.* Those Priests are, as it were, with child (says Origen) who have not yet brought forth spiritual children to grace by the ministry of the word. Again, those Priests are giving suck whose children are indeed living but as yet insufficiently nourished, so that they continually need to give them spiritual milk. Pastors of souls are rightly compared to nurses: "As if a nurse should cherish her children" (1 Thess. ii. 7): or they may be compared to mothers, to whom the Faithful should have recourse as to the bosom of their mother. Now, pregnant women and nursing women must be well nourished, in order that they may communicate healthy nourishment to their offspring; and in like manner Priests, if they are not careful of their own interior life, cannot nourish the Faithful as they ought. As St. Laurence Justinian declares, abundant grace, fervent charity, and more than ordinary wisdom are required in those who endeavour to raise to life the souls of their brethren. They, therefore, who are not careful of their own spiritual life shew themselves unfaithful stewards and watchmen. May Almighty God give us grace to understand these truths, and to profit by them.

"O God, set my soul to live, and suffer not my feet to be moved."—From *Ps.* lxv. 9.

"Thou hast granted me life and mercy, and Thy visitation hath preserved my spirit."—*Job* x. 12.

TUESDAY.

———

THE DUTY OF THE CLERGY IN PUBLIC CALAMITIES.

I. To EXCITE PEOPLE TO PENANCE.
II. To ENDEAVOUR TO APPEASE GOD'S ANGER.
III. To LABOUR TO ASSIST THE SUFFERERS.

———

"And pray that your flight be not in the winter, or on the Sabbath. For there shall then be great tribulation, such as hath not been from the beginning of the world until now, neither shall be. And unless those days had been shortened no flesh should be saved, but for the sake of the elect those days shall be shortened."— *St. Matt.* xxiv. 20—22.

1. *For there shall then be great tribulation.* Public tribulations, which render nations miserable, are the punishment of sin : " Justice exalteth a nation, but sin maketh nations miserable" (Prov. xiv. 34). Famine, inundations, wars, pestilence, earthquakes, are the chastisements with which Almighty God punishes the corruption of a nation ; and therefore He keeps these, as it were, shut up among His treasures, to distribute according to the judgments of His justice : "Are not these things stored up with Me, and sealed up in My treasures ? (Deut. xxxii. 34.) But He promises, when nations amend, that He will remove the scourge : " Cease to do perversely, learn to do well . . . and then come and accuse Me, saith the Lord" (Isaias i. 16, 17, 18). The whole history of the Jewish nation is a continual proof of

sins and consoled through God's mercy (says St. Augustin). Hence it is the office of Priests to stir up nations to penance, to public acts of humiliation, to reformation of manners, to the removal of scandals. They must, indeed, repeat the words of the Prophets, who on such occasions as these exhorted men in God's name to repentance, saying, "Turn to the Lord your God" (Joel ii. 13). When nations are cast down and humbled they listen more readily to the exhortations of God's Ministers, teaching them to acknowledge "those very punishments to be less than their sins deserve," and to believe "that these scourges of the Lord, with which, like servants, they are chastised, have happened for their amendment, and not for their destruction" (Judith viii. 27). Is not the Lord able by our means to bring about the same result as in the case of Ninive, which was converted by the preaching of Jonas alone?

2. *Those days shall be shortened.* Whilst zealous Priests exhort nations to be converted, they must also appease God's anger, so that He may replace His sword in the scabbard, and shorten those days of tribulation. Let them, then, begin by offering the Victim of atonement, and for this purpose purify their hands, "that it may be an atoning sacrifice, and the hands of the offerers may be sanctified" (Exod. xxix. 33). Let them pray fervently to the Lord that "where sin has abounded" He would cause "grace to abound"; saying to Him, "Forgive Thy people that have sinned against Thee, and all their iniquities by which they have transgressed against Thee, and give them mercy" (3 Kings viii. 50). Let them be the first to do penance, in imitation of that king who, when he beheld the sufferings of his people, clothed himself in sack-cloth, so that "all the people saw the hair-cloth which he wore" (4 Kings vi. 30)—or of that other king who, himself giving the example, commanded the people to cry to the Lord with fervour, in fasting and sack-cloth, saying, "Let neither men nor beasts, oxen nor sheep, take anything; let them not feed nor drink water. And let men and beasts be covered with sack-cloth, and cry to the Lord with all their strength" (Jonas iii. 7, 8). Thus has it often come to pass that the Clergy have appeased Almighty God, and He has vouchsafed to turn

the evil which had come upon them, or which they feared would come upon them, into good. And the very uncertainty (says St. Jerome) in which a nation finds itself of obtaining grace incites them to more fervent Penance, so that Almighty God may be more easily moved to mercy. Let the Clergy, therefore, institute solemn Processions, Triduums, Litanies, and other pious exercises to which people are wont to have recourse on such occasions; but let them practise them with groanings of heart and humiliation of spirit. How many examples of this kind may we find in the annals of the Church, and in the lives of holy Bishops and zealous Priests! Let us remember the Angel's answer to St. Paul's prayer—" Behold God hath given thee all them that sail with thee ". (Acts xxvii. 24); for thus the Apostle was the means of delivering two hundred and seventy-six souls from shipwreck, and (according to St. Chrysostom) of bringing them to eternal salvation. Of so great avail are the prayers of one holy Priest in times of public calamity.

3. *No flesh should be saved.* It is not sufficient for the Clergy to pray in seasons of public calamity; it is also necessary for them to labour to the utmost of their power for the salvation both of the souls and bodies of the people thus afflicted. Truly this is the time to devote all our efforts (as St. Laurence Justinian says) to reclaiming and feeding the wandering sheep. This is the time for the Clergy to bear the yoke, like oxen treading out the corn, in the face of all obstacles (to use St. Chrysostom's expression), if they would merit the promised reward, for otherwise the labourer is not worthy of his hire. This is the time for administering the Sacraments, which serve to sooth and bind up the wounds of the people (as St. Augustin says). Moreover, let the Clergy relieve the temporal necessities of those who suffer, so that by their example they may encourage others to assist the people in their distress and misery. The Priest should thus be (as St. Jerome says) "the staff of the blind, the food of the hungry, the hope of the miserable, and the consolation of the mourners." Great is the need that he has to shew compassion for the afflicted, and woe to the Priest who abandons them without being moved to pity them. How often has it happened that Priests have met

death when seeking their own safety in flight! And, on the other hand, how many who, for the love of God, have exposed themselves to danger, have escaped temporal evils, and have enriched themselves with merit for all eternity! How many, again, have met death with courage and heroism, sacrificing themselves for the good of their brethren, as martyrs of charity! This is the maxim which we ought to keep before our eyes in public calamities, and, if we are not able to afford the sufferers all the assistance we wish to give them, let us pray to God to supply our inability, saying with the Church, "Be appeased, and succour those in tribulation." As for ourselves, let us appease God's wrath by holiness of life, by the exercise of our Ministry, and by prayer, in order that God may not reserve for us a season of still greater miseries: "In the morning my prayer shall prevent Thee" (Ps. lxxxvii. 14).

"Wilt Thou, O Lord, be angry with us for ever; or wilt Thou extend Thy wrath from generation to generation?"—*Ps.* lxxxiv. 6.

"Hear Thou from heaven . . . and forgive Thy people, although they have sinned."—2 *Paralip.* vi. 39.

WEDNESDAY.

———•———

ON A SCRUPULOUS CONSCIENCE.

I. Priests must guard themselves from scruples.
II. They must preserve others from them.
III. The most suitable means to attain this object.

———•———

" Then, if any man shall say to you, Lo, here is Christ, or there, do not believe
him. For there shall rise false Christs and false prophets, and shall shew great signs
and wonders, insomuch as to deceive (if possible) even the elect. Behold, I have
told it you beforehand. If, therefore, they shall say to you, Behold, He is in the
. desert, go ye not out ; Behold, He is in the closets, believe it not. For, as l'ghtning
cometh out of the east, and appeareth even into the west, so shall also the coming
of the Son of Man be. Wheresoever the body shall be, there shall the eagles also
be gathered together."—*St. Matt.* xxiv. 23—28.

1. *If, therefore, they shall say to you, Behold, He is in the desert, go
ye not out.* Christ is not to be found in false doctrines, which
(St. Jerome says) are well typified by the dryness, darkness, and
desolation of the desert. Hence the Priest who follows false
doctrines, which are productive of scruples, does not come to
Christ ; he mistakes the road, and will fail in obtaining the consolations promised to those who find our Lord : " Come to Me,
all you that labour, and are burdened, and I will refresh you "
(St. Matt. xi. 28). Nay, Priests of scrupulous conscience become
themselves a " desert," instead of being to the Faithful " like a
watered garden, whose waters shall not fail" (Isaias lviii. 11).
The angel of darkness, transformed into an angel of light,
suggests to them false principles, by which they become always

doubtful, irresolute in deciding cases of conscience, unfit for the work of the Ministry, unable to advance towards perfection, ridiculous in the eyes of the people. The devil, indeed, treats them as Antiochus treated that holy youth whose tongue "he cut out, . . and chopped off the extremities of his hands and feet," so as to render him wholly useless (2 Mach. vii. 4). It is a false principle which leads them to employ so much time in the recital of their Office and in saying Mass, by continually repeating the words afresh; for the Holy Ghost tells us, "Repeat not the word in thy prayer" (Eccl. vii. 15). Cornelius à Lapide, following the interpretation of other great commentators, teaches us, in reference to the above passage, that the scrupulous who on account of distractions repeat the words of their prayer are in error for several reasons—viz., because such scrupulous fears are for the most part groundless and mischievous; because such repetition is irreverent; because thereby the fault and scruples are increased and magnified; because the pronunciation of the words satisfies the obligation of the prayer; and, supposing there are distractions, these distractions are often involuntary, and therefore without sin, or, if voluntary, the sin is blotted out by contrition, not by repetition of the words. Again, a false principle often hinders the scrupulous from undertaking any good and profitable works through a notion of greater sanctity; whereas God tells us, "Be not over just, and be not more wise than is necessary." Lastly, another false principle sets before them the severity of God apart from that infinite goodness which "knows our infirmity, and delights not in the perdition of men," whereas the Apostle enjoins us to "see the goodness and the severity of God" (Rom. xi. 22). Let us, then, put away from us these false principles, considering their absurdity and their fatal consequences.

2. *Behold, He is in the closets, believe it not.* Christ is not found in obscurity (as St. Augustin explains). He is not found in certain fantastical conceits and subtleties which scrupulous Priests make for themselves, and with which they torment the conscience of the just, whereas it is written, "Seek not after wickedness in the house of the just, nor spoil his rest" (Prov.

xxiv. 17). If the director of scrupulous souls be not learned, prompt, and firm—if he allow those who consult him to plunge deeper and deeper into doubts and difficulties—it may easily happen, as it often has happened, that, wearied by so anxious a life, instead of finding safety they will precipitate themselves into vice. Moreover, souls torn by scruples taste not, in their continual sadness, the delights of that "peace" and "joy" which are "fruits of the Spirit;" they do not know by experience how "sweet is the yoke," "how light the burden," which our Lord has put upon our shoulders; and hence to every one of them the words of the Wise Man should be repeated, "Give not up thy soul to sadness, and afflict not thyself in thy own counsel" (Eccl. xxx. 22). The holy Fathers have exposed the evil effects of such sadness, and therefore is it incumbent on enlightened directors to free their penitents from it. Further, the scrupulous are wont to be fiercely assailed by the devil at the point of death, and easily will they who have once been absorbed in the gulf of sadness (as St. Bernard says) be plunged into the abyss of despair. Directors, then, should be convinced that scruples are an obstacle to perfection, and they must strive to the utmost of their power to remove them. But, if in their own case they are agitated by scruples and know not how to cure themselves, let them not act as physicians to others, but rather refer those who apply to them to some one wiser and more prudent than themselves. To them it may justly be said, "What agreement shall the earthen pot have with the kettle? for, if they brush one against the other, it shall be broken" (Eccl. xiii. 3).

3. *Wherever the body shall be, there shall the eagles also be gathered together.* If under the name of "body" is signified our Lord Jesus Christ, dead for us, and under the name of "eagles" the Saints (according to St. Jerome's interpretation), here is the proper remedy for the evils of the scrupulous. We must accustom such souls often to look upon "the Sun of justice"—that is, to meditate upon the consoling mysteries of our Redemption; for He invites us to approach Him in order that He may refresh us and give us peace of conscience. He saith not (as St. Chrysostom points out) "I will save you" only, but (what is much

more) "I will place you in all security." Let us excite such souls to the love of Jesus Christ; let us strive to kindle in them a lively fervour; and this will be the most powerful means of dissipating their vain and cowardly fears; for "perfect charity casteth out fear" (1 St. John iv. 18). Besides this, let us urge the scrupulous to frequent Communion, which is wont to appease the agitations of their conscience; and thus may these words be applied to the Body of our Divine Lord on the Altar. The Body of Christ (says St. Ambrose) is on the Altar: you are the eagles. Lastly, in order that these eagles may fly, let us furnish them with the wings of obedience; let us make them recognise Christ in His Ministers; for this (as St. Alphonsus teaches) is the most effectual remedy against scruples. Let us follow, finally, the rules which the Saints have given for freeing the souls of the Faithful from such perilous torture; and especially let us urge them to beg of Almighty God, through the merits of His Son, perfect docility to their Confessor's commands. Many souls might thus run the way of God's commandments without being distracted by scruples! Let us pray to Almighty God to deliver us and others from this fatal weakness, and to grant us grace to fulfil His law with exactness.

"How long shall I take counsels in my soul, sorrow in my heart all the day?"—Ps xii. 2.

"Thou shalt bring us in, and plant us in the mountain of Thy inheritance, in Thy most firm habitation."—From *Exod.* xv. 17.

THURSDAY.

---

*FULFILMENT OF THE DIVINE WILL THE TRUE
END OF THE PRIESTHOOD.*

    I. For the glory of God.
    II. For the sanctification of Priests.
    III. For the salvation of the people.

" And, immediately after the tribulation of those days, the sun shall be darkened, and the moon shall not give her light, and the stars shall fall from heaven, and the powers of heaven shall be moved. And there shall appear the sign of the Son of Man in heaven, and then shall all the tribes of the earth mourn, and they shall see the Son of Man coming in the clouds of heaven, with much power and majesty. And He shall send His Angels with a trumpet, and a great voice, and they shall gather together His elect from the four winds, from the furthest parts of the heavens to the utmost bounds of them.—*St. Matt.* xxiv. 29—31.

1. *Then shall appear the sign of the Son of Man.* In the Day of Judgment (says St. Thomas) the Cross, with the other instruments of the Passion, will appear; and so brilliant will be its splendour that (as St. Augustin says), because of this light, the sun will be darkened, and the moon will not give her light, and the stars of heaven will be obscured. This Cross will be a sign of the obedience of our great High Priest to the will of His eternal Father; for when He was about to take up His Cross He said, " Not My will, but Thine, be done " (St. Luke xxii. 42). The end of the Priesthood which He assumed in the fulness of time was to obey, and so to glorify, His Father: " I came down from heaven, not to do My own will, but the will of

Him that sent Me" (St. John vi. 38)... "I seek not My own will, but the will of Him that sent Me" (St. John v. 30). This, then, will be the glory of Priests, who, in imitation of our Lord Jesus Christ, have recognised the end of their Ministry—that is to say, the renunciation of their own will, in order to fulfil the will of God. Rightly, then, did St. Francis say to the Priests of his Institute that, since Jesus Christ had given Himself wholly into their hands, it was fitting that they should give themselves wholly to Him. And St. Bernard went so far as to say that the Priest who did not despise his own will was not intent solely on the glory of God and the good of souls. Let us examine ourselves on this point, and let us pray to God for our amendment.

2. *Then shall all the tribes of the earth mourn.* At sight of the Cross, those Priests who have not attained the end of their Priesthood, and who have not sanctified themselves, shall mourn with all the tribes of the earth. But, alas! too late will they thus mourn (says St. Augustin): too late, and in vain, will they confess their error. The sight of the Cross will remind them of all that they might have gained had they but carried the Cross, had they but preached the Cross. They will then perceive that this was the mode in which they should have fulfilled the will of God, which was their "sanctification" (1 Thess. iv. 3). But, on the contrary, they have been enemies of the Cross of Christ, and therefore (as St. Chrysostom says) when they see the Cross they will mourn, because they have derived no benefit from His death, and because by their sins they have crucified Him afresh. Let us, then, enter into ourselves; let us labour earnestly for our sanctification; for (as St. Gregory Nazianzen warns us) not to advance in virtue amounts to vice. Let no Priest fondly imagine that he has attained complete perfection or sanctification, but let us all strive (as St. Gregory of Nyssa exhorts us) continually to advance more and more—to grow more and more holy, more and more perfect, each day of our lives. Let us, then, fulfil the Divine will, in order to our sanctification, and let us be convinced that for this end has Almighty God anointed us Priests.

3. *They shall see the Son of Man.* Priests will behold our Lord ~us Christ, and will know with what truth He said, " For them

do I sanctify Myself, that they also may be sanctified in truth "
(St. John xvii. 19); for the sanctification of both is the end of
the Priesthood. He declared this to be the will of His Father
and the object of His mission, and He fulfilled it perfectly:
" This is the will of the Father Who sent Me—that of all that
He hath given Me I should lose nothing" (St. John vi. 39). On
that great day, then, He will with justice say to men, " For you
I was made man, for you I was bound, and mocked, and blind-
folded, and crucified." Now, what shall we say if, as His Ministers, we have done little or nothing to promote this great
object for which we were ordained ? Let us remember (as St.
Chrysostom tells us) that on this account did He choose us, that
we may be as seed, and may bring forth much fruit. If we fail
in this, how shall we appear in the presence of our Judge, and
how shall we obtain the glorious crown of Priests ? For those
Priests (says St. Gregory) will be without glory when they stand
before the great Judge who shall have failed to promote His glory
in preaching to the souls committed to their charge. On the
other hand, great will be our advantage if we have devoted ourselves to procure the salvation of our brethren ; for this (as St.
Peter of Blois says) is the most efficacious means of saving ourselves, of performing the Divine will, and of fulfilling the end of
our Priesthood. If we do not make use of the wisdom which
God has given us for the benefit of our people, it will be as useless as a hidden treasure: " Wisdom that is hid, and a treasure
that is not seen, what profit is there in them both ?" (Eccl. xli.
17.) Let us pray to our Lord Jesus Christ to enlighten and
strengthen us, before He come to judge us, so that we may understand and put in practice these holy doctrines.

" Teach me to do Thy will, for Thou art my God."—*Ps.* cxlii. 10.
" As it shall be the will of God in heaven, so be it done."—1 *Machab.* iii. 60.

FRIDAY.

___

PRIESTS SHOULD PERFECT THEMSELVES IN THE VIRTUE OF HOPE.

I. SPECIAL MOTIVES FOR INCREASING THIS VIRTUE.
II. SPECIAL REASONS FOR EXERCISING IT.
III. SPECIAL OBLIGATIONS TO PROMOTE IT IN OTHERS.

___

"And from the fig-tree learn a parable : when the branch thereof is now tender, and the leaves come forth, you know that summer is nigh ; so you, also, when you shall see all these things, know ye that it is nigh, even at the doors. Amen, I say to you that this generation shall not pass till all these things be done. Heaven and earth shall pass, but My words shall not pass."—*St. Matt.* xxiv. 32—35.

1. *From the fig-tree, &c.* Almighty God, in bestowing vegetative power on the fig-tree, and in disposing it to bear fruit, shews that He really desires fruit from it, and that summer, the type of the future happiness of the just, is approaching. He foretells a spiritual summer (says St. Chrysostom), and the calm that is to succeed to the present tempest. In like manner (as St. Augustin declares), the particular benefits which Almighty God has conferred upon us are a pledge of the future good things which we expect from Him. Further, Priests being better instructed than other men, know the four solid pillars on which Hope rests— viz., the infinite goodness of God, His omnipotence, His fidelity to His promises, and the plentiful redemption which He has worked for us. These pillars form our anchor, which the Apostle calls " an anchor of the soul, sure and firm " (Heb.

vi. 19). Priests have frequent opportunities for the exercise of this virtue, as in the celebration of holy Mass, in the recital of the Divine Office, and in mental prayer; so that in them is shed abroad what St. Ephrem calls the most powerful consolation of the soul. They have, indeed, better means than other men of understanding the value, the importance, the necessity of this most noble virtue, which is deservedly called by St. John Climacus "the strength of charity, the rest in labour, the treasure which anticipates our eternal treasure." The Priest, from his first entrance into the Church—from the hour that he was regenerated by this holy Mother—has special reasons for hoping in Him, and can say to Him in a special sense, "My hope from the breasts of my mother: I was cast upon Thee from the womb" (Ps. xxi. 10). Let us, then, strive to grow continually in this virtue, which was infused into us in holy Baptism, and let us often repeat the Church's prayer, "Grant to us an increase of faith, hope, and charity."

2. *Amen, I say to you.* Our Lord Jesus Christ added these words (says St. Hilary) in order that the faith of His disciples in future things might be certain. We in like manner ought to be full of confidence in regard to the future good things which our Lord promises us; we ought frequently to stir up in ourselves this confidence, exercising ourselves beyond the laity in the virtue of hope. We, indeed, are exposed to more terrible encounters than are the laity with spiritual enemies who seek our fall, nor is there any more effectual means of keeping ourselves upright than trust in God: " He whose strength is the Lord," says St. Augustin, " falleth not, because the Lord falleth not." Moreover, this is the best means of pursuing the Ecclesiastical career with alacrity, for (as St. Bonaventure says) hope is the source of strength, of freedom, of elevation of mind, of salvation. Scarcely would it be possible to support the labours of our Ministry were they not alleviated by consideration of the eternal recompense (says St. Gregory). How, indeed, could God's ministers endure adversities, persecutions, outrages, the storms of the world, if they did not rest upon this anchor, if they did not exercise themselves in this virtue? And how is it

possible not to fear the wrath of men (asks St. Cyprian) unless we trust in the protection of God? Lastly, it is perfect hope which causes us to undertake great things for God, and to regard ourselves as omnipotent in His strength, saying, "I can do all things in Him Who strengtheneth me" (Phil. iv. 13). These are great truths, and worthy of careful meditation.

3. *My words shall not pass.* The words of our Lord Jesus Christ (says St. Hilary) cannot fail, for they come forth from the bosom of eternity. Meanwhile it is the office of the Clergy to make known to men our Lord's words, and especially His magnificent promises, in order to excite them to hope, saying to them, "Trust in Him, all ye congregation of people; pour out your hearts before Him" (Ps. lxi. 9). Let us, then, stir them up to trust in His promise of hearing our prayers, and of giving us the means necessary for eternal salvation, assuring them that trust in God is one great and necessary means of attaining to the condition of the blessed: "Blessed be the man that trusteth in the Lord, and the Lord shall be his confidence" (Jerem. xvii. 7): "Blessed are all they that trust in Him" (Ps. ii. 13). Above all, let us say to the weak-hearted, and to those whom the devil tempts with vain fears, "Know ye that no one hath hoped in the Lord and hath been confounded" (Eccl. ii. 11). In like manner let us convince such as are tempted to fall into the sin of Cain—the sin of despair—that "hope confoundeth not" (Rom. v. 5). Lastly, let us teach the dying (whom the enemy most frequently tempts to despair) to turn to Jesus, to approach Him, to cast themselves into His wounded side, in the certainty that He will not reject them: "Him that cometh to me I will not cast out" (St. John vi. 37). So shall we prevent them from trusting in themselves, from presuming on their own justice, from placing confidence in human means. Be God thy hope (says St. Augustin), be God thy strength, be God thy firmness, be God thy praise.

"I have put my trust in the Lord, and shall not be weakened."—*Ps.* xxv. 1.
"Although He should kill me, I will trust in Him."—*Job.* xiii. 15.

SATURDAY.

THE PRESENTATION OF THE BLESSED VIRGIN MARY.—II.

THREE FAVOURS TO BE ASKED OF THE BLESSED VIRGIN IN BEHALF OF THE PEOPLE ON THE OCCASION OF THIS FESTIVAL.

I. THE CONVERSION OF UNBELIEVERS.
II. THE FREQUENTATION OF THE CHURCH BY THE FAITHFUL.
III. THE PRESENTATION OF THEIR SOULS IN PARADISE.

" Blessed are they who hear the word of God and keep it."—*St. Luke* xi. 28.

1. *Blessed are they, &c.* In these most significant words our Lord Jesus Christ would teach us that whoever truly fulfils the will of God attains true nobility and relationship to Him. There is one only true nobility (says St. Chrysostom), and that is, to do the will of God. Now, this great privilege has its beginning in Baptism ; for then we enter the true Temple of God on earth— that is, the Catholic Church, of which the Temple at Jerusalem was the type. The Temple represented allegorically the Church militant, says Venerable Bede. Now, Priests ought to present " the children of wrath" in this mystical temple, in order that they may become " children of God, children of the kingdom ;" and for this end they must have recourse to Mary, that by Her most powerful intercession She may obtain for them this blessing. Therefore did St. Germanus, the Patriarch of Constantinople, say to Her, "No one is filled with the knowledge of God

unless by Thee, O most Holy One." The grace with which Mary was filled is diffused throughout the whole world by Her agency (says St. Bonaventure). Let us, then, pray to Her to regard with a pitiful eye those infants who are in danger of losing their life without being regenerated by means of holy Baptism, in order that She may obtain this Sacrament for them, and in this sense may be their " Regeneratrix " (as St. Athanasius calls Her). Let us pray to Her to implore of God strength for Missionaries, light for the many Jews, Turks, and Idolaters, in order that by the water of Baptism they may obtain pardon of all their sins; for thus She is rightly called (by Albertus Magnus) the "universal Baptism of sinners." Let us pray to Her to bring back to their mother, the Church, those many lost children, those heretics and schismatics, who have strayed from her, and so show Herself to be (as St. Ildephonsus calls Her) " the entrance into life." Such prayers are befitting the Clergy, and will be readily granted.

2. *Blessed are they, &c.* When our Saviour answered the woman in these words He desired to show (says St. Chrysostom), not that He neglected His Mother, but that the name of "mother" would have availed Her nothing had She not been perfect in faith and holiness. Hence we must understand that we have always need of faith, and of a life adorned with virtues, by which alone we can be saved. Now, if we desire that the Faithful should be well instructed in the Faith, and lead a holy life, we must induce them to frequent our temples, for there will they hear the Divine word ; there will they more readily obtain grace; there will they receive the Sacraments ; there, in short, will they become just and holy, and will confess that they "have received the mercy of God in the midst of His Temple " (Ps. xlvii. 10). Priests ought, then, to use all their efforts to induce people to flock to the churches, and for this end they should celebrate Festivals with magnificence, adorn the churches with splendour, perform the sacred functions with decorum, bestow a due care on the ecclesiastical chant and music, and cause the word of God to be heard with due fitness. Zealous Priests should be continually saying to the people, "Come and let us go up to the mountain of the Lord, and to the

house of the God of Jacob, and He will teach us His ways, and we will walk in His paths" (Isaias ii. 3). And, in order that our exhortations and our pious efforts may have the happy effect of bringing crowds to the house of God, let us implore the assistance of Mary, Who was on this day presented in the Temple with better dispositions, and more acceptable to God, than all creatures who had ever entered that holy place (says St. Bernardin). We all know by experience that without Her help people listen not to our invitation : " My people heard not my voice, and Israel hearkened not to me" (Ps. lxxx. 12). Let us pray to Her with fervour, and great will be our consolation.

3. *Blessed are they, &c.* They who hear the word of God and keep it are "blessed;" that is, they attain eternal happiness, they attain Paradise : " This man shall be blessed in his deed " (St. James i. 25). Paradise is the temple typified by that which Mary on this day entered (says Cornelius à Lapide). But, in order to present therein souls instructed, directed, cleansed, strengthened, assisted by us, we have need of Mary, by Whose aid the entrance of that blessed mansion is opened to us. She, in fact, holds in Her hand the keys of the heavenly kingdom (says St. Bernardin of Sienna). She causes Her devout children to find mercy in the Day of Judgment, and obtains for them the possession of eternal goods (says St. Chrysostom). Therefore let every Priest direct his prayer to Her, and in Her, next to our Lord Jesus Christ, let him place all his confidence. Then will She answer him from heaven: "Take courage, and be valiant, for thou shalt bring this people into the land which the Lord swore He would give to their fathers " (Deut. xxxi. 7). Thus, under the protection of so great a Mother, will he enable many souls to attain their eternal inheritance, and to conquer the infernal enemy . . " For the saving of the elect of God, to overthrow the enemies that rose up against them, that he might get the inheritance for Israel" (Eccl. xlvi. 2).

" In His Temple all shall speak His glory."—*Ps.* xxviii. 9.
" O Lord, shew to the house of Israel the Temple."—From *Ezech.* xlii. 10.

END OF VOL. IV. AND LAST.

www.ingramcontent.com/pod-product-compliance
Lightning Source LLC
Chambersburg PA
CBHW022125020426
42334CB00015B/767